THE NEW HOME OWNER MANUAL

Shana + George.

Inverness

Tuesday 16TH November 1982

THE NEW HOME OWNER MANUAL

Hamlyn
London · New York · Sydney · Toronto

This edition first
published 1982 by The Hamlyn Publishing Group Limited
London · New York · Sydney · Toronto
Astronaut House, Feltham, Middlesex, England

Copyright © Butterworth & Co (Publishers) Ltd,
1975, 1977, 1979, 1980, 1982

ISBN 0 600 34991 8

Printed in Great Britain

Preface

This is a basic manual for those who wish to keep their homes in tip-top order or to carry out work which will greatly improve them. It is self evident that maintaining your property will pay huge dividends should you wish to sell it, as it will stand up to a surveyor's report and will therefore hold its market value.

The book has been planned in six main sections:

1 Building Construction
2 Woodworking
3 Domestic Plumbing
4 Central Heating
5 Electric Wiring
6 Home Decorating

and it takes a 'beginner's guide' approach to each subject.

Section 1 is a simple introduction to the principles of building construction. It provides the handyman and home owner with the information that is essential for making a success of any building job, whether it be a small home extension or a complete structure, from foundations to the roof and drains.

An introduction to the craft of woodworking is contained in Section 2. Starting from first principles, it is invaluable to the newcomer to the subject and to the do-it-yourself enthusiast who wishes to increase his theoretical knowledge and his practical skill. Constructional techniques are explained in detail from setting out to finishing processes; both simple and more complex methods are dealt with. Other chapters cover the use of power tools and their accessories, and the special tools and techniques required in the craft of woodturning.

Section 3 is intended primarily for the householder who would like to be thoroughly familiar with the hot and cold water systems and the drainage system of his home. It enables him to identify

PREFACE

faults, to discuss intelligently plumbing repairs, alterations and extensions with his builder and, if he is a do-it-yourself enthusiast, to carry out minor plumbing projects competently and safely. It also provides useful background reading to plumbing apprentices, particularly in the early stages of their careers.

Section 4 has been specially written for house owners who wish to install central heating so that they can select the most effective and economic system. The principles and workings of heating systems are lucidly explained. Full details are given of radiators, convectors, boilers, flues, controls, etc.

This section is also valuable to house owners whose heating equipment needs replacing, and it also features guidance on the more effective and economic use of existing heating systems.

With the ever increasing rise in the cost of fuels, it is of paramount importance to find ways of reducing home heating costs, and an appendix shows some ways in which energy can be saved.

The importance of properly installed electric wiring in domestic premises cannot be overestimated, and Section 5 provides a readable yet authoritative guide to the subject. The information is intended to bridge the gap between the layman and electrical tradesman, and will also be of considerable value to first year electrical students on electrical installation courses.

Finally, an introduction to basic interior decoration is provided in Section 6.

Contents

CONTENTS

Section 1

Building Construction

1 Preparation and setting out

Although the majority of us would claim that we know very little about architecture, we are all very interested in buildings, because we have to live and work in them. We get our first introduction to building when as children we are given wooden blocks to play with, or the patent clip-together construction sets. We learn the crude basics of proportion when we find that our out-of-proportion buildings tend to fall down. We teach ourselves to put lintels over openings and we get an idea of bonding the blocks.

Later, when we are the proud owners of our own houses, the urge to build returns; we want to lay bricks, tile walls, build extensions and garages. This is the point at which building begins – when the need for a structure to meet a special purpose is first recognised.

The architect's drawing board is the next stage, when the plans are drawn for official approval and the structure is designed to meet both the requirements of the user and the Building Regulations, which are intended to ensure that the finished structure will be safe and sound.

For the craftsman and the handyman with an urge to build, to create his own environment, building starts with the practical work on the site. Whether the structure is to be a block of offices or a small dwelling house, the first step is to clear and level the site. All vegetation and top soil are removed from the area where the structure is to stand. This can be done by hand for an extension to the living room of a small house, but for a building the size of a house, or larger, mechanical aid is needed. Ground preparation for a dwelling consists usually of digging out the foundations to the specified depth and clearing the earth from the floor area. Even if the ground floor is to be suspended timber, the soil still has to be removed and the site covered with concrete.

At one time, only those trees that would actually interfere with building operations were removed, but since the severe drought of 1976 there has been a lot of panic over the possible effect of trees on the stability of the surrounding ground and, therefore, on the foundations of buildings in close proximity to trees.

Unfortunately, all damage of whatever nature which occurred to buildings during what was probably the driest summer for 200 years, was blamed on trees. Building Research Establishment papers first published in 1947 and based on shallow foundations only 425 mm (18 in) deep were used as a guide to the positioning of trees around buildings some thirty years later in 1977 when shallow foundations were 1 m (39 in) deep.

In 1953 it was suggested that the height of a tree was a rough guide to the spread of its roots and that a house should be kept away from trees a distance equal to the mature height of the tree. Where there were groups of trees the distance was increased to one and a half times the height of the trees. This extra distance was applied to single trees of popular, elm and willow, and in this case, where there were groups of trees, it was suggested that the distance should be two and a quarter times the mature height of the trees.

As shrinkable clay covers a large proportion of the country it is important that the tree problem is kept in perspective. Although a mature tree can take 20 000 gallons of water from the ground in a year, there is evidence to show that much of the damage that occurred during the hot, dry summer of 1976, could have happened even without the presence of trees and there were, in fact, cases of damage where there were no trees at all.

When clearing the site for building it is necessary to remember that if a mature tree is removed, the water table will rise and this will itself bring about some movement of the ground caused by the clay swelling as it takes up the water, and damage can also be caused by this clay heave.

It would seem sensible, therefore, to leave mature trees as they are, if they do not get in the way of the proposed building. They will have already produced a stable ground condition and it will be necessary only to take the foundations down perhaps a little deeper than the usual 1 m depth. Where new trees are planted on the site, it should be borne in mind that they will not reach maturity for 60 to 80 years and by that time the dwelling will be reaching the end of its useful life.

When trees are removed from the building site, it would seem prudent, therefore, to cut them down and clear out the stumps as far in advance of building operations as possible. In this way the ground water can stabilise at a new level and the clay can swell without the pressure displacing the building foundations or the solid floors.

The principles involved in setting out buildings are quite simple and few implements are necessary to carry out the work. A large wooden square, plenty of string and a number of stout wooden stakes about 50 mm × 50 mm (2 in × 2 in), a long level and a long straight edge with parallel sides will be needed. Accurate setting out of large buildings is done by means of a dumpy level which is basically a small telescope that can be swivelled in a horizontal plane. The object lens has a hair-line cross on it so that a level reading can be taken on a surveyor's staff which is marked in feet and inches and placed some distance away. A theodolite can also be used as it is a similar instrument, the telescope of which can also be moved in a vertical plane, but these are not essential for small works like garages and extensions. It is quite possible to set out the average dwelling house without using any sophisticated equipment.

Levelling has to be carried out from some fixed point called the datum. It is usually marked by a wooden peg driven into the ground until the top is at least 150 mm (6 in) above the highest point of the building area, which is of course the damp proof course level. The datum peg can also be set to a given height above the invert of a drain. The invert is the bottom of the drain and is measured in the drain channel where it passes through an adjacent inspection chamber.

The datum peg must be clear of all building work and is

cemented into place to prevent it being moved during building operations.

The large wooden square which is used to set the corners of the building at right angles can be made out of 50 mm × 25 mm (2 in × 1 in) batten, using the 3:4:5 formula well-known to all builders. Any triangle which has sides that bear the same length ratio as the numbers 3, 4 and 5 will have one right angle (*Figure 1.1*). Any unit of length can be used, i.e. centimetres, metres,

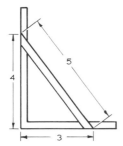

Figure 1.1. A builder's square, made to the 3 : 4 : 5 principle

feet or yards. A handy size of square is 3 ft × 4 ft × 5 ft (or using 300 mm to the foot: 900 mm × 1200 mm × 1500 mm). The three pieces of timber can be cut off to these lengths, or the sides can be made a little longer, provided that the third piece (the hypotenuse) is fixed in the correct place.

A halved joint is made at one end of each side batten and these are then screwed together temporarily using one screw. The hypotenuse piece is then placed on top of the two side battens so that its outer corner is exactly in line with the outer corner of the two side pieces. If the sides have been cut longer than the required unit length, then they must have marks made at the required ratio length and the hypotenuse outer corners placed on them. The joints can then be marked at each end and the halvings cut out. Alternatively, the batten can simply be screwed into place on the top of the side pieces and the second screw driven into the right angle halving.

For a strong job the timber is taken apart and the joints cut and glued with a waterproof adhesive so that the square will not be affected by the weather and will withstand rough usage.

Another simple piece of equipment that can be made is a set of boning rods. These are formed out of two pieces of batten 50 mm × 25 mm (2 in × 1 in), or for a stronger job 75 mm × 25 mm (3 in × 1 in), which are fixed together in a tee-shape (*Figure 1.2*). They may be 1 m (3 ft 3 in) or 1.2 m (4 ft) high with the top cross piece 457 mm (18 in) to 600 mm (24 in) long. A set comprises three rods all exactly the same size. They are used for levelling by standing one on a fixed point such as a datum peg. A second rod is then held on a distant point, level with the datum peg. This point will have been fixed by sighting

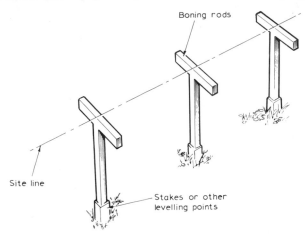

Figure 1.2. Using boning rods to level the tops of stakes

with a dumpy level or by using a spirit level and straight edge. The third boning rod is then used to produce as many other points between these two extremes as required, simply by holding it in place and sighting over the tops of the boning rods (*Figure 1.2*). Boning rods are also useful for lining up drains to the correct falls. A variation is to level a peg, using a straight edge and long spirit level, as far from the datum as possible. Then a boning rod is stood on each of the pegs and, by sighting over them to the third rod, a third peg can be levelled at almost any distance from them.

A long straight edge is another item that can be made to aid setting out. A 2440 mm (8 ft) straight edge has to be at least 100 mm (4 in) wide and if the length is 3 m (10 ft) or more, it will have to be 150 mm (6 in) wide, otherwise it will have a natural sag that will prevent an accurate level being taken.

The wood must be about 25 mm (1 in) thick, straight grained and free from knots or heartwood that would make it twist under site conditions. The edges are planed square and straight. It is tested by using it to draw a straight line on a sheet of plywood, plasterboard or on the floor. The straight edge is then turned over and brought up to the line from the other side. If it is accurate the edge and the line will match. If the straight edge is hollow it will show up by meeting the line at the ends but not in the middle. If the straight edge is bowed then it will cover the line in the middle and a new line is drawn to show how much bow there is. The straight edge can also be reversed end-to-end to get it even more accurate.

Setting out

Setting out begins by fixing the datum peg from which all vertical measurements are taken. This peg must, obviously, be driven into the ground at some point where it will not get in the way of subsequent building operations. Its height is established from some permanent level which should be marked on the plan. It may be a surveyor's bench mark which is chiselled into a wall or on a kerb stone. Another place for obtaining a level is the invert of a drain. This will entail lifting the cover of an inspection chamber and lowering a surveying staff on to the open channel or invert, then taking a reading with a dumpy level.

The dumpy level is basically a small telescope mounted on a tripod. The object glass has crossed hair lines for sighting on to the surveying staff. The level must be set up carefully and levelled in all directions to get a correct reading. It has a spirit bubble and adjusting screws to enable this to be done.

Having taken a reading from the invert, the dumpy level is turned on its pivot and used to level the datum peg which is driven to a given height above the invert. When it has been levelled accurately the datum peg is concreted around to ensure that it will not get moved during the construction work.

Additions and extensions to existing buildings usually employ the damp proof course of the main buildings as the datum point which enables the heights to be matched for floors and window sills. But it is often more convenient to set up the datum peg well clear of the structure than to try to level from the d.p.c. for every measurement that has to be taken later.

The building line is established next. This is a line fixed by the local authority and marks the position of the front main walls of buildings. Only small projections such as porches and bay windows are allowed in front of this line. In built-up areas the position of the building line can be seen by the position of the existing buildings, though in old streets the authority may have moved the line back in order to provide space for future road widening. This must be established before planning the project, otherwise a situation could arise where some or all of the new building would have to be demolished.

In the case of a detached or isolated building, great care must be taken to ensure that the positioning is correct as it may not be possible to line up the new building with existing ones. The position must therefore be checked by measurement from the road, or from other fixed points which are marked on the plans.

Setting out these stages in building is critical, as mistakes would reflect throughout the rest of the operations and it would be disastrous if, because of failure to check with the local authority, it was discovered at some later stage that the building was out of position.

When the datum peg and the building line have been established, the profile boards are set up. These boards mark the corners of the building and are set up well clear of the foundation trenches so that they will not interfere with the building operations. This is especially important if a mechanical digger is to be used.

The boards must be long enough to span the whole width of the foundation trench because on them will be marked the width of the foundation trench and the face of the brickwork and for cavity walls the inside face of the inner wall will be marked also.

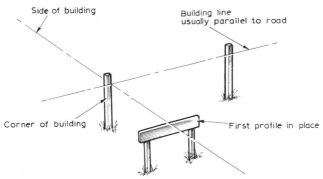

Figure 1.3. Setting out foundations using profiles and string lines. First profile in place

The boards can be set up separately or they can be joined together on one of the pegs so that they form a right angle. Minimum sizes are 50 mm × 50 mm (2 in × 2 in) for the pegs and 100 mm × 25 mm (4 in × 1 in) for the board itself.

First, the front line of the building is marked by a string line (*Figure 1.3*) and then a pair of pegs is driven to mark the front corners of the building. These are used as guides for positioning the profile board. From the front wall line, measurements are taken for the rear wall of the building and a parallel line is set up.

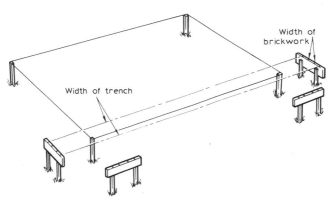

Figure 1.4. Setting out: rear corner pegs in place

17

On this line the rear corner pegs are driven (*Figure 1.4*). Lines are then set up to mark the side walls. These must be at right angles to the front and back walls and are set out by using the large wooden square (*Figure 1.5*). A final check is made by measuring the diagonals of the building. These must be the same, and if they are not, the measurements must be checked to ensure that the front and back lines are parallel and that the sides are also parallel.

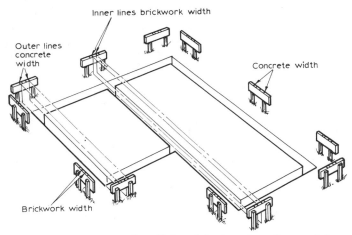

Figure 1.5. Setting out: all profile boards in place. Outer lines mark the trench and inner lines mark the wall

The rear profiles are then fixed and the positions of the brickwork and the foundation trenches are marked on the top edge of the horizontal board. The foundation concrete is marked separately if it is different to the trench width.When the accuracy of all the lines and angles has been checked, the marks are cut into the top of the profile boards with a fine toothed saw, so that they cannot be rubbed out or otherwise obliterated.

This completes the setting out for the main walls of the building. Intermediate walls are set out in the same manner except that they will most likely be half-brick in thickness and only one line marking the face of the brickwork will be needed.

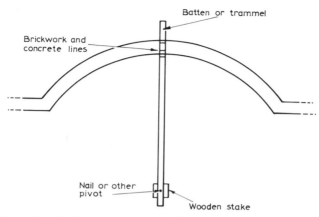

Figure 1.6. Setting out a curved wall using a wooden batten as a trammel

Non-load-bearing partition walls made of lightweight blocks do not need to have deep foundations; they can be built from the concrete floor slab.

At this stage the foundations for the projections such as porches and bay windows are set out. Centre lines are essential for this work if the setting out is to be accurate. Curved walls can be set out with a trammel, which is simply a batten pivoted on a wooden peg driven into the ground at the striking point of the curve (*Figure 1.6*). An alternative is to make a template out of timber (*Figure 1.7*). The curves are cut out of wide boards about 25 mm (1 in) thick. These are joined together and braced with 50 mm or 75 mm (2 in or 3 in) wide struts. A template can only

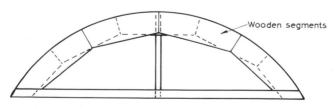

Figure 1.7. Wooden template for checking curved walls

19

provide the outer curve pattern for checking and adjusting the brickwork. A trammel can have all the setting out lines marked on it – the trench width, concrete width if different from the trench width, outer face of a cavity wall and the inner face of the cavity wall.

A trammel is only as accurate as the positioning of the axis peg, which must be perfectly plumb. The higher the peg the more movement will take place making the shape of the curve vary. A trammel is therefore best used in the early stages for setting out the ground and guiding the brickwork up to damp proof course level. From that point it would be better to use a wooden template to ensure the correct shape of the curve.

Foundations

The depth below ground level to which the foundation trenches should be dug depends both on the load to be imposed and on the type of ground to be found below the site. On large building sites, soil investigation by test boring is undertaken and from the results the required depth is calculated.

Loads are not excessive in small domestic buildings and the foundation depth is usually indicated on the plans and then the condition of the subsoil is checked by the Building Control Officer when the trenches have been dug. In all cases, the foundations must be taken to a depth where the earth is not affected by changes in the weather. They must be deeper than the level penetrated by surface water which saturates the ground and then disperses fairly quickly, partly by natural drainage and partly by evaporation. This level of earth is affected by the drying effect of hot sunshine and drought.

Deeper down, below the level to which frost generally penetrates, the subsoil is much more stable and is subject to less movement, it can therefore be relied on to support calculated loads. In general the depth is about 1.5 m (4 ft 6 in) in clay and decreases as the proportion of gravel increases. In firm gravel the foundation depth would be a minimum of 600 mm (2 ft). Soil is in fact graded and the classifications are:

(1) Rock: not inferior to sandstone, limestone or firm chalk; this would need a mechanical pick for excavation.

(2) Compact gravel or sand: this would need at least a hand pickaxe for excavation.

(3) Stiff clay or sandy clay: this also needs a pickaxe for excavation. It is too hard to be moulded with the hands.

(4) Firm clay and sandy clay: this can just be moulded by hand and can be excavated with a spade.

(5) Loose sand, loose silty sand and loose clayed sand: can be excavated with a spade.

(6) Soft silt, soft clay and soft silty clay: fairly easily moulded by hand and is easily excavated.

(7) Very soft silt, very soft clay, very soft sandy clay and very soft silty clay: in winter conditions this soil exudes between the fingers when a sample is squeezed in the fist.

Compact, well graded, sands and gravel-sand mixtures can be expected to carry from four to six tons per square foot. Loose soils of this type could be expected to carry only two to four tons per square foot. Stiff clays could also carry two to four tons per square foot. Firm and sandy clays could be expected to carry one to two tons per square foot.

A typical two-storey house of about 1000 ft^2 floor area with brick cavity wall construction, timber floors and tiled roof is considered to weigh about 100 tons. The load per lineal foot on the front and back walls at ground level is about 0.8 tons. For the party wall it is about 1.5 tons and for the gable walls, it is about 1.2 tons.

It can be seen therefore that provided that the foundations are dug to a depth where they will not be affected by the swelling, shrinking or freezing of the subsoil, most soils (except for made up loose ground and types 5, 6 and 7 or other unstable soils), can support the average dwelling house without resorting to special constructions.

For a grade 4 soil (firm clay or sandy clay) the required width of concrete would be 600 mm (24 in) to support 1½ tons per lineal foot, or 750 mm (30 in) to support 1¾ tons. As this is about the maximum load for house foundations it can be seen that the generally accepted width of 600 mm (24 in) for the concrete foundation is adequate all around the building on most subsoils.

One rule-of-thumb method of determining the width of the foundation concrete is to make it twice the width of the wall it supports (*Figure 1.8*), which again works out about right at not

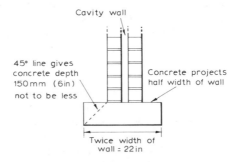

Figure 1.8. Rule-of-thumb method of determining the width and depth of a concrete foundation

less than 559 mm (22 in) for a 279 mm (11 in) cavity wall. The thickness of the concrete is determined by making a scale drawing of a section through the wall and then drawing a line at 45 degrees from the face of the brickwork down through the concrete. Where this line meets the front edge of the concrete denotes the depth or thickness required (Figure 1.8). However, the concrete must never be less than 150 mm (6 in) thick; also the depth of the concrete should be at least equal to the amount that it projects beyond the face of the brickwork.

Levelling the bottom of the trenches can be carried out with the boning rods, and pegs are driven into the bottom of the trenches to mark the thickness of the concrete. These pegs are also levelled with the boning rods.

The top of the pegs in the trenches represents the top of the concrete foundation. So if the base of the foundation is to be 1224 mm (4 ft) below datum level and the concrete is to be 150 mm (6 in) thick, then the top of the peg will have to be 1067 mm (3ft 6in) below the datum level. A straight edge board is packed up level across the trench from the datum peg and beneath it a peg is driven into the bottom of the trench until the top of this peg is exactly 1067 mm (3ft 6in) below the bottom edge of the straight edge (*Figure 1.9*).

Another peg is then driven into the bottom of the trench as far from the first one as the length of the straight edge will allow and the top of this peg is brought to the same level as the first one. This procedure is carried out from one end of the foundation trenches to the other and right around the building.

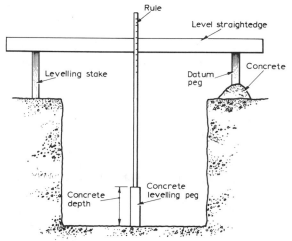

Figure 1.9. Measuring the depth below the datum line

The bottom of the trench is then carefully dug out level to 150 mm (6 in) below the tops of the pegs. The sides of the trenches must be vertical and when all the loose material has been cleaned from the bottom of the trenches, the concrete is poured. No hardcore is ever put into the foundations for walls. The concrete is placed direcly on to the prepared ground.

The concrete mix to use for the foundations is 1:2½:4. That is one part cement, two and a half parts sand and four parts coarse aggregate. The sand should be 'sharp' not the soft building sand used for mortar. It is most important that the materials for concrete making are kept clean, they should not just be dumped on the soft earth where they will pick up dirt. Sand and gravel are washed at the pits and should be kept on a prepared base. Wooden boards will do for small quantities, but large quantities need a base made of weak concrete. Corrugated iron or wooden boards can be used for the sides of the enclosure.

The coarse aggregate can be either gravel or crushed stone which varies in size from 4.5 mm ($\frac{3}{16}$ in) to 19 mm ($\frac{3}{4}$ in). In some parts of the country, especially where there are quarries providing crushed stone, it is possible to get 'all-in' ballast. This is a combined aggregate which can be used where the uniformity of the concrete is not of any importance, such as garden wall foundations, paths and bases for garden sheds. For house foundations and other important work separate aggregates which can be accurately measured to exact proportions must be used.

Use only enough water to make the mix workable so that it can be placed in the trenches and compacted without leaving large air-holes at the sides of the trench. The concrete is not just dumped into the trench and left. It is laid carefully in layers about 100 mm (4 in) thick and each layer is tamped or prodded with a length of timber to compact it. On large building sites this is done with a poker vibrator which shakes the concrete down into a solid mass.

The top of the concrete is tamped level with the top of the pegs, using a straight edge. The pegs are pulled out and the holes filled in. When the concrete has cured sufficiently, bricklaying can start. Below ground brickwork is solid, or if cavity walls are being built the cavity must be filled up to ground level. Ideally, the top of this filling is sloped to the outside face of the wall and one or two open joints are left in the brickwork as weep-holes to let out any water which may collect at the bottom of the cavity. Foundation brickwork is carried up to not less than 150 mm (6 in) above ground level and at that point a damp proof course is laid.

Solid floors

Where solid floors are to be constructed, the floor area is covered with hardcore consisting of broken bricks and stone, coarse gravel or broken concrete, to within about 75 mm (3 in) of the floor level. This hardcore is well tamped and consolidated and a layer of sand is spread over it to form a base for a polythene damp proof membrane. This should be laid in one piece and can be carried over the inner leaf of the cavity wall to form the damp proof course or it can be turned on to the wall and a felt or other type of damp proof material can be laid on the brickwork (*Figure 1.10*).

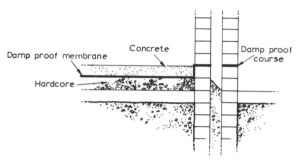

Figure 1.10. Section through a concrete floor

The concrete floor is then laid and tamped with a long board which will reach from wall to wall. There are two ways in which this type of floor can be finished. One is to trowel the concrete smooth and level to form a finished surface on which plastic tiles or other flooring material can be laid. This smoothing is often carried out with a power float which consists of a large rotating metal disc. Without any walls in the way the disc can be moved over the whole of the surface right into corners that would not be accessible if the walls had been erected.

The other method is to lay the base concrete to about 38 mm (1½ in) below the finished level of the floor. Then, when the building is complete and the roof is on and even the glazing completed so that the building is weather tight, a screed of fine concrete is laid and trowelled off by hand.

The mix used for the floor base concrete is the same as that used for the foundations. The mix used for a finishing screed has no coarse aggregate. It is important in both cases that only

PREPARATION AND SETTING OUT

enough water to make the mix workable is used, because not only will excessive water make the concrete weak, it will also cause the finished surface to be permanently dusty.

Load-bearing partition walls are built up from the foundations at the same time as the external walls. They are usually brick or blocks and are bonded into the outer walls. Where suspended timber floors are to be installed (*Figure 1.11*) no hardcore is needed but the ground under the floors is covered with about 50 mm (2 in) of concrete to prevent the growth of vegetation and to prevent the sour smell of damp soil or rotting vegetation arising. This concrete does not have a damp proof membrane under it.

Where suspended wooden floors are constructed, the partition walls are honey-combed below floor level, that is to say 57 mm (2¼ in) spaces are left between the bricks to allow a free passage of air under the floors. Dwarf walls also have to be constructed in the same way to support the joists (*Figure 1.11*) which are only 127 mm (5 in) deep and 50 mm (2 in) thick. These dwarf walls

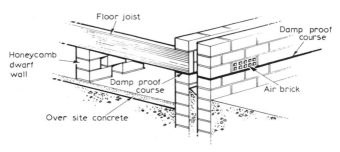

Figure 1.11. Section through a suspended wooden floor

are built at 1828 mm (6 ft) centres. Air bricks are also inserted in the exterior walls to allow fresh air to blow under the floor so that the timber will be protected against rot. Little ducts made of slate or asbestos should be made between the outer leaf of the cavity wall and the inner leaf, because the cavity should be filled with still air (*Figure 1.12*).

These little ducts should also be formed where air bricks have to be inserted in walls to ventilate larders. They are useful too if at a later date the cavity is filled with insulating foam, because they will prevent the ventilation points becoming clogged.

Services for the house should not be forgotten and provision must be made for the entry of water pipes, gas pipes and electricity cables. For this purpose holes are left in the brickwork below ground at the level at which the service will be laid and a

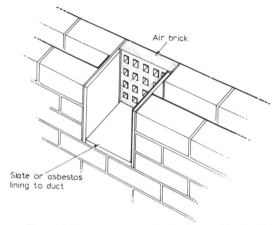

Air brick

Slate or asbestos lining to duct

Figure 1.12. Duct for air vent through cavity wall

small wooden box is constructed inside the building to provide a hole through the hardcore and concrete.

This also applies to the drains, and similar provision is made for the soil pipe. Water services should be brought to the building at least 457 mm (18 in) below the surface of the ground so that they will be below the general frost level.

It is not usual to lay drains until after the heavy foundation work has been completed, because they could be disrupted by heavy lorries carrying the concrete or the hardcore, or the sand and gravel needed for making the concrete on site. In particular, lorries carrying ready mixed concrete should be given a clear and firm access to the site so that they can get right up to the foundation to discharge their load.

2 Brickwork and masonry

The basic size of a brick has remained virtually unchanged for many hundreds of years and its popularity as a building material derives from the ease with which it can be handled by the bricklayer who can hold a brick in one hand and pick up a trowel full of mortar with the other. Bricks also allow the workman to follow his plans with a facility which other materials do not allow.

There is a wide variety of bricks and of names to describe them. The colour, texture and qualities of the bricks depend largely on the clay from which they are made and this varies from area to area. Because of this the names of the bricks often include the name of the area, such as Staffordshire Blue, Accrington Red or London Stock.

Apart from clay bricks there are calcium silicate bricks, sand-lime bricks and flint-lime bricks which are made from a mixture of hydrated lime and sand or crushed stone, or a mixture of both.

In addition to solid bricks there is the type with an indentation known as a frog in either one or both sides. Other bricks have perforations through them, the main object of which is to reduce the weight of the bricks. Standard bricks are rectangular and measure nominally 9 in × 4½ in × 3 in. They are, in fact, made slightly smaller than these measurements in order to allow for the mortar joints. Metric bricks are 225 mm × 112.5 mm × 75 mm nominal size, actual, or work size, 215 mm × 102.5 mm × 65 mm. There are, of course, a number of standard shapes as well; these include bevelled bricks and bullnose bricks, the latter having a rounded corner at either one or both ends (*Figure 2.1*).

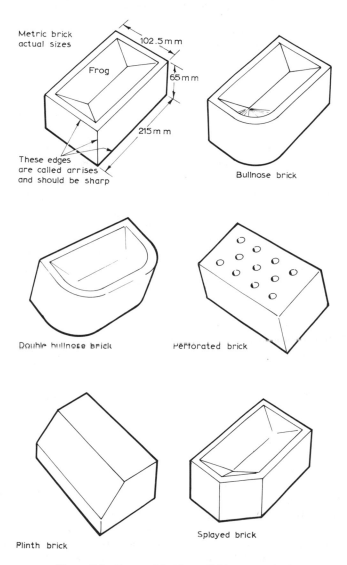

Figure 2.1. Types of brick available as standard

Although the finished product from each type of clay will be different in colour and texture, good bricks of any type will have the same characteristics. They will, for instance, be of the same size and be regular in shape, unless they are of the hand-made rustic type whose charm lies in not only their colour and texture, but also their irregularity. The edges of a good brick should be sharp and when two bricks are knocked together, they should ring with a slightly metallic sound. When broken in two, the inner faces should be uniform in appearance and have a granular texture. When choosing bricks, weathering ability is just as important as the colour and texture.

Commons are bricks which have no particular claim to provide an attractive appearance, but are suitable for general building work. The term is not a guide to quality; many common bricks have excellent properties.

Facing bricks are those which are intended to provide an attractive appearance to the building. They are made in a wide range of colours and textures, some called rustics have the texture imposed by machine. Others like sandfaced have, as their name suggests, sand incorporated on the surface during manufacture.

Flettons is the name given to bricks made from the Lower Oxford clay in the Peterborough, Bedford and Buckingham areas. They are both commons and facings.

Wirecut bricks are those that are made by a process of extruding the clay through a die then cutting it with wire.

Handmade bricks are still produced, although the process is not now entirely by hand, but the bricks still retain a certain attractively uneven finish which in some circumstances is considered to be well worth the high cost.

Clay bricks may also be of the perforated type, that is they may have a number of holes through the full thickness of the bricks. These holes vary considerably in number and size and under British Standard definitions they are called perforated or hollow, dependent on the sizes and total volume of the holes. The perforations do not seem to affect the amount of rain penetrating a wall. There is some reduction in the weight of the wall and a slight increase in the thermal insulation value. Because the holes soon fill with water, unfinished work is vulnerable to saturation and the top of a wall should be covered in wet weather.

Calcium silicate, or sand-lime bricks, made from a mixture of sand, crushed flint, pebbles or rock, or a combination of these materials and hydrated lime are moulded under pressure and hardened in autoclaves where they are subjected to saturated steam under pressure.

These bricks are made in the same sizes as the clay bricks and in the same range of standard shapes such as bullnose, bevelled or squints. They are usually white or off-white, cream or pale pink in colour. Compared with clay bricks they are smooth textured but, of course, the texture varies according to the aggregate used. Facing bricks are made in various pastel shades and are also available with textured surfaces.

Care in handling these bricks is important as the arrises are susceptible to damage, which because of the inherent regularity of the bricks, is very noticeable.

Apart from this their main advantage is the low cost and the accuracy of their size and shape. This makes them easy to lay and to plaster. Being free from soluble salts they do not suffer from efflorescence which can cause the breakdown between the bricks and the plaster.

Calcium silicate bricks tend to shrink as they dry out and this can give rise to cracks in the brickwork. It is therefore important to keep the bricks as dry as possible and to avoid wetting them before laying. If the suction is too great it is better to add more water to the mortar than to soak the bricks.

Long lengths of this type of brickwork should be divided up to permit the movement and dry joints should be made at between 7.5 m (24 ft 6 in) and 9 m (29 ft 6 in) intervals.

The durability of calcium silicate bricks is related to their strength, which is itself variable by adjusting the time the bricks are autoclaved. In general, high compressive strength and low water absorption gives a guide to good frost resistance of clay bricks, but there are some high absorption, low compressive strength bricks which are frost resistant.

BRICKWORK AND MASONRY

Bonding of Bricks

Bond is the arrangement of bricks in the wall so that the vertical joints do not form a continuous straight line. To maintain strength the bricks must be lapped over each other both along the courses and through the thickness of the wall. In housing, cavity walls are now always used and they are formed with bricks laid lengthwise along the wall so that the wall is 112.5 mm (4½ in) or half-brick thick. This is called stretcher bond (*Figure 2.2*). The bond is achieved by starting alternate courses with a half brick. This half brick is formed by the return brick at corners, (*Figure 2.2*), or by cutting a brick in half at the end of a straight wall, or at an opening. Where two walls join, the bond has to be maintained and some cutting has to be undertaken. Pieces of brick are called bats and for bonding at the junction of a half-brick wall two ¾ bats will be needed at alternate courses (*Figure 2.2*).

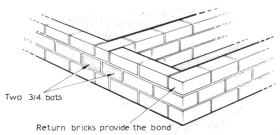

Two 3/4 bats

Return bricks provide the bond

Figure 2.2. Half-brick stretcher bond wall showing use of ¾ bats at junctions and how corners are formed

The two leaves of a cavity wall are held together with metal ties made of galvanised metal and shaped to form a drip at their centres, so that moisture will drip down to the bottom of the cavity and escape through the weep holes provided at the base of the wall. They are spaced at 900 mm (3 ft) centres horizontally and 300 mm (12 in) centres vertically and are also staggered so that they do not form vertical rows.

When 225 mm (9 in) walls are being built, the bonding pattern becomes more complicated and there are a number of patterns

BRICKWORK AND MASONRY

from which to choose. The strongest bond is called English (*Figure 2.3*) and consists of a course of stretcher bricks followed by a course of headers. These are bricks that are laid at right angles so that their ends show at the face of the wall. In order to stagger the vertical joints to provide the bond a brick cut lengthwise has to be placed after the first header of each heading

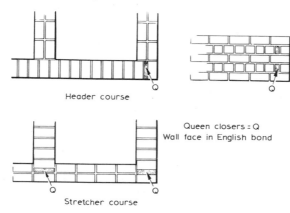

Header course

Queen closers = Q
Wall face in English bond

Stretcher course

Figure 2.3. English bond showing alternate courses and position of Queen closers at corners and junctions

course (*Figure 2.3*). This cut brick is known as a Queen Closer. Closers are bricks which are cut along their length.

Junctions of walls which are built in English bond are not complicated, but they must be carried out correctly or continuous vertical joints will occur in the centre of the wall. They may not be obvious when looking at the face of the brickwork, but they will weaken the structure.

Another bond which is not often used now is Flemish (*Figure 2.4*). This is simpy courses of one stretcher brick followed by one header along the length of the wall. The header must be in the centre of the stretcher of the course above and below and to achieve this a queen closer has to be placed after the first header of successive courses. This bond is weaker than English bond because a straight vertical joint occurs inside the centre of the wall on each side of the headers.

Successive courses in Flemish bond with ends shown stopped

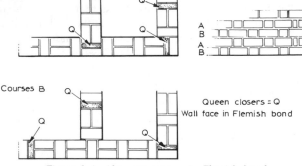

Figure 2.4. Alternate courses in Flemish bond

A variation of English bond, which is more often used, is garden wall bond. This is three courses of stretchers followed by one of headers. Some straight vertical joints occur inside the wall but they are not detrimental. The number of stretcher courses can be increased for simple garden walls where no specific strength is required. It is not usual to exceed six courses of stretchers between the courses of headers. Flemish garden wall bond consists of three stretchers followed by a header throughout each course. A queen closer occurs after the first header in alternate courses.

Gate posts and free-standing piers must be large enough to withstand the strain that will be placed on them; bonding is not their only requirement, as they must have sufficient sectional

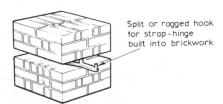

Figure 2.5. Two-brick pier in English bond showing queen closers and a built-in rag-hook for a gate hinge

area or they will break apart at the bed joints, especially at the point where the crook of a hinge is built-in (*Figure 2.5*). The minimum size for the average gate is not less than 330 mm (13 in), that is 1½ brick square (*Figure 2.6*), but a two-brick square pillar 450 mm (1 ft 6 in) square is better and more able to

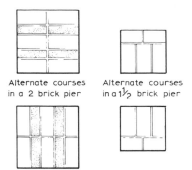

Alternate courses
in a 2 brick pier

Alternate courses
in a 1½ brick pier

Figure 2.6. Alternate courses for 1½ and 2 brick piers in English bond

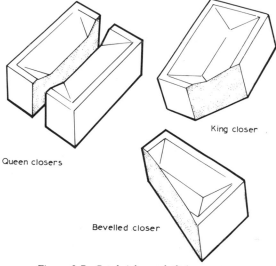

King closer

Queen closers

Bevelled closer

Figure 2.7. Cut bricks and their names

withstand the vibrations of the slamming gate (*Figure 2.6*). A coping or cap should always be provided to protect the top of the brickwork and make the rainwater drip clear.

Bricks are cut to the various shapes (*Figure 2.7*) which are required, by means of a bricklayer's bolster chisel which is like a cold chisel but has a thin blade two to four inches wide and a small club hammer. Final trimming to shape is done with the chisel end of the brick hammer.

Blockwork

Concrete and insulating blocks are made in larger sizes than bricks, the average size being 457 mm × 228 mm (18 in × 9 in) and thicknesses are from 50 mm (2 in) upward. The insulating blocks used for the inner leaf of a cavity wall are 100 mm (4 in) thick and the dimensions must allow each course of blocks to be level with a course of bricks on the outer leaf of the wall. There are usually three courses of bricks to each course of blocks (*Figure 2.8*).

This also applies to the blocks used for partition walls inside the building, as these walls are bonded into the inner leaf of the

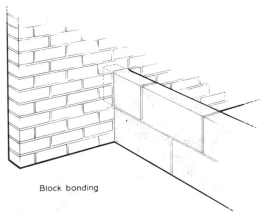

Block bonding

Figure 2.8. Block bonding for brickwork and blockwork

cavity walls whether or not they are bricks or blocks. The method used to bond blocks to a brick wall is to set alternate courses into the brickwork and when the outer walls are being built, holes are left in the brickwork at the appropriate positions so that the internal walls can be bonded-in later (*Figure 2.8*).

Sometimes, stone-faced decorative blocks are used for the outer leaf of cvity walls and these decorative blocks may be of regular size or in random sizes, but whichever type is used they must be made to course up with the inner leaf at regular intervals so that the wall-ties can be inserted in their proper places. These bonding patterns apply to all internal brick or block walls whether load-bearing or non-load-bearing.

Laying the Bricks and Blocks

The art of bricklaying can only be acquired by practice. First, the materials must be prepared properly and placed in convenient positions. The board for the mortar must be reached easily and long walls require a number of boards positioned at intervals which will allow the bricklayer to move along the wall and always be within easy reach of a board full of mortar. Bricks must be stacked in similar convenient positions just an arm's reach from the face of the wall, so that no unnecessary movement is involved. The mortar board is set on a brick at each corner so that it is clear of the ground and the surface of the board and the mortar will be kept clean.

Grasp the trowel firmly with the thumb on the ferrule so that a flexible wrist action is possible. A banana-shaped quantity of mortar is cut out of the heap and picked up on the trowel with an easy sweeping action and is spread on to the wall. Do not make the mistake of laying too thick a bed of mortar as it will only be squeezed out when the brick or block is tapped down to the guide line, with the result that the face of the wall will be stained and the excess mortar will have to be collected on the trowel before it can run further down the wall. With a little practice it should not prove difficult to gauge roughly the right quantity of mortar needed.

The hollow frog of the brick is laid upward, but if hand-made bricks are being laid and they are bent in their length, as they may well be, because this is part of their charm, lay them with their hollow side down, especially where they are used as headers in one-brick or more thick walls.

Engineering bricks are difficult to lay and are not the right type to learn with. Because they are non-absorbent, they tend to 'swim' about in the mortar. This makes it hard to keep them in line with the face of the wall and progress is very slow unless a great deal of skill at bricklaying has been acquired.

In summer, ordinary bricks will need wetting to clear off the dust and to reduce the natural suction of the clay. Engineering bricks do not need this treatment of course. At the end of the work the top of the wall must be covered with sacks in the winter to prevent frost damage and the scaffold boards next to the wall should be turned on edge to prevent rain splashing off it and staining the face of the brickwork.

Brickwork starts by building-up the corners or ends of the walls (*Figure 2.9*). A string-line is set up on the profiles to mark

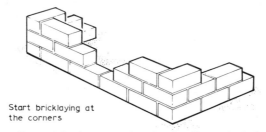

Start bricklaying at the corners

Figure 2.9. Corners and ends of walls are built first

the position of the face of the brickwork. Then mortar is spread on the concrete foundation. A long spirit level is used to plumb down from the string-line and a trowel mark is made to indicate the position of the corner brick.

Three or four more bricks are then laid in each direction, each one being carefully plumbed into position. A straight edge is used to test the front face of the bricks to ensure that as well as being plumb down from the line, they are also in line with each other. Each brick is also levelled on the top surface and again when three or four bricks have been laid they are levelled with the straight edge. Each brick has a small amount of mortar placed on the end to form the vertical or perpendicular joint. These perpends must be fully filled with mortar and not left half empty with just enough mortar at the face to form a pointing finish.

When four or five bricks have been laid on the foundation concrete, the second course of bricks can be laid. The process is exactly the same except that the first brick is laid on the opposite side of the corner, so that a bond is formed by the overlapping bricks.

When the first corner has been raised five or six courses, work can start on the second corner. Plumbing and levelling must be carried out meticulously as the corner brickwork will be used as a guide for the rest of the wall. The common way of holding the string-line for the wall is to wrap it around metal line-pins which

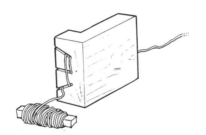

Wooden corner block for holding the line

Figure 2.10. Wooden block for holding the string-line

have a flat blade that can be pushed into the mortar joints. A better way, which is needed when the mortar has set hard, is to make a pair of line blocks (*Figure 2.10*), which are L-shaped pieces of wood with a slot cut in one side for the line to pass through and a couple more to hold the line tight.

The line is fixed so that it is right on the top corner of the brick. When laying bricks to the line always ensure that a trace of daylight can be seen between the brick and the line. This prevents bricks being laid hard against the line, pushing it forward and eventually putting the whole wall out of alignment.

One other tool is essential for good brickwork, and that is a gauge rod. This is a length of timber on which the courses of brickwork are clearly marked. As the corners are built up the rod is tried against them and the courses brought in line with the marks on the rod. By this means each corner is kept the same height and has the same number of courses, because the gauge rod ensures that the mortar joints are the same thickness. If a gauge rod is not used it is possible for the corners to be brought up to the same height, but because of thick mortar joints one could have a course of brick less than the other which would make it impossible for a string-line to be used for lining up the wall between the corners. Building is continued in this manner until all the walls are up to the required height.

Mortar mixes

Mortar is commonly made of cement, lime and sand, the proportions varying, dependent on the type of brick being used. This is because the mortar must never be harder than the bricks. Builder's soft sand is used and if the appearance of the finished work is of importance, ensure that the sand is of a light and even colour, because it will effect the colour of the mortar. Either lime or a proprietary mortar plasticiser can be added to the mix to make it easier to use, or more fatty, as it is called.

A good general mortar mix that is suitable for internal and external walls is composed of 1 part cement :1 part lime : 5 parts sand. If a plasticiser is to be used, simply leave out the lime and add the plasticiser strictly in accordance with the maker's instructions.

The tops of parapets and free-standing walls must be protected. This can be done by laying overhanging coping stones (*Figure 2.11*) or the top of the wall can be finished off with a course of bricks laid on edge, in a slightly harder mortar to resist the frost action in winter. For this a mix of 1 part cement : ½ part lime : 4 parts sand can be used.

This stronger mix can also be used below ground level, especially where the ground is generally waterlogged. Even stronger mixes are used with engineering bricks. With such hard bricks it can be strengthened to 1 part cement : ¼ part lime : 3 parts sand. The amound of water used is largely a matter of common sense, but the mortar should be soft enough to spread easily, but firm enough to be picked up with the trowel. It should not squeeze out and run down the wall when the bricks are bedded into it.

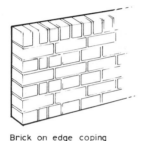

Figure 2.11. Coping for the top of a wall

Brick on edge coping

When using a plasticiser, less water will be needed as the air entrained in the mix reduces the amount necessary, so stop adding water when the mix becomes sufficiently wet to be workable. Do not mix more mortar than you will be able to use in about an hour to an hour and a half. After this time the mortar will have started to set and must not be remixed. On hot days when the sun dries the mortar quickly, an hour may be the limit, but on damp days the mortar may stay workable a little longer.

Mortar must never be stronger than the bricks which are bedded in it, because if it is too strong any natural settlement that takes place can cause cracks through the bricks themselves, whereas softer mortar would let the movement take place along the line of the mortar joints. This would only leave hair-line cracks which would not be detrimental to the wall.

In general, the inner leaf of cavity walls is laid in a 1 : 1 : 5 mix of cement, lime and sand. If calcium silicate bricks are being used then the mix is 1 : 2 : 8, other internal walls are laid in 1 : 2 : 8 mortar whether they are clay or calcium silicate bricks.

External walls are laid in a mix of 1 part cement, 1 part lime and 5 parts sand, but if the walls are sheltered the mix can be 1 : 2 : 8 for calcium silicate bricks. Sills and copings in clay or calcium silicate bricks are laid in a mix of 1 : ½ : 4. Parapets and free-standing walls are built in a 1 : 1 : 5 mix because they are prone to saturation with water and need to be able to withstand frost.

Except for these severe exposure conditions, frost damage to finished buildings is rare. Where the mortar is raked out for subsequent pointing, there may be more risk of frost damage if a strong cement mortar is used for pointing over a weak backing mortar. Risk of frost damage is greatest during the building period and it is essential to take precautions to protect the brickwork from unnecessary wetting and to cover it with sufficient insulation material to protect it from frost. Anti-freeze additives such as those used in concrete should not be used with bricklaying mortar.

For general building there is no need for any fancy finishes, but when building extensions to match existing work and when constructing ornamental brickwork in the garden, there are cement colours that can be added to the mortar to give improved effects. These additives must always be used in accordance with the maker's instructions. Gauge the ingredients accurately if you want to maintain an even colour throughout all the mixes. When the mortar is wet it will be a little different in colour from what it will be when dry, probably a little darker. This means that it will be impossible to match each batch by appearance and newly mixed mortar, when placed against mortar that has started to dry, will be a different colour. These cement colours are obtainable as either powder or liquid.

The mortar joints of the brickwork are finished off in various ways according to the type of building. For a rustic appearance the mortar can be scraped off level with the face of the bricks and left to collect moss and algae.

Structural brickwork of a general kind is given a 'struck' or 'weathered' finish (*Figure 2.12a*). This is done by using the trowel to press the mortar in at the top of the joint so that it slopes slightly towards the face of the wall. By this method a small drip is formed under the top brick and the rain is brought forward by the slope so that it runs down the face of the brick to the next drip, instead of soaking into the mortar.

Among the other ways of pointing the mortar joints is running a piece of pipe about 9 mm (⅜ in) along the joint to form a curved recess (*Figure 2.12b*). Another is to take out the mortar to a depth of not more than 9 mm (⅜ in) (*Figure 2.12c*). This method increases the shadow effect making the mortar joint

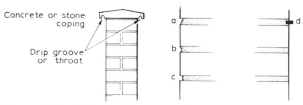

Figure 2.12. Methods of pointing: (a) struck, (b) bucket handle, (c) recessed, (d) tuck pointing, not now in use

stand out more boldly against the bricks, but it also encourages water to stand on the top of the bricks where it can cause damage, especially if it freezes. This type of pointing should therefore only be used in fairly sheltered positions.

For special effects, the mortar is raked out to a depth of not more than 12 mm (½ in) and a mix of coloured mortar is used for pointing to one of the conventional finishes. Although rarely used now, tuck pointing provides an interesting finish. This is a method whereby a coloured mortar is inserted into the mortar joint so that it projects in front of the face of the wall (*Figure 2.12d*). With this method a recess is pressed into the face of the flush mortar joint and then a special tool is used to form a strip of coloured mortar so that it fills the recess and projects a little in front of the wall face.

When preparing pointing mortar, sufficient water is added to the dry-mixed materials to give a stiff doughy consistency. If the mortar is too soft it cannot be handled with the pointing trowel or ironed into the brickwork joints.

Mortar ingredients must be well-mixed before the water is added. Measure out the correct proportion of sand first, then add the lime and mix the two together well. These materials can be mixed in large quantities and left until it is time to make up a new batch of mortar. Then the cement is added in the correct proportion and well mixed until the whole heap is of a uniform colour. Water can then be added slowly while mixing to ensure that the mortar is not made too wet.

Figure 2.13. A Frenchman or pointing knife

Frenchman

Vertical joints are filled first and then the bed joints are filled. Ideally, the ragged edges of the mortar are trimmed off with a tool called a Frenchman. This is simply a thin blade with its end bent at right-angles and filed to a triangle point (*Figure 2.13*). Traditionally it is made of an old table knife, heated so that the blade can be bent at the end. A straight edge is used to guide the tool and it is packed off the brickwork with cork or wood so that the surplus mortar will drop clear of the wall (*Figure 2.14*).

Window and door frames are positioned in the wall when the correct sill height has been reached. The actual brick or concrete sill can be constructed later, in which case the frame is packed up to its required position and is then built into the wall. Metal ties are screwed to the sides of the window and door frames and their

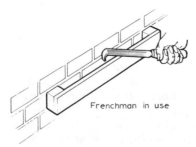

Frenchman in use

Figure 2.14. Using a Frenchman

split ends are built into the bed joints of the brickwork. A vertical damp proof course must be built into the wall where the inner brickwork is returned to close the cavity at door, window or other openings. In exposed positions, the straight joint between the brickwork and the woodwork can be protected from weather by setting the wooden frame in a reveal (*Figure 2.16*).

No wooden frame should carry any of the weight of the wall above the opening, so a lintel must be inserted. This must have a minimum of 150 mm (6 in) bearing at each side of the opening.

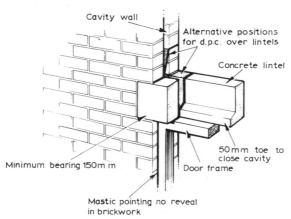

Cavity wall

Alternative positions for d.p.c. over lintels

Concrete lintel

50 mm toe to close cavity

Door frame

Minimum bearing 150m m

Mastic pointing no reveal in brickwork

Figure 2.15. Damp proofing over lintels

It can be made of metal or concrete. Concrete lintels are heavy and large spans have to be cast *in situ*. The metal lintel is most suitable for domestic work and for amateurs, because of its light-weight and because the size and shape are designed to suit the span of the opening.

Where appearance is of no importance, simple square lintels which show on the face of the brickwork can be used (*Figure 2.15*). In order to improve the appearance of the opening a boot lintel can be used (*Figure 2.16*). This has an L-shaped section, the back being as wide as the inner leaf of the wall, 100 mm (4 in) and a reinforced toe at the front takes the outer brickwork and shows only about 75 mm (3 in) at the face. If the lintel is kept back behind the face of the brickwork about 25 mm (1 in) then it will hardly be seen (*Figure 2.16*). The effective load that the lintel is considered to carry is that contained in a 60 degree triangle above it. This, of course, includes any floor joists that may be bearing on the wall in that triangle.

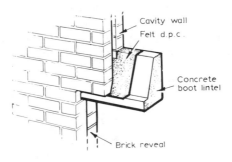

Cavity wall
Felt d.p.c.
Concrete boot lintel
Brick reveal

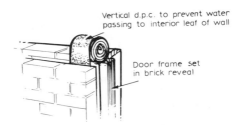

Vertical d.p.c. to prevent water passing to interior leaf of wall

Door frame set in brick reveal

Figure 2.16. Damp proofing course over a boot lintel and the position of damp proofing where the cavity is closed at an opening such as a door frame

Bricklaying can be practised in the garden where the work does not have to be perfect; in fact, the charm of ornamental garden brickwork lies in its imperfections. The uneven courses, chipped bricks and crooked lines have a rustic charm that makes the brickwork seem to belong where it is, especially when moss and algae have become established. This kind of brickwork still needs to be protected against the weather and the inside of a brick planter or a retaining wall should be coated with bitumastic or similar waterproof material to prevent it from becoming, and staying, saturated with water. Open vertical joints must also be left in the lower courses to allow excess water to escape.

The principles for building a coal bunker are the same as those used for building a house; the corners are built up first and the middle of the wall is filled in to a line. The main difference is that the coal bunker does not need to have strip foundations, it can be built up from the concrete floor slab.

A larger structure such as a garden shed should have strip foundations, but it could be built up from the concrete slab if the edges were thickened to take the extra weight.

Brick paths

Apart from building walls, bricks can be used for making paths and for informal gardens they provide a path more in keeping with the style than concrete paving would. The base for laying brick paths is the same as that used for concrete drives and paths. First the vegetation and garden soil have to be removed and although the hardcore sub-base is not needed it can be used to build-up the path to the required level. An alternative is to lay coarse gravel over the area and roll it well to make a firm foundation.

When this base has been rolled firm and solid, about 25 mm (1 in) of sand is laid on it ready for the bricks. Not all bricks are suitable for paths, most of the commons are too soft and it is best to get the advice of the merchant or the makers before buying any bricks.

The face side of bricks makes an attractive path, but if they are laid flat, as in walling, they will cover more ground. An edge restraint is needed because the bricks are only laid in sand, not mortar. The edging is bedded in concrete to hold it in place. If the sand base is levelled and rolled the bricks can be laid straight on to it without any joints being made (*Figure 2.17*). Later sand is brushed over the surface of the path so that it will fill any slightly open joints.

BRICKWORK AND MASONRY

Bricks also lend themselves to pattern making, and instead of straight courses (*Figure 2.17*), herringbone or basket designs can be laid. Herringbone is the most difficult as it needs not only a string-line down the centre of the path to keep the pattern straight, but also a line across the path to keep the pattern level across. This pattern needs a lot of cut bricks too for filling in at the sides of the path.

Figure 2.17. *Patterns and method of laying brick paths*

It is not necessary to level brick paths accurately, because they often look better if they follow the contour of the land. A minimum fall for the paths is 1 in 60, but a more generous fall will help the path to dry out quicker and will also discourage the growth of moss and lichen, which although attractive in many ways, can cause slipperiness.

When bedding the bricks, they should first be set up about 6 mm (¼ in) above the finished level of the path so that they can be tapped down. A straight edge is used to keep the courses in line and to keep the surface reasonably level. A popular form of edging for these paths is to set bricks at an angle of 30 to 45 degrees in concrete down the sides. It takes about 50 metric bricks to lay a square metre when laid flat and about 60 when they are laid on their sides. A square yard takes about 40 imperial size bricks laid flat and about 48 when they are laid on their sides.

Paths near the house must not cover the air bricks which ventilate wooden floors. They must always be at least 150 mm (6 in) below the damp proof course level.

Tools for bricklaying

Not a lot of tools are needed for simple bricklaying (*Figure 2.18*), but as with any other craft, it pays to buy the best that you can afford. The bricklaying trowel should be as large as you can handle. If you are going to do a lot of bricklaying, then learn to use a professional bricklayer's size of trowel, but if you are not doing much of the work you can make do with a smaller trowel, it just means that you will probably work much slower.

A club hammer is needed for use with the bolster for cutting the bricks. Do not get one which is too heavy as it will only tire your wrists. Do not try to make do with the brick hammer, its face is too small and you will hit your hands as often as you hit the end of the bolster. The brick hammer is very useful for trimming bricks to fit in awkward places. A long string-line and metal pins to hold it in place are essential for keeping the courses straight and level. Wooden blocks are better for most purposes.

If a large bricklaying trowel is being used, a smaller trowel will be needed for pointing. You will also need a wooden rule as well as a tape measure for setting out. A long spirit level will be needed for plumbing the work and a short one for levelling individual bricks. A straight edge or two, and a hawk or hand-board will be needed for holding the mortar when

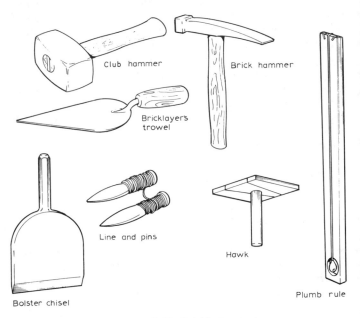

Figure 2.18. Bricklaying tools

pointing. In place of the long spirit level a straight edge and plumb-bob can be used. This is slower than the spirit level as it is affected by the wind when used out of doors, but when used properly it is very accurate.

Finally, keep the tools clean; clean tools make a clean job. A little time spent at the end of the day cleaning tools and equipment will pay off when the next day's work is started.

3 Panelling and sheet materials

There are some finishes which can be classed as part of the structure of a building because they are fixed more easily if they are considered at the design stage and provision for fixing them is made during the construction of the building. If walls are to be panelled instead of plastered, provision for fixing the battens or grounds can be made by building pallets into the joints of the brickwork at regular intervals.

These pallets are made of preservative treated softwood and are about 100 mm (4 in) square. They are the thickness of the mortar joint which will be about 10 mm (⅜ in). It is usual to bed them so that the nails will be driven into the side and not the end grain. They should be made of rough sawn timber to provide a grip in the brickwork.

The alternative to building-in these pallets is to plug the wall after the building has been completed and this can be a long and tedious task. Masonry bits in electric drills can be used, or even the hardened steel masonry pins driven into the wall by hammering or by fixing guns which fire the hardened masonry nails into the brickwork. All this extra work can be avoided if the type of finish to be used is considered at the design stage and proper provision is made during construction.

Grounds, as these supporting battens are called, are usually fixed horizontally, but where wide boards are to be fixed, such as sheets of decorative plywood, vertical grounds will be needed at the vertical joint of the boards. When fixed, the grounds must be plumb and straight, so that it will be necessary to pack them at the nailing points, using a straightedge and a string-line to keep them all in line.

Extra vertical grounds will be needed around window and door openings as well as at angles. The finish at external angles can be a problem when plywood or hardboard sheets are used, because the edge of one of the boards would show unless the two boards were mitred together. This would hardly be practical, as getting a perfect mitre on such thin material over such a long length would take a very great deal of time and patience.

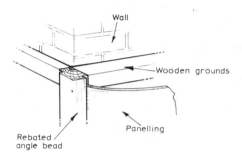

Figure 3.1. The corner treatment of wooden panelling, showing wooden grounds for holding the panelling and the rebated corner bead

The easiest way of overcoming the problem would be to fix a cover strip at the corners, but this may not be acceptable where the rest of the finish is flush. An alternative is to fit an angle bead, either square edged or rebated, so that the decorative sheeting has something to butt up against (*Figure 3.1*). Internal angles do not present the same problem as one board butts against the other.

Spacing between the grounds depends, of course, on the thickness of the sheets being used and as a rough guide the spaces for hardboard would be not more than 400 mm (16 in) centres. Plywood up to 6 mm (¼ in) thick would need spacings of not more than 450 mm (18 in) to 600 mm (2 ft) centres.

It is best if sheet materials are fixed with adhesive, because nails are likely to show, however carefully they are punched below the surface and then filled with a coloured filler. Matchboarding and similar tongued and grooved boardings are nailed through the tongue edge into the grounds, so that the grooved edged of the next board will cover the nail head.

The spaces between the grounds can be filled with either thermal or acoustic insulation. This can be glass-fibre mat or mineral fibre mat, in which case it will need fixing to the battens to hold it in place otherwise it will eventually slide down to the bottom of the cavity. An alternative for thermal insulation is sheets of expanded polystyrene, which is, of course, stiff enough to hold itself in place once the boards have been fixed.

Ideally, the panelling would be made in the more traditional form of a framework with each panel fitting into grooves. This offers more scope for secret fixings. If one or two of the panels are left out at the outer edge of the framework, then the fixing screws can be inserted through the rebates of these panels or the angles can be screwed together through the edge of the frame

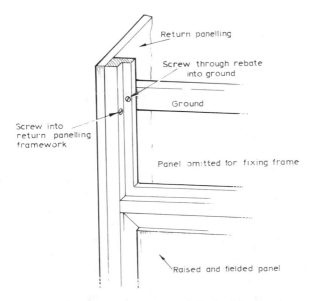

Figure 3.2. Framed-up panelling can be fixed by screwing through the rebate into the grounds and covering the screws by beading the loose panel into place

(*Figure 3.2*). When the whole frame has been fixed, the loose panels are then fitted into the rebates and beaded into place.

Sheet materials are usually faced with hardwood veneers or they have a printed woodgrain pattern to resemble hardwoods, and can have the joints covered (*Figure 3.3*). Close boarding such as matchboard is usually carried out in softwood such as pine or redwood. In this case the knots seem to have some decorative value. Cedar planking and parana pine planking are two other materials which can be used to provide a permanent interior finish, but they have rather straight grain and can be monotonous if used over too large an area.

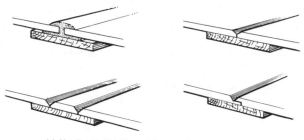

Methods of jointing plain panels

Figure 3.3. Treatments of panel joints

Plastic panelling imitating mediaeval or other historic mouldings can be obtained, along with imitation oak beams, nearly all of which require some form of grounds for fixing them to the walls. Provision made for these fixings during construction will save much time after the structure has been completed; it only takes a little care in setting out.

Where a wall is to be panelled, the door linings must be wide enough to come flush with the finished panels or the framework if the panels are in the traditional framing (*Figure 3.4*). Then the architrave will fit over the joint between the lining or door frame and the panelling in the same way as it is used to mask the joint between the lining and the plaster.

Sheet plastics nearly always have to be fixed by adhesive, as nails would spoil the finished surface. Joints in these hard-surfaced materials are rarely successful and some form of plastic, metal or wooden moulding has to be used as a cover strip. It is better to arrange the flat areas so that they can each be covered with one complete piece of decorative material so that no joints will be needed.

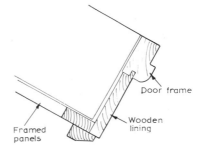

Figure 3.4. Treatment of wooden panelling at a door or window reveal

Where pre-finished panels or timber are being used, secret fixings are called for, if the appearance is not to be spoiled. In many cases the framing can be screwed to the grounds with the heads of the screws sunk below the surface and the hole filled in with a wooden pellet. However carefully the colour and grain of the timber is matched, the pellet will show, if the finish is to be varnish. This method only works successfully when the finish is to be paint.

Among the secret fixing methods, two, nailing through the tongue of the leading edge of matchboarding, and screwing or nailing through rebates before fixing a panel with beads, have already been mentioned. Slot screwing (*Figure 3.5*) is another method, and this is done by driving stout screws into the grounds leaving the heads of the screws projecting about 10 mm (⅜ in).

Figure 3.5. Screw and slot for secret fixing by slot screwing

A dab of paint is applied to the heads of the screws and while it is still wet the moulding to be fixed is packed up about 25 mm (1 in) off the floor and is then pressed against the screw heads so that their positions will be marked on the back.

Holes are then bored at these points about 12 mm (½ in) deep and slightly larger than the diameter of the screw heads. Next, a gauge is made by driving a screw into a block of hardwood allowing it to project exactly the same amount as the screws in the grounds. A slot equal to the width of the shank of the screws is cut upward from the hole in the back of the moulding, so that the hole now resembles an upside-down key hole (*Figure 3.5*). The gauge is put into the hole and driven along the slot so that the head of the screw cuts a dovetail shaped groove in exactly the same position in each of the slots.

The screws in the grounds are given an extra half-turn more and the moulding is placed on the screw heads and driven down to the floor, the screw heads following the grooves in the slots will draw the moulding tightly to the wall. This method of secret fixing is useful for cover strips, architraves and other mouldings as well as for decorative wooden brackets which are not intended to carry any weight.

If skirting boards are fixed to wooden grounds at the top and bottom edges, then the space between can be used as ducting for electric cables or for pipework. These grounds are, of course, fixed before plastering the wall and they are placed just below the top edge of the skirting so that the skirting will cover the joint between the ground and the plaster. Fixing wooden grounds prior to plastering is the best way of providing fixing points for most fittings as there is no need for messy drilling and plugging of the finished wall surface and the nails or screws used for the fitting can be placed at any point along the grounds.

Where pallets are not built into the wall the brickwork joints can be raked out while the mortar is still fairly soft. Where concrete is being cast, dovetail blocks are set into it at the required points (*Figure 3.6*). For instance, lintels over windows need provision for curtain track and casting these blocks into the concrete is a quicker and easier way of providing the fixing points than drilling the hardened concrete after the structure is

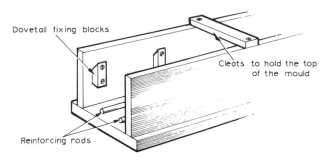

Figure 3.6. Dovetail wooden blocks fixed inside a lintel mould box so that they will be retained in the concrete as fixing points for curtain track or other equipment

complete would be. After the wall is plastered the blocks can be located either by careful measurement or by probing at the approximate place using a thin nail or bradawl. Another method of ensuring that the little blocks are not lost is to drive a small nail partly into them before the wall is plastered. The nail is left protruding through the finished plaster so that the fixing block can be found.

Careful locating of the fixing points will enable decorative fittings to be screwed directly to the wall instead of having to have a wooden strip fitted first. The metal or plastic rose can then be positioned so that the fitting will be in the exact place that it is required as well as being upright. It is because drills often wander out of position when holes are being made in walls, causing fixing plates to be off-centre or even making it impossible to use all the available screw holes, that making early provision for the fixtures and fittings is so important.

Where possible, shelf bearers and cupboard framing are fixed before plastering, as this enables a neater finish to be made without resorting to cover strips or scribing which are needed when the frames are fixed after the plastering is complete.

All the woodwork and preparation carried out before plastering the walls is called the first fixing. Door linings are made up by cutting housings in the head-piece to take the jambs (*Figure 3.7*).

These are then fixed to the wooden plugs or pallets built into the door openings. The linings project at each side of the brickwork, by the thickness of the plaster. They must be levelled and plumbed carefully as well as being checked with a straight edge and packed out accordingly. Where only narrow skirtings are

Barefaced tongue

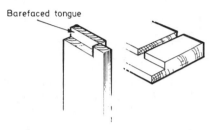

Figure 3.7. How a door casting head is trenched to take the tongue of the jamb

being fixed and grounds are not used, and there are no pallets, the brickwork has to be plugged at intervals using wide plugs to take nails at the top and bottom edge of the skirting. These plugs are cut off so that they project from the wall the thickness of the plaster, a straightedge being used to ensure that they are all in line.

Sound insulation

Complete sound proofing of a structure is very difficult and has to be considered at the design stage so that provision can be made to have main parts of the building disconnected from each other to prevent sound being carried through the structure. Soundproofing an existing building is impossible. Mass or weight is the best means of absorbing sound energy and therefore major structural alterations would be necessary, but even then the amount of sound reduction may not justify the amount of money spent.

It is easier to deal with noise problems at the source and by this means maximum effect at minimum cost is possible. For example, a loud television or record player can be muted as far as the neighbours are concerned by the extensive use of carpets and underlays with heavy curtains and tapestry or acoustic tiles on the walls, as well as acoustic tiles on the ceilings. In new property or extensions these materials can be augmented by sound insulation quilt under the floors and above the ceilings.

Soft furnishings will not eliminate the noise, but will reduce the reverberation so that the airborne sound is reduced. The effect can be compared to a 100 watt electric light bulb in a room painted white and the same bulb in the same room painted black. In the first room the light would be strong and clear as it would be bounced off the walls and ceiling to be reused. In the black room the light would be absorbed to a large extent when it reached the walls and there would be little bounce back so that the room would appear to be dimly lit.

Concrete, brick and stone are materials which are suitable for use as sound barriers. Additional walls built beside party walls would help to reduce sound transmission, but to be really effective they would have to be totally disconnected from the existing structure because sound travels through the actual structure of the building (*Figure 3.8*) until it reaches either a break or a soft absorbent material. Wire ties such as those used

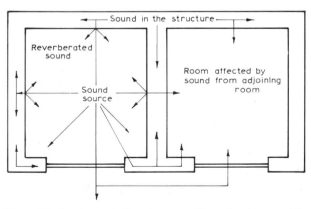

Figure 3.8. A noise created in one room will reverberate around the walls as well as get into the structure and travel to the next room

in cavity walls will transmit the sound from one leaf of a wall to the other. Bricks bonded into party or partition walls also carry the sound through the structure.

Detached walls are not often possible in existing houses and the best that can be done is to increase the mass of the party wall by lining it with one or two layers of 12 mm (½ in) plasterboard. This can be done by the dry lining method already explained in Chapter 6, or the wall can be battened and the plasterboard nailed to it. If this latter method is used, then sound absorbing quilt can be put up between the battens (*Figure 3.9*).

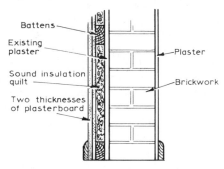

Battens

Existing plaster

Sound insulation quilt

Two thicknesses of plasterboard

Plaster

Brickwork

Figure 3.9. Sound insulation on a wall. It is more effective in the room where the sound is being generated

Any soundproofing treatment must be carried out over the whole of the party wall, it is not possible to soundproof just one room. Even the triangle of the gable in the roof space has to be treated. Floor boards next to the party wall should be raised so that the ends of the joists can be reached and any spaces at the sides of them filled with mortar.

Another method of using plasterboard to reduce sound transference is to form a hanging curtain wall (*Figure 3.10*). This would be better at preventing sound escaping from a music room than it would be preventing sound entering a room from an outside source.

First the existing wall is lined with 12 mm (½ in) soft fibre insulating board. Then a framework of 50 mm (2 in) square timber is made large enough to cover the whole of the wall. This framework is hung on to a timber fixed near the top of the wall. A strip of Neoprene rubber or thick felt is placed between the two lengths of timber, and the bottom of the frame is restrained by being screwed to the wall at about 1 m centres. The framework is clad with 12 mm (½ in) plasterboard. It does not touch the floor or the ceiling. A strip of felt is placed at the top and bottom of the framework. This curtain with the minimum

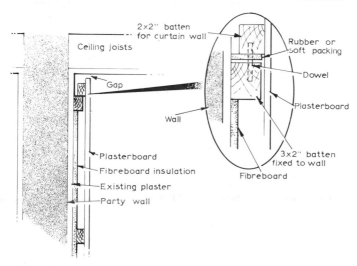

Figure 3.10. A framework of timber being used to support plasterboard and hung from a batten fixed to the top of the existing wall to form a kind of curtain

fastenings to the wall will absorb much of the sound generated within the room. It can be decorated like the rest of the walls and it will therefore not be obvious that it is different from the rest of the walls of the room.

Soundproofing floors can be a problem and the old-fashioned pugging with dry sand on boards fixed about half way up the joists cannot be carried out in existing floors as the extra weight would make it necessary to increase the size of the joists. A floating floor can be constructed in new buildings (*Figure 3.11*) by battening large areas of the flooring into sections like trestle-table tops. Battens are fixed at the same centres as the joists; they are the same width as the joists and are 38 mm (1½ in) thick. The floorboards have to be cramped and nailed to

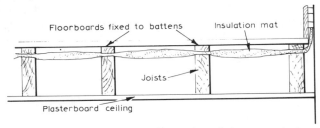

Figure 3.11. A loose or floating floor with insulation mat under it to reduce sound getting into floor joists

them and when complete the sections are placed in position on the top of a glass fibre blanket, which is laid over the joists. These sections are not nailed to the joists, but are held in place by the skirting board which is packed off the wall to allow the glass fibre blanket to go behind it. The bottom edge of the skirting has a strip of felt or rubber attached to it to help break the connection between the floor and the wall which would otherwise carry the sound.

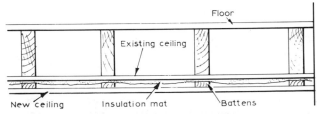

Figure 3.12. Sound insulation mat applied to a ceiling

If the extra height can be accommodated, an existing floor can be treated in this manner and where the floor cannot be treated the ceiling below can be treated by applying the glass fibre quilt to the ceiling and holding it in place with battens on to which a new plasterboard ceiling is attached (*Figure 3.12*).

Soundproofing between floors of new buildings can be achieved by constructing a separate ceiling with joists set between the floor joists so that they do not touch each other and between these joists is threaded the soundproofing quilting (*Figure 3.13*). Extra quilt can also be battened under the ceiling joists before the plasterboard is fixed and also to the top of the floor joists before the boards are fixed. A floating floor can also be used.

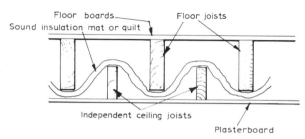

Figure 3.13. Sound insulation between a suspended ceiling and independent floor joists

These soundproofing precautions will have their effects minimised if the structure of the building itself is not designed with soundproofing in mind, with walls detached from each other as far as possible and soundproofing in partition walls.

Soundproofing in partitions is very much the same as for floors. The face of the wall can be lined with soundproofing quilt and battened for plasterboard, or the studs of a timber wall can be staggered so that the quilt can be threaded between them. Again as with ceilings, extra quilt can be battened to the studs before the plasterboard is nailed on to them. Felt or strips of quilt should also be fixed between the ends of the partition walls and the main structure.

Doors and door frames are best insulated by weight. A 50 mm (2 in) thick flush door can be filled with compressed straw. Sand could be used, but it would tend to settle to the bottom and leave a space at the top which would allow the sound to pass through and reduce the value of the door. Also, the sand could make the door too heavy to be practical. These heavy doors must be hung on at least three 100 mm (4 in) butt hinges and they should have the minimum joint all round. Almost any form of weather stripping can be used to help seal the gap.

The doors are hung in frames, not on linings. The frames have to be isolated as far as possible from the rest of the structure and this is done by rebating the back of the jambs so that the partition, whether timber or brick, will fit into the groove. A strip of felt is then fitted into the bottom of the groove and the frame is fixed to the floor and the ceiling with, if possible, no fixings into the partition. This may not be possible on the hanging side because of the weight of the door, which would bow the frame jamb if it were not secured. Heavier doors can be hung in existing property, but there is always the problem of the extra weight where the previous doors have been hung on thin linings.

Soundproofing windows is a different matter; they can be treated at any time either during construction of the building or after it is completed. The thermal insulation of windows has a marked effect on the sound insulation. Those windows which have been fitted with factory-sealed double glazing make a noticeable reduction in the amount of sound entering the rooms from outside. Secondary windows have the same effect, the extent to which they reduce the sound being dependent on the type of inner glazing used, and the frame into which it is fitted.

For soundproofing, the secondary frame should be fitted so that there is a space of at least 150 mm (6 in) between the two panes of glass. The reveal between the windows is lined with acoustic tile or similar material and if the two panes of glass are of different weights a slight increase in effectiveness will be made. Another aid to increasing effectiveness is to alter the plane of one of the windows. Angling it by making the top of the space a bit wider than the bottom is one way of doing this without any structural problems. Secondary windows can be linked to the main exterior sashes so that the two can be opened together. Opening the window does, of course, totally destroy the soundproofing effect, but on closing the windows they should be completely sealed to keep the sound out.

In general, sound insulation is dependent on a number of design factors and the materials used do not matter very much, the most influential factor being the weight of the structure, not just of the party wall but of the flanking walls and the floors. One exception is the double-leaf wall which gives an insulation value in excess of its weight contribution.

Attention to detail is important and this is demonstrated by the fact that a wet plastered wall has a better soundproofing value than a dry construction, because the wet plaster will get into every crack sealing it effectively and stopping sound getting through by closing all air paths.

Cavities between leaves of walls are effective barriers and if possible should be 230 mm (9 in) wide. An increase in efficiency can be obtained if the cavity is filled with a sound absorbent material and for this almost any glass wool or mineral wool quilt will do. The quilt should be at least 25 mm (1 in) thick and the paper lining should be limited to one side of the quilt only. Its actual position in the cavity is not important.

Lead is a material that offers both the limp characteristics which will give better than normal sound insulation and the weight that is necessary. Where the expense has been justified it has been used to good effect.

Much depends on the frequency of the sounds which have to be stopped; for instance, an independent ceiling is not very effective for stopping impact noise or low-frequency noise. A lightweight suspended ceiling would however improve the sound insulation against high-frequency noise. It is at the low frequencies that timber joists are mainly deficient and more weight is needed to remedy the deficiency.

Other points of sound transference are pipes and pipe ducts. Where possible there should be baffles along the ducting to stop or absorb the sound. All holes where the pipes enter the duct should be filled to prevent sounds entering or escaping. Cisterns are particularly noisy fittings, and the installation of siphonic models is the best method of reducing the noise. Lagging pipes to protect them from frost also helps to reduce the noise. Plumbing is a particularly noisy service in a house and there is little that can be done to quieten it other than fit the quieter units.

4 Roofs

Roofs are seen in a great variety of shapes and are made from an equally wide variety of materials. There are pitched roofs, mono-pitched roofs, flat roofs, gable roofs and hipped roofs; they can be covered with felt, asbestos, slate, clay tiles, concrete tiles and translucent plastic. Flat or low pitched roofs can be hidden behind parapets and gable or hipped roofs can have deep overhanging eaves, in fact, the whole appearance of a house can be altered by the design of the roof.

Correct detailing and careful workmanship are needed if gutters behind parapet walls are not to give trouble and constructing a hipped roof requires an understanding of roofing geometry if the double angle cuts around the hips are to be accurate.

Flat roofs which have in fact got a slight fall, and mono-pitched roofs, can overhang the building on all sides so that there is no need for fancy flashings to cover the joint between the roof and the walls.

Mono-pitched roofs are usually covered with corrugated asbestos, corrugated iron or even corrugated translucent plastic. These sheet materials are laid on to purlins which span the width of the building at right angles to the pitch or slope. The distance apart for these timbers depends very much on the type of sheeting being used. Sheets 1800 mm (6 ft) long generally need a purlin in the middle as well as one at the top and the bottom. Longer sheets would need two purlins spaced out along the length. Neither asbestos nor plastic sheets are safe to walk on without first placing a plank on them to span the purlins. Corrugated iron can be walked on, but it is liable to bend.

Roof covering starts at the eaves allowing enough overhang for the sheeting to reach nearly halfway into the gutter. One corrugation is generally sufficient side lap, but on exposed sites two can be given. End overlap should not be less than 150 mm (6 in).

Because corrugated iron is thin, it is simply laid on the purlins and nailed into place. Where the four corners of the sheets overlap there is no need for cutting, just hammer the nail harder so that it goes through. Thick materials like asbestos and plastic must be mitred. The sheets cannot be piled up at the corners or there will be spaces beneath them to let the rain through.

The first sheet is laid as it is, with no cutting, but all the following ones have to be mitred and this cut is the same length as the overlap and the same width as the side lap (*Figure 4.1*).

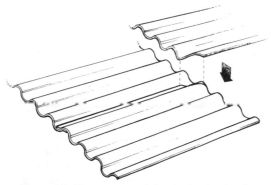

Figure 4.1. How corrugated sheeting is mitred at the top and bottom corners where four sheets meet at a purlin

After the first sheet has been laid the second sheet is laid with its over-lapping edge mitred at the top corner. The next sheet is mitred in the same way and so on to the end of the row. On the next row above, the bottom corner of the sheet is mitred to match the cut on the sheet below. If there is to be a third row, the second row of sheeting will need to be mitred at the top as well as the bottom, but at the opposite corner to the bottom mitre. The top row of sheets do not need mitring at the top, of course.

Specially shaped foam filling is made to fit under the corrugations at the eaves. Alternatively, the openings can be filled with sand and cement mortar. A strip or fillet of sand and cement is applied along the wall under the sides of the sheeting to make a neat finish where the brickwork is cut at an angle under the roofing.

The purlins have metal straps screwed to them with the ends built into the brickwork about 600 mm (2 ft) down the inside of the building. These straps are to hold the roof against wind damage. It is never a good idea to let water drip off a roof so a gutter and some form of drainage must be provided.

Both asbestos and plastic roofing has to be drilled for the fixing nails or screws. These materials can also be fixed to angle-iron purlins by using hook bolts. These bolts must not be overtightened or the sheets will crack.

Boarded and felted roofs can be either flat or mono-pitched, but the treatment is the same. Tiles cannot be used on roofs of less than 22 degree pitch and not all types of tiles are suitable for such a low pitch, so enquiries must be made before deciding to tile a low-pitched roof.

Joists for flat roofs need to be about the same size as those for floors and a table of sizes appears in the Building Regulations. This is because of the weight of snow that may have to be supported. Boarding can be tongued and grooved or square edged. It can be either roughsawn or planed. The roof of a habitable extension would be in planed boarding or chipboard, in order to provide a good surface on which to apply the felt. A garage or shed roof could be clad with rough timber as it would not be so important to have a smooth finish.

The joists must be well anchored down and are set at 400 mm (16 in) centres so that a ceiling of plasterboard or other sheet material can be fixed if required. Herringbone bridging is also required for spans of over 2 m (6ft 6 in). The amount of fall required is a minimum of 1 : 60 which is 50 mm (2 in) in 3 m (10 ft). The fall should not be too slight, because if any settlement takes place, the fall could be reversed.

Tapered fillets called firring pieces are nailed to the top of the roofing joists to provide the fall. If the joists are at right angles to the roof fall, then battens reducing in size for each joist are used. The roofing boards are nailed through these firring pieces.

A wide board or fascia is used to cover the ends of the joists and the roof boarding projects over this fascia to almost halfway over the gutter. The first layer of felt is usually nailed in place with galvanised clout nails and the following layers are laid in either hot or cold laid bitumen. The top layer is mineral faced.

As felt cracks fairly easily it is best to remove all sharp edges of the boards and to provide an angle fillet at the junction between the roof and the adjoining walls. This includes the parapets if there are any.

It is easier to allow the roof to overhang the building on as many sides as possible, because the flashing needed at the wall junction creates a lot of extra work, and if it is not carried out properly the roof will never be thoroughly waterproof. Guttering is screwed to the fascia board and is given a slight fall to the outlet. The insulation may be placed on top of the plasterboard ceiling making the roof itself cold, or a warm roof can be created by fixing the insulation under the roof covering by using insulating slabs for the roof boarding (*Figure 4.2*). A vapour check is always inserted on the warm side of the insulation to

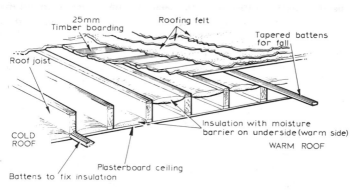

Flat roof construction

Figure 4.2. How the insulation is positioned in a flat roof, showing the position for a warm roof and the position for a cold roof, with the moisture barrier always on the warm side of the insulation

prevent condensation problems within the cold roof space, or within the structure itself where the insulation is above the roof void.

The roof covering is carried over the angle fillet and up the wall to a total of 150 mm (6 in) above the roof surface. A cover flashing of felt or soft metal such as lead or soft aluminium is tucked about 12 mm to 19 mm (½ in to ¾ in) into the first convenient joint above and turned down over the roofing felt and angle fillet, but not on to the flat roof. The flashing is held into the joint by little wedges made of the same material and then the joint is pointed with cement and sand.

Felt or metal sheeting can be used to cover flat roofs and some large tiles can be used on very low pitched roofs, but small tiles need a pitch from 35 degrees upwards. Because the tiles have their heads hooked over battens and their rails resting on the course of tiles below, the actual angle of the tile is slightly less than the pitch of the rafters of the roof structure.

The actual type of roof structure is determined by the span which has to be bridged. A simple lean-to roof is suitable for spans of up to 2.4 m (7 ft 8 in). A simple pitched roof can be used for spans up to 3.6 m (11 ft 10 in). If the ceiling joists are used to tie the rafter feet, the span can be increased to 5.4 m (17 ft 6 in). It is usually sufficient to space the roof rafters at the same centres as those of the ceiling joists, which are themselves governed by the width of the plasterboards for the ceilings. This gives 400 mm (16 in) centres to meet the requirements of a 1200 mm (4 ft) wide board which is the size most commonly used for housing.

A mono-pitch or lean-to roof (*Figure 4.3*) is the simplest type of pitched roof and the top of the rafters are fixed to a wooden plate attached to the rear wall. At the eaves the rafters are birdmouthed over a wallplate carried by the wall. Intermediate support may be given to the rafters by purlins carried on the end walls. This type of roof relies on the fixing at the top of the rafters and the security of the wall plate for its strength. If the fixing at the head gives way the rafters will slide slowly down the wall and either push the lower wallplate off the top of its supporting wall, or it will push the wall over.

Coupled roofs of the double pitch type (*Figure 4.3*) derive their strength from the principle of triangulation, and all struts and hangers are positioned so that triangles are formed. When a triangle is soundly joined it will remain rigid and cannot be distorted. Loads placed on one member are transferred to the others and the bending of members is restricted by placing struts to the purlins and hangers from the ridge which again form triangles. Removal of one of these struts or hangers would weaken the roof and allow one of the triangle sides to bend and possibly break, if its sectional area were not big enough. This is a serious consideration when roofs are being altered to make attic rooms.

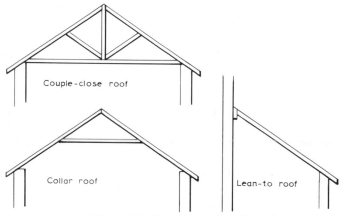

Couple-close roof

Collar roof

Lean-to roof

Figure 4.3. Three types of roof

Roofs have to withstand possible snow loading as well as wind loads and it is therefore important that the roofs of dwelling houses are designed by competent people. Pitched roofs for sheds and gardens are not so important, but as the loads present an outward thrust at the eaves some form of restraint is required. Ceiling joists are not needed usually so collars are placed about halfway up the rafters to tie them together (*Figure 4.3*), and form the required triangle. It is best to have a tie on each of the rafters, but they can be reduced to one every two or three rafters.

When the brickwork has been completed, roofing starts by bedding a timber wallplate (*Figure 4.4*) around the top of the wall. It can be on either the inner or outer leaf of cavity walls, although it is more usual to place it on the inner leaf. The rafters are cut to form a birdsmouth over this plate and are cut at the top to fit against the ridge board. The angles for these cuts are easy to obtain by drawing the roof triangle to a large scale on a board.

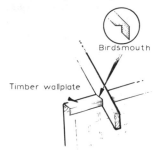

Figure 4.4. A birdsmouth joint at a wallplate

An adjustable bevel can then be set to the required angles. The birdsmouth cut must not be taken more than halfway into the rafter. The amount of rafter beyond the cut depends on the amount of overhang that is required at the eaves of the building. This too can be ascertained from the scale drawing.

To erect the roof, four rafters are made up into trusses by laying them on the ground and nailing a board or gusset across the top, keeping the rafter heads apart just sufficiently to take the ridge board and so that the ridge board will rest on the gusset. A ceiling joist is nailed across the foot of the rafters flush with the top of the birdsmouth. The inside or vertical cuts of the birdsmouth must be exactly the same distance apart as the width of the building between the outside edges of the wallplate. These two sets of rafters, or more if it is a long roof, are then ready for lifting into place.

The wallplate is set out with all the rafter positions carefully marked. Then the two rafter trusses are lifted up and nailed into place. This will be two positions clear of the ends, if it is a gable roof or in line with the top of the hip if it is a hipped roof. They are held plumb using temporary battens.

The ridge board, which is also marked with the rafter positions, using the wallplates as a template so that they are in exactly the same places, is lifted into the slots provided at the top of the rafter trusses and secured. The rest of the rafters are then fixed in pairs at each side of the roof, leaving the two end rafters out to make room for the bricklayers to build the gable walls (*Figure 4.5*).

Roofs for domestic property are built-up using internal loadbearing partitions to take the thrust of the purlin struts. Ceiling joists act as ties and if they are in two lengths they are lapped or cleated together over the supporting walls. Plates are also positioned on top of the ceiling joists over the supporting walls so that the struts can be birdsmouthed over them. Binders are positioned at the centre of the ceiling span and hangers are

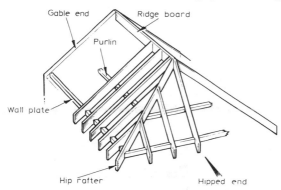

Figure 4.5. The structure of a roof showing the ends finished both as gable and hip

nailed to them and to the ceiling joists to support the ceiling and reduce the size of timber that would otherwise be required. In this way the roof and ceilings are locked into a rigid framework of triangles.

The ties, struts and hangers are all equally spaced at about 1.5 m (4 ft 6 in) to 2 m (6 ft 6 in) centres. If the spacing is increased it will put more load on the purlins and from them on to the struts, hangers and binders, their sizes being related to the spacings.

ROOFS

Rafter feet are cut to receive the fascia and the soffit using the same bevels as those used for the birdsmouth (*Figure 4.6*). The fascia is fixed about 38 mm (1½ in) higher than the rafters to allow for the tilt of the tiles. A special tilting fillet should be fixed to the top edge of the rafters to hold the tiles up, but the fascia is often used and is backed by a piece of angle fillet. It makes for easier repairs at a later date of fascia boards if the weight of the tiles is taken by a separate tilting fillet.

The soffit or level board beneath the eaves is fixed to battens which are nailed to the rafters at one end and to a length of timber fixed to the brickwork at the other end. A wide overhanging eaves not only gives character to the property, but shelters the top of the wall and the upper window frames from a lot of bad weather.

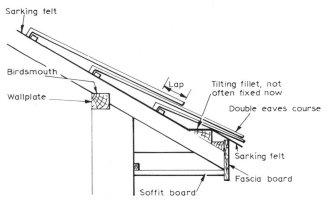

Figure 4.6. Section through the eaves of a roof showing the rafter, wallplate, birdsmouth joint and the treatment of the soffit and fascia. Note the double eaves course of slates or tiles and the lap of the course next but one below

Weather proofing around chimney stacks and other projections through the roof is done by a system of flashings. Trimming around the stack follows the same principle as that for floors. First, a horizontal trimmer is fixed between the rafters that run on either side of the brickwork and then the short rafters are cut and fixed up to the trimmers. At the back of the stack a flat gutter is formed and this is covered with a flashing material such as lead, zinc, felt or other sheet material (*Figure 4.7*). The gutter is 150 mm (6 in) wide and a further 125 mm (5 in) of flashing is taken up the roof under the tiles, and over the top a length of tilting fillet (see also *Figure 4.6*) that is required for the tiles

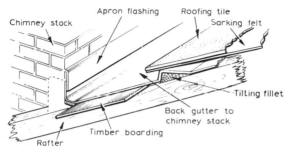

Figure 4.7. Flushing around a chimney stack showing the back gutter tilting fillet and apron

immediately over the gutter. Another 125 mm (5 in) is turned up the face of the brickwork. This back gutter apron has to be fitted before the roof covering is fixed.

Down the sides of the chimney stack soakers are fitted between each course if plain tiling or slating is being used as the roof covering, but the over flashing method is used where contoured tiles or sheet materials are used as roof covering.

Soakers are strips of flashing material which are turned up the brickwork 75 mm (3 in) and under the tiles 100 mm (4 in) (*Figure 4.8*). The length of the soaker is determined by the length of plain tile or slate being used. It equals the gauge of the tile or slate, that is the amount that is exposed on the surface of the roof, plus the lap, which is the amount that one tile or slate overlaps the course next but one below it.

Therefore, if the tile is 266 mm × 165 mm (10½ in × 6½ in) and is laid to a gauge of 95 mm (3¾ in) the length of soaker required would be 95 mm + 75 mm = 170 mm. An extra 25 mm (1 in) can be added so that the top of the soaker can be turned down the edge of the tile batten and nailed to hold the soaker in place.

The cover flashing which cloaks the upturned edge of the soakers is stepped to suit the courses of bricks (*Figure 4.8*). It overlaps the soakers by 50 mm to 65 mm (2 in to 2½ in). The flashing is placed against the wall and the courses are marked on it so that the steps can be cut in it. Then the mortar joints are raked out about 12 mm (½ in) to receive the flashing which is held into the joints by wedges made of the flashing material in

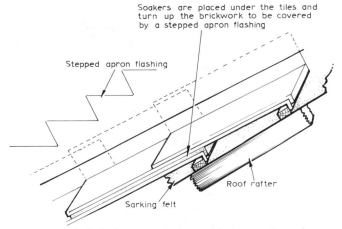

Figure 4.8. Side flashing to a chimney stack showing the soakers tucked under the tiles and the stepped apron flashing

the same manner as the flashing for flat roofs. Where soakers are not used, the cover flashing is made wide enough for it to be dressed down over the roofing material a distance of about 150 mm to 175 mm (6 in to 7 in).

At the front of the chimney stack an apron flashing is necessary and this extends beyond the brickwork by the amount of the side apron or soakers. It is turned up the brickwork about 150 mm (6 in) to the most suitable bed joint, which is raked out to receive it as with the other flashings. It is dressed over the roof covering by 150 mm to 175 mm (6 in to 7 in). The extended ends of the front apron fit under the side flashings, of course.

At the gables, the end or verge of the roof overhangs the brickwork and the tiles are bedded in mortar over the wall so that they project a few inches; the underside then has a sand and cement fillet applied to cover any uneven brickwork and make a neat finish. Where there is a deep overhang at the eaves, it is usual to carry the roof over the verge the same amount and to do this the wallplates and ridge are projected beyond the gable and an extra rafter is fitted outside the wall. This is done by joining the last two rafters together with short lengths of timber like a ladder. The two rafters are then fixed in place with the outer rafter gaining support from the short timbers over the gable wall.

The sloping soffit is lined with the same kind of boarding that is used for the soffit at the eaves. It is nailed or screwed to the horizontal timbers. Wide barge-boards are then cut to the same angles at the top and the bottom as were used for the rafter head and foot cut. These boards are nailed into place and the tiling is allowed to overhang them a few inches. A batten is then scribed to fit under the tiles to make a neat finish.

Dormer window treatment follows the principles applied to trimming for a chimney stack. The rafter at each side of the dormer is doubled to take the extra weight. Rafters are trimmed at the top and bottom of the window opening. The dormer roof is often rested on the top of the window frame, but it is better if a separate timber can be arranged, as window and door frames should not be made load bearing. Side cheeks of the dormer can be either glazed or solid. Glazed side cheeks are frames made up on the bench and fitted into place as a single unit. Solid cheeks have the frame work for the cladding built-up on the site. Flashing is by means of soakers which are fitted under the roof tiles and up behind the cladding of the dormer cheek.

It is never a good policy to let the collected rainwater simply drip off the edge of a roof, so the dormer should either be fitted with a gutter and downpipe, or it should be given a fall to the rear. In either case the roof treatment is similar to the back gutter of a chimney stack. It has a flat area for the collection of water and the covering material is carried up the roof under the tiles and over the tilting fillet.

This will mean that a great deal of water will pour down the roof at the side of the dormer so that flashing between the side cheeks and the main roof will have to be carefully installed.

Roofs for conservatories are either translucent plastic sheeting or glass. The latter is generally the Georgian wired type. Glazing bars which are 75 mm (3 in) deep and 38 mm (1½ in) thick are double rebated to take the glass on either side and are supported by purlins. Where the glass has to be in more than one piece the bottom piece is fitted first and then the next one is bedded into place allowing it to overlap the first piece by about 50 mm (2 in). A tack is driven into the glazing bar just below the bottom edge of the glass to prevent it slipping down the roof. A fillet of putty is bevelled on the top of the glazing bar in the same way as glazing windows.

The wooden bars are birdsmouthed over the bottom plate in the same way as roof rafters, but the glass rebate should not be allowed to come in line with the bottom plate; a space between the bottom plate and the glass is necessary to let the inevitable condensation escape.

Patent metal glazing bars are obtainable and the manufacturer's fixing instructions should be followed. This usually means fixing the bars to the bottom wallplate and to another timber plugged and screwed to the wall at the top of the roof. The number of intermediate supports necessary will depend on the size of the bars and the span of the roof. There is no putty required as the glass rests on a soft strip fixed to the metal and the top seal is generally by means of lead also fixed to the metal bars. This is simply tapped down over the glass using a wooden mallet.

Plastic sheeting is fixed with springhead nails and clearance holes must be bored as the sheets are easily cracked. Mitring at the joints of the sheets has to be carried out in the same way as for asbestos sheets. One corrugation overlap is usually sufficient for the side joint. End overlaps are about 150 mm (6 in). Soft foam infill strips are made to fit the corrugations and stop the draughts at the eaves. Condensation is frequently a problem with these roofs.

It is important to remember in the interests of safety, that glass, plastic and asbestos roofs are unsafe to walk on and will give way without warning. A plank which spans from purlin to purlin must be placed on the roof to walk on, both during construction and afterwards when maintenance is being undertaken. Snow guards are also necessary at the eaves of the main roof above conservatories, to prevent a sudden rush of snow sliding down on to the lower roof and collapsing it under the weight.

Access to windows and gutters above the conservatory roof has to be provided by screwing certain of the sheets in place so that they can be removed reasonably easily on those occasions when painting or other maintenance has to be carried out. With glass roofs the putty will have to be scraped out and the glass removed as required.

Rainwater disposal has to be arranged and in some areas this has to be taken to soakaways and in others, the water can be taken to the nearest drain.

The guttering and downpipes can be made from plastic, asbestos or metal. Asbestos is relatively cheap and is made half-round pattern. Putty or mastic is used for the joints which are held by small, galvanished 6 mm (¼ in) gutter bolts. The half-round gutter is supported on galvanised brackets screwed to the fascia board. Down pipes are screwed to plugs set in holes bored in the brickwork.

Metal gutters can be in half-round or ogee pattern; the joints are also made with putty or mastic and held with gutter bolts. Metal brackets screwed to the fascia are used to support these gutters and the downpipes are fixed to the walls with plugs and screws.

Both asbestos and metal rainwater systems can be painted to suit the colours of the house. Asbestos gutters need to be painted on the inside to prevent water penetrating to the back of the paint and pushing it off. The material needs sealing with emulsion paint on the outside before the gloss paint system is applied. If this is not done the alkali in the asbestos will combine with the paint to make a crude soapy mess that will not dry.

Metal gutters also benefit from a bitumen treatment on the inside, but it is not essential. The appropriate primer should be used on the exterior before the undercoat and gloss are applied.

Both asbestos and metal rainwater goods can be cut with a hacksaw and the holes can be bored with metal cutting drills and countersinks. No special tools are needed.

Plastic rainwater systems are easy to install. The joints are usually sealed with some form of patented Neoprene gasket and the systems simply snap together. The brackets are in plastic and are screwed to the fascia board. In some makes the brackets form the joint between the lengths of guttering. Whatever the material used for the gutters, there should always be a support at the end joints and at least one intermediate support. If the lengths of gutter are more than 2 m (6 ft 6 in) then two intermediate supports will be required. The various systems all make provision for the expansion and contraction of the plastic which would otherwise cause the gutters to buckle in the summer.

Plastic systems can be in the half-round pattern or they can be of the modern version of the ogee pattern which is square at the back and double curved at the front. There are special fittings made so that the plastic system can be jointed to existing metal gutters of half-round or ogee shape.

5 Concrete mixing and casting

Although concrete is considered to be hard, heavy and uninteresting, it is really quite versatile and there are a number of textures and finishes that can be produced to make it more acceptable. Initially it is soft and plastic so that it can be moulded into almost any shape, provided that the correct mix is used, but thin sections may be difficult to reinforce.

The basic materials for making concrete are Portland cement, sharp sand and gravel. Cement is supplied in 50 kg (1 cwt) bags, but it can be obtained loose for storage in silos of large static mixing plants. The fine and coarse aggregate (sand and gravel), are supplied by the cubic metre. The coarse aggregate is graded for most concrete work, but it is possible to get an 'all-in' ballast which is a mixture of sizes from sand to about 19 mm (¾ in) stones. This is suitable for use where the uniformity of the concrete is not important; concreting fence posts into the ground for instance. For quality work the materials must be measured separately.

Bags of ready-mixed dry materials can be obtained and they are useful on sites which are too cramped to provide storage space for both the materials and the mixing machine, and where the quantities needed at any one time would be too small to make deliveries of ready-mixed concrete an economic proposition.

Ordinary Portland cement is grey in colour, but it is possible to get white cement if the job warrants the expense – white cement is much dearer than the ordinary cement. Colouring materials are obtainable either in powder or liquid form and if they are used the maker's instructions must be followed exactly. This applies especially to quantities as the degree of colour can be maintained only by accurate measurement, because the concrete will vary in colour as it dries out. A newly mixed batch will look quite different from that already laid, which itself will look patchy as the area dries at different rates.

Sand bought at the merchants will have been washed to remove the dirt and impurities. It must therefore be stored on a clean, hard base. On a large site a weak concrete mix is laid a few inches thick over the ground, but on a small site old wooden boardings can be used. Wooden sides are needed if large quantities are to be stored, and also to keep the sand from mixing with the large aggregate (*Figure 5.1*). Small quantities can be stored on thick polythene sheeting if care is taken not to cut the plastic with the shovel. The same precautions apply to the coarse aggregate which can be either gravel or crushed rock in sizes between 19 mm (¾ in) and 4 mm (³⁄₁₆ in).

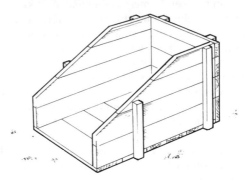

Figure 5.1. An enclosure for storing sand or gravel

Mixing machines are obtainable in sizes to suit most jobs, but where hand mixing is to be undertaken it must be done on a clean, hard surface such as a platform of boards. If the concrete is mixed on a drive or road it will cause stains that will not come off.

A gauge box is required to measure the materials accurately. This can be made out of wood and is about 300 mm cube (1 ft cube). A bucket is the traditional measure, but as they are all different sizes, it makes calculating the total amount of mix being made rather difficult.

A good general mix suitable for strip foundations, not less than 150 mm (6 in) thick, for walls or for drives and garage floors not less than 100 mm (4 in) thick and laid over 150 mm (6 in) of well compacted hardcore, is mixed at a ratio of 1 : 2½ : 4, which is one part cement, two and a half parts sand and four parts coarse aggregate.

When mixed by hand, 2½ measures of sand are placed in a flattened heap on the mixing platform. Then, four measures of coarse aggregate are spread evenly over the top of the sand. These two materials are then blended together by turning them over using a shovel and forming them into a new heap. This process is repeated two or three times when one measure of cement is added and mixed in the same way until the mix is of an even colour, before the water is added.

The usual method of adding the water is to hollow out the centre of the heap to form a crater and pour the water into it, gradually pushing the dry mix into it and as the water is soaked up, the wet mix is turned over to ensure thorough wetting. The problem with this method is that the large quantity of water tends to wash the cement off the aggregate, undoing all the careful coating which has taken place during the dry mixing stage. This cement then forms a slurry at the bottom of the crater and if the sides are breached the slurry runs away off the mixing platform and so reduces the strength of the mix.

A better method of adding the water is to sprinkle it on the dry materials using a watering can. Spray just a little at a time and turn the concrete over between spraying, this way the cement coating will stay on the aggregate where it is needed and there will be less chance of the mix being over wetted.

Whatever method is used, either hand or machine, it is important that only enough water is used to make the mix sufficiently workable to be placed into the casting mould or into the foundation without it forming air holes. The mix is tamped into the mould or trench using a stout piece of wood or a mechanical vibrator to ensure that the mould is filled solid without any honeycombing. Over tamping, or vibrating, a mix that is too wet will bring the cement to the top instead of it being evenly spread throughout the mix. Too much water will cause excessive shrinkage as the concrete dries, crazing the surface with tiny cracks.

Once the concrete has been mixed it must be placed in position within one hour. It must not be allowed to dry too quickly; finished work must be covered. Polythene sheeting is used generally as it is impervious and will keep the moisture in the concrete by preventing it evaporating. When the cast, or drive, is hard enough it can be wetted gently and the polythene replaced. At this stage the sides of the casting mould are removed so that the sides of the cast can be wetted and any surface defects made good.

The amount of making good required will depend on how well the mould has been made and how carefully the concrete has been placed in it. Concrete that has been properly mixed and placed into moulds that have been designed so that they can be taken apart easily, will produce casts that need little or no making good. The sides of casts can usually be removed after 24 hours, but the cast will not be strong enough to be lifted for another three or four days. In the case of lintels or beams cast *in situ*, the bottom or soffit must remain supported for at least a week after the sides have been removed.

Honeycombed surfaces, caused by poor compaction, or using a mix that did not contain enough fine aggregate or which is the result of insufficient mixing, should be made good with a mortar mix of the same proportions as the concrete mix, but without the coarse aggregate. That is, in the case of a 1 : 2½ : 4 mix, the mortar should be made of 1 part cement to 2½ parts sand, but patching should be avoided if at all possible because the patch generally dries darker than the original concrete.

Cement mortar and concrete shrink slightly as they dry and harden, so use the mix as dry as possible, because the amount of shrinkage depends largely on the amount of water present in the mix. Before filling the holes, all loose and thin, fragile material must be removed from the area and if a large patch has to be filled it must first be primed with neat cement grout which is simply cement and water mixed to a creamy consistency and brushed into the surface. Cement mortar is applied immediately and smoothed off with a wooden float. Patches should not be smoothed with a steel float because this would darken the surface making the patch show even more. Patches will need the same curing treatment as the main concrete.

Concrete walling blocks and paving slabs are easy items to cast as they need no reinforcing and can be made in simple square boxes. Planed timber should be used as it will give a better finish and will not stick to the concrete as much as rough timber would.

The most important point to remember when making any kind of concrete mould is that it must be easy to take apart after the concrete has started to harden. For this reason it is better to use bolts to hold the mould together than to use nails or screws. Nails get bent and soon loose their grip and screw heads soon get badly damaged and cannot be reused. These fixings are suitable only if the mould is to be used for just one cast, as when casting a concrete lintel *in situ*.

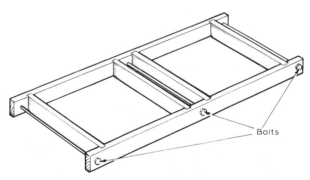

Figure 5.2. Shallow boxes for casting paving slabs

Mould boxes can be made separately or in multiple units (*Figure 5.2*), depending on the number of casts needed and the type of casting. Paving slabs for instance are made flat with the sides of the mould not more than 50 mm (2 in) high (*Figure 5.2*). If the mix is not made sloppy there will not be much outward pressure and 25 mm (1 in) thick timber will do the job. If there is sufficient space a number of slabs can be cast in a long mould.

The dividing battens are housed into the long sides about 6 mm (¼ in), not for strength, but to ensure that they are held in the correct position. The long sides can be held at the ends by long threaded rods with nuts and washers (*Figure 5.2*) or they can be held by wedges driven between them and blocks of wood screwed to the baseboard (*Figure 5.3*). If this wedge method is used, stripping the sides when the concrete has set is simply a matter of knocking the wedges out and lifting the side away.

Avoid making casts too heavy, a 600 mm (2 ft) square slab 50 mm (2 in) thick is the maximum that one person can be

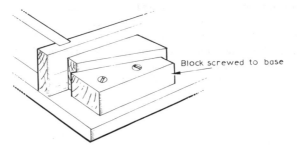

Block screwed to base

Figure 5.3. If the base is timber the side can be wedged instead of bolted

expected to move for laying. A thickness of 38 mm (1½ in) is sufficient for slabs for paths around dwelling houses. Slabs 600 mm × 450 mm × 38 mm (2 ft × 18 in × 1½ in) are better for handling and, used with 300 mm (1 ft) square slabs, can be laid to various patterns.

Building blocks can be made either standing on edge in the laying position (*Figure 5.4*) or they can be cast lying flat. Blocks are usually 450 mm × 230 mm (18 in × 9 in) and in thicknesses from 50 mm (2 in) to 100 mm (4 in). They can be cast singly or in multiple boxes. As the mould will have to be used many times it is worthwhile taking care with its construction. Timber at least 25 mm (1 in) thick is used and the sides are held firmly by bolts, one at the top and one at the bottom at each end. The ends are housed into the sides to ensure that they are fixed in the same position each time the box is used (*Figure 5.4*).

The mould is fixed to the baseboard to keep it firm while it is being filled and the inside of the mould is given a coating of a releasing agent to ensure that the wooden mould will leave the concrete block cleanly, without any sticking. For this reason it is essential that the moulds are cleaned thoroughly between castings.

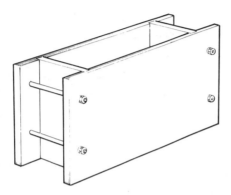

Figure 5.4. A box for casting building blocks

Moulds should be filled with concrete in layers about 50 mm (2 in) deep, each one being tamped well before the next layer is laid. If a smooth-faced block is required a trowel is used with a chopping action at the sides of the mould to compact the concrete and bring the cement forward so that honeycombing is avoided. A bolted box can be removed as soon as the concrete has set as this can be done without shaking and cracking the casting. The blocks must be kept damp and are not moved for a few days after the mould box has been removed.

Apart from making blocks and slabs, concrete can be used for making other building units such as lintels and copings. Lintels need only simple boxes like the building-block boxes, but longer and with centre supports to prevent the sides bowing under the pressure of the wet concrete. This support can be given by wire passed through holes drilled in the sides of the box. The wire is simply cut when the box is removed and the ends snipped off close to the cement.

Moulds for copings are slightly more complicated because the copings must have sloping tops to drain the water off and they must have a groove or throat at each side on the underside to make the water drip clear and run down the wall. They can be cast either the right way up (*Figure 5.5*) or upside-down. If the coping is to be cast the right way up then the mould must have

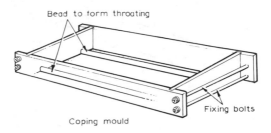

Figure 5.5. Box or mould for casting a coping stone. Beads are fixed to the base to form a throat and the sides of the box are sloping to form the slope of the top of the coping

one side higher than the other and sloping ends so that they can be used as a guide for levelling off the top. Small beading strips must be nailed to the base board to form the groove or throat. Small beadings frequently become so tightly embedded in the concrete that they pull out the nails when the cast is removed, and have to be chiselled out of the concrete.

When copings are cast upside-down in the mould boxes, these little beads are at the top and can be removed while the concrete is still fairly green, so that any nibs that are holding the beads will break off easily and at the same time, any damage can be repaired with a better chance of keying into the concrete than if the concrete were fully cured.

This method of casting means that tapered wooden slips have to be fitted into the bottom of the mould box to form the slope of the coping top. The angle need not be steep – 25 mm (1 in) is sufficient to make the water run off. Saddle-back coping which slopes to each side need be only about 75 mm (3 in) at the centre and 50 mm (2 in) at each side. The coping must over hang the wall by 25 mm to 38 mm (1 in to 1½ in) with the throating about central in the overhang.

In order to get a dense and smooth finish, the concrete is mixed with pea-shingle as the coarse aggregate, or a one-part cement to three-parts sand mix is used. Fine material is spread over the bevel slips and well compacted to make a smooth surface for the finished coating.

A mould box for an upside-down casting needs to be fixed to a flat wooden base so that the sides can be held in place by wedges. Then, when the concrete has hardened sufficiently, the whole box can be turned over and the wedges knocked out and the base and sides removed. This will expose the face of the concrete so that any blemishes can be made good and the surface trowelled to a uniform smoothness. When the cast is made the right way up this operation can be carried out without disturbing the casting at all.

Castings are kept damp while the concrete cures, in the same way as the drives and paths. Spray the surface with water gently so that it does not get pitted, then cover it with polythene.

Reinforcing is not needed in copings and small castings, but it is needed in lintels and gate posts. Lintels for dwellings rarely

Figure 5.6. Why reinforcement is needed at the bottom of a lintel

need more than two reinforcing bars at the bottom edge, and the ends of the bars are bent round to form a hook so that they will be anchored in the cement. Reinforcing is needed because the concrete is not strong under tension, although it has a very high compressive strength.

When a beam supported at each end is loaded, there is a bending action imposed on it. This puts the upper part of the beam in compression and the lower part of the beam, which is stretched, is under tension (*Figure 5.6*). Therefore, the reinforcing is placed in the bottom part of the lintel or beam. It needs 50 mm (2 in) of concrete around it to protect it from the weather which would make it rust. However, the reinforcing bars do not have to be bright metal or even galvanised metal, the patina of rust that they normally carry helps to give a grip on the concrete. No oil or grease must be allowed to get on the bars. The ends of the bars are bent back to form a hook which will anchor them and hold them in place against the tension which is set up.

Where beams are supported in the middle as well as at both ends, the reinforcing has to be bent to rise to the top of the beam where it passes over the central support because the beam will tend to bend over the support and the tension will be at the top (*Figure 5.7*). It can be seen that except for simple lintels, the designing of reinforcing must be done by a skilled engineer.

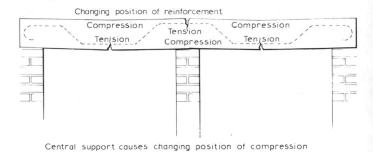

Changing position of reinforcement

Central support causes changing position of compression

Figure 5.7. How the pattern of stress is changed when a support is placed under the centre of a lintel

When posts are cast, four reinforcing bars are better than one in the middle of the post. Place a reinforcing bar at each corner to resist any tendency to bend in any direction. Give the bars as much concrete cover as possible. The bars themselves need to be 6 mm (¼ in) diameter for most posts. Bars 12.5 mm (½ in) diameter are only needed when load bearing columns are being cast, and in this case the reinforcing must be designed by an engineer.

Reinforcing is not usually needed for domestic drives or for the bases of garages and sheds, but where it is needed it is again placed at the bottom of the concrete. The reinforcement for concrete slabs of this nature is in the form of a light metal mesh made of about 4 mm (3/16 in) rods welded at the cross joints to form 75 mm (3 in) squares. The mesh is held about 50 mm (2 in) off the ground or hardcore, by tying 50 mm (2 in) concrete cubes to the underside of it with wire for it to rest on. These blocks can then stay in place when the concrete has been poured.

Only properly cut and shaped reinforcing bars or mesh are effective, it is no use just putting into the concrete any old lengths of iron bar or mesh that happen to be lying around. For domestic work it is easier and perhaps better to use the ready-made pressed steel lintels which are made to the size and shape necessary for the size of opening which they are long enough to span. These lintels are light in weight and can be positioned by one man.

Provision for fixings in the castings must be made before the concrete hardens. One way of providing fixing points is to set dovetail-shaped blocks in the concrete. They can be tacked to the inside of the mould just sufficiently to hold them while the concrete is poured. When the sides are removed later, they will pull off the points of the nails which can be bent over out of the way.

Bolt holes can be made by putting the bolt in place through the sides of the mould and fitting a cardboard sleeve over it so that the bolt can be removed when the sides are taken off the mould. A well greased, tapered wooden peg can be used for forming the bolt hole, but there is always the danger than the wood will swell and become tightly wedged in the casting in spite of its being covered with grease.

One of the best ways to provide holes in concrete castings is to use pieces of expanded polystyrene. They can be held in place by wire passed through small holes drilled in the sides of the mould. When the sides are removed the wire can be cut and then the polystyrene melted out of the concrete, using a blow-torch.

Laying concrete drives and paths

Preparation for laying drives and paths starts with clearing all the soil and garden loam from the site down to firm ground. The depth is perhaps not so important for paths as they have little weight to carry, but drives need to be firmly based because the weight of the car passes over a narrow strip at each side. If the drive is not firmly based this edge load will cause the concrete to break away from the unloaded central area.

A drive needs to be a minimum of 2.1 m (7 ft) wide and the concrete needs to be 75 mm to 100 mm (3 in to 4 in) thick. It is laid on a base of well compacted hardcore made of broken bricks and stones. This layer should not be less than 75 mm (3 in) thick and it is covered with a layer of sand well rolled to compact it.

Wooden formwork is set up along the sides of the path and held in place by 50 mm (2 in) square pegs driven into the ground on the outside of the boards. The formwork should not be less than 25 mm (1 in) thick and the pegs should not be more than 760 mm (30 in) apart. The formwork is set to the appropriate falls so that the water will run away quickly. A drive can be laid with a slight camber to run the water to both sides or it can be given a slight slope to one side. A fall of 12 mm to 25 mm (½ in to 1 in) is sufficient to get the water away.

Large areas of concrete need a proper arrangement of drains and gullies to get the water away without causing ponding in the garden at the sides, but water on drives can usually be allowed to run off the sides and soak into the ground.

Drainage work has to be carried out before any of the drive is laid and where gullies are provided they must be positioned before any concreting starts. A central gully is positioned about 25 mm (1 in) below the level of the formwork so that the concrete can be given a fall towards it. Drainpipes with a diameter of 100 mm (4 in) are given a fall of 1 : 40 and their joints are packed with hemp and then filled with cement mortar neatly bevelled off around the collar. Water which is being taken to a soakaway can be run through unglazed earthenware pipes that are not joined but simply laid end to end. The soakaway must be at least 3 m (10 ft) from any building.

The concrete is laid in sections of not more than 3 m (10 ft) long to minimise the risk of cracking due to thermal movement. A temporary board is set up across the drive at this point to provide an edge to finish the concrete against. The board is removed when the concrete has set and is replaced by a strip of thick bituminous felt when the next section of concrete is laid. This acts as a soft cushion which will take up the expansion of the concrete in hot weather.

When ready-mixed concrete is to be used it is essential that all the joint boards are positioned and that there is clear access for wheelbarrows. It is not often that the delivery truck can get any closer than one end of the drive and as the driver will want to unload and return to base as soon as possible, there will be no time for measuring and cutting timber.

In this case the section boards can be quite thin as concrete will be placed on both sides of them at once and they can be left in place instead of putting in strips of felt.

For drives the concrete mix is 1 : 2½ : 4 and is made just wet enough to be placed and tamped without being too sloppy. The drive is filled to about 19 mm (¾ in) above the level of the formwork and the concrete is tamped down using a board that will reach from one side of the drive to the other. This board is used with a chopping action and needs two persons to operate it. When the concrete is almost level with the formwork they change to a sawing action dragging the board forward cutting the concrete off level with the top of the formwork and drawing the excess material in front of the board. Where a cambered surface is required, the underside of the tamping board must be hollowed to the required camber.

The surface of the drive can be left with the rough ridges across it produced by this method of laying. They will give extra grip if the drive is laid on a steep slope, but domestic drives are usually trowelled smooth after the initial set has started to take place. Trowelling with a steel float will give a fine surface, but it could be too smooth for safety in the winter when it would be frequently wet and often frozen. A wooden float gives a better surface as the finish is slightly roughened, though otherwise flat and even. A fine ribbed finish can be provided by brushing the concrete straight across as it sets. For an exposed aggregate surface the concrete is swept with a soft brush about an hour after it has been placed. The concrete is then allowed to harden until the stones cannot be dislodged. The surface is then brushed with a stiff brush and sprayed with water to clear the stones and leave them standing proud.

Imitation paving slabs can be marked on the surface by rubbing the rounded edge of a piece of 6 mm (¼ in) batten on the concrete to form shallow groves in the required pattern. Crazy paving patterns can be made in the same way.

If real paving slabs are to be used for drives they should be laid on a concrete base of the type described, but they can be laid on firmly compacted sand. The concrete base need be only 75 mm (3 in) thick and the slabs are laid on a bed of mortar made of one part cement and three or four parts sand. A full bed of mortar should be used for each slab, the five pats of mortar generally used for paths would not be sufficient to support the car without the slabs cracking.

Small concrete sets, rather like bricks, can be laid on a base of hard-packed sand using no mortar. Some of these specially made sets are interlocking so that they will hold together under the

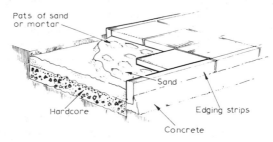

Figure 5.8. Laying paving slabs

movement of the wheels and will not spread at the corners. Edge restraints such as concrete curbs should be provided. A similar method is used for laying paving slabs for paths. When the garden soil has been removed, a hardcore base is laid and this is covered with sand, well-compacted to take the weight of whatever traffic is likely to pass over it. The paving slabs are levelled on to this base by laying a small trowel-full of sand at each corner position and one in the middle (*Figure 5.8*). When the slab is placed on these heaps of sand it can be knocked down to the required level using a heavy wooden mallet or the end of a length of timber.

A string-line down each side of the path will serve as a guide both for direction and for level. The slabs should be levelled individually and a straightedge is used to check three or four at a time to ensure that they are all level or have the desired fall.

In order to prevent the sand under the slabs being washed away in wet weather, an edging must be provided. This can be preservative-treated boarding which finishes flush with the surface of the path, or it can be purpose-made concrete edging bedded in weak mortar. The edging can be finished flush with the top of the path or it can have rounded edges and can stand up above the surface. If this method is used, then some of the joints must be left open to allow water to escape.

Mortar for bedding paving slabs is made of 1 part lime to 4 parts sand. In sheltered places where there will not be much water on the surface of the path, the sand can be increased to 6 parts to make an even softer mix. Where a lot of water is to be expected on the surface of the paving and where cars are expected to use the area, some cement is added to the mix, but it should not be stronger than 1 part cement : 3 parts lime : 12 parts sand. It can be used as a full bed for the paving slabs or as dots.

Whatever method is used to bed the slabs they are best laid with a joint of 6 mm to 12 mm (¼ in to ½ in). These joints are filled when the area is complete. The filling is a dry mix of the same type as the one used for laying the slabs. In sheltered areas, sand can be brushed into the joints and will bed down surprisingly hard. Filling the joints with a wet mix of mortar is not recommended because it is nearly impossible to keep the surface of the paving clean and free from cement stains which will not come off.

The less formal crazy paving is laid in the same way as the whole paving slabs. Pieces with straigh edges are picked out to fit neatly along the edging of the path. If the pieces of paving are laid in a cement : lime : sand mortar mix a formal straight edging need not be provided and the ragged edge of the path can be covered by the plants. The pieces of paving should appear to have been scattered haphazardly, with joints of various widths. If the pieces fit too carefully the path will look like a jigsaw puzzle. Because the joints of this type of paving are much wider than those of formal paving it is best to fill them with a mortar mix instead of just sand. These very wide joints are filled with a wet mix taking care not to get the mortar on the paving.

Paths laid in mortar or which have mortar joints should not be walked on for a day or two to give the mortar time to set. Paths and patios can also be laid in bricks, of special quality or frost resistant types.

Cobble stones make decorative features and, as they are uncomfortable to walk on, they can be used to discourage people from taking short cuts across lawns by placing a wide strip of cobbles alongside paths. The base for these stones is laid in the same way as the base for the path, but the surface of the concrete is kept down about 38 mm (1½ in) below the surface of the path. This allows for the mortar mix of 1 part cement : 3 parts sand in which the stones are set. The cobbles are about 75 mm (3 in) or more in size and are each placed by hand in the wet mortar, bedding them to about half their depth.

Only small quantities of mortar should be made up at each time, the actual amount depending on the rate at which the stones can be bedded. The work should start as soon after the base concrete has set as possible as this will improve the bond between the concrete and the bedding mortar. Keep the tops of the stones as clean as possible during laying operations as they will be difficult to clean after the mortar has set.

Block walls and foundations

The foundations for walls are laid in a concrete mix of 1 : 2½ : 4 which is placed in layers about 75 mm (3 in) thick and tamped with a piece of wood about 50 mm (2 in) square. There is no need to make a neat finish, but the concrete must be levelled off to the tops of the pegs which have been driven into the bottom of the trench. When this has been done the pegs can be pulled out and the holes made good.

Walls built with broken slabs, in order to give a rough stone-like appearance, can be difficult to plumb and much depends on the ability of the operator. Small pieces of wood can be built into the joints so that they project clear of the rough surface of the blocks, each piece projecting by the same amount so that a plumb level can be placed against them to assist the eye

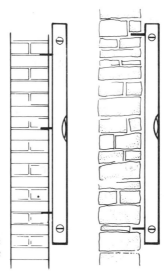

Figure 5.9. Plumbing a rough stone wall using wooden pads as a guide

in keeping the wall vertical (*Figure 5.9*). These building blocks are cast like other blocks, but twice the required width so that they can be broken in two while they are still 'green'. Proprietary blocks are made in shaped moulds and often have a walling pattern cast on the face so that when they are laid it is difficult to see that they are really rectangular blocks, all of the same size.

Ordinary plain building blocks are laid in the same way as bricks, but it is advisable when using blocks under 75 mm (3 in) thick, not to take the wall higher than about 1220 mm (4 ft) without leaving the mortar to set for a day otherwise the wall may buckle.

Where large decorative blocks are used, the mortar mix should be a little stiffer than that generally used for building with bricks, because these blocks are heavier than bricks and will squeeze more mortar out of the joints. Care must be taken to prevent mortar staining the face of decorative work.

The main tools needed for concreting are shovels for mixing and laying, trowels for patching, steel and wooden floats for finishing surfaces. Bending equipment may be needed where reinforcing is involved, and of course, mechanical mixers and vibrators are needed where a lot of concreting is to be undertaken. A strong wheelbarrow will be needed to transport the concrete from the mixing point to the site where it is to be placed. All the tools must be washed in clean water as soon as possible after use to keep them in good condition and ready for future use.

6 Rendering and plastering

External rendering consists of two or more coats of a mixture of cement and sand or cement, lime and sand. The rendering can be applied to brick or block walls as well as other structures such as expanded metal lathing fixed to wooden or metal supports. In addition to providing protection against moisture penetration, the material is used for decorative purposes, either by making patterns on the wet surface or by varying the surface texture by the different methods of application, mixing and finishing. Cement colours can be added, but very careful measurement of the colours and all the other ingredients, as well as careful mixing, would be required to give an attractive appearance, that is not patchy.

In general, the undercoat should be weaker in strength than the walling material to which it is applied, but it should also be stronger than the finishing coat which will be applied on the top of it. Rendering failures are often caused by using mixes which contain too much cement. This leads to crazing and cracking. The addition of lime to the mix will overcome this problem as rendering containing lime will harden to form weatherproof and frost resistant surfaces which will allow structural movement to be absorbed. Small cracks are self-healing.

An external rendering must be durable, it must resist moisture penetration and have an attractive finish. Durability depends on a number of factors such as the type of mix, the bond between the wall and the rendering as well as on the standard of workmanship.

Water is less likely to penetrate through rendering of an absorbent type than it is through the cracks in the surface of a hard, dense coating. Rain falling on a smooth surface which has no absorption does not distribute itself evenly, but tends to run in rivulets down the surface. A rough surface breaks up this flow and therefore avoids concentration of water at any one point.

This means that when cracks appear in impermeable rendering, water may get through them and into the wall behind. When this happens it may cause loss of adhesion, further cracking or even complete disintegration of the rendering through frost action. Complete penetration of solid walls gives rise to damp patches on the interior with the consequent ruining of internal decorations. Serious dampness on the interior of the wall could also bring about the failure of the internal plastering.

Porous rendering will absorb some of the water which falls on its surface and this moisture will be retained until the weather conditions change and the sun dries it out again. In this way the water takes much longer to penetrate right through the rendering into the wall itself so that it rarely appears on the inside.

Water which has penetrated cracks in dense impermeable rendering will be trapped behind it and will only be able to escape to the interior of the building. It will be obvious that the less water that is retained by the surface coating, the greater will be the risk that water will find its way through cracks into the wall. So a rough textured porous rendering will normally be more effective than a hard and impermeable, smooth finish. Appearance can also be a problem with smooth finishes, because they tend to weather unevenly due to stains from sills, copings and eaves. Rough textures help to break up water flow from these places and therefore they weather uniformly. In any case these stains depend to a large degree on the exposure of the site.

Ordinary Portland cement is used for the rendering mix, but white cement can be used if required. In cases where there is severe exposure to the weather or where a low suction is needed, a waterproof cement may be used for the first coat and it can also be used to advantage to provide an even suction on surfaces when white or coloured cement is to be used for the final coat.

RENDERING AND PLASTERING

Lime is added to the mix to improve the workability. As it reduces the strength and density of the mix it also reduces the danger of cracking which could lead to moisture penetration.

Clean, sharp sand is the third ingredient and it should be noted that sands with a strong colour will effect the colour of the mix and this is especially important when white cement is being used. For general mixes and for smooth finishes, the sand is evenly graded. For roughcast and similar finished a coarse particle is introduced. As with concrete, the small particles fill in any spaces between the larger ones and all particles must be covered with the cement slurry. Poorly graded sand takes up a lot of water and too much water in the mix will lead to cracking in the finished surface.

Different types of wall require different types of rendering mix. Rendering should not be applied to dense strong materials like concrete walls, hard, dense, concrete blocks or hard, impervious, clay bricks and blocks which do not have keyed faces, without the provision of an adequate key which must be strong enough to resist separation.

A splatter dash coat can be given to these materials to provide the key and this consists of a mix of 1 part cement : 2 parts fairly coarse sand, with the addition of enough water to form a thick slurry. This mix must be kept well stirred. The wall must be cleaned and damped then the cement is dashed against it to give a thin coating of an even roughcast appearance. This coating is wetted again after about an hour or so to ensure complete hydration.

Concrete can also be given a key by brushing on to it a mixture of 1 part cement : 1½ parts fine sharp sand mixed with water that contains an equal quantity of p.v.a. adhesive. The mixture is vigorously brushed into the surface of the wall and then stippled using a banister or similar brush so that a close textured key is formed. This is then left for at least seven days to harden before the rendering coats are applied.

Special treatment is not necessary for fairly strong porous materials such as bricks made of clay or sand and lime, or most lightweight building blocks, but it is desirable to rake out the joints to a depth of about 12 mm (½ in). It is also important when applying the material that no air pockets are left between the wall and the rendering. Fairly weak, porous materials like aerated concrete, building blocks and soft bricks are not suitable for mixes which are rich in cement. This is because, on drying, shrinkage stresses can be set up which will lead to bond failure between the rendering and the wall.

Where expanded metal is being used three coats will be needed, the first being a dense and relatively impervious mix which will protect the metalwork. This type of metal background is applied over wood, which would otherwise provide an unsatisfactory bond, and over unsound surfaces such as perished and disintegrating brickwork or masonry. The metal should be of 6 mm (¼ in) or 9 mm (⅜ in) mesh and it should be applied with the long way of the mesh across the supports. These should be preservative treated battens set at not more than 400 mm (16 in) centres. Metal packing should be used to hold the expanded metal at least 6 mm (¼ in) from the wooden battens so that the first coating can be forced through the mesh to totally encase the metal.

Good bond depends on mechanical key and on suction. If the background is coarse enough for the rendering to cling to the surface there will be sufficient key, but smoother surfaces need a degree of suction, which is the ability of the background to absorb moisture. Spraying the wall will indicate the degree of suction available, but if the water is soaked in too quickly, then the water in the mix will be extracted rapidly, so that the mix becomes stiff and difficult to spread. Spraying the wall with water will overcome this problem.

New brickwork which is to have a rendered finish should have the joints raked out while they are still green and a good brushing down is all that is required to remove loose material. Old walls, of course, need to be cleaned and free from lichen, mould, soot or paint.

Before applying the first coat, the wall is damped to ensure even suction and where possible the work should be started on the shaded side of the building. If a water repellent is used in the first coat it will not be advisable to dampen the surface before subsequent coats are applied, unless the weather is very hot and dry. In winter, exterior rendering must never be carried out during frost, or if frost is likely before the rendering will have cured sufficiently to resist it.

Straight cement and sand rendering mixes give a strong impervious finish with high shrinkage and cracking; lime is introduced to soften the mix and give the property of being able to absorb moisture which is given off rapidly when the rain has ceased. A mix of 1 part cement : ½ part lime : 4½ parts sand is suitable as a first coat for expanded metal and walls of dense strong materials. If the lime content is increased to 1 part cement : 1 part lime : 6 parts sand it will make a good average mix for the first coat on most other walling materials. It will also make a final coating for expanded metal. A good average final coating for all but severe conditions of exposure would be 1 part cement : 2 parts lime : 9 parts sand.

The hydrated lime is mixed with sand to the required proportions first and then the required proportion of cement is added. Ideally, the sand and lime should be allowed to stand for about 16 hours before the cement is added, but it should be protected during this time to prevent it drying out. If the sand and lime are allowed to stand the resultant mix will be more workable. Once the cement is added the mix should be used immediately.

Two coats are standard practice, but three coats are used when very irregular surfaces have to be levelled up and three coats are always used on expanded metal. The first coat should not be more than 16 mm (⅝ in) thick. This is the 'floating' coat and is given ample time to dry and harden before the second or final coat is applied. The floating coat is given wavy horizontal combings when it has started to set. This is to provide a key for the final coat. These lines should be about 19 mm (¾ in) apart and about 6 mm (¼ in) deep. The final coating is quite thin and should not exceed 9 mm (⅜ in) and in most cases is not more than 6 mm (¼ in).

Roughcast needs a first coat of 1 part cement : ½ part lime : 4½ parts sand. The second coat which is the actual roughcast is 1 part cement : ½ part lime : 1½ parts shingle: 3 parts sand. The shingle can vary from 6 mm (¼ in) to 13 mm (½ in). Sufficient water is added to make a plastic mix which can be thrown on to the wall from a bucket using a scoop or a laying-on trowel. The final appearance depends on the way in which the material is applied and an endeavour should be made to get an even texture with a wide spread of the rendering mortar.

For pebbledash the first coat is 1 : 4½ with a waterproofer added. The second coat 1 : 1 : 5 cement, lime, sand is applied about 12 mm (½ in) thick. This coating is brought to an even and regular surface by drawing a straightedge over it and then while the rendering is still soft aggregate is dashed against it and gently pressed with a wooden float, to ensure a good bond. The aggregate is thrown from a bucket using a laying-on trowel or a scoop, in a similar manner to roughcast and again the object is to get an even and uniform appearance.

Another finish, though not often used, is produced by first applying a mix of 1 part cement : 4½ parts sand with a waterproofer added, followed by a final coat mixed at 1 : 2 : 9. When the final coat has started to set, the surface is scraped with an old saw blade or similar tool. Then the surface is brushed lightly to remove all the loose dust. This method produces a textured finish showing the larger particles of the aggregate.

Whatever the finish to be applied, the method of application of the two coats of rendering is the same. The rough surface of the wall is levelled up by applying bands of the mortar horizontally across the face of the brickwork. These bands of mortar are positioned as wide apart as can be spanned by an 1800 mm (6 ft) straightedge. They are made the same 16 mm (⅝ in) thickness as the finished coating and are straight and smooth. In really first-class work they are plumbed as well. When they have set, they are used as a guide to level off the rendering. A laying-on float is used to spread the mortar mix between these bands and then the straightedge is used with a sawing action to scrape the excess material off the wall and leave a level and even surface.

The second coat which is much thinner and is applied to a level surface does not usually need these bands of mortar as a guide, but there is no reason why a beginner should not use them to help him to get a good surface. In any case when the coating has been spread over the surface to a fairly even thickness it is scraped off level with a straightedge as before.

Scaffolding is, of course, needed for both external rendering and internal plastering, because the wall has to be coated in bands about 1800 mm (6 ft) wide. This is as much as the average man can reach. These scaffolds must be independent; holes where horizontal supports for the planks have been inserted into the wall cannot be made good after the work is finished. The structure should be a minimum of 225 mm (9 in) from the face of the wall to which the rendering is to be applied.

Tyrolean finish is an interesting texture that can be applied to walls by means of a hand operated splatter machine. The mix is 1 part ordinary or white cement : 2 parts sand and a colouring agent can be included if required. Enough water is added to make a creamy mix that can be splattered in layers on to the background. Make up only enough mix to be used in one hour. An alternative is to use a proprietary material called Cullamix made by the Cement Marketing Co. Ltd. This is a dry mix that only needs water adding. It can be obtained in a small range of colours.

There are various methods of preparing a suitable base for the decorative finish and these depend on the type of wall and its exposure. Application can be made direct to cavity walls and calcium silicate bricks, provided that the surface is clean and dry and free from any algae or lichen. All walls should have damp proof courses and overhanging eaves. The material is not suitable for application to previously painted surfaces.

All window frames and other areas which are not to be coated must be masked. The material is mixed in a clean bucket using 5 measures of Cullamix to 2 measures of clean water. Application is in layers to give a honeycombed texture. The interval between the layers will depend on the suction of the surface. If the wall is sufficiently absorbent the process will be practically continuous. Where an area cannot be completed in one day the edge is feathered out to blend in with the next day's work.

The splatter machine should not be overloaded with material, it is better to use small quantities at frequent intervals. Turn the handle so that the maximum amount of material is thrown on to the wall and keep the machine moving with its mouth tilted slightly downwards to avoid overloading the flickers. After the first layer the speed of turning the handle is reduced to allow the flickers to pick up more material which when thrown on to the first layer forms the basis of the texture. The first layer is thrown from as far as possible from the wall but the second layer has to be thrown from much nearer to compensate for the reduction in the spread. A new layer must not be applied while the previous layer is still wet. For the application of the first layer it does not matter whether the machine points squarely at the wall or at an angle to it, but for subsequent layers the material is flicked on at an angle to accentuate the texture.

To provide a protective rendering and decorative finish to most types of brickwork and concrete blocks where there is adequate key, a render coat can be followed by the Tyrolean finish. The render coat is applied about 10 mm (⅜ in) thick using a mix of 1 part cement : 1 part lime : 6 parts clean sharp sand. A proprietary mortar plasticiser can be used in place of the lime. The rendering is applied in the usual way and finished with a wood float. It is not keyed. For exposed conditions the rendering has a waterproofing agent incorporated. The mix is 1 part cement : 3 parts clean sharp sand. It is applied in the usual way, well keyed and allowed to dry for a minimum of five days. Next, a second coat mixed at 1 : 1 : 6 (cement, lime, sand) is applied and then the Tyrolean finish is applied when the rendering is dry.

An alternative finish is to rub down the surface of the decorative finish after it has been left for at least 24 hours to dry. The surface is then rubbed lightly with a carborundum or other suitable stone, using a circular motion to flatten the high points and leave all the valleys and indentations untouched. As the rubbing proceeds, the dust must be brushed out of the textured surface simultaneously, in order to be able to see just how much to rub to obtain an even texture. Mechanical rubbing is too severe and should not be employed. The operation must not be carried out if the surface is wet. Rubbing down can be done to the finish whatever the age, but it will of course take longer, as the finish hardens with time. Another way of obtaining a similar finish is to rub a straight-grain wooden float very lightly over the surface of the Tyrolean finish two or three hours after the application. The effect is to flatten the high points just sufficiently to retain an open texture.

Independent scaffolding must be used for access when carrying out this work and the boards must be turned back during rain or overnight in order to avoid splashing. If the decoration dries out rapidly due to drying winds or high temperature, then it will be necessary to spray the area lightly with water twice a day until the material has fully hardened. The machines for applying the splatter finish can be hired from the suppliers of the Tyrolean finish materials.

Internal plastering

Cement is not often used for internal plastering, internal plasters are based on gypsum which is mixed with sand or used neat. The Thistle brand of plasters made by British Gypsum Ltd, include backing coats and finishing plasters.

All walls to be finished in gypsum plasters must be reasonably dry and protected from the weather. Raked out joints will improve the bond between the plaster and the background. Wooden linings for door openings, cupboard frames and other woodwork must stand proud of the brickwork by about 10 mm (⅜ in) to allow for the plaster. The background must be brushed down with a hard broom to remove dust, loose mortar and salts.

Gypsum plaster does not need a long drying-out period so that the finish plaster can be applied to the undercoat fairly soon after undercoating has been completed. If the finished plaster is applied correctly it will be free from shrinkage cracks. Full strength is attained within a few hours of it setting and special treatment of angles is unnecessary.

Good adhesion is obtained by applying the undercoat with firm pressure. When building up a thick coating a thin layer should be applied first with firm pressure, then it is built up to the required thickness and levelled with a straightedge, against horizontal bands of plaster set up in the same way as those used when rendering surfaces with cement and sand mixes.

Thistle Browning is an undercoat which is suitable for most solid backgrounds and is applied as a floating coat of 11 mm (7/16 in) thick. When brought to an even surface it is scratched to provide a key for the Thistle finish coating. This is applied about 2 mm (less than 1/8 in) thick and used neat. It is trowelled to a smooth surface using a steel plastering trowel.

There are a few problems encountered in plastering and those that occur are due mainly to the incorrect use of the materials. Cracks may be caused by structural movement and most commonly occur on ceilings where they are caused by the movement of the timber joists or shrinkage of concrete lintels. Other cracks which appear on the walls around lintels and window sills may be caused by settlement or by thermal movement. These cracks can be cut out and filled, but as they are likely to reappear the repair should be delayed as long as possible.

Crazing in the form of hair cracks in the finishing coat may be due to using a loamy sand in the undercoating or it could be that the finish has been applied over a cement or lime based undercoat before the undercoat has had time to dry out. The filling of so many fine cracks would be very difficult and the area may have to be lined with wallpaper.

Failure to let a cement or cement-lime based undercoat dry out sufficiently will also cause the loss of adhesion of the finishing coat. Other causes are the failure to key the undercoat properly and also adding too much sand to the undercoat, making it too weak. The only remedy for a poor backing is to strip it off completely and replaster using a stronger mix. Where only the finish coating is affected then it can be stripped off and the undercoat given time to dry thoroughly. Its surface should be roughened and all the dust removed with a damp brush. Then the surface can be replastered in the normal way.

Plasterboard

Ceilings and walls can be lined with plasterboard which is either given a finishing coat of plaster or, if the board is fixed with the

RENDERING AND PLASTERING

ivory side outward, it can be filled at the joints and decorated. If
the boards are fixed with the grey side out then they need to be
given a skim coat of Board Finish Plaster.

Ceiling boards are fixed first and then the walls are dry lined
with the plasterboard. Ceiling joists must be placed so that they
give adequate support to the boards, which for 1220 mm (4 ft)
boards means 400 mm (16 in) centres. The paper covered edges
of the plasterboard need no extra support where they cross the
joist but it is better if the cut edges of the boards are supported
on noggings fixed between the joists where appropriate. The
nails used must not cut through the paper covering and special
galvanised or Sherardised nails are available. A solid fixing is
needed around the perimeter of the ceiling to prevent the plaster
pushing the boards up to make a wavy line when the walls are
plastered. The end joints of the boards should be staggered, not
in a straight line across the ceiling. Before plastering starts, the
joints are filled flush with Thistle Board Finish. All internal and
external angles and the angles between the walls and ceilings are
reinforced with jute scrim not less than 90 mm (3½ in) wide.
This joint filling should be left to set, but not dry out, before
plastering commences.

The skim coat of finishing plaster is applied using a wooden
float to spread the material as evenly as possible over the boards.
The finish plaster is used neat and is mixed with water in a clean
bucket. Add the plaster to the water stirring all the time, beating
out any lumps and bringing the plaster to a creamy consistency.

When the plaster starts to set it is smoothed with a steel
plastering trowel. A small amount of water applied with a brush
just ahead of the trowel will help to ease the setting plaster to a
smooth finish, but do not use too much water or over trowel the
surface as this could make the finished work dusty.

Where it is necessary to plaster over glazed surfaces or walls
finished with oil paints, old brickwork or other difficult surfaces,
Carlite Bonding Coat or Welterweight should be used, in
conjunction with a proprietary bonding agent. The surfaces must
be wirebrushed to remove loose paint and other extraneous
matter. Then they should be washed down with a detergent and
rinsed, and be left to dry out thoroughly.

Carlite is a retarded hemihydrate pre-mixed gypsum plaster made by British Gypsum and requires only the addition of water to prepare it for use. The Bonding Coat is an undercoat for low suction backgrounds and the Carlite Browning is an undercoat for most solid backgrounds which offer an adequate mechanical key. It is applied about 11 mm ($^7/_{16}$ in) thick and brought to an even surface with a straightedge then lightly scratched to form a key for the Carlite finish. The finish plaster is applied at 2 mm (less than $^1/_8$ in) thick as soon as the floating coat has set. It is brought to a smooth surface using a steel trowel.

Dry lining walls

Instead of plastering the walls with wet material in the traditional way, they can be lined with plasterboards which are stuck to the brickwork with dabs of plaster or special adhesive. Normally the system is used to secure 900 mm ($35^1/_2$ in) wide, 9.5 mm ($^3/_8$ in) or 12.7 mm ($^1/_2$ in) thick, tapered-edge boards.

Installation starts by marking the walls vertically at 450 mm ($17^3/_4$ in) centres and then checking them with a straightedge to find the high spots. At these points bitumen-impregnated fibreboard pads are stuck in place with plaster. These pads are used as a guide for fixing the rest of the pads. Two pads are fixed at each angle, one 230 mm (9 in) from the ceiling and the other 100 mm (4 in) from the floor. They are carefully plumbed and then an intermediate pad is fixed half-way betweem them. This process is continued down all the marked lines, making sure that they are all in line horizontally and plumb vertically.

When the pads have set, which takes about two hours, Thistle Board Finish plaster or Gyproc multi-purpose adhesive is applied to the wall in a series of dabs between the pads, about three dabs between each pad vertically. Each dab should be the length of a plasterer's trowel and thick enough to stand pround of the pads. There should be a space of 50 mm (2 in) to 75 mm (3 in) between the dabs and they should be between 50 mm (2 in) and 75 mm (3 in) wide. Only enough dabs should be applied for one board at a time and those at the joints should be set about 25 mm (1 in) in from the line.

Next, taper edged boards are placed in position starting from an internal angle or a window reveal. The boards should be cut not less than 13 mm (½ in) and not more than 25 mm (1 in) shorter than the floor to ceiling height. The boards are pressed back against the pads using a straightedge. After ensuring that the leading edge is plumb and central on the joint pads, double-headed nails are driven through the boards and into the pads. They are generally only required at the edges.

The nails are driven until the first head slightly dimples the surface of the board which they will then hold in position for the critical setting period. These nails can be removed by pulling the second head with pincers. This process of fixing is repeated until the walls are fully lined. Joints should be only lightly butted and at internal angles if a board has to be cut, the cut edge is fitted into the angle.

Window reveals are lined with narrow widths of board cut so that they line up with the pads on the main wall face. These strips of plasterboard are fixed by applying dabs of plaster to their backs and pressing them into position. The lining to the window head will have to be temporarily supported. The main wall is lined from the window opening allowing the bound edge of the plasterboard to cover the cut edge of the reveal.

Dry lining is carried out using the ivory decorating side of the board outwards and the joints are filled with a special compound which is reinforced with a paper tape. The filler comes in 12.5 kg bags and is mixed by sprinkling it into water until a thick creamy consistency is achieved. When a layer of filler has been pressed into the joint the tape is applied and a second layer of filler is trowelled over the top. Before the filler starts to stiffen a sponge is damped and surplus material is wiped from the boards. When the filler has set, any depressions are filled in and smoothed over.

Next, joint finish is applied after the filler has set but not necessarily dried out. This material is applied in two layers allowing the first to dry before the second is applied. Each of the layers is feathered out to mask the joints completely.

Laying a floor screed

A fine topping or screed can be laid on the top of the base concrete of a floor in order to provide a finer surface than may be possible with the coarser concrete used for the structure. This topping, which can be from 25 mm (1 in) to 50 mm (2 in) thick is applied very much in the same manner as rendering. First, strips of topping mix are laid and in them lengths of wooden batten are bedded to make a firm and level guide from which to straighten up the filling between them using a straightedge. The battens are then removed and the hollows filled.

When the cement topping has started to set it is trowelled to a smooth surface using a steel trowel. The mix should be fairly dry having just sufficient water in it to make it possible to lay it. It should be smoothed carefully, trowelling the surface as little as possible because over trowelling will bring the cement to the top and cause the finished surface to be dusty.

7 Drains and rainwater disposal

The basic sewage and drainage system that we know today was devised only about a hundred years ago, after medical science had proved that there was a link between disease and the open sewers and piles of filth that lined the streets in those days. Their discovery provided the necessity which brought about the invention of the salt glazed drain pipe. However, the egg-shaped, butt-jointed pipe, which was the forerunner of our present-day circular salt-glazed pipe was unknown in 1840. Since that time the Victorian engineers devised and installed a drainage system which today forms the backbone of our sewage disposal system. Even so, the glazed, socketed, circular pipe was not in universal use until about 1900.

Water closets had been patented as early as 1775, but without the mass production of suitable pipes the water-carried sewage system was impracticable. The first system was of the combined type in which one large pipe carried all types of discharge from soil and waste fittings as well as taking the surface water. This was replaced later with a two-pipe system in which parallel pipes were laid, one to take the surface water and the other to take the discharge from soil and waste fittings. It was then found that the foul drain often became insanitary because of the lack of flow, so a partially separate system was devised in urban areas where the surface water drain took the discharge from the main roofs and gullies and the soil and waste sewer took the discharge from the back additional roofs and the paved yards to provide the necessary water which would assist the flow in the drain.

Insistance on inspection chambers at every change of direction was not by any means generally adopted and the drain layer often laid pipes to curves by knocking off a piece of the spigot end of a pipe so that it could be forced at an angle into the socket of another pipe. The necessity for calculating the proper falls was understood but every drain layer interpreted this according to his own ideas, so that drains followed their own way underground. Early gullies were inefficient and interceptor traps were incorporated in the drains as a first line of defence against foul air from the sewer, and the traps of the gullies and fittings served as a second line of defence. It has been said that the best period of drainage for surburban housing was from about 1890 to 1914 when the first world war put an end to it.

The joints of the early glazed pipes were caulked with clay and, not surprisingly, this was unsatisfactory. Later, when cement was used there was some difficulty in keeping the pipe central in the socket while the cement was wet. The wet cement would ooze through the joint at the bottom of the pipe and set to form a ridge on the inside and thus cause an obstruction to the flow.

This problem was overcome with the introduction of the tarred hemp gasket, which is inserted all around the spigot end of the pipe and driven into the socket rebate using a special caulking tool. A mix of 1 : 3 cement and sand is used to finish off the joint and this is neatly bevelled to about 45 degrees. Care has to be taken to ensure that the under side of the pipe is well caulked and filled with cement as it can be difficult to get at.

The traditional tarred hemp and cement method of jointing salt-glazed pipes has now given way to more modern methods, which include various patents. These new joints allow a degree of movement to take place without the joint or the pipe cracking. The new joints are based on the old principles of sleeves or O-rings but the materials are polyester or pvc (*Figure 7.1*). Building regulations require joints to remain watertight under all conditions including differential movement between the pipe and the ground.

Fall is of great importance to the design of a drain and it should be sufficient only to carry the sewage and the greatest quantity of rainwater. Where the pipe is used for sewage alone a moderate fall is better than a steep one. The liquid should not

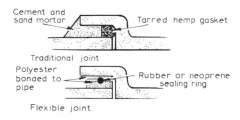

Figure 7.1. Section through part of a drain pipe showing two methods of forming a water-tight seal. The top method is rigid but the bottom method is to some degree flexible

run away leaving deposits to form and adhere to the drain. Fortunately, there is a rule-of-thumb method of determining the fall required and this will be suitable for use when laying domestic drains or extending them. Known as Maguire's rule it consists of simply multiplying the diameter of the pipe in inches by ten. Therefore, a 100 mm (4 in) pipe needs a fall of 1 in 40 and a 150 mm (6 in) pipe needs a fall of 1 in 60.

Inspection chambers (*Figure 7.2*), or manholes as they are sometimes called, are needed for proper access to the drain for

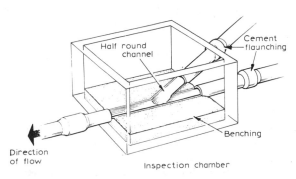

Figure 7.2. An inspection chamber showing the half-round channels and the benching

repair and cleaning. They are situated at each change of direction of the drain and at 91 m (300 ft) intervals along straight runs of drains. There must be room in the chamber for a workman to be able to stoop down or kneel to fit stoppers and operate cleaning rods or other equipment. This is not so important where the invert depth is not more than about 915 mm (3 ft). For depths of 1.83 m (6 ft) the inspection chamber must be at least 1 m × 660 mm (3 ft 3 in × 2 ft 2 in). Extra width will be needed where there are a number of branches entering the chamber.

The chambers are generally built in brickwork and must be watertight. This is important not only to prevent the sewage seeping out, in case of a stoppage that fills the chamber, but ground water is not wanted in the drain so it must not be allowed to enter. The brickwork is built in English bond using a special quality brick, or dpc quality brick and a suitably strong mortar mix. There are also precast concrete manholes obtainable. These are made in circular sections which can be placed one on top of the other to provide the necessary depth. In this type of installation it is important that the joints between the sections are watertight.

All bends and branches into the drain must be in the direction of the flow and the channels are bedded in cement mortar. Benching has to be provided at the sides of the channels and this has to rise up to the height of the top of the outgoing sewer. These benchings are given a slope of 1 in 6 up to the sides of the manhole and they must provide a safe foothold for workmen. The benching is finished to a hard smooth surface using a mix of one part cement to one part sand.

There are also plastic moulded inspection chambers which, if they carry an Agrément Certificate, can be used with plastic, pitch fibre or vitrified clay pipes. The different local authorities take their own differing views of plastic drains and pitchfibre drains so that it is essential that enquiries are made before specifying these two types.

There are two methods of providing domestic drainage, one is the single-stack system (*Figure 7.3*) and the other is the two-pipe system (*Figure 7.4*). In the two-pipe system the soil and the

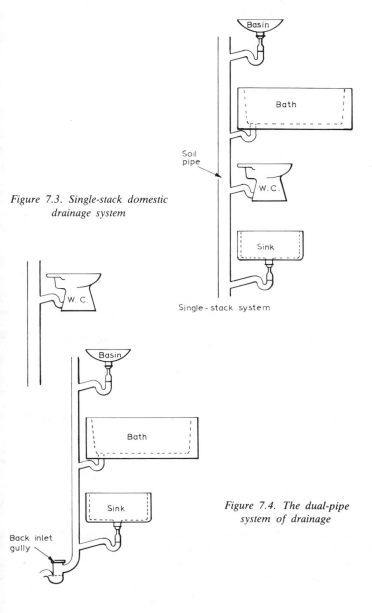

Figure 7.3. Single-stack domestic drainage system

Soil pipe

Single - stack system

Figure 7.4. The dual-pipe system of drainage

Back inlet gully

117

waste water are piped separately and in the single-stack system they are conveyed together. Whatever system is used, the whole object of the plumbing system, if it is to operate satisfactorily, is to ensure that the traps in the various appliances remain sealed at all times. These seals can be broken by the pull induced by siphonage caused by the full flow of the drain lower down the pipe line or by the full flow of the waste through the trap itself.

This self-induced siphonage is used in the siphonic w.c. suites to assist in the clearing of the pan. The traps are deliberately made to run at full bore to cause siphonage, then the siphon is broken so that the final wash of water fills the traps again.

The two-pipe system of domestic drainage is not installed now, but there are millions of old houses which use it. In this system, the soil stack takes the discharge from the w.c. or w.c.s only; the sink, bath and other wastes are discharged separately into hopper heads and downpipes to open gullies. The break at the hopper head and the gully and the ventilated soil stack ensure that the sewer gases do not enter the house. Unfortunately, the hopper head and the gulley can become quite foul and offensive so that some of the effect of the disconnection from the drain is lost.

Soil pipes for a domestic system are usually 100 mm (4 in) diameter, and in the single-stack system the old style hoppers are done away with and waste pipes from the bath, handbasin and sometimes sink discharge into the soil stack which, as with the two pipe system, acts as a vent pipe and is carried up at least 1 m (3 ft 3 in) above the top of any window that is within 3 m (10 ft) of the pipe.

In this system the soil pipe and the waste pipes are situated within the building and are therefore not as unsightly as the old systems which snaked all over the exterior of many buildings. To work correctly, the single stack system needs to be installed carefully in order to prevent the lack of ventilating pipes allowing the traps to become unsealed. The stack itself must be straight and the bend at the bottom, leading to the drain must be slow. The sanitary fittings should be grouped as close as is practicable to the stack pipe which is 100 mm (4 in) diameter cast iron or plastic.

Waste pipes to the fittings need to be fitted with traps giving 75 mm (3 in) seal. The maximum length for a sink waste is 2.3 m (7 ft 6 in) and the pipe should be 38 mm (1½ in) diameter, the self-cleansing gradient for this pipe being between 1 in 12 and 1 in 24; this will also reduce the possibility of self-siphonage in the trap. Baths and washbasins have waste pipes 32 mm (1¼ in) diameter and these need a fall of between 1 in 12 and 1 in 48. The maximum length for a bath waste is 2.3 m (7 ft 6 in) and for a washbasin it is 1.7 m (5 ft 6 in). All the waste pipes must be connected to the soil stack separately above the w.c. connection or at least 203 mm (8 in) below the centre line of the w.c. connection.

In many houses it is more convenient to carry the sink waste to an adjacent gully rather than move the sink to within the limits of the permitted length of waste pipe. If this is done the gully must be of the back entry type so that the waste discharges below the level of the grating and above the level of the water in the trap.

The soil branch for the w.c. must not be more than 1.5 m (4 ft 11 in) long. If there is a w.c. at ground-floor level it must be at least 460 mm (18 in) above the bottom of the bend at the foot of the soil stack. The correct fall for the soil branch is an angle of 104 degrees to the vertical soil stack.

A minimum seal must be kept in the trap at all times and to do this there are various patent traps as well as the ordinary bends. For a single-stack system a seal of 75 mm (3 in) is required for traps up to 64 mm (2½ in) diameter. For traps of 75 mm (3 in) to 100 mm (4 in) diameter the seal has to be 50 mm (2 in) for any system of plumbing.

An efficient trap should be incorrodible and as self cleaning as possible. There should be access for cleaning and the trap should hold as little water as possible while giving the correct depth of seal. A trap is essentially a U-bend in a pipe and the different patterns have different names; when one leg of the bend leads to a horizontal outlet it is called a P-trap (*Figure 7.5a*). If there is a double bend so that the outlet leads vertically downwards it is an S-trap (Figure 7.5b). A running trap is one in which the inlet and outlet are both horizontal (*Figure 7.5c*). Bottle traps have a bend shaped like a bottle with a division down the middle (*Figure 7.5d*).

There are also patent self-resealing traps in which a vent pipe, extra chamber or an enlarged chamber are used to break the siphon caused when the traps run at full bore, and then hold back enough water to reseal the trap.

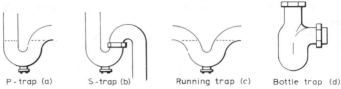

P-trap (a)   S-trap (b)   Running trap (c)   Bottle trap (d)

Figure 7.5. Types of trap for sealing pipes

The w.c. pan can be connected to the soil pipe with the usual hemp and cement joint, but a better method is to use one of the plastic connectors which are simply a push fit over the outlet spigot of the w.c. trap and also a push fit into the collar of the soil pipe. Using this type of connection means that any slight movement can be accommodated without the joint cracking as a cement joint may do. This is an important consideration when the w.c. is situated on a wooden floor, because it will not only be subject to thermal movement of the timber, but there may also be some slight springing of the floor which though otherwise unnoticeable, could bring about damage to a rigid pipe joint.

Waste pipes may be in copper, in which case they can be jointed either with the easily made, though clumsy looking, compression joint, or they can be soldered. The waste pipes are more likely to be plastic and in this case the joints can be simple, push-fit fittings which are sealed by means of a plastic or rubber O-ring or they can be a kind of compression fitting in which a large plastic nut drives a wedge-shaped plastic ring into the fitting to form a seal.

These plastic waste pipes can be uncoupled for cleaning; they are also used in conjunction with bottle traps, the bottom of which will unscrew for cleaning purposes. Where the U-bend type of trap is used there is generally a joint on the outlet leg of the trap which enables the outlet to be swivelled to face in any direction. Plastic waste pipes can also be of the solvent welded type which is a similar method to that used for the plastic soil systems.

Vertical plastic pipes need supporting brackets at about 1220 mm (4 ft) centres and horizontal runs need support at about 762 mm (2 ft 6 in) centres. Because of the amount of thermal movement which takes place in plastic piping, manufacturers make special fittings to accommodate this expansion and contraction and their recommendations must be carefully carried out. They also provide the necessary fittings and instructions for jointing the plastic system to metal or salt-glazed drain pipes.

As plastic pipe and fittings are manufactured to a good quality finish there is no need for any further work such as painting and decorating them. However, colours are limited mainly to grey, brown or black, dependent on the manufacturer, but some white products are also available.

Rainwater systems

When installing a rainwater system it is important that the gutters and downpipes are adequate for the area of roof which has to be drained. The flow capacity for a straight gutter depends on its cross section, its shape and the length, also the fall. The fall will increase the capacity up to a point, but there is a limit because too much slope would make too big a gap between the edge of the roof and the gutter so that much of the water would be blown against the wall before it reached the trough. Although the length does not influence the flow capacity it does determine the area of roof being drained and therefore the quantity of water collected.

A level gutter 11 m (36 ft) long and made of 112 mm (4½ in) half-round sections could carry 68 litres (15 gal) per minute. If the same length of gutter were given a fall of 25.4 mm in

5846 mm (1 in in 18 ft) it could carry 118 litres (26 gal) per minute.

Of course, there are other factors to take into consideration; if there is a right-angled bend near an outlet it will reduce the capacity by about 20 per cent. If the bend is 1.8 m to 3.6 m (6 ft to 12 ft) from the outlet then the reduction in carrying capacity can be reduced to 10 per cent.

The position of the outlet also has a bearing on the gutter capacity. If the outlet is at the centre of the gutter, the gutter capacity required is only half that which would be needed if the outlet were placed at the end of the run. The correct positioning of the gutter depends on the type of roofing material. If it is a slate roof then the gutter is placed centrally under the edge of the overhanging slates and not more than 50 mm (2 in) beneath them. Water running off roof coverings such as clay pantiles behaves differently and spreads out as it leaves the edge. This means that the gutter must be close to the edge and with its centre slightly forward. If the lower edge of the roof is rounded then the gutter must be placed more to the rear to catch the water which will be deflected backwards. The best type of roof edging is one in which the top edge is rounded and the bottom edge is sharp.

It is best if it is possible to have the rainwater discharged into the local authority stormwater drainage system or combined sewer if it is used, but often the water has to be taken to a soakaway. This is a pit dug at some distance from the property and filled with clean rubble (*Figure 7.6*). The rainwater is drained into this pit and allowed to soak away into the surrounding earth, if possible the rainwater is directed to stream.

The soakaway has to be carefully constructed otherwise it will soon fill due to clogging or saturation of the surrounding area. The pit must not be dug within 3 m (10 ft) of the house and twice that distance if the ground is clay, or if the pit has to be in such a position that the dispersing water will affect the foundations of the building.

When the pit has been dug and filled with clean brick rubble, it should be covered with a strong polythene sheet or a concrete slab about 300 mm (12 in) below ground level to prevent the

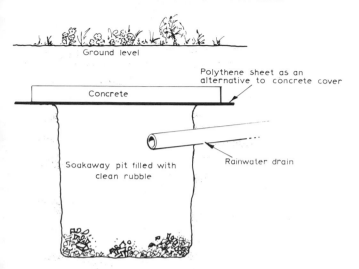

Figure 7.6. A soakaway. It can be covered with either polythene sheeting or a concrete slab

garden soil being washed into the rubble and clogging the pit. The pipes leading to the pit should be 100 mm (4 in) diameter and can be laid to the same fall as the domestic drainage system. In soft ground the soakaway pit can be lined with perforated precast concrete rings, which are dry jointed. The tank which is formed can either be left empty or it can be filled with rubble. In either case it still needs to be covered over the top.

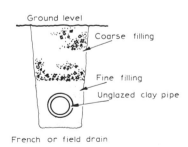

Figure 7.7. A French, or field drain for draining the water off the surrounding land

The drainage of the subsoil is essential on some sites, particularly sloping sites or low lying sites. These drains are known as field or French drains and are simply unglazed clay pipes set to falls and covered with clean rubble or gravel before back filling the trench (*Figure 7.7*). They are usually laid herringbone fashion leading to a slightly larger drain which discharges at a lower level, preferably into a stream.

The trenches for the drains should be dug as narrow as possible and the bottom should be given a fall of about 1 in 100. The distance between the trenches will, of course, vary with the type of soil and can be from 3 m (10 ft) to 9 m (30 ft). The pipes are laid dry with butt joints, the uneven surfaces providing sufficient space for the water to get through. About 380 mm (15 in) of gravel or fine rubble is laid over the pipes before the earth is replaced, loosly at first and then well rammed. On no account should the land drain to be taken underneath a building.

Section 2

Woodworking

1 Introduction

Woodworking has so many facets to it that even dedicated craftsmen continue to learn about it throughout their lives. However, even acknowledged experts in any field of human activity have to start somewhere and this book is for those whose background to the craft is limited, and who are quite willing to call themselves beginners. Before we can use a material or handle tools competently we should learn something about them. Let us start with wood.

Wood

A cross section of a tree trunk, showing main parts only, is given in *Figure 1.1*. The best quality timber is cut from the heartwood (duramen); this is usually darker in colour than the sapwood, which contains living cells and is not so dense. Heartwood gives strength and support to the tree while new growth builds up around the sapwood, from the cambium layer beneath, and protected by, the bark.

Annual rings (growth rings) are formed each year: in the spring when sap is rising, and in the autumn when it is falling. Hence the names, spring wood and summer wood. The age of a tree can be calculated by counting the growth rings. Close annual rings indicate slow growth, wide ones indicate quick growth.

Growth rings of hardwoods are generally much closer than those of softwoods, and often less pronounced. Timber with close rings is usually more stable and less liable to distortion than wide ringed timber. Less than six rings to the inch in softwoods is often unacceptable for structural work.

Trees are divided into two classes: (1) broadleaf trees usually shed their leaves in winter, although some are evergreen. Such

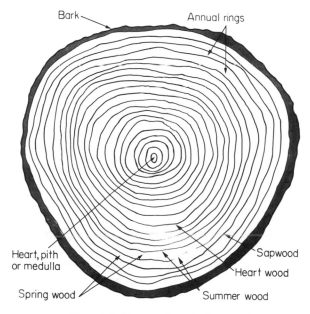

Figure 1.1. Cross section of a tree trunk

trees produce hardwood. Class (2) are the conifers, usually evergreen with needle-like leaves amongst which are produced cones. These are the softwoods.

The terms softwood and hardwood are rather inclined to be misnomers because balsa, the softest wood known and used for modelling, buoyancy aids, some stage furniture (such as a chair broken over the hero's head) etc., is classified as a hardwood while yew, once used to make longbows and now used for fencing, furniture and decorative items, is dense, hard, and very durable; although it is a softwood. A point to observe in these classifications is that softwood and hardwood are each one word. When the term soft wood (two words) is used, it indicates a characteristic of the particular species, not its classification.

Despite the reservations above, here are some general characteristics of hardwoods and softwoods.

Hardwoods	Softwoods
Tend to be harder and denser than softwoods	Tend to be softer and lighter than hardwoods
Slow growing, therefore annual rings tend to be close	Faster growing, therefore annual rings well spaced
Annual rings often indistinct	Annual rings usually well pronounced
Not much resin content	Some species very resinous
Knots can be very large but usually not many of them	Many small knots are common and some large ones
Wide colour range over the hardwood species, with many rich, colourful and dark shades	Mostly pale creamy white to light brown, with the exception of yew

Newly felled timber is taken to the saw mill for conversion, as the initial sawing of the round log into plank and board form is called. The most common method of conversion is 'slab' sawing, also known as slash sawing or sawing through-and-through (*Figure 1.2*). The method of sawing and the part of the trunk sawn has some influence on the timber produced as shrinkage during drying or seasoning takes place. The illustration shows a plain sawn log, which is the easiest and cheapest method of converting. Plank (*a*) would distort by cupping away from the heart side, as would plank (*c*).

Plank (*b*), referred to as a radial plank, would shrink in width but would remain fairly flat.

Planks sawn so that the growth rings meet the face at an angle of not less than 45 degrees are called quarter sawn, the most desirable timber for first class constructional work. When

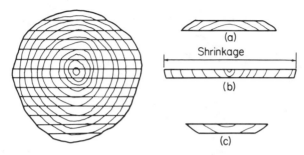

Figure 1.2. Timber conversion. Tangential planks are shown in section at (a) and (c). A radial plank is shown at (b)

the growth rings are at an angle of less than 45 degrees the plank is described as plain sawn. These planks show the fine contour-line oval grain configurations. Plain sawing can therefore produce both types.

Before timber can be used for constructional purposes it has to be dried, or seasoned, to reduce the amount of moisture in the timber (moisture content) to suit the situation where the timber will be used. There are two methods of seasoning.

Natural seasoning

Here the sawn timber is stacked on level ground with spacers or 'stickers' between the planks, to allow a free circulation of air. This is the old way, but it is slow, taking about one year for each 25 mm (1 in) of thickness of material (*Figure 1.3*). Ends of slabs may be painted or otherwise sealed to prevent too rapid drying and weights may be placed on top of the stack to prevent movement.

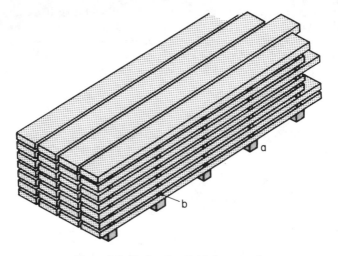

Figure 1.3. Timber 'in-stick', for seasoning

Kiln drying

This is much quicker and a lower moisure content can be
achieved by the carefully controlled conditions it is possible
to create in the kiln. The stacking system is similar to that
used in natural seasoning. This takes place in an enclosed
chamber and by a combination of steam, dry air and fans the
time of drying is reduced from years to weeks.

Often timber bought at a local merchant's yard is only
partially seasoned. This can lead to complications, especially
with regard to shrinkage. Ideally, the timber should be carefully
stacked, as for seasoning, in the place it will be used so that
the moisture content can adjust to the environment. As stated
earlier, timber shrinks unequally: lengthways, with the grain,
nil; with the annual rings (circumferentially) considerably;
across the annual rings (radially) about half as much. Poor or
inefficient seasoning can lead to splitting, warping, bowing and

cupping. Leaning planks against a wall, ladderlike, for long times in sun, wind or rain can also cause bowing and warping, which is practically impossible to rectify (*Figure 1.4*).

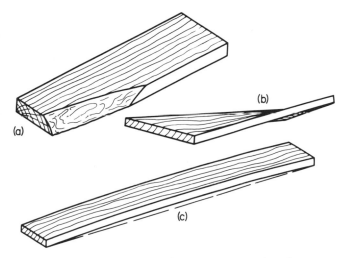

Figure 1.4. Defects in timber planks: (a) waney edge, (b) warped board, (c) bowing

Board (*b*) is twisted and (*c*) is bowed. A part waney edge is shown at (*a*). Waney edge is the outer part of the trunk covered, with bark. Some boards are sold with the waney edge for special use, such as cladding walls, but waney edges are not desirable on finished timber for structural use.

Terms

Already we have used terms which may be unfamiliar. Some of them are illustrated by the drawings but the following simple glossary will introduce a few more. It is good sense to learn the language of woodworking; you will then know what your supplier is talking about and, very importantly, he will know what you mean.

Air-dried	Seasoned as previously described, in open air conditions. Such timber will have a relatively high moisture content at least equal to the ambient climatic humidity. If used indoors and especially in heated rooms, such timber may shrink or deform unless carefully used. Generally such timber is satisfactory for normal constructional use such as roofing timbers, but during long periods of damp weather air-dried timber, and indeed any timber stored under normal climatic conditions during such periods, will have a high moisture content.
Board	Converted timber around 51 mm (2 in) or greater thickness. Manufactured product in sheet form.
Clean	Free from knots.
Clear	Free from visible defects and imperfections.
Density	Weight per unit volume such as lb per cubic ft or g per cubic cm.
Edge	Narrow side of square sawn timber.
End	Cross-cut surface of square sawn timber.
Face	Broad side of square sawn timber.
Figure	Ornamental markings, seen on cut surface of timber, formed by structural features of the wood.
Grain	General direction or arrangement of fibres. Plane of the cut surface, e.g. edge-grain, end-grain.
Lumber	Imported square edged sawn hardwood of random width. Also refers to all forms of sawn timber.
Machined	Having a surface or dimension that has been subject to machine operation after initial conversion.
Nominal	Size before planing. Planing will reduce the nominal thickness of a sawn board by about 3 mm ($\frac{1}{8}$in) and width by up to 6 mm ($\frac{1}{4}$in).
P1E	Planed one edge. P2E, planed two edges.
P1S	Planed one side. P2S, planed two sides.
P1S1E	Planed one side and one edge.
P4S	Planed four sides.

P.A.R.	Planed all round.
P.T.G.	Planed, tongued and grooved.
T. and G.	Re-sawn and machined boards to the general section shown in *Figure 1.5*. Much used for flooring.
Un-edged	Plank with both edges waney.

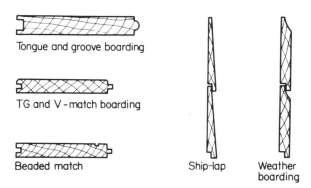

Tongue and groove boarding

TG and V - match boarding

Beaded match   Ship-lap   Weather boarding

Figure 1.5. Varieties of tongue and groove boarding

Man-made boards

Various composite boards are manufactured by quite involved processes requiring complicated machinery, intricate production lines and well organised factories. Probably the most common is fibreboard, which includes the ubiquitous hardboard, so well known it needs no description. Fibreboards range from fairly thick low density boards (insulation board) through various medium density boards to standard hardboard and finally oil-tempered hardboard, which is so dense that it can be used for external cladding and floor surfacing.

Fibreboard

This is made from wood and other ligneous materials after they have been reduced to a fibrous pulp. This pulp is carefully graded, spread on 'mats' to a predetermined thickness, pressed, dried and trimmed to standard size sheets. Various refinements in the general process described are added to produce the different qualities or grades.

Plywood

This is made from three or more thin laminations (or plies) of wood bonded together so that the grain of one ply is at right angles to its neighbour (*Figure 1.6*). Many grades are available according to type of wood used, whether surfaced

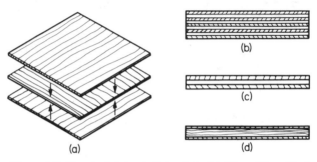

Figure 1.6. Plywood: (a) principle of construction, (b) multi-ply usually has an odd number of laminations, (c) 3-ply equal, which is stronger in one direction than the other, (d) 3-ply 'stout heart', which is of about equal strength in both directions

with a decorative veneer or not, thickness of laminations, quality of exterior surface, and type of glue used. Marine grade is made from best quality materials with water- and boil-proof glue.

Block-board, lamin-board and batten-board

These are composite boards with cores of solid softwood in the form of strips. The narrower the strips the less chance there is of distortion and surface undulations. It usually has birch faces and is frequently sold in veneered form.

Chipboard or particle board

In simple terms this is a board made from graded wood chips bonded together with an adhesive under great pressure and heat. Many manufacturers offer this material with veneered faces and edges in two or more standard lengths and up to ten widths from 152 mm (6 in) upwards. It is also available with melamine and other plastics surfaces. Chipboard, unveneered, is used for constructional work, including floors, and is manufactured to specific standards.

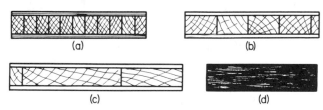

Figure 1.7. Composite boards: (a) lamin-board, (b) block-board, (c) batten-board, (d) veneer faced chipboard

Lamin-board, shown in *Figure 1.7* (*a*), is considered the best and most stable of the composite boards. The core strips, not more than 6mm ($\frac{1}{4}$ in) wide, are bonded together with the heart sides alternating. Lamin-board may have one or two outer plies. Block-board (*b*) has strips up to about 19 mm (¾ in) wide and also has one or two outer plies. Batten-board (*c*) has strips up to 76 mm (3 in) wide.

Veneer faced chipboard is shown in *Figure 1.7* (*d*). Often chips are graded from large ones in the centre to fine particles on the face. A point to watch is that in large particles screw-holding may be affected when edge fixing so it is advisable to use plugs specially made for chipboard.

Fixings and fittings

To assemble woodwork constructions, joints, glues, mechanical fixings and numerous fittings are needed. The most common fixing is the nail.

Wire nails are usually made from mild steel, but other metals are used for special purposes such as brass, gun metal or copper for boatbuilding. Diameter of the nail is referred to as the

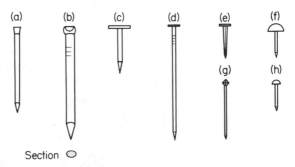

Section ◉

Figure 1.8. Nails: (a) panel pin, (b) oval, (c) clout, (d) wire or French nail, (e) tack, (f) upholstery nail, (g) hardboard nail, (h) escutchion pin

gauge, and nails are sold by weight. The most common nails used today, illustrated in *Figure 1.8*, are now described.

Panel pins

These are used in light woodworking and cabinet making (*a*). Thin nails, with small heads that are easily punched below the surface, they are obtainable from 13 mm ($\frac{1}{2}$ in) to 51 mm (2 in) long.

Ovals

These are oval in section, with small heads easily punched below the surface (*b*). The oval section helps to prevent splitting of thin wood, especially near edges. They are made in many sizes and have many applications in general woodworking.

Clout

This is a round nail with a large head (c). Invariably galvanised to prevent rusting, they are used mainly for fixing roofing felt and similar fabrics to sheds and outbuildings, or underfelts and other membranes before tiling or slating roofs.

Round heads

These are sometimes known as wire nails or French nails (d). Heads are not usually punched in as they are designed to take much of the load and in many constructions the nail heads are not objectional. They can, however, be sunk with a stout punch or 'nail set' and the hole can be stopped prior to painting or other finish.

The chance of splitting wood being fixed is greatly reduced if the point is nipped off a wire nail or pin, or if the head is placed on an iron mass while the point is given a direct tap with a hammer. The nails then tend to punch a hole through the wood rather than force the fibres apart.

Tacks

Usually available from 13 mm ($\frac{1}{2}$ in) long and with a blued finish to prevent rusting (e), they have round heads for gripping fabrics such as upholstery materials or carpets. To make 'starting' easier, tacks have fine, needle-like points. A very thin type of tack, also used for upholstering, is called a gimp pin.

Upholstery nails

About 19 mm ($\frac{3}{4}$ in) long, they have a large, domed head, are usually made of steel and electro-brassed to provide a decorative effect and are used to fix finishing edges or strips in upholstery (f).

Hardboard pins

These are thin, square section copper or cadmium coated pins (*g*) with diamond shaped 'lost head', easily punched in for stopping.

Escutcheon pin

This is a small, domed head nail, usually brass, for pinning small metal plates to a surface (*h*).

Screws

Generally, screws provide a stronger fixing than do nails, but are more expensive and more preparation is required. Screws are the usual means of securing brassware, ironmongery and

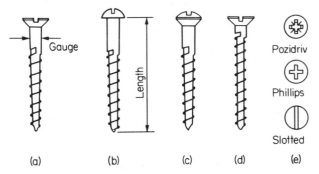

Figure 1.9. Screws: (a) countersunk, (b) round head, (c) raised head, (d) chipboard, (e) screwdriver patterns

other fittings. They are made in various metals, of which by far the most common is mild steel, followed by brass. They are also available in stainless steel and other hard, non-ferrous metals for marine and outside work, and aluminium alloy. Steel screws are sometimes finished with chrome and other deposited metals, or black enamel (japan).

They are made in many diameter sizes and lengths, and with different kinds of head (*Figure 1.9*). Gauge is the diameter of shank and length is measured from the widest diameter of the head to the tip of the point. Four common types of screw are: countersunk (csk) (*a*), round head (*b*), raised head (*c*) and csk chipboard screw (*d*). The extra thread on a chipboard screw provides more grip when fixing thin fittings.

Three screwdriver patterns are used (*Figure 1.9*) but the most common are slotted and Pozidriv. The Phillips is practically obsolete but a Pozidriv screwdriver can be used to drive Phillips pattern screws. A Phillips driver, however, should not be used for Pozidriv screws.

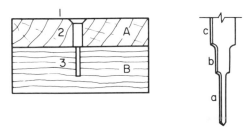

Figure 1.10. Preparation of wood for screwing (see text)

Where possible, screw fixing is done through the thinner material into the thicker (*Figure 1.10*). Preparation of two pieces of wood (A and B) for joining with a screw is shown: (1) is the countersink for csk screws, (2) is the clearance or shank hole and (3) is the pilot hole, which should be drilled first through both pieces if possible.

Special bits for drills, which bore the three sizes in one pass, are available for many screw sizes. The tip of such a drill is illustrated: (a) cuts the pilot hole, (b) cuts the shank hole and (c) the countersink.

Brass screws are soft and can easily shear off when being driven in, especially in a piece of close-grained hardwood. An old dodge is to initially insert a steel screw, then remove it

INTRODUCTION

and replace with a brass one. A scrape of candle wax or soap on the threads of large screws makes them go in much easier.

Pozidriv screws have a star-shaped recess in the head, instead of a slot. Main advantages are neatness, and far less chance of the screwdriver slipping and possibly damaging the surface. As with slotted screws, the correct size of screwdriver must be used in relation to the screw size.

Hinges

Many varieties of hinges are now available, including speciality hinges for step ladders and decorator's pasteboards, chipboard

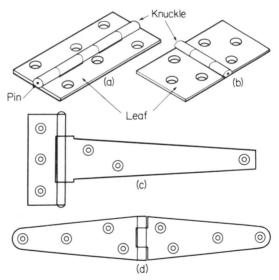

Figure 1.11. Hinges: (a) butt hinge, (b) back flap, (c) tee hinge (d) strap hinge

hinges, lay-on hinges and skeleton hinges which do not have to be housed in the hinged members. The more traditional types are still used every day (*Figure 1.11*). They include the following types.

Butt hinges, or butts   The best are of solid, cast brass and are used as door hinges on high quality cabinet and joinery work (*a*). Lighter patterns are available in pressed or folded brass. Cast iron butts are often used on heavy entrance doors and lighter, pressed steel butts are used for internal, domestic doors and other joinery. In all cases the pins are of steel or harder alloys. These hinges are usually sunk or 'housed' in the members, flush with the surface.

Back flaps   These are used where the wood is wide enough to take the leaves (*b*). This type of hinge, in brass or steel, enables the screws to be well spaced out, thus spreading the load and reducing chances of the wood splitting. They are also housed.

Tee hinges   These are usually in pressed steel, bright, or japanned (*c*). They are used mainly for exterior doors of ledged construction to sheds and outbuildings. Simple and strong, they are easy to fix and do not need to be housed in.

Strap hinges   This type can also be used for doors, but are much used on boxes and chests for storing tools, and so on (*d*).

Piano hinge   This is a thin, light hinge in the form of a continuous strip with leaves of about 13 mm ($\frac{1}{2}$ in) and screw holes every 50 mm (2 in) or so. This is also a surface fixed hinge used for boxes, light cupboard and wardrobe doors, in addition to piano lids.

Fittings

There are literally thousands of fittings made for woodworking, in addition to the usual knobs, bolts, catches and locks. Some fairly modern ones are shown in *Figure 1.12*.

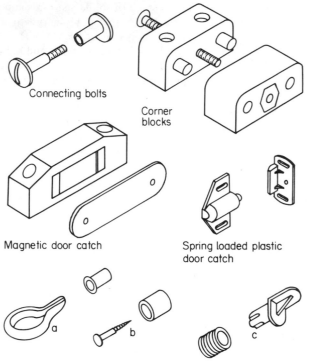

Connecting bolts

Corner blocks

Magnetic door catch

Spring loaded plastic door catch

Figure 1.12. Fittings. Various shelf fittings are also shown: (a) ring stem and sleeve, (b) stud, (c) insert and lug

Connecting bolts   These are used to join two cabinets or box constructions, especially if they are likely to be dismantled at some future date.

Corner blocks   These provide a simple means of making right-angled joints and are especially useful with chipboard constructions. Each half of the fitting is screwed to one of the pieces being joined. The two parts are then held together by a moulded-in nut and set screw.

Shelf fittings Three popular types are shown. The ring stem
(*a*) fits in the sleeve, which is inserted in a drilled hole, two or
more to each side. The shelf is supported by the flat rings. The
stud (*b*) is simply screwed to the upright sides to provide
support and at (*c*) the insert fits in a pre-bored hole and the
lug is pressed into it. Inserts can be fitted in 'ladder' formation;
the inserts can then be varied to suit the shelf space required.

Woodworking terms

Many terms are used in woodworking; some have meanings in
our everyday life but others are peculiar to the craft and may
have different meanings in ordinary usage. Some of the more
common are listed; others will be introduced as they are used
in subsequent chapters.

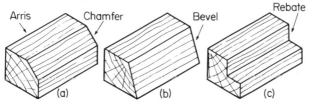

Figure 1.13. Terms applied to various edge treatments

Arris A sharp edge of wood left when an angle is formed
(*Figure 1.13*). It is often rounded off or radiused to avoid
damage.

Chamfer To remove an edge or corner for protection or
decoration. Normally the cut is made at 45 degrees, but this
angle can be varied. A chamfer is shown in *Figure 1.13(a)*.

Bevel In some ways similar to a chamfer and often confused
with it, a bevel is where the whole edge is planed at an angle
other than 90 degrees (*b*).

143

Rebate Where the edge of a member is cut away in the form of a step it is said to be rebated. Surfaces of the rebate are normally parallel to the main surfaces (*c*), but can sometimes be bevelled.

Groove While a rebate is formed on the edge, the groove is formed away from the edge, as shown in *Figure 1.14(a)*, with the grain. Across the grain this cut is called a trench, or dado

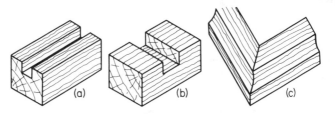

Figure 1.14. (a) Groove, (b) trench, (c) mitre

in American terms (*b*). When two corners are joined to conceal end grain the joint is called a mitre (*c*). This need not be at 90 degrees, as shown in the example.

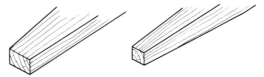

Figure 1.15. Simple tapers

Taper Simple tapers, as used on chair and table legs, are shown in *Figure 1.15*.

2 Tools

Good tools will last a lifetime and it is better to have a few tools of the right type and quality than a mass of third rate ones. Even in this age of machinery hand tools are indispensable and a woodworker's basic kit should include the following items.

Chisels

To start with, choose the bevelled edge firmer pattern (*Figure 2.1*) as this form enables the worker to get in to close corners and angles when trimming off, and paring off thin shavings when 'easing' a sinking, or cut. In the drawing (a) is the handle — these days made principally from high-density plastics material and formerly from boxwood or ash. The ferrule (b) prevents splitting of the handle and (c) is the tang which locates the chisel in its handle. The shoulder (d) prevents the tang from driving further into the handle. The bevel which gives the chisel its name is (e), while (f) is the grinding bevel and (g) is the honing or sharpening bevel. The tip of an ordinary firmer chisel is shown at (h) and (i) is that of the stouter mortise chisel.

Three sizes of chisel, 25, 13 and 6 mm (1, $\frac{1}{2}$, and $\frac{1}{4}$ in) are suggested as starters. New chisels should be sharpened before use; they are sold with only the grinding bevel applied. This is about 25 degrees, while the cutting bevel is about 30 degrees.

Chisels should be stored in a rack — blade guards, if available, should be used. This is to protect the easily damaged cutting edge. If a chisel has to be struck to do its cutting, hit it with a rubber, or wooden, mallet — never with metal hammers.

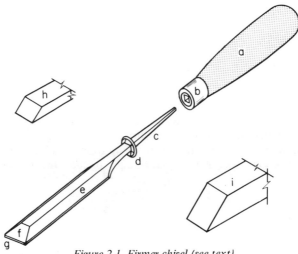

Figure 2.1. Firmer chisel (see text)

Mallet

Joiners' mallets are usually made of beech but other hard and dense woods may be used. Choose a medium size one for general use. Some workers make their own with square, rectangular or even round heads.

Marking gauge

A simple but much used tool for making lines with the grain and parallel to the face or edge of a workpiece *Figure 2.2*. The method of setting the gauge is shown in (*a*) and method of using is shown in (*b*). The stock of the gauge, which slides along the bar, is secured with a thumb screw, shown in (*a*).

Note that the gauge is tilted with the point just touching the work and held against the face edge. It is pushed away

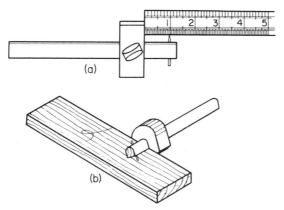

Figure 2.2. Marking gauge: (a) setting the gauge, (b) method of use

from the user and kept tight against the edge. The line should not be drawn over with a pencil. Always double check the setting before use.

Try-square

The traditional pattern, with a steel blade and wood or plastics stock, is shown in *Figure 2.3(a)* and the combination square, with a 305 mm (12 in) blade is illustrated at (*b*). This can be recommended as a tool with many uses without losing its efficiency as a try-square.

It can also be used for angles of 45 degrees and, because the blade is adjustable, it can be adapted for small or confined work which the fixed blade one will not. It can also be used as a marking gauge by holding a pencil against the blade and sliding both square and pencil along the work. Most combination squares have a small spirit level built into the stock.

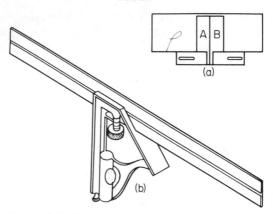

Figure 2.3. Try-square: (a) testing for accuracy, (b) combination square

To test a try square for accuracy, scribe a line with the square held as at A in *Figure 2.3(a)*, then reverse the square as at B and scribe a line again. They should coincide, or be parallel.

Rules

It is advisable to have two types: a folding rule of rigid material opening out to 1 m (39 in) is useful when working on the bench while a flexible one of the steel tape type up to 3 m (10 ft) is very handy when tackling bigger work or when measuring up for a project around the home.

At the present time both imperial and metric units are in use so it is just as well to buy rules with dual scales – metric down one side and imperial down the other.

Tenon saw

This is the general purpose saw used for bench work, including the cutting of most joints in woodwork. Tooth form and cutting action are shown in *Figure 2.4(a)* and *(e)*. As the back of the blade is stiffened with a steel or brass 'back' (hence the general name of back-saw to such tools) it is used only for

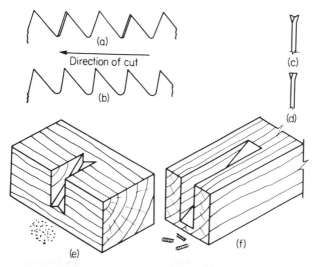

Figure 2.4. Sawing: (a) tenon saw tooth form, (b) rip saw tooth form, (c) 'set' of tenon saw teeth, (d) 'set' of rip saw teeth, (e) tenon saw kerf, (f) rip saw kerf

straight cuts and care should be taken to prevent buckling of the blade. A popular size is one with a 254 mm (10 in) blade and 14 points per inch (PPI). Larger and smaller blade sizes are available.

Angles and shape of saw teeth affect their cutting. Tenon and most other saws have teeth shaped to the cross-cut pattern (*a*). Teeth are bent alternately right and left and the needle-like points scribe a double line across the wood on each stroke. The remaining edges push out the waste matter in the form of 'dust'. This bending is called the 'set' and is shown, exaggerated, at (*c*). In practice the setting is only sufficient to allow the blade to run without binding and varies according to the number of teeth there are to the inch. This tooth form will cut with the grain but for extensive with-the-grain cutting the rip saw and rip-form shaped teeth are used (*b*). Angles are also different, the teeth edges being flat and chisel-like as shown at (*d*) – not needle pointed. These chisel points produce small curly shavings and the cutting action with a sharp saw is quite rapid. The cut made by a saw is called the 'kerf'. The kerf made by a cross cutting saw is shown at (*e*) and that made by the rip saw is shown at (*f*).

All saws should be looked after with great care and blade guards should be used when they are not in use. It is also a good idea to hang them up, by the handle, on pegs or hooks.

When a saw becomes 'dull', points of the teeth look dull. When they become blunt, they should be re-sharpened. This is a fairly skilful operation and the beginner is advised to send his saws to a 'saw doctor' for professional attention. Good hardware stores usually provide this service.

Hammers

The two most popular types of hammer for woodworking are the Warrington pattern and the claw hammer. Although both are available in different sizes or weights of head the Warrington is generally used for lighter work and the claw for constructional work in heavy timbers. The claw is useful for withdrawing nails.

A 6 oz cross pein Warrington for general use and a 3½ oz one for light work – often called a pin-hammer – are to be recommended, and a 10 to 16 oz claw hammer for heavy work.

Planes

Metal planes have now almost completely replaced the wooden planes of former years. There are many different planes, quite a number for specialist use, and there is a range of bench planes – the two most frequently in use being the jack plane, about

356 mm (14 in) long and the smoothing plane, about 230 mm (9 in). Different widths of blade are offered, the 51 mm (2 in) being popular. For a beginner these two can be regarded as interchangeable; apart from the obvious difference in length the other differences are controllable by the user. One is the shape of the cutting edge; some workers have two blades for a jack plane, one for preparing sawn stuff and the other for 'smoothing'.

Part of a typical bench plane is illustrated in *Figure 2.5*. This shows the front of the mouth, which prevents the wood from

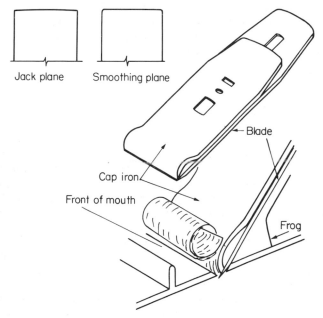

Jack plane   Smoothing plane

Blade

Cap iron

Front of mouth

Frog

Figure 2.5. Bench plane

splitting ahead of the blade. The cap iron creases and coils the shaving, and also stiffens the blade. This prevents the blade from 'chattering' or vibrating. The cap iron is adjustable and is set very close to the cutting edge for a smoothing plane and rather less for a jack. The jack plane blade should be very slightly rounded or curved, while smoothing, block and similar planes have a straight edge. Corners of a smoothing plane are slightly rounded to prevent 'digging-in', caused by tilting the blade sideways when honing.

The mouth on a bench plane is adjustable for size; the smaller the mouth the less chance there is of tearing the grain, thus a better surface is made. A small mouth, however, will only allow the passage of fine,thin shavings. As the jack plane is often used for the quick removal of excess wood the shavings may be thicker; this is done by opening the mouth, a simple operation. After preparing work with the jack plane a smoothing plane may be used to bring up a fine finish. It is also used to clean up wide boards, which is why the edges are rounded slightly.

Sharpening planes and chisels

The sharp cutting edges of planes and chisels are imparted in the 'honing' process, carried out on an oil-stone (*Figure 2.6*), either natural or artificial. This is used with an oil; ideally, neatsfoot oil should be used but a light machine oil (lubricating) is frequently used. Never use an oxidising oil such as linseed. This would form a skin on the stone, clog up the pores and ruin it.

The main purpose of oil is to float away the minute particles of metal as the edge of the blade is worn away, so frequent oiling is needed. The stone may be completely cleaned from time to time with paraffin.

Many grades and shapes of stone are available. For general use a standard flat double-sided stone is best. One side is fine and the other coarse. The coarse side brings the edge up more quickly but it should be finished on the fine side.

For both planes and chisels the grinding angle (G) is about 25 degrees. To produce the cutting edge the angle is increased to about 30 degrees (H). When sharpening, always maintain as low an angle as possible, providing the tip of the edge is in contact with the stone. It is essential that the angle between blade and stone is consistent as even a slight backwards and forwards rocking action with the hands will produce a rounded bevel on the blade. Do not push the blade straight up and back

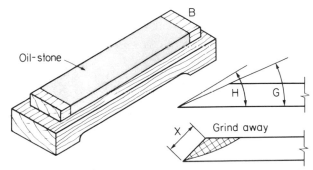

Figure 2.6. Sharpening of planes and chisels (see text)

but use a sideways, figure-of-eight motion which will help to induce even wear of the stone — a stone will wear out in time and a 'hollow' stone will need facing up, a difficult process.

Sharpening should continue until a slight burr is felt on the back of the blade. The blade is then carefully laid flat on its back and pushed across the stone to remove the burr. After many re-honings the grinding angle will be removed and the area being honed will be increased (X). Such a blade will need re-grinding.

Never form a bevel on the back of a chisel or plane blade as this will seriously affect the cutting action and will prevent the cap iron of a plane from seating properly. Stropping on a leather strop will remove any final trace of burr for really critical work but that careful back stroke across the oil stone should be sufficient. Ignore the so-called experts who advise stropping on the palm of the hand — it is a silly and dangerous practice.

An excellent general purpose stone which cuts fast and produces a keen edge is the India medium grit. Preferred size is 203 × 52 × 25 mm (8 × 2 × 1 in). The stone should be housed in a box and provided with a lid. Serious workers usually extend the stone at its ends with blocks of hard wood, fitted perfectly level with the stone surface (B). These blocks enable the stone to be used for the whole of its length, another aid to even wear.

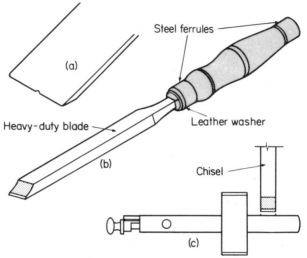

Figure 2.7. (a) Nicked blade, in need of grinding, (b) mortise chisel, (c) setting a mortise gauge

A number of honing guides are available and while they help a novice to keep to the bevel required it is better to practise 'free-hand' honing, maintaining an even pressure near the tip with fingers of one hand and holding the top of the blade or handle with the other. Watch that too much pressure is not applied to one side of the blade. This will cause an out-of-square end to the blade.

The purpose of grinding is simply to remove excess metal behind the honing bevel, otherwise honing will become a long, slow process. Blades which are 'nicked' as shown in *Figure 2.7 (a)*, or otherwise damaged will also need grinding.

The most important point to guard against is the danger of overheating your steel when grinding on a modern high speed wheel. Overheating 'draws' the temper, causing the steel to go soft and lose its ability to hold a keen cutting edge. During grinding the blade should be frequently dipped in water; the whole operation should be carried out slowly, carefully and with gentle pressure. Sparks from a grinding wheel are really white to red hot fragments of metal — so do not make many.

For cutting mortises there are heavy duty chisels and if you intend to make many mortises it is just as well to obtain the ones you will need. A mortise chisel is shown in *Figure 2.7 (b)*. The blade is thicker than that of a firmer chisel and the handle is usually reinforced with a ferrule to take the constant mallet blows it will receive. There is also a shock absorber pad inserted over the shoulder. Note the grinding and honing bevels on the blade. When 'setting' a mortise gauge the pins are spaced to suit the chisel being used (*c*).

Additional tools

There is really no such thing as a complete kit of woodworking tools, so vast is the subject and so wide is the range of tools used to fashion the raw material into the many different projects that can be undertaken. However, the following are some of the tools most likely to be needed to augment the basic kit.

Brace

The two types of brace in use are the 'plain' and 'ratchet' (*Figure 2.8*). A useful size is one with a 254 mm (10 in) sweep. The ratchet mechanism enables drilling in spaces where a complete revolution of the handle is not possible. By adjusting the ratchet drive a forward or reverse movement of the bit is possible, or the drive can be locked to give drive in both directions, like a plain brace.

The jaws of a brace (*a*) will grip normal tapered square shanks of joiners' bits or the rounded shanks of morse pattern ones. Some popular types of bit are: Jennings pattern (*c*),

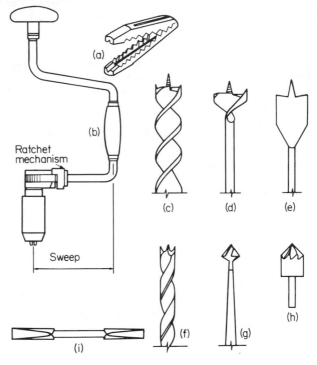

Figure 2.8. Brace and bits: (a) jaws of brace, (b) ratchet brace, (c) Jennings pattern bit, (d) screw-nosed centre bit, (e) flat bit for power drills, (f) lip and spur drill, (g) snail countersink, (h) wood or metal countersink, (i) double ended screwdriver bit

screw-nosed centre bit (*d*), flat bit for power drills (*e*), lip and spur drill (*f*), snail countersink (*g*), wood or metal countersink to fit all drills (*h*) and double ended screwdriver bit for the brace (*i*), which provides a powerful screwdriving force.

Wheelbrace

Although this is strictly an engineer's tool the wheelbrace is useful to a woodworker for boring small holes with standard twist and morse pattern drills. It can also be used for various metalworking jobs associated with woodworking. A chuck size of 8 mm ($^5/_{16}$ in) is to be preferred.

Brace bits

Many different types and patterns are available but the Jennings pattern is a good, all-round boring tool. It cuts a clean, deep hole and does not wander when knots or wild grain is encountered. The spurs, screws and cutting edges of bits must be protected, and kept sharp with a fine file. Wrapping them in baize-lined canvas is a good and simple way of looking after the bits; tool rolls made from canvas and baize can be bought if your stock builds up but bits should be purchased as the need arises — it is possible to buy a large set and never use half of them.

For large holes or occasional use the screw-nosed centre bit is a cheaper alternative to a Jennings but the bit should be withdrawn frequently to clear the hole being bored.

Other types of bit include the expansive, which can be adjusted within a good size range to bore various diameters in soft wood, and the Forstner, used for shallow and over-lapping holes, and for 'blind' holes where a lead screw would penetrate the surface.

Two types of bit have been specially developed over recent years for use in power drills. They are the flat bit (for larger holes) and the lip-and-spur bit, which is particularly suitable for making the smaller holes used for dowel joints. They fit in the various dowel jigs available without wobbling or wandering. It is, however, essential that metric drills are used in metric jigs, and imperial in imperial ones.

Screwdrivers

At least two cross-point screwdrivers and perhaps two Pozidriv ones will be needed. Drivers must be selected to fit the screw size. There is a large range of cross points but only four Pozidriv. Although the drivers are sized according to the length

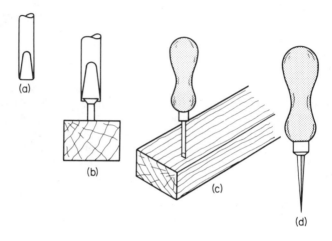

Figure 2.9. (a) Screwdriver blade with filed corners, (b) a blade which is too wide for the size of screw, (c) use of a bradawl, (d) birdcage pattern bradawl

of blade the critical dimension is the width and thickness of the cross-point tip. If too wide, as in *Figure 2.9 (b)*, it can cause damage to the work being screwed, and if too narrow it will not be possible to impart the 'drive' needed. Also, if the fit is 'sloppy' the driver can slip out of the slot, with unfortunate results. It is a good idea to file off the corners of a cross-point driver (*a*) and use a file to dress the tip so that it is a good fit in the screw slot.

With Pozidriv such problems do not arise; sizes 2 and 3 will drive a good range of screws but they should have pilot holes to assist entry.

Bradawls

Rather like a small screwdriver, the bradawl is used to bore pilot holes for smaller screws. To use one, the blade is placed across the grain, then the tool is twisted in the hand and pushed into the wood (*c*). They are easily sharpened with a smooth file. The birdcage pattern, with square, tapered and pointed blade, is preferred by some workers and is especially handy when using small screws (*d*).

Cutting gauge

The cutting gauge illustrated in *Figure 2.10* is used mainly for marking across the grain, while the marking gauge (*Figure 2.2*) is used with the grain, and the mortise gauge is used to mark

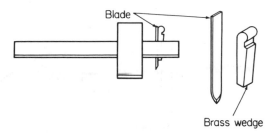

Blade

Brass wedge

Figure 2.10. Cutting gauge

double lines with the grain. Because of its blade profile the cutting gauge can also be used for 'slitting' or cutting strips of veneer and thin plywood.

Dovetail saw

For fine work the dovetail saw is ideal. This is a smaller version of the back saw, but only about 203 mm (8 in) in length and with smaller teeth and thinner blade.

Panel saw

This is used for cutting sheet material such as hardboard, ply-wood and composite boards, or wood which is not too thick. Although the teeth are sharpened and formed primarily for cross-cut use the saw will function reasonably well in any grain direction. Popular size is 560 mm (22 in) long with 9 points to the inch.

Saws for curves

The most useful saw in this group is the coping saw, shown in *Figure 2.11 (a)*, which cuts quite well in wood up to about 19 mm ($^3/_4$ in) thick. The blade is held taut with the spring-steel frame. Lever bars, which can be turned to adjust the

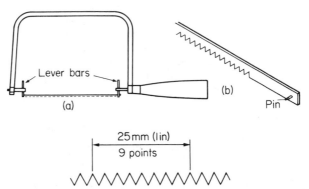

Figure 2.11. Coping saw: (a) general view, (b) blade design, (c) tooth size

blade in the frame, must always be aligned the same way to avoid blade distortion and bad cutting. A section of the blade is shown at (*b*), illustrating the directional slope of the teeth and anchor pin, which fits in a slot in the lever bar. Tension of the saw is given by the handle, which is threaded to the lever bar arm.

Experts argue as to whether the teeth should point away from the handle, thus giving the cut on the forward stroke, or towards the handle, when the cut will be on the backward stroke. In practice users find which method is applicable to a particular job. This saw is well suited to cutting out the waste on common dovetail joints.

Spokeshaves

These are really a kind of planing tool and remove shavings in a similar manner to a plane. They are used to smooth or round

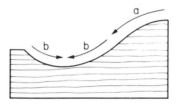

Figure 2.12. Use of spokeshave (see text)

off the edges of curved work. There are many types but are divided into flat-faced and round-faced patterns. As shown in *Figure 2.12*, flat faces are used for straight work and external curves (a) while the round face is used for internal curves (b).

3 Basic Processes

Even though wood is often bought ready planed, or machined, in one form or another it is frequently necessary to prepare the timber to non-standard sizes in the workshop. If the timber is received 'sawn' then it must be prepared before it can be used.

Preparation includes reducing all the wood needed to required sizes by sawing and planing. For as long as can be established the planing and preparation of wood by hand has followed the same basic principles, with the same basic terminology and guide marks.

First the 'face side' is established. The better side of the timber is selected. It is then planed smooth and flat, tested with a straight-edge lengthways, crossways and cornerways until it is right. A face mark is then pencilled on it with the tail starting from the face edge, as in *Figure 3.1 (a)*.

The 'face edge' is next prepared, planed and tested with straight-edge and try-square, held tight against the face side; finally it is marked with the face edge mark (*b*).

Your timber is now gauged and planed to the required width. Gauge from the face edge, across the face side and underside to the required width, holding the gauge stock firmly to the face edge. Plane off the waste, testing frequently as before (*c*).

Now the timber is gauged to the required thickness on both edges, and ends, holding the gauge on the face side. Waste is then planed off, testing as before (*d*).

Usually the next step after planing is to mark out the length, although whether or not the waste at the ends is removed at this stage depends on the nature of the job.

When planing along the grain always plane with it, not against, otherwise tearing and digging-in may occur. The run of the grain is easy to see on the edge of the section. If the wood is planed on the end grain in a similar manner to

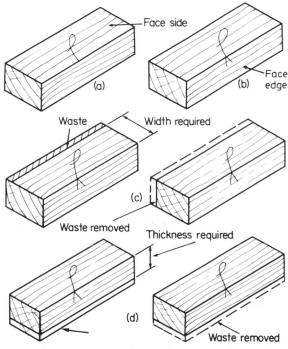

Figure 3.1. Preparation: (a) marking the face side, (b) marking the face edge, (c) gauging and planing to the required width, (d) gauging and planing to the required thickness

how it is planed on the edges then it is almost certain to split at the far edge. This is because the wood cannot adequately resist the pressure of the blade, and the splitting takes place where the wood is weakest — near the edge, as shown in *Figure 3.2 (a)*. If the wood can be supported at the corner, so that the edge cannot be forced outwards, then splitting will not occur.

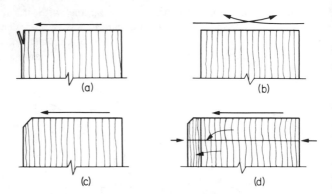

Figure 3.2. Planing on end grain: (a) splitting, (b) prevention by careful use of plane, (c) prevention by corner removal, (d) prevention by addition of scrap piece

When wood is planed on end grain it is usually referred to as 'shooting'. The following methods are ways of doing this which will prevent splitting.

1. Planing in both directions but not allowing the plane to complete the stroke and reach the far corner (*b*).

2. Removing the corner. This can only be done if the removal of the corner is of no consequence, perhaps because of subsequent shaping (*c*).

3. Cramping scrap wood on workpiece. The scrap wood, in effect, extends the width of the wood and any splitting will therefore be in the scrap piece. If the scrap is chamfered then even this is not likely to split (*d*).

4. Using a shooting board. This is a very satisfactory method providing the wood is not too large. If the shooting board is accurate the wood is not only planed, but it is finished square and true.

As end grain offers greater resistance to the plane it is essential for all end grain cutting that the plane is kept very sharp.

Cutting a trench

Making a trench is a fairly simple operation and forms the basis of a number of joints: housing, bridle and half-laps of various kinds. When using a saw to cut joints the cut (kerf) must be on the waste side of the line (*Figure 3.3*).

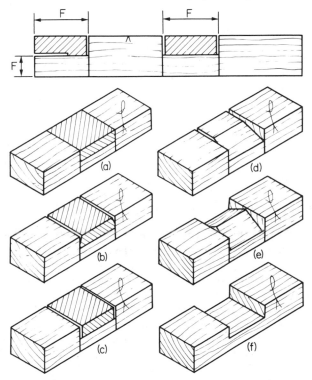

Figure 3.3. Cutting a trench: (a) marking off, (b) chiselling of V-grooves, (c) sawing, (d) and (e) chiselling away waste, (f) levelling off

Dimensions (F) represent the finished size of parts of the joints being made. (Joints are used in woodworking to provide greater mechanical strength, help hold the assembly together, provide greater gluing areas, give smooth flowing lines in design detail and to conceal end grain.)

The width of the trench is made exactly equal to the width or thickness of the part fitting into it, and is best if initially squared in with a pencil. That part of the joint which is actually going to be cut can be gone over with a marking knife. A marking knife lightly cuts the surface and gives a more accurate mark to work from, and working this way also gives an opportunity to check the precise width needed. A gauge is used to mark the depth. Remember to have the stock against the face side when gauging. The sequence of procedure is shown in *Figure 3.3*.

First mark off the trench, squared across, in pencil (*a*). Mark the depth of the trench with a gauge. Go over the lines, where actual cutting is to take place, with a marking knife then chisel in small V-grooves on waste side of lines (*b*). Saw down to the gauge mark, using V-grooves as guides for the saw, which must cut on the waste side of the line (*c*).

Chisel away waste at one side. Use as large a chisel as possible. Keep the flat side of the chisel down to the work and cut by pointing upwards on one side (*d*). Repeat this stage, working from the opposite edge (*e*). Level off the remainder of the waste by working inwards from the edges (*f*).

This is the type of trench used for half-lap joints and is half the thickness of the member. Trenches for other purposes are usually made one third of the thickness.

A stopped trench (*Figure 3.4*) is often used for bookcase shelves and similar work. It is marked out as described for a through trench, using a gauge to mark the limit of the 'stop' (*a*). Marking knife and chisel are used to make V-grooves (*b*), then a mortise is cut with the chisel at the 'blind' end of the trench (*c*). This allows sawing along the V-grooves to be carried out (*d*). Waste is then chiselled away with the back of the chisel down and initial cuts made as in *Figure 3.3 (d)* gradually decreasing the angle of chisel until a good start is made along the trench. Ideally a router should be used to level off the bottom of the trench but this tool has not yet been described and careful use of a sharp bevel-edge chisel should produce a satisfactory 'bottom'. The completed trench is shown at (*e*).

Perhaps the most traditional joint of all, employed by stonemasons and blacksmiths as well as woodworkers, is the

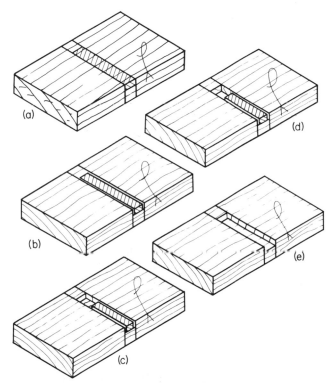

Figure 3.4. Stopped trench: (a) marking off, (b) chiselling of V-grooves, (c) forming a mortise, (d) sawing along V-grooves, (e) completed stopped trench

mortise and tenon. It is probably more widely used than any other joint in woodwork, and has variations of one sort or another that are almost countless. Its basic forms, though, are quite simple (*Figure 3.5*).

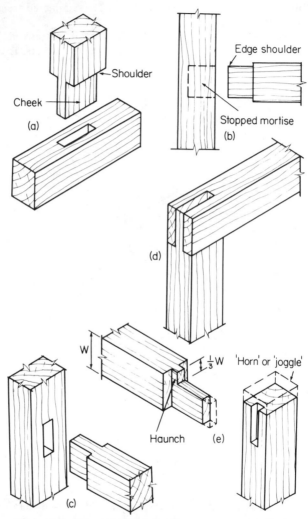

Figure 3.5. Mortise and tenon joints: (a) simple form, (b) stopped, (c) joint for wood of unequal size, (d) open mortise or corner bridle, (e) haunched

For very simple work tenon edge shoulders are not usually included. For furniture projects, edge shoulders are often incorporated as they completely seal, and conceal, ends of the mortise. With wide pieces the tenon is normally made in the form of a double tenon.

The shoulder of a tenon is marked with a marking knife and the location of the mortise is made in pencil. Thickness of the actual joint is gauged with a mortise gauge. Corresponding parts of the same joint should be marked at the same time, while the gauge is 'set'.

Ideally, a mortise gauge should have the distance between the pins set directly from the chisel which will be used for cutting the mortise. This is because chisels vary slightly in size and their widths are frequently not exactly what they are specified to be.

In its most simple form the mortise is cut right through the wood and the tenon has side shoulders but not edge shoulders, as in *Figure 3.5 (a)*. A blind or stopped mortise and tenon is shown at (*b*). Small, usually about 3 mm ($^1/_8$ in), shoulders are also introduced to conceal ends of the mortise.

Where the wood being joined is of unequal size, thickness of tenon can be increased above the usual one third rule, as in (*c*).

An open mortise, also known as a corner bridle, is shown in (*d*). This is a simple joint often used in framing.

More involved, and stronger, the haunched mortise and tenon is also used in frame construction. In practice it is usual to allow a little extra on the length of the mortised member to add strength during handling. This 'horn' or 'joggle' is cut off after assembly or when the frame is positioned (*e*).

Double tenons are made when the part to be tenoned is considerably wider than the part to be mortised, as in *Figure 3.6*. A long mortise, in relation to the thickness of the part, would weaken the joint (*a*). In addition to gluing, the joint can be further secured by wedges (*b*) which should have a slope of about 1 : 7. Ends of mortises are cut on a complementary slope to provide 'wedge' room (W). Screws or dowels can also be inserted (X).

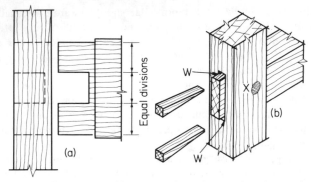

Figure 3.6. (a) Double tenon, (b) addition of wedges and dowel

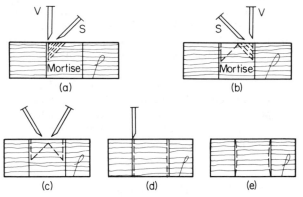

Figure 3.7. Chiselling a mortise (see text)

Mortises can be formed either entirely by chisel or the bulk of the waste can be removed by a chisel after the centre has been bored out with brace and bit. The bit must be smaller in diameter than the width of the mortise and the holes must not touch the sides of the mortise.

The procedure when chiselling out a mortise is shown in *Figure 3.7*. A series of vertical (V) and sloping (S) cuts are made, just inside the lines, about halfway through the wood (a) and (b). Extra sloping cuts are made in the centre part to level off the bottom (c). The work is then reversed and the first three steps are repeated. The chisel is now placed exactly on the line; the remaining waste is trimmed away, as in (d). Check that the ends of the mortise are not rounded (e) as this would give a false sense of tightness, when in fact the tightness is located at the centre. Remember that all surfaces in contact should have parallel sides.

Tenons are normally cut by sawing, with the saw just touching the line on the waste side. It is better to make the cuts with the grain first, followed by sawing the shoulders as, otherwise, some of the marking out may be lost if the side of the tenon is completely removed before all the cuts down the grain have been made. It is better to rasp away any excess rather than cut it away with a chisel.

When sawing a tenon, work is held upright in the vice. The saw is started in a corner on the waste side of the line, as shown in *Figure 3.8 (a)*. The handle of the saw is lowered as sawing continues (b) without the front of the saw cutting any deeper (far line cannot be seen during sawing). Now slope the wood slightly in the vice and continue sawing by lowering the handle until the shoulder line is reached (c). Reverse the wood in the vice, but keep it vertical, and continue sawing, keeping the saw level, until the shoulder line is reached (d). The sequence of cutting on a tenon with edge shoulders is shown in (e).

The bridle joint is in many ways similar to the mortise and tenon, but with the 'opposite' parts cut away, as shown in *Figure 3.9 (a)*. It is the joint usually adopted where a piece has to be jointed to a component which is thinner. Care should be taken to see that the joint is not made too tight, or the forked parts will tend to be forced outwards, which can even result in splitting.

The dovetail joint, when correctly made, is a very strong joint as, by the nature of the slope it resists attempts to pull it apart except in the way it was assembled. A dovetail halving joint is illustrated in *Figure 3.9 (b)*. This is the most simple

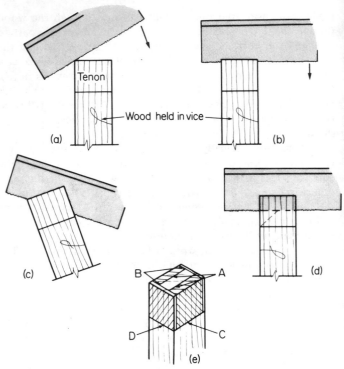

Figure 3.8. Sawing a tenon (see text)

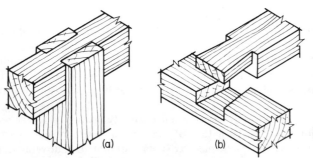

Figure 3.9. (a) Bridle joint, (b) dovetail halving joint

variation of the joint, the basis of which is the sloping part of the joint which resembles the tail of a dove. Because of the slope this joint can only be assembled in one direction and will resist being pulled apart in any other.

The dovetail halving and variations of it are used in frame, or 'flat', construction while the common, or box dovetail — as its name suggests — is used for box or 'carcase' constructions.

Dovetailing is easiest if carried out from a squared off end, as the extent or limit of the joint can then be readily marked

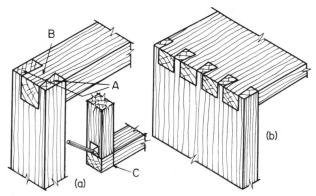

Figure 3.10. (a) Single dovetail joint, (b) common or box dovetail joint

with a cutting gauge. There are more ways of cutting the joint than one but most craftsmen cut the pins first, following the method shown in *Figure 3.10*. By standing the piece with the pins on the opposite member and marking around them with a well pointed pencil the exact size, shape, slope and position of the corresponding tails or 'sockets' can be accurately marked out. This means that for something like a simple box or frame the marking out must be done so that all four pieces will properly fit together. Face side and edge marks on all work and individual labelling of each half of each joint, will help to prevent errors.

The single dovetail joint, shown in *Figure 3.10 (a)*, is much used in framing. Pins are indicated (A) and (B) is the tail. It is usual to cut the pins first. The tail is then marked directly from the pins, as shown, after having squared or gauged in the guide line (C). Corresponding parts of dovetail joints are usually individually 'tailored' in this fashion.

Common or box dovetails follow the same basic pattern (*b*) as do the single dovetails. It is more satisfactory and gives a better joint if a pin is arranged to come at the edge, and not a tail.

The work sequence when forming dovetail pins is shown in *Figure 3.11 (a)*. First shade in the waste to avoid errors in sawing (A). Next, saw down the grain on the waste side of the line (B). Cut out the bulk of the waste with a coping saw (C),

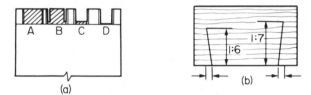

Figure 3.11. (a) Work sequence for forming dovetails, (b) dovetail angles

keeping just clear of the line going across the grain. This line is usually made with a cutting gauge. Chisel away the remainder of the waste, checking that surfaces are flat and square (D).

The angle at which a dovetail is cut must be considered: if it is too slight the joint will tend to slide out, and if it is too great there is a danger that the corners of the tail will break away. By long usage and practice it has been established that the angle should be about one in seven. That is, if the tail is seven units long it should be one unit wider at the end than at the base, as shown in *Figure 3.11 (b)*. If the wood is hard and close grained a slightly smaller angle can be employed, but the limit at all times is considered to be one in eight.

174

4 Workshop Practice

A methodical, disciplined approach to work is essential if accuracy and fine workmanship are to be achieved. Whatever the job may be it has to be 'set out', parts have to be prepared and identified, cut to size and test assembled.

Setting out

In many cases the project will be in the form of a prepared plan, with or without a descriptive article, and a parts or cutting list. Do not rush blindly into cutting parts from a list before first checking carefully. Look over the drawings. Check measurements on them, then check the list. If it is possible, make a full size drawing from the scale details, then check for cutting. Timber is costly these days and an error in cutting can waste a lot of valuable material. There is still an old saying, doubly true these days: 'Measure twice, cut once'.

To give an example of setting out and preparing a job let us consider a typical small project for the home or school workshop. *Figure 4.1* shows the stages of setting out for a small corded-seat stool which has the same elevation on all four sides (*a*). The stool is 305 × 305 × 305 mm (12 in square). Legs are 32 mm (1¼ in square). Top rails are 32 × 19 mm (1¼ × ¾ in) and the bottom rail is 25 × 19 mm (1 × ¾ in) placed 76 mm (3 in) from lower ends of legs.

The basic procedure, which generally is the same on all projects, is first to place all legs together in the vice, with ends approximately level and face sides and edges arranged as shown in (*b*). Then carry out all gauging, squaring, marking and measuring from these surfaces.

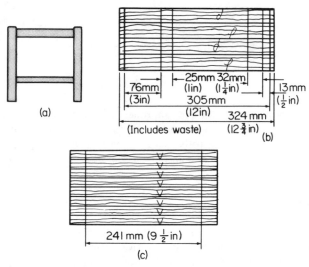

Figure 4.1. Setting out for a small stool: (a) elevation of stool, (b) marking out the legs, (c) marking out the rails

Next, mark out all similar pieces, together, while they are held in the vice or cramps. This is not only quicker but far more accurate than marking each piece separately.

Do not forget that there are often right hand and left hand parts to a job, therefore, when doing the marking out arrange the face marked components in pairs. *Figure 4.1 (b)* shows the legs of the stool arranged in pairs although, in this case, they are all the same. Marking out for the rails is shown in (*c*).

Reference has frequently been made to a marking knife. There is a tool by this name, with a pointed and bevel-edge blade. But a trimming knife of the Stanley type can be used to mark out, and this has other uses. Where sawing has to be done across the grain use a marking knife, or a sharp pencil of moderate hardness, say 2H. Mark out all corresponding pieces for that part of the job at the same time, before doing any sawing.

Remember that the marking out for one part of a joint must correspond exactly with the other part, and not be made slightly bigger or smaller. Always shade in the waste. It is so easy to cut out the wrong part of a joint, or even saw on the wrong side of a line.

Returning to the rails (c), place them in the vice, ends level and face edges up. Square across to the dimension given. This dimension is known as the shoulder length. In this case it is arrived at by subtracting the thickness of two legs from the length: $305 - (2 \times 32) = 241$ mm, or $12 - (2 \times 1\frac{1}{4}) = 9\frac{1}{2}$ in.

Check and re-check all marking out. An accurately cut joint will not fit if it is made in the wrong part of the wood. Acknowledge that old saying 'measure twice, cut once' without having to learn it the hard way!

Slight alternatives are possible in the positions of the rails, and therefore the joints, as shown in *Figure 4.2 (a)*. One is central, the other is offset. The latter gives slightly longer tenons.

With a mortise gauge mark in the tenon size (b), and gauge from the face side, setting the gauge to the chisel you will use. For gauging the legs, pins of the gauge are not changed but the stock must be moved to give either a central mortise or an offset one, as shown in (c).

The kinds of errors that can occur when setting out are shown in (d). Incorrectly squared lines around the work (A) is one. Lines should meet at every corner. At (B) the gauge lines do not align on edge of end, probably because the gauge was not set with pins central, or the gauge was not always kept tight against the face side.

In (e) the gauge lines are correct on the face side but not on the face edge. Correct position is shown dotted. This error arises through failure to keep the gauge stock against either the face side or the face edge.

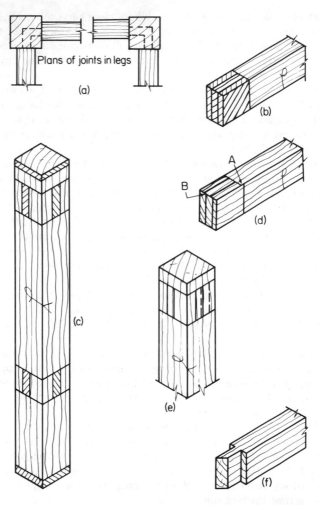

Figure 4.2. Forming the joints for a small stool: (a) plan
showing alternatives for rail positions, (b) marking out the
tenon, (c) marking out the legs, (d) errors which can occur
when setting out, (e) gauge lines are correct on face side but
not on face edge, (f) completed tenon with edge mitred

After tenons have been sawn they must be cut to length and also have their ends mitred (*f*). Both can be done on a mitre block or in a mitre box. Length of tenons must be slightly less than depth of mortise.

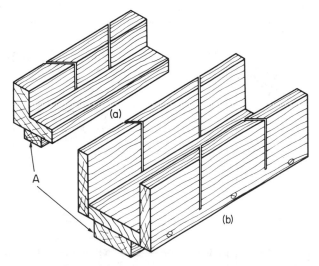

Figure 4.3. (a) Mitre block, (b) mitre box

The mitre block, shown in *Figure 4.3 (a)* can be used for mitring small section material where accuracy is not too critical. A mitre box (*b*) is used for larger size work and provides better control of the saw (which should fit closely in the slots) and is therefore more accurate. Either can be purchased or made in the workshop (see Chapter 5 for construction details). Blocks screwed to the base (A) provide a grip for the vice.

Cleaning up

Assembling the parts, cleaning up, securing the assembly and applying the finishes are stages that logically follow setting out. No matter how well made a joint may be, a light stroke with a plane, rub with glasspaper or some other cosmetic operation is needed to enhance the appearance of the work before applying polish, varnish or whatever the final process may be.

Cleaning up is the process of removing all pencil and other marks from the work, making the surfaces smooth, and

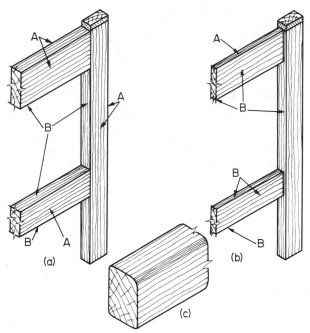

Figure 4.4. Cleaning up procedure: (a) rails same thickness as legs, (b) rails thinner than legs, (c) arris removed

preparing the job for the application of the 'finish'. Broadly, cleaning up is carried out with a smoothing plane, followed by glasspapering, as in *Figure 4.4*.

Joggles or horns are usually left on until after assembly, then removed (*a*) and (*b*). In (*b*) the rails are thinner than the legs so the cleaning up procedure is slightly different.

Rails are cleaned up on their faces before assembly and joints do not have to be levelled as in (*a*). Outer surfaces of legs can be cleaned up before or after assembly.

Removing the arris with plane or glasspaper gives the professional touch, is more pleasant to the hands and lessens the chance of bruising or damage to a corner (*c*), but when

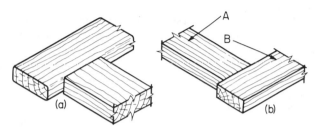

Figure 4.5. (a) Error to avoid when removing arris at a joint, (b) glasspapering around a joint

removing arrises care is needed to avoid the situation shown in *Figure 4.5 (a)* where the arris has been removed at a joint, resulting in an unsightly gap.

When glasspapering around a joint part (A) should be done first, always finishing with part (B). This helps to reduce the amount of cross-grain papering, and therefore scratching.

To do its job effectively the smoothing plane should be kept quite sharp, with the blade, cap iron and mouth prepared as described earlier. The aim with the smoothing plane is to skim over the work so that everywhere is covered, and yet the minimum of wood is actually removed. A close eye should be kept on the surface as planing proceeds to see if there is any tearing of grain. Any tendency of the fibres to tear can usually be corrected by reversing the work and thereby, in effect, planing the opposite way.

Glasspaper varies in its granule size, from 'flour' (00 grade), which is very fine, to 'strong 2' (S2), which is coarse. For most work two grades are sufficient, starting with either grade M2 or F2 and completing with grade $1\frac{1}{2}$ or 1. The following points should be noted when glasspapering.

1. Use a cork, rubber or wood block to support the paper. Do not work over flat surfaces with the paper held in the hand.

2. Hold the work firmly, either in a vice or cramped to the bench top.

3. Apply plenty of pressure; working slowly this way is much more effective, and far less tiring, than trying to do the job hurriedly.

4. Work with the grain whenever possible. Working across the grain, especially with coarse glasspaper, will scratch the surface and this will show up under a clear finish. Direction of working is not so important for a painted finish.

5. Do not glasspaper joints. A poor fitting joint is not improved by glasspaper and a good joint can easily be spoiled.

Other types of abrasive paper are available but they all do the same job and are used in the same manner as glasspaper. An exception is 'wet-and-dry' paper, which should not be used directly on a raw wood surface.

By the very nature of its purpose the cleaning up stage comes towards the end of a job when all the joints, shaping, cutting and fitting have been carried out. However, it cannot always be left until last and, broadly, the following is the procedure:

Before assembly, clean up those parts which cannot be reached after they have been put together. Those parts which can be tackled by plane and glasspaper after assembly are left until the work is glued up. This stage will often include levelling off joints and adjusting surfaces.

Assembling

Occasionally work is assembled without adhesives but for the vast majority of jobs glue of one sort or another is employed.

Scotch, or bone, glue is rarely used these days as it has many disadvantages compared with modern glues; it is still used by some craftsmen for special jobs such as veneering.

PVA (polyvinyl acetate) adhesive, which is a white emulsion that dries to a clear transparent film, is a good general-purpose woodworking assembly glue and is widely used. It is bought ready for use and is applied cold. This adhesive provides a satisfactory bond with materials allied to woodworking such as cork, leather and fabrics, and is clean and simple to use. It is not a waterproof glue however and is therefore limited to indoor use. It will also cope with plastics laminates, but only if pressure is applied over all the surface until the glue sets.

A more satisfactory adhesive for bonding plastics laminates to wood is one of the many 'impact' or 'contact' types. Makers' instructions must be followed and the result should be a bond so successful that it is impossible to break. Impact adhesive can also be used for veneering but it is not the best glue for normal assembly work.

For external work, and boatbuilding in particular, special resin-type glues are used. They are completely waterproof and are usually bought in powder form. They may be 'one-part' which incorporates a hardener, or 'two-part' where the hardener is separate.

Epoxy resins, usually sold in two-tube packs of resin and hardener, are useful for special applications of bonding metal surfaces to wood, or other dissimilar materials.

For most jobs, and especially for the man with little experience, it is advisable to have a trial run of assembling a piece of work with everything fitted 'dry'. This means that the work can be checked to ensure that it will, in fact, go together correctly, and with joints that are not too tight. While so assembled, it is advisable to mark each part of each joint so that when gluing the work will be re-assembled the same way.

For use when assembling, a simple form of squaring lath is shown in *Figure 4.6 (a)*. This is simply a strip of wood with one end pointed. The point fits in one internal angle and the diagonally opposite angle is marked on the other end of the lath. The lath is then reversed to the other angles and if the frame is square the mark will coincide. A better pattern is shown at (*b*) where two pointed laths slide over each other. They can then be held together and transferred to the other angles.

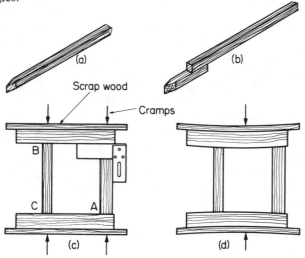

Figure 4.6. Squaring: (a) simple squaring lath, (b) a better pattern of squaring lath, (c) cramping and checking with a try-square, (d) bowing caused by incorrect cramping

Small frames can be checked with a try-square (*c*). Check also corners A, B and C. Cramps should be applied as indicated by arrows and scrap wood should be used under the cramps to protect faces of the work.

Bowing of sides can occur as the result of using a single cramp in the centre of the job (*d*), or when cramps are incorrectly positioned. Thick pads of wood also reduce the chances of bowing.

Being methodical is one of the essential disciplines of assembly work. Such cramps as are to be used should be set out and prepared at the 'dry-run' stage and scrap wood pads collected to place between jaws and work to prevent bruising and marking. Nails, screws, wedges or pegs to be used during assembly should be set out on the bench beforehand. In addition a container of clean water and some cloth swabs should be to hand for wiping off surplus glue before it hardens. Glue, once set, is very difficult to remove and if any smears of glue, however slight, dry out on parts that are to be clear varnished or polished, they will 'grin' through the polish as areas of a different shade to the natural wood colour you hope to achieve.

PVA glue can be applied directly from its plastics container if it has a nozzle, or with a brush or spatula if in a can. Do not be too generous but also do not be 'greedy'. Apply enough to wet all contacting areas without a lot of excess which will have to be mopped off later.

After applying the glue, check and cramp up without delay. Makers specify an 'open' time for their adhesives and usually it is slow enough to allow plenty of time for correct assembly. But the sooner the work is assembled and at rest for setting the better will be the bond. If things do go wrong, dismantle, mop off the glue while it is still wet, and start again. Partially set glue will not give a good bond. By the same token an incorrectly glued up assembly can rarely be put right once the glue has set.

Do not forget that cramps can exert a great deal of pressure. Use just enough to hold the assembly firmly — too much can distort the work.

As shown in *Figure 4.7 (a)* a frame which is out of square can be corrected by the slight re-positioning of one or both cramps, as indicated by the arrows. When the right-hand cramp is tightened it will pull the corner over, thus correcting the misalignment.

In (*b*) a frame which is badly twisted, or 'winding', is shown. Here, ends of cramps must be moved vertically up or down in order to pull the frame free from twist.

To test for correct alignment sight with the eye, as in (*c*). Surfaces of rails are in line. When viewed at right angles to the first observation point the legs should also be in alignment. The whole frame should be flat, or 'out of winding'.

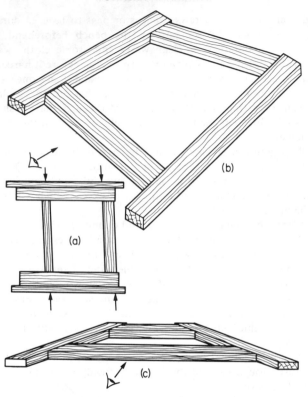

Figure 4.7. (a) Correction of out of square frame by re-positioning of cramps, (b) a badly twisted frame, (c) testing for correct alignment

All this is the counsel of perfection. It may sound formidable but in reality it is not; just the application of some common sense, patience and pride in achievement.

5 Workshop Equipment

Basic workshop requirements

A lot of woodworking projects can be done in a spare room, shed, garage, or even kitchen; for such activities there are many ingenious folding benches, including the Black and Decker Workmate bench. But, for more serious work and certainly if long periods of activity are expected a proper workshop is a necessity. It should have a good, level and dry floor, with walls strong enough to support shelves, racks and storage cupboards.

Figure 5.1 provides some idea of the minimum set-up needed for non-professional use but much depends on what the main interests will be. If large units of built-in furniture are going to be made then an area for pre-assembly is desirable. An outward opening door (A) creates less restriction on floor space than an inward opening door (B). An outward opening pair of doors (C) is advantageous where biggish work is tackled. It is also helpful if the door(s) are positioned so as to open opposite the line of the vice (D). Thus when long timber is worked in the vice it can project through the open door. Small woodworking machines may be acquired later, such as the universal woodworker, circular saw bench, lathe or bandsaw. Floor space will be needed for them. A simple rack, for holding saws, G-cramps etc., is also shown.

Many amateurs work quite comfortably in a shop or shed about 3 m × 2.5 m (10 ft × 8 ft) floor area or even less, but

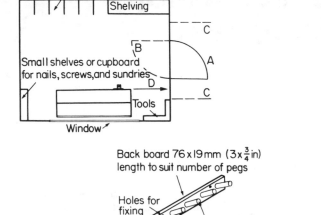

Figure 5.1. Typical home workshop (see text) and a simple tool rack

space to move around the bench from front and sides, at least, will be required.

Making a sawing stool

Before starting to make the bench something to work on, and support pieces for sawing and planing, is a requirement. The carpenter's or joiner's sawing stool, often incorrectly called a sawing horse, is a device with which we can work timber, with cramps to assist in holding if needed.

In any case the sawing stool is a handy piece of equipment to have, especially for anyone who has a lot of work to tackle around the house. It also makes a useful platform on which to stand when working at some height, and can be used in conjunction with a pair of steps to support a scaffold plank.

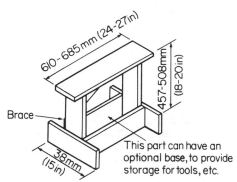

Brace

This part can have an
optional base, to provide
storage for tools, etc.

Top, 152 x 25 mm, (6 x I in)
remainder 127 x 25 mm (5 x I in)

Figure 5.2. Sawing stool

The type of stool with splayed legs is not too easy for a new-comer to woodworking because of the compound angles involved in the joints. A simplified version is shown in *Figure 5.2*, where no formal joints are used and where construction relies very much on the use of screws.

Making a bench

Plans for an easy to make bench are shown in *Figure 5.3*. For a person of average height a bench with its top around 838 mm (33 in) from the floor is about right. Length can be anything from 914 mm (60 in) to 1,829 mm (72 in), but a top of about 1,524 mm (60 in) by 533 mm (21 in) gives a good working area.

The 'well' is a traditional part of the woodworker's bench; and for very good reasons. First, it provides a receptable for tools in use for any particular job and prevents them from being accidentally knocked on the floor. Secondly, wood being worked on, or jobs being assembled, can be placed across the bench without tools getting in the way. Finally,

189

it allows the introduction of a thicker piece of wood for the front of the bench. This is the area that needs to be the most solid, partly so that the vice can be properly mounted, and also it is the front part of the bench where rigidity is most needed.

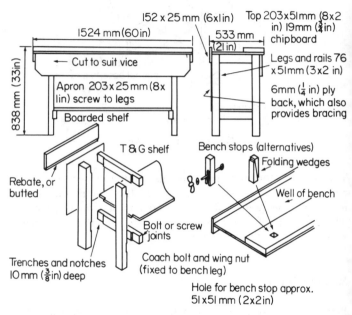

Figure 5.3. Construction of workshop bench

Legs are made from 76 × 51 mm (3 × 2 in) softwood, or 'deal', obtained from the timber merchant as P.A.R. (planed all round). Timber is measured in sawn condition – after machining it is, in fact, rather smaller than the 'nominal size'. There are also these days 'preferred sizes' and all timber is actually cut to metric dimensions within these sizes. So, the measurements of sections are more for guidance and should be taken as approximate. (For softwoods, merchants allow 25 mm as equal to an inch on sections.)

The joints for our bench are based on a simple form of trenching and notching, but without removing too much timber so as not to reduce the strength of the members. A depth of 10 mm ($\frac{3}{8}$ in) is adequate and where possible the legs and rails should be marked out in sets of four (see Chapter 3). Either a single coach bolt of 8 or 10 mm ($\frac{5}{16}$ or $\frac{3}{8}$ in) diameter can be used for fastening each joint, or the rails can be prepared for three screws at the ends. Extra strength is gained if an adhesive is used during assembly.

Chipboard or T. and G. boards can be used for the shelf, the boarding being nailed or screwed to the rails. The ply back, as well as enclosing the bench, provides a great deal of longitudinal rigidity and helps to resist the strains put on the bench, especially during planing and fairly heavy work in the vice. Ideally, the board which provides the lipping at the back should be rebated to receive the ply. The top of this lipping needs to be level with the top of the front part of the bench.

The thicker, main working area of the top of the bench should, preferably, be made of hardwood. In order both to economise and simplify construction the drawings show a variation in the usual method of forming the top. The well of the bench is made from a piece of 19 mm ($\frac{3}{4}$ in) chipboard, but with this arranged to come under the thicker front piece. The top is fixed by securing through from the upper surface but the screws need to be 'counterbored', and the resulting holes are filled with wooden dowels or 'pellets'. The chipboard must also be screwed from the underside to the thicker front member.

Bench accessories and their use

Vice

At this stage the vice should be fitted. Depending on the type and size selected, either a certain amount of recessing of the top or, alternatively, some packing will be required. *Figure 5.4* shows how a standard, Record type of vice is fixed to our bench. Detailed instructions follow at the end of the section.

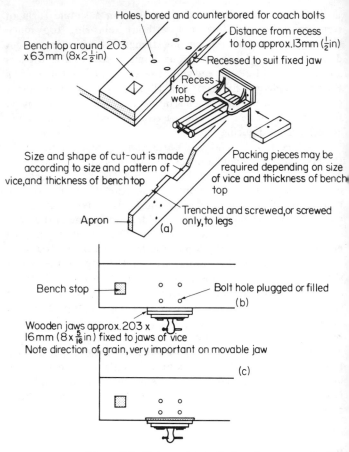

Holes, bored and counterbored for coach bolts

Distance from recess to top approx.13mm ($\frac{1}{2}$in)

Bench top around 203 x 63mm (8x2$\frac{1}{2}$in)

Recessed to suit fixed jaw

Recess for webs

Size and shape of cut-out is made according to size and pattern of vice, and thickness of bench top

Packing pieces may be required depending on size of vice and thickness of bench top

Trenched and screwed, or screwed only, to legs

Apron

(a)

Bench stop

Bolt hole plugged or filled

(b)

Wooden jaws approx.203 x 16mm (8x$\frac{5}{16}$in) fixed to jaws of vice

Note direction of grain, very important on movable jaw

(c)

Figure 5.4. Fixing a vice to the bench

Wooden packing pieces, or 'chops', should be fixed to inner surfaces of the vice jaws before it is ready for use. The packing should be of good, solid hardwood, about 16 mm ($\frac{5}{8}$ in) thick, preferably with the grain running vertically. The outer, movable, jaw is bored and threaded for set screws, which are used to fix the packing. The fixed jaw also has two threaded holes for engineers' machine screws, which are used to fix the inner packing. Packings are fixed level with the top of the bench and screw heads are countersunk.

The apron will have to cut around the vice, although this does not need to be a close fit. Screws are used to fix the apron to the legs, this also adding to the bracing effect needed on the bench.

Bench stop

A bench stop is essential and for this a hole is made in the bench top (*Figure 5.3*) about 51 mm (2 in) square, to coincide with the outer surface of the leg. Two forms of stop are shown: in one the stop is slotted, the vertical movement of the stop being controlled by a coach bolt and wing nut, the bolt passing through the leg and the slot fitting over it. The second pattern is simply a pair of folding wedges, easy to tighten or loosen with a tap of a hammer. Folding wedges is the term given when a pair of wedges slide together so that their outer edges remain parallel.

It is well worth while giving a new bench two or three coats of varnish. Not only does this help to keep it clean, it also means that glue which inevitably gets spilt on the top is more readily cleaned off. Finally, always ensure that the bench is standing on a level surface, and adjust the legs accordingly if necessary to make it stand firmly on all legs.

Sawing board

The most used piece of workshop equipment is a sawing board, also known as a bench hook. It is easily made from three pieces of hardwood. *Figure 5.5* shows how it is made, and approximate dimensions. Sawing boards can be made right-, left-, or dual-handed and by their simple design are double-sided.

Small chamfers should be made where indicated (A). These help to clear the sawdust which may prevent the workpiece from lying square against the board. The blocks should initially

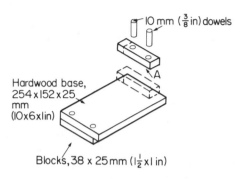

Figure 5.5. Sawing board or bench hook

be simply glued in place, then holes are bored right through and dowels are glued and pushed in, then finished off flush. Until a high standard of proficiency is reached the sawing board should be used with one block clamped in the vice.

Mitre box

A mitre box is another simple working aid which is not difficult to make (see *Figure 4.3*). Overall size is around 305 × 127 × 89 mm (12 × 5 × 3½ in), and construction is of hardwood, glued and screwed. Depth should not be greater than the sawing capacity of the tenon saw that will normally be used. Screws can be used for fixing the parts together so long as their positions are carefully made to be well clear of the saw kerfs. Kerfs should be marked out with an accurately set bevel or a mitre square. They should then carefully be cut with a tenon saw. Once made, it is virtually impossible to correct them if they are wrongly cut.

Shooting board

Chapter 3 referred to the problem of planing end grain, and the inherent risk of splitting unless precautions were taken. One of the commonest ways of tackling this problem is by using a shooting board and *Figure 5.6* shows a basic pattern.

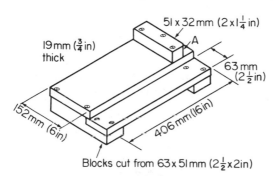

Figure 5.6. Shooting board

This is made from two pieces of 19 mm ($^3/_4$ in) hardwood or multi-ply which are screwed to supporting blocks, as shown in the drawing. Ensure that the top block is fixed exactly at right angles to the edges of the board and, in fact, make the whole assembly quite true on edges and surfaces. It also helps if the block is chamfered at corner (A) to avoid the risk of the block splitting when being used.

As drawn, the board is intended for a right-handed person. For a left-handed worker the top block should be fixed at the opposite end. Alternatively, and for dual use, blocks could be fixed at both ends but in this case the board should be made rather longer.

Cramps

When skills begin to develop and as the woodworker broadens the range of projects he/she undertakes, the need for cramps and other holding devices soon becomes apparent. These include sash cramps, G-gramps and holdfasts, and other more specialised cramps such as corner, or mitre, cramps. They are all available in a large range of sizes and are of various patterns. Patent cramping devices are now quite popular. They are cleverly designed and easy to use but the old-fashioned G-cramp still holds pride of place in most workshops.

Holdfast   Frequently work needs to be held down on top of the bench as, for example, while cutting a mortise or forming a trench. For such purposes the holdfast is ideal. Such a device

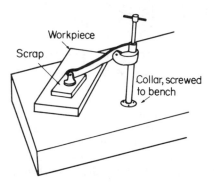

Workpiece

Scrap

Collar, screwed to bench

Figure 5.7. Holdfast

is shown in *Figure 5.7*. The collar is fitted into a hole drilled in the surface of the bench and housed to bring its surface flush. The collar is then screwed down. The holdfast shank is simply a sliding fit in the collar and is held by a combination of ribbed surface and friction. When the clamping arm is placed on the workpiece the turn-screw is tightened down. Combined leverage on post and clamping arm holds the work quite securely with minimum effort and time. Two collars are usually supplied with a holdfast so, with strategic positioning, quite a large area of the bench can be covered.

G-cramps   G-cramps (*Figure 5.8*) are a useful form of small cramp and have many applications in the home workshop. They too can be used to hold work on the bench and are also used on small assembly work. At one end of the available range is the 'junior' pattern — a small lightweight type in

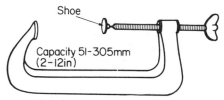

Figure 5.8. G-cramp

different capacities up to 102 mm (4 in). These are handy for toy or model making. In the middle of the range the light/ medium duty varieties can be obtained with capacities up to 305 mm (12 in). The smaller ones are fitted with wings for screwing down but the larger ones have 'tommy bars' or 'drop handles'.

The distance from the frame to the cramping screw is fairly small on most G-cramps, and this limits the distance relative to the edge at which they can operate. In practice, this is not restrictive for most applications but there is a pattern available where the throat depth is about double that of the normal type: they are known as 'deep throat cramps'.

A fairly recent innovation is the 'spring-grip' cramp. This has a small, knurled wheel let into the frame where the screw passes through. In use, the hand holding the cramp can also operate this wheel until the cramp grips sufficiently tightly to support itself, leaving the other hand free to control the work. Greater pressure can then be applied by tightening the cramp in the normal way.

Another modern variety is the edging cramp. This is a fairly small capacity cramp with a second cramping screw introduced in the centre of the frame; that is, at right angles to the main screw. Its main use is for gripping edging strips by means of the side screw once the cramp has been positioned on the work. The cramps can be used on straight or curved edges and is especially suitable for holding lippings to curved surfaces such as table tops and bookcases.

All G-cramps are fitted with swivelling shoes which automatically adjust to accommodate surfaces which are not quite parallel to each other, providing the taper is not pronounced. Scrap wood should always be used between the cramp and the work, or pressure from the screw will cause bruising. The larger the scrap, within reason, the better as this helps to spread the load. Replacement shoes are available if needed.

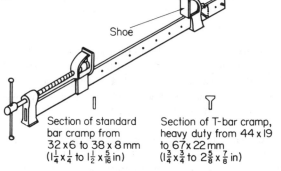

Shoe

Section of standard bar cramp from 32 x 6 to 38 x 8 mm ($1\frac{1}{4}$ x $\frac{1}{4}$ to $1\frac{1}{2}$ x $\frac{5}{16}$ in)

Section of T-bar cramp, heavy duty from 44 x 19 to 67 x 22 mm ($1\frac{3}{4}$ x $\frac{3}{4}$ to $2\frac{5}{8}$ x $\frac{7}{8}$ in)

Figure 5.9. Sash cramp

Sash cramps   Sash cramps (*Figure 5.9*) are used in general assembly work and can be obtained in two main weights. The regular pattern has a bar of rectangular section, but the heavy duty pattern has a bar of T-section. The latter is intended for industrial use. Regular pattern sash cramps are available with capacities up to 1372 mm (54 in) but lengthening bars of 914 and 1219 mm (36 and 48 in) can be used with the cramps, which greatly increases the scope of the work they can tackle. It is also possible to remove the shoes from two cramps then bolt the bars together in order to increase capacity.

Always use sash cramps with considerable care as even moderate pressure wrongly applied can distort an assembly and finish up by doing more harm than good. Take, for example, two or more boards being butt or edge jointed to form a wider piece, and of a length which calls for the use of three cramps.

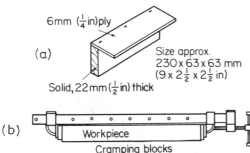

(a) 6mm (¼in)ply

Size approx.
230 x 63 x 63 mm
(9 x 2½ x 2½ in)

Solid, 22mm (½in) thick

(b) Workpiece
Cramping blocks

Figure 5.10. (a) Cramp packing block, (b) use of cramp packing blocks

Two of these should be placed on one side of the boards, near the ends. The third should be placed in the centre, underneath the boards. This will counteract the strain of the end cramps and keep the glued-up boards flat. If all three cramps are placed on the top side the boards will probably bow as pressure is applied.

When a frame is properly assembled and checked it must be correctly left for the glue to set and the work to dry out. This means that the cramped up job should be left on a flat surface for several hours or, if left in a vertical position, checked that it is not under strain from its own weight.

As with all cramps, packing of some sort must be introduced between cramp jaws and the work. It is also desirable to have scrap between the bar of the cramp and the assembly. This eliminates the risk of any part of the cramp causing damage to the work. It also prevents spoiling from a less obvious source. It is normal practice to wash off any surplus glue when the job is in cramps. This often results in the work being wetted. If a cramp is in contact with damp wood a pronounced stain can be the result. This can be difficult to remove and the lighter the wood the more obstinate becomes the stain.

As an aid to cramping, simple cramp packing blocks can be

199

made. These are glued and pinned together as shown in *Figure 5.10 (a)*. In use, the thicker part is positioned under the shoe of the cramp (*b*).

Cramp heads   Perhaps one of the most useful forms of cramp for the amateur is one which is partly home-made, using what are called 'cramp heads' (*Figure 5.11*). These are, in effect, the

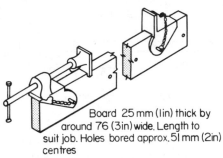

Board 25 mm (1 in) thick by around 76 (3 in) wide. Length to suit job. Holes bored approx. 51 mm (2 in) centres

Figure 5.11. Cramp heads

two working ends of a sash cramp, without the bar. The heads are used in conjunction with a wooden bar 25 mm (1 in) thick, which forms the bar part of the cramp. One big advantage of cramp heads is that cramps of considerable length can be made. Width of the wooden bar should be about 63 to 102 mm ($2\frac{1}{2}$ to 3 in), depending on length but hardwood bars up to about 1220 mm (4 ft) need only be 101 mm (2 in) wide. For the sliding shoe, holes for the fixing pin should be made about 101 mm (2 in) apart.

Corner cramp   A rather more specialised form of cramp is the corner cramp. This has two threaded screws mounted at 90° to one another, applying pressure against a right-angled fence. The two mitred pieces of wood forming the corner (angle of a picture frame, for instance) are gripped under respective pressure screws and are held accurately in relation to each other. There are several variations of this type of cramp.

200

Fixing a standard vice to the bench

Two main dimensions are to be considered in connection with vices: width of jaws or size of clamping face, and distance between the jaws when they are fully opened.

The smallest vice of any real, but limited, use has a jaw width of 152 mm (6 in) opening to 114 mm ($4\frac{1}{2}$ in). This size is also available with a built-in clamp on the underside, enabling it to be fastened to the top of a bench or table.

For the more serious worker a heavier vice should be considered. Such vices are more robustly made, have a deeper capacity from top of jaws down to slides and screws and also open wider. Although there are many sizes, one with 178 mm (7 in) wide jaws opening to 203 mm (8 in) should be adequate for most home undertakings.

This range of vices offers alternative types of screw action. One is a plain screw which has to be turned until the required opening is reached; the other is known as a 'quick action screw'. With this one there is a small lever at the front, near the screw head. When this is depressed the screw is disengaged from the fixed jaw and the movable jaw slides back or forward. When released, the normal clamping action can be made by turning the screw. This is a great time saver when there is a lot of working with the vice. Mounting sequences when fixing such vices are similar in each case.

A medium size vice, such as the 7 in one previously described, is suitable for the bench illustrated in *Figure 5.3*. In *Figure 5.4* we show fixing details for the popular Record pattern vice. The vice should be fitted carefully and rigidly anchored.

The front edge of the bench will need a certain amount of recessing to accommodate the fixed jaw and the two webs which add strength to the frame (*a*). The size and extent of this recess will depend on two main factors: the thickness of the top is the first. A vice should be fixed so that the top of the jaws is about 13 mm ($\frac{1}{2}$ in) below the top surface of the bench. The main reason for this is to keep the metal of the vice well clear of tools being used on work held by the vice. Chisels, saws and planes can easily be blunted or damaged by accidental contact with the metal.

Secondly, the way in which the wooden jaws are attached to the metal ones must be considered. Wooden jaws must always be added to a woodworker's vice, mainly to protect the work. Without this precaution the metal will surely bruise or mark any wooden parts gripped in the vice.

Alternative ways of fixing the jaw faces are shown in *Figure 5.4* at (*b*) and (*c*). In method (*b*) the fixed jaw projects beyond the edge of the bench, but at (*c*) it is flush. Some craftsmen prefer one way while some prefer the other, as each has its merits. For instance, the vice at (*b*) will often cope more easily with partly assembled work while (*c*) is better when planing the edge of a long board because a certain amount of lateral support is offered by the whole length of the edge of the bench top.

In method (*b*) the depth of the recess must be equal to the thickness of the metal fixed jaw. In (*c*) it must be equal to the thickness of the metal plus the thickness of the wooden face — around 16 to 18 mm ($^5/_8$ to $^3/_4$ in). The recess would then need to be extended beyond the edges of the metal jaws to allow for the wooden facing, and this usually has its ends dovetailed into the bench, as shown.

For smaller vices coach screws could be used for securing the vice. They are, of course, driven in from the underside, and are in no way visible from the top. With larger vices and for maximum security coach bolts are better. Although engineers' types of bolts could be used coach bolts, with their large head and square shank immediately under the head are intended specially for use with wood. The heads, however, must be let into the top of the bench. Holes prepared in this way are known as 'counterbored'. Washers should always be used under the nut. Holes in the top should be filled once the bolts are tightened. This can be done either by gluing in dowels of wood or by using a proprietary filler.

Where a fairly large vice is being added to a bench with a relatively thin top, it might well be that packing will have to be introduced between the underside of the bench and the vice. This is to compensate for the thickness of the top so that the jaws of the vice when fixed will be below the top surface, as before explained. *Figure 5.4 (a)* shows one of the two packing pieces which may be needed. The actual thickness of these pieces would, of course, depend on the factors described.

The apron piece will require a certain amount of shaping. This, however, does not have to be precise as there is no need for the apron to be a tight fit around the vice. The exact shape and extent of this shaping will depend on the thickness of the bench top, and the size of the vice. Apron and bench top are usually arranged so that the top overhangs the apron by about 16 to 18 mm ($\frac{5}{8}$ to $\frac{3}{4}$ in). This overhang would then determine the thickness of the wooden faces used in (*b*).

The jaws should be made of hardwood as this best resists the wear to which they are subjected. It is very important that the grain on the moving jaw is vertical: if it is horizontal then the part projecting above the metal can easily split when something is held right at the top of the vice, and the vice is then well tightened.

On most vices the metal jaws are drilled and tapped to accept 'set screws' for fixing the wooden faces. It is, however, possible to use ordinary wood screws from the back of the jaw, into the wood. Set screws pass through holes drilled in the wood faces, and make a much stronger fixing. Whichever way they are fixed care must be taken to ensure that the inner faces of the wood jaws are left smooth and without screw heads that stand proud, or screw points sticking through. The wooden jaws need replacing from time to time and care must always be taken in their fitting so that when the vice is closed the surfaces of the wood remain parallel both vertically and horizontally.

Do not grip metal objects in the wooden faces and take care of the vice, with an occasional drop of oil on slide and screws. When gripping irregular shaped material be sure to place softwood packing pieces at the 'slack' spots so that the pressure is evenly exerted.

6 Portable Power Tools

One of the many changes which have taken place in recent years is the development of small portable power tools for home workers. Woodworking is well catered for, although the tools are not as robust or powerful as their industrial counterparts. The power source is always domestic mains electricity and the tools are as portable as the availability of a power outlet and the length of lead on the tool or added as an extension.

A safety point to stress right away is that extension leads on reels should be fully opened out when used for more than a few minutes, otherwise the wound up cable overheats to an extent which may burn out the insulation.

The power drill and its attachments

Most of the popular power drills have many attachments or accessories available for them, which either fit in the chuck or can be attached to the drive after the chuck has been removed. In general terms an attachment means that the chuck has to be removed – a simple operation – while an accessory fits the chuck. With these, the power drill owner can convert a single tool into a multi-purpose piece of equipment.

Drill sizes and types

The smallest and cheapest drill on the market has a chuck capacity of 6 mm ($\frac{1}{4}$ in). This means that the shank of drill or other accessory being fitted cannot exceed that size. Also explicit in the specification is the warning that attempting to drill in metal over 6 mm diameter will seriously overload the machine and probably destroy it.

This type of drill has a speed of around 2 500 revolutions per minute (r.p.m.) when running free, or unloaded. When the drill is actually under load, or working, the speed will drop. As the load is increased the motor will begin to labour and heat up rapidly until 'stalling' point is reached. Long before this stage is reached the user should have reduced the load.

Chuck capacity and no-load speed are standard specifications for power drills. The speed quoted is quite satisfactory for boring small diameter holes in wood but it is too fast for drilling in steel or masonry. Power output of the motors fitted in these small drills varies from maker to maker but typical working capacities are 6 mm diameter holes in steel and 13 mm ($\frac{1}{2}$ in) in hardwoods.

A very popular drill for home use is one with a chuck capacity of 10 mm ($\frac{3}{8}$ in). The power is uprated above the smaller capacity drill and the 10 mm drill should be able to drill in steel up to 10 mm diameter and 19 mm ($\frac{3}{4}$ in) in wood. With this capacity of drill variations are available in no-load speeds. The first is a two-speed model providing a fast speed suitable for wood and a slower speed intended for drilling in steel or masonry. Typical speeds are around 3 000 r.p.m. and 700/850 r.p.m.

The problem of drill speed and the need to have fast and slow revolutions has been overcome by some manufacturers with various electronic circuits which reduce the current flowing to the motor, thus reducing its speed. Some infinitely variable speed drills can run from only a few revolutions a minute up to maximum by trigger control only, the trigger acting rather like an accelerator.

Speed-changing accessories

Other devices to change the speed of a drill are available as accessories. One is in the form of a secondary chuck which fits into the drill chuck. It is, in principle, a small gear box which reduces the speed by about half. Some patterns can be reversed, thus increasing the speed, while others are arranged so that the drilling is done at right angles to the machine's axis. This arrangement can on occasions be quite useful in awkward or constrained situations.

Another piece of equipment which can be used to vary the speed of a drill is in the form of an electronic variable control which is plugged in line with the drill lead. By operating a knob the speed can be reduced from maximum to minimum, within the control design. The principles on which these gadgets work are, broadly, rapid interruption of the current flow which in effect switches the drill off and on again; makers claim that this system, whether plugged in line or built into the drill itself, does not reduce the torque, or turning power, of the tool.

Drill stands

For most of the time a drill is used it is hand-held and used free-hand. Indeed, for many drilling operations this is the only way it can be used. There are, however, many occasions when a drill becomes far more efficient and easier to use when it is clamped in a drill stand. Repetition work and when drilling metals are two examples of when a drill is more efficient when in a stand. Most leading manufacturers make stands for their own drills and some make stands which will accept other makes of drill. In the domestic range one, at least, makes a stand for drilling which also forms part of a small wood-turning lathe, powered by the drill. There is a certain amount of interchangeability between drills and stands of various makers but this should be checked before purchase.

A drill stand should be robust and smooth in action, with no backlash in the linkages. For safety it should be bolted or screwed to a suitable bench. If this is not practicable it should, at least, be clamped or otherwise secured to the work bench or table.

Mortising bits and attachments

Not only do stands make drilling operations easier to perform, they also open up the way for further attachments to be used. The bigger and stronger stands can be equipped to make mortises, using the very efficient hollow, square mortising chisels and bits, sold by good tools shops (*Figure 6.1*).

This type of tool has a special bit which revolves in the hollow centre of the chisel. When the chisel is pressed down

Figure 6.1. Hollow square mortise chisel and bit

on the wood the bit bores a hole, ejecting the waste through a hole in the top of the chisel, which continues the cut, converting the round hole to a square one. By taking a series of cuts side by side a mortise of any length can be made. For the most satisfactory cutting of mortises, the chisel should equal the width of the mortise.

Because of the limitations inherent in this system, the largest bit which can be used is $\frac{1}{2}$ in. These chisels are not made by the firms who supply the drills but by specialist firms. A leading firm supplies them in five sizes, from $\frac{1}{4}$ to $\frac{1}{2}$ in, but not as yet in metric sizes.

Shaper cutters

A recent development in power tool attachments is the shaper cutter, which fits directly in the chuck. A range of cutters allows cuts such as beading, chamfering, coving, rounding, grooving and rebating to be made, as in *Figure 6.2*. They can

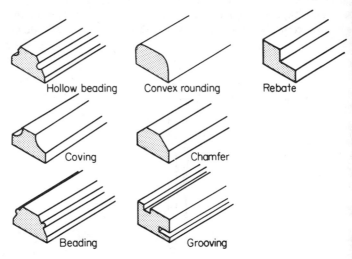

Hollow beading   Convex rounding   Rebate

Coving   Chamfer

Beading   Grooving

Figure 6.2. Cuts which can be made using a shaper cutter

be used in conjunction with a drill stand or in a hand shaper attachment (*Figure 6.3*). One supplier of these cutters produces a universal shaper table, designed for fitting to popular drill stands and providing a fixed work table with an adjustable fence (*Figure 6.4*). The table fits on to the base of the drill stand.

With a slotting type cutter a groove the width of the cutter can be made, or by repeating the cut after some adjustment to the fence a wider groove can be made. This can be repeated to form quite wide grooves. By grooving from two adjacent faces, rebates can also be made.

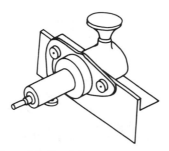

Figure 6.3. Hand shaper attachment

Adjustable fence

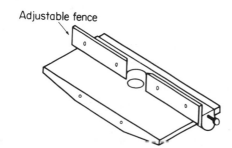

Figure 6.4. Shaper table

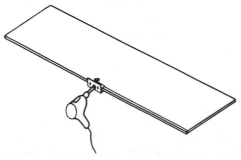

Figure 6.5. With large panels it is better to use the hand shaper, rather than move the wood across the shaper table

The hand shaper attachment performs the same function as the shaper table but, whereas the drill is fixed with the table to the drill stand and the wood moves across the cutter, with the shaper attachment the drill and cutter move across the wood, which is usually held in a vice, or clamped to the bench. The hand attachment is particularly suitable when making a cut in a fairly large piece of wood, as in *Figure 6.5*. It would be far more difficult to move such a piece across the small table in a drill stand than to move the attachment along the timber.

Circular saws

Circular saw attachments for power drills can be used for many jobs, especially ripping and cutting man-made boards. They have blades up to approximately 127 mm (5 in) diameter and can be used at the place of work, with an extension lead plugged in at a convenient socket outlet. The saws are easily attached to the drill and have adjustable depth and angle of cut. The blade is enclosed by a guard when not actually cutting and the guard snaps closed by a light spring when the saw finishes its cut.

Most saws have a ripping fence which can be adjusted to about 300 mm (6 in) from the face and the fence can be removed as required. The sole plate of the saw has a cut-out section at the leading edge of the blade so the operator can see the line of cut and many have a guide line on the sole plate to assist the lead-in to the cutting line.

Saw bench

A small saw bench to which the circular saw attachment can be mounted further increases the scope of a power drill (*Figure 6.6*). The attachment, with the drill, is mounted under or on top of the bench (according to make) with the blade protruding through the table top. Maximum depth of cut is about 38 mm ($1\frac{1}{2}$ in) but thicker material can be ripped by first grooving then turning the timber over and completing the cut. The work should not be forced through the saw, just lightly thrust against the revolving blade and pressed firmly against fence and table.

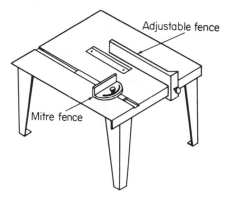

Figure 6.6. Multi-purpose saw table

The ripping fence is adjustable and frequently a mitre and cutting-off fence is provided. This slides in a groove as shown in the diagram, transporting the workpiece through the saw.

Circular saw blades

Most circular saw attachments are supplied with a 'general purpose' blade (*Figure 6.7*). This has coarse teeth of the rip saw profile, for cutting along the grain. Tips of the teeth, however, are sharpened with side bevels as shown, so that the outer tips of the teeth cut first. This is a requirement for cross-cutting as it helps to prevent the grain from splitting on the underside of the wood.

The blade can therefore be used for most wood-cutting functions, but has slight drawbacks. The teeth are quite large and tend to tear the grain, especially on thin sections.

Smaller teeth give a cleaner finish and absorb less power from the drill; the power of the motor tends to govern the speed of the cut, rather than tooth size. Fine teeth blades, as shown in *Figure 6.8 (a)*, are available and should be used for sawing plywood or hardboard or thin sections of timber.

For the person who expects to do a lot of sawing, a tungsten carbide tipped (T.C.T.) blade (*b*) is a worthwhile investment.

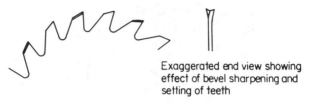

Exaggerated end view showing effect of bevel sharpening and setting of teeth

Figure 6.7. General purpose blade – ripsaw shape teeth but with tips 'bevel' sharpened

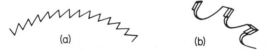

(a)   (b)

Figure 6.8. A saw with smaller teeth will give a much smoother finish

These blades are relatively expensive but have a life between sharpenings of fifty times or more greater than an ordinary steel blade. They also leave a much smoother cut surface. Home users cannot, however, re-sharpen them, and they must be sent to a specialist for servicing.

Jig saw

Another saw attachment available for many makes of drill is the jig saw. This has a short, narrow blade with which curves and awkward shapes can be cut. The blade reciprocates in an up and down movement, with the teeth so shaped that it cuts on the upward stroke. These saws cut quite well on thinner material but the rate of cutting can become rather slow on wood near the saw's maximum capacity, usually 19 mm ($^3/_4$ in).

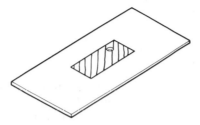

Figure 6.9. Hole bored in waste so that jig saw blade can be inserted

A jig saw is particularly useful when it is required to cut a hole of some sort from the centre of a panel or board. A hole may be needed to introduce the saw (*Figure 6.9*), but with some types of jig saw they will 'work themselves in'. How this can be done is explained in the instruction leaflet.

Woodturning lathe

Mention has already been made of a drill-powered lathe. A woodturning lathe is usually a fairly heavy and robust type of machine, so it may be realised that those which are basically power drill attachments are very much in the lightweight class. In spite of this they are capable of producing satisfactory work so long as it is accepted that they have limitations and that only fairly small work can be turned on them.

Lathes of this type will turn work up to about 457—508 mm (18—20 in) in length and 100 mm (2 in) in diameter. The length of work possible is referred to as 'between centres' capacity. They will cope with face-plate jobs (bowls, plates, etc.) up to about 102 mm (4 in) diameter.

For the beginner who wants to start off on woodturning, there are sets of woodturning tools below the size normally used on standard lathes. A recommended set, made by one of the best known tool manufacturers, comprises three principal tools in the small-size range: a 13 mm (½ in) gouge, same size skew chisel, and a parting tool.

Grindstones

The cradle which holds the power drill, forming the head-stock of the lathe, can be used for other purposes. One is to enable the drill to be used to turn a small grindstone. The maximum size of stone which can be mounted on the drill is about 127 mm (5 in) diameter, by 13 mm ($\frac{1}{2}$ in) thick. It is used in conjunction with a special mandrel, or arbor, on which the stone is mounted at one end, the other going directly into the drill chuck.

Disc sanders

One of the most simple attachments is the disc sander. This is a circular, flexible rubber pad of 127 to 152 mm (5 to 6 in) diameter, mounted on a small arbor. The shank fits chucks of $\frac{1}{4}$ in capacity upwards. A disc of abrasive paper is held by a screw in the centre of the pad, which is dished to keep the screw below the working surface. When in use the outer edge of the disc is lightly kept in contact with the work and constantly on the move – the abrasive action is quite effective, especially if a coarse one is being used.

Because of the circular action much of the sanding is across the grain. As a result, there is a tendency to scratch the surface, leaving circular marks. Because of this the disc sander is only really suitable for work which is to be painted, when slight surface scratches will be obliterated, or when trimming across end grain, edges of plywood and hardboard, or 'fairing off' when boatbuilding.

Abrasive discs

As well as the traditional abrasive paper, other abrasive discs can be obtained which, it is claimed, have certain advantages over the paper. One of these is a thin metal disc, shaped and dished to fit the rubber backing pads. At a stage in the manufacture small particles of tungsten carbide are bonded to the surface. Because of the extreme hardness of the abrasive granules, a very long life is claimed.

Another type of disc is in the form of resin-bonded matting, woven from abrasive-impregnated materials. Although the disc itself is rather stiff the weave is 'open', thus allowing dust to pass through. This means that the disc does not clog up, which is one of the problems of ordinary abrasive papers.

Orbital sanders

A much more gentle abrasive action is achieved with an orbital or finishing sander, also available as a drill attachment. Used correctly and with a fine abrasive sheet, the finishing sander produces a smooth matt surface which is used extensively on modern furniture. With coarse grits, orbital sanders can be used to rub down paintwork but they are not intended to clean off rough or sawn surfaces.

Drill bits

Many other attachments and accessories, not necessarily for woodworking, are available for power drills and, with such a wide range available, it is easy to overlook what the power drill is primarily designed for: to bore holes.

In order to bore holes properly and precisely, the correct type of bit must be used. Bits intended for holding in a carpenter's brace cannot be used as they have square, thick, shanks which cannot be gripped in the power drill chuck.

The most common type of bit used in the power drill is the engineers' pattern, shown in *Figure 6.10 (a)*. There are different qualities of this type — the cheapest are referred to as 'jobbers' quality', suitable for occasional use in soft materials. These drills do not like a high speed and if used in a single (high speed) power drill to bore in metals, they will quickly lose the cutting edge and stop drilling. Jobbers' drills are not made to a high degree of accuracy but they are close enough in tolerances for wood.

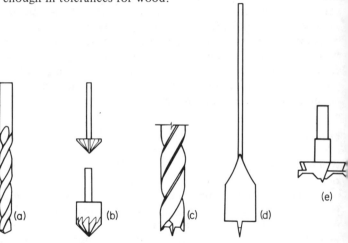

Figure 6.10. Power drill bits: (a) engineer's twist drill, (b) countersinks, (c) lip and spur, (d) flat bit, (e) 'end mill', for use with concealed hinges

A rather better type of drill is made from carbon steel. They also do not like high speeds when drilling metal — especially steel — but are unaffected when drilling wood. High speed when drilling a hard material causes friction, and this in turn creates heat. Only a slight excess of heat is enough to draw the cutting edge temper and once this is lost friction and heat build up until the drill tip turns blue and is useless. Sharpness of drill, slow speed and moderate pressure are essential when using carbon drills.

The best type is the high-speed drill. These can be run at high speed without damage, and with sensible care will give many years of service. Engineers' drills are available in metric and imperial sizes, and also in a 'letter' range. For woodworking purposes these drills are ideal for boring the sort of holes needed for screws, when it is important that the holes should be just the right size to match the gauge of screws. The drills are also useful for drilling pilot holes when using large nails and it is desirable to pre-drill to prevent splitting the wood.

When fixing a drill bit in the chuck (and, indeed, when fitting any attachment or accessory to a drill) first be sure that the drill is disconnected from the power supply. Then check that the bit is properly centred in the chuck before tightening up with the chuck key, usually a lever device which plugs into holes bored in the chuck body. A small toothed wheel engages with similar teeth cut around the chuck. When the chuck is sufficiently tight fit the lever in the next hole and tighten again. Do this in all the holes (usually three). This ensures that the bit is truly central and secure.

Many domestic woodworking jobs involve fixing pieces of wood to the walls. This means drilling and plugging the wall for screws; a power drill with the correct type of boring bit will make quick work of a job which, by hand, would take many times as long and would be extremely tiring.

A masonry drill is essential. Such drills are numbered to match plug and screw sizes, and it is important that they do match for many reasons. These drills must not be driven at a high speed, which leads to overheating but they should have a moderate amount of pressure. Too little pressure means that the tip rubs, rather than cuts.

Although a tipped masonry drill will retain its cutting edge for a good while when properly used, it needs to be sharpened from time to time. For this purpose a special grinding wheel is needed. Tungsten carbide is too hard to be sharpened on an ordinary grindstone or oilstone. For tipped drills the stone to use is known as a 'green grit', and it operates without creating sparks. These drills, however, are best left to specialist firms, unless one wishes to experiment with the smaller, cheaper sizes.

All engineers' drills can be re-sharpened on an ordinary

grindstone, smooth or medium grit. It is essential to retain the original angles and shapes and this can be achieved with a little practice. There are special grinding jigs and machines for 'touching up' engineers' drills and they do not cost a lot.

When holes are made for screws it may be necessary to countersink for the screw head. There are two popular patterns of countersink bit for power drills, as shown in *Figure 6.10 (b)*, but there is nothing to choose between them in their performance. It is always better to slightly over-countersink to ensure that the screw head does not lie above the surface. Sometimes the countersinking is made deliberately excessive so that the head of the screw can be concealed by filling with 'stopping'.

A very efficient bit for boring wood is known as the 'lip and spur', shown in *Figure 6.10 (c)*. These bits have a small central point, slightly longer than the cutter spurs, which are characteristic of many patterns of wood-boring bits. They are made in many sizes up to 25 mm (1 in) but with 6 mm ($\frac{1}{4}$ in) shanks on the smaller sizes and 13 mm ($\frac{1}{2}$ in) on the larger. These bits are excellent for boring holes of the size and type used when making dowel joints.

For the home woodworker, flatbits *(d)* are the cheapest for use in power drills. They are very simply made and were developed especially for portable power drills. They have a large point on which the flat cutting part rotates – the two cutting edges, in fact, scrape rather than cut. Despite this they bore quickly in wood and sharpening is easy, using a fine file. The bits are available up to 38 mm ($1\frac{1}{2}$ in) in diameter and all have 6 mm ($\frac{1}{4}$ in) shanks. Although they absorb little power the largest of these bits may be too much for the cheaper drills with 6 mm chucks.

More specialised bits, which can only be satisfactorily used when the drill is in a stand, include the screw Jennings pattern, the Forstner pattern, and the saw-tooth centre bit. The first two are similar to those used in a carpenter's brace, excepting the shank. Special bits, sometimes called end mills, are now made for machine-boring the holes for 'concealed' hinges used extensively on modern furniture *(e)*.

Single purpose or integral machines

Excellent though most attachments are, they do not perform quite as well, or have the same capacity, as a power tool designed for a single function. With an independent machine power and speed are matched for optimum performance, and this can never be achieved in quite the right balance with a single power source.

Separate, or integral, machines are easier to use, often requiring only one hand compared with two for the equivalent attachment. The range of independent machines is very wide and covers a great many woodworking operations.

Orbital, dual motion and belt sanders

Sanders are possibly among the more popular in this range of integral machines. Most are of the type called 'orbital' because of the circular motion which the rectangular sanding pad makes. The amount of wood they are capable of removing is only slight, therefore a surface should be in a reasonable state before this type of sander is used.

There are some sanders on the market which are classed as 'dual-motion'. They can operate as a normal orbital sander or, by moving a small lever, the movement changes to a straight up-and-down, or in-line action. This means that the sanding can always be arranged to be with the grain – an orbital movement is bound to have part of the stroke across the grain. However, because of the nature of this machine, the extent of swirl-scratching is only slight. The in-line sander does not produce a matt surface, as the orbital one does, so the dual motion sander at least gives a choice of finish.

By far the best type of portable sander is the belt sander. The abrasive is an endless belt about 102 mm (4 in) or more in width. The machines are usually designed so that on one side the belt extends beyond the body, thus allowing the sanding to take place right up to the edges. Belt sanders are capable of moving quite a lot of wood fairly quickly, and because of this the bigger and more powerful machines are fitted with dust bags or dust extraction systems. Cutting action is in one direction only and wherever possible this should be arranged to be with the grain. Belt sanders are very effective but their cost is many times that of an orbital sander.

Abrasives

Machine type abrasive paper or cloth must be used in all power sanders. This is normally bought to suit the size and type of machine for which it is needed. The grit is nearly always aluminium oxide and, although a wide range of grades is manufactured, popular packs are often available in assorted sizes: coarse, medium and fine.

When used on wood which is resinous, there is often a tendency for the paper to stop cutting because clogged with resin and dust, rather than normal wear. A rub with a wire brush will usually clear the surface, and extend the life of the abrasive paper considerably.

Jigsaws

The jigsaw machine is available as a single- or two-speed tool. As with boring holes, a fast speed is needed for wood and a slow speed for metal. Blades have a limited life but are quite cheap and quickly changed, being held in place by a set screw or on some makes, two screws. Various types of blade can be fitted, large or small teeth for cutting wood and very small teeth for metals. Because of the upward cutting action, sawdust is deposited on top of the work, right on the cutting line. Many of the better jigsaws have built-in blowers to clear the dust from the line.

When a hole has to be cut in the centre of a panel, it is necessary to bore a hole in the centre of the panel to 'start' the saw. It is advisable to bore holes at all sharp angles, the diameter equalling the width of the saw blade. Although jigsaws (sometimes also called sabre-saws) are particularly suited to cutting holes inside panels, and for cutting shaped pieces, they can also be used for straight cutting. Some makers provide a guide fence which can be fitted to the sole plate, for sawing parallel to an edge. It is not likely that the fence can

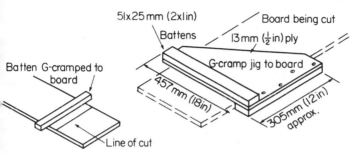

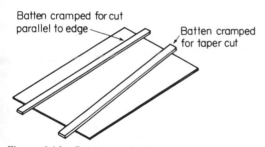

Figure 6.11. Cutting guides for use with jigsaw machines or circular saws

be used for cross-cutting or for cuts well away from the edge but a batten can be temporarily fixed to the board and this used to guide the saw. It is also possible to make a simple jig which can be G-cramped to the board and thus give an accurate, square cut every time. Some ideas and suggestions for cutting guides are shown in *Figure 6.11*. They can also be used for circular saws.

Portable power saws

Portable power saws are capable of quite heavy cutting. Blade sizes range from around 152 mm (5 in) to 229 mm (9 in). A popular size is about 190 mm ($7\frac{1}{2}$ in) and this machine will cut timber up to 63 mm ($2\frac{1}{2}$ in) in one pass. Most of the saws are fitted with a safety clutch which automatically stops the blade from revolving if the motor is being overloaded. In the interests of safety the trigger is spring loaded and returned to 'off' if released. A retractable blade guard is fitted which uncovers the blade as it works into the wood and returns as the saw clears from the cut or the wood.

A fence can be fitted to the sole plate, enabling cuts to be made parallel with an edge. When the cut is at a distance from the edge greater than the operating capacity of the fence then guides or jigs can be used, as in *Figure 6.11*.

Grindstones and their use

Machine driven grindstones are useful in a busy workshop. Small ones are in two main sizes: 127 mm (5 in) diameter by 13 mm ($\frac{1}{2}$ in) thick, and 152 × 25 mm (6 in × 1 in). Most of the machines are double-ended, enabling different grades of wheels to be mounted. Those usually fitted as standard are medium and fine; adjustable tool rests and guards are now a standard requirement on grindstones, with eye shields. If the grindstone does not have eye shields then safety glasses or goggles should be worn when using the machine.

These grinders will cope very adequately with all the general requirements of home and workshop. When grinding cutting tools on these 'dry' grindstones there is the risk of overheating the cutting edge and 'drawing the temper'. This means that the metal in the cutting edge has changed its characteristics and will not retain its cutting edge when used. If the heating becomes excessive the end of the blade turns blue or purple. This burnt area would then have to be ground away to reach unspoilt cutting steel.

Two main points need watching in order to prevent this overheating from taking place. One is to use only gentle pressure. Too much pressure, in a bid to speed up the grinding, creates excessive friction and heat. Secondly, keep a container of water handy so that every few seconds the tool can be dipped in the water to cool it. Many grinders have a container or trough attached to them for this purpose. Although the motors are usually well protected, do not splash water over them — water and electricity are a dangerous combination.

Other precautions are: keep the tool on the move as far as this is possible, and ensure that the grindstone itself is cutting properly. Wheel dressers can be purchased for truing up and resurfacing grindstones.

Bandsaws

Mention should be made of bandsaws. There are some on the market which are portable in the sense that they can be carried to the working area. A bandsaw is a fine, versatile machine which does require careful and considerate handling. After some practice the operation of a bandsaw should present no difficulties and such a tool is worth considering when skills and requirements develop.

Do's and don't's for power tools

All machine tools have an element of danger in their handling and use. Correct wiring up is the first safety check to make. Proper earthing of most tools is essential but an exception is tools classed as 'double insulated'.

We have already warned about having a drill connected to the power source while fitting attachments or accessories. Other 'do's and don't's now follow.

DO learn to understand the tool, what it can tackle, and also its limitations. Read and apply the information given in the instruction booklet.

DO NOT experiment with it or try to perform functions for which it is not designed.

DO keep the guards and safety devices fully operational.

DO NOT tie them back out of the way or jamb them with a match stick or nail.

DO maintain tidy habits, and keep the work area well lit, clear and clean.

DO NOT work in your own light.

DO store tools properly when not in use. Keep them out of the reach of children.

DO NOT allow children to get too close. They are naturally curious but do not appreciate potential danger.

DO use the correct tool for the job.

DO NOT force tools. Experience soon shows at which speed the tool performs best, this being the speed for which it was designed.

DO hold the workpiece firmly with cramps or in a vice. Keep hands away from moving parts.

DO NOT adjust or service a machine with the power supply on — always disconnect.

DO keep tools in good working order. Blunt tools can be dangerous — cutting edges must be kept sharp.

DO NOT put them away while dirty or wet. Clean them up properly.

DO switch off the power source, or disconnect tools when not in use.

DO NOT leave power tools switched on when unplugged from the power supply. This could lead to accidental starting when plugging in again.

DO make sure that chuck keys and other tightening devices are removed before switching on.

DO NOT leave them lying around on the bench or in the workshop but tie or clip them to the machine power lead.

DO be most careful when a machine has been switched off and is being put down. It is very easy to catch the cable or something while the drive is still revolving.

DO NOT place it where it can be knocked off or tripped over.

DO ensure that when extension leads are used they are positioned where they will not be damaged or tripped over.

DO NOT leave a lot of spare cable wound on a reel — open it out but place it tidily.

DO be tidy in your dress. Loose ties and cuffs can easily be caught in moving parts.

DO NOT scorn overalls or protective clothing.

7 Finishing Processes

The terms 'finish' and 'finishing process' have a particular meaning when applied to woodwork and refer to the way in which surfaces are treated. This is usually by the application of a liquid coating material which dries by evaporation of solvents and/or oxidisation of the vehicle in which the constituents are suspended. Reasons for applying a finish are many. They include: preventing (or at least retarding) decay, as in fencing; protecting the woodwork from the elements; introducing bright and attractive colours; protecting the wood surface from wear and abrasion, chemical attack and so on; and enhancing the natural beauty of the wood, which is the aim of a cabinet maker. Finishes also protect the wood surface from dirt, spillages and many other hazards in the domestic and commercial spheres. Where mixed species of wood have been used on a single project the finish selected may be to high-light the colour differences, or to try to bring the mixed woods to a uniform shade.

Preparation for finishing, known as 'cleaning up', has been described previously but it will vary according to the nature of the job and the type of finish to be applied. At one extreme, timber that has to be creosoted will not require any preparation other than ensuring that it is reasonably dry. At the other end of the scale a finely made piece of furniture will require very careful and thorough cleaning up as a preparation for applying the finish, with or without staining.

226

Finishes for woodwork come under two main categories: opaque and clear. Paints of various kinds provide the main types of opaque finishes, which include oil, vinyl, emulsion, cellulose-based and enamels. Generally the type of paint is determined by the liquid vehicle, or solvent (thinner) used in the manufacture.

Clear finishes include wax, oil, shellac, white french polish, varnish, clear cellulose and modern 'plastic' finishes.

It should be understood that while paints have an obliterating effect they do not make up for poor work or shoddy materials. The quality of a painted finish depends partly on the paint itself, and to a much greater extent on the surface to which it is applied. A poorly cleaned up or ill-prepared surface will show through the best of paint. Small blemishes, if carefully filled, stopped and levelled off, properly treated knots and other minor faults, nail and screw holes, can become undetectable under a carefully applied paint.

If a clear finish is required, whether stain will be used or not, then the surface needs even more preparation. A commonly held belief is that any form of finish covers up faults in materials or workmanship. Not only is this wrong but the opposite is actually true. Clear finishes have the effect of highlighting and magnifying defects. The slightest of ridges, which insufficient glass-papering has failed to remove, may be difficult to spot before finishing but can become very noticeable afterwards. By then it is too late to do anything about it.

Preparation for the finish, following the cleaning up process described in an earlier section, includes stopping, filling and staining.

Stopping and filling

Stopping means filling cracks, holes and indentations with a plastic material which dries fairly quickly and adheres firmly. There are many preparations available in powder or paste form. The powders are mixed with water, and pastes are applied as they are supplied. Ideally the stopper should have the same density and porosity when dry as the surface being treated. It is an advantage also if it is of the same colour, but this is of less importance with painted finishes.

Although used extensively at one time, linseed oil putty is not a good stopper. It is slow drying, eventually shrinks and does not have good adhesion. Plaster of paris expands some time after it has set and causes 'blowing'.

Cellulose type stoppings are inert and have good adhesion. They are quite good for preparing wood that has to be painted, but as they are water-mixed they dry slowly. Resin putties are quick drying and special ones for wood are excellent, but not readily available in the domestic market.

The author has used powder stopping mixed with resin into a putty-like paste, then added the catalyst or hardener and used the paste as a stopping for exterior woodwork, with excellent results, including rapid setting. Even car body repair resin paste will make a good and quick-drying stopper, although rather expensive, for painted wood that has suffered some damage.

For varnishing and polishing, open grain needs to be filled. As with stoppings, many types are available, ready mixed or in powder form.

Grain fillers are rubbed in with a damp rag, across the grain. When dry, as with stopping, they are sanded smooth. If required, a further application is made until a satisfactory surface is achieved.

The filler should be near enough the colour of the wood, but light coloured fillers can often be toned down with water-based stains such as Furniglas, even if the woodwork itself is going to be stained during the next stage of work.

Various tools are used to apply stoppings and fillers – a painter's broad-knife is useful – but often enough a wood chisel makes a good applicator for dealing with small holes. The materials can also be scraped on with strips of plastics sheet, scraps of plywood, card etc.

Brushes

Quality of tools and materials used for finishing is important. It is always better to play safe and use the products of a reliable manufacturer. This applies particularly to brushes, where the cheaper 'household' types should be avoided. When buying, choose a brush which has long bristles, and with a good body of them in the head. The bristles should also have a fair degree of spring in them, especially where oil paints are being used.

For shellac polishes and spirit varnishes a softer bristle is to be preferred. Ideally, polisher's mops should be used. These are circular in shape with soft bristles or hairs, having a rounded or slightly pointed tip. They are available in different sizes, number 8 being a good general purpose size, well suited to home use.

Some workers prefer to fit a plywood 'hood' to the mop, holding it in place with a panel pin as shown in *Figure 7.1*. The

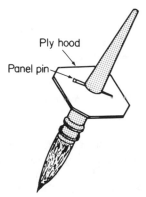

Ply hood

Panel pin

Figure 7.1. Polisher's mop

purpose of this is twofold: the hood acts as a cover for the jar in which the polish is contained, and it prevents the bristles from resting on the bottom of the container, where they would soon spread out and become useless. A paint brush distorted in such a manner is said to be 'crippled'. Signs of a good brush or mop are that the bristles hold together when wet, and keep a good shape.

Brushes need some care and attention if their maximum life potential is to be obtained. If they are going to be used again the following day they should be suspended overnight in a container of the appropriate thinners. After final use, wash out in clean thinners, dry out as much as possible with a clean rag then wash thoroughly with soap and hot water. Bristles should then be manipulated to a good shape and lightly tied with a rubber band before leaving to dry out.

The author prefers to wrap the head lightly with kitchen tissue as an aid to setting the shape while drying out, and wash out brushes after every session, in thinners. To get rid of excess thinners before re-using the brush, hold the handle between the palms of the hands and 'swizzle' the brush vigorously — taking care that the fine spray does not alight on anything vulnerable.

Rag is used during many of the finishing processes, apart from drying out brushes. This always should be clean, soft and most important, free from fluff. Sections of washed cotton garments are likely to be the best, but avoid wool.

Conditions for finishing

Physical conditions under which finishing is done are important. Good light is essential and where possible the arrangement should be to have adequate light on one side of the job being tackled, with the operative on the other, as in *Figure 7.2*. This is to allow the surface being treated to act as a reflector of the light from one side to the eyes of the person doing the finishing, on the other side. The reflection which the surface gives is a very important guide to the way the work is going.

The big enemy of most finishing processes is dust, particularly surfaces which remain tacky for several hours. Draughts must be avoided as far as possible as they create air currents by which particles of dust become mobile. Doors and windows should be kept closed as far as this is reasonably possible to minimise air movement.

Finishing is best carried out in a warm atmosphere of around 65° F, but avoid the use of fan heaters for obvious reasons. Most finishes dry better with gentle warmth, and the flow quality usually improves as the temperature is raised,

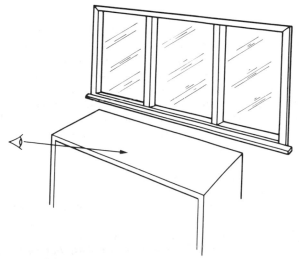

Figure 7.2. Position work near light source so that light is reflected on to the surface being tackled

within tolerable limits. Humidity is not good for finishing processes and the air should be reasonably dry. It is often convenient to carry out the finishing process in the afternoon or evening, when work with wet surfaces can be left to dry overnight in a closed room or workshop.

Finishing with oil paints

With an oil painted finish at least three coats are necessary. Before applying any paint, however, all knots or resin pockets should be coated with 'knotting'. Resin can exude through several coats of paint, and prevent some paints from drying properly. Knotting is a kind of thick, shellac varnish which dries quickly and seals in the resin. It should be feathered off at the edges so as not to cause ridges which will show under the paint.

Primers

The first coat of paint applied to new woodwork is referred to as the primer. Primers can be white, grey or pink in colour but their common quality is the ability to penetrate deeply into the wood fibres, adhere firmly and provide a solid base for subsequent rubbing down and following coats.

Aluminium primers for wood are becoming increasingly popular. It is claimed that they are more effective in sealing knots than the traditional material, and the author's experience confirms this. They should be well stirred before use, and frequently during use.

Standard primer can be thinned with white spirit to increase its penetrative powers in hard, dense wood or to seal off very absorbent surfaces. If this is done it may be necessary to apply another coat, to provide the body required for rubbing down. Primers, nonetheless, should be well brushed out and not applied thickly. If your primer does not brush out easily, thin it slightly with the recommended thinners.

Undercoats

The next coat is the undercoating, usually of a similar shade to the finishing one, but not invariably. This also provides body and a good, opaque base for the top coating. Two under-coats are even better but each one must be lightly rubbed down when dry.

Topcoats

The topcoat, gloss, satin or matt, provides protection to the undercoatings. It is a thin, tough but elastic film which will withstand dirt, many harmful vapours and the elements, and with some makes is slightly translucent to allow the colour of the undercoating to blend with it. Some paint makers advise two top coats for finest results. Satin is usually used indoors, matt invariably so.

A coat of oil paint should be left for at least 12 hours before follow-on treatment, although it may be touch dry before that time has elapsed. On the other hand, do not leave the following coat until the film has hardened. A dry surface and a hard one can be very different. Paint usually dries overnight but may take several days to harden. A fresh film will bond to the dry one but not so readily to it when it has hardened off.

Many modern paints are designed to short circuit the techniques described for oil paint with linseed or other vegetable oil as the vehicle and white spirit for the solvent. Oil paints are returning to favour because of the faults inherent with these modern paints. Craftsmen who make reproduction painted furniture would not use synthetic finishes.

Light rubbing down with fine abrasive should be carried out between one coat of paint and the next. This is known as 'flatting'. The purpose is to level the surface and free it from brush marks, runs and dust pimples, and provide a good 'key' for the next coat. Coarse paper will make scratches on the surface, which will show through the final coat, and may cut the ground back to bare wood. For very hard paint films and enamels wet-and-dry abrasive can be used, lubricated with water. Do not use this on bare wood. After flatting, the surface must be dry and well dusted before another coat is applied.

Paint should be applied relatively thinly. Never overload the brush as this results in runs and messy dripping. The brush is not used merely to apply the paint but to spread it out thoroughly and evenly. Brush tips are used with progressively lighter strokes as the paint is spread out from each brush-load. Only about two-thirds of the brush should be dipped in the paint and tips are then lightly wiped on the container edge to remove excess charge.

Each part of the surface should be brushed over several times, alternating across and with the grain. This is called 'crossing' and helps to ensure even coverage, and the avoidance of thick build-ups which can lead to runs and wrinkled drying.

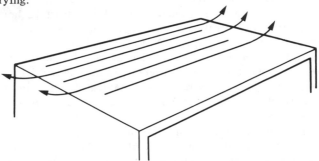

Figure 7.3. Work outwards with the brush, starting the stroke near to one end, and lift the brush off at the other

Figure 7.4. Dragging the brush inwards from the edge will result in runs

When a specific area has been evenly coated a final light brushing, along the grain and with only the brush tips, should be given. This is known as 'laying off' and the brush strokes should be parallel to one another, as in *Figure 7.3*.

Work away from the edge, starting some distance in from it, as arrowed in the drawing. Dragging the brush, fully charged, right from the edge will induce runs or 'tears' over the edge as in *Figure 7.4*. The brush should have lost most of its charge when it sweeps the opposite edge and the tip should be lifted so the bristles leave the work gently as it reaches the edge.

That may seem complicated but it really is quite easy. The manipulative skill with a brush is soon acquired. Just keep a flexible, sensitive touch, from the wrist and hold the brush lightly, as you would hold a pen. Do not apply the paint thickly — one-coat painting is for amateurs, and the results look amateurish.

Staining

Techniques when applying other finishes by brush are similar but results may be different. Most 'clear' finishes have a slight darkening effect on wood, usually similar to the change of colour seen when the wood is mopped with a wet cloth. Sometimes, however, the intention is to make the wood considerably darker than this but without reducing the grain and other patterns. A typical example is an item of reproduction furniture in oak. Time gives oak a beautiful mellow colour ranging from almost brown-black to a rich golden-brown. The rich red of old mahogany is also much simulated in reproduction work.

Producing colours or matching one colour to another is called 'staining'. A quite legitimate process in woodworking is staining strong but poorly coloured hardwoods to resemble better coloured but weaker — or more costly — species. Beech, for example, is often stained to resemble walnut or teak. We must add that the resemblance is only in colour — figure and grain will not be similar. Poorly coloured timber can, however be enriched to match perfect stock and the grain or figure will agree.

At one time stains would be made up by the polisher, as required. Invariably they would be made with powdered pigments obtainable from specialist shops, and mixed with water. Chemicals would also be used, mixed in water; in old books on finishing and in updated versions of old books these pigments and chemicals will still be quoted. They are not now so easy to find, although they are around, but excellent ready-mixed stains are available. Water stains penetrate well and are not 'fugitive' in the finishing material. Some, however, are earth pigments and produce a slight muddiness in the colour which gives the game away to an experienced eye. Pigments and dyes in alcohol are good and do not raise the grain like water stains, which is not much of a fault anyway, but the pigment may flow into the finish if it is also alcohol based, such as french polish. One other disadvantage is that the rapid evaporation of the alcohol makes it difficult to keep a wet edge going when staining large areas, with the result that streakiness and patches can occur easily.

Naptha stains are very common and extensively advertised these days. They penetrate well, do not dry too quickly and hold a wet edge, are intermixable and can be thinned quite readily with white spirit. They are excellent when used in conjunction with modern synthetic varnishes or oil varnishes but do not, in the author's experience, agree with shellac finishes or cellulose.

Thus staining is not just a matter of applying some colouring liquid to your woodwork. The stain must be compatible with the finishing material, and water soluble stains appear to be the nearest to a universal stain that we can find.

When you have the stain, try it out first on a piece of scrap wood of the same type as the workpiece, or in an unseen corner. If necessary, dilute the stain so that it is a little lighter than required — you can always apply some more. When the stain dries give it a coat or generous rub of the finish. Establish that you have the colour required, bearing in mind that it is easy to tone down too light a colour but almost impossible to reduce one that is too dark.

Whatever stain is used the method of application is basically the same. It can be applied by brush or pad of cotton wool wrapped in a cloth, which is easier and gives a more uniform coverage on large areas. Work with the grain and apply fairly liberally so that streakiness is avoided, but bearing in mind the nature of the surface being copied, matched or 'created'. When applying stain, or a clear finish, always keep the wet edge parallel to the grain, which is also the direction of application, as in *Figure 7.5 (b)*. If applied across the grain as in (*a*), marks could be left on the surface.

236

End grain must be treated with care. It is very absorbent and will come up much darker than faces of the timber if the same quantity of stain is used. It may be a good plan to seal

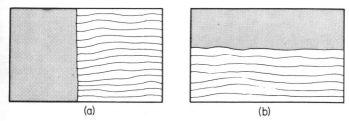

(b)

Figure 7.5. Do not apply stain or clear finish across the grain as at (a), but keep the wet edge parallel to the grain as at (b), to avoid leaving marks on the surface

end grain before staining, with some well diluted finishing material. Then use diluted stain in one or more coats, as required.

Surfaces, also, may be patchy with areas of 'woolly', inter-locked, reversed or soft grain. Areas such as these may take up more stain than the rest, or it may go in more deeply, causing dark patches. Filling may have reduced the risk but a weak sealer coat may be advisable if a stroke with a water-charged brush indicates extra absorbency areas.

If darker streaks have to be introduced deliberately in order to match, use artists' or pencil brushes, after the base coat of stain is dry. When all staining is completed the work must be well rubbed down with the finest grade abrasive, following the grain, and then dusted off until quite clean. Vacuum dusting is best if finishing is to follow in the same room because dust can float around for hours after brushing off.

Staining does no more than change the colour of wood. It is not in itself a finish although there is a range of varnish stains which provides a dual role. There is a proper sequence of applying the stain to a construction: an example of the correct sequence of applying stain (and any type of general

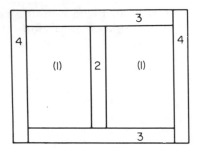

Figure 7.6. Sequence for applying stain to a framed assembly (see text)

finish) is shown in *Figure 7.6*. First treat the panels (1), then muntins (2), rails (3) and stiles (4). This sequence avoids the bad practice of cross-grain brushing where joints occur.

Varnishes

At one time varnishes were considered to have relatively poor drying qualities, especially in colder than normal temperatures. They did not like humid conditions and proof of this would be displayed by a grape-like bloom on a varnished surface affected by damp air. Copal, carriage and similar varnishes are still used for high-class work when appearance, durability and weather resistance are the first requirements.

Modern synthetic varnishes are much quicker drying than the oil types but can also be temperamental. Polyurethane varnishes are tough, resist abrasion reasonably, are easy to apply when atmospheric conditions are favourable (not cold or humid) but appear to lack the penetrative power and adhesion, and the solar ray resistance of older types of varnish. This is, of course, a generalisation and these finishes are still being improved upon and fortified in the light of experience and research by the chemists who created them.

The polyurethanes generally have a good flow and do not need extensive brushing out. They can withstand temperatures up to that of boiling water, many acids and alcohol mixtures.

At least two coats of varnish are needed and up to four, depending on the nature of the wood and the particular type of finish required. As with paint, the first coat should be diluted for extra penetration, but always follow the maker's instructions in this respect. All coats except the final one should be lightly rubbed down and dusted before the next. Some woods, particularly the softer ones, are more absorbent than others and in consequence require an extra coat.

Modern varnishes are available in three distinct types, drying out according to the particular texture required for the finished surface. They are gloss, eggshell (or satin) and matt finish. The first provides a high gloss, accentuated by the quality of preparation, and easy to clean surface. The eggshell finish leaves a pleasing satiny sheen which is nowadays very popular and the third provides a well-bodied surface without gloss or sheen. It is not suitable for outdoor use or in situations where a lot of dirt is produced, as this clings to the matt surface and can be difficult to remove.

When an eggshell or matt finish is required the undercoating should be glossy; with a gloss finish the opposite is the case. Do not apply a finishing coat directly to the wood surface — it will simply sink in, unevenly, and provide a blotchy base for following coats.

Some modern finishes, however, can be applied coat-on-coat and are claimed to provide a one-coat finish. But, they have limitations not immediately apparent yet obvious to anyone who can appreciate a first-class job.

Some manufacturers offer a range of 'coloured' varnishes. The colours are of two broad varieties, one being the shades of traditionally treated furniture woods: dark oak, rich mahogany, teak, and so on. The idea is to combine the purpose of a stain with a varnish and thus colour pale or cheaper wood to imitate the more expensive kind. Such varnishes have their place and are useful, in particular when on restoration work of a domestic nature. They must be applied carefully from the point of the brush to obtain an even flow, as uneven coating will result in patchiness. Each coat applied will make the surface darker so, when the required colour is obtained and a further coat is needed to build up body or gloss, a compatible clear varnish (by the same maker, if possible) should be used.

The other type of coloured varnish is pigmented by the addition of bright dyes in basic colours: orange, green, yellow and many others. They act rather like translucent paint, giving a bold colour to the work but allowing the grain to show through. They are useful on kitchen projects and for nursery furniture or toys.

Spirit varnish offers a quick-drying alternative to oil varnish and is particularly suitable for small jobs. It is made from shellac with the addition of a gum such as sandarac, dissolved in industrial alcohol. Methylated spirit is a thinner or solvent. Because alcohol evaporates rapidly, especially in a warm atmosphere, spirit varnish dries quickly. As a result, several coats can be applied in the time it would take one coat of oil varnish to dry and the freshly applied surface remains tacky for a short while only. It is therefore less likely to be affected by dust in the atmosphere.

The varnish must be applied evenly and quickly, with particular attention to brushing out as it does not flow out so readily as oil varnish. Rubbing down between coats is essential or the final surface will be very uneven.

Polishes

French polish is also shellac and alcohol formulated. Traditional french polishing requires a fair degree of skill on the operative's part and the technique of this process is outside the scope of this book. French polishing can, however, be done in a simplified way, with satisfactory results for the amount of time and skill involved.

Between three and six coats of polish should be applied, thinly and evenly — preferably using a polishers' mop. Rubbing down between coats is an essential part of this process but, as the film of polish is very thin, flatting must be done with the finest grade of abrasive paper: 00 or 'flour'. If a high shine is required the last coat can be left as applied by the mop.

Alternatively the final coat can be flatted like the others and then waxed. A good quality furniture wax will do, applied rather thinly and well rubbed in. The surface is finally burnished with a clean, soft duster.

Some workers prefer to apply the wax with very fine steel wool, which further abrades the shellac and therefore continues to level out the surface. Whatever method is used the final result is a semi-gloss type of finish which is quite popular and pleasant to handle. The waxing can periodically be repeated if the surface needs a tonic and restoration of lustre.

The techniques can be modified slightly to leave a matt finish. Coating is continued, as before, to build up what is called a 'body' and the final, dry coat is rubbed down with fine steel wool, used dry. Rubbing must be with the grain or very fine scratches made by the wool will be visible.

Most shellac polishes and varnishes are orange-brown in colour, depending on the particular type of shellac used. This includes orange, button and garnet. They all have a slight darkening effect on the wood but if the wood is very dark in colour this is insignificant. Problems arise with light coloured or mixed woods, where the work would be spoilt using a polish of this type – as, for example, in inlaying or marquetry work. For any job where the colour of the wood is to be retained as natural as possible, white french polish should be used. White polish is made from orange shellac which has been bleached.

Shellac finishes are only suitable for indoor use as they rapidly break down if exposed to the elements. They also mark very easily, particularly from heat and water, and spillage from alcoholic drinks can ruin the surface.

Wax polishing is a fairly simple process and is one of the oldest methods of finishing woodwork. It is considered especially suitable for oak, leaving as it does a surface with a very mellow 'feel'. Because waxing has only limited qualities of adequately filling the grain, there is a danger that a wholly waxed finish will, after a period of time, tend to pick up a certain amount of dirt. Waxing is therefore not particularly suitable for light coloured woods, and when used now with oak this is usually when the wood has been stained, often quite dark, to simulate an antique finish.

In order to seal off any staining from the effects wax may have and also to act as a foundation and help keep out the dirt, it is common practice with this form of finish to give one or two coats of french polish over the stain, before waxing.

An effective way of applying wax polish is by using a small brush, such as a shoe brush. The wax should be brushed on thoroughly and liberally then left for several hours to harden off. Next, as with shoe polishing, another brush is used to bring up the shine and a soft duster for final burnishing.

Wax polish can quite easily be made at home. The principal ingredients are pure beeswax, a little carnauba wax, and pure terpentine. The wax is shredded into a shallow tin, covered with turpentine and left until the wax disolves. Final consistency should be like soft butter. Slight variations of the above recipe exclude the carnauba wax, which is exceedingly hard, or involve addition of other substances and heating to speed up the process. Turpentine, however, has a low flash point and great care is needed.

Waxing is the sort of finish which improves with the passage of time, providing periodic re-waxing and the all-important burnishing operations are carried out.

Oiling

Oiling the wood as a means of finishing has seen a revival of popularity in recent years. This is probably because of the preference for a natural finish with minimal shine, which is the effect given by oils. It is also quite suitable for teak – an oily wood – and veneered chipboard constructions with their large plain surfaces.

Traditionally linseed oil, which slowly oxidises when exposed to the air, was used but it is slow to dry and picks up dirt easily. Modern oil preparations are usually sold under the name of 'teak oil', but they can be used on almost any timber.

Application is simple: the oil is wiped on generously with a cloth, rubbed well in and the surplus then mopped off. After leaving for several hours a second application is given. Oiling has only very slight grain filling qualities and is more suited to darker coloured woods because of dirt-retaining properties. As with waxing, it can be re-done at intervals and the body of the finish builds up in a similar manner.

Lacquers

Plastic lacquers offer a modern way of finishing home-built furniture projects. Most set by a chemical reaction brought about by the addition of a catalyst or hardener. Only enough for the job in hand is prepared because once the catalyst is added the action is irreversible. Coatings can be generous and they flow out evenly. Setting is entirely by chemical action, not evaporation or oxidisation, so the process is quite rapid. Thorough flatting between coats will result in a beautiful surface finish, and wet-or-dry papers are required for best results, using water or white spirit as a lubricant. Flatted surfaces must, of course, be well cleaned off and quite dry before following coatings are applied. Use grade 400 or 500 to avoid scratching and continue until all traces of shine are removed from the surface, which must be free from ridges or hollows.

The final lustre is obtained by use of a burnishing cream and the shine will be in proportion to the amount of rubbing which the surface receives. A power drill fitted with a polishing bonnet can speed up the burnishing work considerably. As these lacquers are so hard a very high shine can be produced by burnishing. This is known as a 'mirror-finish'. It can also be waxed to a satin sheen or left matt, as in the waxing process previously described.

Because this type of lacquer requires a fairly thick film, built up from relatively liberal coatings, the polish is at its best when applied to flat, horizontal surfaces. It is therefore ideal for table tops, especially as it is highly resistant to scratching and marking from heat and liquids. Some, in fact, will resist the heat of a smouldering cigarette.

Emulsion paints

For certain kinds of toys and nursery projects, decorators' emulsion paints offer a cheap and simple way of providing a finish. White emulsion can also be used as a primer/sealer for hardboard which has to be painted. Emulsions have the advantage of being quick drying and they have good covering properties. For most jobs two coats are sufficient, but to protect the surface from finger marks one or two coats of clear varnish can subsequently be applied.

Creosote

Sometimes wood is given a finishing treatment more to protect it from decay than anything else. By far the most common treatment is creosote. It is still a popular way of protecting garden fencing, sheds, greenhouses and similar outbuildings.

At its simplest creosote is just brushed on, the more coats the better. The treatment is renewed every two or three years. For fencing posts and any timber in contact with the ground a better process is to immerse the lower part in a container of creosote for several days, or even weeks. Timber should be well seasoned as the drier it is the more it will absorb the fluid. Creosote has also a decorative effect as it stains the wood brown. It is available in light or dark shades. Once wood has been treated with creosote it cannot be painted as the 'tar' will eventually bleed through the paint, even though it appears to be dry and fit for painting.

Where it is desired to give a painted finish combined with a decay inhibitor, then one of the proprietory solutions, such as Cuprinol clear should be used. It is applied in the same way as creosote.

So much for finishing. We have only touched the fringe of the subject but hope the object of this Chapter has been achieved. Your woodworking project, whether it be a fencing post or a reproduction piece of furniture, will ultimately be only as good as the finish applied.

8 Basic Constructions

Historical background

Wood is one of man's most widely used raw materials. Such is the great variety of purposes for which wood can be used that, over a long period of time, many quite separate crafts evolved. These divisions of woodworking developed largely according to the nature of the end product. Because of new materials, new ideas, new technologies and changes in social life or customs some of these crafts, which were still thriving at the beginning of the century, have all but passed into history. Carriage and cart building, wheel-making and coopering (making barrels) are three where great difficulty would be experienced in finding a practising craftsman. Yet more wood is now being used than ever before, and through good 'harvesting', re-planting and conservation the supply will continue to meet demand.

Revival of interest has in some cases led to a resurgence of craftsmanship in many areas of woodworking. Marquetry, carving, musical instruments, toy-making, turnery and boat-building again are thriving activities. Indeed, in small boat-building the pendulum of favour has now swung back towards using wood for this most traditional of crafts.

Principal crafts

Despite the many branches of woodworking, the three major ones have always been, and still are, carpentry, joinery and furniture-making. It is true that the nature of the work done under these headings changes as time goes by. For instance, the amount of solid wood used in furniture making has decreased while the amount of chipboard continues to be on the increase. This means a change, or for many an extension, in the skills needed for the craft as the techniques required for the wise use of a different material are learned and mastered.

Carpentry

Carpentry is often thought of as rough work, with only limited skills. This may be true of some individuals but is more likely not to be so. Carpentry does frequently involve using wood 'in the rough' meaning timber straight from the saw and in situations where to plane it would be a waste of time and money. This branch of woodworking tends to use

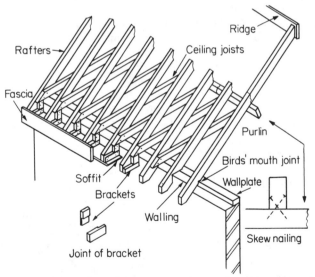

Figure 8.1. Typical carpentry work – roof construction

a large volume of wood in relation to the amount of labour put into it, and building operations still include a lot of carpentry, as in roofing, illustrated in *Figure 8.1*.

Floors and roofs are two of the main parts of a building where the work is classed as carpentry. Even on a building where floors and roofs are no longer of timber it is still very probable that the carpenter has played a significant part.

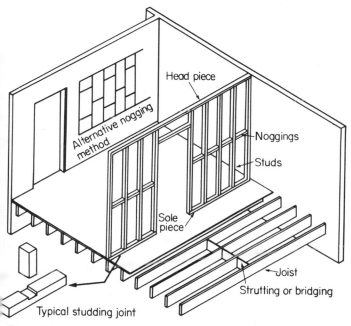

Figure 8.2. Typical carpentry work – construction of floor and partition

Floors of concrete, and roofs and stairs of the same material, need temporary moulds or supports for the concrete in its wet state. Wood is used far more than any other material for this purpose and this is an area of carpentry which has been growing in recent years. This temporary supporting of concrete work is known as shuttering or formwork; it has indeed almost become a sub-branch of carpentry.

In building work, many interior walls which are non-load-bearing are often referred to as partition walls. Frequently these are made of timber in the form of a framing, known as 'studded partitions'. The stud is the vertical member of this framework. *Figure 8.2* shows a typical example, with the various parts named. Vertical timbers are positioned at 406 mm (16 in) centres, as are floor and ceiling joists, because the usual method of cladding such a partition is by plaster board which is nailed to the studding and then 'skimmed' with plaster. Plaster board, and other sheet materials such as plywood, hardwood, wall and insulation board, all have a standard width of 1220 mm (48 in). Joints, therefore, coincide with centres of the supporting timbers without cutting and waste.

Figures 8.1 and *8.2* illustrate typical carpentry work examples (by no means complete) of a building nature, along with the usual names for components involved. Joints in common use for this work are also shown. Trenches, both through and stopped, are frequently used, as are half-laps of one type or another. A simple joint much used on roofing work of traditional nature is a notch cut on an angle to suit the slope of the roof. It is employed where a rafter crosses the wall plate and is called a bird's mouth. Many of the members are nailed together from the side. This is called 'skew nailing', and is illustrated in *Figure 8.1*.

Joinery

Joinery work includes making and fitting doors, windows, staircases and the fitting out of a building to its purpose, e.g. the fitting of counters in a bank and shelves in a library.

Joiners nearly always work with 'prepared' timber, also known as planed, dressed or wrot. Joinery is invariably visible and therefore would go through a finishing process. The most common finish for joinery is paint, although hardwood joinery (another sub-division of the trade) is more often varnished or polished.

Sometimes a craftsman may be described as a carpenter and joiner. This is common in building work where the joinery is usually of softwood. The most common softwood used is red deal, also called redwood. It is sometimes referred to by its country of origin, hence names like Baltic red, Scandinavian or Russian redwood. As with all timbers the quality varies but the best is selected for joinery and is often called joinery quality or joinery redwood.

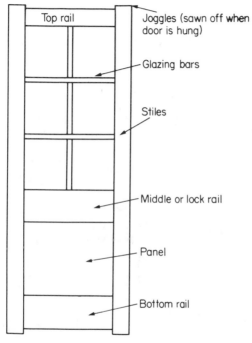

Figure 8.3. Typical joinery work – door construction

Other softwoods used by the joiner include whitewood, hemlock and Columbian pine. The joiner may find himself using the same range of hardwoods used by the furniture industry, and here the range is very wide. Teak, iroko, mahogany, walnut and oak are some of the long established hardwoods to be seen alongside those of more recent introduction.

The door shown in *Figure 8.3* is a typical piece of joinery of the frame type. (We will explain what we mean by 'frame' later on.) In a better class product the joints would be through mortise and tenons. Many doors, however, are imported and these frequently are of dowelled construction. This method, properly applied with sound materials and adhesives, is quite satisfactory for domestic-class doors.

Joggles, or horns, are left on for two reasons. The first is that it is wise to leave on some waste when a mortise is

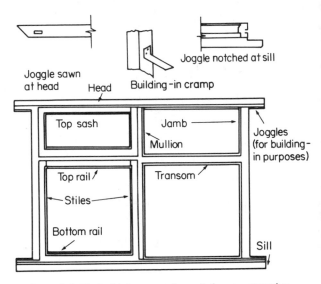

Figure 8.4. Typical joinery work — window construction

being cut near the end. This reduces the risk of the wood splitting at this point, especially if the joint is secured by wedging. The second reason, which applies to all doors whatever the pattern or mode of construction, is that the joggle projecting at a corner protects the door from damage during storage and transporting and before being hung.

Windows are made in almost every conceivable size and pattern, in both softwood and hardwood. Although many windows are mass produced to comply with British Standards specifications governing window sizes, materials and construction, a high proportion of windows outside the area of housing are 'specials' of one sort or another. Most, however, have certain features in common and *Figure 8.4* shows a typical window and the names of the various parts. This is also an example of framed construction.

Fairly large joggles are left on the head and sill of a window frame. They are used for 'building-in' purposes but they also protect the joinery during handling and transportation.

The usual practice on domestic type buildings is for the windows to be positioned into the brickwork as the wall is built. The sill joggles are usually notched to fit around the wall while the head joggles are sawn on the splay so as to allow the projecting part to be built in the wall. Exterior door frames have similar joggles and, while building practices regarding building-in sills vary a little, sides of frames are fixed in masonry joints by hoop-iron or similar cramps screwed to the frames. These features are illustrated in *Figure 8.4*.

An item of joinery that has been around for very many years is the door shown in *Figure 8.5*. This is known as the ledged and braced door. Smaller and cheaper ones are made without the diagonal braces and are called braced doors. While the braces add a great deal to the rigidity of the door this also means that the door becomes 'handed' because, in order to gain full benefit from the braces, these members must slope upwards from the hanging side. This door is also an example of a construction which does not fit into any of the three main types of classification discussed later, although it can be thought of as a fore-runner to the frame.

Ledged and braced doors are a good example of construction which relies almost entirely on nailing. Usually, oval nails are chosen which will penetrate the battens by about 13 mm ($\frac{1}{2}$ in). The nails are driven in from the front and punched well home then the projecting points are hammered flat on the battens. Punching down on the end of the nails ensure that they are

BASIC CONSTRUCTIONS

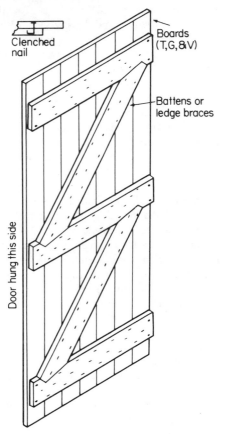

*Figure 8.5. Typical ledged and braced
door*

slightly below the surface. This method of nailing is known as
'clenching', and is illustrated in *Figure 8.5*. For extra strength
ends of the ledges are often secured by a couple of screws. The
braces can have a simple notching arrangement as shown, or
merely be butted against the ledges.

Furniture and cabinet making

Furniture making in this country has its origins going back four or five hundred years to the days when the majority of the population lived in villages or small towns and when one of the principal craftsmen of the community was the carpenter. Chests, settles, tables and sideboard-cupboards were the main items made. Mortise and tenon joints abounded and the most common timber was oak. Decoration, if any, was by relief carving and the finish was oil or beeswax.

Eventually furniture making became a separate craft and English furniture reached its zenith about two hundred years ago in the days of elegant living for the privileged few and miserable poverty for the vast majority.

Most people connected with the furniture industry agree that furniture making went through a bad time in the years between the two world wars. Possibly it was a reflection of the times but the standards of construction, workmanship and finish were regarded as poor. Naturally there were exceptions but the bulk of mass-produced suites during this time were in most cases made with complete regard to a single over-riding factor: price. Quality had to suffer.

Most manufacturers of any note now employ trained designers. This fact alone has elevated the standard of much of what we see offered for sale. New materials introduced a few years ago are now well proven, and this is particularly true of man-made boards. Chipboard has possibly been the biggest single influence on the trends in cabinet making, along with melamine plastics surfaces and laminated sheet, or in the form of other synthetic surfaces coated on to a board during manufacture.

Basic forms of construction

Woodworking constructions are generally of three basic types: frame, stool and box. Many are a combination of two forms while others involve all three. Some projects, however, cannot be conveniently classified into any particular type.

253

The chest is one of the earliest pieces of furniture and in the primitive form was of box construction. This would be made from wide boards, or a series of boards side by side. The earliest jointing would have been by crude nails or wooden pegs. Shrinkage of wood, more pronounced in wide boards, always creates problems. Whichever way the direction of grain was combined there was always a conflict of side grain with lengthways grain. As wood shrinks across the grain, but not

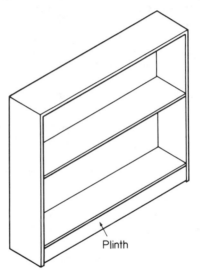

Plinth

Figure 8.6. Small bookshelves – a typical box construction

lengthways, splits and distortion took place. Over the years techniques have been evolved which make allowance for the fact that solid boards, especially wide ones, are likely to shrink and sometimes swell.

Broadly, shrinkage takes place during seasoning but wood can re-absorb moisture under damp conditions and as a result swell then subsequently shrink again when conditions become drier. This is a very significant factor which has influenced

254

construction methods over the last few years in many specific ways, as we shall explain.

Returning to box constructions, they are to be found a great deal in cabinet making. *Figure 8.6* shows a simple example of a set of open bookshelves. Although these days material forming the bookshelves may be of veneered chipboard, the use of other man-made boards does not alter the overall style, only the details such as jointing and methods of adding the back. In this example the plinth is shown as an integral part of the assembly.

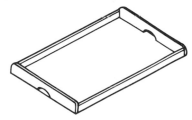

Figure 8.7. Simple tea tray is essentially a shallow box

A simple tea tray is shown in *Figure 8.7*. While hardly an example of cabinet making as such it is another example of box construction. It has four sides and a bottom, and although the sides are narrow it can more conveniently be thought of as a box rather than a frame.

Figure 8.8 illustrates a simple stool, although it is not of stool construction. It is of box form, even though there are only three sides to the box; rails are introduced as alternatives to the sides.

Most stools and tables are based on stool construction. Broadly, stool construction can be thought of as a three-dimensional framework where the members are relatively narrow compared with the overall size involved.

A basic form of stool construction is shown in *Figure 8.9*, where the same arrangement of legs and rails could be used for a dining table, small occasional table or stool. The cross-sectional sizes of the legs and rails, their positioning in relation

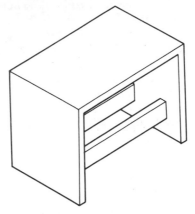

Figure 8.8. Stool of box construction

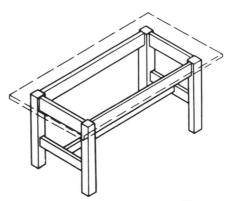

Figure 8.9. Most stools and tables are examples of stool construction

to one another and the range of joints and variations to these joints are almost without limit. These factors, along with others such as proportion and shaping, form the basis of designing, and explain why even for a project like an occasional table the number of designs which can be produced is very large.

For stools, a fairly common variation to the use of legs which are rectangular in cross section is to use dowelling, as shown in *Figure 8.10.* When cabinet- and chair-making were in their heyday many parts of a piece of furniture were produced by the woodturner on his lathe. Chair legs were often turned

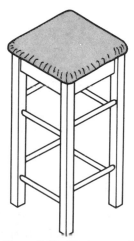

Figure 8.10. Kitchen stool in which all the lower rails are dowels

for at least part of their length and rails frequently for the whole length, when they were sometimes known as spindles. Using a dowel for a rail is a simplified version of a spindle where, in both cases, the rail is joined to the leg by a hole being bored in the leg to correspond with the diameter at the end of the rail. For both functional and appearance reasons it is possible to use metal tubing such as polished aluminium alloy for the lower rails, which also serve as footrests.

The sideboard illustrated in *Figure 8.11* shows a combination of constructional styles. The main part of the sideboard is known as the carcase, and this is of box construction. The same applies to the drawers. The underframing is made up as a separate part and is of stool construction.

Figure 8.12 shows the early chest referred to previously, while *Figure 8.13* illustrates a panelled version, evolved and constructed to overcome the difficulties of using wide boards and the problems associated with this mode of construction.

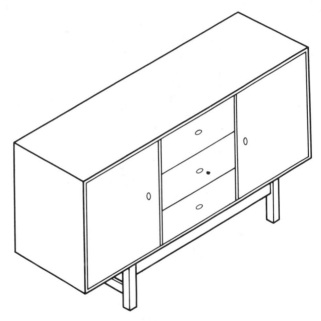

Figure 8.11. Sideboard shows a combination of box and stool constructions

Before the introduction of plywood and other man-made boards the panels were, of course, made from solid wood, but the construction allowed the panels to shrink or swell without this affecting the job overall, and eliminated the likelihood of splitting taking place. Although the chest is in the form of a box the construction shown in *Figure 8.13* is a combination of stool for the body of the chest and flat frame for the lid.

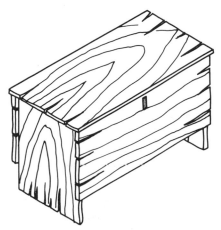

*Figure 8.12. Early plank chest – splitting
was inevitable because of wide boards
and combination of grain direction*

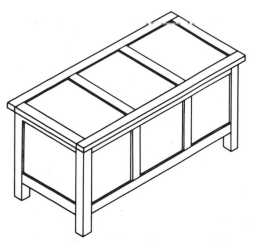

*Figure 8.13. Panelled chest – framed construction
allows for shrinkage of panels*

259

Shrinkage and swelling

The problems associated with the shrinkage of timber during seasoning or drying out were known to early craftsmen but it took time for these difficulties to be overcome. Timber is to some extent hygroscopic. This means it acts in the same way as a sponge and releases moisture to the air during favourable atmospheric conditions, re-absorbing it during very humid

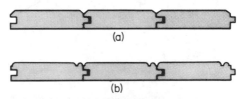

Figure 8.14. Sections through a ledged and braced door: (a) tongue and groove with Vee, (b) tongue and groove with bead

conditions. When this happens the wood shrinks or swells accordingly. This is the reason why external doors often stick in the winter time but operate quite satisfactorily during the warmer and normally drier months of the year.

Figure 8.14 shows a cross section through the boards of a ledged and braced door (*Figure 8.5*). Such doors should be assembled with the boards only loosely fitting; if dry boards are assembled and cramped up under dry conditions, subsequent swelling is almost bound to take place if the doors are used externally, as they usually are, and this would lead to distortion. The tongues and grooves are to hold the boards in alignment, and also to prevent gaps from appearing under conditions of shrinkage. The V and bead moulding is partly decorative and partly to conceal what otherwise might become a very obvious gap.

Weather boarding is often used as a cladding material on sheds and garages, and even houses. *Figure 8.15* shows two popular types. Not only is the method of rebating one piece to

260

the other a form of jointing, it is also the device by which shrinkage is catered for without the weather-shielding characteristics being diminished.

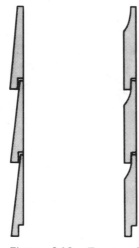

Figure 8.15. Types of vertical weather boarding in section

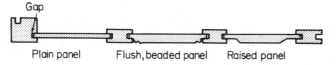

Plain panel   Flush, beaded panel   Raised panel

Figure 8.16. Types of solid panel in section, showing gaps

The principle behind panelled construction is to provide a framework of members which are grooved along their edges. Panels are fitted into these grooves. A panel must not be so tight that it cannot move, and there should be a slight gap between the panel and the bottom of the groove. *Figure 8.16* shows such a panel, along with variations in panelling design.

Ideally, the best kind of solid wood for panels is known as radial sawn. Cross shrinkage is at its least on boards sawn this way and the panels are likely to remain flat. (That is also why musical instrument soundboards are made from radial sawn timber.) Hardwoods, especially oak, have the most attractive grain and figure patterns when radial sawn.

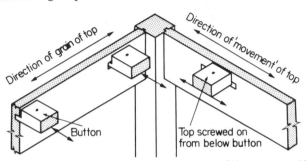

Figure 8.17. Use of buttons for securing a solid top to a table

The use of 'buttons' for securing a solid top to a table is now a very old established way of holding what can be a quite large area of wood (*Figure 8.17*). At the same time they allow the all-important freedom for the top to move, which in a large table could be quite considerable. The small mortises into which the buttons engage are made rather wider than the buttons; this applies especially to the rail which will be at right angles to the grain of the top. Mortises should also be made so that when the button is inserted it is not quite level with the upper edge of the rail. This is to ensure that the screw used to secure the top will hold it tight against the rail. When screwing the top in place the buttons on the rails which are parallel to the grain of the top should not be fully inserted into the mortises, again to allow for free movement.

As a modern alternative to buttons, shrinkage plates can be used. Two patterns are shown in *Figure 8.18*. For one, it is necessary to cut a recess in the rail, as shown. The angled type can also be used for other assembly work, such as fixing a plinth to the main carcase.

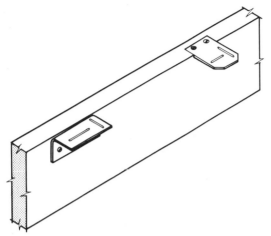

Figure 8.18. Shrinkage plates may be used as an alternative to buttons

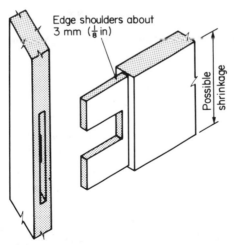

Edge shoulders about 3 mm ($\frac{1}{8}$ in)

Possible shrinkage

Figure 8.19. Edge shoulders are used on wide rails, to prevent formation of a gap due to shrinkage

Where a fairly wide rail is being tenoned into a stile the tenon is often cut with small edge shoulders. The purpose of this is twofold: a wide rail, as shown in *Figure 8.19,* can shrink slightly and if tenons were cut to the edge of the rail a small gap would result. Many craftsmen, however, feel it is good

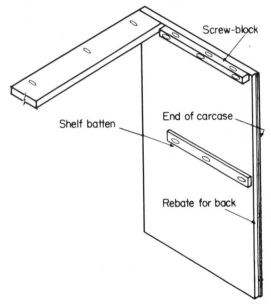

Figure 8.20. Slot-screwing minimises the problem
of wood shrinkage across the grain

practice to cut small edge shoulders wherever this is reasonably practicable, as it always conceals the end of the mortise and makes for a better job.

Edge shoulders are always formed on good quality cabinet work but rarely on softwood joinery. One reason for this is that in joinery the edges of a rail, as shown, would in all probability be either rebated for glass or grooved for a panel. Both of these cuts mean that the edge of the joint becomes hidden anyway. This would be exactly the case in the middle rail of the door shown in *Figure 8.3*, the lower edge being grooved and the upper one rebated.

It is often required to fix a batten across the grain of part of a carcase. Such a situation is shown in *Figure 8.20*. Here again there is a conflict of grain direction, where solid fixing by glue and screws would almost certainly result in trouble. By making the holes for the screws in the form of slots, the solid side with the screws in it is free to move. This technique is known as slot-screwing. The piece supporting the shelf is usually referred to as a batten, while the upper one, fixed to the top, is called a screw-block.

Framing joints

Simple types of framework members can be joined in a number of ways, *Figure 8.21* showing a typical selection. Half-lap joints can be employed in a number of different forms.

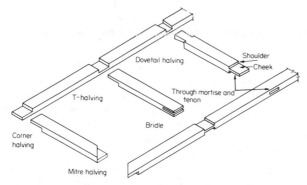

Figure 8.21. A selection of joints for framework members

Corner-halving for the corners and T-halving for the intermediate members are the most straightforward. As the name suggests, half the wood is removed on each part of the joint. Where one side of the frame will be visible, the mitre halving has a neater appearance; where there might be a tendency for the frame to be pulled apart the dovetail version has certain self-locking characteristics.

The dovetailed halving is probably the most basic form of dovetail joint. *Figure 8.22* shows the limits of the slope used in all dovetail joints, a slope of 1 in 6 being considered more suitable for softwoods while a slope of 1 in 8 is generally regarded as being more suited to hardwoods. Some craftsmen settle for a 1 in 7 slope for all timbers.

Also shown in *Figure 8.21* is the mortise and tenon joint in its most elementary form, and a bridle joint. In practice, the

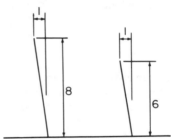

Figure 8.22. Limits of slope for dovetail joints

bridle would not be used in the type of framing shown as it would leave a very thin 'neck' in the rail. The bridle is, however, a useful joint with other applications to be discussed later.

The mortise and tenon joint is the most widely used joint in woodwork. It has been estimated that the number of variations of this joint run into thousands but some basic forms are shown in *Figure 8.23*.

For a joint which is at the corner of a framework such as a door the haunched joint (*a*) is usual. The haunch (H) is made about one-third the width of the wood (W), while the thickness of the tenon is one-third, or slightly more, the thickness of the wood. The haunched mortise and tenon has itself a number of varieties. It can be 'through' or 'stopped', with or without a rebate, with or without a groove, and so on. An ordinary through joint is shown at (*b*).

A blind mortise and stub tenon joint (*c*) are really the same type of joint. It is also known as a stopped mortise and tenon. The proportional length of the tenon can vary. For location purposes only, the tenon can be quite short, but for maximum

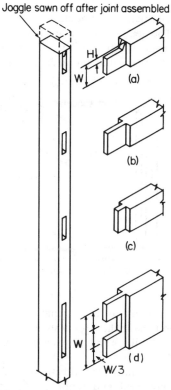

Figure 8.23. Some basic forms of mortise and tenon joint

strength the mortise should be cut as deeply as possible without penetrating the member and the tenon made fractionally shorter than this depth. For all blind mortise and tenon joints there should be a slight gap at the end of the tenon in order to ensure tightness at the shoulder.

Hard and fast rules cannot be laid down to decide at what point the tenon in a wide rail should be made into double tenons (*d*). The governing factor is the mortise: too long a mortise in a thin member will weaken it, particularly if it is a through joint. Where the width of the wood (W) exceeds about 4 times its thickness, double tenons are used with a centre haunch. The length of a haunch from the shoulders equals the thickness of the tenon. The purpose behind a double tenon is to make the tenon in two parts with solid

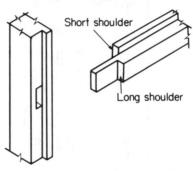

Figure 8.24. Long and short shoulders, for rebated members

wood left between them so that strength is not impaired. The tenon is continuous haunched for a shallow depth in order to keep the member 'in-line' and provide a clean, tight joint in the finished work.

It is frequently required to rebate the edge of material which is to be mortised and tenoned. The rebate must be allowed for in both parts of the joint. *Figure 8.24* provides an example. Shoulders of the tenon are not level, the one on the rebated side must be made nearer to the end by an amount equal to the depth of the rebate. The rebate will also cut away part of the tenon, so reducing its width. The extent of the mortise must, therefore, be diminished accordingly. This tenon is said to have 'long and short shoulders'.

A rebate does not necessarily line up with the edge of the tenon as in *Figure 8.24*, but may come part way across the tenon as in *Figure 8.25 (a)*. In this case the tenon must be further cut to the form shown at (*b*) and the mortise made to suit this.

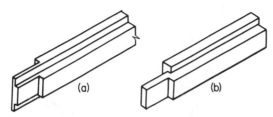

Figure 8.25. Where a rebate coincides with a tenon, as at (a), the tenon must be further cut as at (b)

For a panelled frame edges of the material have to be grooved as a means of holding the panels. Here again the joint will be affected. Because it is very much easier to form grooves from end to end wherever this is feasible, the mortise and tenon have to be adjusted to suit. *Figure 8.26 (a)* illustrates this type of joint as required for a corner. The groove on the rail cuts away part of the tenon, so the mortise is made narrower by an amount equal to the depth of the groove. Because the mortised member is grooved right through, the tenon has to be prepared with a square haunch. This serves to fill what would otherwise be a gap. For a wide rail in such a frame, as often occurs at the bottom, double tenons may be desirable as shown in *Figure 8.26 (b)*. If so, the tenons and the spaces are made approximately one fourth of the width available. If the groove is narrower than the joint, adjustments have to be made in a similar way as for rebated material.

It is generally considered easier and more straightforward in work of this kind to cut the joints first, then make the grooves or rebates. Rebates in doors and frames are the usual way of supporting and holding glass, bedded in putty and retained by glass sprigs and putty or wooden beads which may be pinned or screwed to the frame.

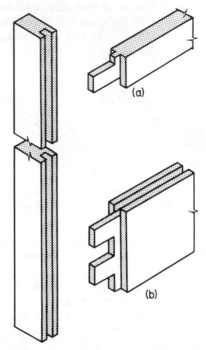

Figure 8.26. (a) Joint for corner of grooved frame, with square haunch to fill groove, (b) double tenons formed in wide rail, with haunch in centre and at edge

Sometimes it is necessary to form a mortise and tenon joint on the face of the wood, rather than on the edge. *Figure 8.27* shows this sort of situation. This type of joint is known as twin tenons. Note that the twin tenons are side by side, as distinct from the in-line double tenons.

Where a thinner member is being jointed to a wider one, as in *Figure 8.28,* it is wise to increase the thickness of the tenon above the usual one-third rule. This provides for a stronger

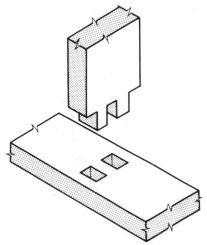

Figure 8.27. Twin tenons

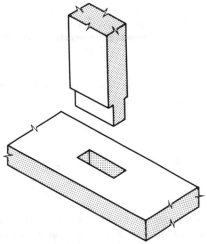

Figure 8.28. Where a thinner member is being jointed to a wider one, the thickness of the tenon may be increased

tenon, and therefore a stronger joint. Thus the shoulders are kept quite small to provide a tenon around half the thickness of the member. If the piece being tenoned is very thin, as in

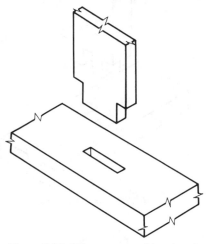

Figure 8.29. Where a very thin piece is being tenoned, edge shoulders only are made

Figure 8.29, it might be impracticable to form shoulders in the normal way, so edge shoulders only should be made, as illustrated.

Stool and box joints

The corner of a table, as shown in *Figure 8.30,* illustrates the application of the type of tenon called 'bare faced'. This has a shoulder on one side only. If the tenon were to be positioned in the centre of the rail it would mean that the mortise in the leg would be very near the edge of the wood, thus creating a weak spot. Where two tenons meet at right angles, as they do in a leg of the type illustrated, the usual way of obtaining

272

maximum length for both tenons is to mitre the ends but always so as to leave a small gap between the mitred edges. In the example shown a small edge shoulder is included in the

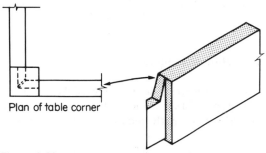

Plan of table corner

Figure 8.30. Bare-faced tenon, with sloping haunch and mitred end, suitable for a table corner

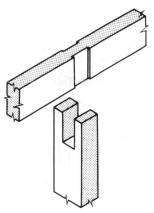

Figure 8.31. Bridle joint, used where a wide piece is being jointed into a thinner piece

lower edge but it does not matter whether the top haunch is square or sloping.

In work such as small tables and plinths it is often the case that a wide piece of wood has to be jointed to a narrower one.

273

Here the mortise and tenon joint would not be suitable and *Figure 8.31* shows a typical arrangement of the bridle joint, which is applicable to this situation. To minimise loss of strength the trenches need only be fairly shallow but the actual depth would depend on the sizes of the parts being jointed.

Box construction techniques

A wide variety of jointing methods is available for constructions of the box type. Actual choice depends on the nature of the job, amount of strength required and the importance of

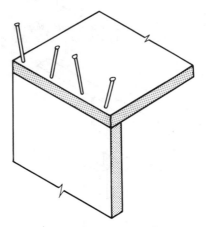

Figure 8.32. Dovetail-nailing

appearance, to name only three. All the joints shown are suitable for solid wood, but those of an intricate nature, such as the comb joint or the dovetails, are not suitable for chipboard although, with care, they can be cut on plywood.

Figure 8.32 illustrates the simplest form of corner joint. The wood is merely butted together, with the strength coming very much from the nails employed. Ovals, roundheads and panel pins are all used for this purpose but it is usual to slope the nails as shown. This is known as dovetail-nailing and the arrangement resists being pulled apart more than it would if the nails were driven in straight. In any case, nails do not hold so well in end grain as they do in side grain so dovetailing is a good compromise.

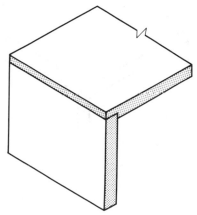

Figure 8.33. Rebated joint

The rebated joint in *Figure 8.33* is an improvement over the plain butt joint although it has little mechanical strength. The area that can be glued is slightly increased, but again the joint needs reinforcing with nails.

A form of tongue and groove joint is shown in *Figure 8.34*. It is wrong to make the tongue too long or too thick as this would result in a weakness between groove and the end of the wood, where splitting could occur because of the short-grain situation. Carefully cut and with a good adhesive, this joint will hold without nails or screws.

The finger or comb joint shown in *Figure 8.35* has the advantage of some mechanical strength, plus a wide area for gluing. It is a joint which is increasing in popularity, partly because it can be quickly cut with the aid of an attachment working in conjunction with a small circular saw, or with a power drill.

275

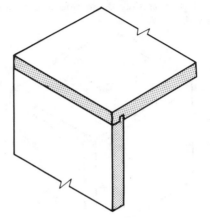

Figure 8.34. Tongue and groove joint

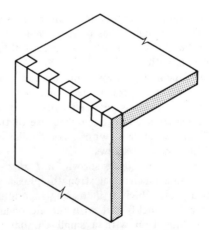

Figure 8.35. Finger or comb joint

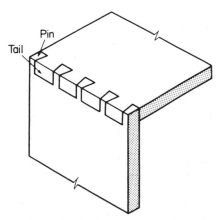

Figure 8.36. Common or box dovetail

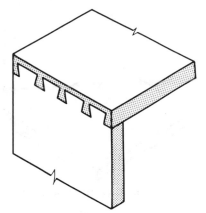

Figure 8.37. Lap dovetail

The common, or box dovetail, shown in *Figure 8.36*, is a strong joint that can only be assembled and pulled apart in one direction. The basic principles of the mating slope of pins and tails is that the joint cannot be pulled apart against the slope as, in fact, force applied in this direction makes the

277

joint tighter. For this reason it is quite important on which member the pins should be cut. For instance, they should be made on the horizontal parts of a tool box which has to be carried, and on the front of a drawer. Such joints should always be glued.

In order to conceal the joint on one face, lap dovetails are used (*Figure 8.37*). This is the traditional joint for a drawer front and is sometimes referred to as a drawer-front dovetail. The piece with the lap is often thicker than the part with the tails.

Other dovetails which can be used for corners include the double lapped dovetail, where the joint is almost completely

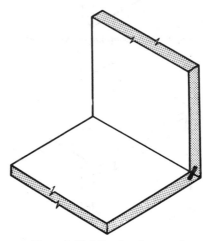

Figure 8.38. Mitred and tongued

hidden and the mitre dovetail, where the completed and assembled joint has the appearance of a plain mitre. Both require considerable skill to make properly.

A joint which is both neat and strong is shown in *Figure 8.38*, where the two members are mitred. For both maximum strength and appearance the tongue should have the grain running crossways, when the tongue becomes inconspicuous at the edges. This is a popular type of machine-made joint but can be tedious when made by hand.

The screw block method shown in *Figure 8.39* can be used on its own, or as a way of strengthening the methods shown in

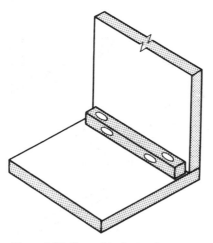

Figure 8.39. Screw blocked — slot-screws are not necessary with man-made boards

Figures 8.32 and *8.33*. As already mentioned, the screws must be slotted if the wood is solid, but this is not necessary with man-made boards.

There is a wide range of metal and plastics devices on the market nowadays, designed to simplify and speed up assembling construction of the type under discussion, especially in the commercial field. Many are of the K.D. (knock-down) type designed for furniture which can be packed flat in a carton and assembled at home. The most common of these is the corner block shown in *Figure 8.40*. It is a two-part fitting, each half being screwed to the respective pieces forming the joint, then the assembly is held together by a set screw joining the two half blocks.

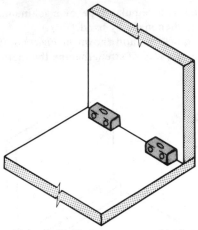

Figure 8.40. Modesty or corner blocks

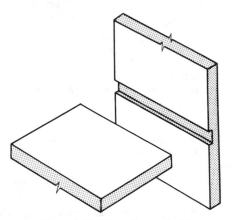

Figure 8.41. Through trenched joint

With many box constructions it is often required to have components which sub-divide the area formed by the four main sides. Through-trenching is a simple way of doing this and *Figure 8.41* shows the joint. Trenches of this nature are often made about one-third the thickness of the material.

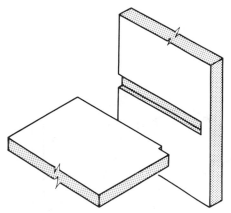

Figure 8.42. Stopped trench

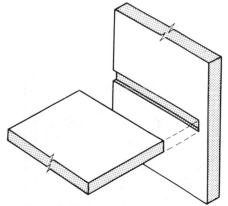

*Figure 8.43. Stopped trench with division
fitting as far as the stop*

In order to conceal the front of a trench when used, for instance, in a set of book shelves, a stopped trench as shown in *Figure 8.42* is often used. Frequently it is desired to have the edge of one piece deliberately not level with the other, as in *Figure 8.43*. The stopped trench is used. The double-stopped trench, as in *Figure 8.44*, is another variation of the joint.

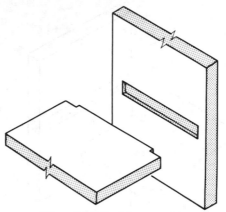

Figure 8.44. Double-stopped trench

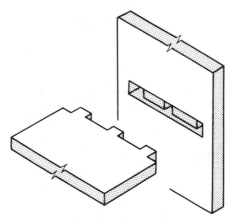

Figure 8.45. Combined trenching with mortise and tenons

Where maximum strength is needed the joint illustrated in *Figure 8.45* can be used. This is really a combination of a double-stopped trench with mortise and tenons. Details of the arrangement can vary considerably regarding number and position of the tenons, and whether the trench is double or single stopped. This joint is sometimes used as a decorative feature, with the option of inserting wedges of a contrasting colour to secure the tenons.

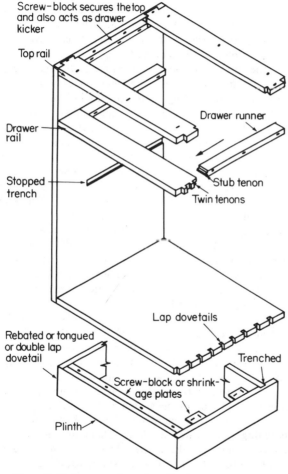

Figure 8.46. Construction of small cabinet, showing joints

BASIC CONSTRUCTIONS

The construction shown in *Figure 8.46* shows a small cabinet of the bedside type. This combines a great deal of joint applications and furniture-making practice. It can be regarded as typical of traditional techniques, but there are many alternatives depending, for instance, on appearance. For example, the top can be secured directly to the sides by rebating, tonguing or some form of dovetail, and the plinth can be of the integral pattern shown in *Figure 8.6*. Alternatively, small legs could be added to the underside.

Where the top is to be added separately to the main carcase, top rails are employed. The usual method of jointing these to the ends is by dovetailing. Note how the tails are off-centre: this is to prevent the corner of the carcase from being weakened and maybe splitting as a result. It is usual to add a screw through the joint. The back top rail is positioned to be level with the rebate. Screw blocks between the rails serve a double purpose and must be the same thickness as the rails. They act as part of the means of securing the top and also help to control the movement of the drawer. The kicker, which prevents the drawer from tipping when it is pulled out, must never be made a tight fit between rails because an allowance is needed in case of shrinkage.

The rail immediately below the drawer is called the drawer rail and the use of twin tenons is a way often used to joint the ends. Dowels can also be used as a quicker method. Tenons would normally be stopped.

Runners, which are the main components on which the drawer slides, are best if stub-tenoned into the back of the drawer rail. This joint is really for location purposes only, to ensure that the alignment necessary on the top surface for the smooth action of the drawer is achieved.

Cabinets of this nature often contain a shelf, and there are many ways of supporting such a part. For the more simple constructions the batten shown in *Figure 8.20* can be used, but trenching is a neater method. There are many fittings available for supporting the shelves. These are often used when there is a need to make the shelf adjustable for height.

A separate plinth is a common feature on small cabinets, and alternative ways of jointing the parts are available. In addition to the ones indicated on the drawing the tongued and mitred joint can be used at the front, and the rear part of the plinth positioned right at the back and jointed by rebating, tonguing or lap dovetails. Often on parts that are

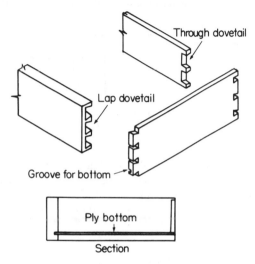

Figure 8.47. Drawer construction

completely out of sight, like the inside of a plinth, blocks are glued to the internal corners of the joints to add strength. These are known as 'glue blocks'.

The drawers illustrated in *Figure 8.47* indicate the time-honoured way of making a drawer, although again there are slight variations in how the bottom, nowadays invariably of plywood, is held in at the sides. Note how the dovetail on the front is lapped to conceal the joint, with the pins themselves arranged so as to resist the pull of the drawer. The back of the drawer is positioned to be level with the grooves in the sides, so that the bottom can be slid in after the sides are assembled.

This is seen in the sectional view. Not shown are the glue blocks usually added to the underside of a drawer. Glue blocks add a lot to the rigidity of a drawer and also increase the area on which the drawer slides.

Plywood is a very satisfactory material for the backs of cabinets. Two ways of adding this to the carcase are shown in *Figure 8.48*. A minor disadvantage of grooving (*b*) is that there

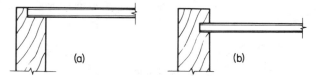

Figure 8.48. Fixing plywood backs to carcase: (a) rebated, (b) grooved

is a slight loss of internal depth. When rebated (*a*) fixing can be by glue, with pins or screws. Sometimes, to facilitate the finishing process, the back is not actually fixed until the finishing is completed. The back is then screwed or pinned in place.

Adhesives

We now have a great range of adhesives produced synthetically. Many of them are impervious to moisture, and some are boil-proof. Others bond on contact, after first being applied to both mating parts, others even bridge small gaps in jointing surfaces. These are called 'gap-filling' adhesives. The subject of adhesives alone is a big one but for general woodworking the many general purpose woodworking adhesives are suitable and makers provide full instructions. They are usually used cold; animal glues generally have to be heated, applied hot and the assembly must be cramped up before the glue cools.

There are some points to be considered when using glues and adhesives: wood is much stronger with the grain than across it, it varies in cell structure and moisture content. These things have an effect on the type of adhesive most suitable for the work.

Face grain to face grain or edge to face and edge to edge produces very strong bonds. End grain is, however, difficult because of the thousands of ends of hollow fibres that are involved. Adhesive must be applied generously to end grain and allowed to soak into the fibrous structure. Dowel joints are a big help with end grain.

When clamping glue joints together while setting the pressure should be firm enough to hold the parts close but not so firmly that all the glue is squeezed out of the joint. Any that does should be mopped away while still wet.

9 Wood Turning

Basic theory

Woodturning is one aspect of woodworking which is now exceedingly popular as a hobby, source of supplementary income or full-time occupation. There is a large range of wood-turning lathes on the market, from tiny machines for modellers to huge ones on which really large work can be performed. In between these extremes there are many makes of the most popular size for serious work — 762 mm (30 in) between centres. Such a machine will accept work up to 762 mm in length, which is long enough for table legs.

In Chapter 6 reference was made to drill powered lathes. They are limited in capacity and capability but they can produce many useful but smaller examples of the turners' craft, and can provide a good jumping off point for any one anxious to try out or develop his skills at turning.

There are also reasonably priced universal woodworking machines which include a lathe. With a much greater capacity than the drill-powered lathe, they also provide other operations such as band or circular sawing, planing and slot mortising. Some are basically a lathe, with the other operations carried out by attachments which can be added as the need arises. They are a sound investment for the keen woodworker.

Another term which relates to the size of a lathe is referred to as the swing. This is the distance from the lathe bed to the centres, which determines the maximum diameter that can be turned on the right-hand side of the headstock (see *Figure 9.1*).

A lathe with a 102 mm (4 in) swing will turn work up to a maximum diameter of 203 mm (8 in). Thus the term 'swing' indicates the maximum radius of work.

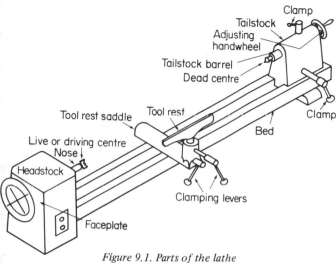

Figure 9.1. Parts of the lathe

Many lathes, however, are designed and equipped so that faceplate turning can be carried out on the left-hand side of the headstock, a facility known as 'rear turning'. Because there are no restrictions imposed by the lathe bed the diameter of work which can be done with rear turning is up to three times the diameter possible on the right-hand side.

Basic principles

If a block of wood is held horizontally between points on which it can be made to revolve it is possible to hold chisel-type tools, on a suitable rest, against the wood and gradually shape it in the form of a cylinder with parallel sides, or cut to give an elaborate profile. Similarly, if a block of wood is fixed to a revolving plate the tools can be used to hollow out and shape the block to make a bowl, platter, vase, table lamp and so on.

The lathe (*Figure 9.1*) has a headstock in which revolves the spindle. Almost invariably the machine is powered by an electric motor. Usually there are stepped pulleys on both spindle and motor which enable different speeds to be provided as the drive-belt is re-positioned on the pulleys. Speeds usually range from around 750 r.p.m. for large diameter work to 3,000 r.p.m. for work of small diameter.

When wood is being turned it is really the speed of the wood at its periphery which is important, rather than its r.p.m., i.e. the feet per minute speed of the wood as it passes the cutting tool. Too high a speed should be avoided, as this will result in dust being removed rather than shavings, which should be the aim. Ideal speeds cannot be achieved, especially for faceplate work. If, for example, a fairly large bowl is being turned, then the speed at which the wood passes the tool at the rim of the bowl is very much greater, for a given r.p.m., than the speed at which the wood passes the tool near the centre of the bowl.

For turning between centres, or spindle turning, a device called a live centre is placed into the hollow spindle in the headstock. This live centre grips one end of the wood. The other end is held on a fixed point or dead centre, on which the wood revolves. The dead centre is held in the tailstock, which is a sliding fit on the base, or bed, of the lathe. The headstock is fixed to the bed. An adjustable tool rest is mounted on the bed. It can be moved along the bed and locked in any position within the maximum capacity of the machine.

The live centre, also known as the driving centre, can be removed from the spindle and a faceplate screwed onto the threaded nose of the spindle. On this can be fixed a wood block of roughly circular shape. The tool rest can be adjusted to allow for both the hollowing of the block, and exterior shaping.

When wood is mounted between the centres it has its grain parallel to the axis of rotation. This is known as spindle turning. When wood is mounted so that the grain is at right angles to the axis of rotation it is referred to as faceplate turning. There are subtle differences in technique between the two, especially with regard to tool sharpening and handling.

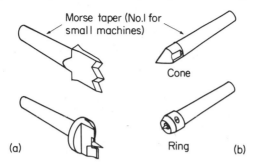

Morse taper (No.I for small machines)

Cone

Ring

(a)

(b)

Figure 9.2. (a) Prong centres, (b) dead centres

Figure 9.2 shows different patterns of both driving and dead centres. They have a tapered shank, known as a morse taper. Tapers are number-graded according to their size. Most lathes up to 762 mm (30 in) between centres size take a number-one morse taper and the headstock spindle and tailstock barrel are bored with a tapering hole to suit. The mechanical principle of the morse taper is the circular wedge, and even a small amount of end pressure creates adequate friction for a positive grip between the two surfaces.

Work is also held on chucks, of which the most common is the screw. Small screw chucks are mounted on morse tapers but a better pattern is shown in *Figure 9.3*. This has a fairly heavy gauge wood screw which is both renewable and adjustable, so that the amount of projection can be varied. Screw chucks of this type can be used for mounting wood where the grain is parallel to the axis of turning, or at right angles to it. Because the wood is held by a single screw its capacity is limited, and this applies especially to the length of a piece of wood when it is being held at its end. The greater this projection the greater is the levering effect of the cutting tool — the screw in end grain has limited holding power.

Other types of chuck include collet chucks, one which incorporates a coil spring to grip the work and one, recently introduced, where it is claimed that the work piece can be held by one of six different methods.

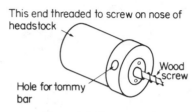

Figure 9.3. Screw centre

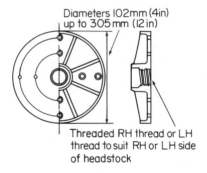

Figure 9.4. Faceplate

A typical faceplate is shown in *Figure 9.4*. This type of faceplate is drilled for screw, the usual way of mounting work on a faceplate. Different handed threads are used at the centre of such faceplates according to which side of the headstock they are to be used: standard clockwise thread for right-hand side of the headstock and anti-clockwise thread for left, or out-board side.

Engineers' type dividers or the more traditional woodworkers' wing compasses are used frequently before and during actual turning operations. Prior to mounting a block for faceplate work it should be cut approximately to circular shape to eliminate projecting corners and reduce vibration during preliminary turning. The wing compasses are a convenient means of marking out for this. During turning they are used to scribe out circles indicating where cuts are to be made. The compasses are set to the required diameter, one leg is placed on the centre of the revolving work, and the other lightly trailed against the work in order to scribe the working line.

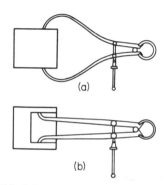

Figure 9.5. Calipers: (a) outside, (b) inside

Outside calipers are used far more than inside ones but both have their place in the turner's tool kit. They are shown in *Figure 9.5*. Simpler patterns of calipers are available without the screw adjustment. Lateral marks, required on a piece of wood during turning to indicate shoulders, steps, sinkings and similar features, are done by pencil, the marks being transferred directly from the rule to the work while it is revolving.

Tools

Tools used by the turner are relatively few but they are made in many sizes and weights. For the drill-powered lathe small tools are available and for larger machines tools called 'long-and-strong' are quite popular. The principal tool is the gouge.

WOOD TURNING

This is sharpened in a number of different ways according to the type of work it has to perform.

For the initial shaping in spindle turning a fairly large gouge of about 32 mm (1¼ in) should be used. This is sharpened with its end square. Although all turning tools need grinding from time to time it is not usual to have a second bevel in the

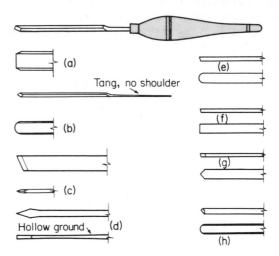

Tang, no shoulder

Hollow ground

Figure 9.6. Turning tools: (a) square-ended gouge, (b) round-ended gouge, (c) skew chisel, (d) parting tool, (e) round-nose scraper, (f) square-nose scraper, (g) diamond-nose scraper, (h) gouge sharpened for faceplate work

same way that bench chisels and planes have. A typical turning gouge is shown in *Figure 9.6 (a)*, while at *(b)* is shown one sharpened with its end rounded. This type of sharpening is required on a gouge for concave shaping on spindle work.

The third manner of sharpening is shown at *(h)*. This gouge is prepared for faceplate work and has a bevel of 45 degrees. It can be steeper without loss of efficiency. Only relatively narrow gouges are used for faceplate work, rarely more than

13 mm ($\frac{1}{2}$ in). Patterns known as long-and-strong are popular for bowl turning, when 10 mm ($\frac{3}{8}$ in) is considered to be an ideal size. Many turners use gouges straight from the grindstone, and gain the cutting action from the burr so produced.

The parting tool, shown at (d), is included in all sets of turning tools and is in frequent use. It is used for squaring off ends, forming shoulders, and reducing diameters at specific points on the work. It is a very useful tool but it does not cut cleanly because of the nature of its cutting action. An end squared off with a parting tool would need attention from a skew chisel if the end of the work is to be seen.

A skew chisel (c) is used to make smoothing cuts for finishing and for cutting shoulders, beads, vees and convex curves. The exact angle at the end is not important but it is always policy to use as large a skew as possible, depending on the nature of the work. The heel of the chisel is used to bite into the work and the toe must trail, allowing the waste to curl off in a thin shaving. This is because in use there is the ever present danger of the toe digging into the work. Therefore, the wider the chisel the further the toe is away from the wood.

Tools shown at (e), (f) and (g) are classed as scrapers because they scrape the wood rather than cut it. They are used more on faceplate work. The most common of the scrapers is the round nose, used for finishing hollowed out work where a gouge cannot operate. Scrapers are ground with a steep bevel and work best when used straight from the grindstone.

Cylinder or spindle turning

Spindle work can, and should, be carried out entirely with tools that cut the wood. Such tools are gouges and skews. When used properly both are capable of removing long, continuous shavings from the wood — to the delight of the turner and amazement of the onlooker. The ability to remove very long shavings does depend to some extent on the species of wood as some respond to this technique better than others. When the wood is properly cut with the gouge and skew the surface is usually left smooth, and does not require much sandpapering.

Using the gouge and skew correctly is a knack acquired by experience, and until the proper way of using these tools is mastered the beginner will in all probability resort to scraping. This is, undoubtedly, easier and safer but scraping does not cut the wood anything like so cleanly as the gouge and skew.

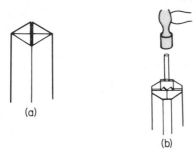

(a)

(b)

Figure 9.7. Preparing headstock end: (a) saw-cut in end, (b) prong centre tapped home

This has the result that the surface is left fairly rough, necessitating a lot of work with glasspaper. On long, slender work scraping can cause the wood to bow while revolving, as the wood will tend to resist the pressure and lower cutting efficiency of the scraper.

Stock to be turned between centres usually starts off by being square. Sufficient waste must be provided at each end for mounting and subsequent parting off. First the diagonals are drawn in at both ends, as in *Figure 9.7*. These locate the centres for mounting in the lathe. It helps if a diagonal at one end has a small V-cut sawn in it, as shown, and the centre of the other emphasised with a bradawl. It is also worth while, and saves time in the long run, if the corners are planed off the wood to reduce it to octagonal section. This lessens the work turning tools have to do, and also reduces vibration.

WOOD TURNING

If the wood is rather hard, a pronged centre can be tapped home with a hammer, as shown. Live centre and wood are then returned to the headstock, and the tailstock positioned so that the dead centre engages in the small hole made by the bradawl at that end. The tailstock is then locked in the bed and the barrel is screwed up and tightened to drive the centre into the wood, then slackened off a little to permit free rotation. A spot of oil at the tailstock end reduces friction and prevents the possibility of burning, but a rub from a candle is even better as it will not penetrate and discolour the wood.

Figure 9.8. Position of gouge on work

Gouge pointed slightly in direction of movement

Figure 9.9. The gouge is pointed slightly in the direction of movement

The tool rest is now adjusted to within 3 mm ($^1/_8$ in) of the wood, and about the same distance above its centre. As a precaution, the work should be revolved by hand to ensure it does not touch the tool rest.

Tools should be held firmly with the left hand near the end of the blade, fingers gripping the tool and palm of the hand partly on the tool rest so as to control lateral movement. The right hand is used to control the handle; that is, to provide: the angle of tool to the work, as seen from the side in *Figure 9.8*; the angle of the tool to the work in plan, as shown in *Figure 9.9*; and rotational twist to the tool to determine actual cut.

Note that the tool is placed fairly high on the wood (*Figure 9.10*), the aim being to have the bevel rubbing the surface so that it forms a tangent to the cylinder. The tool should also be pointed slightly in the direction of cutting.

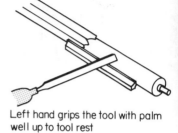

Figure 9.10. Left hand grips the tool with palm well up to tool rest

Left hand grips the tool with palm well up to tool rest

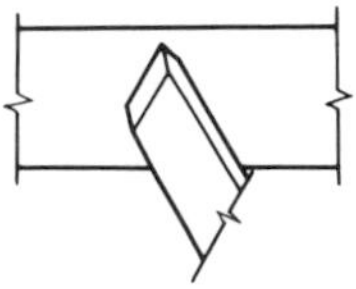

Figure 9.11. Using a skew chisel to smooth the surface

First stage of the cutting is with a fairly large gouge; this procedure is known as 'roughing down'. It matters little whether the cutting is from right to left or left to right but it will probably be necessary to move the tool rest as roughing down continues. The work should be checked frequently with calipers, set to a little more than the required diameter. It is safer to stop the machine when calipers are being used.

Smoothing a cylinder, and arriving at final diameter, is done with a large skew. *Figure 9.11* shows its position on the wood. It is placed high on the cylinder and positioned so that the centre part of the cutting edge is in contact with the surface. The handle is then lifted and rotated to enter the heel of the cutting edge to the depth of cut required, after which the tool is moved along the work. The skew is held in a similar manner to the gouge and, also like the gouge, it is better to move off at the ends, rather than on to the work.

The bevel of the skew acts as a fulcrum and the handle hand controls the actual cut. Point of contact with the work should be at the approximate centre of the cutting edge, or slightly nearer the heel. If a point too near the toe is used, the wood has a habit of taking control over the chisel, the toe digs into the wood and a piece is split out. Cutting can be carried out in either direction, the chisel merely being turned over.

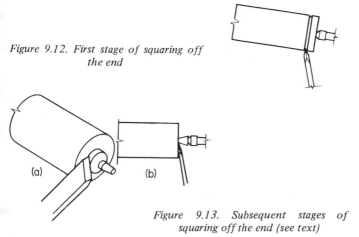

Figure 9.12. First stage of squaring off the end

(a)

(b)

Figure 9.13. Subsequent stages of squaring off the end (see text)

To square off an end, either the parting tool or skew chisel can be used. With the skew, a light nicking cut is made with the toe of the chisel, pushing the point directly into the work a trifle outside the required dimension, as shown in *Figure 9.12*. This cut cannot be made very deep so the chisel is now placed flatways on the wood, and pushed forward and downward at the same time. *Figure 9.13 (a)* shows this cut being made. To finish off the cut exactly to the line the chisel must be held as shown in (*b*). The essential point here is that the bevel of the skew adjacent to the end being cut must be nearly parallel to this end surface. There should be just a fractional variation from this plane, only enough to allow the toe to cut.

As an alternative to the skew, a parting tool can be used to square off an end in a similar way to that shown in *Figure 9.14 (a)* for forming a shoulder. For a shoulder with a tenon or a pin, the parting tool is used close to the shoulder line, and a

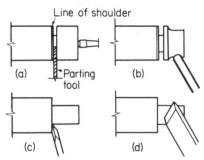

Figure 9.14. Stages in forming a pin, or tenon, at the end (see text)

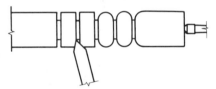

Figure 9.15. Beads formed with a scraping tool

cut made to within about 1.5 mm ($^1/_{16}$ in) of the required diameter. Waste is then removed with the gouge, as at (*b*). Next, the shoulder is trimmed back to the line with the skew, held as described for squaring an end, and as shown at (*c*).

The horizontal cut is also made with a skew. This is seen at (*d*) and only very light cuts should be taken, with frequent checks using calipers. Such a pin, or dowel, is often intended to fit into a hole so it is therefore wise to check it in a sample hole bored in a piece of waste wood.

Small beads are made with a convex cut and *Figure 9.15* shows a simplified way of forming the beads. Their locations are pencilled in and the parting tool is used to form grooves between the beads. Depths of the grooves should be made equal, about half the width of the bead, and checked with calipers. A diamond point scraper is then used to form the profiles.

Scrapers are initially held horizontally on the tool rest, and the handle moved slightly upwards until the tool is cutting the wood rather than just rubbing it. The edge of the scraper should be on, or slightly below, the centre line. If little more than dust is being removed the tool probably needs sharpening, but scrapers will never remove shavings as do cutting tools.

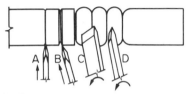

Figure 9.16. Beads formed with a skew chisel

Figure 9.16 shows a more professional approach to cutting beads and is carried out entirely with the skew. The point, or toe, of the skew is thrust into the work as at A. This incision is enlarged to form a Vee by making the following cuts first at one side, then the other, of the Vee, as shown at B. Depth of cut is increased a little as subsequent rounding is carried out. This must be done carefully in order not to sever the grain as, otherwise, there may be a tendency for some slight surface splitting along the grain. Actual rounding is done from the centre of the bead downwards into the Vee, as in C. This involves quite a compound movement of the tool, controlled from the handle.

The chisel does not move laterally along the tool rest but, for the left-hand side of the bead, the handle moves to the right and is raised so that the cutting edge is lowered around the curve of the bead, and at the same time the tool is rotated slightly so that as it completes the cut the flat surface of the chisel is almost upright, as at D.

WOOD TURNING

As with the bead, alternative ways of forming a cove, or concave cut, are practised: one by scraping, the other by cutting with a gouge. For the more simple method of scraping a round nose scraping tool is used and the method of working is shown in *Figure 9.17*. It is always better to use a scraper that is smaller than the size of the hollow required, and the tool is moved in the manner shown.

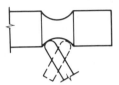

Figure 9.17. Cove or concave cut made with a round-nose scraper

Forming a cove with the gouge involves rather more skill when compared with scraping, but has the advantage that, when correctly executed, the surface is left very much smoother. This is because, with a sharp gouge, the wood is cleanly cut and with no tendency for the grain fibres to be torn out of the surface, which is always a possibility with scraping methods.

To cut a cove with the gouge, start in the centre part with the tool on its edge as shown in *Figure 9.18*. As the gouge is

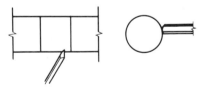

Figure 9.18. Start of cove or concave cut using a gouge

moved forwards, the right hand moves to the right while the left hand rolls the gouge over onto its curved back. This cuts the right-hand side of the cove. The action is reversed for the other side. *Figure 9.19 (a)* shows the cut well advanced the gouge always working from the periphery downwards into the hollow, and the turner always starting the cut with the gouge well over on its side. The position of the gouge at the end of the cut is seen at (b).

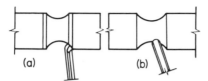

Figure 9.19. Forming a concave cut
(see text)

For maximum control the bevel of the tool must always be rubbing on the work. This also produces the most efficient cutting, and therefore the cleanest surface. Approaching the work with the gouge pointing towards the axis of the wood can be compared to using a plane with a vertical blade. The plane would scrape the wood, not cut it, and a gouge used in this manner is reduced to carrying out the inferior action of a scraper.

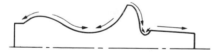

Figure 9.20. Direction of working on
compound shape

Most turning work involves curved profiles and as these are either convex or a combination of convex and concave, a lot of woodturning is based on the two fundamental cuts of beads and coves, although the degree of curvature might be much different. Figure 9.20 shows the sort of combinations of curves which may be found on typical turned parts. The arrows indicate the direction of working, the rule being to work from the large diameter to the smaller one whenever this is possible. Hollow curves must be cut with a gouge or round-nose scraper while convex curves and flat surfaces are formed with the chisel, or square scraper.

Hollowed or faceplate turning

Faceplate turning has an inherent problem associated with it in connection with grain direction. This trouble is at the edge of the turning rather than the face. Reference to *Figure 9.21* shows the nature of the difficulty. Because of the combination of grain direction and rotation of the wood, two opposite

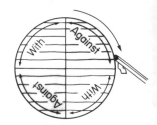

Figure 9.21. The problem of working against the grain with faceplate turning

quarters are inevitably cut against the grain. There are techniques to minimise the effects but the problem cannot be eliminated. When a piece of faceplate turning such as a bowl is examined it will invariably be found to have two areas opposite one another which are darker than the rest. This is because they are cut across the grain, exposing open pores which are more absorbent of light, reflect less, absorb more polish and so on, and are of a different general structure to the smoother, more reflective parts cut with the grain. This does, however, add to the character of good turnery and highly decorative wood.

Many turners prefer to have a piece of plywood sandwiched between the work and faceplate, and this is really essential when the wood being turned is smaller than the faceplate. In practice the ply is fixed to the work, then both pieces are screwed to the faceplate. Small screws may be used to fix the ply to the block but it can be brushed with a white resin type glue then covered with a piece of thick, rather soft, paper. The paper is then similarly glued to the block and the whole allowed to dry. The plywood is, of course, screwed to the faceplate. When the work is finished the ply and turned article are parted quite easily with a sharp chisel, and remains of paper and glue are washed or sanded off.

Figure 9.22 shows the use of ply packing, where the wood being turned is an ashtray. A recess is formed in the centre in order to take a brass or glass dish. For this the diameter of the sinking is marked out with compasses or dividers.

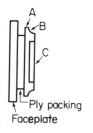

Figure 9.22. Section of simple faceplate work, such as an ashtray

It is usual to commence a piece of faceplate turning by truing up the edges to produce a disc of the required diameter, or a little larger to allow for further shaping, as at A in *Figure 9.22*. This can be done with the scraper or, more properly, with the gouge. The gouge is used well over on its side and pointing upwards so that the bevel is tangential to the surface.

Figure 9.23. Scraping tool sharpened on end and also partly at the side

This operation is best done by working from the flat surfaces towards the centre, so eliminating the chances of slight splitting at edges.

A square-end scraper is used for forming the recess indicated at C. This tool, however, needs 'relieving' on the grindstone on the left-hand edge, near the end. This is shown in *Figure 9.23*. There are two reasons for this: without the edge the scraper will not clear properly when cutting the outer edge of the sinking; the smaller the diameter of the recess the greater the need for this edge grinding. The second reason for the edge treatment of the scraper is that it creates a sharp edge, therefore the recess can be enlarged by moving the tool sideways and allowing the edge of the tool to do the cutting (*Figure 9.24*).

The edge of the ashtray can be shaped in a number of ways; the design shown at B in *Figure 9.22* can be formed with either a round-nose scraper or a small gouge.

Figure 9.24. Face of ashtray showing initial groove to form a recess, and the need to have left-hand side of scraper ground at an angle

One faceplate job which is always a favourite is a bowl. Bowls can vary considerably in shape but those shown in the illustrations are fairly typical. After mounting on the face-plate, shaping is commenced by using a square-nose scraper to form a recess as at A in *Figure 9.25*. This is made about 3 mm ($\frac{1}{8}$ in) deep or slightly more, after which the surface B is

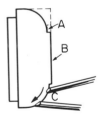

Figure 9.25. Early stage of turning a small bowl. Note that the bevel of the gouge is rubbing on the work, and that the gouge is fairly high on the surface of the wood (see text)

skimmed and also made very slightly concave. The curve to the lower part of the bowl is tackled next, preferably with a small gouge. The tool is kept over on its side and is pointed sideways and upwards so that the bevel is kept rubbing on the surface. This is illustrated at C, which also shows the movement of the gouge.

With the outside shaping completed, the bowl is reversed on the faceplate, making sure that it is concentric. Lengths of screws being used have to be watched carefully to make sure they do not penetrate into what will be the inside of the bowl.

306

The outside is completed with the gouge so that the curve blends in with the initial shaping. A gouge is preferred for the hollowing out process, or at least for the bulk of it. As hollowing progresses the tool rest is moved as in *Figure 9.26,* so that

Figure 9.26. Work reversed on faceplate for hollowing. Wood is removed using a round-nose tool, or a small gouge used largely on its edge. The tool rest is always kept close to the work

it is always only a short distance from the work. This is to reduce the overhang of the tool, and also explains why long-and-strong gouges are recommended for this type of work.

Depending on the exact shape of the bowl, it is sometimes difficult for even the experienced turner to make proper use of the gouge at the bottom of the bowl, near the sides. Here a

Figure 9.27. Completing the hollowing with a round-nose scraper

scraper often has to be employed. *Figure 9.27* shows this area of difficulty, with the tool rest once again adjusted so as to be fairly close to the work.

Finishing processes

Turned work, like most other woodworking projects, has to be glasspapered in order to prepare it for polishing or other type of finish. Before glasspapering, or sanding as it is more often called, the tool rest should be removed from the lathe bed.

Sanding is done with the work revolving, but fingers can be trapped if the tool rest is in position.

The glasspaper is held under the rotating work so that the frictional pull is away from the worker; if held the other way a sudden snatch from the work could break finger nails, or fingers. Medium pressure is applied and the glasspaper is moved slowly along the wood. In the case of spindle turning, too rapid a lateral movement could result in spiral scratches appearing on the work, as this sanding is across the grain. Progressively finer grades of paper are used until a smooth, scratch-free surface is produced.

Polishing is also done on the lathe. A simple way of polishing is by waxing. However, as in the case of cabinet work, it is helpful to give a sealing coat of french polish first and allow this to dry. Do not overlook the fact that this polish will have the effect of darkening the wood, so for light woods use white or very pale polish. Button polish gives a nice glow to darker woods.

Canauba wax is popular with turners. This is a very hard wax which is held, in block form, under some pressure against the rotating work. Frictional heat melts the wax surface and the wax sinks in and coats the work face. This is then burnished with a soft cloth, the lathe rotating at a slowish speed, until the polish is achieved.

Plastic type lacquers are useful for turned work as the effort in rubbing down and the burnishing required are done by the lathe itself. It is not too difficult with plastic lacquers to obtain an extremely high-gloss finish which is hard-wearing and resistant to most domestic hazards. If a tough finish without the gloss is required then fine wire wool, dipped in wax polish and held against the revolving wood, will leave a satin-like surface.

Only the basic outline of woodturning has been covered in this section. Many turners create their own designs as they turn the work, while others follow printed designs or copy items. If you intend to copy, make a card templet and check the work with it as you go along; alternatively, special templet formers can be purchased from craft suppliers.

Section 3

Domestic Plumbing

1 Cold Water Services

Prior to the reorganisation of local government that took place on 1 April 1974, the responsibility for the provision of water supplies rested either with the local Borough or District Council or with one of the many statutory water undertakings. Since that date all-purpose Regional Water Authorities have been responsible for water supply, sewerage and sewage disposal. In many areas however the former water authority continues to act in that capacity as agent for the regional authority.

Water is distributed from the Authority's reservoirs by means of underground water mains, usually of iron suitably protected against corrosion. A branch communication pipe connects the main to a Water Authority stop-cock at the boundary of each property (*Figure 1.1*). It is at this stop-cock that the householder's responsibility for his water services begins.

The stop-cock will be found in a purpose-made pit, 3ft or more deep, with a hinged metal cover (*Figure 1.2*). Unlike the stop-cocks within the house, this one will probably have, instead of the conventional crutch or wheel head, a specially designed shank that can be turned only by means of one of the Authority's turn-keys. This enables water supply to be turned off when the house is unoccupied, or in the event of the occupier failing to pay his water rate!

From this stop-cock a service pipe (usually 15mm or ½in in diameter) is taken to within the house curtilage. This pipe should rise slightly throughout its length to permit any air bubbles to escape but, as a frost precaution, must be kept at least 0.82 metres (2ft 6in) below ground level.

The material of which the pipe is made will depend largely upon the date of its installation. Prior to the mid-1930s it would certainly have been of lead. Nowadays it is more likely to be of dead-soft temper copper tubing or even of polythene.

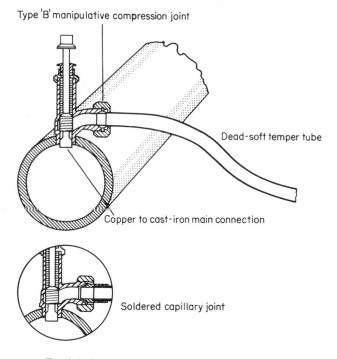

Type 'B' manipulative compression joint

Dead-soft temper tube

Copper to cast-iron main connection

Soldered capillary joint

Fig. 1.1. Connection of communication pipe to main

Where the service pipe passes under the foundations of the house it should be threaded through lengths of drain pipe to protect it from possible damage as a result of settlement. The service pipe usually enters the house through the kitchen floor. Where this is of hollow boarded construction special

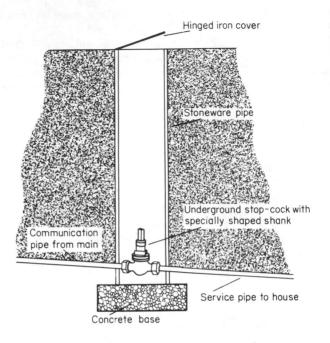

Fig. 1.2. The water authority's stop-cock

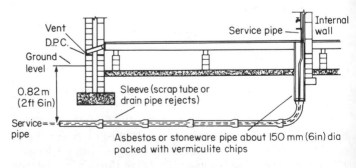

Fig. 1.3. Service pipe entry under suspended floor

precautions must be taken to protect the pipe from exposure to the icy draughts that may whistle through the underfloor space. An effective method of protection is to thread the pipe through the middle of a 150mm (6in) drain pipe and to pack it round with vermiculite chips or some other similar inorganic lagging material (*Figure 1.3*). From the point at which the service pipe enters the house it is often referred to as the 'rising main'. In a modern home it is likely to be of half-hard temper copper tubing, though stainless steel or p.v.c. tubing may also be used.

Immediately above floor level the rising main should be provided with a stop-cock—the householder's main stop-cock. Immediately above this should be a drain cock (*Figure 1.4*).

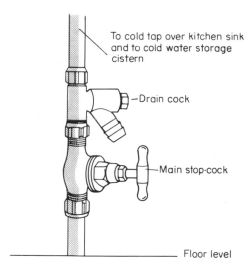

Fig. 1.4. Stop-cock and drain cock as rising main enters house

These two fittings permit the water supply to the house to be cut off and the entire length of the rising main drained when required.

COLD WATER SERVICES

In the past it was quite usual for all cold water services, including the bathroom cold taps and the w.c. flushing cistern, to be connected direct to the rising main. Today however, the regulations of most Water Authorities, and good plumbing practice, permit, at the most, four connections to this pipe.

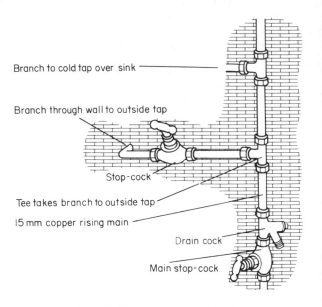

Branch to cold tap over sink

Branch through wall to outside tap

Stop-cock

Tee takes branch to outside tap

15 mm copper rising main

Drain cock

Main stop-cock

Fig. 1.5. Mains supply to outside tap

The first of these is to the cold tap over the kitchen sink. This is the tap that supplies water for drinking and cooking purposes and it is essential, on health grounds, that it should be supplied direct from the main and not from a storage cistern. A second connection *may* be made to the rising main at about the same level as the branch supplying the kitchen sink. This is for a branch supply pipe to serve a garden or garage tap (*Figure 1.5*). Such a tap can be provided only with the permission of the Water Authority who will usually make an extra charge on the water rate for its installation and use.

COLD WATER SERVICES

Typically, a garden supply pipe is taken through an external wall and turned over into a wall-plate elbow. A bib-tap, preferably fitted with a hose connector, is screwed into the outlet of this elbow. It is important that a separate stop-cock should be inserted into a garden supply branch pipe of this kind. At the onset of winter the stop-cock can be closed

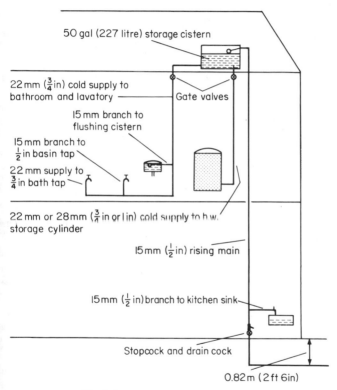

50 gal (227 litre) storage cistern

22 mm ($\frac{3}{4}$ in) cold supply to bathroom and lavatory ——— Gate valves

15 mm branch to flushing cistern

15 mm branch to $\frac{1}{2}$ in basin tap

22 mm supply to $\frac{3}{4}$ in bath tap

22 mm or 28 mm ($\frac{3}{4}$ in or 1 in) cold supply to h.w. storage cylinder

15 mm ($\frac{1}{2}$ in) rising main

15 mm ($\frac{1}{2}$ in) branch to kitchen sink

Stopcock and drain cock

0.82 m (2 ft 6 in)

Fig. 1.6. Domestic cold water services

without affecting the other household services. The supply pipe can then be drained and the garden tap left open to eliminate the risk of frost damage.

315

From the kitchen the rising main will pass upwards to supply, via a ball or float valve, the main cold water storage cistern. This will probably be situated in the roof space. In its journey to the roof space the rising main should preferably be fixed to an *internal* wall though, in a modern home with central heating and cavity wall infilling, this is less important as a frost precaution than it formerly was.

The fourth, and final, branch that may be taken from the rising main of a well-designed modern plumbing system is also taken from within the roof space. It is to the ball valve supplying the small feed and expansion tank of an indirect hot water system, possibly used in conjunction with a central heating installation.

All other cold water services should be supplied by means of distribution pipes taken from the cold water storage cistern (*Figure 1.6*). There will usually be at least two, possibly more, of these. They should connect to the storage cistern at a level about 2in above its base to reduce the risk of grit and detritus from the water main being drawn into the distribution pipes.

Where there is a cylinder storage hot water system (whether direct or indirect) a supply pipe at least 22mm (¾in) and preferably 28mm (1in) in diameter must be taken from the cistern to connect to the cold supply tapping near to the base of the cylinder. Where the hot water system is a conventional indirect one (see Chapter 3) a drain cock should be provided in this supply pipe near to the cylinder connection to enable the cylinder to be drained.

It is very important that no branch supply pipe to any other draw-off point should be taken from the pipe serving the hot water storage cylinder.

Another cold water distribution pipe—again, at least 22mm (¾in) in diameter—is taken from the cold water storage cistern to provide bathroom cold water supplies. This is taken direct to the ¾in cold tap of the bath and 15mm (½in) branches are teed off it to supply the w.c. flushing cistern and the cold tap over the bathroom wash basin.

If an independent shower or a 'through rim' bidet are installed, separate 15mm (½in) cold water distribution pipes must be taken, direct from the storage cistern, to supply them with cold water. The reasons why *separate* supplies must be taken to these fittings will be explained when their installation is considered.

It is obviously to advantage to be able to isolate individual distribution pipes (to renew tap or ball-valve washers for instance) without affecting the rest of the household water supply system. This can be done by fitting gate valves into the distribution pipes close to the storage cistern. Make sure that these are the right size for the particular pipe-line (a 22mm gate valve for a 22mm distribution pipe) and that, when not in use, they are left *fully* open. A pipe is only as wide as its narrowest point! Alternatively each individual draw-off point can be isolated for servicing by fitting a small isolating stop-cock in its supply pipe just before connection to the tap or ball-valve concerned.

Stop-cocks and gate valves

The purpose of both stop-cocks and gate valves is to control the flow of water through water supply pipes. A screw-down stop-cock resembles in every way a conventional bib-tap set in a run of pipe. Turning the crutch or wheel head raises or lowers a washered valve or jumper onto a valve seating (*Figure 1.7*).

By far the commonest defect to which screw-down stop-cocks are prone is that of jamming in position after long periods of disuse. A sudden emergency such as a burst pipe or leaking cold water storage cistern sends the householder hurrying to the main stop-cock, only to find that it is immovable. A jammed stop-cock can usually be freed after applying penetrating oil and attempting to turn it, perhaps over a period of several days. It is however far better to stop it from jamming. This can be done by opening and shutting it several times, about twice a year. Finally, open the stop-cock fully and then give a quarter-turn towards closure. This will not affect the water flow but will prevent jamming. Make sure that all the family know where the main stop-cock is and that turning it off should be the first course of action in practically any plumbing emergency.

Stop-cocks, like taps, may occasionally need rewashering. To do this the water supply to the stop-cock must first be cut off. With the main stop-cock this will mean seeking the assistance of the Water Authority. The headgear of the stop-cock

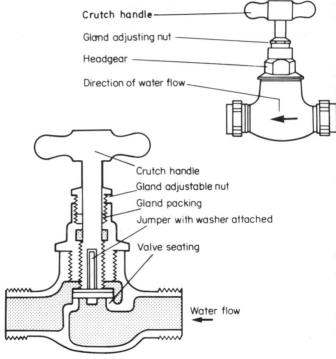

Crutch handle

Gland adjusting nut

Headgear

Direction of water flow

Crutch handle
Gland adjustable nut
Gland packing
Jumper with washer attached

Valve seating

Water flow

Fig. 1.7. Screw-down stop-cock

is then unscrewed and removed (*Figure 1.8*), the small nut holding the washer in place on the valve removed and a new washer—of the right size—fitted.

Failure of the gland packing is a rather more common defect. It will make itself known by water dripping from the

318

stop-cock spindle. This demands immediate attention. A constant drip onto a wooden floor—particularly in the badly ventilated situations in which stop-cocks are often situated—can be the prelude to dry rot.

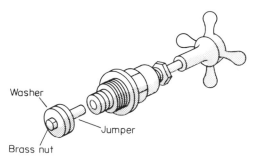

Washer

Jumper

Brass nut

Fig. 1.8. Stop-cock headgear with jumper and washer

It may be possible to stop the drip by giving the gland adjusting nut—the first nut through which the spindle of the stop-cock passes half a turn or so in a clockwise direction. Eventually however all the adjustment will be taken up and it will be necessary to renew the gland packing. Turn the stop-cock off—there is no need to cut off the water supply to it. Unscrew and remove the grub screw holding the crutch or wheel head in place and remove the head. Unscrew and remove the gland adjusting nut. Pick out the old gland packing with the point of a penknife blade and repack using household wool steeped in petroleum jelly. Caulk down hard. Re-assemble the stop-cock and open it.

When fitting a new screw-down stop-cock make sure that it is fitted so that the arrow engraved on the stop-cock's body points in the direction of the flow of water. If it is fitted the wrong way round water pressure will force the valve down onto its seating and it will remain permanently closed.

Gate-valves closely resemble stop-cocks in external appearance but, when screwed down, a metal plate or 'gate'

Hand wheel

Gland —

Head nut

Gate

A

B

Fig. 1.9. Gate valve

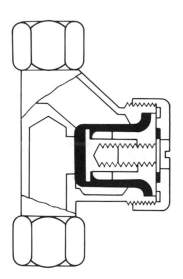

Fig. 1.10. Mini-stop-cocks for isolating taps or ball valves; upper, the Markfram; lower, the Ballofix

Connects to water supply pipe

Connects to tail of tap or ball valve

closes the waterway (*Figure 1.9*). Screw-down stop-cocks are normally used in pipe-lines subject to mains pressure and gate valves in situations, such as in the distribution pipes from a cold water storage cistern, where the water pressure is low.

Isolating stop-cocks are small, unobtrusive control valves that can be fitted into a pipe-line at any point to isolate a particular tap or ball valve when required (*Figure 1.10*). They therefore permit tap washering or renewal with the absolute minimum of disruption to the remainder of the domestic water services. They are opened or closed by means of a screwdriver.

Drain cocks

A drain cock should be fitted at the lowest possible point on any pipe that cannot be drained from a tap—immediately above the main stop-cock, at the base of the cold water supply pipe to an indirect cylinder or to a direct cylinder heated by an immersion heater only, on the return pipe, beside the boiler, of a hot water or central heating system.

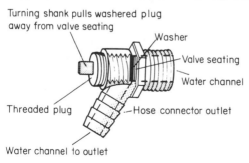

Fig. 1.11. A drain cock

The drain cock is opened by turning, with a spanner, the square shank protruding from the body of the fitting (*Figure 1.11*). This unscrews a washered plug from a valve seating and allows the pipe to be drained. Drain cocks have a hose connector outlet to permit drainage to an external gully. Drain cock outlets may become blocked with grit and the products of corrosion. They should therefore be opened, with a bucket placed underneath them, from time to time, to make sure that they are still working properly. If, when a drain cock is opened, water fails to flow, probing with a piece of wire will usually clear the obstruction.

2 The Cold Water Storage Cistern

The cold water storage cistern can be regarded as the 'heart' of the domestic hot and cold water services. Usually situated out of sight it should never be out of mind. It deserves regular inspection and maintenance.

Failure to fill properly can result, at the worst, in failure of all the domestic plumbing appliances. At the best it can result in intermittent supplies of water and recurring airlocks. A leak or overflow at a time when the family is away from home can result in hundreds of pounds worth of damage to carpets and furnishings.

Householders not infrequently query the necessity for the very existence of this potentially dangerous piece of equipment. They point out that it is technically possible to supply all cold water draw-off points direct from the rising main and that there are nowadays water heaters capable of providing a whole-house hot water supply that are designed for mains connection. Nevertheless the provision of a substantial cold water storage cistern offers real advantages both to the Water Authority and to the householder.

Demand for water is not constant throughout the day. There is a peak period of demand between 7.00 a.m. and 9.00 a.m. that few Water Authorities would be capable of meeting if all connections were made to the main. The cold water storage cistern provides a 'shock absorber' against peak period demand. At 7.00 a.m. all domestic storage cisterns are full. As the demand for water increases water pressure falls in the mains. Stored water is drawn off from storage cisterns which refill slowly during the peak period and more quickly as it passes.

From the householder's point of view a major advantage is that it makes possible (by providing a supply of water under constant, relatively low, pressure) the installation of that most versatile means of domestic hot water supply, the cylinder storage system. The fact that water in the distribution pipes is at low pressure from a storage cistern reduces the possibility of leaks and, if they occur, makes them less devastating. A low pressure supply to w.c. flushing cisterns helps to reduce the noise of refilling. Above all though, the provision of a substantial water storage cistern means that temporary failure of the mains water supply does not immediately paralyse the domestic plumbing system. All householders receive, from time to time, a brief official notification from the Water Authority that, in order to carry out repairs or alterations to the main, water supply will be cut off for a few hours.

For a household without a storage cistern such a notice means the immediate filling of every available bucket and water container for lavatory flushing, food preparation and cooking. The householder with a storage cistern of reasonable capacity can view a notification of this kind with equanimity. He knows that, provided that water supply is resumed within a few hours, only the cold tap over the kitchen sink will fail.

Where should the cold water storage cistern be situated? The traditional site is in the roof space though in recent years it has been suggested that, as a frost precaution, it is better situated at a lower level, perhaps in an upper part of a hall or bathroom airing cupboard. On balance the storage cistern is probably better retained in its traditional position and other measures taken to protect it from frost.

In an airing cupboard a storage cistern can create annoyance from noise (no ball valve is *entirely* silent in operation) and trouble can result from condensation of moisture from the warm damp air of the airing cupboard on its cold surface. Then too, a reduction in height inevitably means a reduction in water pressure. Flushing cisterns will refill more slowly, pressure at hot and cold bathroom taps will be reduced and

324

the provision of a conventional shower on the same floor as the storage cistern will become impossible.

Within the roof space the cistern should be sited well away from the eaves, preferably near a partition wall that will help to support the weight of the cistern and the water it contains and, if possible, immediately above the hot water storage cylinder. However well the latter may be lagged *some* warmth will seep upwards to help to protect the cistern from frost. If it is intended to install a shower on the floor below it is wise to raise the level of the storage cistern. This can be done by constructing a substantial wooden platform for it, so as to raise it three feet or so above the roof timbers.

In the past it was usual to install cisterns of relatively low capacity—25 gal where a hot water system only was to be supplied and 40 gal where the cistern was also intended to serve bathroom cold taps and the w.c. flushing cistern.

Domestic demands for water have increased in recent years as a result of the popularity of washing machines, dish washers and (perhaps) more frequent bathing. Nowadays domestic cold water storage cisterns are standardised at a capacity of 227 litres (50 gal) though smaller sizes are available. It should be noted that this refers to *actual* capacity; that is, to capacity when filled to normal water level, about 4½in from the cistern's rim. The accompanying table gives a guide to the capacity of existing galvanised steel cold water storage cisterns. The figures, which are given in imperial measurements only, since

Nominal capacity (to rim) (gal)	Actual capacity (gal)	Length (in)	Width (in)	Depth (in)
25	15	24	17	17
40	25	27	20	20
60	42	30	23	24
70	50	36	24	23

an existing cistern will certainly have been installed before metrication, illustrate the very considerable difference between 'nominal' and 'actual' capacity.

When faced with the need to replace an existing storage cistern with one of a more appropriate capacity, the dimensions of the trap door giving access to the roof space may appear to present an insoluble problem. A full sized cistern will not pass through many existing trap doors and to enlarge the access makes a substantial increase to the size (and cost) of the replacement job.

Round polythene cisterns can often be flexed through relatively small openings but, if all else fails, storage capacity can be increased by linking two smaller cisterns together by means of a 28mm (1in) pipe 2in above the bases of the cisterns. Where this is done it is important to ensure that the distribution pipes are taken from one cistern and that the ball-valve inlet is connected to the other. This will ensure a steady flow of water through both cisterns and avoid any risk of stagnation.

The traditional cold water storage cistern is constructed of galvanised steel. Cisterns of this material are tough, generally long lasting and offer good support to the water supply pipe. They are however heavy, not too easy to clean thoroughly and —above all— are subject to corrosion.

Members of the older generation of plumbers frequently express surprise and disgust at the fact that in a modern home, a galvanised steel cistern may show serious evidence of corrosion within four or five years of installation whereas they have known similar cisterns, installed in pre-war houses, to remain untouched by rust for half a century. This is not entirely due, as they probably imagine, to the inferiority of modern manufacturing methods. It is explained by the almost universal post-war substitution of copper for lead or iron supply and distributing pipes.

If connected rods of zinc and copper are immersed in a weak ácid (an electrolyte) a simple electric cell is produced. Electric current passes from one rod to the other. Bubbles of hydrogen gas form in the electrolyte and the zinc dissolves away. Similar conditions are produced when copper tubing is connected to a galvanised steel storage cistern. The water in the cistern will, if slightly acid, act as the electrolyte. The zinc coating of the galvanised steel will dissolve away and permit water to attack the steel underneath. This process is called electrolytic corrosion.

One way of preventing this process is to ensure, by protective internal painting, that water does not come into direct contact with the galvanised steel. When installing a new cistern cut the holes for the pipe connections and apply the treatment before making the actual connections. Roughen the entire internal surface of the cistern with abrasive paper to form a key and then apply two coats of a *tasteless and odourless* bitumastic paint. Several manufacturers produce a paint suitable for this purpose. Make sure that the entire internal surface is coated, paying particular attention to the areas in the immediate vicinity of the holes cut for the pipe connections. Install the cistern when the paint has dried thoroughly.

This method of protection can also be used to prolong indefinitely the life of a cistern that is already showing serious signs of corrosion. Drain and dry the cistern thoroughly and preferably disconnect the supply and distributing pipes. Remove every trace of existing rust with abrasive paper or by wire brushing—use goggles to protect the eyes when using a wire brush. This process may well leave deep pit marks in the metal, possibly even holes penetrating right through it. Such holes and pitmarks may be filled with one of the many epoxy resin fillers now on the market used in accordance with the manufacturer's instructions.

When the filler has set apply two coats of bitumastic paint as suggested for a new cistern. It is not generally necessary to roughen the internal surface of an old cistern to form a key. This treatment will prolong the useful life of the cistern for several years and can be repeated when it becomes necessary.

Galvanised steel cisterns which are not already showing signs of corrosion can also be protected by means of a sacrificial anode. This method makes use of the same principle that is responsible for electrolytic corrosion. All metals have a fixed electric potential and, when electrolytic action takes place, it is the metal with the higher potential that dissolves away. Anodic protection takes advantage of the fact that magnesium has a considerably higher potential than either zinc or copper.

A sacrificial anode is a lump of magnesium suspended in the water of the cistern and maintained (usually by means of a piece of copper wire clamped to the cistern rim) in electrical contact with the metal of the cistern (*Figure 2.1*). The magnesium dissolves away (is sacrificed) and the zinc coating of the galvanised steel is protected. Anodic protection has been

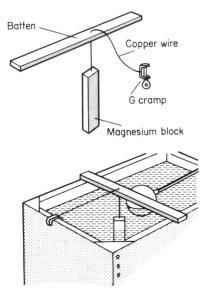

Fig. 2.1. Preventing corrosion by means of a sacrificial anode

found to be most effective in hard water areas. Unlike internal painting it can be adapted to protect galvanised steel hot water storage tanks as well as cold water storage cisterns. Although, as we have seen, galvanised steel cisterns can be protected from corrosion, cisterns made of non-corrodible materials have obvious advantages.

328

THE COLD WATER STORAGE CISTERN

Non-metallic cisterns

Asbestos cement cisterns come into this category but they are not without their drawbacks. They are heavy—a cistern with a capacity of 50 gal weighs 104 lb. They are liable to accidental damage and to damage from frost. They must be handled with care. Holes should not be cut nearer than 4in to the base of the cistern and, since the material of which they are made is ½in thick, hole cutting can present difficulties.

Cisterns made of modern plastic materials have the advantages of asbestos cement cisterns without their disadvantages. They are, of course, quite non-corrodible and have smooth and easily cleaned internal surfaces. They are light in weight so that one-man installation is a practical possibility. Since the plastic of which they are made is a poor conductor of heat they offer a measure of built-in frost protection.

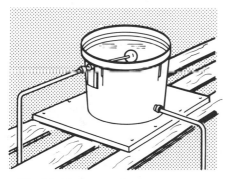

Fig. 2.2. Marley round polythene cistern

Round, flexible polythene cisterns (*Figure 2.2*) have already been mentioned. There are as well a number of rectangular plastic cisterns (*Figure 2.3*) on the market, some reinforced with fibreglass for extra strength. The author's home has a plastic/fibreglass storage cistern that was installed more than fifteen years ago and is, quite literally, 'as new'.

Plastic cisterns are easily installed but there are a number of important points that must be borne in mind. Plastic cisterns must rest on a flat, level base—never just on the roof timbers. A piece of chipboard or two or three pieces of floor board spiked to the roof timbers are quite satisfactory. Cut the holes for the tappings with a saw hole cutter fitted into a

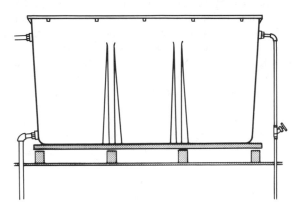

Fig. 2.3. An Osmaflow plastic cistern

drill or brace. Cut from inside with a block of wood placed under the cistern wall for support.

Make sure that all pipe connections are taken squarely to the cistern walls so as to avoid stressing the plastic. For each connection use two large washers—one metal and one plastic—on each side of the cistern wall. The plastic washer should be in direct contact with the cistern wall, followed by the metal washer and back nut. *Never* use boss white or other water-proofing material in direct contact with the walls of a plastic cistern. It is quite unnecessary and could damage the plastic.

Remember that a plastic cistern does not offer the same support to the rising main as does a galvanised steel or asbestos cement cistern. When fitting a ball-valve to a round polythene cistern always use the metal supporting plate supplied with the cistern. Secure the rising main firmly to the roof timbers. Failure to observe these final points can lead to intolerable noise and vibration as the cistern fills with water.

THE COLD WATER STORAGE CISTERN

Whatever the material the cistern is made from, it should be fitted with a dust and vermin-proof but not airtight cover. This is both a frost precaution and a safeguard against contamination. The water from the cistern will not be used for drinking but it will be used for teeth cleaning!

The walls, but not the base, of the cistern should be lagged with fibreglass tank lagging material or—in the case of rectangular cisterns—with purpose made expanded polystyrene or strawboard lagging units (*Figure 2.4*). This precaution is less essential with plastic cisterns than with those of other materials.

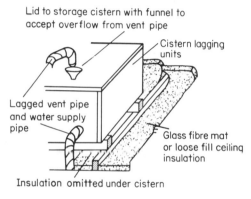

Fig. 2.4. Roof space frost protection

The base of the cistern should not be lagged and if, to conserve warmth in the rooms below, a fibreglass blanket or loose fill lagging material, has been laid between the joists, this should be omitted from the area immediately beneath the cistern. There is, in fact, something to be said for extending the lagging material downwards from the base of the cistern to the ceiling below, to provide a channel via which slightly warmer air can be funnelled up towards the base of the cistern.

One other vital frost precaution relates to the one connection to the cold water storage cistern that has not so far been mentioned—the overflow or warning pipe. This pipe, which should be at least 22mm (¾in) in diameter, connects to the cistern below the level of the ball-valve inlet and about 1in above normal water level. Its purpose is *not* to give indefinite protection against overflow in the event of a ball-valve failure but to give warning that this has occurred. It should therefore discharge in plain view in the open air. A steady drip—much less a full-bore flow—from this pipe should never be ignored.

The warning pipe obviously provides a route by which icy draughts can penetrate to the vulnerable plumbing fittings of the roof space unless proper precautions are taken. The traditional method of protection is to provide a hinged copper flap at the external end of the overflow pipe (*Figure 2.5*).

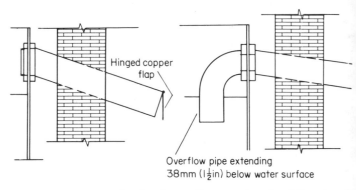

Fig. 2.5. Frost protection for the overflow warning pipe; left, external protection; right, internal protection

Wind blowing against the end of the pipe will close the flap and will be prevented from entering the pipe. Unfortunately, through disuse, these flaps often jam open and fail to function when required.

A better and more modern method of protection is to continue the warning pipe *inside* the cistern and to bend it over so that its open end is a couple of inches or so below the water surface. A trap is thus formed which prevents cold air from blowing up the pipe. Plastic screw-on extension pieces are available to enable this form of protection to be given to existing warning pipes.

332

THE COLD WATER STORAGE CISTERN

Ball-valves (or float-valves)

Strictly speaking the word 'cistern' should be used to describe water storage vessels open to atmospheric pressure—the main cold water storage cistern, w.c. flushing cisterns and the small feed and expansion cistern that supplies the primary circuit of an indirect hot water system (see Chapter 3). 'Tanks' are enclosed vessels and the use of this word, in domestic plumbing, is restricted by the purists to galvanised steel hot water tanks sometimes used for hot water supply.

As however these tanks are increasingly being replaced by copper hot water storage cylinders and can therefore be regarded as obsolescent, there is a growing tendency to refer to the main cold water storage *tank* and, particularly, to the feed and expansion *tank*. However much this may irritate traditional plumbers—and writers of plumbing text books!—this change of use is part of the evolution of the English language and to ignore it is to cause confusion.

Cisterns and open tanks are supplied with water by means of ball-valves or float-valves. Like many other plumbing fittings these valves have experienced revolutionary changes of design over the past half century. Depending upon the age of the installation the householder, or plumber, may find any one of five ball-valves of quite distinct design in current use—and there are a number of sub-species.

All ball-valves operate by means of a float (not necessarily a 'ball') fixed to the end of a rigid float arm of brass or plastic. As water is drawn off from the cistern the water level falls and the float falls with it. This movement is transmitted via the float arm to the valve itself which opens to allow water to flow into the cistern. When the water in the cistern—and the float—reach a predetermined level, the float arm closes the valve and flow of water ceases.

The oldest, simplest—and least satisfactory—kind of ball-valve likely to be encountered today is that of the *Croydon pattern*. As can be seen from *Figure 2.6* this valve has a vertical outlet, closed by a washered plug connected to the float arm. As water level in the cistern falls the plug is pulled away from the valve seating and, noisily and with a great deal of splashing, water flows into the cistern via two channels constructed on either side of the valve body. The inherent, and incurable, noisiness of this kind of valve is its main disadvantage. It is

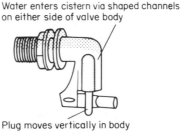

Water enters cistern via shaped channels on either side of valve body

Plug moves vertically in body

Fig. 2.6. The Croydon ball valve

quite suitable, and is often used, for cattle watering troughs and for static water storage cisterns on municipal allotments. Few people nowadays would wish to have one in the home.

The ball valve in commonest domestic use—certainly in installations dating from before the 1960s—is that of the *Portsmouth pattern*. These valves are quieter than Croydon

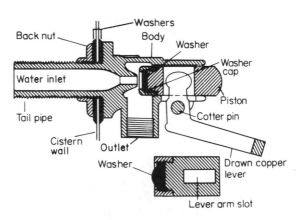

Fig. 2.7. The Portsmouth pattern ball valve

valves if for no other reason than that water flows from the valve outlet in a single stream. As can be seen in *Figure 2.7* the washered plug of the Portsmouth valve moves horizontally in the valve body. A slot in this plug accommodates the angled end of the float arm and the plug therefore moves to and fro as water level rises or falls.

It used to be the practice to enhance the silent action of this valve by screwing a 'silencer tube' of metal or plastic into the valve outlet so that incoming water was discharged into the cistern below the level of water already there. Water Authorities now forbid the use of these silencer tubes because of the risk of back siphonage in the event of a failure of mains pressure, which could result in mains water being contaminated by water from a storage cistern. This prohibition will undoubtedly hasten the changeover from the Portsmouth valve to those of more inherently silent action.

Common faults to which both Croydon and Portsmouth valves are prone are as follows.

Plug sticking in valve body resulting in failure to open or close properly—This is common in hard water areas and is due to the formation of hard water scale on the plug and the interior surfaces of the valve body.

To remedy first cut off the water supply to the valve. Pull out the split pin on which the float arm pivots and remove the float arm. The plug of a Croydon valve will now fall out into the hand.

Some Portsmouth valves have a screw-on cap at the end of the valve body. This cap must be unscrewed and removed. Then insert the blade of a screw driver into the slot under the valve body from which the end of the float arm has been removed. Push the plug out of the open end of the valve body.

Clean the plug and the interior of the valve body with fine abrasive paper. Smear the plug lightly with petroleum jelly and reassemble.

Valve fails to close properly because of washer failure— This is indicated by a steady drip of water from the overflow or warning pipe of the cistern. To renew the valve washer dismantle the valve and remove the plug as indicated above.

335

THE COLD WATER STORAGE CISTERN

The plug is in two parts—a body and a retaining cap. The body should be held securely in a vice and the retaining cap unscrewed with a pair of pliers. The old washer can then be replaced with a new one. The retaining cap of a long-installed valve can be extremely difficult to remove. Rather than risk damaging the plug it is better to pick the old washer out from under the rim of the retaining cap and to force the new washer under this rim. If you take this course of action you should make sure that the washer lies flat in its seating before reassembling.

Continued dripping from the overflow pipe after the ball valve washer has been renewed suggests that the valve seating is scored by grit from the main. Although it is possible, with a special tool, to reseat the ball valve it is usually as cheap (and easier) to renew the valve.

Slow filling or leaking past the valve despite the fact that washer and seating are sound—Either of these faults suggests that a valve of the wrong pressure classification has been installed. Ball valves are classified as 'high pressure', 'medium pressure', 'low pressure' or 'fullway' according to the diameter of the nozzle orifice. They are usually stamped HP, LP etc. on the valve body to indicate the pressure for which they are intended.

Except where mains pressure is unusually low, ball valves serving cisterns supplied direct from the main should be high pressure. Those serving flushing cisterns supplied from a main storage cistern should be low pressure. Where a flushing cistern is supplied from a low level storage cistern—perhaps in the upper part of an airing cupboard only a few feet above the level of the w.c. suite—a fullway valve will ensure rapid recovery.

Noisy filling—Noise may arise both from the sound of inflowing water and from water hammer and vibration in the plumbing system. Water hammer and vibration arise from ripple formation on the surface of the water as water flows into an almost full cistern.

These ripples may make the valve bounce on its seating to produce water hammer. They may also shake the float arm up and down and to and fro. This movement is transmitted to the cold water supply pipe which, particularly if it is of copper, will act as a sounding board to amplify the vibration out of all recognition. It used to be the practice to use the silencer tube already mentioned to reduce ripple formation and the consequent noise. This has now been prohibited but there are still measures that can be taken to improve the situation.

Purpose made stabilisers are available in the form of a plastic disc and a short plastic arm that clips onto the float arm so that the disc is suspended in the cistern a few inches below the level of the float. This will do something to ensure that the float does not bounce on every ripple. Make sure that the rising main is securely fixed to the roof timbers and is not supported solely by the wall of the cistern. This is particularly important where the cistern is of plastic material.

Yet another course of action is to cut out the final metre (3ft) or so of the rising main and replace it with polythene tubing. This will not amplify the sound as copper tubing does. Or, of course, one can fit a ball-valve of a different pattern.

Equilibrium ball valves are particularly useful in areas where mains water pressure is subject to fluctuation because they operate quite independently of the pressure of water behind them. They are also very helpful in eliminating water hammer. A great deal of the 'bounce' that causes water hammer is due to the conflicting forces of water pressure within the main and the buoyancy of the ball valve float.

Equilibrium valves can be made in either the Croydon or the Portsmouth pattern and a Portsmouth pattern equilibrium valve is shown in *Figure 2.8*. The essential feature is that the plug of the valve has a channel passing through it to a water-tight chamber at the rear of the valve. The plug therefore has to have a second washer at the rear to ensure the watertightness of this chamber. The effect of this design is that water pressure is equal on each side of the plug. Mains pressure is not continually trying to force the valve open and the plug moves *solely* in response to the rise and fall of the float. This enables the valve to have a wide nozzle orifice which ensures rapid replenishment of the cistern even when pressure is low.

Some years ago, at the Government's Building Research Station at Garston, a new and revolutionary ball valve was

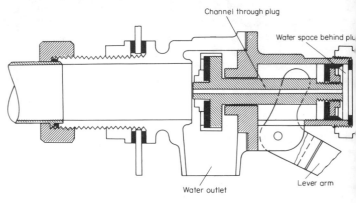

Fig. 2.8. Portsmouth pattern equilibrium valve

developed with the intention of reducing the noise and other drawbacks to which traditional valves are subject. These are sold under various trade names and are referred to generally as *Garston, B.R.S.* or *diaphragm ball valves.*

The moving plug was completely eliminated and the silent and score-resistant nylon nozzle is closed by means of a large diameter rubber diaphragm. The end of the float arm presses a small metal or plastic plunger against this diaphragm to close the valve. There are few moving parts and these are protected from the scaling effect of contact with water by the rubber diaphragm. Another useful feature of this kind of valve is that it can be dismantled by hand, by turning the large knurled retaining nut.

B.R.S. valves are manufactured in brass or plastic. They all incorporate some means of adjusting the water level in the cistern without recourse to bending the float arm. Early models were fitted with a silencer tube (*Figure 2.9*). Since these have been prohibited manufacturers have produced models with an overhead outlet and a device by means of which water enters the cistern in a relatively silent spray (*Figure 2.10*). Another feature of recently manufactured B.R.S. valves is the demountable nozzle. This permits any valve to be dismantled and rapidly converted from high pressure to low pressure operation or vice versa as required.

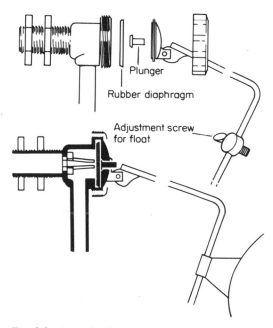

Fig. 2.9. An early Garston or diaphragm ball valve with silencer tube

The very latest design of ball valve is the diaphragm/equilibrium or diaphragm/servo valve, of which the first model on the market was the Torbeck made by Ideal Standard Ltd. This incorporates some of the features of the conventional equilibrium ball valve and some of the diaphragm or B.R.S. valve.

THE COLD WATER STORAGE CISTERN

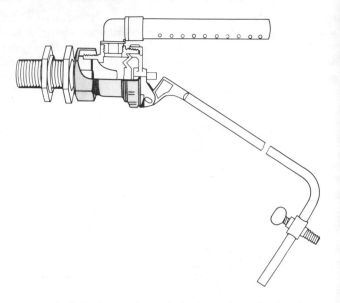

Fig. 2.10. Peglers diaphragm ball valve with overhead outlet

The Torbeck, like a conventional equilibrium ball valve, has a water chamber—the 'servo chamber'—behind the diaphragm closing the nozzle aperture (*Figure 2.11*). Water flows into this chamber via the metering pin opening but is prevented from passing through into the cistern, when this is full of water, by a sealing washer on the float arm which closes the pilot hole. When water level in the cistern falls, the descent of the float arm opens the pilot hole and water can flow out, reducing the pressure in the servo chamber. Pressure of water on the inlet side of the valve then opens the diaphragm and water can pass through the outlet.

The Torbeck has an overhead outlet. This is fitted with a collapsible plastic silencer tube, which reduces the noise of water delivery but—because it is collapsible—is immune to the risk of back siphonage. The design of the valve has permitted the use of a very small float and short float arm. It has a wide

340

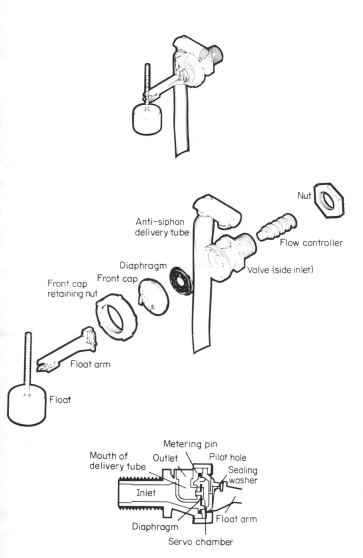

Fig. 2.11. The Torbeck equilibrium diaphragm valve

nozzle aperture, permitting rapid filling. A flow controller is provided for use where the valve is connected direct to a mains supply.

Failure of all types of diaphragm valve is most likely to occur as a result of debris from the main entering the space between the nozzle and the diaphragm and blocking it, either partially or completely. Diaphragm/equilibrium valves can also fail as a result of quite small grit particles from the main obstructing the metering pin hole or the pilot hole.

At the time of writing this type of valve could be regarded as being still in the experimental stage and it is probable that later models will overcome this vulnerability to obstruction.

3 Domestic Hot Water Supply

Plumbers and heating engineers are sometimes asked by anxious householders, 'What is the *best* means of hot water supply?'.

The only honest answer to this question is that there is no *best* means universally applicable to all situations. In deciding upon the best means of hot water supply for his client the installer should consider the design of the house and, perhaps, the way of life of its residents. The best system for a family where there are a number of children and the housewife is at home all day may well be quite uneconomical for an identical house where husband and wife are both at work and are likely to require hot water only for relatively brief periods in the morning and evening.

In some homes—not necessarily particularly large ones—the best solution to the problem of whole-house hot water supply may be to use one means for part of the house and another means for heating water for, for instance, a shower or a wash-basin in an external or otherwise remote w.c. compartment.

There is no doubt that some form of cylinder storage system provides the most popular and most versatile means of domestic hot water supply. Systems of this kind can be operated by electricity, solid fuel, gas or oil or by a combination of these. A cylinder storage hot water system can also be used in conjunction with a central heating system, using the same heat source.

Cylinder storage systems depend for their efficiency upon the fact that water expands in volume when heated while its weight remains unchanged. Thus a gallon (or a litre) of hot water weighs less than the same volume of cold water. Hot water therefore 'floats' on top of cold, or cooler, water. This principle is used to ensure continuous circulation between the boiler and hot water storage vessel. It also ensures that the hottest stored water remains in the upper part of the vessel, immediately available for use.

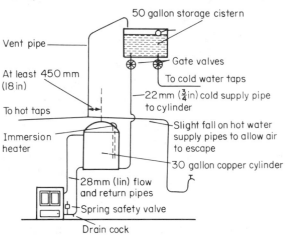

Fig. 3.1. A simple direct cylinder hot water supply system

A simple 'direct cylinder' hot water system is illustrated in *Figure 3.1.* Cold water flows from the cold water storage cistern to the cylinder through a 22mm (¾in) or 28mm (1in) supply pipe connected to the cylinder horizontally at a point near to its base.

Hot water distribution pipes to the various hot taps are taken from another 22mm (¾in) or 28mm (1in) pipe connected to a tapping at the apex of the cylinder dome. This pipe is continued upwards to terminate open ended over the cold water storage cistern and thus to serve as a vent pipe for the hot water system. It should be noted that the system then forms an open ended 'U' tube and that the level of water in the vent pipe will be the same as that in the storage cistern.

If the cylinder is to be heated solely by means of an electric immersion heater there will be no other plumbing connections to it. The boiler flow and return tappings in the side of the cylinder will be blanked off and a drain cock must be provided at the base of the cold water supply pipe to the cylinder to permit it to be drained if required.

If, on the other hand, a boiler is to be used to heat the water this should ideally be situated as close to the cylinder as possible but at a lower level. A 28mm (1in) flow pipe is taken from the upper connection of the boiler to the upper, or flow, connection of the cylinder. A similar return pipe is taken from the lower, or return, cylinder connection to the lower connection of the boiler. In a well-designed system the flow and return pipes will be quite short and will rise steeply all the way from the boiler to the cylinder tappings.

A drain cock should be provided at the lowest point of the return pipe adjacent to the boiler. It is also wise to provide a spring loaded safety valve on either the flow or return pipe as close to the boiler as possible.

It is usual to position this safety valve on the flow pipe but the return pipe is equally appropriate and this position does, in fact, offer a slight advantage. Scale formation, which *could* produce a build-up of pressure, is more likely to occur at the flow tapping than at the return tapping. Such a build-up of pressure would not affect a safety valve fitted to the flow pipe but it would be released from a valve fitted into the return pipe.

When the boiler is first lit water in it is heated. It expands and becomes lighter. Colder and heavier water from the return pipe flows into the boiler beneath it and pushes the heated water up the flow pipe into the upper part of the cylinder. This phenomenon is often described by saying that 'hot water rises' which is not quite true. To understand the principle of circulation it must be appreciated that hot water does not rise of its own volition. It is pushed upwards by colder and heavier water flowing into the boiler beneath it.

Circulation will continue for as long as the boiler fire is alight. Hot water stored in the cylinder will spread downwards until this vessel is full of hot water. As this is drawn off from the hot taps cold water will flow into the lower part of the cylinder from the cold water storage cistern. This will, in its turn, pass down the return pipe into the boiler to be heated.

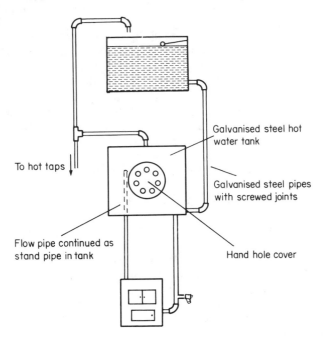

To hot taps

Galvanised steel hot water tank

Galvanised steel pipes with screwed joints

Flow pipe continued as stand pipe in tank

Hand hole cover

Fig. 3.2. Typical arrangement of a direct cylinder hot water system using galvanised steel pipes and tank

Many dwellings built before 1940 will be found to have a hot water system similar to that already described but with galvanised steel, instead of copper, circulating and distributing pipes and with a rectangular galvanised steel hot water storage *tank* instead of a copper cylinder (*Figure 3.2*). A rectangular tank of this kind may be easier to accommodate in an airing cupboard. It may also be easier to lag effectively to prevent heat loss. There are however serious disadvantages.

The rectangular shape means that it is more liable to distortion or damage from internal pressure. Where a hot water storage tank is installed the cold water storage cistern must usually be situated no higher than the floor immediately above. It is not possible—as it is with a cylinder—to have the hot water storage vessel on the ground floor of a two-storey house and the cold water cistern in the roof space. Then too, since hot water is more corrosive than cold, galvanised steel hot water tanks are even more subject to corrosion than galvanised steel cisterns. Nor can they, like cold water cisterns, be protected by internal painting.

Because of the risk of electrolytic action (see previous chapter) extensions to a galvanised steel hot water system should never be made with copper tubing. Where extensions are required it is best to use modern stainless steel tubing. This is scarcely more difficult to use than copper and does not present any risk of electrolytic action.

When fitting a replacement galvanised steel hot water tank an essential precaution against corrosion is to ensure that every trace of metal dust or shaving—resulting from cutting the holes for the pipe connections—is carefully removed. Any such metal fragments, however small, left in the base of the tank will unfailingly become a focus for corrosion and will lead to rapid tank failure.

Galvanised steel hot water tanks are provided with a circular hand-hole, sealed by a rubber gasket and a bolted-down hand-hole cover, to give access to the interior of the tank. Should it be necessary to remove this cover, never overlook the fact that, with all hot water storage systems of this kind, the hot water distribution pipes are taken from the top of the storage vessel. When water has been cut off to the cold water storage cistern and the hot taps opened and drained, *the hot water storage tank or cylinder is still full of water.* It cannot be drained from the hot taps. Before attempting to unbolt the hand-hole cover drain from the drain-cock beside the boiler—or at the base of the cold water supply pipe.

Installers are often faced with the problem of providing a piped hot water supply to a pre-war house that was previously without this amenity or, where such a house has been divided into two or more self-contained flats, providing a separate hot water system for each flat.

To meet this need cheap and space-saving 'packaged' hot water systems have been produced. These consist of a hot water storage cylinder and cold water storage cistern combined in one unit—sometimes called a two-in-one tank. These preserve the essential features of a cylinder storage hot water system but, of course, with much shortened cold water supply and vent pipes.

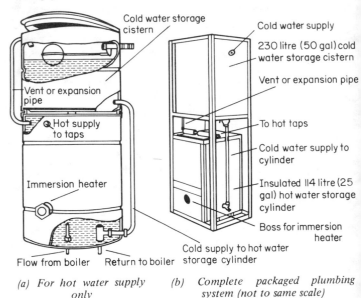

(a) *For hot water supply only*

(b) *Complete packaged plumbing system (not to same scale)*

Fig. 3.3. Packaged 'two-in-one' systems

One such unit has a 25 gal or 30 gal capacity hot water cylinder with a relatively small (15 gal or 20 gal) round copper cistern immediately above it (*Figure 3.3a*). A small cistern of this kind is capable of supplying only the hot water storage cylinder and is therefore of little value in areas where the Water Authority forbids the connection of w.c. flushing cisterns and bathroom cold taps direct to the main. Other units have a full-sized 50 gal capacity storage cistern (*Figure 3.3b*). These may be regarded as complete 'packaged plumbing systems'. They need only provision of a heat source and connection to supply and distributing pipes.

Such packaged plumbing systems must, of course, be situated so that the base of the cold tank is above the level of any draw-off point. It will, for instance, be impossible to install a conventional shower on the same floor as such a unit though, of course, one could be installed on the floor below.

Although direct cylinder storage hot water systems provide a reliable and trouble-free hot water supply in a great many homes, they are subject to damage and deterioration from two causes—rust and scale. Rusting may take place within the boiler. This will be indicated when discoloured, rusty water flows from the hot taps—particularly when a considerable volume of hot water has been drawn off.

Boiler scale can present an even more serious problem. Hard water will be discussed in some detail in a later chapter. Here it is sufficient to say that when hard water (which means most water supplies in southern and central Britain) is heated to a temperature of about 70°C (160°F) calcium carbonate—boiler scale or fur—is deposited. This can be seen on the interior surfaces of any kettle in regular use in such an area.

The first indication of scale formation in a domestic boiler is loss of efficiency. Scale insulates the water in the boiler from the heat source and the water takes longer to heat. Later, as scale deposits increase, hissing, bubbling and banging sounds will be heard as overheated water is forced through ever-diminishing channels. Scale does not *only* insulate the water in the boiler from the heat source. It also insulates the metal of the boiler from the cooling effect of the circulating water. Deprived of this protection the metal of the boiler will slowly burn away and, eventually, one of the most disastrous of plumbing emergencies—a leaking boiler—will result.

Another problem arises when a direct cylinder storage hot water system is used to heat a radiator or towel rail. Modern pressed steel radiators should *never* be connected to such a system as they will very rapidly corrode. It was considered permissible to connect a cast iron or copper radiator to a direct system and it is not unusual to use a system of this kind to heat a towel rail of non-corrodible material. This never works very satisfactorily in practice as the purpose of the storage cylinder is to conserve the heat in the stored water and the purpose of the radiator or towel rail is to dissipate it. When a large volume of hot water is drawn off for a bath—the time that the towel rail is most required—the towel rail will run cold.

Indirect cylinder storage hot water system

These difficulties can be overcome by the provision of an *indirect* cylinder storage hot water system (*Figure 3.4*). With a system of this kind the water heated in the boiler passes through the cylinder in a closed coil or heat exchanger thus heating the domestic hot water *indirectly*.

The flow and return pipes, together with the heat exchanger, are referred to as the primary circuit. It is supplied with water from a small 'feed and expansion' or header tank and it is a vital design feature that the domestic hot water and the water in the primary circuit are kept entirely separate. As its name indicates the purpose of the feed and expansion tank is to accommodate the expansion of the primary circuit when it is heated as well as to ensure that this circuit is supplied with water. For this reason the ball-valve feeding this tank should be adjusted to give only two or three inches of water in the tank when the system is first filled. When heated the water in the primary circuit will expand into the tank and rise above the level of the ball valve float.

Water from the primary circuit is never drawn off in normal use and only the very small losses arising from evaporation are made up from the feed and expansion tank. This accounts for

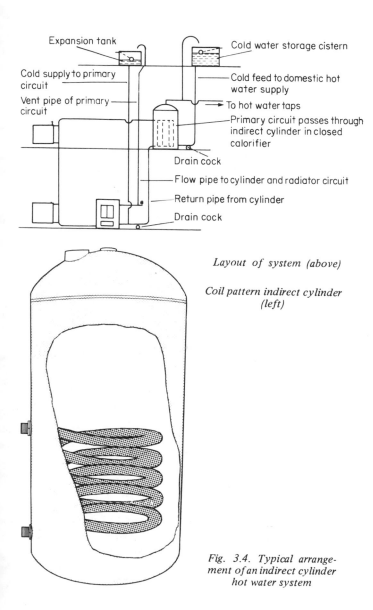

Expansion tank

Cold water storage cistern

Cold supply to primary circuit

Cold feed to domestic hot water supply

Vent pipe of primary circuit

To hot water taps

Primary circuit passes through indirect cylinder in closed calorifier

Drain cock

Flow pipe to cylinder and radiator circuit

Return pipe from cylinder

Drain cock

Layout of system (above)

Coil pattern indirect cylinder (left)

Fig. 3.4. Typical arrangement of an indirect cylinder hot water system

351

the relative freedom from corrosion and scale of indirect hot water systems. Dissolved air gives water its corrosive quality. This is driven off from the water in the primary circuit when it is first heated. Similarly, any given volume of water contains only a given quantity of scale-forming chemicals. These are precipitated on the internal surface of the boiler when it is first heated and, thereafter, no more scale will form. Any towel rail, radiator or central heating circuit should be connected to the primary circuit. The effect of drawing off a large volume of hot water will have far less effect upon it.

Although central heating is treated separately in Section 4, it must be mentioned here, however, that where central heating system is installed in conjunction with an indirect hot water system, freedom from corrosion is only *relative*. Some air will always be present in the primary circuit as a result of minute leaks too small to permit water to escape and as a result of air dissolving into the surface of the water in the feed and expansion tank.

Where pressed steel radiators are used with copper circulating pipes a form of electrolytic corrosion can take place. The metal of the radiators slowly corrodes away and hydrogen and black iron oxide sludge, or magnetite, are produced. These obstruct circulation and the corrosive qualities of the magnetite are a common cause of early circulating pump failure. This corrosion can be prevented by the introduction of a reliable chemical corrosion inhibitor into the feed and expansion tank.

The conventional indirect hot water system requires a separate feed and expansion tank. There are however on the market patent self-priming indirect cylinders, of which the primatic is the best known, which require no separate feed tank.

A purpose made heat exchanger or 'inner cylinder' permits water to spill over from the domestic hot water system into the primary circuit when the system is first filled (*Figure 3.5*). It is prevented from returning to mix with the domestic hot water by an air lock that is automatically produced.

Some scepticism has been expressed about the effectiveness of self-priming cylinders of this kind. Experience suggests that they provide effective separation of the primary and domestic water so long as the boiler is never permitted actually to boil (this should, in any case, always be avoided) and the particular

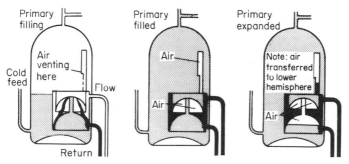

Fig. 3.5. How a primatic self-priming indirect cylinder works

model of self-priming cylinder is large enough to accommodate the expansion of the primary, and any radiator, circuit when heated.

Electric water heating

An electric immersion heater is frequently fitted into a hot water storage cylinder served by a boiler to provide a supply of hot water during the summer months. On the other hand one or more immersion heaters may be fitted into a storage cylinder to provide the sole means of hot water supply. Most manufacturers of electric appliances manufacture cylinders, complete with immersion heaters, designed to meet this need (*Figure 3.6a*). Usually installed under the draining board of the kitchen sink they are, for this reason, often called 'under draining board' or UDB heaters.

Typically, UDB heaters have very heavy built-in insulation and are provided with two horizontally aligned electric immersion heaters. The upper element is kept permanently switched on to meet the small, but frequent, demands of hot water for washing up, washing and shaving and so on. The lower element is intended to be switched on an hour or so before greater volumes of hot water are required for baths or laundry purposes. Most UDB heaters need a separate cold

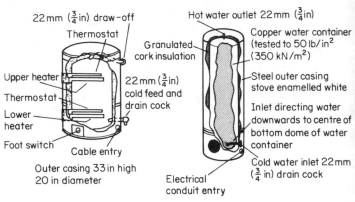

The 'under draining board' (UDB)   Off-peak electric water heater
water heater

Fig. 3.6. Two methods of providing hot water by electric heating

water storage cistern in the same way as an ordinary cylinder storage system does. There are however 'cistern heaters' which incorporate their own small, cold water supply cistern in the upper part of the unit.

A variant of the UDB water heater is the off-peak electric water heater designed to take advantage of the cheaper off-peak electricity (*Figure 3.6b*). These are usually tall and slim to encourage the stratification of the heated water. A spreading device at the cold water inlet ensures that incoming cold water spreads evenly over the base of the cylinder and does not mix with water already heated. Off-peak heaters usually have a large capacity—50 gal instead of the 25 gal usual with a UDB heater. Fifty gallons is said to meet the daily demand for hot water of an average family. The heater is switched on overnight, to take advantage of the off-peak rates. During the day the electric element is switched off and the stored hot water is used by the family.

DOMESTIC HOT WATER SUPPLY

Heat loss

Electricity is a very efficient, but very expensive, heat source. When it is used either as the sole or as a supplementary means of heating stored water there are important design considerations that must be observed if the system is to operate economically. A basic requirement is that the storage cylinder should be *effectively* lagged. Effective lagging is built into the construction of UDB and off-peak heaters but must be provided by the installer or householder for an ordinary copper cylinder.

It has been established that the insulating material used is less important than its thickness and that maximum economy is achieved with a thickness of 3in. An insulated copper cylinder 18in in diameter and 36in high, with a nominal capacity of 30 gal, will lose 86 units of electricity per week if the temperature of the water is maintained at 140°F and the air temperature is 60°F. Raise the water temperature to 160°F (the usual storage temperature in soft water areas) and the loss will be 115 units per week. The same cylinder, provided with a 2in thickness of glass fibre lagging, will lose 8.8 units per week. Increase the thickness of the lagging to 3in and the loss will be only 6 units.

The avoidance of long 'dead legs' is another important design consideration. 'Dead legs' are lengths of pipe from the storage cylinder to the draw-off points. After water has been drawn off the water left in the dead leg will rapidly cool and its heat will be wasted. A dead leg of 15mm (½in) copper tubing carrying water at 140°F to a sink or basin tap will waste about 0.19 units of electricity per foot run per week. A similar 22mm (¾in) copper tube will waste 0.38 units per foot run per week.

Modern architectural design usually eliminates long dead legs by situating the bathroom and kitchen in close proximity. Where hot water is required at any draw-off point more than about 20ft distant from the storage cylinder it is wise to consider the provision of a small, separate water heater to serve that point only. Above all, electrically heated water must never be permitted to circulate. Circulation of this kind can produce really crippling electricity bills.

Electrically heated water circulating through a 15mm (½in) copper tube at 140°F will waste 1.36 units of electricity *per foot run* per week. The wastage from 28mm (1in) copper tubing will be 2.33 units per foot run per week.

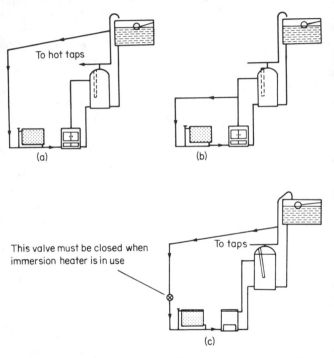

Fig. 3.7. Circulation of hot water through a towel rail or radiator circuit

There are a number of ways in which circulation may take place. The most obvious one is through a towel rail or radiator circuit. Where a towel rail is fitted into a direct hot water system the flow pipe is frequently taken from the vent pipe, above the hot water cylinder. It is dropped onto the towel

356

rail and the return pipe is taken, falling all the way, to the return pipe from the cylinder to the boiler (*Figure 3.7a*).

This arrangement ensures rapid circulation and the elimination of bubbles that could produce an air-lock. It may be permissible where the cylinder is heated only by a boiler but is quite unacceptable where an immersion heater is fitted. In such a case any towel rail circulation should, preferably, be taken from the flow pipe to the cylinder below the level of the electric heating element (*Figure 3.7b*). This will permit the circulation of water heated by the boiler but prevent the circulation of electrically heated water. Where this arrangement is impossible an alternative might be to fit a gate valve into the towel rail circuit and to make sure that this valve is kept tightly shut when the immersion heater is switched on (*Figure 3.7c*).

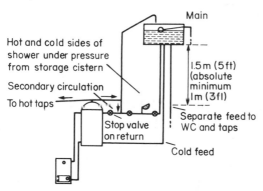

Fig. 3.8. Hot and cold water supplies for a shower installation

Sometimes where there is a long dead-leg serving a shower, for instance, a secondary circulation is arranged as shown in *Figure 3.8* to reduce the delay in the arrival of hot water at the draw-off point. When fitting an immersion heater into a cylinder with a secondary circulation the return should be cut out and eliminated or, alternatively, a gate valve provided to prevent circulation when the immersion heater is switched on.

Reversed circulation may, under certain circumstances, take place between a hot storage cylinder and a cold boiler. This may occur where the cylinder is at only a slightly higher level than the boiler and there is a long horizontal run of flow pipe. It can be prevented by taking the flow pipe to the cylinder at low level and then taking it up to the cylinder flow tapping close to the cylinder wall and within the cylinder lagging jacket (*Figure 3.9a*).

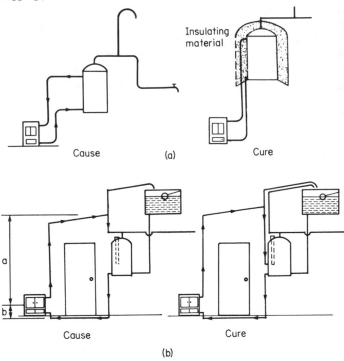

Fig. 3.9. Reverse circulation causes and cures

Sometimes, because of an intervening doorway, the flow pipe from a boiler is taken to connect at high level to the cylinder vent pipe. The return pipe is taken back to the boiler under the floor boards (*Figure 3.9b*). This arrangement will inevitably lead to reversed circulation if an immersion heater is installed.

The best remedy is to reposition either the boiler or the cylinder so that both are on the same side of the doorway. A 'second best' alternative is to provide the flow pipe with an additional vent and to connect it to the cylinder at a point below the level of the immersion heater. This will result in a loss of efficiency and delays in heating the cylinder from the boiler. It will however cut out circulation of electrically heated water.

Finally, there is a risk of 'single pipe circulation' within the vent pipe itself. If this pipe rises vertically from the apex of the cylinder dome currents of hot water may flow up its centre and, cooling, descend against its walls (*Figure 3.10*).

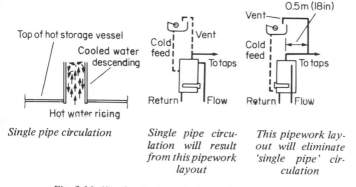

Single pipe circulation

Single pipe circulation will result from this pipework layout

This pipework layout will eliminate 'single pipe' circulation

Fig. 3.10. 'Single pipe' circulation and its prevention

Single pipe circulation can be prevented by bending the vent pipe over as it leaves the cylinder dome and taking it horizontally for a distance of at least 18in before permitting it to rise to the cold water storage cistern.

Instantaneous hot water

Other means of providing domestic hot water supply include 'instantaneous' water heaters and open-outlet water heaters.

The heat source for these appliances may be either electricity or gas. They are generally designed for direct connection to the rising main and thus make it possible (where this is permitted by the Water Authority) to eliminate both the cold water storage cistern and the hot water storage cylinder. Gas still has the advantage for the provision of instantaneous hot water. Small instantaneous heaters are available to supply hot water at a single point and large multipoint models can provide a 'whole house' hot water supply.

The invention and development of the 'balanced flue' has overcome a problem that formerly faced all installers of gas appliances—the safe disposal of the products of combustion. Balanced flue appliances can be installed in any room with an external wall. They involve none of the risks that were associated with the old fashioned gas 'geyser'. Balanced flue appliances are available for both space and water heating. The appliance has its combustion chamber sealed off from the room in which it is fitted. Air intake and flue outlet are situated adjacent to each other on an external wall (*Figure 3.11*). Because they are adjacent they are 'balanced'. Air

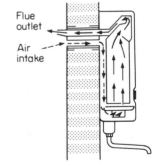

Fig. 3.11. Balanced flue gas water heater

pressure against the flue outlet will be equalled by air pressure against the inlet. The appliance should continue to work satisfactorily no matter how hard the wind may be blowing against the flue outlet.

DOMESTIC HOT WATER SUPPLY

Electric instantaneous water heaters are a relatively new development but the suspicion with which early models were received has now been largely dispelled. They have the advantage of quick and simple installation in virtually any situation where a water and a power supply are available (*Figure 3.12*).

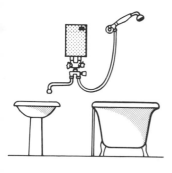

Fig. 3.12. Electric instantaneous heater supplying basin and shower

They are particularly useful in providing a hot water supply for wash basins in w.c. compartments remote from the main house hot water system and in making possible the provision of a shower in situations where this would otherwise be impossible.

The great advantage of instantaneous water heating is that only water actually *used* is heated. There is no stored water slowly losing its heat and requiring more fuel to restore it. A multipoint gas water heater can therefore be particularly useful to a working husband and wife who require hot water only for relatively short periods in the morning and evening.

A limitation of this kind of appliance that is not always appreciated is the fact that it does not, by its nature, raise a given volume of water *to* a required temperature. It raises the water that passes through it *through* a range of temperatures. During very cold weather, low temperature of water at the inlet will result either in a reduced flow of hot water or a supply of water at a lower temperature. Flow of hot water in gallons per minute is, in any case, generally less than from a storage hot water system.

Open outlet heaters are (usually) small storage heaters designed for direct connection to the rising main (*Figure 3.13*). They may be used over sinks and wash basins where there is no cylinder system or where the use of the storage cylinder would involve an unacceptably long distribution pipe or dead leg.

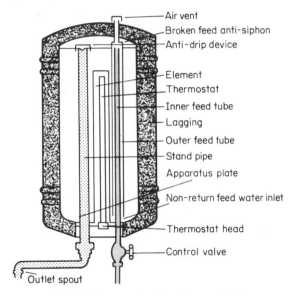

Air vent
Broken feed anti-siphon
Anti-drip device

Element
Thermostat
Inner feed tube
Lagging
Outer feed tube
Stand pipe
Apparatus plate
Non-return feed water inlet

Thermostat head
Control valve

Outlet spout

Fig. 3.13. Open outlet electric water heater

The essential feature of the open outlet heater is the position of the control valve. This must be on the inlet side— *not* on the outlet—of the appliance. When hot water is required the inlet control is opened. Cold water flows in to the base of the appliance, displacing stored hot water which overflows through an internal stand-pipe connected to the outlet spout. Modern variations of this kind of appliance may be installed under, instead of over, the sink or wash basin. These must still comply with the essential requirement of a controlled inlet and a free outlet.

DOMESTIC HOT WATER SUPPLY

Solar heating

Rapidly rising fuel costs in recent years have led heating engineers to give serious consideration to the use of a free source of energy—the sun—to supplement traditional means of water heating. Heat transmitted *by radiation* from the sun is unaffected by air temperature. Even on a cold winter's day the sun's rays can be used to transfer heat to water passing through a purpose-made and specially protected solar panel.

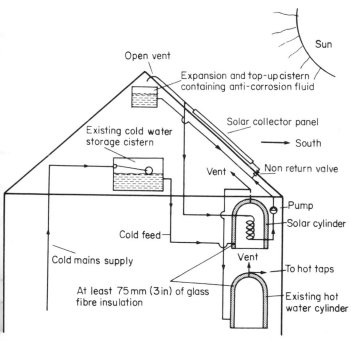

Fig. 3.14. One method of utilising solar heating

Various means of trapping and transmitting this free heat source have been attempted. The one illustrated in *Figure 3.14* is, in my opinion, among the more promising. It is, in effect, an indirect hot water system in which the solar collection panel, heated by the sun, provides a supplementary 'boiler'. A complication is added by the fact that, unlike a conventional boiler, the solar panel must of necessity be situated above the hot water storage cylinder.

This difficulty is overcome by providing two cylinders, one above the other. The upper cylinder is a conventional indirect one in which water from the storage cistern is pre-heated by means of a sealed heat exchanger connected to the solar panel. The lower cylinder may be either direct or indirect and can have, as its main source of heat, either a boiler or an electric immersion heater. Pre-warmed water flows from the top of the upper cylinder to the lower one, from which it is drawn off in the usual way to the hot taps. Water is pumped, in a closed circuit, through the solar panel situated on the southern aspect of the roof's slope. Water passes through the solar panel in small bore copper tubes on a black bed, designed to absorb the radiant heat of the sun.

The solar panel has a glass face, which must be hosed down from time to time for maximum efficiency. This affords protection from the cooling effect of the wind and also has a 'greenhouse' effect, permitting the short wavelength heat rays from the sun to enter but confining the longer wavelength rays reflected from the interior of the solar panel.

Solar heating is still in its infancy but it is not unreasonable to suppose that improved collection, distribution and storage systems will be developed in the years to come. It may well be that financial necessity will dictate that, at least during the summer months, solar energy will, in the future, provide the main heat source for domestic hot water supply.

4 Taps and Mixers

The tap is the basic piece of plumbing equipment. A plumber of the early 1900s, confronted with the taps of today, would find that the differences between these and the old brass taps to which he was accustomed, are more apparent than real.

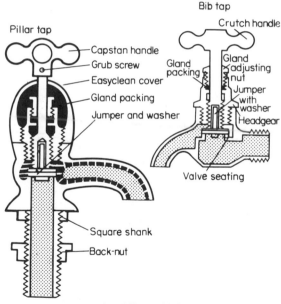

Fig. 4.1. Pillar and bib taps

Although there have been tremendous changes in appearance and design, most modern taps operate in exactly the same way as the bib-cocks that can still be seen protruding over the kitchen sinks of 1914 houses.

Taps are described as 'bibs' or 'pillars'. Bib taps have a horizontal inlet and pillar taps a vertical one (*Figure 4.1*). Pillars are now used for most purposes within the home while bibs are most likely to be found nowadays providing a garden or garage water supply. Water flows into the body of the tap via a threaded 'tail' connected to the distribution pipe. It passes through the valve seating and leaves by the spout. Into the tap body is screwed the 'headgear', a fibre body washer between the two parts of the tap ensuring a watertight joint. The spindle, with a crutch or capstan head, passes through the headgear. Turning the spindle opens or closes the tap by raising or lowering a washered valve or jumper onto the valve seating. When the tap is turned on water is prevented from

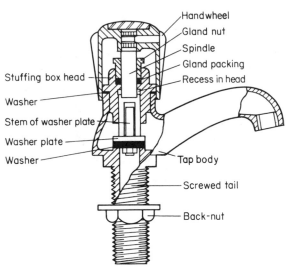

Fig. 4.2. Pillar tap with shrouded head. The section illustrated is the Nuastyle 2 BSS type pillar tap

escaping up the spindle by a gland or stuffing box, packed with greased wool, through which the spindle passes.

Most modern taps have an easy-clean cover that conceals the headgear and many have 'shrouded heads'. With such taps the headgear and the head or handle appear to comprise a single unit (*Figure 4.2*).

Bath and basin mixers are, in effect, two taps with a single spout. Adjusting the two heads produces a single stream of water at the required temperature. Many bath mixers incorporate an upper outlet to supply a flexible shower hose (*Figure 4.3*). A switch is provided to direct the mixed water

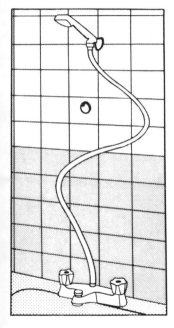

Fig. 4.3. Bath/shower mixer by Barking Brassware Co.

either upwards to the shower or downwards into the bath as required. Some modern basin mixers incorporate a 'pop up' waste. These units dispense with the usual waste plug and somewhat unsightly chain. Pressure on a knob in the centre of the mixer activates a rod and causes the waste plug to 'pop up' and allow the basin to drain (*Figure 4.4*).

Sink mixers are different in design from those used for basins and baths. This is because it is illegal to mix in one fitting water direct from the main (the cold water supply to the kitchen sink) and water from a storage cistern. Consequently sink mixers have separate channels for the hot and cold water passing through the tap body and spout. Hot and cold water mixes *in the air* after leaving the spout.

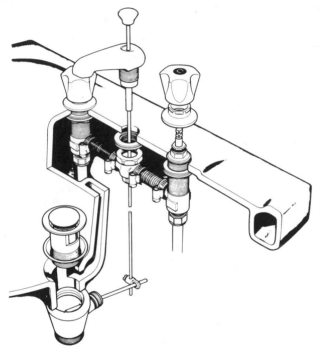

Fig. 4.4. The Bourner basin mixer with pop-up waste plug

Rewashering is the most common maintenance job required on taps. The need for rewashering is indicated when the tap becomes more and more difficult to turn off fully. Eventually, however hard the head is turned, there will still be a steady drip from the spout.

To rewasher any tap of the kind described above the water supply to it must first be cut off. With the cold tap over the sink this is done by turning off the householder's main stop-cock (see Chapter 1). It may be possible to turn off the supply to the hot taps and the bathroom cold taps by turning off any gate valve or stop-cock in the supply pipe. If there is no such control valve the best course of action is to tie up the float arm of the ball valve supplying the main cold water storage cistern and drain this cistern and the distribution pipes. This can be done from the bathroom taps.

Where both hot and cold bathroom taps are supplied from a storage cistern there is no need to drain the hot water from the hot water storage cylinder even if it is a hot tap that is to be rewashered. Turn on the bathroom cold taps and leave to drain. When no more water flows from them turn on the tap to be rewashered. Only the few pints of water in the distributing pipe will drain away. The storage cylinder will remain full of hot water.

Unscrew and raise the easy-clean cover. It should be possible to do this by hand. If it is necessary to use a wrench pad the jaws to avoid damaging the chromium plated surface (*Figure 4.5*). Insert the wrench under the easy-clean cover and turn the hexagonal nut at the base of the headgear. This will unscrew to permit the headgear to be lifted off the tap body. When the headgear is removed the valve, with its washer attached, of a kitchen sink cold tap will be found to be resting on the valve seating. A small retaining nut holds the washer onto the valve. This must be removed or (if this proves difficult) a new washer and jumper complete can be used as a replacement.

Valves of hot taps and bathroom cold taps may be found to be 'pegged' into the headgear of the tap. The valve will turn freely but cannot be removed without breaking the pegging. In such a situation every effort must be made to unscrew the washer retaining nut. A drop of penetrating oil will often loosen it sufficiently to enable it to be unscrewed with a spanner of the correct size. If this proves to be absolutely impossible the valve *can* be removed from the headgear by inserting a screw driver blade between the valve plate and the headgear to break the pegging. The stem of any replacement valve should be scored with a rasp to give a moderately tight fit.

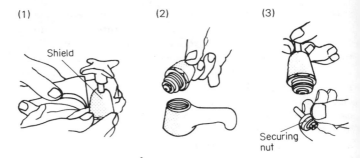

1. Turn off water supply and open tap or valve fully. Fit waste plug in sink. Wrap rag round shield and loosen it with adjustable spanner if there are flats – if not use a pipe wrench very gently. 2. Unscrew the shield fully and loosen hexagonal nut securing head using adjustable spanner. Unscrew the nut by hand and lift the head of the tap out of the body. 3. With some taps the jumper can be removed – on others it fits loosely. The washer is usually held against the jumper plate by a small nut. Some taps used a domed washer fixed to the jumper – in this case the jumper is replaced.

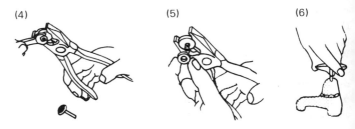

4. Grip the edge of the jumper plate with pliers and undo the nut with a small spanner. Turn the nut gently – it often gets fouled with fur and scale. If the nut cannot be removed the whole jumper will have to be replaced. Either the same type or a domed jumper (inset) can be used. 5. Remove the nut and the metal washer. The old washer is replaced by the new one, fitted with the side with the maker's name against the jumper plate. Replace the metal washer and nut and tighten securely. 6. Reassemble the head into the body as it was removed, screw down carefully by hand and tighten with the adjustable spanner. Screw down the shield – hand tight only – and turn on the water supply

Fig. 4.5. Fitting a new washer

Continued dripping after a washer has been renewed suggests that the valve seating has been scored and scratched by grit from the main. The tap can be reseated using a special tool or, alternatively, a nylon washer and valve seating kit can be used to fit a new nylon seating over the old brass one.

The way in which the head of a shrouded head tap is removed to give access to the interior for rewashering depends upon the make of the tap. Some models have a retaining screw concealed under the plastic 'Hot' or 'Cold' indicator. Prise off this plastic disc, undo the retaining screw and the head will lift off, revealing a headgear similar to that of the traditional tap. Other models have a small grub screw (resembling the grub screw retaining a crutch or capstan head) in the side of the shrouded head. The shrouded head of one of the taps in the Deltaflow range is removed by turning the tap fully on. Then the head is given a final turn and can be pulled off in the hand.

A number of taps have been produced with the object of eliminating the need to cut off the water supply before re-washering. Only one of these—the supatap—has stood the test of time. Supataps are turned on or off by turning the nozzle of the tap itself. Ears of kemetal plastic are provided to enable this to be done easily and comfortably.

Supataps are rewashered by first unscrewing and discon-necting the retaining nut at the top of the nozzle. Then open the tap and keep on turning the nozzle. At first water flow will increase but will then stop—just before the nozzle comes off in your hand—as a check valve within the tap falls into position (*Figure 4.6*). Tap the nozzle end on a hard surface—*not* the glazed surface of a ceramic sink or basin!—and turn it upside down. The anti-splash device, into which the valve and washer is fitted, will then fall out. Prise out the valve and fit a replace-ment. When re-assembling the tap remember that the nozzle screws in with a left hand thread. It must therefore be turned in the opposite direction from that dictated by instinct.

Leakage up the spindle of a tap when the tap is turned on indicates failure of the gland or stuffing box. It may be accom-panied by water hammer—since the tap can be 'spun' on and off much too easily—and often results from the connection of a garden or washing machine hose having been connected to a kitchen tap so as to produce back pressure.

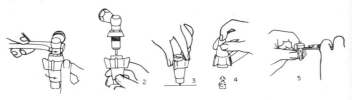

1. Hold the nozzle in one hand and loosen the gland nut with a spanner. 2. Hold the gland nut and unscrew the nozzle fully. See that the check valve drops into position. 3. Tap the nozzle on a firm surface to loosen the anti-splash. 4. Turn the nozzle upside down and push out the anti-splash. 5. The jumper may be stuck in the anti-splash, but can be gently levered out with a coin or blade

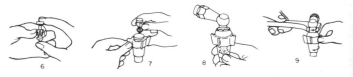

6. Put a new jumper into the anti-splash and make sure it clicks home. 7. Drop the anti-splash into the nozzle, washer uppermost. 8. Refit the nozzle to the tap and screw up by hand. 9. Holding the nozzle, tighten the gland nut and ensure that the tap works properly and does not drip

Fig. 4.6. Replacing the washer on a Supatap. It is not necessary to turn off the water supply to do this as a check valve does it automatically when the tap is dismantled

First try adjusting the gland nut. This is the first nut through which the spindle of the tap passes. It may be possible to reach it, without removing the tap head, by opening up the tap fully and raising the easy-clean cover as far is it will go. Half a turn, or a turn, in a clockwise direction may remedy the leakage (*Figure 4.7*).

Eventually all the adjustment will be taken up and the gland will need repacking. There is no need to cut off the water supply to the tap to do this. Unscrew the grub screw retaining the crutch or capstan head and tap the head upwards to remove it. Remove the easy-clean cover. Unscrew and remove the gland nut and pick out all existing gland packing material with the point of a penknife blade. Repack using household wool steeped in petroleum jelly. Caulk down firmly and reassemble the tap. In some modern taps an 'O' ring seal replaces the conventional gland. It is interesting to note that

If water leaks out between the spindle and the shield the gland nut may be loose. Release the shield and tighten the nut. 1. Open the tap fully. Do not shut off the water supply. Using a small screwdriver, remove the grub screw holding the cross head on the spindle. 2. Unscrew the shield. Using an adjustable spanner, lever under the shield to force the cross head up off the spindle.

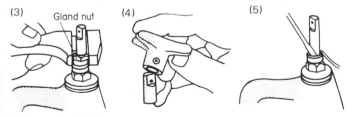

3. When the shield is removed the gland nut can be seen. Tighten the nut half a turn with the adjustable spanner. 4. Replace the cross head temporarily in order to check that the tap is easy to turn on and off. If it is too tight slacken the gland nut a little. When satisfied that the tap turns easily and does not leak reassemble the tap. 5. If the tap still leaks, shut off the water supply and remove the gland nut. Remove the packing and replace with household wool steeped in petroleum jelly. Caulk down firmly and reassemble the tap. Some modern taps have an 'O' ring seal

Fig. 4.7. Tightening a leaky gland nut

the modern shrouded head was not, in the first instance, introduced for the sake of its appearance, but in an attempt to prevent gland failure. It had been noted that housewives frequently turned taps on and off with hands dripping with household detergent. This detergent ran down the spindle of tap into the gland, from which it quickly washed the grease out of the packing.

Poor or intermittent flow, particularly from hot water taps, is more likely to be due to an air lock in the distribution pipe than to a fault in the tap itself. Air locks can usually be cured by connecting one end of a length of hose to the cold tap over the kitchen sink and the other end to the tap giving trouble. Turn both taps on and the mains pressure from the kitchen cold tap should blow the air bubble out of the system (*Figure 4.8*).

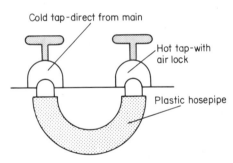

Cold tap-direct from main

Hot tap-with air lock

Plastic hosepipe

Fig. 4.8. Clearing and air lock in the hot tap over the kitchen sink – the same principle can be used in the bathroom if necessary

Constantly recurring air locks are caused by design faults that should always be investigated and remedied. The commonest single cause is too small a cold water supply pipe from the cold water storage cistern to the hot water cylinder. If this pipe is only 15mm (½in) in diameter it will be incapable of replacing hot water drawn off by a ¾in bath tap. Water level will fall in the vent pipe until air is able to enter the distribution pipe to produce a blockage.

Sometimes the supply pipe is of adequate diameter but a gate valve of a smaller size has been fitted into it. Alternatively a gate valve of the correct size may have been left partially closed after a piece of maintenance has been carried out. Other possible causes of recurring air locks are a cold water storage cistern of inadequate capacity or one fed by a sluggish ball valve. All 'horizontal' lengths of distribution should, in fact, slope slightly upwards towards the cold water storage cistern or the hot water vent pipe. This will permit any bubbles of air that may gain access to escape.

At the time of writing taps have not yet been metricated and are still to be found in builders merchants' catalogues designated as ½in (for sinks, basins and bidets) and ¾in (for baths). There is however a growing tendency to refer to them metrically by the metric size of the copper tubing to which they are to be connected. Thus sink and basin taps are given a nominal size of 15mm and bath taps one of 22mm although these dimensions represent no actual measurement of the taps themselves.

Before fitting a pillar tap a plastic washer is slipped over the tail of the tap to protect the surface of the fitting from the metal base of the tap (*Figure 4.9a*). Alternatively the tap may be bedded onto linseed oil putty or a non-setting mastic such as the plumber's mait. Another plastic washer should be provided under the fitting before the back nut is tightened up. For fittings of thin materials (for example sinks and basins of stainless or enamelled steel) a special spacer washer— sometimes called a 'top hat' or 'cap' washer—is needed to accommodate the protruding shank of the tap (*Figure 4.9b*). The tail of the tap is then connected to the water supply pipe by means of a tap connector or 'cap and liner' (*Figure 4.9c*). This incorporates a fibre washer to ensure a watertight connection. The cap and liner may have a compression or capillary joint outlet for connection to copper or stainless steel tubing or a plain outlet for connection, by means of a wiped soldered joint, to a lead supply pipe (see Chapter 12).

Bib taps are most likely to be fitted into a wall plate elbow. The wall must be drilled and plugged and the elbow screwed to it. Before screwing in the tail of the tap p.t.f.e. plastic thread sealing tape should be bound round the thread of the tap's tail to ensure a watertight joint.

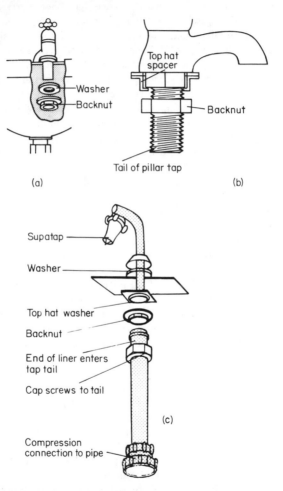

Fig. 4.9. Methods of protecting surfaces when mounting taps

5 Some Plumbing Fittings; Baths and Showers, Sinks, Basins and Bidets

Baths

Baths come in all shapes and sizes nowadays but the standard rectangular panelled bath ranging in overall size from 1500mm to 1800mm (about 5ft to 6ft) in length and from 700mm to 800mm (about 2ft 4in to 2ft 8in) in width is likely to remain the most popular choice for the average British householder.

Size will be dictated by the space available though the prudent purchaser will also bear in mind the additional fuel cost of filling one of the larger baths with warm water. Colour —and there is a wide colour range available—will depend upon the overall decor of the bathroom. It is with regard to the material of which the bath is made that the purchaser has greatest freedom of choice.

The traditional material is enamelled cast iron (*Figure 5.1*). Any bath installed more than twenty to twenty five years ago will certainly be of this material. The fact that there are still so many of them installed and in regular use is a tribute to their strength and toughness. They have disadvantages though. They are extremely heavy. Installing (or removing) one is certainly not a one man job. The thick iron of which they are made tends to conduct away heat, quickly cooling the water run into them. Once the enamelled surface is damaged renovation can be extremely difficult, if not impossible, and corrosion can attack the metal underneath. They are also, by most people's standards, very expensive.

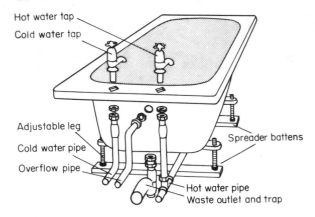

Fig. 5.1. Detail of enamelled cast iron bath with lead water supply pipes

For all of these reasons the cheaper, lighter and more easily installed enamelled pressed steel bath enjoys considerable popularity. A disadvantage is its liability to accidental damage in storage, transport or installation. To overcome this objection, one bath manufacturer (the Curran Engineering Co. Ltd.) has produced a 'supersteel' bath, backed by guarantee, made of 2.5mm gauge steel. This is 50% thicker than that used for standard enamel steel baths but baths made of this material are still only half the weight of cast iron baths of the same size.

The third material of which baths may be made is acrylic plastic. These baths show a steady increase in popularity and offer many advantages to the householder and to the professional or d.i.y. installer. Tough and hard wearing, they are also extremely light in weight and easy to handle. It is well within the capacity of one man to unload one from the

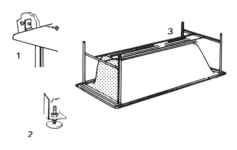

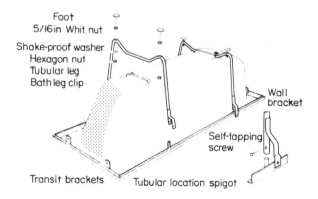

Foot
5/16 in Whit. nut
Shake-proof washer
Hexagon nut
Tubular leg
Bath leg clip

Wall
bracket

Self-tapping
screw

Transit brackets   Tubular location spigot

Fig. 5.2. Cradles for acrylic baths. A universal wall fixing bracket (1) may be used at the side, or over the lip, of the bath. Screw adjustments (2) at five points will allow for uneven floors. Metal cradles as at (3) can be assembled allowing for support for the bath and for fixing side panels

SOME PLUMBING FITTINGS

delivery vehicle, carry it upstairs to the bathroom and install it single-handed. They are available in a wide range of colours and the colour extends throughout the material. Small surface scratches can be polished out without trace. Acrylic plastic has good insulating properties retaining the heat of the bath water and remaining comfortable to the touch. It is possible to purchase acrylic plastic baths with a flat, non-slip, base that eliminates a frequent cause of home accidents among the elderly.

Acrylic plastic baths are supplied with strong metal or wooden frames and cradles (*Figure 5.2*) that should be assembled and secured to wall and floor exactly as indicated in the instructions of the manufacturer. Felt padding is provided at points of contact. These padded cradles eliminate the sagging and creaking when filled that occurred with early models of this kind of bath.

Acrylic plastic can be permanently damaged by extreme heat. When working with a blow torch in a bathroom fitted with a bath of this material keep the blow torch flame well away from the bath. Similarly the householder should make sure that all members of his family, and visitors, are made aware that placing a lighted cigarette, even briefly, on the bath rim, can cause irreparable damage.

When fitting a bath of any kind the cramped space available at the end of the bath should be borne in mind. Carry out as much of the plumbing work as possible before moving the bath into position. Fit the taps or mixer as described in the previous chapter and bed down the waste outlet in non-setting mastic, tightening up the back nut beneath the bath. Have the hot and cold water supply pipes in position with their tap connectors fitted. The trap should be connected to the waste pipe with its flexible overflow pipe ready for connection to the bath overflow. It is wise to use a plastic trap and waste pipe with an acrylic bath. There will be some movement as the bath fills with hot water and a rigid metal trap and waste pipe could cause damage.

Having moved the bath into position, make the plumbing connections in logical order so as to make the most of the limited space available. First connect the trap to the waste outlet (*Figure 5.3*). Then connect the further tap to its supply pipe. Next make the overflow connection and finally the

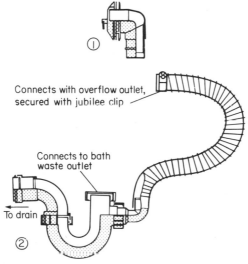

Connects with overflow outlet, secured with jubilee clip

Connects to bath waste outlet

To drain

Fig. 5.3. Bath overflow (1) and waste (2) outlets

connection of the supply pipe to the nearer tap. All that will then remain is to fit the bath panels and to fill the gap between the side of the bath and the wall with a suitable mastic filler.

Showers

A shower may be provided either in connection with a conventional sit-down bath or as a separate facility in its own shower cabinet. There can be few people nowadays who are unaware of the advantages that a shower has to offer. They save both time and money. Five or six showers can be taken with the same amount of hot water—and in scarcely more time—than would be required for one sit-down bath. They are more hygienic and mean less work for the housewife clearing up afterwards. A shower cubicle will be easier and safer for an elderly or disabled person to enter than a sit-down bath.

Where a house is being converted into self-contained flats an independent shower can be provided in any space, on a landing, in a hallway or even under the stairs, where there is a space at least 3ft square. 'A fixed bath *or shower*' is one of the amenities for the provision of which the owner of an older house can claim an improvement grant from his local council.

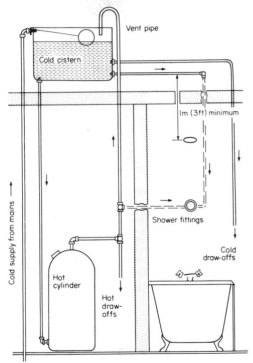

Fig. 5.4. Design requirements of a shower installation

A shower can usually be provided without difficulty in any home with a cylinder storage hot water system. There are however certain, quite specific, design requirements that must be met.

The first is that to ensure safe and efficient mixing, the hot and cold water supplies to the shower must be under equal pressure. With a cylinder storage system the hot water supply will be under pressure from the main cold water storage cistern. The cold supply must therefore also be taken from this cistern (*Figure 5.4*).

It is illegal, and impracticable, to connect the hot side of a shower to a hot water supply from a cistern and storage cylinder and to connect the cold side to the rising main. Pressure must be adequate. This depends upon the height of the cold water storage cistern above the shower sprinkler. Best results will be obtained if the base of this cistern is 5ft (about 1500mm) or more above the sprinkler. However if pipe runs are short with minimal bends a vertical distance of 3ft (about 900mm) may be sufficient.

Finally, the cold supply to the shower should be taken in a separate distribution pipe direct from the storage cistern, not as a branch from some other cold water distribution pipe. This is a safety precaution. If the shower cold supply is taken as a branch from another distribution pipe, flushing a w.c. cistern or running a basin cold tap could reduce pressure on the cold side of the shower. Pressure on the hot side would remain constant and serious scalding could result.

The design of some hot and cold water supply systems may make it impossible to comply with all of these requirements. Nevertheless there can be few homes in which it is absolutely impossible to install a shower.

Where the cold water storage cistern is not sufficiently high above the shower sprinkler to provide the minimum 3ft (900mm) head of pressure the simplest solution is usually to raise the level of the cistern. This may involve moving it from the upper part of an airing cupboard into the roof space or constructing a wooden platform for it above the roof timbers. This cannot be done where there is a 'packaged plumbing system' (see Chapter 3) in which the cold water storage cistern and the hot water cylinder comprise one unit. It may be impossible too in flats and ground floor maisonettes where there is no access to the roof space. There are however available electrically operated shower pumps which will effectively boost pressure to the shower sprinkler (*Figure 5.5*). These operate on a flow switch and are brought into action when the control valve of the shower is turned on. They do, of course, make an appreciable addition to the cost of the installation.

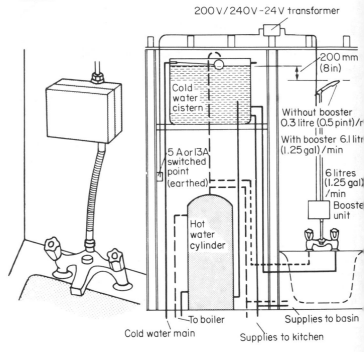

200 V / 240 V - 24 V transformer

200 mm (8 in)

Cold water cistern

Without booster 0.3 litre (0.5 pint)/r

With booster 6.1 litr (1.25 gal) /min

5 A or 13A switched point (earthed)

6 litres (1.25 gal) /min

Booste unit

Hot water cylinder

To boiler

Cold water main

Supplies to kitchen

Supplies to basin

Fig. 5.5. Installing a shower using a booster unit

Where bathroom cold supplies are direct from the main it will be possible, in many cases, to bring the cold supply to the shower from the cistern supplying the hot water cylinder. In some instances though this will have too small a capacity to do more than supply the hot water system. In others, where all hot and cold water supplies are direct from the main, there may be no storage cistern at all. It is under these circumstances that the instantaneous electric shower units that have been developed in recent years can prove invaluable. They need only connection to a mains water supply and a suitable source of electric power to provide an 'instant shower'.

Apart from electric instantaneous showers, which incorporate their own control valve, all showers need to have some kind of mixing valve to blend the hot and cold water to the bather's requirements. The bath taps themselves can provide the simplest kind of shower mixer. They may comprise the bath/shower mixer referred to in the previous chapter with facility for diverting the flow of water into the bath or up to the shower sprinkler at the flick of a switch. A portable rubber shower, with push-on tap connectors, can be used to convert any pair of bath taps into a shower mixer. These basic shower kits work perfectly satisfactorily provided that the design requirements already mentioned are met by the hot and cold water systems of the house.

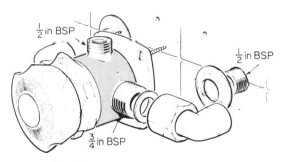

Fig. 5.6. Fixing a manual mixing valve

It usually takes considerable adjustment, and some discomfort, before a 'mixing valve' of this kind produces a stream of water at exactly the temperature required. Better control is achieved with a single unit 'manual shower mixing valve' (*Figure 5.6*) which gives control of the shower temperature and, in some instances, flow control as well, by turning a single control knob. Manual mixers of this kind are installed in most independent shower cabinets and there are over-bath versions available too.

Finally there is the 'thermostatic shower mixing valve' which is capable of dealing with fluctuations of pressure in the hot or cold supply pipes and providing a mix of constant temperature. These valves are naturally more expensive. They are particularly useful in hotels, schools and similar institutions where a number of showers are run from single hot and cold water distributing pipes. They are also of value in domestic situations where providing *separate* distribution pipes from the cold water storage cistern to the shower presents difficulties. Early thermostatic mixing valves needed a considerable head of pressure, perhaps as much as 10ft (3m), to work effectively. There are however present day models that will operate satisfactorily on the minimal 3ft (900mm) head required by a manual mixing valve.

It should be realised that a thermostatic valve cannot increase pressure on either the hot or the cold supply. It can only reduce the pressure on one side to match that on the other. If therefore, cold water pressure is reduced to a thermostatic valve already operating on minimal head, the shower will simply dry up until pressure is restored.

A shower fitted over a bath needs some means of preventing water from splashing onto the bathroom floor. Plastic shower curtains provide the cheapest means of doing this but glass panels, which may be hinged or detachable, provide a neater and more professional solution. Shower trays may be of ceramic material, of acrylic plastic or of enamelled steel. Waste and trap are fitted and connected to the branch waste pipe in the same way as are those of a bath except that shower trays are not normally fitted with an overflow.

Sinks

Houses built between about 1920 and 1950 were almost invariably fitted with glazed fireclay, 'Belfast pattern', sinks

(*Figure 5.7a*). These were supported by heavy iron cantilever brackets built into the wall. They had a built-in weir overflow and a separate, hook-on, wooden draining board. Water supply was from bib-taps protruding from the tiled wall surface behind the sink. These sinks have been superseded, for

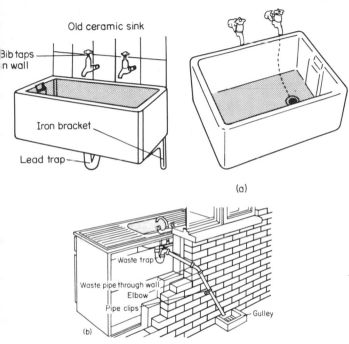

Fig. 5.7. Kitchen sinks. The 'Belfast' pattern ceramic glazed sink (a) is usually mounted on iron brackets fixed to the wall; these must be removed or cut back when replacing with a modern sink. The modern sink unit (b) is fairly simple to fit

both new and replacement work, by sink units with a stainless steel or enamelled pressed steel sink and integral drainer (*Figure 5.7b*). Sinks of either of these materials are more attractive in appearance, more easily cleaned and less damaging to accidentally dropped crockery than those of glazed fireclay.

Enamelled steel sinks are available in a number of colours but suffer from the disadvantage that the enamel is liable to accidental damage. For this reason a stainless steel sink is the modern housewife's most usual choice.

Stainless steel sinks designed for sink unit installation are provided with tap holes to take pillar taps or a sink mixer. They may have a built-in overflow but are nowadays more likely to have an overflow hole only provided. The overflow pipe is intended to be a flexible one fitted into the trap in the same way as the overflow of a modern bath (*Figure 5.8*).

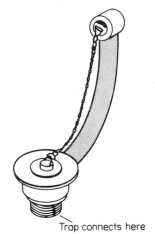

Fig. 5.8. Sink waste incorporating overflow pipe

Trap connects here

Since both stainless steel and enamelled pressed steel are thin materials a spacer or top-hat washer (see previous chapter) must be slipped over the tail of each tap before the back-nut is screwed home. When installing a new sink unit the taps should be fitted before the unit is placed in position. Waste, trap and overflow are fitted as for a bath. Where the unit has a double sink a trap is fitted only under one outlet—the one nearer to the waste pipe. The waste from the other section of the sink is taken untrapped to connect above trap level.

If a sink waste disposal unit (*Figure 5.9*) is to be fitted the sink must have a 3½in (87.5mm) waste hole instead of the standard 1½in (38mm) hole. The waste holes of stainless steel, but not enamelled steel, sinks can be enlarged to this size with a tool obtainable from the supplier of the unit. Waste

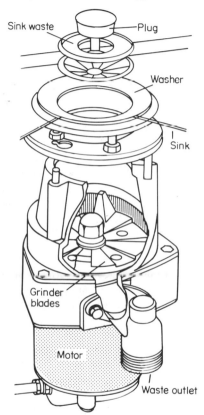

Fig. 5.9. Sink waste disposal unit (garbage grinder). The unit is easy to fit, but an electrician should be employed if new wiring is necessary

disposal units are fitted by placing a rubber or plastic washer round the outlet hole and inserting the flange of the unit. The unit is then connected beneath the sink by means of a snap fastening. The outlet of the disposal unit connects to a trap in the usual way. Waste disposal units are operated by an electric motor and will grind soft household and kitchen waste to a slurry that can then be flushed into the drain by running the cold tap.

Basins

Although wash basins, or lavatory basins as they are referred to in builders merchants' catalogues, may be made of enamelled pressed steel or of plastic materials the traditional ceramic basin retains its popularity and is the kind most likely to be chosen for new or replacement work.

Ceramic basins may be either wall hung or pedestal in design. Pedestal basins are often preferred for bathroom use because of their appearance and their capacity for concealing water supply and waste pipes. Modern pedestal basins are always provided with concealed hangers or wall brackets to help support the basin's weight.

The height of a pedestal basin is, of course, decided by the pedestal. Wall-hung basins may be fitted at any height convenient to the user. Since one bends over a basin to wash it should be set at a lower level than the kitchen sink—32in (about 81cm) from floor level to rim is usual. Particularly with wall-hung basins it is important to check that the wall is capable of supporting the weight of the basin and someone leaning on it. Breeze partitions offer a somewhat dubious support and it is wise to use a pedestal basin in such a position.

Taps, or a basin mixer, are fitted in the same way as they are in a sink unit. The thicker material of a ceramic basin makes it possible to use a flat plastic (instead of a top-hat) washer between the back-nut and the material of the basin. Do not overtighten the back-nut. Ceramic basins are very easily damaged in installation. Basins of this kind have a built-in or 'secret' overflow (*Figure 5.10*). The waste fitting must therefore incorporate an overflow slot. When this fitting is bedded down into the waste outlet, care must be taken to ensure that the overflow slot coincides with the outlet of the built-in overflow. The basin must, of course, have a trapped outlet. Chromium plated brass or plastic bottle traps are space saving and neat in appearance. They can be obtained with adjustable inlets that permit easy connection to an existing waste pipe in replacement work.

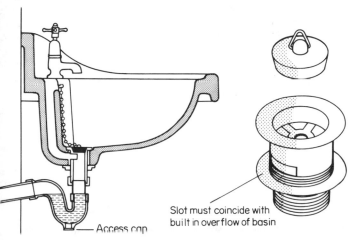

Slot must coincide with built in overflow of basin

— Access cap

Fig. 5.10. Ceramic basin waste fittings

(a)   (b)

Fig. 5.11. Vanity units fitted (a) in the bathroom, (b) in a bedroom

Enamelled steel or plastic wash basins are usually inset into a toilet table to form a 'vanity unit'. Such a unit may be installed in either a bathroom or a bedroom (*Figure 5.11*).

391

In the latter situation they constitute an extremely attractive, and useful, piece of bedroom furniture. A vanity unit may be regarded as the ablutionary equivalent of a sink unit. Apart from the cold water supply—which will normally come from a storage cistern and not from the main—it is plumbed in in exactly the same way. Hot water supply to the wash basin will probably be taken from the household domestic hot water system. However, where the basin is used for hand washing only and is remote from other plumbing fittings, the provision of an instantaneous electric water heater providing a spray for hand washing can be an economy. A heater of this kind can be very useful for a basin in a cloakroom or w.c. compartment used only occasionally.

Bidets

Bidets are specially shaped, low level, wash basins designed for cleansing the lower parts of the body. Virtually unknown in the United Kingdom prior to World War II they are gradually gaining acceptance in this country. It may well be that the well-appointed bathroom of the future will contain a shower cubicle, a wash basin and a bidet rather than, as at present, a wash basin and sit down bath.

There are two, quite different, designs of bidet. The differences between them result in differences in means of installation that should be clearly understood by both the plumber and the householder. In an identical situation the cost of installing one pattern of bidet is likely to be considerably greater than that of installing the other.

The simpler pattern, which is cheaper both to purchase and to install, is usually described as an 'over rim supply' bidet. Apart from its shape it is identical to a bathroom wash basin. Holes are provided for pillar taps or, more probably, a pillar mixer. There may be a pop-up waste or an ordinary chain secured waste plug. The bidet is filled with warm water before use in the same way as a wash basin. Bidets of this kind can be plumbed into existing bathroom hot and cold water supplies without any special precautions being taken. If there are 22mm (¾in) hot and cold distribution pipes supplying ¾in bath hot and cold taps, reducing tee junctions 22mm to 15mm may be inserted into these distributing pipes and taken to the bidet taps or mixer.

The other type of bidet is described as 'rim supply with ascending douche'. This has a rim not unlike the flushing rim of a w.c. pan and a douche directing a spray of warm water to those parts of the body to be cleansed (*Figure 5.12*). Warm water flows into the bidet via the flushing rim which it thereby warms and makes comfortable for use. When required the water flow can be diverted to the ascending douche.

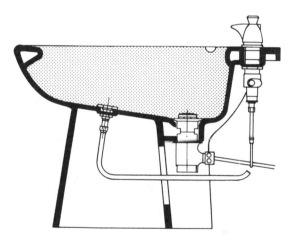

Fig. 5.12. Section through a rim supply bidet

It is the ascending douche, with its outlet below normal water level, that complicates plumbing installation. With any water inlet of this kind precautions have to be taken to ensure that other water supplies, especially mains water supplies, cannot be contaminated by accidental back-siphonage. The purpose for which the bidet is used makes this particularly important in this case.

To avoid this danger the hot and cold supplies to a 'rim supply with ascending douche' bidet must *not* be taken as branch supplies from pipes supplying any other draw-off point. They must be taken, as separate distribution pipes,

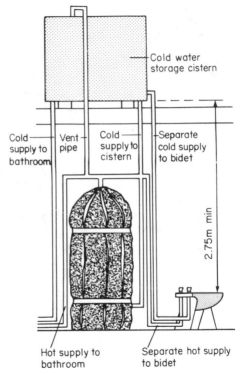

Cold water storage cistern

Cold supply to bathroom

Vent pipe

Cold supply to cistern

Separate cold supply to bidet

2.75m min

Hot supply to bathroom

Separate hot supply to bidet

Fig. 5.13. Design requirements for a rim supply bidet

direct from the hot water storage cylinder and the cold water storage cistern (*Figure 5.13*). As a further precaution the base of the cold water storage cistern should be at least 2745mm (9ft) above the level of the bidet inlet.

Where there is a two-pipe drainage system (see Chapter 7) a distinction is made between 'soil' and 'waste' fittings. 'Soil appliances' such as w.c.s are connected directly to the drain or soil pipe. 'Waste appliances'—baths, sinks and basins—are disconnected from the drain by means of a gully.

Plumbers sometimes argue that, because of the nature of the use of bidet, it should be regarded as a 'soil appliance' and connected direct to the drain. This is incorrect. A bidet is a waste or ablutionary appliance and, where a two-pipe drainage system is installed, it should be disconnected from the drain in the same way as other waste and ablutionary fittings.

6 The W.C. Suite

From many points of view the w.c. suite is the most important and critical item of the householder's plumbing installation. A bad choice of suite can lead to embarrassment. Faulty installation can produce a positive risk to health.

It is not always realised that there are three different kinds of w.c. suite in common use, and they they depend upon quite different principles for their cleaning and recharging with water after use.

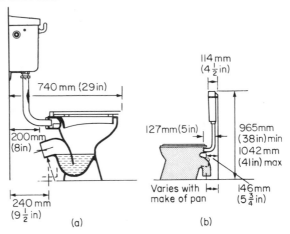

Fig. 6.1. Conventional low-level suite (a) and low-level suite with flush panel (b). Both types are wash-down pans

Commonest (and cheapest) is the straightforward wash-down suite (*Figure 6.1*). This depends for its flushing and cleansing action solely upon the weight and momentum of the two gallons of water released when the flushing cistern is discharged. Wash-down w.c. pans may be used in both high level and low level suites. For efficient cleansing—particularly with low level suites—the following conditions are essential.

(a) The float arm of the ball-valve should be adjusted so that the water level of the cistern when full is at the mark indicated on the inside of the cistern wall, usually about ½in below the overflow of warning outlet.

(b) The flush pipe (often called a 'flush bend' with a low level suite) should be of the diameter and length recommended by the manufacturer. It is best (though not absolutely essential) when installing a low level suite to buy pan, flush bend and cistern as one unit from the supplier.

(c) The flush pipe must connect absolutely squarely to the flushing horn of the w.c. pan and no jointing material must be permitted to obstruct the flush inlet. The old-fashioned way of connecting a flush pipe to a w.c. pan was with a 'rag and putty joint'. Apart from the fact that a connection of this kind is thoroughly unhygienic, the nature of the joint frequently resulted in putty obstructing the flush. Some modern w.c. pans are provided with a patent 'O' ring connector for the flush pipe. The alternative is to use a push-on rubber cone connector.

(d) There must be no obstruction—from putty, flakes of rust, hard water scale or other debris—within either side of the flushing rim. This can be checked with a mirror or by feeling with the fingers.

(e) The pan must be set dead level. This should be checked with a spirit level. If necessary, the pan can be made level by packing slivers of wood, or pieces of linoleum, under the lower side.

(f) The pan outlet must be set squarely into the socket of the branch drain or soil-pipe and, when fitting, care must be taken to ensure that any cement or mastic jointing material is not extruded into the connection between pan and socket to reduce its effective diameter.

When a wash-down suite is properly installed flushing water should flow evenly from each side of the flushing rim, the flushing water should meet in the middle of the front of the pan and there should be no marked rise in water level and no 'whirl-pool effect' as the pan empties.

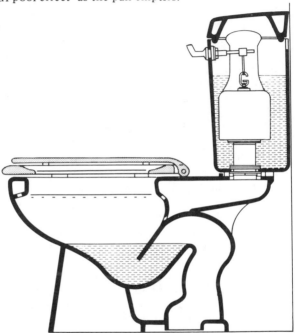

Fig. 6.2. The single-trap siphonic suite (close coupled). At the start of the flush water rises in the bowl and then rapidly discharges over the weir of the trap. This completely changes the upper portion of the trappage drawing air with it and a strong siphonic action is created

Wash-down suites are suitable for most domestic, industrial and commercial purposes. Where a more positive cleansing action is required or where the position of the w.c. suite (a compartment just inside the front door of a house or immediately outside an executive office suite, for instance) makes silent, unobtrusive action a prime consideration, then one or other of the two kinds of siphonic w.c. suite should be installed. These depend, to a greater or less extent, upon the weight of the atmosphere to push out the contents of the pan by siphonic action. Since they do not depend upon the weight and momentum of the flushing water for their cleansing effect they permit the use of 'close coupled' w.c. suites in which the flushing cistern and the pan comprise one unit without even the short 'flush bend' required for a low level wash-down suite. This markedly reduces the noise of flushing.

The simpler 'single trap' siphonic suite depends for its effectiveness upon the design of the outlet of the pan (*Figure 6.2*). Immediately behind the trap the outlet is first constricted and then widened. When the flush is operated, water overflowing from the trap completely fills the constricted section of the outlet and then enters the wider section carrying air with it. This creates the partial vacuum upon which siphonic action depends and the contents of the pan are pushed out by atmospheric pressure.

When a siphonic closet of this type is flushed water will first rise slightly in the pan. The contents will then be quite forcibly ejected. The siphonic action will cease when water level within the pan falls to a level at which air can pass into the trap. Single trap siphonic suites are rather prone to accidental blockage—usually as a result of misuse. Although they flush silently the passage of air into the trap to break the siphon can produce a somewhat noisy gurgle.

A more positively silent action is provided by the double-trap siphonic w.c. suite. A suite of this kind is, in my opinion, always to be preferred where silent, unobtrusive and efficient action is of greater importance than the initial cost of installation.

As its name implies a double trap siphonic suite has two traps built into the outlet (*Figure 6.3*). The air space between the two traps is connected to the flushing inlet by means of a short pipe or 'pressure reducing device'. When the flush is operated, water flowing over this pressure reducing device aspirates air from the air space in the same way that the wind,

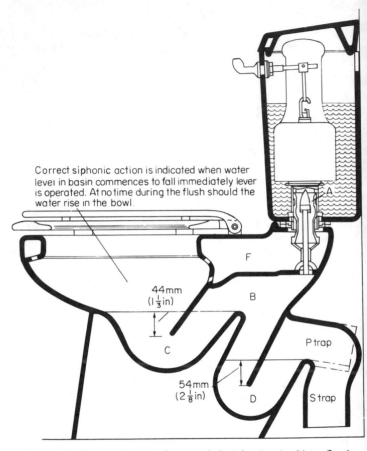

Correct siphonic action is indicated when water level in basin commences to fall immediately lever is operated. At no time during the flush should the water rise in the bowl.

44mm (1⅓ in)

F

B

A

C

P trap

54mm (2⅛ in)

D

S trap

Figure 6.3. The double-trap (close coupled) siphonic suite. Water flowing down the leg of the siphon passes through the pressure-reducing fitment A. This lowers the air pressure in chamber B and a powerful siphonic action is set up which draws the contents of the basin through sealed traps C and D into the soil pipe. Simultaneously the sides of the bowl are thoroughly washed by streams of water from the perforated rim E. After flushing, complete resealing of the two traps is ensured by after-flush chamber F.

Correct siphonic action is indicated when the water level in the basin starts to fall immediately the lever is operated. At no time during the flush should the water rise in the basin

blowing across a chimney stack, will aspirate air up the flue from the room below. This action creates a partial vacuum in the space between the two traps and the pressure of the atmospheric pushes out the contents of the pan. Where a double-trap siphonic suite has been properly installed the water level in the pan can be seen to fall *before* flushing water actually reaches the pan. Having set the siphonic action into operation the main purpose of the flushing water is merely to recharge the pan.

Apart from its silent action a further advantage of this kind of w.c. suite is the fact that the large water area that its design makes possible, reduces the risk of the sides of the pan becoming fouled. Unlike most sanitary appliances the trap of the w.c. suite is built in to the fitting itself. Ground floor w.c.s usually have an 'S' trap with an outlet connected directly to a

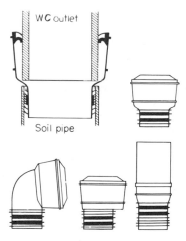

Fig. 6.4. Push on plastic w.c. connectors

branch underground drain. Upstairs w.c.s are usually connected to a branch soil pipe and have a 'P' trap with a horizontal outlet. A variety of angled 'P' outlets are available for installation in difficult situations.

It is usual nowadays to connect both ground floor and upstairs w.c.s to the drain or soil pipe by means of some kind of flexible joint (*Figure 6.4*). This may be a patent push-on plastic joint such as the 'multikwik' or may be made in situ using a non-setting mastic filler such as 'plumber's mait'.

In the past ground floor w.c.s were always connected to the stoneware drain socket by means of a cement and sand joint using two parts of cement to one of sand. A grommet of tarred hemp, or a wad of dampened newspaper, was first caulked into the space between pan outlet and socket to prevent jointing material entering the drain and causing a partial obstruction. Upstairs w.c.s were sometimes connected to iron branch soil pipe sockets in the same way. This was never a satisfactory arrangement however. Vibration or movement of the wooden floor to which the w.c. pan was screwed inevitably resulted in a cracked and leaking joint.

Remedying a leak in the joint between w.c. outlet and drain or soil-pipe socket is a common maintenance job. A radical remedy is, of course, to disconnect the w.c. pan and to replace the existing joint with a push-on plastic one. This may not be convenient or even possible. An alternative is to rake out the existing jointing material and to bind two or three turns of a waterproofing building tape such as 'sylglas' round the w.c. outlet, caulking it down hard into the socket of the soil pipe or drain. Fill in the space between outlet and socket with a non-setting mastic such as 'plumber's mait' and complete the joint with another couple of turns of waterproofing tape.

When fitting a new w.c. pan onto a solid floor it should *not* —as was usual in the past—be set in a bed of sand and cement mix. It has been established that the setting of the cement can produce damaging stresses. The pan should be screwed down with non-corroding screws. Place the pan in position. Mark through the screw holes with a ball-point refill. Remove the pan, drill the floor and plug. In order to make sure that the pan is placed in exactly the correct position over the plugs it is a good idea to insert short pieces of wire (straightened out paper clips will do) into the plugs. The pan can then be lowered over these pieces of wire which are removed before the screws are inserted. Slip a lead washer over each screw before insertion to avoid the risk of damaging the ceramic surface of the w.c. pan.

Although direct-action flat bottomed flushing cisterns are in universal use for new and replacement work there are still many thousands of the older Burlington or 'bell' high level cisterns in use, particularly in external w.c. compartments in older properties (*Figure 6.5*). Their function and failings

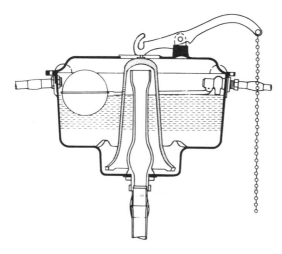

Fig. 6.5. Bell pattern well-bottomed flushing cistern

should be clearly understood. Burlington pattern cisterns are invariably made of iron. Their essential feature is a well in the base in which stands a heavy iron bell. A stand-pipe connects to the flush pipe and rises, within the bell, to terminate open-ended an inch or so above 'full' water level. The bell has lugs cast into its base to permit water to pass freely.

To operate the flush the bell is raised, usually by means of a chain, and is then suddenly released. Its weight causes it to fall rapidly back into the well of the cistern and its conical shape forces the water trapped inside it up and over the lip of the stand-pipe. This water, falling down the stand-pipe into the flush-pipe, carries air with it thus creating the partial vacuum upon which siphonic action depends. Atmospheric pressure then pushes the water in the cistern under the base of the bell and into the flush-pipe to flush the w.c. The siphon is broken when water level falls to the base of the bell and air can enter.

Burlington cisterns are always noisy in operation. There is the clank of the descending bell, the rush of water from high level and the gurgle as the siphon is broken. Since they are usually connected directly to the main refilling, under mains pressure, is also noisy.

Another fault to which Burlington cisterns are prone, particularly after they have been in use (as most of them have) for many years, is continuing siphonage. After the cistern has been flushed the siphon fails to break. Water continues to flow into the cistern through the ball-valve and there is a continuous flow down the flush-pipe that can be stopped only by 'pulling the chain' again at the end of the operation. A number of circumstances contribute to the this failing. After years of use the lugs at the base of the bell become worn, reducing the gap between the base of the bell and that of the well. Rust from inside the cistern and grit and debris from the water main accumulate in the well, further reducing the space through which air must pass in order to break the siphon. Coupled with a high water pressure and an efficient ball valve these two factors result in the rim of the well being continuously covered with water. The siphon can be broken only by pulling the chain and raising the bell again.

This trouble can usually be cured by the simple expedient of cleaning the rust and debris out of the well. In some cases it may be necessary, by turning down the stop-cock on the water supply to the cistern, to reduce the flow of water through the ball-valve. In others it may be possible to 'build up' the lugs on the base of the well with an epoxy resin filler such as 'plastic padding' or 'isopon', or to drill a hole through the metal of the bell an inch or so above its base to permit air to enter. A better solution is, of course, the more radical one

of replacing the old and obsolete cistern with a modern
'direct action' one.

Direct action cisterns normally have a flat base though
there are well-bottomed models available to facilitate the
replacement of old bell pattern cisterns with the minimum of
alteration to the plumbing. Like bell pattern cisterns, direct
action ones have a stand-pipe connected to the flush-pipe that
rises from the base of the cistern to a point an inch or so above

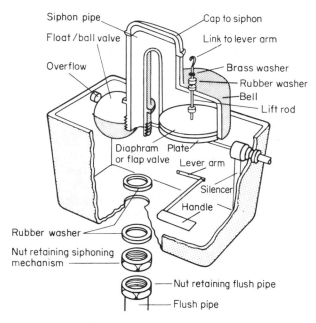

Fig. 6.6. Direct action flushing cistern

water level. This stand-pipe is not however open-ended at
this point. It is bent over in an inverted U and widened to
form a dome with an open base extending almost to the
bottom of the cistern (*Figure 6.6*). A rod connected by a
metal link to the flushing handle passes through the dome to
connect to the centre of a circular metal plate. The metal

plate has a hole, or holes, in it to permit water to pass freely upwards but a kind of non-return valve, usually a plastic disc, closes these holes when the plate is raised.

These cisterns are often loosely referred to as 'low level cisterns' though they may, of course, be installed at low level, at high level or as part of a close-coupled suite. High level cisterns of this kind are operated by pulling a chain in the same way as a Burlington pattern cistern. Flushing takes place as the chain is pulled not, as with a Burlington cistern, when it is released. The most usual method of operating a low level direct action cistern is by depressing a lever. However press button operation is becoming increasingly popular and there are also pedal operated models on the market. These are particularly to be commended in commercial food premises where every means by which the operatives can avoid contamination of the hands should be encouraged.

Whatever the means adopted to induce flushing the action within the cistern is the same. The metal plate within the dome of the siphon is raised throwing water over the inverted U into the flush pipe. This falling water carries air with it to create a partial vacuum thus inducing siphonic action. Once siphonic action has begun water flow raises the plastic diaphragm or 'flap valve' on the plate to permit water to pass through freely.

Failure of this plastic diaphragm is the commonest fault encountered in direct action cisterns. The user finds that, whereas originally the cistern flushed promptly at the first attempt, several sharp jerks are necessary to induce siphonic action. The diaphragm is no longer blocking the holes in the plate and, when the plate is raised, water passes back into the cistern instead of being thrown over into the flush pipe.

To renew the diaphragm the flushing siphon must be removed from the cistern. First of all, tie up the arm of the ball-valve to prevent water from flowing in and flush to empty. Next unscrew the nut securing the external flush pipe to the threaded tail of the siphoning mechanism protruding from the cistern's base. Disconnect the flush pipe. With some makes of cistern the siphoning mechanism is secured by bolts within the cistern itself. In most cases however the siphon can be withdrawn after unscrewing and removing the large nut immediately below the cistern's base. As you loosen this nut the pint or so of water remaining after flushing will be released. Be prepared for this!

Once the siphon has been withdrawn the plate can be removed after disconnecting it from the 'link' connection with the flushing handle. It is important that the replacement diaphragm should be of the correct size. This will normally be purchased before the cistern is dismantled. If in doubt about the size required choose the largest—it can easily be cut to size with a pair of scissors. The diaphragm should overlap the plate and touch, but not drag on, the walls of the siphon dome.

Slow refilling is another fault that may be encountered with any kind of flushing cistern. After flushing the cistern should refill and be ready for use within two minutes. Failure to refill promptly is usually the result of the cistern being fitted with a high pressure ball valve where a low pressure or fullway model is required. Cisterns fed direct from the main normally require a high pressure valve. A cistern supplied from a roof storage cistern will probably fill sufficiently quickly if a low pressure valve is installed. Where the storage cistern is below roof level, perhaps in an airing cupboard only a few feet above the level of the flushing cistern, a full-way valve may well be needed.

If a valve of the correct type has been installed slow filling is almost certainly the result of the valve jamming because of an accumulation of hard water scale. The valve should be dismantled and cleaned as suggested in Chapter 2.

Condensation is another trouble to which all w.c. flushing cisterns are prone. Iron Burlington pattern cisterns may be treated with two or more coats of an insulating anti-condensation paint but this treatment cannot be used to prevent condensation on the external surfaces of modern plastic or ceramic cisterns. As with all condensation problems the best remedy lies in warmth and ventilation. Consideration should be given to the provision of a radiant heat source directed towards the cistern and to improved means of ventilation, perhaps an electric extractor fan fitted into the window of the w.c. compartment.

It is worth bearing in mind that plastic cisterns, being of a self-insulating material, are less subject to condensation than ceramic ones. Cisterns supplied from the marginally warmer water of a cold water storage cistern are also less prone to condensation than those supplied direct from the main.

Bathroom w.c.s are more likely to have condensation troubles than w.c.s installed in a separate compartment. Here there are one or two steps that can be taken to reduce this nuisance. Refrain from drip-drying clothing over the bath. Always run one or two inches of cold water into the bath before turning on the hot tap. It may even be worth connecting a length of rubber tubing to the bath hot tap so that incoming water enters below the level of water already in the bath.

As a last resort consider insulating the inside of the cistern. Empty the cistern and dry it thoroughly. Then apply strips of expanded polystyrene wall paper lining to the interior of the cistern using an epoxy resin adhesive such as Araldite to retain the lining in position. Do not refill until the adhesive has set.

Finally there is the problem of noise. A w.c. that makes its presence known by its noise is a source of annoyance and embarrassment to the householder. Noise may arise from the cistern refilling, from the flush itself or from the contents of the w.c. flushing into the soil pipe. Noisy refilling depends upon the ball-valve and has been dealt with in Chapter 2. So far as the noise of the flush is concerned it should be remembered that a low level suite is more silent in action than a high level one and that a close coupled suite—particularly if it is a double trap siphonic one—is the most silent of all.

The connection between w.c. outlet and soil pipe should always be of mastic or plastic material that does not readily transmit sound. In some cases it may help if a hard rubber pad is interposed between the base of the w.c. pan and the floor or if dry sand, or a layer of vermiculite chips, is run onto the ceiling of the room immediately below the w.c.

THE W.C. SUITE

Attempts to silence a noisy w.c. are rarely *wholly* satisfactory. For reasons that lie within the province of a psychologist rather than a plumber, once a householder has become aware of a nuisance from noise the volume of the noise can be reduced many times but, to the hearer, will remain a source of annoyance.

For this reason it is important that the installer should foresee, and forestall, this problem before or during installation.

7 Above-ground Drainage

Leaky and insanitary drainage systems, coupled with equally unsatisfactory sources of water supply, were directly responsible for the epidemics of typhoid fever and cholera with which Britain was plagued until towards the end of the nineteenth century.

Victorian sanitary and social reformers noted the coincidence of bad drainage and disease but, lacking modern knowledge of the means of spread of infection, they drew the wrong conclusions. They became obsessed with the idea that bad drains were responsible for all the ills to which the flesh is heir. Not only the diseases already mentioned were attributed to this cause but such unlikely candidates as diphtheria, scarlet fever, smallpox and tuberculosis were blamed upon the malign influence of 'drain air'.

The results of this misapprehension were almost wholly beneficial. The provision of watertight, self-cleansing drainage systems prevented the contamination of water supplies and water-borne cholera and typhoid were virtually eliminated. Improved domestic ventilation—intended to get rid of 'drain smells'—did something to reduce the incidence of air-borne droplet infections such as scarlet fever and diphtheria.

However, their determination to 'keep drain smells out of the home' resulted in the cumbersome and obsolescent 'two pipe' system of drainage which remained with us until well on into the 1960s. It is, in fact, only in the last few years that the modern 'single stack' drainage system has ceased to be regarded with suspicion by at least some plumbers and environmental health engineers. The purpose of the two-pipe system was to keep as much of the drainage system as possible outside the walls of the house. Barriers were interposed to remove the least possibility of gases from the drain or sewer entering the home. Since the majority of houses in this country were built prior to the 1960s, the two-pipe system of drainage is the one most likely to be encountered in existing buildings (*Figure 7.1*).

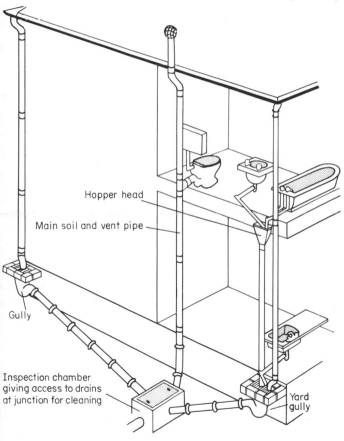

Hopper head

Main soil and vent pipe

Gully

Inspection chamber
giving access to drains
at junction for cleaning

Yard
gully

Fig. 7.1. Two-pipe drainage system

The two-pipe system makes a firm distinction between 'soil' and 'waste' appliances. W.c.s, urinals and slop-sinks are soil appliances although, of course, only the first of these is likely to be found in the home. Soil appliances could be connected directly to the drainage system. The trap built into the appliance afforded a barrier against 'drain air'. A further precaution is that the w.c. compartment must be adequately ventilated—by means of a window opening to the external air or by mechanical means ensuring at least three air changes per hour. Furthermore there must be an 'intervening ventilated space' between the w.c. compartment and any room used for living, sleeping or for the cooking and preparation of food. In most homes a passageway or landing provides this intervening ventilated space though in some instances a separate lobby has to be provided.

These provisions relating to ventilation must still be observed in modern building design. Most authorities today would accept that these requirements are essential for aesthetic, rather than for health, reasons. Ground-floor w.c. outlets connect, by means of a branch underground drain, to the nearest drain inspection chamber. Outlets of upper floor w.c.s are joined to an external soil-pipe by means of a short branch. The soil-pipe is continued, open-ended, to above eaves level to provide the drain with means of ventilation.

Waste appliances—sinks, baths, showers, wash basins and bidets—could be situated in, or immediately adjacent to, habitable rooms. Two barriers are therefore provided by the 'two pipe' system against the possible ingress of drain air. There is the trap provided at the outlet of the appliance and, as a further precaution, the waste pipe from the appliance is required to discharge over an external, trapped yard gully. Only the gully outlet could be connected directly to the drain.

At one time indeed the byelaws of some local authorities went even further. Waste pipes from sinks, baths and basins were not permitted to discharge directly over a yard gully but into an open channel, at least 18in long, connected to the gully. The simpler the plumbing system the more satisfactory the two pipe system of drainage was, and is, likely to prove.

ABOVE-GROUND DRAINAGE

In the 1920s and 1930s the great majority of houses intended 'for the working classes' (a phrase in common use in Acts of Parliament and elsewhere between the wars!) had just two plumbing fittings—an external w.c. and a shallow stoneware kitchen sink. If a bathroom was provided it was likely to be on the ground floor adjacent to the kitchen. The w.c. outlet connected directly to the underground drain. The sink and bath wastes discharged over a yard gully outside the kitchen. There were no problems. Difficulties arose when upstairs bathrooms became commonplace. An upstairs w.c. could discharge into the external soil/vent pipe, but how should the bath and wash basin wastes be dealt with?

The usual solution, in the provinces, was to run a length of rain water down-pipe discharging over a yard gully up the external wall of the house to a point just below the floor of the upstairs bathroom. A rain water hopper head would be inserted into its open upper end and the bath and basin waste pipes would discharge over this hopper head.

This was never a satisfactory arrangement. Soapy water would dry and decompose on the internal surfaces of the hopper and down-pipe. Smells resulting from this process (and smells from the yard gully below) would be carried up the down-pipe to discharge within a few feet of bathroom and bedroom windows. Thus, the very drain smells that the two pipe system was designed to eliminate would find their way into the house. The risk to health may have been minimal but the nuisance from smell was undeniable.

Recognising the defects of the rain water hopper head, the drainage byelaws of some local authorities (notably those of the former London County Council) forbade their use. They required the main waste pipe to discharge over a gully but insisted that the upper end should be treated in exactly the same way as the soil/vent pipe—it had to be taken open-ended to above eaves level. Branch waste pipes were connected to it in the same way that branch soil pipes were joined to the main soil and vent pipe. This arrangement was acceptable for one and two storey buildings with basic plumbing fittings.

413

Its disadvantages for multi-storey blocks of flats and hotels are obvious.

Prior to World War II, what was known as the 'one pipe' system of above-ground drainage was becoming commonly adopted for buildings of this kind. With the 'one-pipe' system —as with the 'single stack' system that has superseded it—the distinction between soil and waste appliances is abolished and all branch soil and waste pipes discharge into a single main soil and waste pipe. The danger that attends any installation in which a number of appliances drain into a single pipe is that of loss of seal from the trap beneath the appliance.

All sanitary fittings are provided with a trap at their outlet which retains sufficient water to prevent smells from the waste pipe or drain (the Victorians' 'drain air') from escaping. W.c.s and yard gullies have a built-in trap that forms an integral part of the appliance. A separate metal or plastic trap is fitted to the waste outlet of sinks, baths, basins and bidets (*Figure 7.2*).

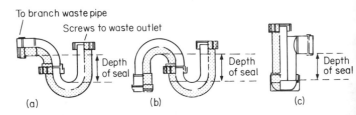

Fig. 7.2. Traps for sinks, basins, baths or bidets. (a) Tubular swivel trap with P outlet. (b) Tubular swivel trap with S outlet. (c) Bottle trap with P outlet

The simplest kind of trap is a U bend, usually made of copper, brass or lead, having an access eye with a screw-in cap fitted into its base. More attractive in appearance is the bottle trap, the whole of the lower part of which can be unscrewed for cleaning or clearance. Traps are described as 'P' traps if they have a more-or-less horizontal outlet and as 'S' traps if they have a vertical outlet. The 'seal' of the trap, that prevents the passage of drain air, is the vertical distance between the outlet of the trap and the upper part of the bend. With the two-pipe system it was usual for traps to have a 1½ in (37 mm) or 2in (50mm) seal. In order to ensure that drain smells cannot pass the trap it is essential that this seal should be maintained at all times.

Loss of seal may occur from momentum—a bucket of water thrown quickly and accurately down a w.c. may go straight through the trap leaving the seal broken—by evaporation, by 'waving out', by self-siphonage, by induced siphonage or by compression. Momentum and evaporation rarely present serious problems. Waving out is also a relatively rare phenomenon though it may be observed at times when a gusty wind is blowing across the top of a soil and vent pipe. The aspirating effect of the wind reduces pressure in the soil pipe and the water level in any w.c. attached to it can be seen to rise and fall with the gusts of wind. This movement creates its own momentum which, in time, can break the seal of the trap.

The connection of a number of appliances to a single drainage stack substantially increases the risks of self and induced siphonage and compression—and the unpleasantness that can result from these phenomena. *Some* self-siphonage occurs when any sanitary appliance is discharged. Water overflowing from the trap of a bath, sink or basin completely fills the waste pipe, taking air with it and producing the partial vacuum that induces siphonic action. This is not too important where baths and sinks are concerned. They have a relatively wide diameter—37mm (1½in)—waste pipe. After the siphon has been broken by air passing under the trap sufficient water will flow from the appliance to remake the seal. Basins are another matter. They have a small diameter—31mm (1¼in)—waste pipe that quickly fills with water as the basin discharges. There is relatively little subsequent drainage of water to recharge the trap.

With a two pipe drainage system temporary loss of seal from the trap of a waste appliance will not have serious consequences. The second line of defence, the seal of the yard gully, will remain intact. Only air from a relatively short length of waste pipe will be able to enter the room. With a one pipe or single stack system the situation is very different. Loss of seal can mean that smells from the main soil pipe, the underground drain and, in all probability, the sewer, can pass into the house.

'Induced siphonage' means siphonage of the water in the trap of one appliance resulting from the discharge of another appliance. Supposing, for instance, that a short length of branch waste pipe from a wash basin is connected to a waste pipe from a bath. The bath waste pipe will fill as the bath empties and water, flowing past the junction between the two waste pipes, will aspirate air from the basin branch. This will produce a partial vacuum within the branch and atmospheric pressure will push the water our of the basin's trap, breaking the seal.

'Compression' can result in a temporary loss of seal. It can also produce some extremely disconcerting results! Suppose that a combined soil and waste pipe connects to the underground drain with a sharp 'knuckle' bend. The discharge of a bath or w.c. may completely fill the pipe at the base of the bend, if only for a few moments. The discharge of another upstairs w.c. at that time will compress the air in the soil pipe

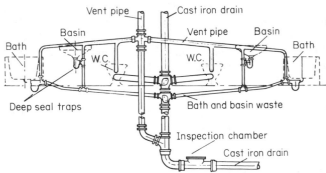

Fig. 7.3. One-pipe drainage system in cast iron

between the point of discharge and the point at which the soil pipe is temporarily obstructed. Air pressure within the pipe can then blow out the water seal of the trap of any appliance —perhaps a sink or a ground floor w.c.—connected to the soil pipe at low level.

Self-siphonage, induced siphonage and compression are prevented from occurring in a properly designed one-pipe system by ventilating the trap of each appliance (*Figure 7.3*). A small diameter vent pipe is taken from a point immediately behind each trap. This is connected to a main vent pipe which may be carried up to terminate open-ended above eaves level or, alternatively, connected to the main soil and vent pipe at a point at least 1m (3ft) above the highest soil or waste connection. Other precautions normally insisted upon in one-pipe drainage were deep seal (75mm or 3in) traps and an easy bend connection between the soil pipe and the underground drain.

A typical one-pipe system installed prior to about 1960 would have been constructed in heavy iron pipe, suitably protected against corrosion, with caulked lead joints. The main soil and waste stack and the main vent pipe would normally have been against an exterior wall though there was a tendency, particularly in good class hotel construction, to situate these pipes in service ducts within the structure of the building. A first class early example of this kind of installation is to be found at the Cumberland Hotel, Marble Arch, London.

The 'single stack' system of above ground drainage is a natural development of the one pipe system. First introduced into this country from the U.S.A. in the years immediately following World War II it was used experimentally, and somewhat hesitantly, for some multi-storey building construction during the 1950s. Two factors that have led to its almost universal adoption for all above-ground drainage work are the development of plastic soil and waste systems and the requirement of the Building Regulations that all soil and waste pipes must be contained within the fabric of the building.

This regulation has led to a revolutionary change in the external appearance of British buildings. Virtually any building constructed before the 1960s will be seen to have its walls festooned with soil and waste (or soil and vent) pipes. The back walls of suburban domestic properties have the down-pipe and hopper head arrangement of the two pipe system (*Figure 7.4a*). In contrast, the only visible evidence of drainage that can be seen on a building erected since the advent of the Building Regulations will be the rainwater guttering and downpipes and a short length of capped plastic vent pipe protruding a few inches above the surface of the roof (*Figure 7.4b*).

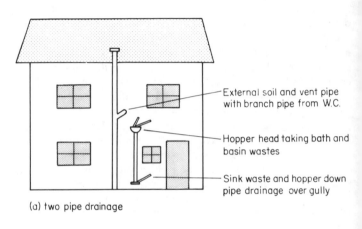

External soil and vent pipe with branch pipe from W.C.

Hopper head taking bath and basin wastes

Sink waste and hopper down pipe drainage over gully

(a) two pipe drainage

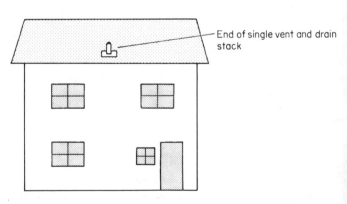

End of single vent and drain stack

(b) single stack drainage

Fig. 7.4. Two-pipe and single stack drainage compared

The essential difference between one-pipe and single-stack drainage is the elimination of trap ventilation. It has been found that, provided proper attention is given to design, the risk of siphonage and compression can be eliminated without the need for an extensive, and expensive, complex of ventilating pipes.

For really successful single stack installation the building should virtually be designed round the plumbing system. Branch waste pipes should be short and laid at minimal falls. This is particularly critical where the wash basin waste is concerned. The maximum length of the wash basin branch waste pipe should be 1.68m. Where a longer branch is unavoidable it is usually necessary to ventilate the trap of the wash basin as with a one-pipe system. A small vent pipe is connected immediately behind the trap and taken upwards to connect to the main soil and waste stack at least 1m (3ft) above the highest connection to it. Possible alternatives might be the use of a patent self-sealing trap or the expedient of taking the outlet of the trap into a 40mm or 50mm diameter waste pipe instead of the 30mm pipe usual for basin wastes.

Deep seal (75mm or 3in) traps should be used for all fittings. The w.c. branch connection should be 'swept' in the direction of flow and there should be an easy bend (minimum radius 200mm for 100mm stack pipes) between the main stack and the underground drain.

Measures must also be taken to ensure that there is no risk of bath, basin or bidet outlets becoming fouled or obstructed by discharges from the w.c. No connection to the main stack should be made for a distance of 200mm (8in) from the centre of the point at which the w.c. branch connects to the main stack (*Figure 7.5a*). This can pose a problem where bath, shower or bidet wastes are concerned. One solution is to offset these wastes so that they connect to the main stack below the level of the floor on which the appliance is situated. This is always inconvenient and can make a considerable addition to the cost of installation. It can be overcome by the use of the Marley collar boss. This fitting permits bath or bidet wastes to be discharged into an annular cavity between the collar and the connection taking the w.c. branch (*Figure 7.5b*).

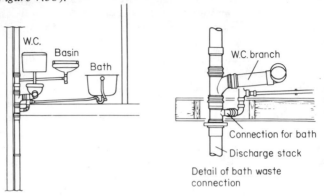

(a) Without Marley collar boss

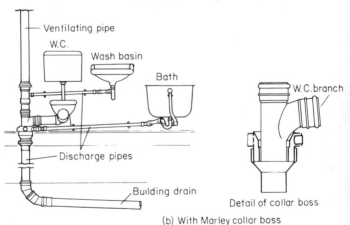

(b) With Marley collar boss

Fig. 7.5. Single stack drainage

Although single stack drainage is now commonly used for all waste drainage from all kinds of building it has few, if any, advantages over two pipe drainage for single storey (bungalow)

420

development. Many designers prefer to limit the use of the single stack to upper floors in two or multistorey buildings.

Ground floor sinks, baths and basins can still discharge by means of short waste pipes over yard gullies. A very sensible provision of the Building Regulations requires that such waste pipes shall discharge above the level of the water in the gully but *below* the grid. This means that yards cannot flood with drainage water as a result of grids becoming blocked with leaves and other debris and also ensures that the full force of the waste pipe discharge is available to cleanse the gully.

Back and side inlet gullies are available to permit easy compliance with this requirement. Alternatively gully grids are available with slots in them through which the waste pipes can be passed.

8 Roof Drainage

Rainwater drainage from roofs is an important aspect of domestic plumbing for the design of which, in the past, rule of thumb methods have always been applied. On the whole rule of thumb methods have proved to be satisfactory.

'A little learning' might suggest that, since rainfall varies tremendously throughout the United Kingdom, gutter sizes and the number of downpipes provided should vary correspondingly. The roof of a house built in the Lake District, for instance, may be expected to receive, during the course of a year, three to four times as much rain as a house built in north-east Essex.

Design of roof drainage does not however depend upon total annual rainfall but upon rainfall intensity—and this varies very little from one part of the country to another. The average intensity recommended as a basis for rain water drainage design is 3in per hour. This has been found to occur, in any given locality, over a period of five minutes about every other year. It will occur over a period of ten minutes only about once in eight years. As an indication of the safety factor that is provided by designing on this basis it may be mentioned that an intensity of rainfall of 4in lasting for five minutes occurs only once in five years, for ten minutes only once in about nineteen years. For roof pitches up to $50°$ the actual area of the roof surface is taken as a basis for calculation. The pitch and the angle at which the rain falls is ignored. At 3in per hour the flow load will be $0.026 \times$ actual roof area in square feet, giving a result in gallons per hour.

Prior to World War I rainwater gutters were almost invariably made of cast iron, painted internally and externally, in either half-round, square or ogee pattern. Downpipes were made of the same material. For a brief period during the post-war years asbestos cement gutters and downpipes enjoyed a certain popularity because, since they needed no painting, they materially cut the cost of house maintenance. They were however rather heavy, clumsy in appearance and subject to accidental damage.

P.V.C. (vinyl) guttering and downspouts are now in standard use for both new and replacement work. The smooth internal surface of p.v.c. gives a better flow. No painting is required either for decoration or for protection against corrosion and the lightness in weight of the material makes for easy installation without the risk of damage to the material or injury to the installer.

The *only* disadvantage of rainwater systems of this material is that p.v.c. guttering does not offer adequate support for a ladder. When access to the roof is required the ladder must be placed against either the fascia board or the wall below it. Although p.v.c. guttering is available in a number of sizes and shapes 100mm (4in) wide, half-round gutter has become the standard choice for general domestic use.

On the basis of the design considerations already set out a gutter of this size, set dead level, will drain a roof having an area of approximately 425 sq. ft. Where the gutter is laid to a fall of 1in in 50ft (note that this is a fall of 1 in 600—not 1 in 50!) the area that can be drained is increased to 600 sq. ft. 68mm (about 2¾in) downpipe is used with 100mm guttering and a downpipe of this size, centrally situated, will cope with the drainage of a roof area of 1200 sq. ft. For all practical purposes this means that 100mm half round guttering draining into one 68mm downpipe will cope with the drainage of the front roofs of a pair of terraced or semi-detached houses and that similar provision will be needed at the back. 100mm guttering with 68mm downpipes at front and back will cope with the roof drainage of all but very large detached houses.

As has been suggested, rainwater guttering can be fixed dead level. However the slight fall of 1in in 50ft improves drainage capacity and guards against the possibility of a slight accidental back-fall—perhaps the commonest cause of overflowing gutters.

All manufacturers of plastic waste and soil drainage systems include roof drainage systems within their range and supply full installation instructions. The details given below relate to the Marley system of 100mm half-round guttering with 68mm down-pipes. The first thing that must be established is the position of the gutter outlet. In a new building this will be decided by design considerations bearing in mind the effect of appearance of the downpipe on the facade of the building. For replacement work the deciding factor will be the position of the existing yard gully. A plumb-line dropped from the fascia board to the centre of this gully will establish the position of the gutter outlet.

Working back from this point with a line at a fall of 1in in 50ft the position of the supporting brackets can be determined (*Figure 8.1*). Brackets must be fitted in close proximity

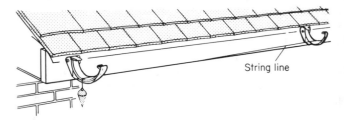

String line

Fig. 8.1. Aligning the gutter brackets

to and on either side of the gutter outlet. They must also be fitted closely to both internal and external angles of the roof (*Figure 8.2*). For straight runs of guttering, brackets should be fitted at 1 metre centres with Marley heavy gauge guttering and at no greater than 900mm centres for the lighter 'System 2' guttering. Brackets should be fixed to the fascia board with 1in × No.8 gauge zinc plated or sherardised round head screws.

Marley 'heavy grade' roof guttering is provided with one socketed end and one notched spigot end. 'System 2' guttering

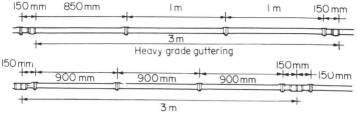

System 2 guttering on straight runs

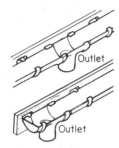

In close proximity to outlets

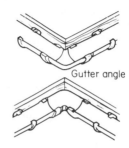

In close proximity to external and internal angles

Fig. 8.2. Position of gutter brackets

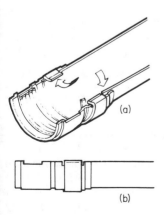

Fig. 8.3. Assembling a Marley gutter joint. To assemble a joint, clip the gutter strap round the gutter socket or the fitting socket between the notches. Turn the end of the gutter into the socket so that the back edge of the strap fits into the notch (a). Press down the front edge of the gutter until it snaps under the front of the strap. This compresses the rubber seal to form a watertight joint. Finally, line up the notches so that the strap is in the centre of the notches (b)

425

has notched spigot ends only and separate Marley gutter joints must be used for connecting lengths of gutter. In both cases however the method of connection is the same.

The flexible plastic gutter strap is clipped round the socket of the gutter or of the separate gutter joint. The spigot of the other length of gutter is then placed in the socket and turned so that the retaining projection of the back edge of the gutter strap fits into the notch of the spigot (*Figure 8.3*). The front edge of the spigot is then eased down into the socket until its notch snaps under the front projection of the gutter strap. This has the effect of compressing the spigot against the prefixed synthetic rubber seal to give a watertight joint.

It will be seen that the notch in the spigot of the gutter is an essential feature of the patent Marley joint. Where it is necessary to cut a length of gutter a similar notch must be made in the cut end. The gutter should be cut absolutely squarely with a fine toothed saw and a notch 40mm wide and 3mm deep made 10mm from the end (*Figure 8.4*). A special notching tool is made for this purpose but it is possible to make the necessary notch with a file.

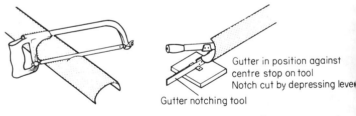

Gutter in position against
centre stop on tool
Notch cut by depressing lever

Gutter notching tool

Fig. 8.4. Cutting and notching a length of gutter. The gutter must be cut perfectly squarely with a fine toothed saw (a). The notch is then cut 40 mm wide, 3 mm deep, 10 mm from the end using a fine toothed saw and a file. A special notching tool can also be used (b)

The first task to be undertaken in connection with the fixing of the downpipe is assembly of the offset. Marley offsets have three components—an offset end socket for connection to the gutter outlet, an offset end for connection to the downpipe and a length of offcut rain water pipe to connect the two (*Figure 8.5*). The offset is made into one unit by means of solvent welding. This technique, which is used for connecting p.v.c. water supply and waste pipes, is described fully in Chapter 12. The instructions set out below relate solely to rain water offsets.

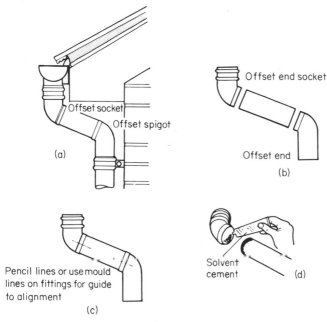

Fig. 8.5. Assembling the offset using solvent welds. The offset (a) can be made up using an offset socket, an offset spigot and an offcut of pipe (b) as follows. (1) Cut the pipe to length and remove all rough edges. (2) Using a dry cloth, clean the outside of pipe ends and the internal surfaces of sockets. (3) Assemble the offset and draw pencil lines to ensure correct alignment (c). (4) Apply a thin layer of solvent cement to the ends of the pipe and inside the sockets (d) and fit sockets and pipe together, ensuring that the pencil marks line up

The offcut length of rain water downpipe must be cut squarely to length and all rough edges removed. Wipe internal surfaces of the solvent weld sockets and the outside of the pipe end perfectly clean with a dry cloth. Next assemble the offset dry and draw a pencil line along pipe and offset ends to ensure correct alignment. Withdraw pipe from offset ends and apply solvent cement evenly round the spigot ends of the offcut and the inside of the offset sockets. Press pipe and offset sockets quickly and firmly together taking care to line up with the pencil guide lines that have already been made. Leave the completed offset for several minutes before fitting into position to ensure that the joints set properly.

Various offset components are available to overcome the problems that may arise from, for instance, a deep fascia or a corbel projection. Rainwater downpipe components are provided with ring seal sockets but the ring seal is not normally inserted in external rainwater work. Since the downpipe should

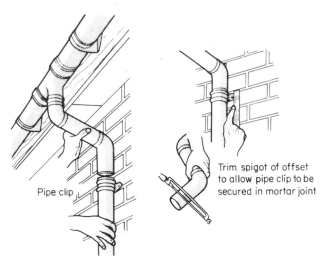

Pipe clip

Trim spigot of offset to allow pipe clip to be secured in mortar joint

Fig. 8.6. Aligning the pipe clip with a mortar joint

never run full a ring seal is normally unnecessary and the absence of such a seal makes it possible to locate quickly any blockage that may occur.

However, where an eaves projects more than 600mm there will be a tendency for the weight of the offset to pull the offset away from the gutter outlet. To counteract this tendency a ring seal should be provided for large eaves projections.

The offset spigot for connection to the rainwater downpipe is 112mm long. This allows for adjustment of the position of the first pipe clip. Offer up the socket of the first downpipe to the spigot of the offset. If the holes of the pipe bracket back plate do not align with a mortar joint, measure the amount of spigot that needs to be cut off in order that the pipe clip can be fixed to the next joint up (*Figure 8.6*).

Two kinds of pipe clip are available. A one-piece clip and a two piece unit in which the plastic strap that supports the pipe socket is bolted to a back plate secured to the wall. In both cases the mortar joint should be drilled and plugged with purpose made fibre or plastic plugs and the back plate—or the clip itself in the case of the one-piece unit—secured to the wall with two 1½in or 1¼in by No.10g zinc plated or sherardised round head steel screws. A clip should be located at the socket of each length of rainwater downpipe and an intermediate clip provided for any length of downpipe exceeding 2 metres. An important point to note is that an expansion gap of 10mm should be left between the end of each pipe and the bottom of the socket into which it is fitted. This is done by inserting the pipe to its fullest extent into the socket, withdrawing 10mm and marking the point to which it has been withdrawn.

Various means of connecting the rainwater downpipe to an underground drainage system are illustrated in *Figure 8.7*. A trapped gully should always be used where the rainwater is disposed of into a sewerage system. Where discharge is into a soakaway or ditch an untrapped connection is permissible.

Ultimate disposal of the rainwater will depend upon the policy of the sewerage authority. In some areas some, or all, rainwater from roofs is permitted to flow into the normal household drainage system and thence to the public sewer. This results in the sewerage authority having to provide unnecessarily large sewers to cope with the surge that occurs at times of intense rainfall. It means too that the sewage arriving at the treatment works will be highly concentrated in times of drought and very dilute during periods of heavy rainfall.

These factors have led many authorities to require separate provision for rainwater drainage. In some areas a separate

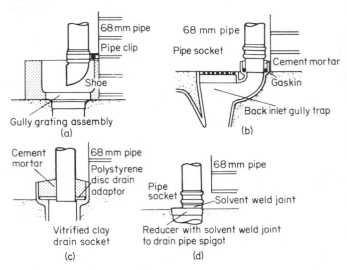

Fig. 8.7. Connecting the rainwater downpipe to the underground drain. (a) With a shoe above the grating of a trapped gully. (b) Joined to the back or side inlet of a gully trap. (c) or (d) Connected direct to the drain with an adaptor

surface water sewer is provided. In these areas it is *very important* that the builder should make the ultimate connection, of both the foul and the surface water drain, to the right sewer. Connection of the foul drain to the surface water sewer can result in untreated sewage flowing into a stream or ditch. In other areas the householder is required to provide a soakaway for the reception of rainwater drainage from roofs.

Typically a soakaway consists of a rectangular pit about 5ft deep and 5ft square in plan. This is filled with brick rubble to within about 1ft of the surface and the top soil is then replaced. The snag about a soakaway of this kind is that, after a few years, the interstices between the rubble will become full of silt and the soakaway will then have to be dug out and remade. This eventuality can be delayed by laying a sheet of polythene over the brick rubble before back-filling with top soil.

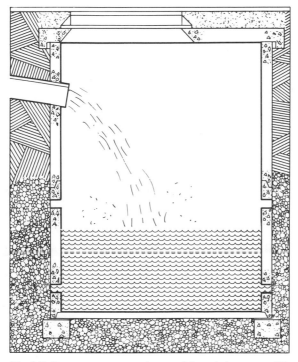

Fig. 8.8. Precast concrete soakaway. Where it is not possible to dispose of surface water by a drainage pipe system it can be done by a system of soakaways, provided that the soil is permeable

There are nowadays precast concrete soakaways available into which rainwater can be discharged (*Figure 8.8*). These resemble cesspools but have holes in the sides from which water can escape into the surrounding soil. A manhole gives access to enable the silt to be dug out when required.

It should perhaps be added that soakaways are rarely very successful except where the soil is light and friable and there is a low subsoil 'water table'. Few soakaways will cope adequately with long periods of continuous, heavy rain.

9 The Underground Drains

The basic principles involved in the design of underground drainage systems have remained virtually unchanged for over half a century. Underground drains must be laid in straight lines, to a constant self-cleansing fall. They must be watertight and must remain watertight even if there should be slight soil settlement. Every point of the drainage system must be accessible for rodding in the event of a blockage occurring.

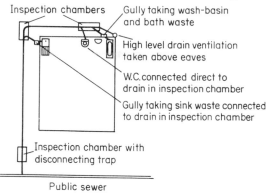

Fig. 9.1. Plan of traditional house drainage

Branch connections must join the main drain obliquely in the direction of flow. The drainage system must be adequately ventilated (*Figure 9.1*). The development of new materials has however resulted in revolutionary changes taking place in the way in which these principles are observed.

Up to about 1950, only two materials were used for underground drainage work—either salt glazed stoneware pipes or heavy iron pipes suitably protected against corrosion. Glazed stoneware pipes were commonly used for domestic drains. They were 4in in internal diameter and 2ft in length, and were usually laid upon a 6in thick 'raft' of concrete to give them some stability in the event of ground settlement (*Figure 9.2*).

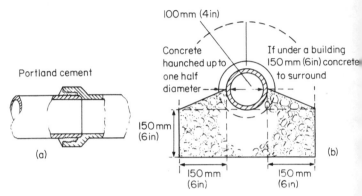

Fig. 9.2. Jointing of stoneware drain pipe (a) and base of a stoneware drain (b)

The multitudinous joints—each a potential point of leakage—were made by caulking a tarred rope grommet into the space between spigot and drain socket and completing the joint with either neat portland cement or a mixture of two parts cement to one of sand. The purpose of the rope grommet was to prevent the jointing material entering the drain to impede free flow and establishing a cause of blockage.

To be absolutely certain that no jointing material had leaked through it was usual to draw a sack through the completed drain by a length of rope. The inspector of the local authority would, before passing the drain for use, check on this point by observation with the aid of a mirror and an electric torch and, perhaps, by rolling a ball through the drain. After the drain was laid it was usual to haunch it over with concrete to increase its strength. Where a stoneware drain

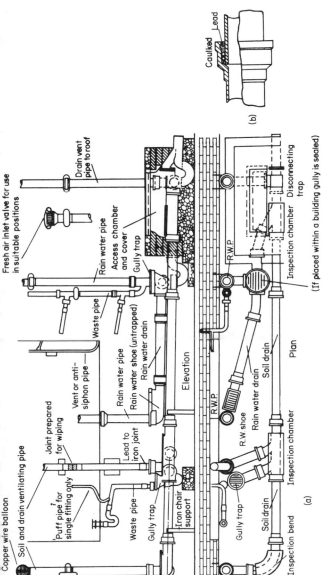

Caulked

Lead

(b)

Drain vent pipe to roof

Fresh air inlet valve for use in suitable positions

Rain water pipe

Access chamber and cover

Gully trap

Waste pipe

Disconnecting trap

R.W.P.

Inspection chamber

(If placed within a building gully is sealed)

Plan

Soil drain

Rain water drain

R.W. shoe

R.W.P.

Inspection chamber

Gully trap

Soil drain

Inspection bend

Vent or anti-siphon pipe

Rain water pipe

Rain water shoe (untrapped)

Rain water drain

Elevation

Copper wire balloon

Soil and drain ventilating pipe

Joint prepared for wiping

Puff pipe for single fitting only

Lead to iron joint

Waste pipe

Gully trap

Iron chair support

(a)

Fig. 9.3. Layout of iron drainage system (a) and jointing of iron pipes (b)

435

passed under a building it was covered entirely by a layer of concrete 6in thick.

Iron drainpipes were considerably more expensive and were used in good class industrial and commercial work (*Figure 9.3*). They were obtainable in 9ft lengths, thus reducing the number of joints. These were made by caulking lead wool into the space between spigot and socket. Iron drains were not required to be laid on a concrete base.

It has been established empirically that drains are self-cleansing when water flows through them at 3ft per second when one third full. A universally adopted rule of thumb allowed for a fall of 1 in 40 (3in in 10ft) for the usual 4in drain and a fall of 1 in 60 for the 6in drains that might be used where a number of houses were drained in combination.

Even with the many-jointed stoneware drains this gave a flow in excess of 3ft per second if the drain were laid to a steady fall and it should perhaps be stressed that too steep a fall is almost as undesirable as a too shallow one. If the fall of the drain is too steep there is a tendency for liquid to flow on in advance of solid matter that may be left behind to form a blockage. However, for most purposes, the 1 in 40 rule worked well enough.

Access to every part of the drain was ensured by the provision of inspection chambers or 'manholes' at every change of direction of the main drain and at every point where a branch drain connected to it. Inspection chambers were constructed of brickwork on a 6in concrete base and it was usual to render the internal surfaces of the inspection chamber walls with a sand and cement mixture. The drain flowed through the inspection chamber in a half-channel built into the base and concrete was haunched up on either side of the half-channel and trowelled to a smooth sand and cement surface. Purpose made 'three quarter bends' could be built into the haunching to permit branches to connect in the direction of flow.

Access to the inspection chamber was obtained by raising a cast iron manhole cover set into a frame of the same material. On the rare occasions that it was necessary to construct an inspection chamber within a building the cover would be 'double sealed' and set into the frame in a bed of grease to prevent gases from the drain escaping.

The inspection chambers of iron drains did not need to be made watertight as special access sections were manufactured with bolted down iron covers. The bolts could be unscrewed and the cover removed when access was required to the drain.

In the final inspection chamber before the connection of the drain to the sewer (usually situated near the front boundary of the property) it was common practice to provide an intercepting or disconnecting trap (*Figure 9.4*). The purpose of this trap was to prevent gases, and perhaps rats, from the sewer from entering the house drains.

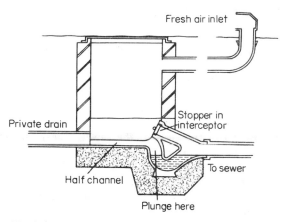

Fig. 9.4. Inspection chamber with intercepting trap and fresh air inlet

The value of the intercepting trap was questioned as early as 1912 by the Departmental Committee on Intercepting Traps and House Drains. A well constructed and maintained sewer should contain neither rats nor offensive gases. If the intercepting trap were omitted the sewer would be ventilated very thoroughly by means of the soil and vent pipe of each individual drainage system. There would be no need for separate sewer ventilators. Furthermore, the intercepting trap was and—where it is installed—still is, the commonest site of drain blockage. The trap inevitably impedes the flow of water and tends to permit solid matter to accumulate in its base. To make intercepting traps rather less liable to blockage they were constructed with a sharp weir inlet and an easy outlet 2in lower than the inlet. For this design to have the desired effect of making the trap more or less self-cleansing it was, of course, essential that it should be set dead level.

Intercepting traps are provided with a rodding arm to permit the clearance of that section of the drain that lies between the trap and the sewer. The rodding arm has a socket inlet closed with a stoneware stopper. This stopper is a common cause of a particularly unpleasant form of partial drain stoppage that can sometimes remain undetected for months.

Any increase of pressure within the sewer—arising from, for instance, a surge of storm water—is liable to push the stopper out of its socket. It will fall into the inlet to the intercepting trap immediately beneath it and will promptly cause a blockage. The blockage will not however be discovered in the usual way because sewage will rise in the inspection chamber until it reaches the level of the, now open, rodding arm and will be able to flow down this arm to the sewer. The liquid in the bottom of the inspection chamber will, in the meantime, become steadily more and more foul until the defect makes itself obvious by the unpleasant smell that greets visitors near the front gate of the property. Complaints of 'drain smells' in front gardens are nearly always attributable to this cause.

Where this trouble has arisen it is usually better *not* to replace the stopper in the socket of the rodding arm. Cut a disc of slate or glass to size and cement it lightly into this socket. On the rare occasions that it may be necessary to rod through to the sewer the glass or slate can be broken with a crow bar and can then be replaced after the blockage has been cleared.

If a drain has an intercepting trap it will usually also be provided with a low level drain ventilator connected to the same inspection chamber. This consists of a length of drain-pipe connected to the inspection chamber and protruding a few inches above ground level. Into the open end is inserted a metal box with a grille at the front. A hinged mica flap is suspended inside the ventilator against this grille. In theory air passing over the top of the open soil and vent pipe would aspirate air out of the drain. The reduction in pressure would result in the outside air pushing open the hinged flap and flowing into and through the drain from low level. In the event of a back pressure within the drain the mica flap would press tightly against the grille and drain air would not escape.

Unfortunately low level ventilators are particularly susceptible to accidental damage and to vandalism. Before long the grille becomes damaged and the mica flap either damaged or jammed in position. A glance into the front gardens of any suburban street developed during the 1920s or 1930s will confirm this. It will, in fact, be found that many householders have removed and sealed off the low level ventilator or 'fresh air inlet' as serving no useful purpose and being a recurring source of unpleasant smells. If the intercepting trap is omitted there is, of course, no need whatsoever for a fresh air inlet.

Modern underground drains are likely to be of p.v.c. or pitch fibre with push-on ring seal joints. Both the drains and the means by which they are joined are sufficiently flexible to absorb slight ground settlement without damage. A concrete base is therefore unnecessary. Proper preparation of the bed on which the drains are to be laid remains important however. Where the subsoil consists of heavy clay or chalk it may be necessary to prepare an imported bed of gravel to form a base. Infilling of the drain trenches must also be undertaken with some care to avoid the risk of accidental damage. Drain gradients may be considerably less than was considered necessary with many-jointed stoneware drains. Falls of 1 in 60 or 1 in 70 are in common use.

Inspection chambers are no less necessary than they were in the past and they may still be built of brickwork in the traditional manner (*Figure 9.5*). They should not however be rendered *internally* with sand and cement to make them watertight. Experience has shown that internal rendering is liable to crack and flake off the walls, causing drain blockages.

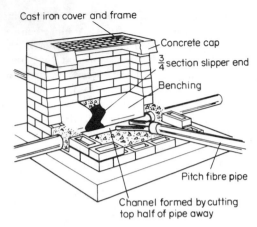

Cast iron cover and frame

Concrete cap

$\frac{3}{4}$ section slipper end

Benching

Pitch fibre pipe

Channel formed by cutting
top half of pipe away

*Fig. 9.5. Pitch fibre drain taken through brick
built inspection chamber*

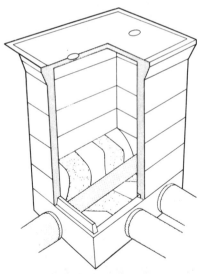

*Fig. 9.6. Pitch fibre drain pipes taken
through sectional concrete inspection
chamber*

If an inspection chamber is to be rendered it should be to the external walls, before the soil is filled in round the chamber.

Complete prefabricated inspection chambers made of fibre-glass reinforced plastic are now available and can speed up installation work. Alternatively inspection chambers can

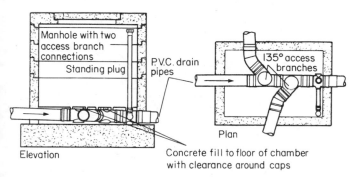

Fig. 9.7. Marley sealed access drainage system. As the drains are sealed inspection chambers need not be watertight. The standing plug allows any ground water to be drained away into the drain

be constructed on the site from precast concrete sections (*Figure 9.6*). Marley Extrusions have now produced a sealed access p.v.c. drainage system resembling in many respects the sealed iron systems referred to earlier in this chapter (*Figure 9.7*).

Blocked drains

Blockages may occur in any part of the drainage system, either above or below ground. Above-ground blockages are most likely to occur in the traps of baths, basins or sinks. The waste stopper is removed and the fitting fails to empty. The immediate course of action should be to try plunging with a sink plunger or 'force cup' (*Figure 9.8*). In the great majority of cases this will produce a speedy remedy.

A force cup is a hemisphere of rubber or plastic usually mounted on the end of a wooden handle. Hold a damp cloth

441

firmly over the overflow outlet of the fitting. Place the force cup over the waste outlet and plunge down forcibly three or four times. Since water cannot be compressed the force of this action is transmitted to the obstruction to move it. The purpose of the damp cloth held over the overflow outlet is to prevent the dissipation of this force.

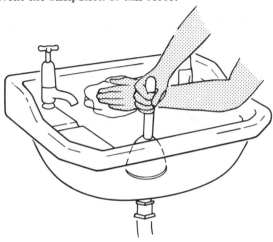

Fig. 9.8. Clearing a blockage in a basin, bath or sink waste with a force cap or sink waste plunger

If plunging fails to clear the blockage gain access to the trap. The traditional U bend trap has an access eye at or near its base from which the stopper can be unscrewed. The entire base of a bottle trap can be unscrewed and removed. Before attempting this place an empty bucket under the trap. Probing with a piece of wire after having gained access to the trap will usually dislodge the cause of the blockage.

A poor flow from a sink, bath or wash basin when the stopper has been removed suggests the presence of a partial blockage. This could be due to hair or other debris clinging to the waste grid. In this case the remedy is obvious. A build-up of grease on the interior surfaces of the waste pipe is another possibility. One of the proprietary chemical drain cleaners can be used to clear this. These chemicals usually have a caustic soda base and should be handled with care.

There are two ways in which a blocked underground drain may come to the attention of the householder. A gully may flood or drainage be seen escaping from under the cover of an inspection chamber; or a w.c., when flushed, may fill almost to the brim with water which will then very slowly subside.

If a flooded gully is the first indication first raise the grid to make sure that the trouble is not due simply to leaves or other obstruction on the grid itself.

Having cleared this point raise the drain inspection covers to establish the position of the blockage. If, for instance, the chamber nearest to the house is flooded but the one near the boundary of the property is clear, then the obstruction must be in the length of drain between these two inspection chambers.

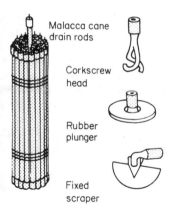

Malacca cane drain rods

Corkscrew head

Rubber plunger

Fixed scraper

Fig. 9.9. A set of drain rods with useful alternative heads

A set of drain rods, or sweeps rods, are necessary to effect a clearance (*Figure 9.9*). Screw two or three drain rods together, plunge one end into the flooded inspection chamber and feel for the half-channel at its base. Push the end of the rod along this half-channel and into the underground drain in the direction of the blockage. Screw on more lengths of drain rod as necessary and continue to thrust into the drain until the obstruction is encountered and cleared.

443

A variety of tools are available that can be screwed onto the end of drain rods to clear difficult obstructions. Twisting the rods will make it easier to push them into the drain and to withdraw them afterwards. Be sure to twist clockwise only. Twisting in the other direction will result in the rods becoming unscrewed and lost in the drain.

If all inspection chambers are flooded and the drain has an intercepting trap, the probability is that it is in this trap that the obstruction is situated. It can be dealt with by plunging. Screw two or three drain rods together and screw a 4in drain plunger onto the end. This is a 4in diameter rubber disc with a screwed socket for connection to drain rods.

Lower the plunger into the inspection chamber containing the intercepting trap. Feel for the half-channel at its base and move along this channel until the drop into the trap is encountered. Plunge down sharply two or three times. The chances are that there will be a gurgle as the obstruction is cleared and water level in the inspection chambers will fall quickly as water flows through freely into the sewer.

In an emergency an old fashioned household mop on a long handle—or even a bundle of rags *securely* tied to a broom stick—can be pressed into service as a drain plunger.

After clearing a drain the sides and benching of the inspection chambers should be washed down with hot soda water, and taps should be left running for half an hour or so to flush out the drain and half channels.

Some legal considerations

House owners should be aware of the fact that their responsibility for their house drains does not end at the boundary of the property. It extends to the public sewer usually situated in the highway.

Blockages and other defects in the length of drain between the property boundary and the sewer are fortunately rare. Remedying them can be very expensive especially when it is necessary to excavate to expose the defective drain. Builders should therefore exercise extreme care in laying this length of drain, in making the actual connection to the sewer and in back-filling.

Other, somewhat complex, considerations arise where (as is very frequently the case) a number of houses are drained in combination (*Figure 9.10*). This obviously saves initial costs.

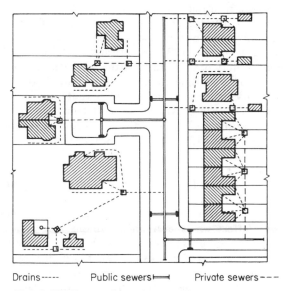

Drains-----   Public sewers ⊨═══⊣   Private sewers ---

Fig. 9.10. Houses drained in combination—drains, private sewers and public sewers. The lengths marked as 'private sewers' in the plan would in fact be 'public sewers' if constructed before 1 October 1937

There is only one deep excavation to the sewer, only one sewer connection and only one reinstatement of the road surface. The difficulty arises when a section of 'combined drain' becomes blocked or otherwise defective and responsibility for remedying the defect has to be determined.

The legal position is that combined drains of this kind, constructed before the coming into effect of the Public Health Act 1936 on 1 October 1937, are 'public sewers'—

but they are public sewers with a difference. The sewerage authority is responsible for any repairs, maintenance or 'cleansing' that may be necessary but can recover the cost of maintenance and repair (but not of 'cleansing') from the owners of the properties concerned. 'Cleansing' is generally taken to include the clearance of blockages and, except in the case of a recurring blockage due to a defect in the 'public sewer' this will usually be undertaken free of charge. Drains serving more than one property that were constructed subsequent to 1 October 1937 are 'private sewers' and are wholly the responsibility of the owners of the properties concerned.

Details of the connection to the private sewer and the responsibility that this entails should be (but rarely are) set out in the deeds of each individual house. It cannot be stressed too strongly that owners of properties connected to such a sewer should establish, with the other owners concerned, responsibility for repair, maintenance and clearance *before trouble actually occurs.*

It is not unusual for as many as ten or twelve properties on a new housing estate to be connected to a single private sewer. A blockage or other defect near to the public sewer may have no visible effect whatsoever on the drainage of properties at the head of this private sewer though their sewage may be flooding the gardens of houses at a lower level. It is far too late to attempt to explain the situation once this has occurred.

When in doubt consult the Environmental Health Officer of the local District or Borough Council. His advice may lack legal authority but is likely to be based on common sense and experience of a score of similar situations.

Rural drainage

Everything so far written in this chapter has assumed the existence of a public sewer to which the house drains will be connected. This is by no means necessarily the case. There are many rural areas where no public sewerage system exists and many isolated houses to which a public sewer can never economically be taken. Such houses, if they are to have a water carriage system of drainage, must be connected either to a cesspool or a septic tank.

Details of the construction of a cesspool or septic tank system are hardly appropriate to a *beginner's* guide to plumbing but it is important that all householders and builders who may be concerned with such installations should be aware of the differences between a cesspool and a septic tank and should be familiar with the principles involved.

A cesspool is simply a watertight underground chamber intended for the reception and storage of sewage until such time as it can be pumped out and disposed of. Cesspools may be constructed of brickwork rendered watertight with sand and cement (*Figure 9.11*), of precast concrete rings set into a concrete base or of fibreglass reinforced plastic (*Figure 9.12*).

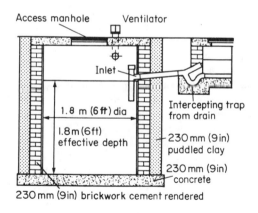

Fig. 9.11. Typical cesspool serving pre-Building Regulations cottage

Capacity may be as little as 500 gallons or may be 4000 gallons or more. The Building Regulations prescribe 4000 gallons as the minimum capacity of a modern cesspool but, of course, the great majority of existing cesspools were constructed long before the Building Regulations came into effect.

Cesspool owners are constantly surprised at the speed with which their cesspools fill and require emptying. A little thought will establish that there is nothing very surprising about this.

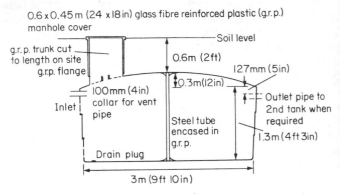

Fig. 9.12. 2000 gallon capacity plastic/glass fibre cesspool (Rokcrete Ltd, Clacton-on-Sea)

It has been estimated that water consumption for all domestic purposes—drinking, cooking and preparation of food, baths, laundry, w.c. flushing and so on—amounts to between 20 and 25 gal per person per day. Taking the lower of these two figures a family of two adults and two children might be expected to use at least 80 gallons of water a day. Every drop of this water passes into the drain, and thence into the cesspool, in one form or another. Such a family could therefore fill a 500 gal cesspool in less than a week and a 1000 gal cesspool (the usual size prior to the Building Regulations) in under a fortnight!

The fact that cesspools do not often require to be emptied *quite* as frequently as this is usually attributable to the fact that few cesspools are wholly watertight. This too however can be a mixed blessing. A cesspool that permits its contents to leak out will permit subsoil water to leak in. A leaky cesspool, in an area where subsoil water level is high, may, during prolonged wet weather, fill up again almost before the Council's cesspool emptier has returned to its depot.

THE UNDERGROUND DRAINS

The prospective purchaser of a property with cesspool drainage should check the capacity of the cesspool and the availability and cost of the local cesspool emptying service. The local authorities of districts in which unsewered properties are situated normally operate a cesspool emptying service. If they do not do so the Council's Environmental Health Department will certainly be able to suggest a local private contractor. These are matters that deserve very careful consideration. Cesspool emptying is, at the best, a smelly and unpleasant operation. It can also prove to be a very expensive one for the householder.

A septic tank system is quite unlike a cesspool in that it offers a permanent solution for the *disposal* of sewage—not merely for its storage. It is, in fact, a small private sewage treatment plant. Small septic tank systems may serve individual houses while larger ones can be used to cope with the sewage of isolated groups of houses. To understand the operation of a septic tank installation it is essential to know something about the chemical and bacteriological processes of decomposition.

In the public mind bacteria or 'germs' are generally thought of as being malign organisms responsible for the spread of disease. In fact the bacteria responsible for disease are the exceptions. The overwhelming majority of the myriads of bacteria with which the world teems are wholly benevolent to other forms of life. Neither vegetable nor animal life could continue without their activities. These activities consist of the breaking down, or decomposition, of dead organic matter into its basic chemical constituents. The action of bacteria breaks down organic matter, first into offensively smelling ammoniacal compounds and then into harmless nitrites and nitrates. The nitrates provide nourishment for plants, some of which become the food of animals—including ourselves. Animals, and of course dead and dying plants, produce dead organic matter which is again broken down into its chemical constituents by bacterial action. This cyclical action is described as the 'nitrogen cycle'. All life on this planet depends upon the continuation of this cycle in which bacteria play a vital role. The purpose of a septic tank installation is to ensure that the bacterial process of decomposition takes place rapidly and under controlled conditions.

The septic tank itself is an underground chamber designed to retain sewage for at least twenty four hours. Sewage enters and leaves by means of dip pipes extending well below the level of the liquid in the tank when full. The surface of the liquid therefore remains undisturbed. A baffle, or system of baffles, may also be provided within the tank to prevent the rapid flow of water from inlet to outlet when, for instance, a bath is discharged. Within the septic tank sewage is liquefied by the action of anaerobic bacteria—bacteria which cannot live in the presence of free oxygen. A scum forms on the surface of the liquid in the tank, retaining the unpleasant smells, and a sludge forms at the base. The sludge must be pumped out from time to time. Twice yearly desludging has been recommended but this is probably a counsel of perfection. It is not unusual for septic tanks to operate satisfactorily for several years without desludging.

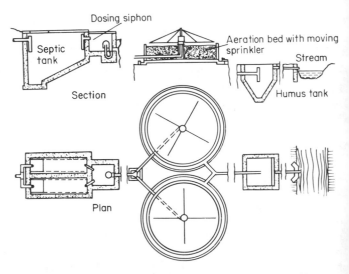

Fig. 9.13. Large septic tank installation suitable for groups of houses

Anaerobic action within the septic tank is only the first part of the bacteriological process of purification. The liquid effluent from the tank must next be submitted to thorough and systematic aeration to encourage aerobic bacteria (bacteria which thrive in the presence of free oxygen) to complete the process. This is usually done by permitting the effluent to percolate through a 'filter' bed of clinker or granite chippings. One cubic yard of filtering or aerating material is required for every forty gallons of estimated daily flow.

Arrangements must be made to ensure that the effluent is distributed evenly over the filter bed. Larger installations will be circular and the effluent will be distributed by means of revolving arms activated by the weight of the liquid leaving the septic tank (*Figure 9.13*). Simpler arrangements are

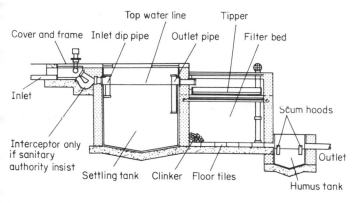

Fig. 9.14. Septic tank and filter system designed by Burn Bros. Ltd

permissible with smaller installations. A tipper device may be used to spill the effluent onto perforated corrugated asbestos sheets, first on one side of the filter and then on the other (*Figure 9.14*). The Gibson-Ingol annular septic tank and filter unit (*Figure 9.15*) has a septic tank, circular in plan, in which

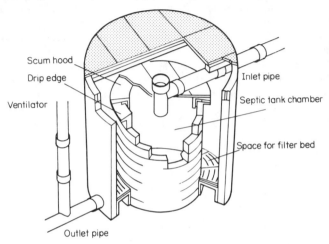

Scum hood

Drip edge

Ventilator

Inlet pipe

Septic tank chamber

Space for filter bed

Outlet pipe

Fig. 9.15. Precast concrete septic tank and filter by Gibson-Ingol Ltd, Preston

the inlet to the tank is at its centre and the effluent spills over onto a circular filter bed provided round the outside wall of the tank. The effluent from the filter can usually be discharged directly into any convenient ditch or stream. With large installations however a further small settlement tank, with baffles, may be provided to trap the small particles of black 'humus' present in the final effluent.

Where there is a light and absorbent subsoil, no sources of water in the vicinity and a sufficient area of land, it may sometimes be possible to dispense with the filter section of the septic tank unit and to dispose of the effluent by subsoil irrigation. Land drains for this purpose should be laid flat, or almost flat, on a 1ft deep bed of clinker or brick-bats. There should be a further 1ft of this material on each side of the pipe line and above it. To reduce the risk of the irrigation system becoming clogged with grit washing down from the soil above it is a good idea to cover the bed of clinker with a polythene sheet before back-filling the trench.

Traditionally, land drain pipes are of earthenware and are laid butt jointed. However perforated pitch fibre or p.v.c. land drainage pipes are obtainable in long lengths and offer a much more satisfactory modern alternative.

It is usual for the effluent from the septic tank to flow directly into the pipes of the irrigation system. This tends to result in the soil in the immediate vicinity of the tank becoming very heavily charged with sewage while little or no effluent reaches the further end of the pipe line. The provision of a final dosing chamber with an automatic siphon

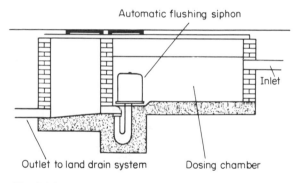

Fig. 9.16. Automatic flushing siphon for effluent disposal by subsoil irrigation

will prevent this (*Figure 9.16*). The level of effluent will rise in the dosing chamber until it reaches the inverted U bend of the siphon. Siphonic action will then take place, emptying the dosing chamber and distributing the effluent throughout the land drainage system. This ensures even distribution of the effluent, prevents the soil in the immediate vicinity of the septic tank from being overloaded and soured and ensures a period of time, after each flush, in which the soil bacteria can act upon the discharged effluent. A properly designed septic tank installation requires little or no maintenance beyond periodic removal of sludge from the septic tank.

Excessive use of disinfectants should be avoided within the home since these will destroy the bacteria upon which septic action depends as well as the germs of disease. For the same reason the salt wash from a mains water softener should not be permitted to flow into a septic tank. Brine has antiseptic qualities.

For a rather different reason the *excessive* use of household detergents should be avoided in a house drained to a septic tank. These tend to emulsify the fats present in sewage. Instead of a scum forming on the top of the septic tank and a sludge at the bottom, the tank will be filled with a liquid of soup-like consistency that will be washed through to clog the filter or land drainage system.

Rain water, whether from roofs or yard surfaces, should of course be rigidly excluded from any cesspool or septic tank drainage system.

10 Hard and Soft Water

Whether a water supply is 'hard' or 'soft' depends upon the nature of its journey from raincloud to the Water Authority's reservoir.

Water has the capacity to take into solution some part of practically any gas or solid matter with which it comes into contact. Even during its brief journey from the clouds to the earth it will take into solution measurable quantities of carbon dioxide and, where it falls over a town, sulphur dioxide and other pollutants of the atmosphere. If it falls onto mountains or moorland it will acquire acid characteristics as it flows, via streams and rivers, to the reservoir. Such water will be soft and will have a tendency towards plumbosolvency—the characteristic of dissolving lead from the surfaces of water pipes.

If, on the other hand, it falls on a chalky soil, or seeps through the various strata of the earth into natural underground storage reservoirs it will dissolve the bicarbonates, sulphates and chlorides of calcium and magnesium from the rock and soil surfaces with which it comes into contact. These are the chemicals that are responsible for hardness in water. Virtually all water supplies in southern England, the south Midlands and East Anglia are hard or very hard. Water supplies in Wales, Scotland and the north of England are predominantly soft though, even in these areas, pockets of hard water supply are to be found.

Hardness is usually expressed in terms of the equivalent of calcium carbonate in the water in parts per million though 'degrees of hardness' on Clark's scale are sometimes used. One degree of hardness on this scale is equal to 14 parts per million or p.p.m. Water containing the equivalent of more than 100 p.p.m. of calcium carbonate is reckoned to be 'moderately hard' and water containing over 200 p.p.m. is 'hard'. Some 65% of the homes in Great Britain are supplied with water that would be classified as hard or moderately hard.

The householder who writes to his Water Authority enquiring about the hardness of the local water supply will probably be given three figures; 'temporary hardness', 'permanent hardness' and the sum of the two, 'total hardness'.

'Temporary hardness' is hardness that can be removed by boiling and is the kind that is most serious from the point of view of the maintenance of water heating systems. It is caused by the bicarbonates of calcium and magnesium whereas 'permanent hardness' (hardness which cannot be removed by boiling) is caused by the dissolved sulphates and chlorides of these chemicals.

When water containing the bicarbonates of calcium and magnesium is heated to temperatures of $70°C$ ($160°F$) and above, carbon dioxide is driven off and the dissolved bicarbonates are changed into insoluble carbonates which are precipitated out as boiler scale or kettle fur. A glance into the inside of any domestic kettle will establish whether or not temporary hardness is a problem in that particular area. If it is, the electric element and the base and sides of the kettle will be coated with creamy white scale. This scale will not have formed only on the inside of the kettle where it can at least be readily seen. It will also be present in the boiler and flow and return pipes of any 'direct' hot water system (see Chapter 3) and adhering to the element of any electric immersion heater.

Scale acts as an insulator and prevents the heat of the boiler fire, or of the electric element, being transferred to the water in the boiler or cylinder. Loss of efficiency is often the first, and frequently unnoticed, indication of a scale build-up. Later, as scale continues to build up, hissing, bubbling and banging sounds will be heard as water is forced through ever-diminishing water channels. Unfortunately, scale does not only insulate the water from the heating effect of the fire or electric element. It also insulates the surface of the boiler, or of the element, from the cooling effect of the circulating water. Eventually the metal of the boiler will burn away until a leak develops or the electric immersion heater will overheat and fail.

Boiler scale, like the fur in the domestic kettle, can be removed by chemical means. The system is partially drained and a descaling chemical introduced into it via the cold water supply pipe to the hot water storage cylinder. After the introduction of the chemical the boiler is lit and the water encouraged to circulate between boiler and cylinder to enable the chemical to act upon the scale accumulation. This treatment must, needless to say, be followed by very thorough flushing.

Permanent hardness does not affect hot water systems in this way but it has other harmful effects. Both forms of hardness prevent soap from dissolving and lathering properly in water. Insoluble, sticky deposits of lime soap or scum are formed that leave dirty 'tide marks' round baths and wash basins, matt woollens and damage other clothing washed in the water. Evaporation of hard water leaves the chemicals of both permanent and temporary hardness behind to produce marks below the taps of baths, jammed ball-valves and clogged up shower sprinklers.

Treatment of hardness and its effects will depend upon the particular aspect of the effect of hardness that is causing concern in individual circumstances. If, for instance, the main concern is the protection of boilers and immersion heaters from scale there are a number of mechanical measures that can be taken.

(a) Check the setting of the thermostat of the immersion heater. In soft water areas it is usual to set the thermostat at $70°C (160°F)$. In hard water areas the setting should be $60°C (140°F)$. It is only when the temperature of water rises above $60°C$, which is quite hot enough for domestic purposes, that scale begins to form.

(b) Endeavour to control boiler temperatures so that the water does not rise above 60°C. This should be practicable where gas or oil are used though solid fuel boilers are less easily controllable. A dial thermometer clamped to the boiler flow pipe will permit the water temperature to be noted.

Never allow the water in a domestic 'boiler' to boil.

(c) Convert a 'direct' hot water system to 'indirect' as suggested in Chapter 3. The water in the primary circuit of an indirect is used over and over again, only the minute losses from evaporation being made up from the feed and expansion tank.

Any given volume of water contains only a given quantity of scale producing chemicals. The scale from these chemicals is deposited when the system is first heated and after that no more scale can form.

Some scale may still form in the hot water storage cylinder. This is however of less importance as it will not impede circulation.

There is also a chemical means by which, without actually softening the water supply, scale formation can be prevented. Certain phosphates of sodium and calcium (sold commercially as Micromet), when released in minute quantities into a hard water supply, stabilise the chemicals of temporary hardness so that they do not precipitate out as scale when the water is heated.

Micromet is prepared in crystalline form. The usual method of introduction into a hot water system is to suspend the crystals, in a purpose made plastic basket, inside the cold water storage cistern, as close as possible to the ball-valve inlet (*Figure 10.1a*). The crystals will slowly dissolve and (for the average household) need to be renewed at six monthly intervals.

Micromet can also be used for the threshold treatment of water passing, direct from the main, to instantaneous gas or electric water heaters. A special container, filled with the crystals, is introduced into the pipe-line leading to the

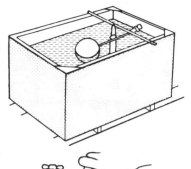

Fig. 10.1. Using Micromet to prevent scale formation: (a) by introducing it into the cold water storage cistern and (b) with a dispenser plumbed into the cold water supply pipe

1. Turn off water at main stop-cock. Fit 6 in (150 mm) of pipe to each side of dispenser head using compression joints and adaptors. Fit a stop valve to the outlet side of the head

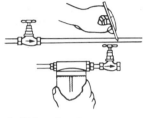

2. Using the dispenser as a guide, mark and cut the pipe. Remove the cut piece of pipe by undoing the stop-cock coupling

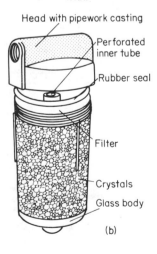

Head with pipework casting

Perforated inner tube

Rubber seal

Filter

Crystals

Glass body

(b)

3. Place the dispenser in position and secure with compression joints. With both cocks still closed, unscrew the dispenser body, fill with crystals and replace. Turn on both stop-cocks and check for leaks

appliance (*Figure 10.1b*). It is, of course, essential to provide a stop-cock on either side of the Micromet container to enable the crystals to be renewed when required. Micromet, it must be stressed, does not *soften* water. Its purpose is to stabilise the chemicals that cause hardness and to prevent them from precipitating out as boiler scale when the water is heated.

Any domestic water supply can be softened completely—reduced to zero hardness—by the installation of a base exchange or, as they tend to be called nowadays, an ion exchange water softener. Water softeners of this kind are usually plumbed into the rising main so that every drop of water flowing into

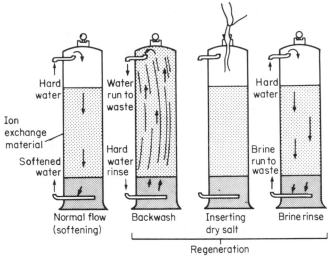

Fig. 10.2. The cycle of regeneration

the house is softened. Synthetic sodium compounds are used in modern base exchange water softeners but the principle was discovered by observing the way in which water could be softened by passage through a bed of natural zeolite sand.

460

The hard water chemicals 'exchange bases' with the water softening material. Calcium and magnesium are left in the softening material and *sodium* bicarbonate, which does not cause hardness, is to be found in small quantities in the water flowing out of the softener. After a period of time the water softening chemical becomes exhausted but can readily be reactivated by passing a solution of sodium chloride (common salt) through it (*Figure 10.2*). Complaints about mains water

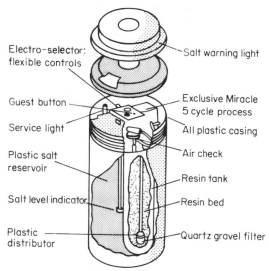

Fig. 10.3. Modern 'Sofnol Satum' automatic mains water softener

softeners usually relate to corrosion from frequent contact with salt water and to the rather tedious weekly task of reactivating the appliance with salt. Modern softeners overcome both of these objections. The body of the appliance is made of corrosion free plastic and the softener reactivates itself automatically from a large salt container at the prompting of a clock control (*Figure 10.3*).

Mains water softeners are somewhat expensive appliances and take up what may be considered to be an unacceptable amount of space in a compact modern home. They may too, be considered to be somewhat wasteful since they soften every drop of water passing into the home including, for instance, that used for w.c. flushing where soft water offers no advantage. Nor is soft water wholly without disadvantages. Many people consider that tea made with soft water is less palatable than that made with hard. Then too, a statistical relationship has been established between soft water supplies and the incidence of cardiovascular disease.

No-one really knows the reason for this. It *could* be that the chemicals responsible for hardness form a part of the body's natural defence mechanism against disease of this kind. It is more likely though that soft water's capacity to take into solution iron, copper or lead from the pipes through which it passes may be responsible. The first two of these metals are harmless enough if taken into the body in the tiny quantities likely to be found in a water supply.

Lead, on the other hand, is a dangerous and cumulative poison. Amounts well in excess of those considered to be acceptable have been found to be dissolved in water (in soft water areas) passing through lead pipes, particularly where water has stood in the pipes overnight. This need not deter the householder from installing a mains water softener or the water engineer from advising installation. Lead pipes are rarely, if ever, used in modern plumbing work. Where a water softener is installed into the lead pipework of an existing plumbing system it is probable that the internal surfaces of the pipes will have acquired an eggshell coating of scale that will prevent the lead going into solution.

To be absolutely safe there is perhaps something to be said for installing the mains softener into the rising main *after* the branch to the kitchen sink cold tap has been teed off. This will mean that softened water will be available for washing purposes and for the hot water system but will not be used for cooking and drinking. If a house has a naturally soft water supply the householder might be well advised to run off, every morning, the few pints of water that have been standing in the pipes overnight. Hot water dissolves metals more readily than cold. One should never be tempted, particularly first thing in the morning, to fill a kettle to make tea from the hot tap.

As well ?` the large mains base exchange water softeners already mentioned there are available small, portable softeners which can be used to supply limited quantities of softened water for hair washing, laundry purposes and so on (*Figure 10.4*). These small softeners operate on the base exchange

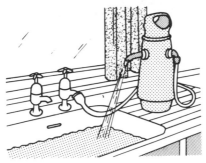

Fig. 10.4. Small portable water softener. This is coupled to the hot-water tap by a rubber hose and refilled with common salt after every 150 gallons of water

principle. They have a hose inlet with a connector suitable for pushing on to any domestic tap. A salt cap at the top of the appliance can be unscrewed to permit salt to be added for regeneration when required.

Small quantities of water can also be softened by the addition of chemicals to the water after it has been drawn off. Most of these chemicals, which are used (among other things) as bath salts, are based on washing soda. They have the effect of causing the chemicals causing hardness to become insoluble, precipitating out and leaving softened water behind. Disadvantages of these chemicals include the fact that the precipitate may harm clothing and the alkaline nature of the softened water can cause some dyes to run and may irritate sensitive skins.

Another chemical water softener, sodium hexametaphosphate (sold commercially as Calgon) works in a rather different way. This is a fine white powder, used straight from the packet, which when added to a hard water, links up with the chemicals causing hardness and neutralises them, so that they do not prevent soap from dissolving.

Calgon does not form a precipitate. Nor does it make the water alkaline. It can be used with confidence for laundry purposes, hair washing, washing and shaving—in fact for softening, for any purpose, any relatively small quantity of hard water.

11 Frost Precautions

Under normal atmospheric pressure water freezes and turns into ice at $0°C$ ($32°F$). As it freezes it expands, increasing its volume by between 9 and 10%. These two facts explain the importance of adequate frost protection in plumbing installation.

Great Britain usually enjoys relatively mild winters. Even so, there are few years in which air temperatures do not fall below $0°C$ on at least some occasions. It does not require a very long memory to recall winters during which sub-zero temperatures and bitter north-easterly winds were maintained for days or weeks at a time.

Because a really hard winter is something of a rarity installers and householders tend to regard frost protection rather casually. Thus, when a prolonged freezing spell does occur, thousands of homes are without water and the thaw brings flooding from a thousand burst pipes. To many people frost protection simply means efficient lagging. Yet intelligent design and installation can do far more to prevent freeze-ups and burst pipes than any amount of lagging.

Some aspects of frost resistant plumbing design have been referred to briefly in earlier chapters. Frost rarely penetrates deeper than about 2ft into the soil in this country. The service pipe bringing water supply into the house from the main should therefore be at least 0.82m (2ft 6in) underground *throughout its length*. The last three words are stressed because it is by no means unknown for an enthusiastic landscape gardener to reduce the effective depth of the service pipe to 1ft 6in or less by constructing a sunken garden or sunken lawn above it.

If the service pipe rises into the house via an open sub-floor exposed to draughts from air-bricks, it should be threaded through the centre of a 6in (150mm) length of drainpipe packed with vermiculite chips. The service pipe or rising main should preferably rise up into the roof space via an internal wall. Where this cannot, or has not, been arranged this pipe should be thoroughly protected from the cold external wall.

Interposing a ½in (12mm) wooden slat between the pipe and the external wall would probably be sufficient protection so far as frost precautions alone are concerned but problems would then arise from the condensation of moisture from the warm, damp air of the kitchen onto this pipe. It is therefore better to protect the pipe both from frost and condensation by thorough lagging (*Figure 11.1*). Use an inorganic lagging material and make sure that it extends behind the pipe so as

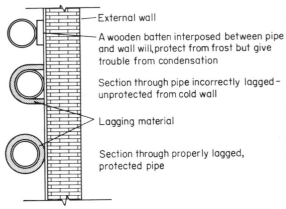

Fig. 11.1. Protecting water pipes against frost

to protect it from the cold wall. Foam plastic pipe lagging units, such as Armstrong 'Armaflex', are suitable for this purpose. New pipework can be threaded through these units as it is installed. Armaflex can also be used to protect existing pipework by slitting it and snapping it over the pipes (*Figure 11.2*).

FROST PRECAUTIONS

It is best if the rising main can enter the roof space as far as possible from the eaves. If it rises against an outside wall it will enter the roof space in the immediate vicinity of the eaves where it will be exposed to draughts and inaccessible for thorough lagging and, if necessary, for thawing out.

Flexible foam plastic lagging is made to fit any pipe up to 3 in (75 mm) dia and is sold in 3 ft (914 mm) and 6 ft (1.8 m) lengths. It can be cut with sharp scissors. The lagging is fixed with waterproof plastic adhesive tape

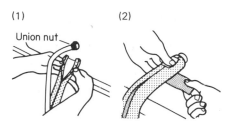

1. Starting at the tank, open the lagging and place it round the pipe and nut touching the tank wall. 2. Ensure that the edges are touching round the pipe and wrap adhesive tape round to secure the lagging

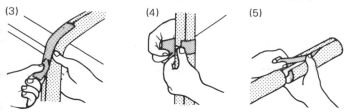

3. At the bends make sure the edges touch and seal lengthways with adhesive tape. 4. At joins in the lagging wrap adhesive tape overlapping both pieces of lagging so that there is no gap. 5. The final piece of lagging must be cut to fit exactly between the last piece and the wall. Use tape at the join and at the wall

Fig. 11.2. Lagging water pipes with foamed plastic

The roof space is a particularly vulnerable area so far as frost damage is concerned and plumbing installations in this area in a modern home with a conscientious and intelligent occupier may be at even greater risk than those in an older house with an occupier of a different kind.

In a modern home the bedroom ceilings will be insulated against heat loss by means of a fibreglass quilt or loose fill insulating material. The rooms below will be warmer but the roof space will be that much colder. There will be no escape of warmth from the rooms below to give the plumbing installation that little extra measure of protection during icy weather.

The roof space therefore demands special attention. The lengths of service pipe and distributing pipes within this area should be kept as short as possible and should be particularly thoroughly lagged. The bodies of ball-valves, gate valves and any other control valves should not be overlooked. These too should be thoroughly lagged so that only the handles or heads protrude from the lagging. Do not omit to lag the vent pipe of the hot water system. It will be filled with water to the same level as that of the water in the storage cistern.

The means of protecting the cold water storage cistern from both frost and contamination have been discussed in Chapter 2. If the house has a solid fuel boiler for a hot water or central heating system the storage cistern is best situated against the flue serving this boiler. Ideally, the boiler, hot water storage cylinder and cold water storage cistern should be arranged in a vertical column so that there will be a continuous flow of warm air upwards towards the vulnerable cistern. Prevent cold draughts from entering the roof space via the overflow or warning pipe by turning the internal end over, as suggested in Chapter 2, so that it dips an inch or so below water level when the cistern is full.

In a modern, effectively heated and thermally insulated home, no special precautions need to be taken for the protection of water distribution pipes below the level of the roof space. They should be kept away from external walls or, where this unavoidable, thoroughly lagged.

It is largely as a frost protection measure that the Building Regulations require waste and soil pipes to be contained within the fabric of the building. Where a house has external waste and soil pipes the important point to remember is that an empty pipe cannot freeze. Every householder's routine autumn frost precautions should include the renewal of the washers of any taps showing a tendency to drip. A waste pipe, dripping all night into an exposed hopper head, can produce a hopper head and down-pipe choked solid with ice on the morning following a night of severe frost.

Lagging, however thorough and efficient, cannot *add* heat to the plumbing system. It can only reduce the rate of heat loss. Careful positioning of the storage cistern above the hot water cylinder can actually add heat to the system. This too can be done in other ways. Lagging units incorporating a low power electric heating cable can be bound round vulnerable pipes and switched on when severe frost threatens. It may be possible to protect the flushing cistern of an external w.c. by thoroughly draught proofing the compartment and then, by means of an extension lead plugged into the electric light socket, suspending a 60 watt electric light bulb outside the cistern a few inches below the ball valve inlet (*Figure 11.3*).

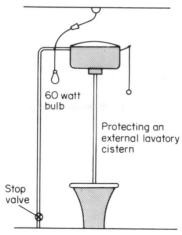

60 watt
bulb

Protecting an
external lavatory
cistern

Stop
valve

Fig. 11.3 Protecting an external lavatory cistern

Under more or less draught free conditions the heat generated by a bulb of this kind will be sufficient to afford protection from quite a severe degree of frost.

The fact that lagging does no more than reduce the rate of heat loss must be borne in mind when a house is unoccupied for more than a few days during severe winter weather. Continued occupation of a dwelling and continued use of its plumbing system are, in themselves, important safeguards against frost damage. The interior of the house is maintained at temperatures well above freezing point and this warmth is transmitted to the water pipes contained within it. Water enters the house from the main at a temperature a few degrees above freezing point. In the roof space it may begin to cool down but, before it can reach danger level, it is drawn off through the taps or flushing cisterns and replaced by marginally warmer water from the main.

The fabric of an empty, unheated house quickly chills off. Water stagnates in the supply and distributing pipes and in the storage cisterns. During a prolonged spell of freezing weather—no matter how thoroughly the pipes are lagged—an ice plug will eventually form and spread through the system. Unless you protect the plumbing system before departing on, say, a winter ski-ing holiday, you may well return to find it frozen and in a thoroughly dangerous condition.

The steps to be taken depend largely upon the nature of the domestic hot water and space heating system, but in every case it is wise to turn off the main stop-cock and to drain the rising main and the cold water storage cistern from the kitchen and bathroom taps. This, of course, will not empty the hot water storage cylinder, the boiler and flow and return pipes, or any central heating system that may be installed.

If you have a 'direct' cylinder hot water system (Chapter 3), drain the system completely. Let out the boiler and turn off the immersion heater. Then connect one end of a length of garden hose to the draincock beside the boiler or, if your cylinder is heated by an immersion heater only, at the base of the cold supply pipe to the cylinder. Take the other end to an outside gully, open up the drain-cocks and leave to drain. After draining leave a large and conspicuous notice on the boiler and beside the immersion heater switch to remind you that the system has been drained and that the boiler should on no account be lit or the heater switched on before it has been refilled with water.

FROST PRECAUTIONS

Refilling after drainage can produce troubles from air-locks. Leave all taps open until water starts to flow through them. It is often helpful to refill by connecting one end of your garden hose to the cold tap over the kitchen sink and the other end to the boiler draincock. Open up the tap and draincock, and the system will fill *upwards,* driving air in front of the rising water.

Central heating systems and the primary circuits of indirect hot water systems (Chapter 3) should *not* be drained. Particularly in central heating systems, water drying on the internal surfaces of radiators, valves and the circulating pump could result in serious damage from corrosion. With a modern gas central heating system the best course is to leave it switched on under the control of a 'frost stat'. This is a thermostatic device (usually positioned in the garage or the roof space) that will bring the system into operation when air temperature falls to a predetermined level.

Systems that do not lend themselves to this degree of control may be protected by the introduction of a suitable antifreeze solution into the feed and expansion tank. Automobile antifreeze should not be used. The manufacturers of Fernox corrosion-proofing products (Industrial Anticorrosion

Fig. 11.4. Rubber tube with stoppered end passed through w.c. trap

Services Ltd, High Street, Waltham Cross, Herts) manufacture suitable antifreeze solutions and will be pleased to advise. Don't leave the introduction of antifreeze solution until the last moment before you leave. It must have time to circulate through the system.

Do not omit to flush the w.c. cistern or cisterns before leaving the house. Water in w.c. traps and other traps must not, of course, be drained off. Throwing a handful of salt into the water in the traps will generally afford adequate protection. A more positive means of protection for the vulnerable w.c. trap is to fix a stopper into the end of a length of rubber tubing and pass the stoppered end into and round the w.c. trap (*Figure 11.4*). If the water in the trap freezes and expands the expansion will then be accommodated by the rubber tubing.

If a freeze-up occurs

The first indication that water has frozen in the plumbing system of an occupied house will be the failure of water to flow from one or more of the taps or into the w.c. flushing cistern.

At first the ice plug will be a small one, easily dealt with. Action should be taken quickly to prevent stagnation of cold water in the pipe affected and the inevitable growth of the plug.

Identify, as accurately as possible, the point at which the blockage has taken place. If, for instance, water is flowing freely from the cold tap over the kitchen sink but is not flowing into the cold water storage cistern, the ice plug will be in the rising main, probably within the roof space.

Strip off the lagging and apply cloths, wrung out in hot water, or a hot water bottle, to this pipe. Modern copper tubing is a good conductor of heat and application of heat in the way suggested will thaw a small ice plug several feet from the point of application. An electric hair dryer, or even a vacuum cleaner operating in reverse, can prove useful in directing a stream of warm air to an otherwise inaccessible pipe.

Dealing with a burst pipe

The idea persists that pipes burst with the thaw. This is, of course, incorrect. Pipes burst when they freeze, but the burst only becomes evident when the ice thaws and water can flow again.

FROST PRECAUTIONS

The first indication of a burst is usually water dripping from a ceiling or into an airing cupboard. Rapid and intelligent action by the householder immediately this occurs can limit the damage and save furniture and furnishings from being spoiled.

Immediately the householder should turn off the main stop-cock and open up all the taps in the house. This will cut off the water supply to the house and drain the storage cistern. There is no need to put out the boiler fire though it might be wise to keep it as low as possible. The hot water storage cylinder will still be full of water. Only after taking this action should the householder seek out the point at which the burst has occurred and consider the remedy.

If the house has copper plumbing joined with compression or soldered capillary joints, the chances are that the 'burst' will merely be the result of one of these joints having pulled apart. The joint can be remade simply and easily as described in the next chapter.

Copper tubing may sometimes split under internal pressure from expanding ice. A burst in a lead pipe will almost certainly take the form of a split. It must be mentioned that householders are sometimes led into a state of false security by the fact that a lead pipe may have frozen on a number of occasions and has never burst. Each time the pipe has frozen the ice plug, on expanding, will have increased the bore of the pipe—and reduced the thickness of the pipe walls. Since lead lacks elasticity the pipe will not resume its former dimensions on thawing out. This process may be repeated several times before internal pressure finally splits the pipe wall.

The remedy in the case of a split pipe is to cut out the damaged section of the pipe and replace it with a new length. If the pipe is of lead the new length will be connected to the old by means of two wiped soldered joints. The technique of making a joint of this kind is described in the next chapter but it does require considerable practice and will certainly be beyond the capacity of an inexperienced householder in an emergency. Professional help should be obtained.

However a temporary repair can be made with the use of

one of the epoxy resin fillers such as Isopon or Plastic Padding. The edges of the split should be knocked together and the area thoroughly dried and cleaned with abrasive paper. The filler is then made up according to the manufacturer's instructions and buttered round the area of the split. Before setting a length of fibreglass bandage is bound round the area affected and a further layer of filler applied to the fibreglass bandage.

Boiler explosion and cylinder collapse

Any period of prolonged severe weather produces at least one report in the national press of fatalities from a boiler explosion. This creates a great deal of anxiety among householders, particularly the elderly who will sometimes take the

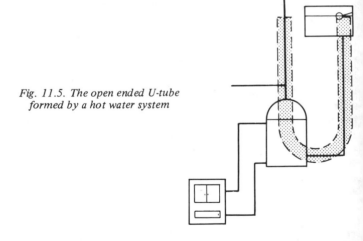

Fig. 11.5. The open ended U-tube formed by a hot water system

'precaution' of letting the boiler fire out during frosty weather —the worst possible course of action under the circumstances. Boiler explosions are, happily, extremely rare. It is, after all, 'the exception that makes the news', as any journalist will confirm. When they *do* occur their results can be catastrophic.

FROST PRECAUTIONS

An understanding of their cause should do a great deal to allay totally unnecessary anxiety.

A cylinder storage hot water system, whether direct or indirect, resembles a U tube, with two open ends—a larger version of the kind of U tube found in every school physics or chemistry laboratory. The two ends, open to the atmosphere, are the vent pipe and the cold water storage cistern (*Figure 11.5*). Provided either one of these ends remains open and unobstructed, no boiler explosion can take place. A spring loaded safety valve, situated close to the boiler in most hot water and central heating systems, provides a final line of defence.

Typically, boiler explosions take place when a family has been absent from home during a prolonged cold spell, without

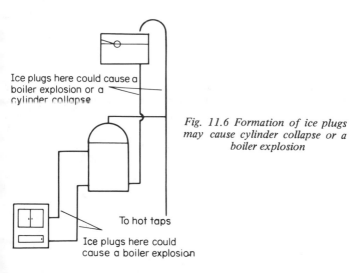

Ice plugs here could cause a boiler explosion or a cylinder collapse

To hot taps

Ice plugs here could cause a boiler explosion

Fig. 11.6 Formation of ice plugs may cause cylinder collapse or a boiler explosion

taking the precautions suggested earlier in this chapter. Ice plugs have formed in the flow and return pipes between boiler and cylinder or in the upper part of the vent pipe and the upper part of the cold water supply pipe to the cylinder

(*Figure 11.6*). The boiler fire is lit but, of course, the water in the boiler can neither circulate nor expand upon heating.

Boiling depends upon temperature and pressure. The temperature of the water in the boiler rises to above $100°C$ but the water cannot, because it is confined within the boiler, turn to steam. Pressure increases until, ultimately, something gives. In an instant the superheated water in the boiler is converted to steam, occupying thousands of times more space than the equivalent volume of water. The system explodes like a bomb with catastrophic results.

Cylinder implosion or collapse is rather more common. It can occur where pipework in the roof space is inadequately lagged and where the householder, perhaps through fear of a boiler explosion, has let the boiler fire out at night during icy weather. A small ice plug forms in the vent pipe and in the upper part of the cold supply pipe to the hot water cylinder. Meanwhile the water stored in the cylinder, originally hot, cools—and contracts.

Copper hot water cylinders are constructed to withstand considerable internal pressure but very little external pressure. As the cooling water contracts a partial vacuum is created within the cylinder and it collapses like a paper bag under the weight of the atmosphere. Typically, cylinder implosion occurs first thing in the morning when the householder turns on the hot tap to draw off some water. The additional loss of water proves to be the final straw that breaks the camel's back.

The best safeguards against boiler explosion, cylinder collapse and, indeed, all troubles arising from frost, are intelligent lagging, particularly in the roof space, keeping the boiler fire alight and the house warm during frosty weather and taking the precautions suggested earlier in this chapter if the house is left unoccupied for more than a few days during a period when icy weather might reasonably be expected.

12 Materials and Methods

Many plumbing textbooks begin with a study of the materials used by the plumber and the means by which pipes and fittings of these materials are joined together. It is the author's opinion that, for the beginner at any rate, this is the wrong approach. The student of plumbing, whether he hopes to become a professional plumber or is 'merely' an intelligent householder, first needs to familiarise himself with the principles of water supply and drainage. Only when he has thoroughly mastered these principles should he attempt the practice by which they are put into effect.

Plumbing practice, so far as it relates to domestic water supply and drainage, consists of the means of manipulating pipework of different materials and connecting these pipes to others of the same or different material or to plumbing fittings such as taps, ball valves, cisterns and cylinders.

Materials used in plumbing installations today include copper and its alloys, stainless steel, galvanised steel and iron, lead and its alloys, pitch-fibre and a variety of plastics.

Copper

Copper is one of the most versatile and easily handled modern plumbing materials. It is used for water supply pipes, hot water storage cylinders and for waste drainage. Alloys of copper, brass and gunmetal are used for the manufacture of taps, stop-valves, ball-valves and indeed, all plumbing joints and fittings.

Copper tubing used for domestic water supply and central heating is supplied in 'half hard' and 'dead soft' temper. Half hard temper tubing is obtainable in straight lengths and is the kind generally used for above-ground water services. Dead soft temper copper tubing is sold in long coils and is particularly useful for underground service pipes where joints, potential points of leakage, are undesirable. Dead soft copper tubing is also used in microbore central heating as it can easily be threaded through and under floorboards to make for un-obtrusive installation.

The commonest means of jointing copper tubing for domestic water supply and waste drainage are by the use of non-manipulative (Type 'A') compression joints, manipulative (Type 'B') compression joints or by means of soldered capillary joints. All these joints are easily made with a minimal tool kit and are suitable for both professional and amateur use.

Joints and fittings for use with copper tubing may be made either of brass (an alloy of copper and zinc) or of gunmetal (an alloy of copper and tin). Joints and fittings of the latter material are recommended in areas where the water supply has corrosive characteristics and the phenomenon known as 'dezincification' is liable to occur. Dezincification is a form of electrolytic corrosion which results in the zinc of the brass alloy dissolving away to produce a fitting, unchanged in external appearance, but totally without structural strength.

Non-manipulative (Type A) compression joints and fittings

These provide the simplest, though not the least expensive, means of joining copper tubing and connecting to it fittings such as stop-cocks, taps and ball-valves.

A Type A compression joint comprises a joint body, a cap nut and a soft copper ring or 'olive' (*Figures 12.1* and *12.2*). To connect a compression joint to one end of a length of copper tubing the procedure is as follows (*Figure 12.3*).

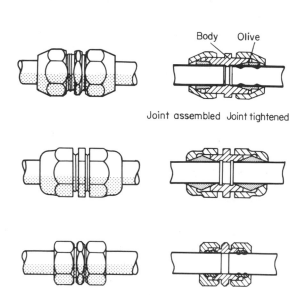

Joint assembled   Joint tightened

Joint assembled   Joint tightened

Fig. 12.1. Non-manipulative (Type A) compression couplings

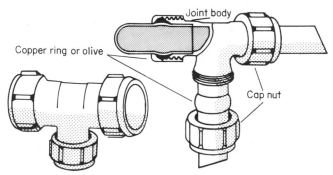

Fig. 12.2. A Conex Type A compression tee joint

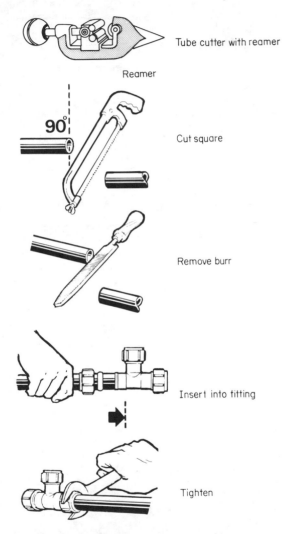

Tube cutter with reamer

Reamer

90°

Cut square

Remove burr

Insert into fitting

Tighten

Fig. 12.3. Making a Conex compression joint

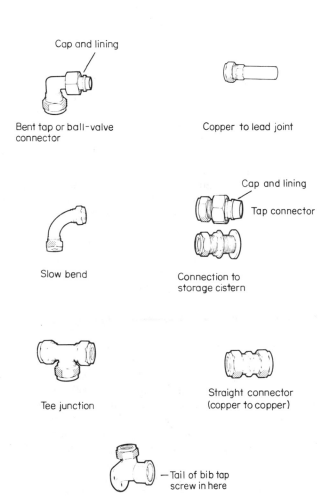

Cap and lining

Bent tap or ball-valve connector

Copper to lead joint

Slow bend

Cap and lining

Tap connector

Connection to storage cistern

Tee junction

Straight connector (copper to copper)

—Tail of bib tap screw in here

Wall plate elbow for outside tap

Fig. 12.4. Some Prestex compression fittings

Cut the tube end square and remove all trace of internal and external burr. This operation can be done with a hacksaw and a file but, where a number of joints are to be made, the use of a wheel tube cutter, preferably incorporating a reamer to remove internal burr, will save time and ensure a squarely cut end every time.

Some manufacturers recommend that, in order to make the joint, the cap nut, followed by the olive, should be slipped separately over the pipe and this end thrust into the body of the joint as far as the pipe stop. Others say that there is no need to dismantle their joints before making them. Simply loosen the cap nut and push the tube end home. In either case the tube end must be pushed in to the pipe stop and the cap nut tightened. This action compresses the olive against the outer wall of the tube to make a watertight joint.

Tighten with the fingers and complete the tightening process with a spanner. Provided that a spanner, rather than a wrench, is used, it is virtually impossible to overtighten. Most professional plumbers smear a little boss white or other waterproofing compound over the tube end and the interior of the compression joint before making the joint. Although this should not be necessary it does accommodate any unevenness in the tube and ensures a watertight joint at the first attempt.

Manufacturers of Type 'A' compression joints publish illustrated catalogues of their products which show the very wide range of fittings available (*Figure 12.4*). Stop-cocks and drain-cocks are made with compression inlets and outlets for direct connection to pipes. There are also easy and elbow bends, equal and reducing tees for inserting branch pipe lines, fittings with compression inlets and cap and lining outlets for connection to taps and ball-valves and fittings with compression inlets and threaded outlets, male or female, for connection to cylinders, cisterns and pipes of materials other than copper.

Manipulative (Type B) compression joints and fittings

These differ from Type A joints in that the tube end has to be 'worked' or manipulated and is itself an integral part of the completed joint.

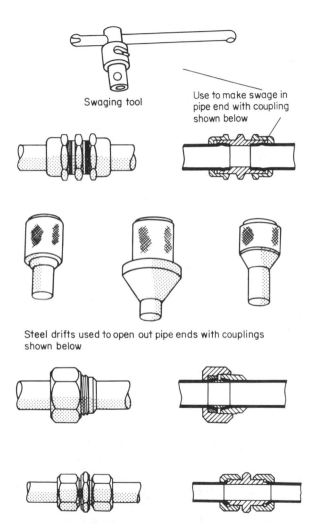

Swaging tool

Use to make swage in pipe end with coupling shown below

Steel drifts used to open out pipe ends with couplings shown below

Fig. 12.5. Manipulative (Type B) compression couplings

To make a Type B joint the tube end must first be cut squarely and all burr removed as with a Type A joint. The cap nut must then be unscrewed from the joint and slipped over the tube end. *After* this has been done the tube end must be manipulated (*Figure 12.5*).

This is usually done by hammering in a steel drift to expand the tube end. However, one well-known make of Type B joint (the Kingley, made by the Kings Langley Engineering Co.) requires the tube end to be manipulated in a rather different way. A special 'swaging tool' is inserted into the pipe end and turned. Turning this tool forces a hard steel ball to make a ridge or 'swage' round the pipe end. The pipe is then placed against or into the body of the joint as the case may be and the cap nut screwed on and tightened. It is wise to apply boss white to the pipe end when making a Type B joint.

As can be seen, once the pipe end has been manipulated, the cap nut cannot be removed. This means that the pipe is much more positively secured than with a Type A joint. The joint cannot pull apart as a result of ground settlement or expansion of ice. For this reason Water Authorities usually insist upon the use of Type B joints for underground work. A disadvantage, which is probably not a serious one in most situations, is that the joint cannot be dismantled as easily as a Type A joint.

Soldered capillary joints and fittings

The effect of capillary action—the property of liquids that causes them to flow into any confined space between two solid surfaces—can be demonstrated by means of a simple experiment. Take two pieces of glass, separate them by about 1½mm ($^1/_{16}$ in) and dip their edges into a vessel filled with coloured water. The water will be observed to flow upwards to fill the space between the two sheets of glass.

Capillarity has its disadvantages. It is, for instance, the cause of rising damp in buildings. The plumber however can take advantage of it. The effectiveness of soldered capillary joints

MATERIALS AND METHODS

depends upon the fact that molten solder, like water, will flow to fill any confined space between two solid surfaces.

Soldered capillary joints and fittings are smaller, cheaper and less obtrusive than compression joints and fittings. They are scarcely more difficult to make though a blow torch is, of course, an essential.

There are two kinds of capillary joint—the integral ring and the end-feed (*Figure 12.6*). Integral ring capillary joints (often called Yorkshire fittings after the name of one well-known brand) incorporate sufficient solder to make the joint.

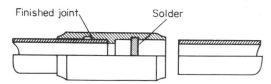

Fig. 12.6. Integral ring soldered capillary joint. End-feed fittings are identical but have no ring of solder

Preparation of the tube end begins as with a compression joint. Cut the end dead square and remove all burr. Next clean the end of the tube, and the internal bore of the capillary fitting, thoroughly with steel wool or fine abrasive paper. Apply an approved flux to both these surfaces (*Figure 12.7*). Thrust the tube end into the fitting as far as the tube stop. Apply the flame of a blow torch, first to the pipe in the vicinity of the fitting and then to the fitting itself. The solder in the integral ring will melt and flow to fill the narrow space between tube and fitting. The joint is made when a bright ring of solder appears all round the mouth of the fitting. It should then be left undisturbed until cool enough to touch.

Solder wire is used to feed solder into the cheaper end-feed fittings. About ½in of wire is needed for a 15mm fitting, ¾in for a 22mm one and 1in for a 28mm one. It can be helpful to bend this length of wire over before beginning the operation. Cut, clean and flux as before and apply the blow torch flame to the tube end and fitting. Feed in the solder when flux can

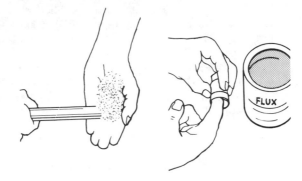

1. clean end of tube and bore
of fitting with steel wool

2. flux bore of fitting and tube
end. With phosphoric acid
flux use a brush!

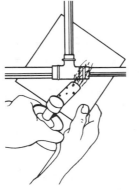

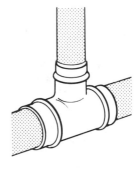

3. apply heat with blow torch
(note asbestos sheet behind
fitting)

4. leave completed joint
to cool

*Fig. 12.7. Making a 'Yorkshire' integral ring soldered
capillary joint*

be seen to be boiling at the mouth of the fitting. The joint is complete when all the bent over piece of wire has been melted and fed into the fitting and, as with an integral ring joint, when a ring of bright solder appears round the mouth of the fitting.

Where more than one joint is to be made to a fitting, as in a straight coupling or a tee connection, it is best if both or all joints can be made at the same time. If this is impossible a piece of damp cloth whould be wrapped round joints already made to prevent the solder in them from melting.

Always remember the fire risk when using a blow torch. Interpose a sheet of asbestos or a piece of fibreglass between the joint and any wooden, or plastic, surface in the vicinity.

Other jointing methods

Other means which may be used by the professional plumber for jointing copper tubing include silver or hard soldering and bronze welding. These methods involve the application of considerably more heat than can be obtained from a conventional blow lamp or blow torch. For bronze welding oxy-acetelene apparatus is required and the techniques involved are not considered suitable for a beginner's guide.

Metrication

Imperial sizes of copper tubes in common use in domestic plumbing are: $^3/_8$ in, ½in, ¾in, 1in, 1¼in, 1½in and 2in. Metric equivalent sizes are: 12mm, 15mm, 22mm, 28mm, 35mm, 42mm and 54mm. These equivalents are not exact translations of Imperial into metric measurements. The reason for this is that Imperial measurements of copper tubing are of the *internal* diameter. Metric measurements are of the *external* diameter of the tube.

When connecting new metric tubing to existing Imperial sized tubing 12mm, 15mm, 28mm and 54mm compression joints can be used, without adaptation with $^3/_8$ in, $^1/_2$ in, 1 in and 2 in tube. Adaptors are required for the connection of $^3/_4$ in, $1^1/_4$ in and $1^1/_2$ in Imperial tube to 22mm, 35mm and 42mm metric tubing. These adaptors are readily available.

Capillary joints demand a much more critical fit than compression joints and, where new metric tubing is to be connected to existing Imperial sized tubing by means of capillary joints, an adaptor should always be used. An alternative, where $^3/_8$ in, $^1/_2$ in, 1 in or 2 in tubing is concerned, is to deal with any metric extension by using a compression joint for the actual connection between Imperial and metric tubing and then to continue the job using capillary joints.

Bending copper tubing

All manufacturers of compression and capillary joints and fittings include a variety of bends within their range of products. Easy bends can however be made in copper tubing either by hand or with the aid of a bending machine and use of this technique can provide a neater, and considerably cheaper, installation.

If a piece of copper tubing is simply bent over the knee it will be noted that the inside or throat of the bend is kinked and the outside or back is flattened while, at the bend, the tube will be elliptical instead of circular in section. To prevent this from occurring the walls of the tube must be supported as the bend is made.

One way of doing this is by means of a bending spring. Steel bending springs are made for all sizes of copper tube. They have an eyelet in the end into which a tommy bar can be inserted. Alternatively, where the bend is to be made in the middle of a length of pipe an extension rod can be hooked into this eyelet.

The spring should be greased to facilitate easy withdrawal and inserted into the tube to the point at which the bend is to be made (*Figure 12.8*). The tube is then bent over the knee, overbending by a few degrees at first and then bringing back to the required curve. To withdraw the spring insert a tommy bar into the eyelet, twist to reduce the diameter of the spring, and pull.

Bending spring inserted

Spring supports tube
walls as bend is made

*Fig. 12.8. Bending copper tube with the aid of a
bending spring*

*Fig. 12.9. Small hand bending
machine*

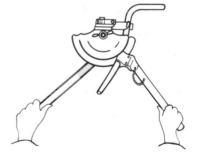

A bending machine provides an alternative means of bending copper tubing and will probably be preferred by the professional (*Figure 12.9*). The essential difference between spring and machine bending is the fact that in spring bending the walls of the tube are supported internally, while a bending machine provides external support.

489

Easy bends in small diameter copper tubing may be made cold. For sharper bends or for easy bends in large diameter pipe, sand or lead loading may be necessary to support the walls and the metal of the tube may need to be annealed— heated to a red heat to change the temper of the copper from half-hard to soft.

Stainless steel

Stainless steel is widely accepted as a first class material for the manufacture of sinks and other kitchen equipment. Although stainless steel tubing has been available in this country for over a decade as an alternative to copper tubing it has not earned the popularity that it deserves.

Stainless steel tubing is obtainable in the same sizes as copper tubing. It can be used in any situation where copper could be used and in some situations where it would be unwise to use copper.

In Chapter 2 reference was made to the danger of electrolytic corrosion that arises where galvanised steel and copper are used in one plumbing system. There is no such risk involved in the use of stainless steel. This material can be used in conjunction with copper tubing or, provided that it is not already rusting, old galvanised steel plumbing. It is therefore the obvious choice when extensions are planned for an existing galvanised steel plumbing system. Stainless steel, as a home product, has a relatively stable price that compares favourably with that of copper tubing.

Like copper tubing, stainless steel tubing may be joined with either Type A or Type B compression joints or by means of soldered capillary joints. There are however one or two points that should be noted when jointing stainless steel tubing. Although a wheel tube cutter can be used with stainless steel tubing this material is best cut with a high speed hacksaw blade having 32 teeth per inch. This is especially important if Type B compression fittings are to be used. A tube cutter will work harden the tube ends and make them liable to split when manipulated. Stainless steel is a harder material than copper. For this reason a little more pressure may be required when tightening the cap nut of a compression joint to ensure a watertight joint.

When using capillary fittings with stainless steel tube a phosphoric acid, *not a chloride,* based flux should be used. The supplier of the tubing should be able to suggest a suitable flux. The flux should be applied to the tube end and the interior of the fitting with a brush, not with the fingers. In making a capillary joint with stainless steel tubing a gentle flame from the blow torch should be applied to the fitting itself, not to the tube. As with copper tubing the joint is complete when a ring of bright solder appears round the mouth of the fitting.

Stainless steel tubing is less easily bent than copper tubing. Tubing of up to 22mm diameter can be bent using a bending machine. Spring bending is suitable for tubing of 15mm diameter or less.

Screwed iron and steel pipes and fittings

Because of their weight, clumsy appearance and the fact that they cannot be bent, screwed iron and steel tubing, usually protected against corrosion by galvanising, are rarely if ever used in new plumbing work today.

These materials were however in common use between about 1920 and 1940. It is not unusual to find pre-war sub-urban homes with hot and cold water systems wholly of galvanised steel—cold water storage cistern, hot water storage tank, flow and return pipes and distribution pipes. It may therefore be required for replacement or extension work. Pipes of this kind have threaded ends and are joined by means of the screwed fittings illustrated (*Figure 12.10*). To ensure watertight joints p.t.f.e. plastic thread sealing tape should be bound round the male thread before it is screwed home.

It not infrequently happens that the galvanised steel hot water storage tank of a hot water system constructed of this

491

material fails through corrosion while the remainder of the system is still sound. In this event the temptation to replace the tank with a modern copper hot water storage cylinder should be resisted unless it is proposed, at the same time, to replace the galvanised steel tubing that comprises the remainder of the system with either copper or stainless steel tubing. The risk of electrolytic corrosion is even greater in hot water systems than in cold systems.

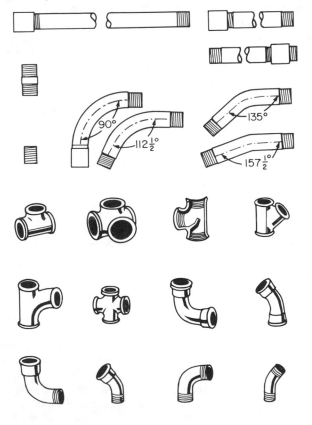

Fig. 12.10. Examples of screwed iron pipes and fittings

MATERIALS AND METHODS

The metrication of iron and steel tubing has resulted in rather less confusion than has the metrication of copper and stainless steel tubing. Measurements are still of the internal diameter. The equivalents are set out below:

Imperial size	Metric equivalent
$^3/_8$ in	10mm
½in	12mm
¾in	20mm
1in	25mm
1¼in	32mm
1½in	40mm
2in	50mm

For all practical purposes there is no change between the sizes of Imperial iron and steel tubing and their metric equivalents. The British Standard Pipe (BSP) thread form has now been accepted internationally and its dimensions will not change. This, of course, relates to the tails of taps and ball valves as well as to iron pipe fittings.

Lead pipes

Lead is the traditional plumbing material. It is, of course, from its Latin name that the word plumbing is derived. Its expense, and the expertise and experience that is needed to handle it efficiently, ensures that it is never nowadays used for new hot or cold water services or drainage. There are however a great many lead, or partially lead, plumbing systems in existence. The professional plumber at least, must know how to cope with lead pipe for replacement and maintenance work.

Lead pipes are joined together by means of a wiped soldered joint. In the introduction it was stated that the technique of making such a joint is far easier to describe that to put into practice. The beginner will probably need to make several attempts before he produces a wiped soldered joint of which he can feel proud. He may console himself with the thought

493

that it is a skill, like riding a bicycle, which, once acquired, is never lost. Before examining the technique, we should look at the properties of solder.

Solder is an alloy of lead and tin, and a small percentage of antimony. Its value lies in the fact that it has a lower melting

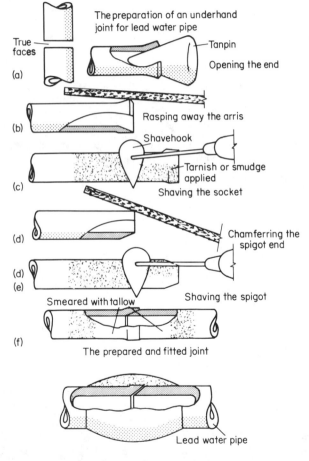

Fig. 12.11. Making a wiped soldered joint

point that any of the elements of which it is composed. Hence the fact that it can be used to join lead pipe without the risk of the lead itself softening and becoming deformed. Solder used with the soldered capillary joints discussed earlier in this chapter has a relatively high percentage of tin and a low melting point—between 170 and 190°C or 340 and 370°F. Plumber's wiping solder on the other hand contains roughly two parts of lead to one of tin and has an appreciably higher melting point—230°C or 440°F.

Careful preparation of the pipe ends is the first important step in the making of a good wiped soldered joint. Ends should be cut squarely and cleaned of all burr. A socket is then formed in one pipe in a tanpin, or hardwood cone (*Figure 12.11*). The external edge, or 'arris', of this opened-out end is then rasped away. The other pipe end is formed into a spigot by rasping to the angle of taper of the tanpin. This will ensure that it fits closely into the socket prepared in the other pipe end.

To limit the extent of the completed joint each pipe end is now coated with tarnish or plumber's black, to which molten solder will not adhere. Mark the limit of the joint on both spigot and socket ends and, with a shavehook, shave away the tarnish *and the surface coating of lead oxide* from the area of the joint, leaving bright, bare metal exposed. The cleaned surfaces must immediately be protected from further oxidation by smearing with tallow. Assemble the joint and fix firmly for wiping.

There may still be some traditional plumbers who make wiped joints with a solder pot and ladle, splashing molten solder onto upright joints with a splash stick and moulding into shape with a wiping cloth. Most modern plumbers prefer to use the solder stick method which is easier, safer and can produce just as satisfactory results.

The flame of a blow torch is applied to the lead pipe on each side of the joint, slowly traversing to and fro until the lead has reached a temperature above that of the melting point of solder. Rub the solder stick lightly onto the shaved surface of the lead pipe so that it 'tins' the entire surface and runs, by capillary attraction, into the confined space between the spigot and socket of the joint.

As more heat is applied the solder stick will soften and blobs of solder will be released. These must be built up round the joint with the moleskin wiping cloth to a neat finish.

The length of a wiped soldered joint will depend upon the sizes of the pipes being joined.

Internal bore	Length	Internal bore	Length
10mm	70mm	40mm	75mm
12mm	70mm	65mm	80mm
20mm	70mm	75mm	90mm
25mm	75mm	100mm	90mm
32mm	75mm		

As with galvanised iron and steel tubing, lead tubing is still designated by its internal diameter and there is no change, for all practical purposes, between the sizes of Imperial lead tubing and their metric equivalents.

The wiped soldered joint described is most likely to be needed in connection with the replacement of a burst or leaking length of existing lead pipework. This should be a relatively rare occurrence.

What the modern plumber is more likely to need is a means of connecting new copper or stainless steel tubing to existing lead pipe. This situation frequently arises in modernisation and improvement work. An obsolete and leaking lead plumbing system has been ripped out and a new copper or stainless steel system is to be installed. The first task is to connect copper tubing to a cut-off length of lead tubing projecting from the floor boards.

All manufacturers of compression and capillary joints and fittings include lead-to-copper connectors within their range of products. There is no difficulty in connecting the copper end of the connector to the copper or stainless steel tube. The lead end has to be connected to the lead tube by means of a wiped soldered joint similar to that described above. The projecting end of lead tube will form the 'socket' of the new joint (*Figure 12.12a*). It must be opened up with a tanpin, rasped and cleaned as though another length of lead pipe were to be connected to it.

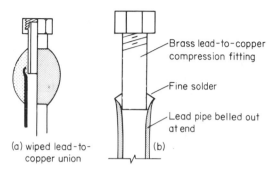

(a) wiped lead-to-copper union

(b)

Brass lead-to-copper compression fitting

Fine solder

Lead pipe belled out at end

Fig. 12.12. Joining copper compression fittings to lead pipe

The lead end of the lead-to-copper union must now be prepared. Its tail must be thoroughly scored with a medium cut file to remove the dull coating of chemical impurities arising from oxidation. The filed portion must be lightly smeared with tallow and plumber's black applied to the other end of the fitting to mark the limit of the joint.

The scored end of the union must then be 'tinned'. This means covering with a coat of fine general purpose solder, composed of equal parts of lead and tin. The solder is best applied to the tail of the union with a large copper bit. When the union has been tinned its end is placed into the socket of the lead pipe and secured with wooden splints. The wiped soldered joint is then made as previously described.

A simpler copper to lead connection can be made with a cup-and-cone joint (*Figure 12.12b*). This is acceptable for waste pipes and gas fittings but cannot be used for pipes carrying water under pressure. The end of the lead pipe is belled out by driving in a hardwood cone or turn-pin until the spigot end of the union can be accommodated to a depth equal to about half of its diameter. The spigot end of the union is rasped and tinned and fixed firmly into the lead socket. Fine solder is then run into the cup, the space between the union spigot and the lead socket, to fill it.

Polythene

Polythene may be used in plumbing for cold water storage cisterns and feed and expansion tanks. It may also be used for cold water supply and distribution pipes and was one of the first plastics to be used for this purpose. Polythene tubing is obtainable in long coils. It can easily be connected to copper tubing and has a built-in resistance to frost.

Its disadvantages are its thick, clumsy appearance and its tendency to sag which necessitates continuous support on horizontal runs. It cannot be used for hot water under pressure but is suitable for waste pipes taking warm wastes from baths, sinks and basins. Its chief value is as an easy and relatively cheap means of taking an underground water supply to a point distant from the home. It can be used to provide a garage supply or to supply a stand-tap at the end of a large garden.

The long lengths in which it is obtainable eliminate underground joints and it can be brought above the surface of the ground to supply a stand-tap without special frost precautions being taken. Polythene is a poor conductor or heat and cold and will provide a considerable measure of frost resistance. If the water in a polythene pipe *does* freeze the pipe will not burst. Polythene has sufficient resilience to accommodate the expansion of the ice and will revert to its original size when the ice thaws. These considerations make polythene tubing extremely valuable to, for instance, the proprietor of a caravan or camping site who must take a water supply to stand-pipes at various points throughout the site.

Polythene tubing is joined by non-manipulative compression joints and fittings similar to those used with copper tubing. Because polythene is a relatively soft material, a metal insert, provided by the manufacturer of the fitting, must be fitted into the tube end to prevent collapse when the cap-nut is tightened (*Figure 12.13*). Unscrew the cap-nut of the compression joint and slip it, followed by the olive, over the end of the tube. Push the metal insert into the end of the tube. Insert the tube end into the body of the fitting as far as the tube stop and tighten up the cap-nut. Tighten as far as possible with the fingers and then give a further one and a half to two turns with a spanner.

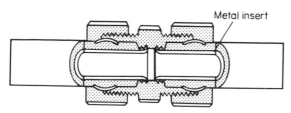

Fig. 12.13. A compression joint connecting two lengths of polythene tube

Polythene has not, at the time of writing, been metricated. Because of the thickness of this material it is usually necessary to use a compression fitting one size larger than the nominal size of the equivalent copper tubing. ½in polythene tubing will probably require a 22mm (¾in) fitting. It is however wise to take a sample of the tube along to the supplier to make sure that the right size of fitting is purchased.

Polythene tubing can be bent cold to easy bends but will revert to shape unless firmly secured. Permanent bends may be made by softening the length of pipe by immersion for ten minutes in water that is kept boiling or by *very gently* playing the flame of a blow torch along it.

Unplasticised polyvinyl chloride (u.p.v.c., p.v.c. or vinyl)

Unplasticised polyvinyl chloride is the most versatile of modern plastic materials so far as the plumber is concerned. Pipes of this material may be used for cold water supply, for above and underground drainage and for roof drainage. It is light, tough and easily handled and joined.

P.V.C. cannot be used for hot water under pressure. For this reason there are two, nominally cold water supply pipes which should never be of P.V.C. These are the cold supply pipe from the cold water storage cistern to the hot water cylinder and the cold supply pipe from the feed and expansion system of an indirect hot water system (*Figure 12.14*). Water in these pipes can become very hot at times and, for this reason, metal pipes should always be used.

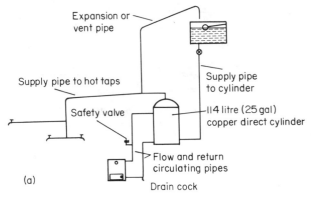

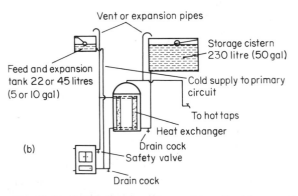

Fig. 12.14. P.V.C. pipes may be used for all cold water pipes except those shown here. (a) A direct hot water system and (b) an indirect hot water system

MATERIALS AND METHODS

P.V.C. tubing can be joined either by solvent welding or by ring seal jointing. Solvent welding is always used for cold water supply pipes. For waste and drainage pipes a mixture of the two methods is often used; solvent welding for the small diameter waste pipes and for the connection of junctions and fittings, ring seal jointing for long lengths of the larger diameter stack and drain pipes.

Manufacturers supply fixing instructions which vary slightly with each brand. The following instructions apply to the fixing of Osmflow p.v.c. water supply and distribution pipes.

Cut the pipe to the required length with a hacksaw or other fine toothed saw. Make sure that the pipe end is square and clean off any swarf or burr. With a fine rasp or coarse file chamfer the pipe end to an angle of approximately $15°$.

Roughen the external surface of the pipe end and the internal surface of the socket with a medium grade abrasive paper. Do *not* use steel wool as this will polish the surfaces.

Apply a coat of approved spirit cleaner and degreaser to the inside of the socket and to the pipe end for at least the distance that it will fit into the socket.

Wipe off with clean tissue and apply to both surfaces an even coat of solvent cement. Stroke the cement along, and not round, the surfaces. Thrust pipe end into socket, twist and hold in position for a few seconds. The joint may be handled after two to three minutes but should not be put into operational use for about 24 hours.

Key Terrain Ltd. give similar instructions with their p.v.c. water supply and distribution system but say that the pipe end should *not* be twisted when thrust into the socket. They also suggest that a thicker coat of solvent cement should be applied to the pipe end than to the interior of the socket.

Marley Extrusions Ltd., in their extremely well illustrated instructions for pipework installation, give rather different advice in connection with the solvent welding of their above ground drainage systems (*Figure 12.15*).

The pipe end is cut square, cleaned and degreased in the same way as described earlier but it is not chamfered to an angle. They suggest that, after application of solvent cement to

501

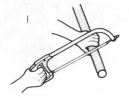

1. Cut the pipe straight and square with a hacksaw. 2. Clean off all swarf and burr inside and out

Half round file

3. Assemble the fittings and check for length and alignment making pencil mark to ensure accuracy. 4. Apply solvent cement to the outside of the pipe and the inside of the socket, spreading it evenly with a spatula

5 Distribute solvent evenly with a spatula if necessary, after application from tube

5. Push the fittings out the end of the pipe with a slight twisting motion until the pipe is fully inserted. 6. Remove surplus cement immediately with a clean dry cloth

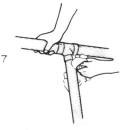

7. Hold the assembled joint in position for about 15 seconds to ensure it stays correctly aligned

Fig. 12.15. Solvent weld jointing of Marley p.v.c. tubing

pipe end and socket interior, the pipe should be thrust into the socket 'with a slight twisting motion' and held in position for about 15 seconds.

A 4m length of p.v.c. pipe will expand by over 13mm when subjected to an increase in temperature of 39°C. For this reason, where a total straight length of waste pipe exceeds 1.8m in length, an expansion coupling should be introduced at 1.8m intervals. The Marley expansion coupling (*Figure 12.16*) has a solvent weld connection at one end and a ring

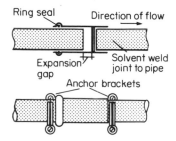

Ring seal   Direction of flow

Expansion gap   Solvent weld joint to pipe

Anchor brackets

Fig. 12.16. Marley expansion joint

seal joint at the other. An insertion mark made 57mm from the pipe end ensures that accommodation for expansion is provided.

An advantage of ring seal jointing is the facility that it provides for the accommodation of thermal movement due to the passage of hot and cold water through waste and drain pipes. Preparation for ring seal jointing is similar to that for solvent welding (*Figure 12.17*). A fine toothed saw or hacksaw must be used to cut the pipe end absolutely square. Draw a line round the cut end of the pipe 10mm from the end and chamfer back to this line with a rasp or special shaping tool. Insert the pipe into the socket and mark the insertion depth with a pencil. Make another mark 10mm nearer to the pipe end than the first mark. It is to this second mark that the pipe end will finally be inserted, thus leaving 10mm for expansion.

Clean the recess within the pipe socket and insert the sealing ring. Lubricate the pipe end with a small amount of petroleum jelly and push the end firmly home into the socket past the joint ring. Adjust the pipe position so that the insertion depth mark is level with the edge of the socket.

Manufacturers provide a variety of means by which p.v.c. water, waste and drain pipes may be connected to taps and ball-valves, copper or galvanised steel tubing and to stoneware and iron drainage systems.

1 Cut tube squarely with fine tooth saw

4 Insert ring joint in socket

2 Chamfer tube end

5 Apply petroleum jelly to tube end

Ring seal in specially shaped recess

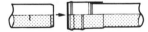

Socket solvent welded to pipe in factory on standard socket and spigot pipe lengths

6 Align tube end to socket and push home

3 Mark depth of tube in socket

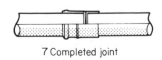

7 Completed joint

Fig. 12.17. Ring seal jointing of p.v.c. pipework

MATERIALS AND METHODS

Polypropylene tubing

Polypropylene tubing resembles p.v.c. in many respects. It may be encountered in domestic drainage work but is of greatest value for the drainage of high temperature and chemical wastes from industrial and commercial premises.

The important point of difference between polypropylene and p.v.c. is the fact that the former cannot be joined by solvent welding. Ring seal joints must be used in all situations.

Expanded polystyrene

Expanded polystyrene is used in plumbing as an extremely valuable lagging material. It is obtainable in pipe lagging units which can be fitted round pipes during or subsequent to installation. Tank lagging sets for cold water storage cisterns are also available. Despite its 'porous' appearance it does not, in fact absorb water in any appreciable amount. It can therefore be used to protect underground pipes when required.

Fire risk should always be borne in mind when expanded polystyrene is used. It can burn, giving off dense and potentially lethal fumes.

Pitch fibre pipes

Pitch fibre pipes are sometimes used for above-ground waste and soil stacks. Their most common use however is for underground drainage work.

The simplest method of jointing is undoubtedly the snap ring joint. The snap ring is placed over the end of the pipe, care being taken to ensure that the ring is square to the axis of the pipe and that its flat surface is in contact with the pipe. The coupling is then pushed home over the ring and pipe end so as to force the ring to roll along the pipe (*Figure 12.18*). Due to the shape of the ring's section it is compressed and jumps into its final position. This can be distinctly felt and is an indication of a sound joint.

MATERIALS AND METHODS

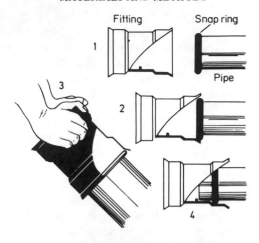

Fig. 12.18. Making a snap ring joint to pitch fibre drain pipe

Pitch fibre pipe can be cut with an ordinary wood saw. Keeping the blade lubricated with water will prevent clogging and speed the operation. As with p.v.c. waste and drain pipes a variety of means are provided for the connection of pitch fibre pipes to pipes and fittings of other materials.

Section 4

Central Heating

1 Introduction

Before studying any subject it is necessary to establish guide lines, to define it. This is as true of central heating as anything else. For the name proves, on examination, to have been used quite loosely.

Central heating was first called 'central' for the best of reasons, that it was heating from a central source, usually a coal fired boiler. This compared with the unsystematic methods which had been in use since the end of the Roman occupation, often one open coal fire in the house, or in the last 150 years the coal fired range, which cooked as well. Larger houses with better-off occupants would generally have several open fires, quite often one in each room, which accounts for the multiple chimney stacks in buildings of the period.

The earliest domestic central heating was cumbersome, usually wholly dependent upon the meagre forces of gravity for its circulation, which made it equally dependent upon a good standard of installation so as to offer a minimum of resistance. Otherwise unexplained noises in the house were customarily and usually justly attributed to the central heating.

This state of affairs ended abruptly following work done by a research association in 1956. They showed, in the course of finding more outlets for coal, that a lot of heat could be obtained from a small boiler, with small pipes, if the water were pumped around to the radiators. This was the 'small bore' system, whose advent led to a wide range of activities. For instance pump manufacturers were forced to look into the availability and reliability of suitable models, and controls manufacturers came to life. But it was the oil industry which seized upon the system and gave it a high market rating. Only later did gas join in seriously, in due course to establish a lead as suppliers of fuel for boilers. Solid fuel, through coke and special coals, maintained a steady but low market share.

INTRODUCTION

Meantime, it was not to be expected that the electricity industry would sit by and watch its competitors making hay in such a potentially vast market. They could not compete in the boiler market, and had to look elsewhere. This led to the development of the off-peak storage heater, which also offered some solution to their own generating problem, of what to do with plant necessary during the day but standing expensively idle at night. Electricity as heat energy could be stored in massive receivers overnight, so that it would leak out during the day and warm the house. The first efforts led to underfloor heating, in which concrete floors formed the heat reservoir.

Underfloor heating could rarely be applied to any but new housing, which was too limiting. So there arrived the unit heater (or storage radiator among other names) which was, and is, a rather heavy free standing unit of manageable size, incorporating a heating coil and heat absorbing material, and scientifically insulated to permit a calculated rate of heat leakage to air.

At that stage the electrical effort was just as surely random and non-central as the old coal fire had been. But it was sold quite firmly under the central heating banner, which is why the name has assumed a portmanteau quality. Only later did electricity produce the central unit, Electricaire, which is in effect a very large unit heater with ducts to other rooms and a fan to distribute warmed air.

We have often had a pedantic urge to give up using the term 'central heating' but the difficulty lies in knowing what will take its place. 'Whole house heating' is tempting but fails because it is untrue in the case of partial central heating, itself a respectable and well documented variant of central heating. To refer to 'modern heating' is too vague, too reminiscent of someone's advertising. So in the end we come back to Central Heating, which despite its imperfections is widely understood.

There is a way to classify heating systems broadly, which divides them into 'wet' and 'dry'. All the systems to be described in this book fall into one of those categories and, broad as they are, they are very important in one respect. With a wet system it may be assumed that the domestic hot water supply, i.e. hot water to taps, is taken care of, or at any rate can be covered without additional fitments. On the other hand with a dry system additional equipment is necessary to supply domestic hot water. More of that in Chapter 11.

Wet systems employ water as the heat conveying fluid. Water is extremely suitable for this duty. It is cheap, usually freely available, not outstandingly corrosive (a point to return to later), is relatively harmless if it escapes from the system, and it has a high capacity for heat. It must of course be confined within pipes, and we have already mentioned that large pipes began giving way to small pipes from 1956. More recently, small pipes have been sharing the market with very small pipes, called microbore, and this indicates how the pump industry has progressed.

Wet systems have a boiler, which puts the heat into the water. We will discuss boilers in Chapter 3. In order to take the heat out of the water at points where it is required, the most common device is the radiator. Everyone knows what a radiator is, and it is important in installation and in room furnishing to remember that it does radiate anything up to half of its total heat output. For that reason it must always be able to 'see the room', never hidden away in an alcove or behind heavy furniture. For the rest it is however a convector.

But a convector by that name is a device which gives next to no radiation, only a stream of warm air. Convectors may be natural, i.e. without fan assistance; or they may be fan convectors, which give very little warm air when not at work, but a lot when a thermostat or similar device switches on the fan. A skirting heater, which the Americans tend to call a baseboard heater, is a form of convector, and a very efficient one in terms of maintaining even room heating, horizontally and vertically. An interesting application of a wet system is that in which it serves as the heat source for a dry system. This is covered in Chapter 5.

Dry systems are, not too surprisingly, all those which do not use water as the heat conveying fluid. (It would be inaccurate to describe them as systems which use air, since nearly *all* heating systems ultimately depend upon air movement.)

A high proportion of dry systems depend upon the direct

heating of air, which is then circulated. Having pointed out the advantages of water as a medium, let us list the advantages of air. It is even cheaper and more readily available than water, it is entirely non-corrosive, is not only beneficial but essential to life (in uncontaminated form), is not a hazard if it leaks from a conveying pipe or duct, and *it does not freeze*. Against those qualities the only negative is that it has a low capacity for heat.

Though we will deal with warm air systems in more detail later (Chapter 4) it may be noted here that there are two broad types. There is the random type, in which warm air is generated and left to find its own way around, mainly by drift, possibly with a little assistance. This system can be quite satisfactory in certain styles of dwelling, principally those which have a substantial vertical factor. It is not very well suited to most bungalows, which have no noticeable vertical factor. The other type is the ducted system, which conveys warmed air to specific points for discharge, and then arranges by means of return air ducts to bring most of it back for reheating.

The dry systems which do not employ air directly as the heating medium are principally electrical. That is to say, electricity is used to heat a solid or a liquid, and in one way or another this material passes on its heat to the surroundings. In most cases it does so by creating a current of warmed air, which then circulates. This includes oil filled electric radiators; storage radiators (or unit heaters) which are mainly based upon natural circulation but may be obtained with plain damper control or with fan control; underfloor heating, which is no longer being installed but deserves a mention. Storage radiators qualify for a reduced tariff, off-peak or White Meter.

A form of electric heating in which air circulation plays no direct part is the low temperature radiant panel. This is generally a structural item and may be fitted to wall or ceiling. It constitutes a large area source of low intensity radiation which is invisible but can be sensed by anyone in its path.

So far we have classified central heating according to fuel and method of operation, but there is another division – by its scope. There are degrees of central heating and some of the terms used are full, partial, background and selective heating.

INTRODUCTION

These phrases were coined early in the development of modern central heating, and although they are not written into any legal definition or standard they are well understood in the heating trade. Let us look at them more closely.

Full central heating: a term applied to a system which will maintain all rooms at their specified temperatures simultaneously, when the outdoor temperature is $30°F$ or $-1°C$.

Partial central heating: will maintain specified rooms at their specified temperatures simultaneously, when the outdoor temperature is $30°F$ or $-1°C$. The specified rooms are those with heat emission apparatus installed.

Background central heating: similar to full central heating but the specified temperatures are much lower; the assumption being that other measures will be taken to boost the temperature at particular points.

Selective central heating: will maintain only a proportion of the rooms at full central heating conditions simultaneously. This assumes that the whole house is equipped with heat emitters, so that the disposition of rooms chosen to be heated may vary. This is a very sensible and economic system for a house which is, as most are, not fully occupied at almost any time.

Clearly one may ring some changes on this basic list, for example with partial background heating, or selective background heating. The important thing is that if a contractor is being employed the type of heating chosen shall be written into the contract. In all the cases mentioned there is one other factor to be detailed, and that is the specified temperatures. These are for the client to select, though some guidance is offered below. In specifying temperatures it is necessary to consider the cost of higher temperatures on the economy of running the system. The salient fact is that the cost of unnecessary heat grows out of proportion to the average cost, and the rule should be therefore to have

(1) *as much* heat (temperature) as necessary, but no more
(2) heat *when* wanted but at no other time
(3) heat *where* wanted but nowhere else.

INTRODUCTION

Points 2 and 3 show the importance of good thermostatic control and on/off controls of heat emitters. Point 1 requires an assessment of reasonable temperatures, and reasonable values may be gathered from the following list.

Living rooms	70 – 75°F (21 – 24°C)
Dining room	65 – 70°F (18 – 21°C)
Bedrooms	55 – 65°F (12 – 18°C) (Fashion varies widely and rapidly between cool and warm bedrooms)
Bathroom	65°F (18°C)
Hall	60°F (16°C)

Kitchen, if not receiving sufficient 'free' warmth from cooking etc, to be kept at approx 65°F (18°C).

Three things must be stressed about this list: first that it is for guidance only; secondly that a decision must be made about the maximum required temperature in each room, and either built into the contract or used by the client doing his own design. The third factor, which deserves to precede all others in timing, is the basis of good running economics, and the way to contribute to the national effort to conserve energy. It is, in short, to *require* less energy for a given result, by losing less. This means, insulate! Insulate to the maximum extent, knowing that money spent at an early stage on insulation will mean less outlay on heating equipment since smaller units will be needed; and it will mean savings on running cost for ever more. We shall have more to say on that important topic later. The reason for thinking of insulation even before heating is that the heat balance must be made on the *insulated* structure in order to secure all the economies in apparatus.

Before leaving the subject of preferred temperatures, and the desirability of avoiding too much warmth, we can deal with another offshoot of this. Heating 'dries the air'. A rise in temperature brings about a fall in relative humidity, so that the air feels drier. In moderation this is no more than a passing nuisance to healthy people, who acclimatise as they would if they moved to, say, the Transvaal where the prevailing humidity is very low but the climate excellent. The effect of dryness increases as the temperature rises, and it is an additional reason for keeping the temperatures down.

The word 'humidifier' is often mentioned, and it describes a device which adds water to the air. We would certainly oppose the proposition that all central heating should be accompanied by humidification, and instead we list three categories where it is usually justifiable.

(1) For people who suffer from sinus complaints. We go no further than that, and recommend that they seek medical advice by way of confirmation.

(2) Where antique furniture is involved. Furniture, unlike people, cannot adapt, and antiques might be spoiled due to shrinkage.

(3) In some cases, in older type timber framed buildings. Although the changes in temperature and humidity which take place are no more than those which occur seasonally (though these occur daily) and rarely do any harm, they do very often cause quite alarming noises to issue from the structure. It is solely to mitigate these that humidification might be considered.

Humidifiers are sold in three classes, cheap, moderate and expensive. The first is little more than a wick or similar evaporative device, though almost always made quite attractive in appearance. The prototype is a towel hanging from a radiator into a bucket of water. Commercial models of this type are suitable for most purposes, and bring about quite good results. At the extreme end of cost are models of considerable complication, extensively instrumented, electrically operated. The moderate range falls somewhere between those two extremes.

So much for shortage, or apparent shortage, of moisture in the air. But what about the times when there seems to be too much, when it forms as condensation, stains wall paper, ruins paint and curtains, mists windows and turns clothes mouldy in wardrobes?. There is no magic machine which will *reduce* the relative humidity irrespective of temperature, but there are two ways to avoid condensation. One is to prevent wall surfaces, in particular outdoor wall surfaces, and windows from becoming cold enough to cause it. The other is to ventilate, to remove enough of the moisture laden air as it forms to keep the concentration within manageable limits. These matters we will deal with when we come to Insulation.

There is no such thing as a best heating system. What is best for any one situation depends upon such things as what it is expected to do, where it has to go, and what may not be available (such as a ready fuel supply).

One such, and a common feature, concerns the space required compared to the space available. An outstanding example of this is a warm air system with full ducting. Ducts average about 250 x 200 mm or 10 x 8 in. Very few houses can tolerate apparatus of such a size running down a corridor or across a ceiling. For that reason, a full warm air duct system is always regarded as something to be built into a new house, not added to an existing one. At construction stage ducting can be built into the structure and 'lost'. Warm air systems put into existing property tend to use stub ducting, i.e. short runs leading only into rooms adjacent to the heat unit. Underfloor electric heating was of course associated with new building, since it was almost wholly incorporated in concrete floors. Its successor, the storage radiator, is sometimes described by owners of rather small rooms as bulky or cumbersome. Some manufacturers have gone as far as the natural limitations of the subject will allow in reducing the depth of projection into the room. In such cases an unbiased observer might say that the unit takes no more space than would a small bookcase, and it has a safe surface temperature. It can therefore be assimilated into the room.

Still considering forms of electric heating, radiant wall and ceiling panels take no noticeable space, but like warm air ducting must be thought of as structural items (though the upheaval in fitting them into existing premises is often within reason).

Let us examine the space and facilities demanded by wet systems. Until quite recently the boiler would stand alongside the refrigerator or the washing machine and look very like either.

Or, still the same size, it might be situated under the stairs, or in a spare room. The criterion was often where it could get access to a flue, either of the conventional or the balanced type (see Chapter 3). Nowadays, a boiler may be hidden behind the gas fire, so taking no useful room at all; or hung on the kitchen wall like a moderately sized cupboard.

Radiators cannot be reduced in size since surface area is fundamental to their performance. Within that context however they have been streamlined, brought as near to the wall as possible without impairing their efficiency, and have had projections smoothed away. The old pattern column radiator is scarcely available now, though it, and the double and treble panel versions of the panel radiator, continue to supply the answer to that other problem, of where there is enough space for projection but too little wall area for the required size of single panel. Radiator manufacturers do their best to meet problems of wall space by offering a choice of heights of radiator. For example the heat emission from a radiator measuring 4 x 1 is just about the same as that from a panel 2 x 2. Shortage of wall space may be overcome in two other ways. The skirting heater increases the projection of a normal skirting board but otherwise uses no wall space at all, and the fan convector may be assumed to occupy a wall area only one sixth or less of the area of a panel radiator of comparable output.

In an extreme case, where the wall width was only two feet, but the height ample, we have known a long radiator of limited height to be fitted vertically instead of horizontally in order to get the required area into a room. It shows what can be done, but for technical reasons this ploy is not highly recommended.

The problem of fitting an appropriate type of system to a given set of conditions has other aspects besides space. Some may be overcome. For instance, no gas main within miles? Then there is bottled gas. Some are not overcome so easily, if at all. Take for instance a flat in a multistorey block. It will almost certainly have no conventional flue. Whether a balanced flue would be allowed to pass through the building wall must be determined by reference to the conditions of sale, or lease, or let. Such a flat would quite certainly not be able to accommodate an oil fuel storage tank, and that limitation is much more widely applicable, covering all premises which have no garden or very little garden.

When we come to the point of deciding which form of central heating to choose, the choice is not so wide and bewildering as might at first appear. Let us begin by supposing that the whole of available heating stretches from A to Z. Then, by the time we have eliminated those sections of the market which cannot be accommodated by us, the market has shrunk to, say, A to P. Then, we find that we do not much care for, it may be electricity, or gas. That would reduce the choice to A to J. Within the new short range we must then be careful to see that what we look at has earned the Approval of the appropriate authority: SFAS for solid fuel, British Gas for gas, DOBETA for oil, either BEAMA or the Electricity Council for electricity, MARC for radiators. All goods which are sold in appointed places, such as gas and electricity showrooms, can be taken for granted. Nowhere else should one fail to enquire about Approval. There are, it is true, cheapjack wares about, but decreasingly so. More to the point are the imported items which are reaching us. There are of course many excellent items being imported, but an item is usually designed for the conditions it will meet in its home country, which are not necessarily those of the UK. It could therefore be successful at home but not here. Any item which is both reputable and suited to UK conditions will have been submitted for UK approval (just as UK items must be tested by countries importing them). You will see therefore that whether an item is British made or imported, you need to satisfy yourself that it has Approval. More than that, if you place your heating contract in the hands of an installer, make sure that he chooses and uses Approved items on your behalf.

Practical points to emerge from this chapter are:
(1) Not all types of heating system can be accommodated in every home.
(2) There are two broad types of system – wet and dry.
(3) The range of choice within 'wet' and 'dry' allows for at least one example of each to be suited to any home.

(4) Before setting out to acquire a heating system (or even a simple gas fire) the householder should be quite clear about the standard of heating he is seeking, e.g. whether full, partial or background; and the maximum temperatures to be maintained.

(5) When buying apparatus make sure that it complies with an official Approval scheme wherever appropriate.

2 The Wet System

For far too long central heating has been known by the fuel which supplies the heat energy. We have for instance gas central heating, or oil central heating. This is entirely due to the efforts of advertisers, of whom the biggest and most persistent spenders have been the fuel interests.

The truth of the matter is that the important aspect of a system is the heat emission side. Suppose you have radiators installed, and a wet system, with a gas boiler. It is a couple of hours work to remove the gas boiler and fit instead a coke or oil boiler. But to take out the radiators and fit instead ducting or some other type of system is a major operation. Equally, substituting a boiler makes no difference at all to the heating, whereas any departure from the radiator system will cause some noticeable change, probably introduce a new method of control for comfort. That is why we are going to consider wet systems before going on to boilers.

In spite of a few half hearted attempts to make changes, the wetness of wet systems is water. Partly with car practice in mind it is possible in a closed circulation system (q.v.) to introduce an antifreeze solution. Another additive is aimed at reducing internal corrosion, and this is vehemently defended by its suppliers and supporters but by no means universally accepted.

The operation of a wet system is entirely dependent upon circulation. Water is heated in the boiler, is piped to the heat emitters (radiators etc.) and returns, partly cooled, to be reheated. In earlier days, and to a very limited extent nowadays, heating circuits operated by gravity. A warmed column of water is lighter than a cold column, and so the one rises and the other falls. A system based upon this natural movement has to have a substantial vertical component. The rise and the fall must be fully established in order that any sideways movement, into radiators etc., can take place with continuing circulation and so with renewal of heat introduction.

The principle of gravity circulation is still the one most used on the domestic hot water side of combined systems. The pipes, known as the primaries, flow to and return from the cylinder, which must be at a higher vertical level than the boiler.

But heating circuits cannot rely upon finding a high vertical to horizontal ratio, except perhaps in a lighthouse. Most gravity inspired heating circuits were either sluggish or failed to circulate. Those that worked were characterised by a wide difference between flow and return temperatures (due to slowness of travel) so that radiators became progressively cooler along the line. The gravity circuit has passed, therefore, without regret. Its successor is the pump assisted, or pumped, circuit, which began seriously with what became known very quickly as Small Bore. Small bore employs pipes mainly in the range 15 or 22 mm, occasionally 28 mm (which used to be ½, ¾ and 1 inch). Gravity systems could never fall below 1 inch pipe.

The reduced diameter, the extra mobility contributed by the use of copper instead of iron, the design freedom due to pumping, have all led to small bore being widely and readily applicable. It is no more difficult to make work in a single storey barrack style building than in a conventional semi. It can of course be made to misbehave, for example by having too much pump power, or by using pipes inadequate for the designed load at any point in the system. But those are matters to be sorted out during design, as we shall be showing in Chapter 12.

Microbore

After twenty years of adherence to small bore we have more recently come to microbore, in which the pipework is almost entirely smaller than 15 mm or ½ in, being more of the order 10 mm. This material can be installed in the same fashion as medium weight electric cable, which makes it a good deal easier, quicker and therefore cheaper to handle than small bore tube. The material used is copper, though nylon is on offer. The latter must be viewed with some reservation, since its only real advantage is in first cost.

The pump to be used with microbore develops more pressure than a small bore pump, since the system still has to carry the same weight of water in unit time. Microbore circuits have another notable difference, compared with what has gone before. In other sizes of circuit the pipe goes from one appliance to the next, giving up as much as each requires. In microbore circuits there is no reserve for such tributary treatment. The total amount of heat for the system, as hot water, is led to a central distributing point called a manifold, by a flow pipe of standard (not microbore) size. The manifold (*Figure 2.1*) should

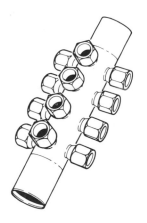

Fig. 2.1. A typical micro-bore manifold. This is fitted under the floor or in a cupboard and distributes pipes to the various radiators

have as many connecting points as there are heat emission appliances. From this central distribution point a pair of microbore pipes is led to each appliance, by the shortest route, and connected to the inlet and outlet. The microbore pipe connected to the appliance outlet is then connected, back at the centre, to another (return) manifold (*Figure 2.2*), which in turn is connected to the return pipe to the boiler.

In spite of the ease of pipe running and other advantages of microbore, it is not destined to take over the market, though it will achieve a share. To give only one reason: a gravity circulation system could be brought to a standstill by almost anything — a dip in a supposedly horizontal pipe, or an air bubble; a clean small bore system will fight on through most disturbances, short of having scale or similar foreign matter choke up

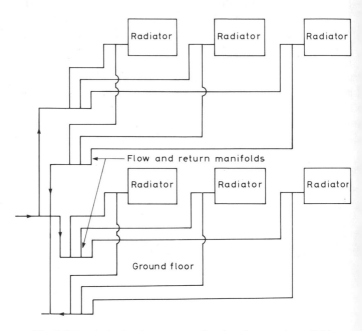

Fig. 2.2. Typical microbore system showing the use of manifolds

the pump; the cross section of microbore pipe is so small that it can be blocked by quite small pieces of foreign matter. We mention this because there is always a tendency to imagine that the latest of anything is about to become the only one. In the end anything of value assumes a reasonably constant share of the market after a settling in period.

Small bore

Small bore is likely to dominate the wet system market for quite a while. It is split into two categories, single pipe and two pipe systems, which we will examine. At present the balance lies in favour of the single pipe system, but only on account of first cost. The two-pipe system, which is technically a much better job, uses almost twice as much pipe. Perhaps we can do something, in the next few pages, to swing the balance in favour of the better system, by pointing out how the results of recent investigations can lead to overall savings, thus bringing the cost of two-pipe to the level once expected from single-pipe. But first, to see what single and two-pipe systems are. The differences are readily apparent from *Figures 2.3* and *2.4.*

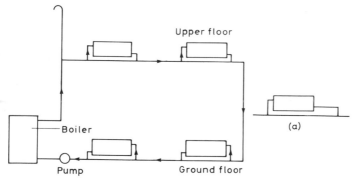

Fig. 2.3. A typical single-pipe system

Taking *Figure 2.3* first, showing a single-pipe system, the flow pipe will be seen to leave the boiler and travel along the upper storey floor. Each radiator is connected so as to take water from, and return water to, this pipe. The process is repeated on the ground floor, until eventually the single pipe, now known as the return, enters the boiler.

At any one radiator there are two important things to note. First, any water which passes through the radiator gives up heat and so drops in temperature. Consequently the water in

523

the flow pipe, just after the point at which the radiator returns to it, will be cooler than before due to the cooling effect of the water from the radiator. But that same water is of course the water which enters the next radiator, and so there is a progressive cooling of the heating medium, as the flowing water is called, along the circuit. This same thing occurred, of course, with gravity systems, and the only benefit of the new system is that thanks to pumping the temperature drop is roughly halved.

The second thing which should be noted is that, while the system is pump circulated, the circulation *within each radiator* depends upon natural forces. The force causing flow to start within a radiator is the very small difference in pressure in the flow pipe due to the frictional resistance of the length of pipe between radiator inlet and outlet. That is why, in some cases of reluctant circulation, a cure has been made by transferring the radiator outlet connection to a point further downstream on the circulation pipe (*Figure 2.3a*). Reluctance, it may be added, is rarely so fundamental. No radiator should be bought without an air valve key, unless an automatic air vent is fitted. That key should be used whenever sluggish behaviour is noticed, and at regular intervals if there seems to be a tendency to accumulate air.

The two-pipe system is shown in *Figure 2.4*. It can be seen that the flow pipe goes only as far as the inlet to the last

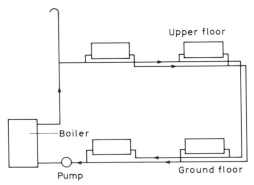

Fig. 2.4. A typical two-pipe system

radiator in the circuit, and that the return pipe begins at the outlet of the first radiator. Thus, in the *Figure 2.3* scheme, a single pipe acts for most of its length as both flow and return. But in the two-pipe system the flow and return functions are kept apart, the return coping only with that water which is waste, or spent, from the heating process.

It will be obvious from this that, subject only to a small practical loss, each radiator receives its water at the same temperature, which is the predetermined boiler temperature. This in turn means that (a) the heating system has more chance of being fully effective, and (b) it can actually save money on radiators, since to get a given heat output from a radiator operating at a lower temperature (as those later in the single-pipe circuit would do) calls for a larger radiator.

The second thing to be noticed about *Figure 2.4* is that each radiator is connected, inlet to flow, outlet to return. There is thus a wide differential pressure causing flow though the radiator, and the manner of flow is much nearer to being positively pumped. This means that the velocity of water flow through the radiator, hence the rate of warming and the response to change, are all more rapid.

A further advantage to come from the two-pipe system and its near-positive water flow is that we need no longer rely upon gravity circulation within the radiator, as was the case with a single-pipe system. Consequently we can get away from the 'top and bottom opposite ends' method of connection shown in *Figure 2.3*, and use any of the much tidier arrangements. Typical is that shown in *Figure 2.4*, of both connections at the bottom; or a later version which employs only one radiator tapping into which both connections enter.

Indirect Systems

All systems, whether single or two-pipe or microbore, are capable of being installed in two ways – direct and indirect. They should certainly not be installed as direct systems, but we must at least consider the possibility in order to see why not.

THE WET SYSTEM

A direct system is the basic one, in which water passes from boiler to pipework and back to boiler. It goes, too, usually through a cylinder, to hot taps. So every time hot water is drawn off, more water enters the system and passes through the boiler. Raw water is a mixture of many things, depending upon its source, but most of the ingredients can be harmful to a heating system, in or after going through a boiler. Hard waters will deposit scale in and beyond the boiler; reducing waterways, coating heating surfaces so that they must be forced to higher temperatures and in the end break from heat fatigue, or burn out. Many soft waters act in quite another way. Their reaction being acid, they attack metal surfaces, and bring about corrosion. This usually destroys a system more quickly than the scale build-up in hard water systems.

Direct systems give a choice, therefore, between the devil and the deep blue sea, and the safest course is to have no dealings with them. The way out is by an indirect system, in which water drawn from taps does not pass through the boiler, but gets heated indirectly. The key apparatus is an indirect cylinder. In appearance like any other cylinder, it contains a heat exchanger, in the form of a coil or other suitable type. Boiler water passes through the heat exchanger, and the domestic hot water for taps passes around the outside of the heat exchanger.

Thus it is that in a leak-free indirect system the primary circulation, which is the water passing through the boiler, heating system and heating coil in the cylinder, never changes. It is the same water going round all the time. If we suppose a system to contain 45 litres of water, and the water in raw condition to have in it 100 parts per million of scale forming or acid ingredient, the total weight of that ingredient to enter the system is 4.5 grams, which is negligible. Raw water must of course enter the cylinder on the secondary side, i.e. outside the heat exchanger, with its scaling or corrosive potentiality unchecked. But this is nowhere near as detrimental because

(1) under the less drastic heating conditions it does not behave so badly;

(2) it is easier and cheaper to clean or renew any apparatus on the secondary side, if this should ever become necessary; and

(3) it may be avoided entirely, since water treatment, most often softening, can be applied to the supply to the cylinder secondary side.

Water Treatment

Water in this context is rarely treated for acidity, mainly because acidity under the gentler conditions is rarely a great problem. Water softening however is often practised for a number of reasons, if nothing more than the supposition that hard water is bad for washing hair. There are really two levels of softening treatment. There is that which employs a softener, a piece of apparatus interposed in the line. Permutit is a long established example of this. The other method consists in treating the water in the feed/storage cistern, by suspending in it a container of crystals which dissolve slowly in the water and inhibit any scale material from depositing in crystalline form. Calgon or Micromet is obtainable, in suitable containers, from builder's merchants.

Let us pause and think what we know so far about a preferred type of system. It is very likely small bore, and a two-pipe system. It is indirect, perhaps with water softening applied to the secondary water supply. There is something else, which has become possible only in quite recent times. It may be open or sealed. The system which we all know in the UK (*Figure 2.5*), which has one or sometimes two cisterns in the roof, is an open system. It is precisely at these cisterns that it is open – to atmosphere. This means that in the ordinary way it cannot build up more pressure than that which is due to the 'head' of water measured up to the cistern level. If there were a surge of pressure it would vent off safely at the cistern.

The open type of system, though it proves satisfactory to most people, has been an irritant to some technical workers for a long time, partly because its supporters have claimed for it blessings which, apparently, the rest of the world cannot see. For it is almost exclusive to us. Not least of the complaints is that it forces us to store a large amount of water in our attics, and, some might say, makes us nationally dependent upon the ball valve.

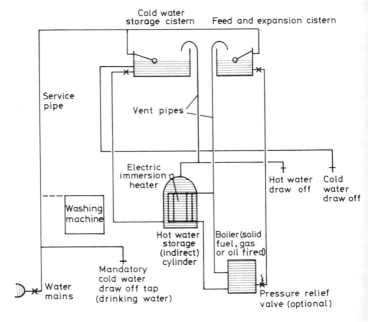

Fig. 2.5. Typical British domestic water installation

The alternative to an open system is a closed or sealed system, and this may be accompanied by either cistern fed or mains fed domestic hot water. The differences are shown in *Figure 2.6* and *2.7*.

It must first be understood that sealed systems are capable of building up pressures beyond those of an open system. This means that most of the apparatus — boilers, cylinders etc, supplied for open systems may be neither suitable nor safe. It means too that the general standard, even of making joints, must be higher; and that certain extra items must be fitted, which low pressure systems do not require. Thus in cost terms any economies due to saving a cistern and pipework are wiped out.

If we couple that with a warning, that sealed systems are not yet through the wood in terms of total acceptance by authorities; that high pressure appliances are not yet easy to come by; that the installation work is not for amateurs and not yet for a lot of professionals; we hope that readers will accept that in ordinary circumstances there is a lot of useful life left in open systems.

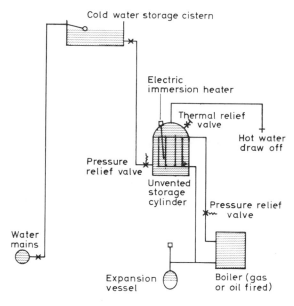

Fig. 2.6. Cistern fed unvented domestic hot water system with a sealed primary circuit. At the present time there are no bylaw requirements for the provision of a pressure relief valve, a thermal relief valve or an expansion vessel. The precautions shown are those recommended by the P.H.W.S. committee

A *sealed primary system* is one in which only the primary system is sealed, the secondary continuing to be supplied from a cistern. This is shown diagrammatically in *Figure 2.6* and includes the all-important expansion vessel. This vessel, in which a rubber diaphragm separates the water in the system from a cushion of air or nitrogen, takes the place of the expansion cistern in absorbing any expansion taking place during heating of the water.

The advantages claimed for a sealed primary system are:

(1) No cold feed/expansion cistern and consequently no freezing problems.

(2) No need for the head (vertical elevation) of a header tank, and the whole system can be accommodated on one floor level. Note that this is advantageous *only* in a system solely for heating. If domestic hot water is added, a loft cistern *is* required.

(3) It follows from (2) that if convenient the entire system may be accommodated in the loft to save useful space, subject to the same condition as (2).

(4) Sealing eliminates oxygen pick-up, thus reducing one source of corrosion.

(5) A sealed system can operate at higher temperatures since the boiling point of water is raised according to the amount of pressure imposed upon the system (determined by the control instruments). This means that smaller heat emitters may be used for a given duty. It will eliminate any tendency to boiling noises which afflict some installations.

It is a fact, but not an advantage, that if higher flow temperatures are used, conventional radiators cannot be used since they will develop unsafe surface temperatures. Convectors must be used instead. A distinct disadvantage of these systems is that, at the present time, they may not be connected to the mains water supply. They must be inspected regularly to see whether there is a loss of water, and if necessary topped up by manual means.

A *mains fed sealed system* as shown in *Figure 2.7* is fully pressurised, in that the domestic hot water supply is taken direct from the mains. This, it is fair to predict, will be the common pattern of the future, and not only on technical grounds. But to look at the technical factors first, this system begins by claiming those advantages listed for the sealed primary

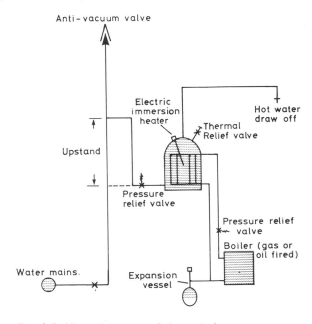

Fig. 2.7. Mains fed unvented domestic hot water storage system with a sealed primary circuit. Precautions shown are those recommended by the P.H.W.S. committee. Some of these are mandatory in continental Europe. The combination of anti-vacuum valve and upstand is required to prevent the water heater from draining down; similar protection can be afforded in other ways

system. It goes on to claim, for the pressurised secondary or domestic hot water side, that:

(1) it overcomes complaints about low pressure systems not giving sufficient flow or pressure at appliances. The

outstanding example of this is the shower, which in the UK is on average so much worse than continental practice;

(2) it makes possible a high performance total water installation on one floor, without need of gaining height (as in a loft);

(3) it clears the way for much smaller and neater water terminal fittings, taps and mixers, and for interconnections of smaller pipe diameter.

A. Cistern fed unvented hot water storage and sealed primary circuits — see fig 2·6

B. Instantaneous water heaters

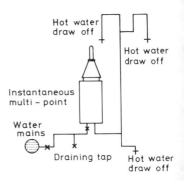

C. Water jacketed tube heaters

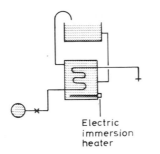

D. Mains fed storage heaters (each up to 68 litres)

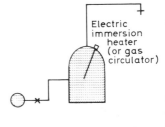

Fig. 2.8. Examples of unvented hot water apparatus which comply with the model water bylaws

The third point is an important one, with economic as well as technical issues involved. If UK water fittings can conform to continental standards in size and performance, which is to say an E.E.C. standard, we can use imported fittings and our manufacturers can make for continental markets without the extra cost of making 'specials'.

The sealed primary system is being installed, to a limited extent, and if a gas boiler is involved the gas industry is able to set out the limiting conditions for a safe installation.

At the time of writing a lot of high level activity is taking place in an effort to spell out the basic requirements of a wholly pressurised system. This involves the National Water Council and the regional Water Authorities, the Department of the Environment, and interested bodies such as the Institute of Plumbing. The impetus and the ingenuity will come from industry, who will design and make apparatus capable of performing right up to − and sometimes beyond − the limits to be laid down by the legislative bodies.

Pumps

The heart of a modern heating system, the pump, is still referred to at times as an accelerator or a circulator. More important to the user is the improvement in its reliability. In the early days of small bore the pump was the most temperamental item in view, if not actually breaking down then noisy. Nowadays all that a pump needs is to be protected from too much foreign matter in the circulating water and it will generally go on working indefinitely. We will not attempt to explain the internal arrangements of a pump since this is rarely relevant to the user or even the installer. Pumps may be 'in line' fixed, and consequently supported by the pipework and brackets; or they may stand on the floor. The former arrangement is by far the most common, particularly since pumps have become more compact. They do require adequate support, usually achieved by pipe bracketing but it is not necessary to use flexible connections as was being advised little more than 10 years ago! Makers' recommendations should be followed. For example some makers require that their pumps shall run with the spindle horizontal, which means fitting the pump in a vertical pipe line.

Many modern pumps have variable output adjustment, so that the pump, up to the limit of its capability, may be adjusted to suit the requirements of the installation. Broadly speaking a pump must be able to achieve the design requirements, which may be measured as causing a drop of 10 degC or 20 degF across the circuit. It must not do so much that it tends to push water right out of the circuit through the vent pipe. This condition, known as 'pumping over', encourages the water to dissolve air before it returns to the system. In that state it is responsible for massive internal corrosion of the system.

A pump which does not have adjustment built in may be suitably controlled by regulating the gate valve on the *outlet*. All pumps should be fitted with gate valves on inlet and outlet, so that the pump may be serviced without draining down the system. If an outlet gate valve is used as a regulator it is very helpful to attach a label to it, stating the amount of closure applied, e.g. ¾ turn, so that if shut for any reason the gate valve may be reset without a trial-and-error period.

Other forms of pump now available are the two-speed pump and the twin pumps in parallel. The first may have some application as a slow speed runner when the system is, relatively speaking, idling, as in late spring. Otherwise, the claim that it is suited to both large and small systems is not likely to benefit the householder if he has to pay for such versatility but never needs it. The other, the twin pumps, may suit those of a nervous disposition who believe in being prepared. It is however a development which would have been much more welcome ten or more years ago.

An important, indeed fundamental decision in circuit design is where to put the pump in relation to the boiler; and since the purpose of this concern is to relate the pump correctly to the vent and the cold feed, the decision really involves all three. Let us first dispose of one theory which was devised more as a money saver than on technical grounds, namely that it is satisfactory to combine the vent and the cold feed. It is not satisfactory and is bad practice.

The pump is more often fitted in the return than in the flow. In a small bore unit which comes fully equipped including a piped-in pump, the pump is almost always connected to the return. The return-fitted pump suits the average installation, in which the feed/expansion cistern is in the loft, and the highest point of the heating circuit is no more than about 0.6 metres above the bedroom floor level. There is then a distance between the cistern and the highest point in the circuit greater than the head of the pump. This creates a positive head of water sufficient to counteract the 'suction' effect which the

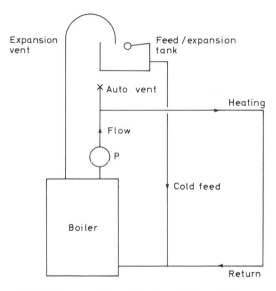

Fig. 2.9. Pump position where head of water is limited, for heating only

pump has on a considerable length of circuit, which would otherwise encourage air infiltration. If the vertical distance between the water level in the cistern and the highest point of the circuit is small, and less than the pump head, then the pump must be fitted in the flow pipe (*Figure 2.9*).

The cold feed and expansion or vent pipes must then be connected both on the same side of the pump. A useful arrangement with pump in the flow is shown in *Figure 2.10*. The air vent pipe is taken off the second boiler flow tapping and is an extension of the hot water flow primary. Like the

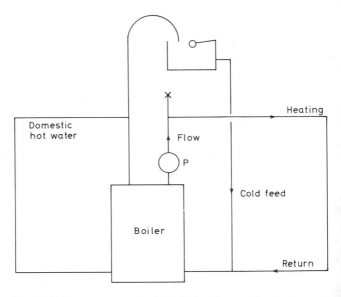

Fig. 2.10. The arrangement of Fig. 2.9 with provision for domestic hot water

cold water feed it is effectively on the pump suction. *Figure 2.11* shows a comparable system but with the pump in the return. This is an appropriate point at which to mention another detail of design. In both *Figures 2.10* and *2.11* it will be noticed that the heating return enters the boiler opposite to the hot water return pipe. (In boilers which do not have tappings opposite this does not apply.) We have already mentioned that the force causing gravity circulation is a very small one. It does not take a lot to neutralise or even to reverse it.

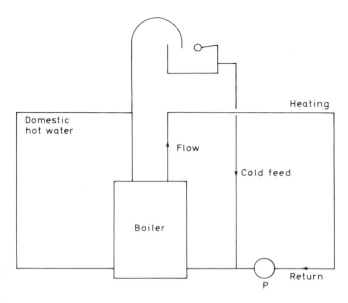

Fig. 2.11. A similar system to that of Fig. 2.10, but with the pump
in the return pipe

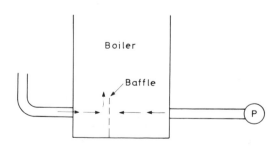

Fig. 2.12. Position of baffle in boiler to separate
flows of heating and hot water circuits

The situation, when the pump is running, is illustrated in *Figure 2.12* and this can in most cases promote reversed circulation in the hot water primaries for at least as long as the pump works. If the pump works for, say 10 minutes in every 20 or 30 minutes, the hot water circuit is unlikely to settle down to work. In some boilers this is recognised, and a baffle as shown in *Figure 2.12* is put in to keep the two streams apart.

Where no such arrangement exists the solution is to make both returns enter on the same side of the boiler, which means using a common pipe. The scheme shown in *Figure 2.13a* would

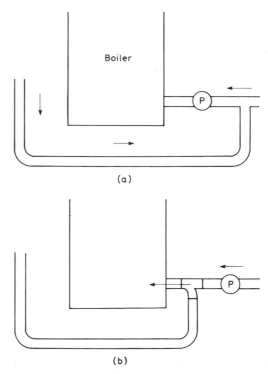

Fig. 2.13. Natural circulation is prevented in (a) when the pump is not in use, but possible with the arrangement shown in (b)

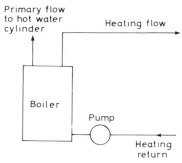

Fig. 2.14. Boiler and pump connections for a small-bore heating system

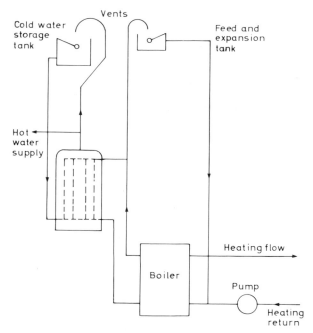

Fig. 2.15. Main features of a typical combined small-bore heating and hot water supply system

be excellent in lending pump suction to the hot water primary and so giving it a useful tonic, but it would effectively stop any circulation when the pump is off, which is all the summer. Consequently we come to arrangement *Figure 2.13b*. By the use of a swept or pitcher tee the flow of water from the pump is used to induce a flow in the other pipe, and if the pump is not running a natural circulation can carry on.

We must now come to consider the appliances which are placed in a wet system circuit as heat emitters, and we start with the most common one, the radiator.

Radiators

Most radiators nowadays are of the panel type. This means that they are almost flat but are grooved or dimpled or in some way wrinkled in order to increase the surface area within the total size which is called the 'picture frame' area (*Figure 2.16*). On this surface area their output depends.

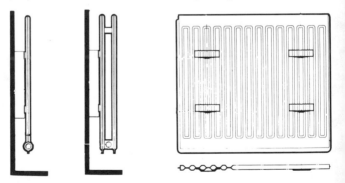

Fig. 2.16. Typical panel radiator which may be single or double panels (by courtesy of Thorn Heating Ltd.)

The other traditional design, called the column radiator, is rarely good looking, being designed for high output in a given space, and often known as the hospital radiator. Although not likely to be considered now for domestic use, it is if met the only radiator normally equipped with feet for floor standing. (This excludes some oil filled panel radiators for electric heating, which are fitted with feet.)

An imported style of radiator which is different in design is that which has a plain front face, e.g. of aluminium, with a heating coil closely soldered or brazed to the back. Radiators of this type offer a high resistance to flow and *must* be supplied through a two-pipe system or microbore, not a single-pipe system.

If other types and designs crop up from time to time they must be examined on their merits and it is up to the suppliers to say what those merits are — and to give some proof of what they claim, in particular the nominal heat output upon which all calculations must depend. The safest procedure is to insist upon buying only what has received MARC approval. (MARC is the Manufacturers' Association of Radiators and Convectors).

All radiators, being vessels which are capable of collecting air, should be equipped with an air release tapping, to be fitted with an air cock or automatic air vent. All radiators should be supplied with the proper means of support, which usually means wall brackets.

Radiators may be finished in enamel or left in primer to be finished by the customer. In the latter case, and for subsequent redecoration, it makes very little difference what type or colour of paint is used, with the one exception that so-called metallic paints, such as aluminium and bronze, must not be used since they reduce the heat output substantially. It is worth noting here that after repainting three or four times the thickness of paint film will become a barrier to heat movement and the paint should then be stripped before repainting again.

The output of a radiator is one aspect examined by MARC. It is measured as the heat emission from the panel when there exists a temperature difference, between the water inside the panel and the air just outside it, of 55 degC or 100 degF. Obviously the emission will be higher if the differential is greater, less if it is lower. Perhaps less obviously, a radiator will give of its best when first coming to work in a cold room. As the room warms the output rate will slow down in proportion, this occurring naturally, without the use of instruments or controllers. Though we must rely upon MARC for a definitive output it is often convenient to get a rough idea of how big a radiator is going to be needed before the design is finalised.

In rough figures, then, a single panel radiator will give 0.6 $kW/m^2/55degC$ or 190 $Btu/ft^2/100$ degF: while a double panel will give 0.5 and 160 respectively.

Using those figures to find out just how big a radiator is in wall or picture frame area, take the dimension figure, square metres or feet and remember that all radiators have two sides. So, suppose a radiator surface is given as $1m^2$ ($10ft^2$), the side you see is only $0.5m^2$ ($5ft^2$). For approximation this may well suffice, but it will be a trifle on the high side. The surface area of a panel, you will recall, is artificially increased by the use of profiling. To get a nearer idea of the picture frame area you could knock 10% off the nominal figure, in this case giving $0.45m^2$ (4.5 ft^2). Steel radiators are recommended for use with indirect systems only.

Where to Put the Radiator

We must start any such consideration by knowing how a radiator — any radiator, whether water or oil filled — works. It delivers heat as natural convection, a rising warm air current, and as radiation. Since the radiation content can be up to half the total, its importance cannot be overlooked. This leads to the first basic conclusion, that wherever the radiator is situated it must be able to 'see' the room. That is to say that it must not be hidden, either permanently behind a sideboard or similar, or effectively by having an easy chair usually pushed back against it. As well as shielding the radiant warmth from the room such treatment will result in overheating the adjacent furniture, with rapid deterioration of textiles and plastics.

We must then think about the radiation from the back side of the radiator. Radiators are always fitted to walls or panels, and usually by brackets supplied. Tests have shown that there is an appreciable loss of heat from the room, through the wall, for this reason. Further tests, interposing insulating slabs and reflective insulation between radiator and wall were not encouraging. The first showed no real change, while the second reduced heat loss but also reduced radiator output.

The logical conclusion is that the radiator would be best placed in the middle of the room. In practical terms it means that it should be fitted to an inside wall, and if this is done overall heat savings of the order of $5 - 10\%$ can be expected. In addition there will usually be a significant saving in pipe runs. This location is in obvious conflict with what we have come to accept, that radiators should be fitted under windows. We must remember however that there was just one reason for that, namely to counter descending downdraughts off the cold glass, with reduction of condensation. That remains a valid reason, except that it ceases to apply where double glazing is fitted. The under-window position has always introduced contention with ladies whose attachment to their full length curtains has assumed greater importance than the technical refinements of heating practice.

Having established that there is an equal case for fitting radiators on inside walls or under windows, we come in the former case to ask where. Within broad limits this is not important. It calls for a small amount of imagination, a visualisation of how the warm air will flow as it rises off the radiator. For example, given only one radiator in a room which is long and narrow one would not fit the radiator at one end, but roughly central — unless occupation were to be confined to one end. The situation chosen for the radiator must allow not only for the radiator to 'see' but for a free air flow to have access to it. Radiators must not be boxed in, for appearance or any other reason, unless it is fully appreciated that this can result in a serious fall in heat output.

A more widespread move to take radiators away from the window position will draw new attention to the radiator shelf. This device has a strictly limited purpose. It prevents or mitigates wall staining above the radiator, which is justification enough. Its effect upon radiator output is usually to bring about a slight decrease, and care must be taken to fit it in the right relative position, not for instance sitting down tightly upon the radiator.

The conclusions about situation reached for radiators do not apply to convectors, fan convectors or unidirectional radiators (such as electric fires). All appliances which are predominantly convectors will have positions which suit their warm air output whether natural or forced. It is a pity that warm air cannot be coloured, since this would greatly assist the imagination when choosing the best sites.

Connections to Radiators

Having examined the general form of the system, and expressed a preference for the two-pipe version, we come to the detail of radiator connection to any type of system.

The wall brackets must be securely fastened to the wall, in positions so that the radiator is suspended true and level. The final connections should be made between circulating pipes and radiator so as to impose no strain upon the brackets or the radiator.

Each radiator should have two valves fitted. It is bad practice to skimp in this respect, for even removing a radiator to paint it will involve the cost or inconvenience of draining down the whole system. One of the valves should be of the lockshield pattern, i.e. to be turned only with a special key. This valve is used for balancing when commissioning the system, as we shall explain later. The amount of opening should be recorded in case it is closed for any reason.

It is a good rule to fit the lockshield valve on the outlet end, the other valve for on/off control being on the inlet. The only time that order becomes obligatory is when the control valve is of the thermostatic type, since this type is almost always made for unidirectional flow. The on/off control is there to be used. It is the means of achieving warmth only when and where needed. The use of thermostatic radiator valves is explained in Chapter 8.. In general the angle pattern valve is preferable to the straight pattern. Not only does it make for a neater job, with less pipe showing, but the radiator may be removed from service without having to spring the pipes apart.

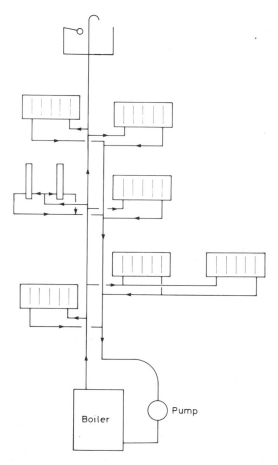

Fig. 2.17. Illustrating the benefit obtained by running flow and return pipes by the most direct route. Only the radiator circuits are shown

The Close-coupled System

The growing practice of double glazing has greatly reduced the significance of radiators under windows. It opens the way for considerable reduction in installation cost, particularly in premises which tend to be long and narrow, in either a vertical or a horizontal direction. As *Figure 2.17* shows, the benefit is achieved by running the flow and return out and in by the most direct route, taking off connections to radiators by the shortest pipe runs. In some cases radiators may be fitted back to back, the ultimate in pipe economy. A system may combine this type of run with longer runs made inevitable by the house plan. *Figure 2.17* shows a vertical system, but the principle applies equally to a horizontal run. Also, the diagram shows a two-pipe system but it can apply to a single pipe system.

Skirting Heaters

The radiator, however much it is styled, is an alien object in any home. If it were not wanted for heating no one would have it. But everyone has skirting boards, and heaters which closely resemble skirting boards must be widely acceptable. That is just one of the advantages of skirting heating. Others are that it does not take up wall space, that it encourages a better vertical temperature gradient (difference between temperature at floor and ceiling level). The reason that we do not see more of it in the UK is that it costs more than radiators, but another answer might be that we sometimes run out of wall. Walls are often used to back sideboards, bookcases, cupboards, thus effectively making those skirtings unusable.

For a rough check, once the heat requirement of the room has been calculated, an average skirting heater will give 450 watt/metre or Btu/ft length of heater. This is based upon a mean temperature difference of 55 degC or 100 degF. In marginal cases a search of the market might show that one make offers significantly more output per unit length.

The skirting heater is, in effect, a tube whose heat emission characteristic has been greatly increased by a number of fins brazed to it. This is encased in a panel structure fitted with a damper (*Figure 2.18*). The damper controls the amount of air able to flow over the fins, hence the heat output of the unit. A closed damper will generally bring the output down to about 30% of the rated value. A more satisfactory method of construction is that which employs a bypass pipe with valves on the finned tube, so that when not wanted in circuit it may be isolated.

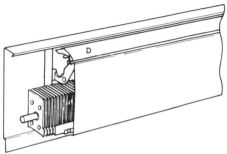

Fig. 2.18. Typical skirting heater in section. D is the damper

These notes, on skirting heaters and similar apparatus, are necessarily general in character, and aimed to explain the nature of the items. Each manufacturer introduces his special feature, which may add something to ease of operation, or appearance, or ease of maintenance. Once the reader is aware of the broad facts he or she must judge the various special claims on their merits in relation to the job in hand.

Skirting heaters emit a certain amount of radiant heat, though the proportion is much lower than in the case of radiators. Both because of this and because of the rising convection, it is not advisable to stand solid objects permanently in front of the heaters at close range.

Convectors

Convectors form a class of appliance whose heat output is almost entirely in the form of a warm air current. There are two forms of convector, natural and fan assisted, and they deserve to be considered separately. The natural convector resembles the radiator in size and in being wall hung. It is particularly useful in situations where a high radiant factor is not required, or where a high convected output is best. A library or an art gallery is an example, requiring a good level of

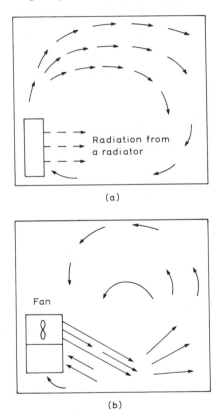

(a)

(b)

Fig. 2.19. Convected warm air pattern from a radiator or natural convector (a) and air travel pattern from a fan convector (b)

ambient warmth but absence of high spots caused by direct radiation.

The convector is capable of giving an output well above its rated value, since it can be connected to a pressurised system working at a temperature in excess of that which an atmospheric system can achieve. The front face remains at a safe temperature.

The detailed design of convectors varies considerably between makes, but all those worth considering have in common that they should be able to claim MARC approval.

The low level of radiant heat output of a convector brings another difference from radiators. We have been at pains to stress that radiators must not be crowded by furniture, which would intercept the radiant heat, with loss of useful efficiency and possible damage to the furniture. The only prohibited area around a convector is above it. For instance one would not hang a picture or a mirror over a convector (*Figure 2.19a*).

The fan convector is very different, because of its powered output (*Figure 2.19b*). It is usual to fit this item within about 0.3m (1ft) of the floor, allowing space for the circulating air to return to the lower half of the unit. Then the discharge, which in some cases has some directional adjustment, is angled downwards at the floor some 2m (6ft) distant. In this way it effectively prevents natural layering, the stratification which allows colder air to collect at floor level. The fan convector correctly installed can promote the lowest room temperature gradient of all heat emitters, no more than 2 or 3 degC difference between head and foot level.

To be able to do so it requires two conditions. First, it must have an uninterrupted distance in front of it of at least 3 m and preferably more, so that the 'throw' pattern can develop along with its secondary entrainment pattern. Then, it should be in a central position on a wall in order to obtain full advantage from the secondary entrainments which occur at both sides of the main air stream. A unit fitted near the end of a wall will lose that effect on one side.

The heat exchanger in a fan convector is a concentrated one. This means that a fan convector has an output equivalent to a natural radiator of at least six times its wall or picture frame

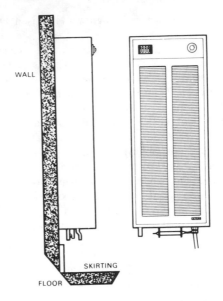

Fig. 2.20. A vertical fan convector (by courtesy of Myson Group Marketing Ltd)

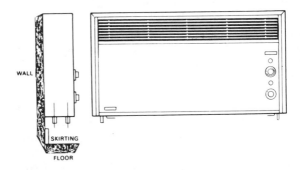

Fig. 2.21. A horizontal fan convector (by courtesy of Myson Group Marketing Ltd)

area. It means too that the unit offers a quite high resistance to flow and must be fitted in a two-pipe circuit.

A fan convector is almost entirely dependent upon the fan for its output. Consequently its on/off control is very easily carried out, by means of an electric switch. Additional controls include a speed changing switch, to adjust the output to the *range* of temperature required, for example high speed for cold weather or quick warm-up, with medium or low speed for milder times or when the room is just about up to temperature. The final adjustment, to achieve a close control of room temperature, is brought about automatically by a built-in thermostat which senses the temperature of the air returning to the unit. Best running results are obtained by using the speed change switch so that the thermostat keeps the unit running most of the time. It is for example better for room temperature control to have the unit running 20 minutes out of every 30, than 10 in 30.

The aim in this chapter has been to present a broad picture of what goes to make up a wet system (excluding the boiler, which calls for special treatment). Certain patterns emerge. For instance:

A two-pipe system is better than a single-pipe system, but either is vastly better than a gravity system

Except in a couple of small areas in Britain where the water is relatively harmless, no one should be allowed to fit a direct water system for heating.

Radiators, convectors and fan convectors can be installed relatively cheaply in many properties, using the close-coupled type of system.

The best temperature gradient results come from skirting heaters and fan convectors.

Fan convectors use very little wall space, are recommended for living rooms, not bedrooms (on account of the slight 'click' as the thermostat switches).

Radiators remain simple, easy to clean; their radiant output of some benefit.

There is room for all types of heat emitter, not only in the market but in any one house. For example, matching unit to duty, one could choose a fan convector for the living room, radiators for bedrooms, a natural convector for the hall.

3 The Boiler as Part of the Wet System

To repeat an earlier statement, the precise type of boiler or the fuel it uses is rarely a matter of any great importance, except to those who sell fuel. The only example of boilers which are not completely interchangeable is that of a system of heating only (with no domestic hot water) having all the heat emitters capable of shutting down at the same time. Such a system could not have a solid fuel boiler, which *must* have a buffer, usually the hot water cylinder, to mop up surplus heat during the slowing down period.

Pressure jet oil fired boilers are not often tolerated indoors, and to that extent are not fully interchangeable with other types. But that is only because of their operating noise, and not relevant to the present context. It is convenient when listing the principal types of boiler available to put them in fuel categories.

Gas: There is the free standing type, with smart casing if it goes in the kitchen, without case if it will go under the stairs or in the attic. The back boiler is allied to a gas fire and is not seen, but is generally much the same boiler as the free standing one, perhaps shortened. The wall hung boiler represents a new breed, with its own technology.

Oil is represented mainly by free standing types, of which there are three: pressure jet, wall flame and vaporiser, depending upon the type of combustion. Oil is taking from solid fuel some of the job of heating combination ranges of the Aga type, and there is even a unit fired by oil which closely resembles a gas fired back boiler with fire.

Solid fuel i.e. a grade of coal (see Fuels, Chapter 7), coke or prepared smokeless fuel. Without access to statistics, if such exist, it is probably true to say that there are more back boiler type appliances than any other type using solid fuel domestically. The choice among bigger and more instrumented appliances is now quite limited, and for an assessment at any given time one should consult the Solid Fuel Advisory Service, Hobart House, London SW1. Solid fuel has many admirable qualities, but it lacks the ability to be instantaneously controlled which its competitors have, and it is not therefore always best suited to work in systems which depend upon quick positive control. In the open fire/back boiler combination, where the only control is a manually operated damper, it does well.

The open fire/back boiler, even the closeable fire with back boiler, has been victimised over the years. Far too often it has, no doubt because of its relatively low cost, become associated with other forms of cost cutting which in these enlightened times should not be tolerated. The most usual is the direct system which we have seen to be responsible for bad internal troubles inside systems. By all means have a back boiler unit if you wish, but do not skimp the system on that account. Also, be aware of what you are buying in quantitative terms. Remember, *as much* heat as you need?

A typical boiler for a typical house would be rated at least 13 kW or 45 000 Btu/h for full central heating. A typical open fire/back boiler is rated at about 7.5 kW or 25 000 Btu/h. It is unlikely that this or any solid fuel appliance will maintain its rated output through all the changes of fuelling and clinkering, burn up and run down of fire bed intensity and so on. So this unit is necessarily associated with an installation with limited requirements, perhaps partial heating, or selective heating.

Gas Boilers

To look at boilers in the sort of detail which might count when deciding to buy, let us start with that which is numerically most in demand — the gas boiler. If we are to look for a reason for this success, perhaps the foremost is that a gas boiler is easy. It is so easy that it will go for a year entirely unattended. No fuel to order, store, carry; no lighting procedure; rarely any noise or temperamental behaviour. These are points which will appeal to those who are planning for retirement and an easy life.

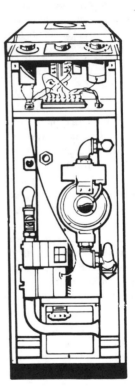

Fig. 3.1. A typical gas fired small bore unit for heating and hot water (by courtesy of Thorn Heating Ltd)

In spite of the growing variety, the standard gas boiler is still based upon a cast iron heat exchanger. This is the free standing boiler, with or without stove enamelled steel case, usually situated in the kitchen or under the stairs (*Figure 3.1*). There is no real limit to the places where a boiler may be placed,

though bedrooms should be avoided on account of the disconcerting 'click' a thermostat can make in the quiet small hours.

It is customary to make the boiler casing to standard kitchen
unit height. In spite of this being the subject of a British
Standard, it is surprising how ideas vary about what an
acceptable height is. The safe course, in order to match kitchen
furniture already in place, is to determine the actual height. A
short boiler can be stood on a metal plate, or tile, to increase
its height.

Most manufacturers try to keep the back-to-front dimension
down as well, still pursuing the elusive 'kitchen unit' standard.
But the real stress is laid upon width, and with certain essential
components to be housed it is obvious that the makers cannot
go on cutting down all three dimensions. So, in the end, it may
take some juggling to get the kitchen looking uniform.

A word of warning against too much emphasis upon neatness
of packaging of kitchen cabinets etc. with the boiler. Read the
boiler instructions carefully. It is very likely that there must be
50mm (2in) space at one or both sides. Some boilers take their
essential air in at the back, and it is therefore vital for ample
air to be available at the back of the boiler. The flue, if it goes
away from the back, must not be in contact with any com-
bustible material. The free space in front of the boiler, if
necessary through an opening door, must be equal to the total
length of the boiler, so that the burner may be withdrawn
during servicing.

It is *not* a part of the responsibility of anyone employing an
installer to decide between the merits of conventional and
balanced flue. This is a matter which tends to decide itself, in
relation to the site. If there is a good flue or chimney, and if
the boiler may conveniently be joined to it and be acceptable
in that position, then a conventionally flued model is the
obvious choice. A balanced flue should not be regarded as an
equal alternative, but as the second choice if a conventional
flue is not available. This advice is strengthened by the fact
that balanced flue models cost more to buy. Chapter 6 deals
with flue characteristics but it is appropriate here to note that
a balanced flue appliance takes its combustion air direct from

outdoors, making no demands upon the room where it is situated. So if for any reason there is likely to be difficulty in getting an adequate air supply to the boiler, good conventional flue notwithstanding, then in that case a balanced flue model would be preferable.

The basic controls on a gas boiler are nowadays almost exclusively electrical. Despite the degree of dependence implied, the risk is small and the benefits, in crisp positive action, considerable. Thus, the boiler thermostat and the gas control valve, and the programmer if fitted, are all electrical. But it is comforting to note that the most basic safety device, the flame failure mechanism, does not depend upon current electricity. It works entirely off the pilot flame, which heats a small bimetal junction, generating an electromagnetic potential which holds open a key gas valve. If the pilot goes out that key gas valve cannot remain open, and nothing can open it. So however much the boiler instruments call for heat, no gas will flow unless the pilot is alight to ignite it.

A boiler which is engaged in heating is a part of a circuit which itself has to be controlled. There is a good deal of sense and usefulness in lumping most of those controls on to the boiler, so that it becomes the 'engine room' of the system. The commonest such addition is the programmer, whose principal duty is to control the starting and stopping times of the boiler, whether it is required to give domestic hot water only or a full service of hot water and central heating.

There are simple programmers with four or five programmes on offer, and there are magnificent units with a great many choices. We will not attempt to indicate which is preferable, and indeed it is a matter for personal choice, influenced perhaps by consideration of how the household operates in its coming and goings. The only pertinent observation to make from experience is that people with say ten programmes to choose from rarely use more than three or four.

A fully equipped boiler usually houses a junction box, into which are wired such external services as the pump and the room thermostat which, along with the clock in the programmer, controls its activity.

It is appropriate at this point to mention the use of the boiler thermostat. Some quaint ideas persist about this, for instance that using a very low temperature setting helps to keep the boiler from wearing out. Unfortunately for this theory the truth is quite opposite. A setting below 60°C (140°F) encourages the boiler to wear out since it permits condensation in the flueways. When direct systems were common, the problems connected with going to higher temperatures were just as serious. In hard water areas, the higher the temperature the more troublesome the scale deposition. That is why the 140°F was first selected, as a compromise. But now that systems are indirect the prohibition is removed, and we recommend the use of the thermostat for seasonal modulation of boiler output. In hard winter set it high, not less than 80°C (180°F), and indeed up to 90°C (190°F). This enables the boiler, and the heat emitters, radiators etc, to give their maximum output. In moderate winter weather this temperature may be relaxed, perhaps to the $70-75^\circ$C ($160-170^\circ$F) range. The milder beginning and end of the heating season are the times for the lower setting. Such attentions are not strictly necessary, but one should never forget the usefulness of the upper range. Instead of getting annoyed with the inadequacy of the boiler, turn up the thermostat to make it work harder.

Ignition

A distinction must be made between first lighting, and the routine automatic lighting of the main burner which occurs under the influence of the boiler thermostat. The second is standardised, employing a small pilot flame which also heats the thermal junction — the flame safety device. The adjustment of the pilot is a part of the boiler design and should never be altered except by an expert. Spark ignition is becoming more common, but is not an alternative, since a given model or make of boiler has one or the other built in. Spark ignition saves the surprising annual cost of running a pilot. Pilot ignition has no moving parts to wear out. The lighting of the pilot introduces some variety of method, though too much should not be made of this, for it will normally occur only once or twice in a season. The room sealed appliance, i.e. balanced flue or Se-duct, is never nowadays lit manually. In anything like an on-terminal wind it is impossible. In the earliest days models were made for manual lighting, and users were advised to hang their hat over the terminal temporarily. But six floors up? With that exception, the main methods of lighting a pilot are:

(1) Manual, using a taper or match, never a bulky spill of paper.

(2) By glow coil, mains fed through a transformer. Many multifunctional controls operate at 12 volts, and the transformer handles everything. The glow coil method is losing popularity, partly because like all incandescent coils it has a measurable life.

(3) By piezo-electric igniter. The quite unexpected result of hitting a certain crystalline chemical a sharp blow is to produce a very high voltage, which can be made to jump a gap as a spark. This is the piezo effect and is built into a small triggering device in the form of a pull or push button. It is entirely independent of any outside source of energy. Piezo igniters are now being sold as hand held units, like the old flint lighter for cookers. They could therefore be used for manual lighting.

Servicing

The routine servicing of a gas boiler involves partial dismantling, removal of burner and of any cleaning cover necessary to enable the heat exchanger to be thoroughly brushed or scraped. A particular area for attention is in the gas injector and at the burner tips. The entrainment of air can lead to a collection of air borne dust and fibres, and a condition called 'linting' can occur. This interferes with the designed air/gas ratio, hence with good combustion. The prohibition against using a paper spill for lighting is to keep paper ash out of the burner.

THE BOILER AS PART OF THE WET SYSTEM

All electrical connections should be examined, and so far as possible instruments and controls checked for operation. It is however usual in routine servicing to assume that if controls are known to be operating satisfactorily they are not in need of detailed attention. Servicing includes taking care of anything specifically mentioned as being in need of attention. Cover plates almost always have a gasket, of asbestos or similar, to form an air tight seal. These gaskets should be renewed.

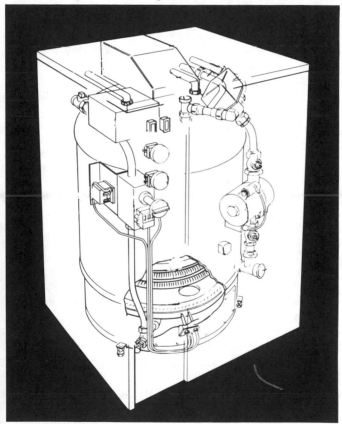

Fig. 3.2. The Worcester Delglo boiler, balanced flue model

A good service engineer will always leave the appliance at work, unless instructed otherwise, and will draw the owner's attention to anything he should know, such as a particular item which ought to receive attention at the next service visit.

Change and innovation are characteristics of a progressive technology, and there is always something happening in the total field of gas boilers and the like. Frequently it is not greatly significant, just enough to give a manufacturer a talking point, but one fairly recent change seems to be in a more significant category, in part because it has to do with that important household commodity, space. The innovators named it Mighty Mouse, though a change of company ownership resulted in the less memorable renaming to Worcester Delglo.

The ex-MM is based upon a gas fired boiler, output 13.4 kW or 45 000 Btu/h. Instead of serving a hot water cylinder in some remote airing cupboard, it incorporates its cylinder within the case, thus saving not only space but heat loss from pipework (*Figure 3.2*). More than that, it employs a larger than usual heat exchanger, giving a high heat make-up rate into a reduced volume of stored water. The makers claim that it will serve a bath every 12 minutes.

It has conventional and balanced flue models, and is British Gas approved.

The Gas Fired Back Boiler

Unlike the free standing boiler, which may be made in any size, the back boiler has limits imposed upon it by the aperture available. The free standing boiler is made right up to the generally accepted but arbitrary limit for domestic equipment of 44kW or 150 000 Btu/h. A back boiler is still struggling to beat 13kW or 45 000 Btu/h. But in terms of usefulness that is only a part of the story. The gas fire will almost always give ample warmth for the room in which it is situated, and the total effective output of the unit could be placed at say 4.5kW (15 000 Btu/h) higher.

The problem of how to get more than a pint into the pint pot of a British Standard chimney opening is almost the only technical problem left. Details of flue sharing with the fire, remote lighting of the pilot or burner, controls for the boiler incorporated in the fire, have all been satisfactorily settled. It must be noted however that the pairing of a fire and a boiler is fundamentally work for a manufacturer. If you have a gas fire you cannot go out and buy a boiler, and couple the two together. In case it is not obvious, this application is for conventional flue only, and it is noteworthy for two reasons. First, it makes the most of the limited space in modern dwellings, by taking no space at all. Second, it forces upon the user a source of radiant heat. This is in some respects superior to convected warmth though impractical as a source of 'central' heat.

All the comments already made about ignition and servicing apply, with (in the case of the latter) the extra proviso that the fire must be removed (and so serviced) in order to get at the boiler.

Wall Hung Boiler

A development even more recent than the back boiler is the wall hung boiler (*Figure 3.3*), another concession to the urge to save space. Weight was very much in mind at the start, and in some cases no doubt still is. Cast iron was abandoned in favour of alloy coated copper for the heat exchanger, and a fair comparison would be with an oversized Ascot type water heater. With this went very small waterways and an entirely new concept of urgency, necessary when applying a lot of heat to a little water. This had to be kept moving rapidly, and so was continuously pumped. A change in control methods had to be made, to ensure that the burner would not light unless the pump were working, and that the pump would stay working for long enough after the burner went out to purge the 'after heat'.

But now ways have been found to blend the old technology into the new package, and we have wall hung boilers which have cast iron heat exchangers and are suited to gravity circulation as well as to pumped primaries.

561

It must be kept in mind however that though the conditions may be relaxed they are most carefully worked out. When fitting one of these, or indeed any boiler, the maker's instructions should be read and followed very carefully. These

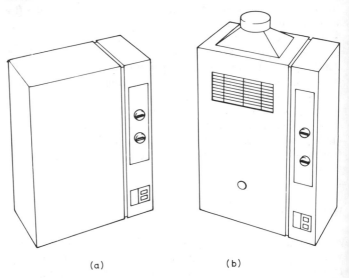

Fig. 3.3. Typical wall hung boilers, (a) with balanced flue, while (b) has a conventional flue

instructions are a part of the official approval and always a condition by which the guarantee is valid. In other words if you do not fit it as instructed you cannot expect any sympathy if it misbehaves.

Boilers on Bottled Gas

In theory — and we stress that point — there is no reason why almost any gas appliance ever devised should not be made in a bottled gas version. But in practice the list is quite short, for two reasons. One is that manufacturers are under no obligation to work out the necessary design characteristics in fulfilling their prime obligation, which is to the approvals authority, British Gas. Some do, and no doubt other makers would if they could command the very considerable work force needed. A second reason may be that conversion characteristics have been worked out as a laboratory exercise, but no parts manufactured. If anyone is interested in converting an existing appliance, or is particularly taken by one model of a new one, the only sure way to find out if parts or even information are available is to ask the technical staff of the manufacturer concerned. Given the information, the gas supplier might be able to do the conversion.

In spite of the difference in combustion and combustion equipment, bottled gas appliances are operationally similar to those using natural gas in all relevant respects. The technicalities are already built in and do not concern the user. Installation might be slightly different in that the required size of the gas pipe supplying the appliance can be smaller for bottled gas.

Some notes on bottled gas appear in Chapter 7. The only query likely to arise concerns the size of storage container, which may depend on the number and type of appliance to be supplied. This is best resolved by taking the advice of the supplier, which will be based upon national experience. The aim is to strike a balance between keeping the cost of hire down, and taking advantage of any bulk discount obtainable – and getting a reasonable time of running out of one container.

Oil Fired Boilers

Perhaps the most important distinction between types of oil boiler divides those which can be used indoors or out from those which are best suited to be away from the house. The latter are the pressure jets, and perhaps the name jet will suggest why this type of burner is best given a place of its own to operate in. Of the rest, those which depend entirely upon natural operation are silent, the rest make some noise however slight. It is always worth asking, in any given case, whether there is a history of the model making more noise as it ages and wears.

The principal types of vaporising burners, as they are called, are the wall flame (*Figure 3.4*) and the pot type, for natural or fan assisted draught. The wall flame and the fan assisted pot type must have electricity, but it is usual nowadays to electrify all types, because as in the case of gas it makes control so much easier and so much more standard.

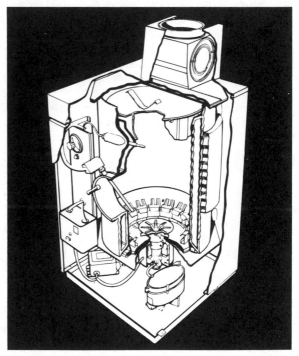

Fig. 3.4. A typical wall flame oil-fired boiler

Another common feature of these boilers is that they burn kerosene, which is 28 sec or Class C fuel oil. They operate in a routine way under the control of a boiler thermostat, and it depends upon the detail of the controller whether the burner works on/off or on high/low flame.

The incorporation of other controls, a clock or programmer for instance, present no difficulty so long as the boiler is electrified, for controls of this kind simply control electric circuits. A clock, for instance, is only a means of switching on or off, and so stopping or starting an operation.

We will not make a serious attempt to describe how these boilers operate. They are not suitable subjects for amateur adjustment or even servicing, and so the details are not relevant. It should be sufficient to know that all the vaporisers have a method of converting the liquid fuel to a vapour, in which form it burns. The method of conversion differs considerably from one type to the next. It is most important that the boiler is not neglected. For instance signs of sooting might indicate that a primary air port has become blocked, perhaps by something falling across it. Irregularities not understood should be reported, and as with gas boilers it is desirable to have an understanding, if not actually a service contract, with a trusted engineer.

Not all models of this type of boiler are available over the entire domestic range, nominally up to 44kW or 150 000 Btu/h. The starting range is about 8 kW or 27 000 Btu/h. Forced draught vaporisers go up to about 23 kW or 80 000 Btu/h, and there are wall flame or rotary vaporisers up to the maximum.

A point to watch for and to get settled at the earliest stage concerns the type of combustion control and the maker's instructions about the system. Boilers of the vaporising type which have on/off control are in general in line with any other instantaneously controlled boiler unit, such as gas. They are safe for use in a 'heating only' system if necessary. But boilers which have high/low flame control, in which the low flame may be compared to an exaggerated pilot, generate an amount of heat in their 'at rest' position, which must be dissipated if overheating is to be avoided. It is customary to employ this surplus warmth usefully, through the primary circuit which feeds the domestic hot water cylinder, the cylinder being an essential part of such a circuit. The heat emitter is a towel rail or small radiator, usually in the bathroom, which is always in circuit. Being in the hot water primary it is independent of any circulating pump which may be on the heating circuit proper. The need to know about any such requirement *before* ordering materials and running pipes, will be obvious.

We have already described the pressure jet boiler as a type unsuited to being indoors, and this is bound to bring pained reaction from some manufacturers. Operational noise occupies a major part of their development engineers' attention, and someone is always claiming to have beaten the bogey. But in the end it is the owner's sensitivity of hearing which settles the matter, and we would advise anyone in doubt to ask for a practical demonstration. But let us add one other note of caution. The site can sometimes influence the nature and level of noise. There are cases of a pressure jet being connected to a

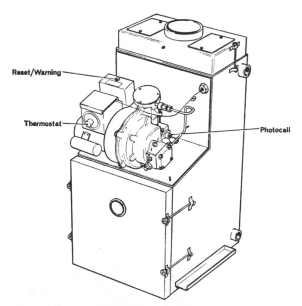

Fig. 3.5. A down fired pressure jet oil-fired boiler, without case (by courtesy of Thorn Heating Ltd)

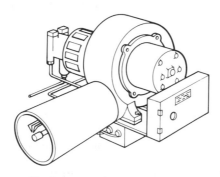

Fig. 3.6. Typical pressure jet burner

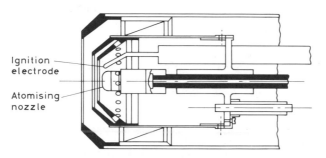

Ignition
electrode

Atomising
nozzle

Fig. 3.7. A typical combustion head used in a pressure jet burner

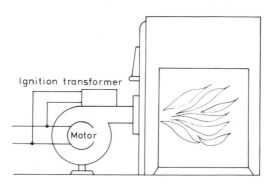

Ignition transformer

Motor

Fig. 3.8. How a pressure jet burner fires

chimney which runs by a bedroom, where the flue gases have to make a sharp change of direction. The effect, particularly in the quiet of night, is of distant battle, muffled but insistent. It is a clear warning to pay attention to the flue as part of the whole installation.

Pressure jets differ from other forms of combustion, in that the flame is not divided between a number of burner jets or spread over an area. It is concentrated in one jet, rather like the water from a fireman's hose, and like that example it issues under pressure. The fuel oil is ejected under pressure from the pump which is incorporated in the burner, and at the point of release is atomised by being given a swirling motion as it passes through a very finely machined and calibrated nozzle. The combustion air, also under pressure and controlled, is admitted and admixed in a very precise way, within the burner assembly. By choice of nozzle, by adjustment of the pump pressure and the air inlet damper, a high degree of precision is obtainable. One of the principal objects of regular service is to ensure that the set conditions are maintained: to keep the nozzle free from foreign matter which might have got past the filters; to see that there is no interference with the air ways.

Pressure jets are on/off burners, and ignition is by spark from a pair of electrodes bridging the exit of the fuel nozzle.

The brain and heart of a pressure jet is the control box. It houses the boiler thermostat, for instance, and when this is satisfied it cuts the current to the burner pump and fan. When the thermostat again calls for heat it sets the spark ignition going, as a preliminary to starting oil pump and fan. If the burner does not light it persists for a given number of seconds, then stops. There is then a pause, known as a purging period, to allow unburnt oil vapour to escape. The control box will then initiate another firing period of similar length to the first. If this fails the burner will shut down, and a red light will show. It is a signal to see what might be wrong, and nothing can be restarted until the user has manually reset the burner by pressing a green button.

At this stage someone is sure to ask how it is that the control box knows that the burner has not lit. Well, it has an eye, a photo-electric cell which is inserted into the combustion chamber. When it sees a flame it generates a very small electric current, enough to inform the control box. If that information is missing the control box reacts in the way described. If it does, the first and most obvious step to take is to make sure that the 'eye' is clean. Quite often a shut-down is due to nothing worse than a thin film of carbon or soot on the glass. But, such is the overall reliability of the device, the second most common cause of flame failure is running out of fuel. This might be due to a blocked filter or pipe line rather than an empty tank.

Pressure jet boilers are generally less sensitive about flue conditions than the vaporising types, for the very good reason that they create a pressure in the combustion chamber to start the evacuation process going.

The smallest pressure jet boilers are in the 14 kW or 50 000 Btu/h range, but they then go on into sizes far above the domestic range. They belong therefore to the larger installation.

Pressure jet burners may be specified for one class of fuel only, i.e. Class C or D, which is kerosene or gas oil. Or they may be classed as suitable for either. In that case it is necessary to see that all the conditions relative to the class of fuel being used are observed. These conditions usually refer to the rating of the nozzle, the oil pump pressure, and then during setting up the correct adjustment of the air damper to go with the oil input. It must not be expected that a change can be made from one grade of oil to another without such adjustments.

If the fuel oil store happens to be buried, or at a lower level than the burner, the pressure jet burner offers one advantage. When considering fuels reference is made to the two-pipe system for getting a supply of oil to the burner. The pump for the purpose is the oil pump on the pressure jet burner, with only a simple adjustment to be made during installation.

Combined units

Oil, like gas and solid fuel, has its hearth fitted unit with a fire in the front and a boiler at the back. The similarity with gas is the more obvious, since the fire resembles a gas fire in appearance. A typical model is as described below.

The boiler is a natural draught vaporising type, with high/low control, and the notes about installation and dissipation of surplus heat apply to it. The total rated output of the model shown is 10.9 kW or 37 400 Btu/h, of which the amount going to water may be varied, from 5.1 kW to 9.3 kW, the rest of course going to the room as radiation and convection. The method by which this ratio is determined could not be simpler.

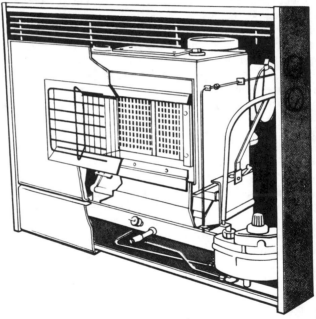

Fig. 3.9. A combination boiler/room heater unit

By means of a knob at the side, the angle at which the radiant section rests is varied, to bring more or less of it into direct heat. The whole of the section is glass fronted.

Because of the limitations imposed by the chimney size, this type of unit is unlikely to exceed 12 kW or 40 000 Btu/h rated output. Within that total will be ample output for most rooms in which the unit is likely to be situated. The oil supply is usually piped in from outdoor storage. But it might interest in particular anyone seeking a 'can take it with you' unit to find one which has an incorporated fuel tank.

Flue Stabiliser

A flue stabiliser is usually in the form of a flap damper which is free to swing, from shut to some way open, under the influence of changing chimney draught or 'pull'. Its purpose is to stabilise the amount of draught at the base of the chimney, when the natural draught emanating from the top of the chimney is fluctuating. A surge of draught causes the damper to swing open, and air enters through the open damper, sufficient to satisfy the extra demand caused by the draught increase. In consequence the extra demand is not passed on to the base, and so to the boiler or other appliance fitted to the chimney.

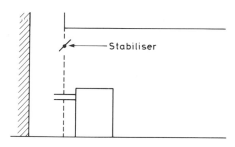

Fig. 3.10. Draught stabiliser fitted in boiler room

Oil fired appliances in particular work best in stable draught conditions, and of those the vaporising type are most sensitive. They are generally fitted with an integral draught stabiliser in the flue offtake (*Figure 3.10*), and this should be able to swing freely.

Pressure jet boilers, due to the start they get from having a slightly pressurised combustion chamber, do not often have a built-in stabiliser, and makers commonly state that in normal conditions none is needed. But in extreme conditions, such as one might meet on an open site in, say North Cornwall, high winds might cause high and fluctuating draughts in a chimney. In such cases, and in cases where vaporising boilers are not already equipped, a separate stabiliser would have to be fitted in the chimney.

When this is done, *it is imperative* that it shall be fitted in the same room as the boiler or appliance. It cannot be for instance in the room above. It is usually put up near the ceiling. The reason for this condition is that it must share the conditions which apply to the burner, on both sides of the damper, inside and outside (*Figure 3.10*).

Solid Fuel Boilers

The breadth of choice of heating equipment with solid fuel is more than with other fuels. In consequence of this there is a greater responsibility upon the seller of apparatus to declare the maximum performance, or rating, of every appliance. It is when this responsibility is avoided, and too much emphasis placed upon the simple evocative phrase 'central heating' that troubles can start. The law recognises that the buyer has a duty to look after himself, and in this market a potential buyer should always enquire, first, what is the official rating of an appliance.

Then, except in the case of automatically fed hopper charged boilers, he should allow for the difference between test conditions, charging every 1½ hours, and the real life conditions into which the appliance would fit. It would not be unreasonable to take 10% off the rated output for that.

Because the result of such a preliminary enquiry will be to narrow the field of choice at the outset, let us start there.

(1) The open fire with back boiler will have a boiler output in the region 3 kW or 10 000 Btu/h. If described as high

output this could go as high as 7 kW (23 000 Btu/h) or even higher. This is 'rated output' of course. Except in the smallest house this is for partial or background or selective heating only.

(2) The closed or closeable room heater with back boiler. We must consider this working as a closed unit since the opening of the front causes a significant drop in performance. The maximum rating for such a unit is 13 kW or 43 500 Btu/h which if sustained could satisfy a good proportion of dwellings. To that output must be added the convection and radiation from the heater which is probably adequate for the room where it is situated. We would recommend that for practical purposes the output be taken to be below the rated figure, to avoid disappointment.

(3) The free standing manually fed boiler. This is probably the type with which older people are most familiar, perhaps when it was in the form of a cylinder, of cast iron with a lid on the top. Originally coke boilers, they will burn any smokeless fuel, the correct size grade being that recommended by the manufacturer. The use of bituminous or house coal is allowed only if the firebed is specially formed as a 'Smoke Eater'. This type of boiler is frequently used as an incinerator of kitchen rubbish. We cannot stop that practice merely by disapproving of it, but may we urge moderation. Years ago we were puzzled by the lady who complained that whenever she burned cabbage stalks she got excessive clinker formation. It did not seem like a common property of cabbage. After a time it was traced to the fact that the cabbage stalks tended to damp the fire down, and the owner opened the damper wide to brighten it up again. Hence the heavy clinker. Manually fed boilers for domestic use fall into a category roughly between 5 and 15 kW, or 17 and 50 000 Btu/h rated output.

(4) The free standing hopper fed boiler is way ahead of the others in operational ease and efficiency (*Figure 3.11*). It provides the working conditions in which the purest of the solid fuels, anthracite, will burn, and in return gives steady output and very limited interference from ash. It is a demanding

boiler, in that it must have a good flue and that size of fuel is critical. The price of anthracite is matched to the size, and most of the hopper fed boilers currently available use peas or grains. The density of packing of these sizes means that a small electric fan is needed to force air through

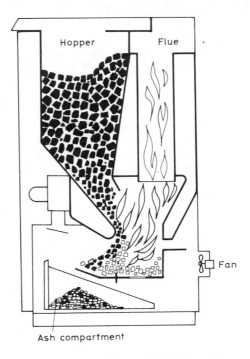

Fig. 3.11. How a hopper fed boiler works

the fuel bed. This offsets any saving on fuel cost but gives an extra measure of control over combustion. One side benefit is to extend greatly the length of time the boiler can stand idling, without the fire going out. A clock is wired into the fan circuit, timed to cut in for a short period at intervals, in order to brighten the fire. If there is a natural draught

574

boiler available at the time of going to print, it will use a larger fuel, probably beans. Any boiler in this class which is allowed to burn bituminous fuel will have a Smoke Eater grade.

The frequency of filling the hopper, and of removing the ash, are competitive features between makes. But bearing in mind that there is no poking or riddling to do — and indeed it would be wrong to do it — then attention once daily should not be excessive. In most models it is arranged that the ash when withdrawn is nearly cold, and so not giving rise to air borne dust.

These are the larger boilers, from about 13 kW or 40 000 Btu/h upward and into the commercial sizes. They are therefore readily available for full central heating in any domestic premises.

We have already commented upon what might be called the social grading of these types of boiler, but it bears repeating. There is *no* justification for the belief that the first two, and perhaps the third, can satisfactorily be connected to direct water systems. The need for an indirect system is as urgent for them as it is for the last, the hopper fed boiler. It is the heat, not the type of boiler, which damages the system.

Despite their wide differences, the four types of boiler have two things in common:

(1) They all have to be lit manually. This may not be the paper and sticks method, and it is quite common to use a gas poker, or an electric poker which generates a stream of very hot air to blow on to the fuel. Or again there are patent fire-lighters. The manufacturer will almost always have something useful to say on the subject, in his instructions.

(2) They all have the phenomenon of response lag, which causes unwanted heat to be generated after the command to stop. Consequently they all must be provided with a buffer or heat leak. In most cases, certainly where the outputs are in the lower range, the hot water cylinder will absorb the normal surplus. But in case of doubt, and for

larger boilers, it is desirable to include a radiator or towel rail in the hot water primary circuit, to be left on continuously.

At the top end of the domestic range is a class of boiler which is industrial in design, and unquestionably needs to be given a boiler house. It requires an independent hopper, facing the boiler, the two being connected by a screw feed mechanism which provides a slow but constant supply of fuel to the base of the fire. This is called under-feed stoking.

The smallest size likely in this would be about 24 kW or 80 000 Btu/h. Apart from the amount of space needed, it may be claimed for this type of boiler that it does away with even daily attention such as a gravity fed hopper boiler needs. Offsetting that is the cost of operating the screw feed.

In comparison with other fuels, the lighting of solid fuel is a chore, and one to be avoided for as long as possible. There is the added disadvantage that an appliance which has gone cold takes a relatively long time to warm up again, because the fire is slow in getting hold. It is of considerable importance therefore to know how long any appliance will keep going between refuellings, so that it may be left and not go out. The obvious and recurring period of neglect is overnight.

Though it is clear that the period will depend upon the rate of burning, whether the boiler is working hard or idling during the period, it is usual to assume that we are considering an idling period, overnight being again typical.

The hopper fed boilers present no problems in fuel availability, since the hopper capacity is almost always capable of riding over at least a day, usually longer at low or nil load. In fact the problem with such boilers is more to prevent them dying of inaction.

The manually fed free standing boiler and the closed room heater are usually designed to have enough room for fuel so that with a nearly closed damper they will idle on for many hours.

The open fire rarely has any such provision, even though the need for continuity of combustion is there. Consequently the makers, if in doubt, supply a deepening bar, a removable plate which is slipped in at night to increase the height of the front of the fire, so creating a larger pocket for fuel. The nature and usefulness of the deepening bar if supplied are examined by the approval authority, and if satisfactory are included in the approval. Intending purchasers might like to note that they have a perfect right to see the precise terms of any approval granted to an appliance and the seller should make this available to them.

It is usual to remove the deepening bar during normal usage hours, not least because it will shield off some of the radiation from the room. Along with its use as a means of prolonging an active fire goes partial closing of the damper which is below the fire bed. This greatly reduces the amount of air able to get under the fire bed, while one role of the deepening bar is to deflect off the air which otherwise would sweep across the top of the fire — both being responsible for some fuel comsumption.

Many modern units have one more damper, fitted in the throat or go-away flue of the appliance. The purpose of this damper is to control by throttling the amount of draught or 'pull' which the chimney is exerting upon the fire, which in practical terms means the amount of air it is persuading the fire to use. One operation in preparation for idling is to part close this damper, so reducing the demand made by the chimney. All the preparations are designed to reduce activity, and not for nothing is a fire in this condition said to be slumbering. The maker's instructions will generally give an indication of the best settings for dampers, though it will be obvious that no absolute values can be given since chimney draughts vary from place to place and from time to time. Fully shutting dampers will almost always result in the fire going out.

Electric Boilers

Electricity does not come readily to mind when talking about boilers. Nevertheless there are two kinds of electric boiler which must be mentioned in the domestic field.

One, the electrode boiler, seems never to have become a serious item on the market, and may be disregarded. The other, known as the Centralec system, is available and would be of particular interest to those who are debarred from having any kind of flue on their premises. Centralec is basically a storage heater of the storage radiator type, which instead of passing its stored heat into the air passes it into water, under control. The water is, of course, the wet heating system, which after it leaves the Centralec unit is exactly the same as any other wet system.

The heater being of the storage pattern qualifies for the use of cheap off-peak current, which is charged at off-peak hours. The capacity of the unit is then made to match the heat requirements over the whole 24 hours. The unit may be obtained with a fitted circulating pump, or an external pump may be used.

One of the advantages of a wet system over a storage radiator system is in greater precision of control over heat output. In Centralec we find electric storage allied to finer control, another advantage.

The Size of the Boiler

A custom has grown up, from father to son as it were, of calculating the size of boiler required for a job, and then adding 10% or even 20%, and we have known even more. It is a practice so well dug in that even text books quote it. But it is neither necessary nor good practice. It arose originally because the waywardness of the solid fuel boiler in the user's hands was recognised, and an allowance made for that. As a cover against bad calculations it was welcomed by some workers, who usually excused it as a hedge against extra bad weather.

We have already mentioned that in the case of manually fed solid fuel boilers one should take a conservative view of the real output in comparison with the rated output. But that is the only case. In all other circumstances oversizing — for that is what it is — is wrong, leading to waste of money and early wear on the boiler. Since the greater part of the heating season is far from being as severe as that on which the calculations are based, we already have a situation, with a boiler of correct size, where it takes a number of rest periods during working hours because it has done its job quickly. Every time it goes off, which it might do for a total of say 30 minutes every hour, things start to cool, and heat is dissipated mostly uselessly. When it goes on again that heat has to be made good, and all this counts against the running cost. Consequently, to make the boiler even bigger is simply to add to the down times, the cooling and the loss.

To anyone tempted still to think of the extreme case of bad weather let us say this. Life is almost wholly made up of quite ordinary weather, bad though it may be. When the wolves are howling outside it is a crisis situation in which you can afford to make a temporary concession. Decide to see it out by having heating in only say two rooms, instead of four or five or six. For that limited duty the boiler will be adequate. But do not live the rest of your life paying extravagantly for the remote possibility that some such crisis might occur.

4 Warm Air Systems

In the Introduction we mentioned the benefits of using air as the heating medium. There is some similarity between wet and dry systems, in that both are capable of being left to Nature to operate, or may be given a mechanical boost. The one fact to be remembered about Nature, apart from the fact that it costs nothing, is that while it is inexorable it is slow and comparatively weak. For instance nothing will stop warm air at ground floor level from rising to the upper floor. But shutting a bedroom door will prove a serious barrier, and it could take a week for the warm air to get through. That is hardly a practical proposition, but it serves to show incidentally that free flowing warm air is most likely to succeed with open planning.

In a dwelling so constructed that free flowing warm air can circulate, there could be a lot of sense, and of economy in first and running costs, in having such an arrangement — it can scarcely be called a system. For best operation it calls for a good standard of loft insulation, and for double glazing in bedrooms. Anyone who does not fancy a well warmed bedroom has only to keep the bedroom door shut to stay out of the circulating zone. We have seen figures of quite unbelievable accuracy for temperatures in rooms warmed by drift in this way, but they are all rather beside the point. The human body is not seeking a specific temperature, but a comfortable zone of temperature above the minimum level of acceptance.

The principle upon which all air heaters are based is that there is a heat exchanger. Fuel is burned on one side of it, and air passes over the other side, becoming warmed (Electricity is of course the odd man out, having no need to be segregated from the air by an independent heat exchanger.) The manner in which the principle is applied illustrates mainly the ingenuity of manufacturers. The commonest of the free flow units is still the so-called 'brick central', because that is what it is, both brick and central. It can house quite a large unit, which calls to mind that in the USA the air heater is called the furnace. No doubt the use of a brick chamber was first employed to make safety obvious, giving some thermal storage as a bonus. In later times units were built in which the chamber was more lightly constructed, for example of asbestos cement sheets. The cladding, brick or otherwise, is *not* a part of the heater. There is a flue, and grilles at high level to allow warmed air to escape. At low level, apart from the combustion air inlet, there is at least one inlet for cool air to be warmed, and a measure of control is exercised over the output by the extent of opening of lower air dampers.

In cases where the brick central was not situated in a way to give warm air an easy passage upstairs it became customary to add a short duct from the top of the unit to a convenient discharge point. The decline in popularity of the brick central is no doubt due to its massiveness, both real and apparent. But that apart it is capable of doing a good job.

The same function is being performed, for much less space taken, by an appliance which looks very like a large gas fire. Using fuel oil, which may be piped in or contained in an attached storage vessel, this unit must be connected to a chimney, so that choice of location is limited. Some models have a radiant section (like a gas fire), even a back boiler (also like some gas fires) but the bulk of their output is in warm air, discharged into the room where the chimney is. In some cases this warmed air is able to travel freely. Where it is not, its passage is aided by a simple extractor fan, let into the wall of the room at high level, and discharging for preference into a hall or passage way by which the warm air may go on its travels to the rest of the dwelling. Reports from users seem to be predominantly favourable.

For warm air heating which qualifies as a system we must turn to ducted air. It obeys all the rules laid down for heating

description, in that it may be a full heating system, or partial, or selective or background. The full range is available only to full duct systems. A stub duct or abbreviated duct system cannot fulfil the requirements of full central heating in terms of individual room control.

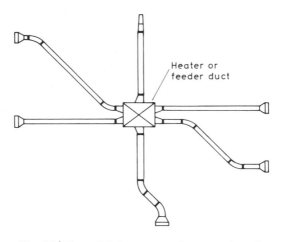

Heater or feeder duct

Fig. 4.1. The radial duct system, for cases where the heater can be centrally located. No branch pipe should exceed 6 m (20ft) or leave more than two bends in the run

The heart of a ducted system is the fan, almost always incorporated in the unit. The fan may be compared directly with the pump in small bore systems. It provides positive flow, speed, assurance, and it frees the system from the annoying limitations which Nature imposes upon a system without artificial power. Notably of course, in natural systems warm air must always be travelling in an upward direction. With fan power, it will travel for long distances horizontally, and even go downward, as into an underfloor duct system.

Ducting is large, not often an item which can be added to an existing house without becoming a nuisance. Consequently a full duct system is usually built into a new house, and the architect or builder should be given early notice so that he may plan it in. Ducting may be run under floors or in lofts, in walls. It may house the required cross sectional area in various shapes. A 6 x 8, for instance, giving an area of 48, may be made as 12 x 4 if it has to disappear in a four inch wall. Although the object is to make duct runs direct, short and economical, all flow ducts are insulated to guard against much unplanned heat loss.

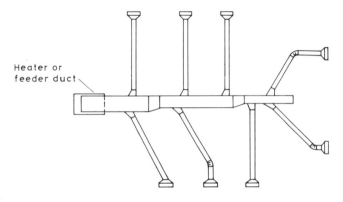

Fig. 4.2. The stepped duct system. This may be in the elementary form shown, with only one main duct. Or the heater may supply more than one main duct and, up to the capacity of the heater, form a radial system as above. The difference between that and the radial system of Fig. 4.1 is in scale. Note that the offtakes from the main duct are 'swept' to assist flow in the changed direction

Another feature of long flow ducts is that the cross section undergoes gradual reduction. Each length of duct is sized according to the amount of air it has to carry, in order to maintain a steady air velocity. This is necessary in order to achieve a certain velocity of air delivery at the outlet points. It will be seen that as draw-offs are made from the main air duct, the quantity diminishes and the area of the duct must be reduced to suit the new reduced volume. Such calculations are made on the basis of all discharge points at work. In any other event if the discharge rate seems too strong it may be adjusted at the damper which controls the discharge.

It has already been suggested that an arrangement by which warm air goes where it pleases does not constitute a system. A system is a logical development, with beginning and end, and the logical development of a ducted system is to return the air, or at least a good deal of it, to the starting point. Thus, a ducted system includes a return air duct, and it is upon this recycling that the economy of the system mainly depends. By comparison with the flow ducting, a return air duct is a simple affair. Usually it collects from main points only, is not insulated, and not made leakproof to more than an elementary degree. The exception to the last point occurs within the heating chamber, or where the heater is situated. There the return air duct must be very effectively sealed in itself and into the heater. If the heater is a conventional flue type it relies upon access to a continuous supply of fresh air for combustion. It cannot tolerate strong competition such as would occur if there were an aperture in the return air duct, already under strong fan suction.

More than that, if incomplete combustion were to occur, with probably the formation of carbon monoxide, it would get into the duct system and be distributed throughout the house.

The fact that a duct system necessarily forms a communication channel from room to room has not escaped the attention of fire prevention officers, and it is advisable to check with the local authority in case their interpretation of the Building Regulations bears upon your proposals.

Sound also passes readily along this type of communication channel and this seems to be particularly true of the return air duct, no doubt because it is intentionally straight. Fan noise will travel in it unless checked, and the most effective check is a bend.

At this point we should mention that anyone seriously intending to install ducted warm air would need to go into the subject in greater depth than this book can, for ducted warm air has never been regarded as a very suitable matter for the amateur. Perhaps, with its new building context, it rarely offers the chance. However, all the leading manufacturers of warm air units, who together form the Warm Air Group of the Society of British Gas Industries, have collaborated in producing a design manual (published by Ernest Benn, 1976), which sets out the current British practice.

Anyone who objects that it is a gas document should be reminded that systems are more important than fuels. The majority of the manual concerns duct systems, which do not alter just because the fuel does.

We have seen how main ducts are stepped, i.e. progressively reduced in cross sectional area as the volume diminishes, in order to maintain a reasonably steady air velocity. If more than one main duct is run from the plenum (which is in effect the distributing box attached to the heater) then the design intention should be to give roughly equal duty to each main duct.

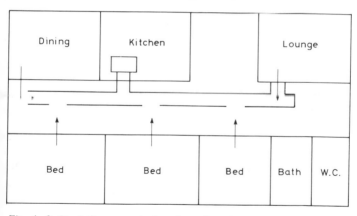

Fig. 4. 3. Typical return air duct in a three bedroom bungalow. The duct runs wholly in the passage. Grilles at high level allow air to pass from bedrooms and dining room to passage, and grilles let into the duct continue the communication. The lounge, having more to contribute, and generally for longer, is given a stub duct connection. The unit is in the kitchen in this case.

Note that under no cirumstances is provision made for pick-up from w.c., bathroom or kitchen. It will be appreciated that what enters the return air duct will emerge eventually at registers, and the system is not intended to distribute cooking smells throughout the dwelling

585

This intention can rarely be achieved in practice, and it is customary to add the final adjustment, known as balancing the system, by means of dampers. The comparison with wet systems, and balancing valves on radiators, will be apparent. Sometimes the need for an incorporated damper will be obvious. For instance if a radial system were to consist of one short duct and a number of longer ducts of about equal resistance, the short duct would have an advantage, and this would require a damper to neutralise it.

On a more general level, it is good practice to include a damper in every register. (A register is an outlet with some form of adjustment; return air inlets and the like, plain apertures with no adjustment, are grilles.) Formerly this called for a separate device, a stack damper, but nowadays it is much more common to include a balancing damper in the total structure of the register. This is independent of any modulating mechanism, including an 'off' position, which is provided for the user to control. Balancing dampers once set should never need alteration.

Where to put Registers and Grilles

Registers or diffusers are the terminal fittings through which warm air is discharged into the room. They should bring about as uniform a room air temperature as is possible, by low speed draught-free air movement. Their relationship to the room, and if more than one to each other, is therefore of first importance. Their ability to project air sideways and forward is limited by the air velocity, which must not create a draught, but their influence is greatly extended by secondary means, by disturbance and by entrainment of air surrounding the ejected warm air stream.

As a convenient rough rule we may assume that one register will deal effectively with a room, or part room, which has a small to medium square plan area. This would include such rooms as 4 x 4m (12 x 12ft), 5 x 5m (15 x 15ft) or 4 x 5m (12 x 15ft). Rooms which are distinctly elongated (e.g. 4 x 7m,

12 x 20ft) or irregular (e.g. L shaped) are best treated by being visualised as squares, and each square treated separately (see *Figure 4.4*).

The decision whether to fit the diffusers in the floor, at low or high level in the wall, or in the ceiling, is in part dictated by local circumstances, in part by local custom. British preference

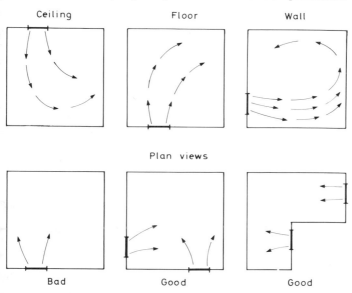

Ceiling   Floor   Wall

Plan views

Bad   Good   Good

Fig. 4.4. Positions of registers and air patterns

has always been for the low level wall diffuser, and if this is arranged to give an angular downward deflection to the issuing air it can achieve very good mixing, with even temperature throughout the vertical gradient. It requires the ability to conceal the ducting in the wall, but that is a common condition. Floor diffusers require that an insulated duct can be accommodated in the floor.

High level diffusers, and in particular the ceiling type, are not for general application, since their natural trend would be to promote a great temperature gradient, hot at ceiling level and cold at the feet. They would be well suited to a place where the floor is already well warmed, possibly by being over another warm room.

It must be pointed out that the air flow from a register must be unimpeded, furniture being the most likely impediment. But in nearly all cases it should be possible to accommodate the furniture to the heating, not the other way round.

Return Air

The number of grilles used will be less than the number of registers, and the system does not even call for a grille in every room. But if a room is equipped with a register but no grille, then there must be a permanent opening at high level through which air can escape to the nearest grille. The typical site is one in which a central grille in a hall or passage collects from one or more adjacent rooms. The permanent opening is most easily provided by relieving the top of the door, though an opening may be made in the wall. No such arrangement must be made with the bathroom, kitchen and toilet, and if these abut a hall equipped with a return air grille steps should be taken to see that they cannot contribute accidentally to the return air supply. Their ventilation should be arranged separately, possibly via a window ventilator.

When grilles are fitted in the same room as registers it will be seen that the zone of negative pressure (the suck) in their vicinity will influence the air flow pattern. This fact can be used with advantage if the grille is situated with this in mind to create air flow in the required direction.

Since the object is to involve as much of the room as possible in the warming current of air, it may be taken that broadly the air will enter at one end of the room and leave at the other.

The Compromise System

We have considered the free flow unit, which uses no ducting; and the full duct system, which is best suited to new building.

It is often possible to obtain many of the advantages of the second, in application to existing property and with a minimum of disturbance. The compromise is called a stub duct system, and as the name indicates it uses only short duct lengths. These should be long enough to send the warmed air in the main directions it is required to go. The feasibility is very largely dependent upon the layout of the house, and the ingenuity of the designer. If there is more than one position where the heater could go, the object is to choose the one which gives most chances to run effective stub ducts.

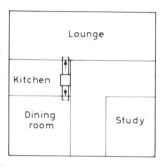

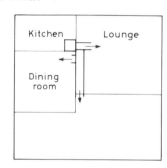

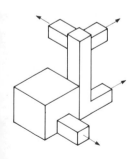

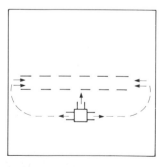

Fig. 4.5. Typical stub duct layouts for different house plans. The diagram bottom left shows a stub duct system on two floors, while the bottom right diagram illustrates the idea of influencing air travel from a stub duct system by means of the return air duct

We have tried to show, in sketch form, ways of achieving this in differing house plans. For houses of two storeys the object may be to transfer part of the air ouput to the upper floor by a single duct, then taking stub ducts from this riser to convenient nearby points.

The conditions imposed upon a return air duct are, as we have seen, not too onerous. A return air duct could for instance be run across a loft, which might well be unsuitable for the flow ducting. In such a case the return air duct could well be more extensive than the stub duct system, and so arranged that by putting grilles at negative pressure at the extreme ends to which it is hoped air will travel, it will induce air travel. *Figure 4.5* illustrates the principle.

Another very important matter concerned with ducting is fan power. Clearly it takes less fan power to operate a stub duct than a full duct system. Even nowadays, when the matter has been fairly well regularised, it is still desirable to ask, when buying an air heater, not only the rated heating power but also the fan power, whether for stub or full duct system.

Control of Warm Air Systems

In free flow units there is only the heater to control. This may be given automatic control in one or more respects, in addition to any fundamental controls, e.g. for flame safety, which may be incorporated in the burner assembly. A room thermostat, for example, may be situated in perhaps the living room, wired back to stop and start the burner. A clock will also decide when the unit is to be started or stopped.

Both these controls are applicable to ducted unit systems too, the room thermostat being more likely to give a sensible response in a system which is positively fed with predetermined amounts of warmth via ducts, than in conditions which can be affected by a draught from an open door.

It is possible to obtain thermostatically operated registers, though it is doubtful whether these contribute enough to the end result to justify their inclusion. The most important part of a duct system for the user, if only in the all-important matter of relating comfort to economy, is the register. It should become as much a routine to shut a register when leaving a room as it is to turn off the light.

Refreshing Warm Air

A warm air system was once regarded as one of diminishing vitality, in which the oxygen content grew less, the carbon dioxide, tobacco smoke and so on increased, presumably to a point at which it would not support life. To offset this, arrangements were made to introduce a controlled quantity of fresh air from outdoors into the circulation, and this would displace an equal volume of stale air.

Experience quite quickly showed that what might be called a laboratory view of the system at work had little relevance to what happened in practice. This is, to put it crudely, that a typical house leaks like a basket at most of its joints, floor boards and so on. The real problem became not one of introducing fresh air but of excluding too much of it, for it will be seen that fresh air is cold air and the need to treat it lowers the efficiency and therefore the economy of the system at work.

Although the introduction of fresh air receives a mention in the latest official document on ducted air design, our recommendation is to ignore it, unless you are convinced that you have a remarkably well constructed and weatherproofed house entirely free from draught leakage at any point.

The Nature of Warm Air Heating

Wet systems, we have seen, work ultimately by warming air, but it is an indirect process and, particularly in the case of radiators, the total effort is divided to give a radiant factor. By their nature they are, too, rather slow, even in spite of pumped circulation. It can take half an hour or more from starting the system before an improvement is noticed in the room temperature. Even then the convected or warm air part of the improvement lags behind the radiant one.

A warm air system is quite different. It is direct, the warm air coming 'from factory to user' with no intermediate process. It is simple in action, being convected only, and it is rapid. The room near to the register will begin to feel warm minutes after the apparatus goes to work, and it is quite possible to have the room up to temperature in about 15 minutes. But that is conditional upon limiting heat loss.

So in return for good insulation you will save money and will get the greatest benefit from a warm air system, in speed of response. The good sense and economy of insulation apply of course with equal force to wet systems. But for anyone specially interested in taking advantage of the speedy action of warm air it might pay to think about the detail of insulation. We shall go into the subject more fully later on, but a brief mention here is not out of place.

Cavity wall insulation is a very important part of house treatment, since it achieves a spectacular heat saving over the greatest surface area the house offers to the outside world. It is also very convenient. The cavity is a ready made former for the insulation, giving it standard thickness but not allowing it to take up any useful room whatever.

Cavity wall insulation stands in the way of that heat which used to pass through the inner brick leaf, over the air gap, through the outer leaf and away on the wind. Now most of the warmth passes through the inner leaf, and is stopped. Consequently the temperature of the inner leaf gradually builds up until it is approaching room temperature. This is both good and open to question. It is good because it is saving heat, also because once the wall is warm it begins to act as a low temperature radiant panel, giving back to the room in acceptable form that heat which it has absorbed.

It is open to question because it has a built-in time lag. The inner wall or leaf weighs several tons and will soak up a lot of heat, which during the warming period is not available for the main job of warming the room.

If heating is continuous over several days at least then the incidence of that amount of heat in the total output diminishes. But if the heating is on for long enough to warm the wall, then shut off for quite a time, the warmth in the wall will gradually dissipate into the room and be lost in air changes and the like.

Perhaps it will be clear, then, that in spite of our gratitude to cavity wall insulation, there are times when we would like to exclude even the inner leaf from our heating system. Such times are particularly bound up with speed of response, and this brings us back to air heating. The way to bring insulation right into the room is by the use of a thermal inner lining. This in its most elementary form may be seen in expanded poly-styrene tiles, about 3mm ($^1/_8$ in) thick, which can be stuck to the walls. They do a very useful job, and one should always buy a fireproofed grade.

A full scale inner lining is usually a little more thermally resistant than that, also more mechanically strong. It need not make more than one inch difference to wall projection, and a good way to construct one is to fix 15mm ($^5/_8$ in) or 25 mm (1 in) battens to the wall and then clad the wall in hardboard, with mineral wool packing in the gap. The wall must not be subject to dampness, though any such wall may be lined if damp is first totally excluded by a heavy and continuous coating of a bitumen compound or other wholly waterproof substance. The hardboard may then be treated as the wall surface, and papered or painted.

Tests carried out by a firm now unfortunately defunct showed that a warm air system could be shut off overnight, the room temperature falling only a few degrees by morning, and within 15 minutes of starting the room temperature was back to its prescribed level. The overnight maintenance of temperature could be due in part to the fact that the furniture in the room had acted as the heat buffer or reservoir. It was a remarkably good demonstration of comfort with economy.

5 Air Heaters

Enough detail was given in the last chapter to cover the subject of free flow air heaters. They have a place in the total heating scene, in providing a source of maximum heat required while leaving its distribution to nature. In return for this elementary service, which often provides remarkably satisfactory results, is a lower first cost than for a more comprehensive system. It will continue to find support, but this book is mainly concerned with systems which are controllable in greater detail.

The majority of air heaters are gas fired, and an estimated million are installed in this country. They take two forms, floor standing and wall hung. Unlike boilers they do not require or. use cast iron heat exchangers, since they do not have to resist water action. Although the air heater does not supply domestic hot water it is now usual for a small and independently operated water heater to be included, possibly as an optional item, within the case. It will share the fuel supply, flue etc.

Both the size and the independence of the water heater are very satisfactory features. It means that the water heater is just right for the job it has to do, unlike a large boiler which in summer is expected to work at low efficiency simply to supply hot water. The independence of both units means that water heating is not dependent upon space heating. More, it allows the air heater to be used for an opposite purpose, for circulating a stream of cooling air in summer, simply by allowing the fan to work while the burner is shut off. In this connection, it is quite common practice for the control system to include a reverse acting thermostat, which will not allow the fan to start until the heat exchanger is up to temperature. In order to promote ventilation without heating this device must be by-passed by means of a ventilating switch, which must of course be returned to 'off' before heating is required.

Another device which is standard equipment on most air heaters is an air filter. Air is no less surprising than water in its capacity for carrying impurities. Much of what is carried in air is invisible to the eye until it accumulates in bulk on a filter. But it is important both to keep the filter in place and to keep it clean.

There are two types of air borne matter which concern us. One is partly what we would call dust, inorganic matter, i.e. ash from a coal fire, plaster from a wall, etc. and partly organic but not living, e.g. lint, minute particles from textiles, plants and so on. The second class of substance is living matter, air borne bacteria and larger organisms. Both classes have a tendency to stick to the hot surface of a heat exchanger, the second class forming a plastic substance which adheres firmly to the surface. The worst result of this is to lower the efficiency of heat exchange progressively. A second result can be a slight tang in the ejected air from the 'cooked' living organisms. While the mechanism is not fully explained, any dust which passes through after heating seems to have an enhanced property for creating a dry feeling on the mucous membrane. Filtration of the air is therefore very desirable.

Cleaning the filter is necessary in order to keep the plant at work: a choked filter can shut it down. A device known as a filter flag is often used. It is a pressure operated indicator, which it is possible to connect to a light or buzzer, which shows when the resistance of the filter has reached a point demanding cleaning. Filters are of two types, washable or throwaway. Instructions are given for care of washable filters, and generally these, after washing, are shaken to remove excess water but put back in a wet condition. Attempts to dry them might cause damage.

All units of this type include the air fan which creates air flow over the heat exchanger and supplies the pressure necessary to cause flow through the duct system. This may lead to an arrangement which is up flow, down flow or even cross flow, referring to the direction of air flow across the heat exchanger. The purchaser cannot usefully become involved in such technicalities, all units of an approved type being capable of achieving a given standard of working efficiency. It might however be relevant to duct connections, and so be preferable for the air outlet to be above, or below, or at the side, in a given case.

It is worth enquiring about the extent and the needs of servicing. Time is money, and ready accessibility saves time. Such features as a bolt-on cover plate which comes away with burner complete, or with instruments, are worth more than a unit which has to be taken apart item by item. Another feature which must be kept in mind is the space needed. A unit may be fitted in a cupboard or under stairs, suitably lined with insulating material but leaving little room to spare. With this in mind, units are often designed to be dismantled from the front, and it is therefore necessary that the unit shall face the openable door, so that with the door open there is ample space in front of the unit. But it should also be ascertained whether side or back access would be required, which could only result in the complete removal of the unit every time it had to receive attention.

Although the pressures employed in a fan powered duct system are very low, it is necessary to take great care with jointing of the flow duct runs generally, and where both the flow and return ducts join the heater. Joints are usually of the socket/spigot type and after putting together are taped. Leakage on the flow side is wasteful, but leakage on the return side, around the heater, can be dangerous, since fan suction can deny combustion air to the burner. If a slide-in filter is fitted, it should be pushed firmly home after cleaning, to leave no air gaps.

Quiet operation has always been one of the makers' aims, and in its way this becomes more important with air heaters than with boilers, because if a unit is noisy its noise can very easily be carried along the large ducts. Although a burner is capable of being noisy this is not often the real worry. It is the fan which has received most attention, and a look across the range of models now on offer shows that makers have abandoned the small fan working with frantic haste, in favour of the much larger, lazier fan, which works at lower speed to achieve the same result. This brings other benefits, such as lower wear, better pattern of air flow over the heat exchanger, and slower fouling rate on the fan itself. (Dust collects on fan blades and must be cleaned at service time.)

Figure 5.1 shows a typical floor standing air heater, the Sugg 25/30M (7.34 to 8.8 kW). It is a down flow unit, the fan being fitted to a slide-out plate in the top compartment. The tall centre compartment houses the burner equipment and heat exchanger, and if required the small water heater which has a branch off the gas supply and one back into the air heater flue. The plenum base, though optional, is necessary, and is not supplied standard in this case because the unit might act as a replacement on an existing installation. This unit, concentrating upon width reduction, measures approximately 1200 mm (48 in) high (without plenum base) by 600 mm (24 in) deep, by 300 mm (12 in) wide.

Figure 5.2 shows an upflow air heater which is designed to accept as much optional equipment as is desired, up to the point at which it qualifies for the makers' description of a Total Comfort System. The illustrations show it acting as a simple heater, air flow entering from below: then as a unit complete with cooling coil, humidifier and electronic air cleaner. Any of the extras may be applied independently.

This unit has a heat output of 15.8 to 45 kW (54 000 to 154 000 Btu/h) and is wholly accessible from the front.

It will be seen that air entry, in the right hand illustration, is not from below but at the side. This is the method which has to be adopted when the unit is situated in a cellar, or on a ground floor of solid construction. It is comparable with the type of unit long known as a basement heater, in which the external connections to both flow and return air are at the top of the unit. Upgrading to a comfort system is of course a special function of the unit shown here.

A unit fitted in a basement or cellar, whether it be an air heater or a boiler, can present a special kind of problem which

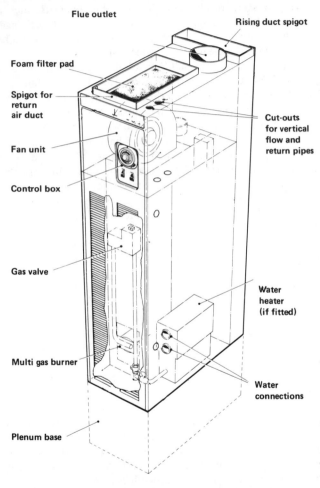

Flue outlet

Rising duct spigot

Foam filter pad

Spigot for
return
air duct

Cut-outs
for vertical
flow and
return pipes

Fan unit

Control box

Gas valve

Water
heater
(if fitted)

Multi gas burner

Water
connections

Plenum base

*Fig. 5.1. An example of a downflow air heater unit with optional
water heater (by courtesy of Thorn Heating Ltd)*

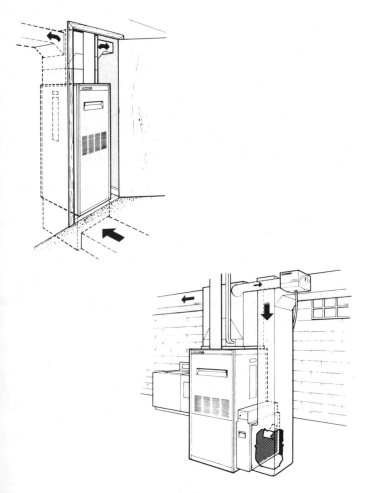

Fig. 5.2. A typical arrangement of a wall mounted upflow air heater (by courtesy of Lennox Industries Ltd)

deserves mention. It must be of the conventional flue pattern (except in special cases of extended duct balanced flue, which is rare) and so the burner draws its air from around the unit. A basement does not have a natural air supply in the way that above-ground rooms have, but the basic minimum need (see Chapter 6) is no less important. It should not be left to chance, to the likelihood that enough air will find its way down via the stairs, even through a shut door. The way to handle this is to run a vertical duct, of 100 mm (4 in) diameter or greater depending upon the heater. The upper end of the duct should be well clear of ground level, and fitted with a mesh cover. The lower end should terminate in the vicinity of the air inlet to the burner.

The free standing and wall mounted units broadly described so far are typical products of those firms which are members of the Warm Air Group of SBGI, the Society of British Gas Industries. Enquiry at any gas showrooms will produce more details of such units. It should be noted that each manufacturer makes a range of heaters, in size of rated output, and almost always offers some variation in physical size and shape, to fit varying installation conditions. For that same reason there will be a choice of connection positions, for air flow and return, perhaps for water connections to a water heater.

In many cases what are structurally the same heaters may be equipped for oil firing instead of gas, and such details may be obtained from the major oil companies or their local agents.

We will not take a great deal of space over units which are thoroughly catered for in readily accessible quarters. But perhaps we can devote more space to what might be called minority types, simply because they are less well known. There are two which deserve mention.

There is Afos, a combined air and water heater. It has two sections, boiler and air heater, usually allied within one casing but capable of being fitted separately. After the burner, which may be gas or oil, the heating medium is water, and a generous supply of domestic hot water is said to be available. The heat exchanger in the air heater differs from that in a direct fired unit, in being at much lower surface temperature. Consequently it avoids most of the charring of dust and microbe particles mentioned earlier. Heat into air is controlled by modulation with room thermostat operation, and this is a feature which

*Fig. 5.3. An example of a combined air and water heater
(by courtesy of Afos Ltd)*

compares well with the more usual on/off mode of operation. The fan, protected by a washable filter, is appropriate to a full duct system, and in addition to having variable fan speed control the unit may be given a programmer.

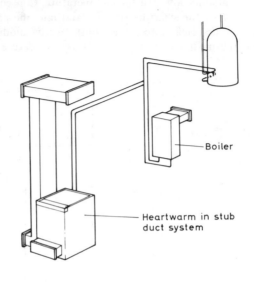

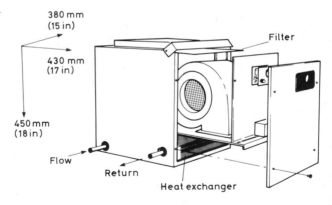

Fig. 5.4. The Heartwarm air and water heater system in a stub duct system (upper) (by courtesy of Massrealm Ltd)

AIR HEATERS

The other type of unit relies upon the existence of an independent boiler, and like the Afos it warms air in a water-to-air heat exchanger, with the same physiological benefit. The unit is the Heartwarm of Massrealm Ltd. In dimensions it is an exact fit as a replacement unit into one of the original Sugg air heaters (coming from the same source) and is therefore tailor made to avoid having to make duct modifications. But more than that it is quite suitable to act as a unit in its own right, with enough fan power for a full duct system.

As a replacement unit it assumes that the old burner and heat exchanger are both in need of replacement — hence a new boiler, and a heat exchange section complete which takes far less room than that which it replaces. As a new unit it emphasises the principle that a heater needs a flue, and a warm air generator needs a good position relative to duct work, and the two are not necessarily coincidental. With Heartwarm each may be given its own best situation, and simply connected by hot water pipework. The system may be regarded as a normal wet system in which the entire heating load is concentrated at one point, in the heat exchanger of the Heartwarm. Domestic water will be available in the usual way. In some circumstances it may be claimed that this is a variant of a wet system with no long circuits capable of suffering damage, or frost when idle.

Electric heating by warm air systems is dealt with in Chapter 9. The principal unit concerned with duct systems is Electricaire, the large storage heater working on off-peak current. Individual storage radiators achieve much the same effect but not centrally and by duct.

The use of electricity at standard tariff to provide warm air, by oil filled radiator or by fan convector, cannot be included in a list of standard recommended methods. It is bound to be expensive and if adopted should be done in full awareness that the basis is convenience, not economy. The weekend cottage might be a suitable place for such a system, where the 'on tap' element is worth a lot.

Solid fuel is no longer a serious contender in this market, except in the following respects. Room heaters have a substantial part of their output in the form of warm air rising off the appliance, and kept in the room by strict control of the chimney opening. This is a valuable part of the total efficiency, but it is, as it were, freelance, not a part of a system. A solid fuel boiler may be used to supply the hot water fed to the Heartwarm unit just described, provided that the system includes a hot water cylinder or other buffer for excess heat.

It was not unknown for a solid fuel stove to form the heat generator in a brick central unit, and so long as all the safety precautions against fire and overheating are observed this remains valid. But the decline in brick centrals has almost eliminated that type of heat source.

6 Flues

All the so-called fossil fuels, plus other substances such as wood and wood products, which contain carbon, burn to give off gases, the products of combustion. Our ancestors, and we are led to believe the North American Indian, mastered this elementary fact when they left a hole in the top of the dwelling so that the smoke could escape.

Nowadays we have flues of varying degrees of complexity, which may be broadly classified as conventional and other. The conventional flue is in most cases the traditional chimney, an integral part of the house structure, a tube conveying waste gases from the fireplace to the open air above. It works because the column of warmed gases inside is lighter than an equivalent column of colder air outside, and the lighter column rises. But this is a delicate balance, and easily upset. A down draught caused by some vagary of the wind will make the chimney 'smoke'.

Some chimneys smoke continually, or always when the wind is in a certain direction. The first may be due to a structural fault or to a permanent adverse condition. The second can sometimes be corrected by neutralising the wind effect. A high building, tree or hill will sometimes cause a wind to lift then to plunge, unfortunately, on to the chimney. There are various types of cowl which are claimed to remedy this or other fault, and would-be purchasers would apply a worthwhile safeguard if they were to insist upon a cure-or-money-back guarantee in writing before buying.

It should be evident that a good chimney will not have a lot of bends. It will, if of any age, be far bigger than is necessary, and the worst offender in this respect is the much praised ingle-nook type of chimney, with ample room in it to accommodate the chimney sweep. Such a chimney is disastrous in modern conditions and almost always smokes. To examine the reason it does so will outline some principles which can be more widely applied.

The ordinary chimney, the nominal 230 mm (9 in) square one, can evacuate up to ¼ *ton* of air per hour. Imagine the appetite of the big one! But what is just as bad, it starts at a high level, perhaps 2 m (6 ft) from the floor. That was all right when wood was burned as huge logs. But nowadays it is

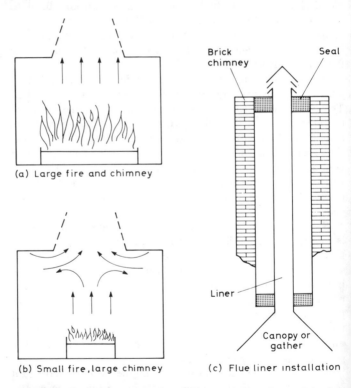

(a) Large fire and chimney

(b) Small fire, large chimney

(c) Flue liner installation

Fig. 6.1. The chimney must be efficient and properly sized for its job. With a large chimney and a large fire (a) it works, but with a small fire and a large chimney (b) the balance is wrong. This can be improved by using a flue liner (c) and a canopy or 'gather'

more often expected to cope with a small basket grate or something on that scale. If we assume that in both cases the chimney is at work, having a rising current in it, then the difference in the two cases can be seen in *Figure 6.1*.

In the first case the fire is large, its waste gases voluminous and over a large area. They monopolise the entry to the chimney base. In the second case the chimney, as always, taking what is most ready to hand, satisfies its appetite with air from the neighbourhood of the entry. Being satisfied, it turns away the legitimate exhaust, the smoke from the fire. Hence, the chimney smokes.

Part of the solution is to bring the entry nearer to the fire. The only way in which this can be done with such a chimney is by means of a canopy, an artificial extension. But a canopy or extension of the same cross sectional area might fail because it is too large, pulling in diluting air from the sides and so failing in the middle. So there has to be a reduction in area as well. The easy modern way to achieve this is by having a flue liner. This is in effect a new flue which uses the run of the old one for convenience. The old one must be rendered ineffective by sealing off the annulus between old and new. A flue liner can have several beneficial effects.

(1) It concentrates the flue upon the job in hand, leaving no margin for adventitious air evacuation.

(2) It bypasses any troubles due to deteriorating joints in chimney brickwork.

(3) It evacuates flue products at higher velocity, giving more positive results, less condensation in the flue, better carry-off of flue products from the terminal. A higher exit velocity will often overcome a tendency to down draught.

These comments upon the use of canopies etc. were designed to show the difference between a suitable modern chimney and an unsuitable one, and were not strictly relevant to the matter in hand. But it allows us to point out that all modern appliances of the types we are considering require to be connected directly and positively to a chimney or flue, and not left with an open ended pipe discharging in the general direction of a chimney base. That fact underlines the sense and logic of a flue liner, which avoids great changes in cross sectional area as the flue gases go from appliance to terminal.

The appliances themselves have stub flue pipes of the correct diameter, pointing either upward or backward, usually depending upon whether they are intended to stand against but outside of the hearth or chimney wall, or to be at least partly let into the hearth so that an upward flue pipe points in the right direction.

Boilers which incorporate a flue stabiliser have upward pointing stub flues for that reason, and it is expected that to couple into a flue behind, a bend will be used. When flue runs are given a change of direction it is preferable to use slow bends, of the order of 45°, and not right angles.

Gas fires often have a closure plate, a sheet of metal or other material which shields the fireplace opening, and has two holes in it; one for the flue to pass through, and one at or near the bottom which acts as a static draught stabiliser. The closure plate must be firmly secured to the hearth, to avoid unsafe conditions arising. But the gas fire/back boiler, which concerns us, has the gas fire flue transferred backwards to a common flue manifold over the boiler, the lot finishing in a spigot designed to fit straight into a flue liner.

If an appliance is fitted so that a backward facing flue enters a larger brickwork chimney at right angles, care must be taken to see that the stub flue is correctly set. As *Figure 6.2* shows it should project a little beyond the inner near wall, but still leave the greatest distance from the back wall. Failure to attend to this, for instance in the case of a pressure jet oil fired boiler, can result in a very disturbing amount of muffled reverberation, as the jet cuts in and during working.

When flue pipes pass through walls, plates and the like, and have to be sealed in, due allowance must be made for the frequent expansion and contraction which takes place. It is useless to make the joint with cement, even with fire cement or fireclay. A soft heatproof jointing must be used, and the most obvious one is asbestos string or asbestos rope depending upon the size of the annulus. If there is any objection to the use of unshielded asbestos then it may be shielded by a collar which is attached to the flue pipe but not to the back brickwork or metal.

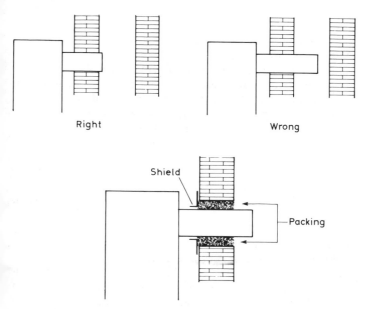

Fig. 6.2. Installation of an appliance with a stub flue into the chimney

Damp patches on bedroom walls are often the result of condensation inside a flue, itself resulting from slow lazy flue gas travel, and the condensation penetrating bad brick joints. A flue liner cures this.

A flue terminal should always be fitted to a flue liner, and advice upon both is obtainable from the representative of the fuel to be used (Gas Region etc.).

The chimney with an open fire, the culprit which can take away ¼ ton of air every hour, was in some respects better behaved than a more modern combination would be. The effect of all that air was to dilute the flue gases, often to the point at which condensation would not take place. But now, consider a gas or oil fired boiler, or modern solid fuel appliance, with a flue spigot of correctly designed size. In most gas boilers for instance this is 100 mm (4 in) in diameter, giving a cross sectional area of about 78 cm^2 (12.5 in^2). That is the size the flue should be, all the way up. If the spigot discharges through an aperture in a blanking plate into a conventional 230 mm (9 in) square flue, area 529 cm^2 (81 in^2), it has more than six times the area it needs and will dawdle. Worse, because of the blanking plate there will be no huge volume of excess air to dilute the flue gases, and condensation will be very much more likely to occur. The evidence all points therefore to the advantages of having a flue liner fitted in an existing flue or chimney to go with a modern appliance.

Because of the way in which wind is affected by high obstructions, it should always be the aim to carry the flue terminal above the roof ridge by about 0.6 m (2 ft). Any wind striking the ridge will then be rising at that point, which is beneficial.

Having more chimneys than are needed, as in older houses with one open fire per room, is undesirable because of their property of whisking away air, often air which has been expensively warmed. The permanent way to deal with them is to cap them off at the top with a waterproof and windproof cover. Then, just in case the exposed brickwork is porous, do not wholly seal the lower or fireplace end. Instead, perhaps after removing the old grate and surround, fit a sealing plate but leave in it a slot, mesh covered and no more than 150 x 25 mm (6 x 1 in). This will prevent stagnation. To remove the breast and associated brickwork is builders' work and should never be undertaken without full professional appraisal of the consequences to the rest of the structure.

At the other extreme is the home without a chimney. It may be a mews conversion, or a new house built with wholly electrical heating in mind. In most cases a conventional flue can be added. One way is to use asbestos flue pipe, double walled to keep condensation to a minimum, with a terminal. Such a flue may be run indoors, in which case there are strict provisions in the Building Regulations about the path it will take. In particular it must be kept away from structural timbers. Alternatively it may be run mainly outdoors, where the asbestos double wall really comes into its own.

The easiest way to run an outdoor flue and still conform with the need to have the terminal above ridge level is to run it up the gable end, other things being suitable. In that way it may be supported off the wall for most of its run.

A more robust, and in most cases better looking job is made by the use of proprietary precast flues such as TrueFlue make. These are in the main consciously styled, have all the necessary insulation built in, and do not need the same degree of support.

The best advice that can be given is: if you have a good working chimney, use it, in preference to any of the other methods of flue gas removal mentioned here. When coupling a modern appliance to a traditional chimney, follow the instructions given by the makers of the appliance. Some measure of sealing in will almost always be required.

There are of course nowadays types of dwelling in which even one chimney per dwelling would be quite out of the question. Multistorey blocks of flats are an example. If these

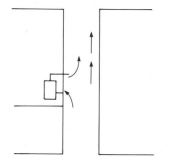

Fig. 6.3. Fitting an appliance into a Se-duct or U-duct

are to be used for other than electrical (unflued) appliances, then one way is to incorporate a Se-duct or U-duct. We need not give much consideration to these here. They are large centrally placed flues into which appliances from adjacent flats pass their combustion products and from which they draw combustion air. Se-ducts and U-ducts are an integral part of the main structure. Unlike the domestic chimney they cannot be added on at any time, but they are not domestic items except in the collective sense, as in flats.

The balanced flue

This is applicable mainly to gas fired appliances, occasionally to oil fired ones, never to solid fuel. The balanced flue forfeits dependence upon the traction effect of a chimney in return for the assurance that any disturbing influences acting upon the flue outlet will act equally upon the air inlet and so cancel out (*Figure 6.4*). This is achieved by ducting the flue outlet and air inlet to a common terminal. Then, if we suppose that a head-on wind is blowing, which would cause an ordinary chimney to reverse, its effect here is counteracted by the same force blowing upon the air inlet and so through the system. It is of course a condition that the combustion chamber must be sealed, hence appliances with a balanced flue are often called room sealed.

The theory of the balanced flue is as follows: suppose that the discharge pressure is p and the suction is s, then the differential causing flue operation is $p + s$. Now suppose a wind of force P blows on the terminal. The discharge pressure becomes $p - P$ and the suction becomes $s + P$. The differential is $(p - P) + (s + P) = p + s$, i.e. it is unchanged by P.

Balanced flue appliances are usually situated against an outside wall, though some will if required work with extended ducts between appliance and terminal. There are a few rules about the placing of balanced flue terminals, social and technical, which must be observed. A terminal must not be placed near an openable door or window, or at low level near a public right of way. It must be covered by mesh or similar to keep out intrusive objects. For good operation it must be kept away from building corners, and from too near bushes or other buildings. Such features can cause non-homogeneous wind effects.

Traditional flues, Se-ducts, U-ducts and balanced flues have one thing in common. They work for ever for nothing, being dependent upon natural phenomena. Such items as the balanced flue have gone a long way to destroying the

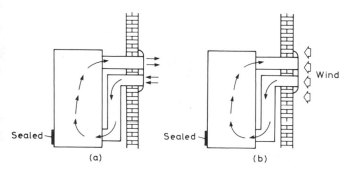

Fig. 6.4. How a balanced flue works

monopoly of the hearth as the focal point of the room. But there are still cases in which it may be impossible or undesirable to put an appliance anywhere suitable for connection to a natural flue. It must not be supposed that there is yet a universal answer to that, but in some cases, to be ascertained by enquiry, an appliance may work with an unnatural flue, e.g. a long horizontal run, to which the power is applied artificially. Such flues are 'assisted'. They include quite complicated controls for safe working, which ensure that (1) the fan starts before the burner lights, and stops after a purging period when it goes out; and (2) if the fan fails to start the burner cannot light.

There is, clearly, a linking of controls between appliance and flue which makes it necessary for the appliance maker to be involved. It scarcely ever happens that a domestic situation cannot be adapted to match a natural flue, but anyone who believes that his does not should consult the gas authorities, or the representative of a major oil company.

A much simpler and cruder device may be used with solid fuel appliances attached to a chimney which is reluctant to work. This is a propellor type fan, let into the chimney, often at an angle, which assists the upward movement of air in the chimney and so creates draught. It carries no special conditions,

Fig. 6.5. A fan assisted flue for a solid fuel appliance

may be switched on or off at any time and without regard to the state, or even the existence, of a fire. Its greatest benefit is probably in cases of marginal or intermittently bad draught. A fuel supplier, particularly if accredited by the SFAS (Solid Fuel Advisory Service) should be able to advise.

Care of flues and chimneys

With the coming of the Clean Air Acts domestic chimneys no longer carry and discharge such volumes of heavy smoke, loading the walls with soot. One must however expect a certain amount of soot to collect, from solid fuels and from oil burning. In addition solid fuels may give rise to mineral dust (fly ash) which will rise part way up the flue. Another reason for occasionally inspecting a traditional chimney is that solid materials, parging and the like, have a tendency to come adrift and fall to the bottom. In time these could build up and choke the applicance stub flue, leading to a dangerous condition. Therefore, chimneys which used to be cleaned every six months should now be at least inspected once a year. The most that a balanced flue terminal on gas needs is occasionally to make sure that the outside of the terminal is clear. Little boys do try to 'post' sticks and things into any such opening, hence the terminal guard. A balanced flue system used with an oil fired appliance should be examined for soot formation during the routine servicing of the appliance.

Assisted flues of the complicated type should be looked at to see that all joints are tight, all controls working as they should (by simulating the conditions which make them work), and that flue runs have not sagged and developed collecting points for condensation. This is best done by experts.

Ventilation

It is most appropriate when considering flues, which take away products of combustion, to consider also the rules which deal with the supply of air to the burner – without which there would be no products to take away.

The most thorough investigation into all aspects of ventilation we owe to the gas industry, and them we will quote. But the principles, and in the main the figures, can be applied to other combustion processes.

Perhaps as a reaction against generations of suffering cruel draughts, people have become very draught conscious. This has led to many cases of over-reacting, and draught stopping to a total extent. Such operations have too often ended in the coroner's court. The gas industry, whose products of combustion are invisible, unlike the recognisable vapours from bituminous solid fuels, is particularly vulnerable to such happenings and so is most concerned by them. They have therefore specified the minimum requirements for the areas of permanent free openings into any room in which an appliance is at work. A full list is available at the gas showroom, but the main points are given below.

For boilers and similar central heating units with conventional flue the *minimum* opening at *high* level into the next room must be 6.5 cm^2 (1 in^2) for every 0.58 kW (2 000 Btu/h) of maximum rated output. At *low* level the minimum is 6.5 cm^2 (1 in^2) for every 0.29 kW (1 000 Btu/h). Half these areas are needed if the openings connect directly to outdoors.

Room sealed models require the same areas at high level, but at low level only half the allowance for conventional flue models. Room sealed appliances are those having a balanced flue or Se-duct.

The minimum areas given above are permanent free areas, i.e. in a typical grille they are the *openings*, not the total face area. Although the proportion of permanent opening varies from grille to grille, it would be unwise to assume that the area of opening is more than 30% of the total, and it would be wise to choose generously sized grilles.

The principles, and to a large extent the details, given by the gas industry may be held to apply to any fossil fuel which is burned under controlled conditions (this excludes the open solid fuel fire). If in doubt be generous, for it is most necessary that air shall be freely available to the combustion process. If the flame is starved of oxygen there is trouble ahead. Most of the complaints about open fires smoking arise through air starvation (brought on by draught proofing) which is caused by the phenomenal appetite of that appliance for excess air. It is an unbeatable spiral, showing how unsuitable uncontrolled combustion processes are in the modern home.

With the accent so much on supplying air for combustion, it might be asked why room sealed or balanced flue appliances require air openings. The answer is that they are what they claim to be, namely for ventilation. Combustion appliances emit a certain amount of warmth, and unless this is removed by deliberate ventilation it can build up a local temperature.

This could become uncomfortable, in some circumstances even dangerous.

Ventilation control

The operative word is control. A lot of houses can be shown to leak like baskets, with air movement taking place between floor boards, through window and door jambs, up unused chimneys, from room to room and away in the attic, and so on. A serious effort should be made to stop all of these, because they carry away a lot of the air so expensively warmed by the heating system. Only when stray and unofficial draughts have been stopped can we realistically set about controlling air movement. Control has two meanings. There is the air allowance for the room containing the fuel burning appliance, while for other rooms it is generally accepted that there shall be 1½ air changes an hour, not least to avoid building up a concentration of carbon dioxide in occupied rooms.

The stopping of unregulated draughts is usually thought of as a part of an insulation programme, and we will treat it as such and discuss it in Chapter 10.

The deliberate provision of air movement we will look at in two ways. First there is the air for combustion: if it is admitted, for example via a door, and the appliance is against the opposite wall, there is bound to be a draught cutting across the room. But if the air opening is on the same wall, even adjacent, then the body of the room will experience no direct draught. A way to achieve this may be seen in the Baxi type of fire with an air duct from outdoors, under the floor, emerging beneath the grate (*Figure 6.6*). But it could, by travelling under the floor or on the floor, discharge near to the fire, just as readily. An opening made in a wall for such a purpose rarely needs more protection than that which excludes wild life. Although a flap may be fitted, the fire when out will not exert any pull on the duct since it is making no demand for air.

If this simple scheme is not possible, or not welcomed, a ground floor room with suspended floor might even benefit by having a mesh covered air opening cut into the floor. So long as the floor is well covered, for instance using good quality under-felt, it will not noticeably increase heat loss. But it will ensure the ventilation under the floor which is necessary to combat dry rot.

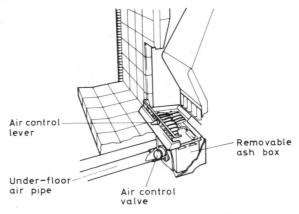

Air control lever

Removable ash box

Under-floor air pipe

Air control valve

Fig. 6.6. A typical underfloor draught fire

If in the end we come back to the door as the source of fresh air, do not rely upon air entering under the door. It not only gives the worst draught, it is also possible for someone else to stop it off, for example by fitting a thicker carpet. The proper way to use the door is to have a deliberate opening at the top, perhaps by cutting an inch off the top.

Or one might borrow a trick from warm air practice, and let a ventilator into a wall which communicates with another part of the house. This is the kind of detail which ought to be decided on personal grounds, for example is it preferable to encourage air movement to or from a room other than that to which the door leads, or should air movement take place in some other than the door-to-fireplace line?

A special example, open to be borrowed for special circumstances, comes from warm air heating of the 'natural convection' type. It involves fitting an extractor fan at high level in a wall,

618

in order to move warm air from one room to another or to a hall for onward travel.

It is difficult to think of any case in which the last example would be required. The general rule is that combustion processes will grab all the air they need, so long as the air is free to travel their way. This means leaving ample area of grille etc., but in one connection there must be a warning. It is by no means unusual to have an extractor fan fitted in the kitchen, with the sole purpose of removing moisture laden air from the kitchen. Very often the boiler is in the kitchen too. In that case the air inlet allowance of 6.5 cm^2 per 0.29 kW (1 in^2 per 1 000 Btu/h) is inadequate, since it has to supply air for both boiler and extractor, and the latter is more powerful. There is then no rule about the size of opening, but it must be judged according to the results of a 'spillage test' which an expert can carry out. This involves putting everything to work, including the fan, and then finding out whether air travels continuously forward, or whether there is any tendency for flue gases to 'spill' back into the room.

Finally, we cannot put too much stress upon the need for air openings to be *permanent*. They must not be closeable at any-one's whim or for any reason.

7 Fuels

The fuels used in domestic practice may be listed as:

Solid fuel: coal (including anthracite); coke; wood; peat. The last two are rare in the UK and we will not pursue them in any detail.

Oil: two grades, kerosene and gas oil (also known by other names).

Gas: mains distributed gas is, except in some remote regions, now entirely natural. Bottled gas, as propane or butane or a mixture is readily available.

Electricity: now almost entirely standardised in characteristics, but sold under a variety of tariffs.

One of the more impressive facts about the technological evolution of domestic heating appliances is that the combustion apparatus is no longer a sort of indoor incinerator, a place to burn any old rubbish. True, an open fire will still burn nut shells if required, but its principal fuel must be selected with care, both for technical and for legal reasons. The same is true of all oil and solid fuel appliances, where there exists a choice.

The manufacturer of an appliance will name suitable fuels for use with his appliance, and the choice should be made from such a list, not only as to type of fuel but also to size and grade where applicable.

On such detail depends the efficient performance of the appliance, and in certain cases one's immunity from prosecution under the Clean Air Acts. Let us look a little more closely at the choice of fuels.

Solid Fuel

Bituminous coal is familiar to most people as 'house coal', whose unregulated use was a considerable factor in causing smokeless zones to be declared. Any appliance which sets out to burn bituminous coal in a smoke control area must be specially designed to be what has become well known as 'a smoke eater' and must have gained exemption under the Clean Air Act 1956. Bituminous coal must not be used in boilers, where it would deposit soot on the heat exchanger surfaces and so ruin the efficiency of heat exchange. It would indeed be fair to say that bituminous or house coal, now far from being the commonest of all solid fuels, is hedged in with special conditions which greatly restrict its use.

Two ranges of smokeless solid fuels have grown up. One consists of naturally occurring fuels, the other of manufactured fuels which are derived from coals in the bituminous range by removal of most or all of their smoke producing constituents.

All these fuels are dearer per ton than house coal but not necessarily dearer per unit of heat output since they lend themselves to more efficient use. This in turn warrants the design of more efficient appliances, and sharpens the attention to be paid to correct size or grade of fuel, upon which the best operation of the combustion process depends.

The natural smokeless fuels are anthracite and Welsh dry steam coal. Anthracite is a relatively pure form of carbon, with very little ash or volatile matter. Because of the latter it is not easy to light, and anthracite burning appliances are often equipped with a gas poker or other device with a similar purpose.

The common sizes of anthracite, in descending order, are: French Nuts; Stove Nuts; Stovesse; Beans; Peas; Grains. The last two, occasionally the last three, have a fan assisted fire bed to overcome the denseness of packing due to the small size of the fuel. Such a fan performs a secondary role as a combustion controller. When the fan is off the fire will idle.

Welsh dry steam coal has a low enough volatile content to be acceptable under the Clean Air Acts without special dispensation, but not so low that it is difficult to light. It is customarily supplied in the larger size range, as Large and Small Nuts. It is incidentally known variously as Welsh Nuts, Welsh Steam, Dry Steam, or Welsh Boiler Nuts.

FUELS

There are three classes of prepared or manufactured smoke-less fuels. These are: coke, semi-coke and briquettes. Since the passing of gasworks there is no more 'soft' or gasworks coke, and the only coke now available appears under the name Sunbrite, in sizes called Singles, Doubles and Trebles. The appliance manufacturer will state which size you need. Some assistance with initial lighting of a Sunbrite fire bed is desirable.

The semi-cokes, familiarly known as 'solid smokeless fuels', the best known being Coalite and Rexco, are the result of giving raw coal only a part of the treatment which would yield a coke. They therefore retain enough of the original volatile matter to assist ignition and to give some flame movement in a visible fire; but not enough to make them offensive under the Act. Both Coalite and Rexco bear a resemblance to the original coal substance and are sold in the larger sizes mainly.

The third class, briquettes, are reconstituted into a con-venient size and usually an ovoid shape. Phurnacite and Home-fire are both made by the National Coal Board. They are made from selected grades of coal ground very fine, and passed through a press to give the form required. Phurnacite briquettes include a proportion of pitch added as a binder, while Home-fire starts with a coal of higher volatile content and relies upon heat generated by the press to employ some of the inherent tar substances as a binder.

There is a further difference, that Phurnacite is carbonised, i.e. heat treated to drive off excess volatile matter (including that which was contained in the binder) *after* being briquetted. But Homefire is made from a char, which is coal substance already partly devolatilised in a fluidised bed. Anyone interested in pursuing these matters in a not-too-technical way will find a clear presentation in a book called *Solid Fuel in the Home*, published by the Women's Solid Fuel Council from Hobart House, SW1X 7AE.

For the average reader it will probably be sufficient to know that Phurnacite is very well suited to solid fuel cookers, room heaters and independent boilers. Roomheat is suited to modern open fires and to glass fronted and other types of room heater.

Any discussion of solid fuel must touch upon storage. Solid fuel of all kinds should be stored in the dry, the importance of this increasing as the surface porosity of the fuel increases. Thus, most of the rain will run off the hard surfaces of natural fuels of all but the very small size. But coke and semi-coke will be able to absorb a very high proportion of its own weight as water, which will have to be driven off by the fire bed when it is charged, with considerable loss of efficiency.

Then we come to handling. All solid fuels degrade to some extent when handled, and even when under the weight of their own heap. Degradation leads to size reduction, and the production of fines and dust which are usually thrown away – a complete waste of money. Handling, moving from one place to another, shovelling over, even walking on top of the heap, should be avoided. And to minimise the slow degradation at the bottom of the heap it is desirable to draw off fuel from ground level so that the bottom layer does not remain unchanged for a long time.

The tendency to degrade is higher among the prepared fuels than it is in the natural fuels. Thus, long after the chemical and combustion features of briquettes had been settled, scientists were still wrestling with the question of mechanical strength. The principal problems were overcome, of course, but a briquette should still be regarded as needing care in handling and storage.

Solid fuel differs from all of its competitors in that it will not obey instantaneous commands. It cannot be switched on and off with immediate effect as can gas, oil and electricity. This feature brings with it other considerations, some good and some less good.

The kitchen based boiler, the hearth fitted appliance and the combination range, when their dampers have been shut either by thermostat or by hand, continue to 'tick over' at a reduced rate of combustion and when the next command comes to start work the fire picks up slowly to a full working condition. The noticeable feature, living with one of these units, is that it is always comfortably warm in the vicinity of the apparatus, which makes its own rather involuntary contribution to house heating in this way. A secondary facet of the same phenomenon is that even though the fuel may be difficult to ignite, it is a job rarely required, in some cases only at the start of the heating season.

A more limiting aspect of the lag in answering to controls is that there has to be allowance made for it, and particularly when it is being ordered to cool down. Consider a boiler, with thermostatically operated damper, which is working at normal high capacity in a small bore heating system in which the room thermostat operates the circulating pump. The house warms up, the room thermostat becomes satisfied, and stops the pump. No more hot water is going to the heating system. The boiler thermostat quickly senses this, and closes the boiler damper (and stops the forced draught fan if fitted). But the boiler does not stop its heat output. It may even increase it temporarily, but will in any event go on delivering heat in considerable quantity for quite a time. If this heat had nowhere to go outside of the boiler it would have to be absorbed into the quite small quantity of water which the boiler holds, and almost certainly would lead to boiling and in most cases to a state of considerable danger.

In such a situation there must therefore always be a substantial buffer available, a large source of heat transfer permanently connected to the boiler which cannot be isolated from it. This is the domestic hot water system, the cylinder of water containing over 100 litres (or about 25 gallons) which can safely be raised about 40 degF or 20 degC.

Thus it will be clear that a solid fuel boiler cannot power a heating system only, but must include domestic hot water. It shows too that the domestic hot water system must not be fitted with a cylinder thermostat, which could stop the primary flow into the cylinder and so isolate the boiler from the cylinder.

Fuel Oil for Domestic Use

There are two grades of fuel oil sold for domestic heating. They are known traditionally as kerosene and gas oil, but it is not uncommon to find them called 28 sec and 35 sec oil (a measure of their viscosity) or the first as domestic fuel oil. The latest, official system, by which they will be recognised in an approvals document, is as Class C and Class D fuel. We will call them C and D; C being the lighter kerosene and D the gas oil.

They are not fully interchangeable. Some appliances will burn only one of them. Other appliances, which have a ready means of varying a component of the burner, can be adapted to burn either but the adjustment is a job for an expert. Broadly speaking, boilers of the pressure jet burner type will be found using Class D, other appliances Class C. But in the first case there is often scope to adjust to the other fuel. The arrangement quoted does however fit neatly into another aspect of modern thought, namely that pressure jets are not acceptable indoors (because of their noise level) and Class D fuel is not welcomed indoors because, in the event of leakage, or spillage during filter cleaning, etc, its smell has a lingering quality beyond that of Class C. Class D and pressure jets are therefore relegated to an outhouse together.

Fuel oil is almost always fed to the burner by gravity, i.e. the storage tank is at a higher level. If not − if for instance it happens to be below ground − then the oil must be delivered to the appliance by pump. In the case of a pressure jet boiler this can be arranged, by a slight modification to the oil pump which forms part of the burner, plus extra pipework to form a two-pipe system. For any but a pressure jet an independent pump must be fitted, and again a two-pipe system is required. The system operates by the pump taking fuel from and returning it to storage, the burner taking off what it needs at any given time. The system will be explained in detail when necessary by an authorised agent of one of the major oil companies − the one chosen to supply the oil, most likely − or by a competent installer. The general principles will be seen in *Figure 7.1*. It is usual to find that practical limits are assigned to pump performance, which in the case of gravity feed are the maximum and minimum heads. Typical values for these might be 8 and 1 m (24 and 3 ft). The limit at which suction can occur in a lifting system is of the order of 3m (10 ft).

All pipe runs should assist flow by having true falls, and freedom from dips. Great stress is placed upon having a filter of the right type in the line. It is customary nowadays for this to be outdoors where it is more easily cleaned. Whether or not a fire valve is to be fitted as a compulsory feature is a matter for the local authority to decide in terms of their building regulations.

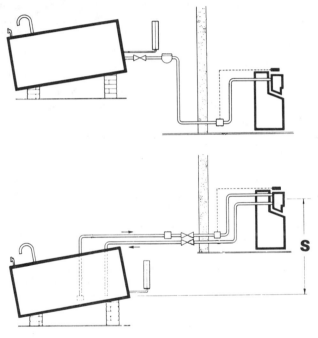

Fig. 7.1. Single-pipe and two-pipe oil supply system to a pressure system jet boiler

The size of the storage tank, and the shape for a given size, are sometimes determined by the limitations of the space available. When that factor is absent, the size of tank is usually balanced between the way tank cost increases with size, and the way oil prices can decrease in relation to the size of each consignment. It is not a matter which requires the services of a chartered accountant on each occasion. Everyone in the trade can now give sensible advice based upon long practice, and only special circumstances should be allowed to overturn this advice. If for example you live on a track which is impassable to lorries for three months each winter then your *minimum* capacity must be that which will last for more than 3 months.

Routine attention starts with cleaning the filter, and opening the drain cock to release any water which (seemingly against all the odds) has collected there. Sludge too may come away, but if what comes is run into a bucket, the good oil after settlement may be returned, so run off generously.

The tank itself will need some maintenance from time to time. Rusting of a steel tank occurs quite readily when paraffin type oils are about, and it is necessary to remove all the rust, dirt and oil, and repaint, using a hard skinned top coat which will resist oil penetration for the greatest length of time. Another point to be noted about oils and metals concerns pipework. Never use galvanised pipe to convey fuel oil. Copper remains best, but any other of the usual metals may be used.

Oil, irrespective of which class, demands quite precise conditions for correct burning. Incorrect burning can lead to smell, sooting of flueways with increasing loss of heat exchange, and general loss of efficiency. Modern appliances are a long way from the old wick burner heating stove, and even that was prone to smoke if the wick was not trimmed.

The best safeguard, and really an essential feature of ownership, is skilled servicing at regular intervals to be agreed with the service engineer. If a service contract can be arranged it saves having to remember and could save money. Beyond that, the owner should be prepared to look occasionally at the appliance, in order to see that operations are normal. If for instance the flame cannot be seen through the inspection window because of soot a more thorough inspection is required.

Gas

Gas is available to all of us, in one form or another. In the form of natural gas it is expected to last until the end of the century, which is long enough for our purposes. With the exception of a very few remote districts, mainly in northern Scotland, manufactured gas is no longer distributed. There remain many places in the UK which are not within economic distance of a gas main, though in total of dwellings they do not amount to much. For them gas can be supplied in containers, principally by Calor.

Manufactured gas, natural gas, Calor gas, are all different, but the differences are really no concern of the public. Two facts alone concern the user or potential user of gas.

(1) The gases are not interchangeable. An appliance, such as a boiler or a cooker, may remain structurally the same for any gas, but it will be given a wholly different set of combustion parts for each.

(2) In order that the preceding point does not cause despair, the whole matter of interchangeability, the right bits for the job, and the overall safety and efficiency of the unit, are very jealously and zealously guarded by the suppliers, either British Gas or the commercial organisations. The proper functioning and safety of a domestic installation is now insisted upon by law.

There is still some noticeable reluctance to use bottled gas as an automatic alternative to a non-existent piped supply. Yet it is almost wholly equivalent, and the price shows no significant difference. In place of a perpetual on-tap situation one may enter into a contract or arrangement with the supplier for regular refills. This is best organised by having two cylinders or containers. The one is used until empty, the supply changed over to the other, and the empty one is replaced by a full one. The only slight chore is to transfer the supply pipe from one to the other cylinder, and rural life offers far worse tasks than that. Natural gas and bottled gas are not lethal in the way that town gas was, since they do not contain carbon monoxide. In heavy enough concentration they can asphyxiate by excluding air, but that takes some doing.

The products of combustion could contain carbon monoxide if combustion is interfered with and not allowed to proceed to its normal conclusion, which merely emphasises the need for ample combustion air, as detailed in Chapter 6, and also the need to keep flue ways unobstructed. But, as has been pointed out, fatalities from this cause are of the order of those due to being struck by lightning; and *we* would point out that reasonable care gives greater chances of avoidance in the case of gas.

In all matters to do with mains gas the authority is British Gas, acting through the appropriate region and local showroom. Advice at least is free, and they make it clear that they will make no charge if summoned to attend to a situation, usually a leak, where safety is involved. Any action subsequent to the first aid might of course become chargeable. Loosely allied to the gas industry there is for installers the organisation called CORGI, the Confederation of Registered Gas Installers. Membership of CORGI gives reasonable assurance that the installer has proved his competence to deal with all matters concerning gas.

Gas appliances, like oil burning ones, should be given regular skilled service. Though sooting is not an endemic problem, gas burners can develop faults of their own, like linting, which alter the carefully arranged gas/air ratio and affect combustion efficiency.

Gas appliances are in the main capable of working without a flue or chimney, and flueless room heaters and geysers were once quite common. In recent times however the practice has become restricted to appliances of low thermal capacity, and we do not recommend it. One of the bad features of an unflued appliance, gas as well as the crude portable paraffin heater, is the amount of water vapour it produces. Sometimes installed partly to combat condensation, it does in fact encourage it. In flue matters gas is the most versatile fuel, for as well as being able to manage without, it is equally at home with conventional, balanced, Se-duct, U-duct and assisted flues.

Though gas runs second to electricity in being easy to control in a great variety of ways, it is first in modulation. This is the type of control which can vary anywhere between on and off, smoothly.

Electricity

Electricity does not 'burn', is not a fossil fuel and so does not require a flue. But it is a fuel, since it is consumed and gives off energy as heat. In spite of the bitter warfare which occurs commercially between the fuels there is little going on in modern heating in which electricity is not present, even in a small capacity. Most control systems, for instance, are now electrical. A solid fuel boiler may be quite independent of it, but the circulating pump on the attached small bore system is not. Most oil fired boilers are wholly dependent. The point is worth making since, even nowadays, some people will weigh up electricity in terms of reliability – a throwback to the days when grid lines were often coming down. But it will be seen that failure of electricity will bring to a halt almost any central system, and perhaps the best way to insure against such a happening is to have at least one gas fire fitted.

Electricity is quite an expensive fuel. In compensation it is usually relatively cheap to install the necessary wiring; and it is very convenient, in being flueless, in appliances which are portable, and so on. There is a choice of tariffs for electricity users, and one, the off-peak tariff, owes its inception to electrical incursion into the central heating market. One other unique and disadvantageous feature of electricity is that it is unstorable. It must be made as required. But means can be found to turn it into heat first, and then store the heat. A suitable store must have several properties, which include mass and tolerance of high temperature. The first medium chosen was a concrete floor, from which came underfloor heating.

But the very mass of the subject rendered it difficult to control, almost impossible to do anything about a floor well warmed for a chilly day if Spring suddenly burst out – except open the windows wide. The system has therefore lapsed, to be replaced by the storage radiator and its big brother Electricaire. This type of heater in its variants is described at length in Chapter 9.

The ease of manipulation of electricity, the fact that anyone can run a cable and that the degree of expertise needed to run a gas pipe is not called for, has led to a good deal of controversy.

We have in mind particularly the type of system which is often claimed to be in some fashion Scandinavian, consists of several wall mounted heaters with controls, which will run for very low cost. If further identification is needed, it is sold by door-to-door salesmen, more often than not. And more often than not it is found to have two drawbacks. One is that the true running cost proves to be prohibitive, the other is that the instantaneous demand for electricity is beyond the capability of the average domestic service.

There may be genuine offers in this kind of system. But never, never commit yourself on the doorstep. Say that you will give a decision after you have shown the technical details to your local Electricity Board. No reputable seller can object to that.

Every electrical appliance has an opportunity to be tested for approval, and it follows that those most worth considering are the ones which have received approval. Look for the BEAB or Electricity Council label. When it comes to imported items, as increasingly it will, there is another consideration, that the item is suited to the characteristics of our current. It is not only having voltage in the range 230 to 250 volts a.c., but also having a frequency of 50 Hz (cycles), if there are moving parts.

There is no question but that electricity is not for taking risks with. Is it clear which connection is for earth, which for live? Does it have a fail-safe cut-off or similar device incorporated? If you are not absolutely sure about items of this kind, and did not buy the appliance from the Electricity Board (or even if you did and are still unsure) do go and ask their advice before making any sort of connection.

Electric heating of the heat storage type, which employs solid floors or storage radiators of the individual or central type, is designed for use with off-peak current. This is electricity generated in 'off-peak' hours, taken to be 11 pm to 7 am (or 2300 to 0700) with (in some areas) extensions beyond that period. It must be separately wired indoors, with its own meter, and unlike the standard supply does not have socket outlets. Each appliance designed for off-peak current is wired into the circuit.

Since the domestic hot water in a house with storage radiators is usually made by an immersion heater, and since this at standard tariff is more convenient than cheap, there would be considerable advantage in making hot water on the same off-peak tariff. This can be done, by arrangement with the Electricity Board. Since the basis of off-peak use is storage capacity, it follows that hot water made during the night must be sufficient for the day's use, and this almost always means a larger than normal cylinder. It is possible that arrangements can be made for a cylinder to be warmed by off-peak current, with a standby heater working at standard tariff in case some top-up heat is required during the day.

A much later tariff, the White Meter, is a very different type. It might almost be called a challenge. As though the electricity people were saying 'You've got a chance to win. But if you don't get thoroughly organised it is more likely that we shall win.' This is no bad thing, because getting organised is a sure step to economy — not only in gaining the advantage of the tariff, but in an all round saving of fuel. Getting organised means several things, the first of which, particularly for anyone with electric heating, means good insulation. It is greatly helped by planning for the automatic washing machine to perform in the small hours.

Cooking, for anyone with an electric cooker, is rarely other than an on-peak activity and weighs heavily on the wrong side of the balance. We have no figures which would show how the score stands, but we do emphasise that the White Meter tariff gives an incentive to do all the sensible things which perhaps would otherwise get put off.

Electric heating by low temperature radiant panels is not a form of storage heating and so does not qualify for the off-peak tariff.

Electricity has proved that it is capable of competing with the other fuels on their own grounds. But in addition, electricity has two special characteristics. One is the way other fuels are dependent upon it. The other is its self-contained, flueless role, which makes it specially convenient for the type of dwelling which is necessarily self-contained and with no outlet but its door. This describes the modern flat of the sort not served by an overall heating system, or a bed sitter.

Central heating by storage radiators is the only form of central heating of which it may be said, with practical truth, that you *can* take it with you. The value of the circuit, which you leave behind, is a very small part of the total.

Other Fuels

Two other fuels must be mentioned because they exist and are a practical proposition to someone, but in truth both are in a special and comparatively rare category.

There is wood, which used to be the only fuel available to our ancestors. Wood is nowadays in three classes. Anyone with access to woodland can get logs and sticks. Even when broken or sawn they are large units and best kept for the open fire. They are not suited to modern controlled apparatus such as a boiler, for several reasons.

(1) The density, i.e. weight of fuel per unit of volume, is low, and refuelling must be frequent.

(2) The absolute need to conform to a maximum size and often shape could impose an intolerable burden upon fuel preparation.

(3) Wood usually gives off during partial distillation a light tar, which coats heat exchange surfaces and lower flues.

Next to logs there are cases where someone has access to standard offcuts as a byproduct of some process. While this might relieve the second condition listed above, it leaves the other two unchanged.

Finally there is sawdust, a much more common industrial byproduct. This has a use as a boiler fuel, but not seriously on the domestic scale. Because it is tightly packed it needs a supply of forced air for combustion, and it is usual for factories producing sawdust to use it as fuel for their own boiler plant.

The short answer about wood is that it is not suitable for burning in standard solid fuel apparatus (other than the open fire) of the kind we are discussing in this book. But there are answers for those who are lucky enough to have supplies available at little or no cost.

Sawdust we have mentioned. But larger wood is still a standard fuel in parts of Scandinavia, and from there we import a limited amount of apparatus. There is at least one importer of Norwegian stoves, with a base in Wales and one in Scotland. And from Denmark at the time of writing there are two known to exist, one at least of them in Eire. The answer to wood must be, use suitable apparatus.

The second of the indigenous fuels is peat, widely associated with Ireland but still quite common in other areas, for example the 'mosses' around Manchester. Peat, like wood, is not suited to apparatus designed for coal and coke. It tends to be dense in the same way as sawdust is, but perhaps it may also be described as sluggish. There is a slow inevitability about peat which makes it easy to believe the tales of fires which have been burning for three or four hundred years. The Irish are taking a commercial interest in peat, but as a boiler fuel it must stay in the commercial and industrial region. It will not concern us here.

8 Automatic Controls

To anyone approaching the subject of central heating there are two kinds of controls. There are those you *must* have and so there is no decision to be made. And there is the other sort, which may again be put in two ranks, those which are to be strongly recommended, and those which if fitted will make some contribution.

The most anyone needs to know about the first category is how best to use them to obtain the most benefit, since like a willing horse they may need to be given guidance. The second category is more complicated since it brings in choice, decision making about whether to spend money, and so one needs to know what each type can contribute to comfort or economy or both.

Controls which are obligatory are built into the appliance. For example it is not possible to buy a gas fired boiler without a boiler thermostat and flame failure device; nor a pressure jet boiler without a control box and boiler thermostat. A further safeguard lies in the fact that if these parts were somehow to be removed from those boilers lighting would be impossible, because they are inextricably built into the lighting process.

A similar degree of interdependence exists in a free standing solid fuel boiler of comparable status. But it does not extend to the more elementary type of unit represented by the back boiler to either open or openable fire. This appliance always has a damper but it is manually controlled in most cases, offering no automatic safeguard against too much or too little fire. There are, however, models with thermostatic damper, and a model which has fan assisted draught is very readily controlled by thermostat. In the same type of appliance, where there exists a choice in the ratio of heat to air and heat to water, the controlling damper is manual.

Among obligatory controls the boiler thermostat is the only one which offers a chance to make routine adjustments. The easy solution is to ignore it, and leave it always on one setting, for example 70°C or 160°F. It can however be used with advantage, in the following ways.

(1) It must never be set below 60°C or 140°F.

(2) It should rarely be set above 90°C or 190°F, or in the case of solid fuel boilers 80°C or 180°F.

(3) Within those limits it may be used to spread the boiler's working time over the total 'on' time, to avoid long periods of being shut down on the thermostat. It is better for a boiler to work for 40 minutes in every hour than 20 minutes. To achieve this, adjust the temperature setting to the climate, for instance with maximum temperature in hard weather, tailing off to near minimum at each end of the heating season.

(4) If the system does not have a cylinder thermostat on the hot water cylinder, and there are very young or very old residents who might be at risk, avoid high temperature settings (in spite of (3) above) so that the domestic hot water stays at a hot but not scalding level.

(5) But note, in relation to (4), that if the dependents have the use of a thermostatic hot and cold water mixing valve, this works best when supplied with really hot water.

The cylinder thermostat is a device which senses the temperature of the stored water, and when it reaches the required figure shuts off the heat source. The thermostat which is incorporated with an electric immersion heater is a simple example. But the device is very often fitted separately, to control the water heating activities of a gas or oil fired boiler. This it does either by being wired back to the appliance so that it shuts it off when the water is up to temperature; or it operates a solenoid valve in the flow or return primary, thus preventing the flow of any more water into the cylinder.

The first method is neater, though on the face of it open to the objection that a satisfied hot water cylinder would shut down the central heating. By various ingenious ways not to be explained here, this is avoidable. The second method avoids it without prearrangement but introduces an extra solenoid valve, which would usually be fitted somewhere in the vicinity of the hot water cylinder. Referring back to Chapter 2 however, it will be clear that with solid fuel there must be no possibility of stopping flow in the primaries, since the cylinder, with or without towel rail, is the buffer or safety outlet against after-heat and over-run on the boiler thermostat control. It would be possible to arrange diversion through a three-way valve at such times, so that the primaries continued to flow through the towel rail only. But the cost and complication would rarely justify such a step.

A cylinder thermostat when fitted has a specific job, that of allowing the stored hot water temperature to be at its own best temperature, not dependent upon what seems best for the central heating. This means in broad figures that the hot water will stay at, say, $60°C$ or $140°F$ while the heating ranges up to, say, $80°C$ or $180°F$. It was a shock and an unresolved puzzle to become involved in an American offshore contract calling for exactly the reverse of that situation!

If the holding of a safe temperature of stored water is not important, it should be remembered that in times of heavy demand, as when a lot of guests want baths, that it is *thermal* storage that counts, not just gallonage. Thus, hot water at $80°C$ or $180°F$ will go about 25% further than the same water at $60°C$ or $140°F$, and if a cylinder thermostat is not fitted, this is a crisis which justifies using the boiler thermostat to boost the hot water storage.

The programmer serves both heater and heating system, and is a device of more or less operational complexity usually attached to the boiler, though it may be supplied detached, to fix to a convenient wall. The essentials of a programmer are a clock, boiler thermostat, wiring to pump and multiswitching. It is usual nowadays to use it as a junction for other items; for example the room thermostat which controls the pump and would otherwise be wired directly to it; cylinder thermostat; frost or low limit thermostat.

Usually the clock has four levers or tappets, which enable the user to choose two periods during 24 hours when the boiler shall start itself up and later shut down. The switching, reduced to a single knob, permits the user to decide whether, during the two working periods, he will have domestic hot water and central heating, or domestic hot water only. Note that unless the boiler has pumped primary flow (in which case the hot water system is effectively just like another radiator or heat emitter) the programmer will not permit heating without hot water. We have stated elsewhere our belief that most people manage very successfully with very few programmes.

Elementary facts about using a programmer include such matters as noting the difference between night and day on the clock face, and turning the dial in the direction shown when altering the time setting. After a shut down for any reason, or a power cut, failure to reset the clock could lead to unexpected working hours.

The most commonly met control away from the boiler is the room thermostat. In most domestic premises there is one only, and it therefore has to act as the representative of the rest of the premises while being answerable only to the room in which it is fitted. This is not as chancy as it sounds, since the design will have allowed for the fact that while it may be set at say $15°C$ or $60°F$ in the hall, the emitters in the living room are of a capacity to bring that room up to $20°C$ or $70°F$, and conversely, supposing the roomstat to be in the living room and set to $70°$.

There are elementary common sense rules about the precise location of a roomstat. It must sense average conditions, not being tucked away in a corner where little air circulation takes place; not being chilled by being near a draughty door or window; not being artificially warmed by an adjacent lamp or television set or direct sunlight — or of course a radiator! Although the traffic through doors is a factor against using the hall, it nevertheless remains a very useful place, on the grounds that it is the one part of the house which should always be warmed. If the thermostat is in the living room this can never be allowed to go cold, without having an effect on the rest of the house.

The ordinary roomstat is an on/off device. But there is another, called a setback, which instead switches from normal to a low setting. It gives the user the ability to choose what the high and low settings are, and also the period of the setback, usually up to about 10 hours, after which it reverts to the high or normal setting. When there are special reasons for some warmth to be maintained all night, perhaps through illness, then the setback thermostat is well worth considering. The effect it produces with refined fuels, of a low level of maintained temperature, is almost precisely what occurs as a matter of course with solid fuel heaters which work at low level instead of going out.

Anyone who has a programmer has a clock, to control the times of operation. But for those who do not, a clock may be obtained separately, and for convenience wired into the room-stat circuit, since both are doing the same job, of controlling the boiler on/off. Other applications of a clock may be made, such as controlling the pump only if for any reason it is desired to keep the boiler always at work. Another example is that of zone control. This must start with the pipe runs, so that each zone is self-contained as a circuit off the main flow and return. A typical zone might be the first floor, the bedrooms, which have different needs from the living rooms. In that example, all heating would be cut off the first floor at, say 7 a.m. This would be the job of the clock, operating a solenoid valve. Such an arrangement is made into a unit in the Satchwell Minival.

Although the commonest clock is the four tappet type, variations abound. There is for instance day omission, which allows everything to stay dormant perhaps over a weekend, but brings it on automatically on Monday morning. Then there is the over-ride, a simple means of making a change of routine for one occasion only. Thus, an unexpected call out when an evening at home was planned, and the 'on' of heating can be over-ridden by a push button or similar. Next evening the heating will come on as usual without further action by the user since over-ride changes are self-cancelling.

Next on the list of instruments which are wired back to the boiler is the low limit thermostat, often called the frost stat. This is of great value to anyone in the habit of leaving the house untenanted for weekends or longer in mid-winter. One can of course keep the heating wholly at work, with thermostats set low. Over a week or two this is not the most economical of measures. The frost stat arranges that only when danger threatens will the system come on to work. The sensor is fitted at the most vulnerable place, where the first freezing might be expected, and the thermostat is usually set to a safe margin, such as 5°C or 40°F. When this temperature is reached it cuts in, bypassing all other controls such as roomstat and clock, until the house is warmed sufficiently to satisfy it. A boiler which is fitted in an outhouse is an example of one which warrants a frost stat.

The radiator thermostat deserves serious consideration, because it makes up for the deficiency which we have seen in the single roomstat, that it controls all the house, except its own setting, by inference. If each radiator has a thermostat each room can be positively controlled. There are those who claim that this automatically leads to fuel economy, but there is an element of nonsense in that. It certainly gives the opportunity, but from that point on it is entirely up to the user. Since one result of intending to use a radiator thermostat is that radiators may safely be oversized (with a view to some temperature crisis) the user has the power to use more than normal heat. A pleasant feature of thermostatic radiator operation is that it is modulating. The water flow is progressively cut down to control the temperature, and this compares with the on/off operation in which a radiator alternates between hot and cold.

Radiator thermostats may have integral or remote sensing, but in either case it is necessary to keep this as far as possible from the influence of untypical temperature conditions.

The influence on the rest of the system must be taken into account. The use of radstats goes with a continuously running pump, stopped only by the clock during 'off' periods. One cannot after all have two controllers trying to do the same job. But there are installers who believe in putting a roomstat into the system as well, getting over the objection by setting it just above the highest temperature which would be expected from the system working normally on radstats. Presumably the roomstat then acts as a watchdog or longstop. Running experience of this method is hard to come by, and against it is the fact that radstats are not cheap, and the roomstat is an extra cost on top. Otherwise there seems to be no objection.

We must refer to the modulating or mixing valve which attracts a very mixed reception. The essential feature of this device is that it takes the boiler water, at boiler temperature, and allows it to pass to the heating system after mixing with a proportion of the cooler return water from the heating system. To put this another way, only a proportion of the water in the heating circuit is passed to the boiler for reheating at any given time.

In principle this is quite good, since if the proportions are right it is a means of adjusting the warmth input gradually to suit changes in ambient temperature. It is in effect a continuous operation of the kind we have suggested might take place seasonally, adapting the circulating water temperature to suit the prevailing weather.

It is plain that the mixing valve is not suited to being adjusted manually. That would be a full time job for someone. It must therefore be automatically controlled, by a thermostat. Where will the thermostat get its routine orders from? The logical answer is that since it is controlling the indoor temperature it will have its sensor indoors. But, say the objectors, this is too slow. The sensed change has already taken place, the corrective action will take time to work its way around and become effective. By that time it may not be needed and an opposite movement must be made, resulting in continuing oscillation of temperature, which is most certainly not the object of the system.

So those who favour the device now claim that the proper place for the sensor is outdoors, where its function is anticipatory. It feels a change in the outdoor temperature, and passes the information indoors so that the system picks up in anticipation of the effects being felt indoors. There is some initial difficulty in finding the best place for the sensor. Use a north wall, say the books, so that it is not foxed by direct sunlight. But suppose the house has a predominantly southern facing aspect, as it might do with a high pitched single pitch roof? Wind is as disturbing in its way as sunlight, so there must be some protection afforded — which the house cannot share though almost equally affected.

But the greatest objection, ignored by those who favour mixing valves, is a matter of timing. The indoor thermostat may be too slow in responding. But the whole of modern practice, as outlined in Chapter 10 (Insulation) is aimed at preventing outdoor conditions from reaching indoors — ever. What it succeeds in doing is to prolong the time taken and to modify the result when it does happen. Meantime the delay between the system receiving a signal and its effect becoming apparent is unchanged.

So it amounts to this: that a man may have a mixing valve at work which gives every satisfaction, bringing up the indoor heat release just in time to meet the oncoming cold spell. He then undertakes a big programme of insulation, which doubles the time of cold penetration and halves its intensity. And still the system reacts as before in response to the outdoor sensor. The result is bound to be at least as much overcompensating, and temperature oscillation, as the indoor sensor might give.

It might be possible to introduce a form of calibration into the system to compensate, though no one has offered to do this. The safest conclusion is that mixing valves seem a good idea but are perhaps best left out because of practical problems.

We do not include such items as automatic air vents in controls, since these are as fundamental as, say, the pump. Most of the useful forms of control are included in the above list, and if we may mention one other device which deserves to be omitted, it is the thermometer to measure air temperature. The only criterion of heating should be comfort, not a mathematical symbol unrelated to health, time of day or any personal factor.

9 Storage Heating

It is interesting to note that the principle employed in electric storage heating is likely to be applied to a much greater extent in the future. The principle is that of converting 'instant' energy, which if not captured when generated will be lost, to a form which can be stored, mainly as heat. Sources of instant energy include solar heat, wind, wave and tidal power and some more obscure sources. These will become more important as the supplies of natural gas and oil are depleted.

The reasons differ a little, though. Natural sources occur naturally, for instance the sun shines by day. But electricity is the same by day or night, except in cost of production. Hence it is cheaper to make it at night to use by day, for those applications in which this can be done; space heating is one of them. Electricity can be stored as chemical energy, which is the principle of the battery, but that is in another context.

The conversion of electricity takes place by 'burning' it, by hot wire as in an electric fire, in a situation in which all the heat generated passes into the storage medium. There is every good reason why the storage material shall be as compact as possible, if only because storage heaters already have a reputation for being on the bulky side. The two factors which govern the heat capacity are the weight and a heat retention factor called specific heat. Water, which has a very good specific heat, has been used, and iron billets, also lime and other substances for which some virtue has been claimed. But in the end practically all models come back to a ceramic material, which is either firebrick or silica brick. The latter has more of a tendency to spall or break with continual heating and cooling. Ceramics are not the best materials thermally but they are very robust and without noticeable expansion/contraction problems.

Thermal storage in its earliest form did not employ ceramics, but quite ordinary cement mixtures, used in the construction of solid floors. *Figure 9.1* shows the heating coil elements set between a solid concrete base below and a heavy screed above, with a layer of insulation defining the lower limit of heat storage. If less total storage capacity were required the insulation could be raised to the top of the concrete section if necessary.

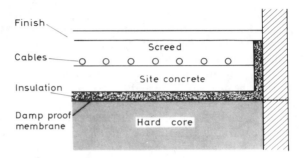

Fig. 9.1. Typical section through a heated floor

But of course such a decision could be made only once. Quite a lot of experience has been gained about the composition and application of screeds which resist the stresses of heating and cooling.

The more ingenious members of the public developed methods of operating which were very flexible (or so they claimed) but there is no doubt that underfloor heating has, in a changeable climate, the outstanding disadvantage of being inexorable. This combines badly with the anticipatory nature of the means of putting in the heat. If you decide that tomorrow will be cold you arrange for a greater charge to go in overnight. And if, as is by no means uncommon, tomorrow is not at all colder, the floor is still going to give off its stored heat, and there is nothing you can do about it, except leave all windows open or go out for the day. In converse conditions you are left to shiver.

This is not to decry underfloor heating for what it was – a pioneer effort which brought a lot of comfortable warmth to a nation shedding its spartan traditions.

The storage radiator is in many respects a notable advance upon the storage floor. It is not a constructional item, and so is available to anyone. It does not bring with it rules about avoiding the use of heavy carpet. Against it in small premises is that it is a piece of furniture, which the floor was not. But principally it is not, at least not necessarily, inexorable. There are in fact three classes of storage radiator. There is the common one, the cheapest, in which the heat leak is scientifically controlled by the amount of insulation given to it during construction, but is not otherwise controllable. This is comparable to the floor.

The other two classes of storage radiator have a common feature, that they are more heavily insulated so that random heat leakage is much reduced. Then, in the one type the heat output when required is damper controlled, usually manually. A damper is opened which allows air to pass from below through a passage or flue in the ceramic mass, where it becomes heated and passes out at the top. The second type of controlled unit is inactive until, under the influence of a room thermostat and probably a clock, a fan starts passing air through the heated core of the unit.

Either of the controlled types of unit is a great advance upon the first, in particular for quite common cases of a living room which is not much occupied until evening, by which time a natural unit is well past its best. The natural unit is quite well suited to halls, stores, libraries, and other situations in which bursts of warmth alternating with much cooler periods do not provide suitable conditions.

Another advantage to be claimed for controlled outlet models is that they relieve the user of a good deal of reliance upon a crystal ball. Whether tomorrow is going to be colder or warmer is less of a crisis if one may take the safe view and turn up the heat input, knowing that if it is not needed a lot of it will stay inside the unit until it is wanted, or it will form a substantial nucleus of heat so that the amount put in next night will be less. The maximum input is of course controlled automatically by a thermostat, adjustment of which is input control.

Inevitably the unit storage radiator grew up, into a central unit called Electricaire, big enough to provide warmth for several rooms. It is a large unit, and some are vertically disposed while others are horizontal. They are of the well insulated fan controlled type, the fan being powerful enough to propel the warm air through a duct system into the rooms to be warmed. In this connection it should be noted that standard units almost always have a stub duct system in mind, the fan being not powerful enough for a full duct system unless specifically stated.

Comparing an Electricaire unit with a stub duct unit using different fuel, the Electricaire has what might prove to be a decisive advantage in not needing a flue. As a heat unit it could suffer from its ability to become exhausted. That is, if given specially heavy duty during the day its heat charge could become used up before it is due to come on charge again. Instantaneous producers do not have this problem.

As a system it should be pointed out that it is unusual for an Electricaire unit to be connected to a return air duct, and return air is more usually allowed to find its own way back, if it wishes to do so. While this may work out quite well, it does tend to rely upon leaving certain doors open and is not therefore entirely automatic in its operation.

Electricaire units incorporate an air filter, usually on the inlet to the fan, and this should be kept clean. If it becomes choked, or even partly choked, it will affect performance and could be bad for the fan.

If we compare the warming action of a storage radiator with that of a hot water radiator, the nearest is the storage unit with uncontrolled output. Having less insulation it develops a generally higher surface temperature, and so is able to give off a higher proportion of invisible radiant heat. While this is an advantage it cannot outweigh the disadvantage of the uncontrollability of output; but when we speak of surface temperature we are speaking always of temperatures within safe limits. A part of the approval testing for any such unit is to ensure that its surface temperature cannot exceed a given standard figure. It should be noted, though, that some build-up can occur locally if normal heat dissipation is prevented, as it might be if say a pile of clothing were to be placed on the unit. Such units should always be kept clear.

We need to know what to do about the place where the unit stands. As a general rule nothing has to be done unless there are quite clear instructions given to the contrary. It is usual for all kinds of heating appliances to be tested for their effect upon the floor on which they stand, and in particular for the temperature which they will create below the unit. A storage radiator needs no special floor preparation. But while it is no doubt safe there is still the possibility that more or less continuous warmth will have some effect upon the floor covering. This may be most marked when the material is in the plastics or man made category, which includes floor tiles and many carpets. The way to avoid a tendency to softening of tiles, or embrittlement of fibres, is to use a protective sheet of asbestos millboard or similar under the unit.

The case of an Electricaire unit might be somewhat different, in that its gross weight might need support. We can only advise that in any given case the electricity people or the vendor must say what is needed, since larger units have greater weight. A suspended floor at ground floor level could for instance be given local support by means of brick piers taken off the under-floor: or the flooring could be cut out and a concrete base put in instead. In any case we recommend the use of an insulating plate under any such unit on a wooden floor, but stress that this is not for safety but to avoid any deterioration of the underfabric.

It is quite common for units of the Electricaire type to have an air duct between fan and heating elements at the bottom of the unit, thus forming a good insulator.

Boilers are a class of appliance which require some base protection, unless otherwise stated, and even then if there is a need to protect floor coverings. But the whole matter of boiler standing is covered by Building Regulations and to be on the safe side these should be consulted. The Regulations draw a distinction between solid fuel and oil fired appliances (Class 1) on the one hand, and gas fired appliances (Class 2) on the other.

The operation of storage units is, as already mentioned, anticipatory. Instead of using a crystal ball one may rely upon the weather forecasts, or if thought more reliable one's corns or piece of seaweed. But whatever means are used to predict the following day's temperature pattern, today is the day to do something about it. The input controller of a storage unit is usually marked in numbers, say 1 to 8. It takes a little while to discover, by trial and possibly error, whether a forecast of fairly cold justifies an input of number 5, or of 6. But this is what it amounts to, and any practical difficulties which may be met are rarely associated with that aspect. The input setting must be made before retiring for the night, since it controls what happens during the night.

The method is the same whether the unit is an individual one or a large Electricaire. The total reliance upon forecasting is greatly relaxed, as we have pointed out, by having units which do not rely upon natural heat discharge but to a very large extent upon extracting the heat required. The real responsibility then rests upon the owner to make sure that he programmes sufficient storage. To err on the generous side does not imply waste and loss since most of the surplus heat is retained by the insulation until it really is wanted. Prudence, economy and a proper regard for the conservation of energy require one not to be extravagant in the production of heat. But the logic of having a heating system in preference to putting up with the cold leads to the supposition that one will do what is needed for comfort. The guide line through this apparent dilemma is that which is set out in the Introduction, namely to have as much warmth as is needed, when and where needed; and outside those limits, nothing.

The service or maintenance on a storage unit may fall into more than one category, from ridiculously simple to the other extreme. Cleaning of the air filter on all fan controlled units should be done as regularly as inspection shows to be necessary; this will vary from unit to unit depending upon external conditions and the amount of dust which is in the air.

Beyond that an annual inspection may be thought desirable. Shut the main switch even though the current is off-peak and the time is on-peak. Remove sections of the casing and look in particular at the controller. Make sure that it is free from dust and that the points or contacts are not burnt. Check that electrical terminals are tightly screwed down.

In the extreme case that a heating element has broken, this can always be renewed in the case of a storage unit, whether single or Electricaire. In many cases it can be done without dismantling the core, though much of the casing must be removed. In the case of floor heating replacement is dependent upon construction. A floor may be made with a solidly embedded heating element, in which case nothing can be done. Or it may have a withdrawable element, with points at which withdrawal may take place. If taking over a house with this form of heating it is desirable to find out which type of element is fitted. Breakage of a heating element is an uncommon occurrence, but if it should occur with an embedded one there is little point in considering whether to dig up the floor. The easier course would be to change the type of heating, if only to storage units or Electricaire, retaining the off-peak meter and tariff.

10 Insulation

Whether you are more concerned to save money or running cost without loss of comfort, or to contribute to the urgent matter of conserving dwindling fuel supplies, the answer lies in insulation. It is not too much to say that it is more important than heating. If near-perfect insulation were possible, heating would not be required. Establishments such as the Centre for Alternative Technology at Machynlleth show how it is possible to save huge percentages of what might be considered normal household fuel bills, by a little planning in advance. This does of course include some planning in advance of building the house, a stage not available to everybody, but not to be neglected by anyone in that lucky position.

Insulation is a form of detective work, which to a large extent has been brought down to simple rules. Heat tries to escape, and the householder must find out where the leaks are, and stop them. We are by now fairly familiar with the tell tale, the house where snow does not settle on the roof in winter. The owner pays dearly to melt that amount of snow, and we all know that roof insulation would prevent it.

Roof insulation in the typical house or bungalow with pitched roof means insulation on the loft floor. It would take about twice as much, and a special rigid type, to insulate the pitched sides, though if the attic is brought into the occupied part of the house that is the way to do it. But if the attic is a place of dust and spiders then mineral wool or glass fibre, cut into widths to tuck cosily between the joists, is very suitable. It must not be laid under the cold water cistern, but may be carried up the sides and also tacked on to a wooden lid, as an extra precaution against the cistern freezing.

Vermiculite, a lightweight substance sold in granules, is another suitable material to be poured between the joists. After pouring it must be raked level.

INSULATION

The thickness of any such layer must be decided. When the subject was first popularised, those who advocated it were pleased if they could get people to accept a one inch thickness. Then it went on to become the 'economic thickness',

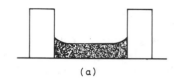

(a)

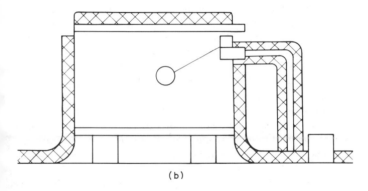

(b)

Fig. 10.1. Insulation in the roof space: blanket insulation (a) tucked between joists. The cold water cistern is contained within the insulated space (b). Wire netting holds the insulation in place

the amount you could put in and still recover the cost within reasonable time. It should be understood that the thicker the insulation the greater the saving, except that the benefits tail off a bit as the thickness increases. After all, if the first 50 mm (2 in) save say 60% it stands to reason that the second 50 mm cannot do the same. For a time economic thickness dictated the use of about 65 mm (2½ in) in the south, up to over 80 mm (3 in) in Scotland. That was before fuel prices soared. Now we may take it that a 100 mm (4 in) blanket is a good economic thickness, and it is of course a much better proposition than the original inch.

But insulation must be properly installed. This means being well tucked in, and in particular not allowing the wind, which always seems to blow in under eaves, to get under it or under any part of it and so carry away heat.

Suppose that you have to fit your insulating material on the pitch of the roof, it is possible to cut rigid or semi-rigid materials to fit between the joists as you would do for the floor. That is not however the best way to do it. Instead, take whole spreads of material and fasten them to and across the joists, so forming a complete surface of the material, as you would if fitting plaster board to a ceiling. By doing it this way you get the extra benefit of the air space between the material and the slates: or you may use that space to tuck in a non-rigid insulating material such as recommended for the loft floor. Or yet again you may use a cheaper front board, such as hardboard, and backfill the cavity formed with the insulating material.

After the roof come the walls, whose importance to heat loss lies mainly in their area. There are various ways of obtaining some benefit, even for instance planting a line of trees which shelter the wall from a strong prevailing wind, for wind encourages heat loss. A more uniform way of giving outside protection to a wall is by some form of cladding, it might be timber in the form of tiles or barge board, or slate or tile hanging. While these are not themselves outstanding insulators, they encourage the formation of a layer of still dry air, which is. In putting emphasis upon both 'still' and 'dry' we underline important principles. Referring to dryness, wall treatment will be less than satisfactory for any wall which suffers either from an inadequate damp course or from excessive porosity of the bricks. The damp course is rarely a problem with newer houses, and can be inserted, physically, or by chemical or electrostatic processes in older houses which do not have one. But brick porosity is relative, and is encouraged by driving rain and by north facing. It is only moderately expensive to apply a colourless preparation which will act to seal the front face of the brickwork.

INSULATION

Most houses nowadays are of cavity wall construction, having a cavity of approximately 50 mm (2 in) between the inner and outer leaves of brick or other building material. A ventilated cavity does not do much as an insulator, since it does not fulfil the condition regarding still air. An unventilated cavity is better from that respect, but does not always succeed in keeping the air still. If the cavity is wide enough there is room for an up-and-down circulation. The air in contact with the inner or warm wall will rise, causing the air in contact with the outer and cold wall to fall. The warmed air has to travel down the cold wall, where it loses its warmth, and in this way transfers indoor warmth to outdoors. Thus, good though air is at insulating, it is not as docile a subject as some solid material. This is where we arrive at cavity wall insulation, which in existing houses is injected through holes drilled in the wall and later plugged. The filling can take the form of a plastic material which after injection sets like a rubber sponge, being riddled with holes. It is the holes, which are not in contact with each other, which are still and dry and do the insulating, the plastic compound acting as a carrier for the holes.

The other type of material, used by Rentokil, is a mineral wool fibre which is blown into the cavity and packs it, doubtless with air entrainment. The plastic injection method can go wrong, for such reasons as having the wrong mix, and in spite of the great value of cavity insulation it is not cheap. Intending users would be well advised therefore to deal only with contractors who belong to the trade association, the National Cavity Insulation Association.

We cannot overlook walls in older houses which have no cavity but instead are perhaps 230 mm (9 in) or 330 mm (13 in) brick, but if we are to treat them by interior insulation it is even more important that they are not excessively porous. In the case of an inhabited house in normal use, with a single skin wall, the wall acts as a battlefield in winter. On one side is water trying to get in, and creeping through the pores. From the inside comes warmth to drive it out again; and somewhere about halfway, with luck, the battle reaches stalemate. The warmth has given up and become cold, but its efforts have halted the forward progress of the damp. That is why such a house, left empty for a few weeks, often shows damp on the walls, because no heat is being passed through from the inside. If we put insulation on the inside it will have the same effect, and damp can come right up to the insulation, unless it is checked at source. We have already described thermal inner linings when discussing warm air systems in Chapter 4 and there is nothing more to add.

The treatment of windows reached a ridiculous peak when it was taken up by people whose real interest does not lie within the heating industry. Ridiculous figures, like 50% saving, were freely bandied about, despite the fact that these would be obtainable only in a greenhouse, and then only with scientifically constructed double glazing. Anything with two panes of glass in it was and still is sold as double glazing for heat retention.

The ideal is still a sandwich of still dry air, which calls for a means of drying the air; and a sandwich width which offers a substantial depth of air but not enough to allow an internal circulation to set up, as we described happening in a cavity wall. The best distance apart for the two glass panes is in the neighbourhood of 18 mm (or from ½ to ¾ in). At that, the heat loss can be considered halved. The saving falls off somewhat as the gap decreases or increases, and by the time it reaches 100 mm (4 in) it is much more useful as a sound insulator than for heat. Since the price of proprietary double glazed units is so high many people are tempted to make their own, by adding an extra pane of glass. To be effective it must be done well, and the gap figure is given above. The handiest method of drying the trapped air is to introduce a little silica gel, a dehydrating agent, into the cavity. If this is properly sealed there will be only the original moisture to remove, not a continuing amount.

Questions are raised about triple glazing, which is not uncommon in parts of Scandinavia where the weather becomes really cold. But the diminishing usefulness of the extra pane or panes is very marked, and considering the current cost of even double glazing it could not achieve an 'economic' justification in this country. It should not be forgotten, though, that during the winter a good half of every 24 hours is darkness, and windows have no functional use. There is nothing to prevent us, then, from bringing in the equivalent of quadruple glazing, or more, for half the winter, by means of shutters, internal and external, by heavy curtains well tucked in, by any means we can devise to put a heat barrier across the gap in the brickwork.

The real importance of windows as a source of heat loss can often be exaggerated. In some houses they constitute a quite small proportion of the total wall area, and their greatest nuisance value comes from the condensation which forms on them. Double glazing, and of course the other steps mentioned, greatly reduce this. The greatest problem from windows comes to those who plan their homes with perpetual summer in mind, with great areas of glass as picture windows, french doors and the like. Almost prohibitive to double glaze, they can certainly do with ample heavy curtains. It is wise, when planning to incorporate such expensive items as large picture windows, to consider at that time incurring some additional expense and having double glazed units from the outset.

In the average house a quite surprising amount of heat is lost through the ground floor. In the case of a suspended floor this can happen in two ways: by conduction downwards and by the infiltration of cold air from below through gaps in floor boards. It should be remembered that a suspended floor must be kept well ventilated and no restriction placed on the access of air to it through the air bricks.

It will be apparent therefore that a solid floor offers more chances of success. It will not suffer from cold air infiltration, and during construction can have an insulating material built into it.

But for most people, who have to put up with what is provided, the first thing to do with a suspended floor is to stop up all the gaps through which air can travel. This may entail carpentry, or moderate gaps may be filled with papier mâché. Another sealer, possibly in addition, is to clad the whole floor in hardboard, wall to wall, sealing the joints with adhesive paper tape. Then in the case of suspended and solid floors, use floor coverings with a view to retaining heat; heavy quality underlay, and either good carpet or, if lino, then plenty of thick mats.

That deals with the top, sides and bottom of the box which effectively comprises any house, leaving the openings into that box, the doors and windows. To find a really well fitting frame to either door or window is exceptional, and again if the discrepancies are too great it may call for carpentry to put things right. This does not of course apply to metal fitments, which should fit unless warped by fixing stresses during erection. But sometimes metal doors and windows do not marry for the very simple reason that a blob of paint has destroyed the smoothness of the mating edge. It is worth going round each fitting to look for this. For moderate aberrations of fit in doors and windows the cure, in the form of some type of draught excluding strip, is fortunately not very expensive.

It was mentioned in Chapter 4, when discussing a fresh air intake to a warm air system, that the average house already lets in more than enough. It may well continue to do so even after treatment, but the probability has decreased. That is not a matter of vital importance, but the supply of air for combustion to any device in the house which burns a fossil fuel — coal, coke, oil, gas — whether it is the boiler or cooker, fire or warm air unit, is important. This gives us an opportunity to do things properly: instead of hoping that we live in a place so bad that in spite of ourselves it is self supporting in fresh air, we can now arrange to deliver fresh air to the exact place that it is needed, and in roughly the right amount.

There need never be serious misgiving about making a purpose built hole in a dwelling. Suppose that you put in an air brick or grille adjacent to the boiler. When the boiler is at work it will draw on it. When the boiler is not at work there will be no other force persuading air to enter through that aperture. If air is to enter, some must leave from somewhere, and you have already seen to it that there are no stray outlets. Indeed, the only stray air to enter a well treated house should be what comes in through the unavoidable opening of the front or back door.

It is quite easy to run a ducted air supply from a grille in the outside wall to a point adjacent to the appliance needing the air, but it is by no means certain that one should do so. A factor to be kept in mind is that in addition to heating there is ventilation to consider. In a sealed house we should gradually use up all the oxygen, and perish, and while there is little likelihood of this happening because of the near impossibility of achieving that degree of sealing, we must recognise it. In fact we do, numerically, since an allowance is made in heating calculations for a change of air in each room 1½ times an hour. Air movement within the house takes place of its own accord, by thermal currents and by the boosting caused by opening and shutting doors, and by the movement of people. The only critical aspect of this subject arises in providing minimum standards for combustion appliances, and figures for this are given in Chapter 6.

Continuing our search for sources of unofficial air leakage we come to the chimney which is not connected to a modern appliance with a sealed in flue connection. It may be that the chimney is not in use. In that case the least that should happen is that the register plate should be closed, and if no register is fitted then a blanking plate in lieu should be placed in the throat. The permanent way to deal with such chimneys is described in Chapter 6.

A fireplace which is still used occasionally should, if of the open fire type, first be reconsidered in case its importance warrants fitting a modern close-coupled appliance instead. If this is not done then quite clearly this chimney must be closed off in periods of non-use, either by a closeable register plate or by fitting a close screen across the opening. The amount of loss due to an uncontrolled chimney can be quite colossal. The effect of controlled leakage on the other hand is to give just that amount of room ventilation which is needed.

There is no doubt that a total programme of insulation, on the lines suggested here, will cost quite a lot. It is an unexciting subject, and unlike heating there is nothing to look at, nothing to burst into life at the turn of a switch, and a fairly common attitude is 'We'll have the heating this year, and do that next year − if we can afford it.' That is to put things in quite the wrong order, for if one had to make a clear choice insulation should win. We mentioned earlier that with ideal insulation heating would be redundant, and if we go only half way, we can say that with good insulation heating is less important. The other fallacy in the 'this year next year' argument is that heating plant needed *before* insulation is bigger and therefore more expensive than that which is needed *after* insulation. Further, if it becomes too large for the job its working efficiency goes down and creates another source of unnecessary running cost.

That argument was put into some very impressive figures recently, and it happened that experiments were carried out independently at about the same time by two quite unconnected organisations. Briefly what happened was that in each experiment two identical houses were built, but one was turned out in 'standard' form and the other was given a full insulation treatment. Each was then equipped with central heating, and since they were in the same area they experienced the same local climate. The two results showed remarkable accord, both indicating a saving of about 41% for the insulated house.

We would be surprised if any of our readers could emulate this, for this experiment was, as they say, under controlled conditions. But is there anyone who may at this moment be looking with disgust at his fuel bill who would reject the chance to knock even 25% off it? The matter does not end there. If the insulation is done first, the system will need a boiler or heater 25% (or 41%) smaller than it would have done, and the same will apply to radiators or other heat emitters. And cost goes along with size, so right at the start there is a chance to recover some of the cost of insulating.

Then there is an uncostable factor, the physiological one. Indoor warmth arrives in two forms, radiant and convected. Convected warmth is what is due to the circulation of warm air. Radiant warmth is a form of emanation which is not dependent upon being air borne. It may be visible, as from a flame or gas or electric fire, or it may be invisible if at low temperature. Equally important, it may be positive or negative in relation to the human body. That is, we may feel cold radiation as well as warmth, and both are more noticeable and more effective than convected warmth. Now, if we find ourselves in an uninsulated room with radiators, in which the temperature on a thermometer has just got up to the specified figure, we might still feel discomfort, and it is due to cold radiation off the still cold walls. Only the air is as yet up to temperature, and it will take quite a long time before the walls begin to absorb and retain warmth. But in a well insulated room, not only is the warming time for the walls less, but there is a much greater chance that the walls still retain a good deal of warmth from the last period of room occupation. That slight shiver in spite of the thermometer might never occur with insulation.

Just in case we ever get another prolonged spell of very hot weather, it is worth recalling that insulation also keeps out heat.

11 Domestic Hot Water

At various points throughout this book, where it was relevant to the matter in hand, we have mentioned domestic hot water. This is the hot water which is piped to bath and shower, to wash basins and to kitchen sink; very likely to washing machine and dishwasher too.

If the domestic hot water comes from an instantaneous gas fired water heater, or indeed from any existing plant such as a storage water heater which is in good condition, the rest of this chapter is unlikely to be of interest to the lucky owner. But for the rest we must bring under one heading what people should know about domestic hot water before choosing other equipment which might have a bearing upon it.

We could begin by asking how much water you need, and the answer lies of course with how many people use it, and for what purposes. It is less concerned with the size of the establishment, for we may find a castle holding only perhaps four people, while in a three-bedroom semi there might be seven or eight. Babies seem to need a lot of water. So do people who bath generously, while those who shower instead use far less. The main purpose in thinking about this is to make sure that you do not depart far from the average, and if you do you must do something about it. Do not neglect to include uses other than washing. A lot of people could mean a lot of laundry, and by hand or machine this uses water. A dishwater is also somewhat extravagant in its demand for hot water.

But having set that out, there is a figure which seems to suit the average premises, which we may take as being three-bedroom with what passes for an average family (2 parents and

2.3 children?). This is represented by a hot water cylinder of 170 litres (35 gal) capacity, with a heat supply of 3 kW (10 000 to 12 000 Btu/h). Obviously if we think about 4 and 5 bedroom properties with appropriate numbers in residence then we move to a 214 litre (45 gal) cylinder and up to 6 kW (20 000 Btu/h) make-up rate. For present purposes it is sufficient to think of 3 kW (10 000 Btu/h), and we would not recommend dropping below this level even if the premises is only a one-bedroom flat. With plenty of insulation on the cylinder the supply will last longer.

Ignoring some losses, 3 kW (10 000 Btu/h) will raise 45 litres (10 gal) of water through 55 deg C (100 deg F) in one hour. If we are starting with cold water, which is by no means to be taken for granted, then the recovery rate in the cylinder is 45 litres an hour. People may well ask why we do not aim for a better rate, to avoid so long a wait between baths. But first it would not just be a case of putting more heat in, for there are times when a central heating boiler of say 15 kW (50 000 Btu/h) rating is working only for the cylinder, and the rate does not improve. The limiting factor is the rate of heat exchange possible in the cylinder. Secondly, how much are you prepared to let hot water encroach upon central heating? Or in a slightly different way, how much extra would you be prepared to pay for a bigger boiler (and of course a cylinder with a special heat exchanger)? For in the first case, when both heating and hot water systems are at work, to take another 3 kW for hot water is to lose it from heating. We think we know the answer to those questions, which is why we now accept as general the 3 kW figure.

It is this which gives us that hardy standby, the electric immersion heater. With very few exceptions (of 2 kW or 2.5 kW) this is rated 3 kW (or it may be 3 kW/3 kW). The 3 kW/3kW is a very useful form of heater, suited only to cylinders which have the boss at the top, and it is made of two heater elements, one long and one short. These are separately wired to a change-over switch so that only one is at work at any one time. They are usually labelled Bath and Basin or something similar. When only small amounts of hot water are needed, as for washing up for instance, the short or Basin heater is switched on, and it heats only the upper part of the cylinder. For baths, or larger demands, the longer or Bath element is switched on and it heats water over most of the cylinder's height, as is usual with this type of heater.

Electric immersion heaters are the only form of heater which may be considered suitable for a direct cylinder, and indeed they would very often fail to enter fully a cylinder which contained an internal heat exchanger (*Figure 11.1*). Proprietary immersion heaters have a thermostat incorporated, and this is usually preset by the manufacturer. Some provide a knob for temperature adjustment.

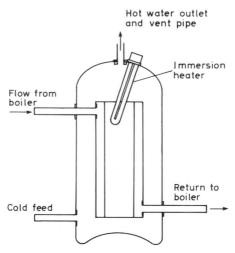

Fig. 11.1. Typical indirect cylinder into which an electric immersion heater has been fitted

There is little to say about the installation of this simple device, except that all wiring and switching must conform to IEE Regulations and these will be allied to local Building Regulations. But there is a feature of operation which crops up year after year, and with no hope of finality we deal with it now. The question is, is it more economical to leave an immersion heater on all the time, or to switch it on only when required? The answer is the latter. It may well be more *convenient* to leave it on all the time, but convenience is not economy. The reason is simple. Heat loss from one body to another proceeds at a rate proportional to the difference in temperature between them, in this case the cylinder and the surrounding air. Loss is also proportional to time: a cylinder which is always running is always (less a few operational dips) at maximum temperature and therefore at maximum heat loss. A cylinder is left to go cold loses no heat at that time, and proportionately less than maximum when cooling and warming.

The electric immersion heater owes its continuing existence to its great convenience. It has a low first cost, takes up next to no room, and is operated merely by switching on. Those factors count against the running cost, which is unquestionably high. But if we have a heating system of the electric storage type, which is charged at off-peak tariff rate, then it is advisable to ask that hot water be put on the same tariff, being another facet of storing. This will entail a change of method of operation, for off-peak current is available only during off-peak hours, say 11 — 7. All the hot water for next day must be made overnight, if the cheap tariff is to be enjoyed, and in most cases this calls for greater storage capacity, and a very determined effort to retain by insulation the heat which is received. These matters can be arranged by discussion with the local Electricity Board. It is not usual for the user to be left entirely at the mercy of his own operational calculation, though. The cylinder may have a second immersion heater fitted, connected to standard tariff current in the usual way, which may be switched on in case the hot water stock becomes depleted. Regular use of that device deserves to be looked upon as an admission of failure, and will certainly cut into any savings made on running costs after the expense of buying a larger cylinder.

This is an appropriate time to kill off another bogey concerning hot water cylinders. It is quite usual, and sensible, to build a cupboard around the cylinder, which has no visual attractions, and to make it into an airing cupboard. It is then not uncommon to assume that since it is now an airing cupboard some provision must be made to introduce warmth. This often results in part or all of the insulation around the cylinder being removed or omitted. There was never a more blatant case of taking a steam roller to crack a nut. Three simple facts must be appreciated.

(1) The cupboard is for airing, not for drying.

(2) With the best quality insulation it is likely to get, the cylinder will still lose enough heat to keep a mild atmosphere inside the cupboard.

(3) What most airing cupboards need most and lack most often is ventilation. This means, foremost, openings at top and bottom, so that warmed moist air can escape and be replaced by fresh air. It also means giving those items which are supposed to be 'airing' a chance to breathe, as they have when on the clothes line — not folded flat and bundled deep in a solid heap.

So do not skimp on the insulation for well intentioned but wrong reasons. This applies with equal force to any hot water cylinder, irrespective of the method by which it is heated.

The electric immersion heater with direct hot water cylinder is appropriate either to the special case of electric heating, preferably by off-peak storage, or to the very unspecialised area in which no other issue such as heating is involved. That is, the area in which a direct cylinder with immersion heater giving hot water is the only amenity.

When we come to consider the provision of hot water as a byproduct of a wet central heating system with boiler, taking our own advice and using an indirect type of cylinder, it is unlikely that an immersion heater could be used even if it were wanted. If it is desired as a standby it could be attempted, if the cylinder has a top entry boss. But you may ask why should it be wanted? Surely the boiler solves the problem of hot water quite satisfactorily?

It solves it, certainly, but not with entire satisfaction, as we shall show in a moment. But first to look at the physical details, which have already been touched upon in Chapters 2 and 3.

Hot water cylinders in this context may be indirect, or semi-indirect or self priming. If you already have a cylinder, the way to find out which of those two you have is to count the cold water cisterns which are connected to it. A fully indirect cylinder requires two cisterns, one for the primary circuit, which is continuous circulation of the same water, through boiler to cylinder and heating system and back to boiler; the other is the supply cistern for the domestic hot water, and in most houses cold water too (except at the kitchen sink).

A self-priming cylinder has only one cistern and one water supply, which sorts itself out inside the cylinder. It goes primarily to the secondary or hot water side, of course, but contributes make-up water to the primary circuit if this is wanted.

There is a structural difference which accounts for this difference in intakes. An indirect cylinder has full separation of the primary and secondary circuits, the former running through a coil or annulus which acts as a heat exchanger, the secondary water being on the outside. In a self-priming cylinder separation of primary and secondary is undertaken by a buffer of air, which is quite stable and adequate to keep the two apart over the whole range of normal operating temperatures and pressures. By the nature of the device however it must be recognised that a physical disturbance well outside the normal range could have the effect of breaking the seal, with temporary mixing of the two water supplies, primary and secondary. This would be very undesirable, since it would in effect return the system to all the drawbacks of a direct system. A disturbance which could bring about such a breakdown would be boiling, perhaps through thermostat failure on a boiler. Another possible cause could be a circulating pump which is far too powerful for the installation, creating great turbulence. It must be stressed however that such trouble-some factors are rare, and that self-priming cylinders correctly sized for the job they have to do are in very wide use and quite satisfactory. They are for open topped systems only, and cannot be used with sealed systems such as are described in Chapter 3.

For anyone who has a direct cylinder and wishes to change it there is a conversion set made, a coil type heat exchanger which is fitted into the cylinder by way of a boss intended for an immersion heater (which the coil is, though not electric). Such an arrangement is a regular part of a microbore system.

A fully indirect cylinder has four pipe connections: the flow and return from the boiler, the cold feed and the hot water offtake and vent pipe. In most cases the primaries connected to the boiler work by gravity. It is necessary therefore to see that their vertical progress is maintained. A pipe must never rise, then fall again before rising, for that way lie air locks which will soon shut the installation down. Even horizontal runs are to be avoided, partly because they can so easily lean a little the wrong way, partly because they absorb energy from the flow system. If some horizontal run is unavoidable it should be offset by at least three times the length of vertical run.

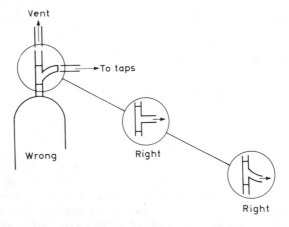

Fig. 11.2. The right and wrong ways of fitting the tee for hot water supply to the cylinder outlet

DOMESTIC HOT WATER

Another place to be on guard against an air lock is on the secondary flow pipe. The vent pipe must go upward as straight as possible, with no horizontal run at all. It must never be fitted with a valve. The domestic hot water is usually taken off this rising pipe, and it would seem quite natural to help this flow on its way by using a swept or pitcher tee, as shown in *Figure 11.2*. This is wrong, and will encourage air locking at that point. The correct fitting is either a straight tee or a reversed swept tee.

Now we will examine why domestic hot water as a byproduct of central heating is not the ideal system. We have already arrived at a figure of 3 kW (10 000 Btu/h) as the rate of heat input into the cylinder. We know that the present value of the rating of an average domestic boiler is in the range of 13 to 15 kW (45 to 50 000 Btu/h). This excludes the open fire with back boiler, referring to independent boilers mainly. Suppose we take a figure of 13 kW, then during the heating season the boiler is presumably well occupied, having to make 3 kW for hot water and 10 kW for space heating. Its work pattern on an average winter day may be 45 minutes on during every hour that it is at work.

The outstanding difference between the heating and hot water loads is that the latter is almost unchanged across the whole year. Whether the boiler is left for long periods in a potential on position, or whether it is switched on only for an hour or two each day, the fact remains that it is unable to deliver at a faster rate than 3 kW, or less than 25% of its rated output. It will therefore have long periods of inactivity in which to cool off, losing heat through dissipation and having then to reheat the structure of the boiler before coming into fully effective work.

The overall efficiency under these conditions is appalling. The reason why we put up with it is the common one, that it is convenient to do so. Although the logical answer is to separate the water heating function, and give it its own heater rated at 3 kW or thereabouts, this would (a) cost more initially; (b) take up more space, which is perhaps not available; (c) require another connection into the flue; so we do not do it.

Yet the objections are answerable, at least in the case of gas. The cost would be offset by the lower cost of a smaller heating boiler. A circulator, as a small gas boiler is called, may be wall mounted, and it may be obtained in balanced flue form.

A look at Chapter 5 will show that those air heaters which incorporate a means of making hot water already follow the recommended path, since the incorporated water heater is (with about one exception) operated quite independently of the heating, and is of the right size for the job.

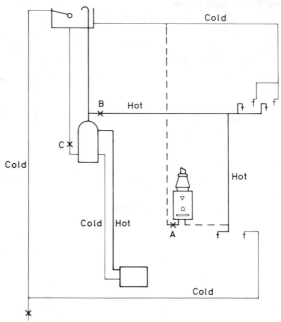

Fig. 11.3. The method of connecting in an auxiliary heater (for summer use, for example)

A variant of that method, and again the one which belongs to gas, is as before to keep the main boiler for space heating only: but to give water heating to an instantaneous heater, so doing away with the need for a hot water storage cylinder. It should perhaps be noted that this type of heater is forever heating and cooling off, but it is of very light weight construction and so not responsible for heavy losses as is a cast iron boiler.

Yet another method of dealing with the summer load combines both the others, and is shown in *Figure 11.3*. An instantaneous heater is piped into a boiler hot water circuit so as to be in parallel with the regular boiler. Heater and cylinder have valves fitted on one of the connections, so as to be able to stop any flow in one of the circuits. Thus valve A stops the inlet to the heater, valve B the outlet from the cylinder, and in each case the one valve is sufficient, and easiest to understand. This last is an important qualification, since there must always be reservations about handing out responsibility for valve operation to an unknown and generally inexpert public.

The method of connecting the instantaneous heater is preferably as shown by the broken lines, the water supply coming from the cold supply from the cistern. But there are bound to be cases in which the pressure, or vertical head, from such an arrangement is inadequate to work the heater, which has automatic valves and safeguards built in. In such a case the heater, being suitably constructed, may be connected direct to mains. But if that happens it cannot any longer be piped back into the existing hot water system. This would constitute making a cross connection between a high pressure and a low pressure supply, which is very properly contrary to the bylaws of the water authority. The existence of an isolating valve does not affect the matter. The requirement, that from the outlet of the heater a separate supply must be run to all outlet pipes, with their own taps, tends to make the thing so cumbersome as to be unacceptable. It would be better to go back to the scheme proposed, of removing hot water from the boiler altogether and giving it to an instantaneous heater.

The best working temperature for stored hot water, and the use of a cylinder thermostat to control that temperature, are matters dealt with in Chapter 8. Here we will repeat the warning that any means of totally isolating the primary circulation through the cylinder must not be used unless the boiler is capable of instantaneous automatic response to its own thermostat.

While so far we have shown how a gas fired system can be used to achieve better than average efficiency, we must come back to the fact that we live with the average, and that oil and solid fuel do not offer that degree of adaptability. Looking at solid fuel first, there are two levels of appliance. Numerically the most important is the fire back boiler, and there are undoubtedly many people who are forced to light a fire in midsummer because that is their only means of getting hot water. For them the standby immersion heater is the most convenient solution, though they would be able to use the *Figure 11.3* scheme if the conditions allow the heater to work.

The free standing and more controllable boiler is more adaptable. If the load is sufficient to keep it alight it may be left to slumber with occasional bursts of energy which keep the fire going. It is not in any better case than the fully automatic boiler in terms of working efficiency. It does not dissipate heat by intermittent cooling, but on the other hand it is always consuming fuel at some rate, however small. Although it would be difficult to obtain anything resembling an accurate costing, there is nothing here which justifies us in dismissing the electric immersion heater as a uniquely costly device to run. It does after all operate at 100% efficiency, near enough. A solid fuel boiler mainly slumbering, or a gas or oil boiler spending a lot of time shut off on its own thermostat, may well do no better than 50% efficiency. If we take a rough guess that electricity costs twice as much as any of those other fuels, the net cost comes out the same. The net cost ought perhaps to take account of extra wear and tear on the boiler, which is greater particularly under on/off conditions.

Although the purpose of this section is to consider hot water only from the heating point of view, leaving the plumbing work for Section 3, it is relevant to mention one aspect of hot water plumbing. This is the size of pipe to be used to convey hot water to taps. When the tap is open this pipe carries hot water; when the tap is shut the pipe is full of hot water, which slowly cools. When the tap is reopened the first stream of water is cold. This is called 'dead leg.'

All the rules of fluid flow indicate that we should use pipes of fairly generous proportions, so that friction is reduced and the tap is able to give a rapid discharge rate. But the more generous we are, the greater the volume of 'dead leg', with its accompanying inconvenience and sheer waste. Consequently hot water pipes are always calculated to be big enough but in no way generous in diameter. The desirability of planning to cut down the length of runs will also be obvious.

All the comments made about boilers apply to those mainly full scale back boilers built into combination units for gas or oil firing, and to the larger capacity hearth units which are the closed or closeable solid fuel room heaters with back boiler.

Instantaneous heaters are available for bottled gas, and are much in demand for mini-domestic conditions, in caravans and yachts. The only practical application for a domestic electric instantaneous water heater is in a shower, in which a very small quantity of water can be fashioned into a useful spray by a well designed rose. The limitation upon this type of heater is the electric loading which would be needed for say basin or bath filling — well beyond the capacity of a normal domestic meter.

Though we are considering domestic hot water as a service based upon a central heat source and a pipe network, this image does not have to be pursued regardless of common sense. It can often happen that a house or other type of dwelling is so constructed, or modified, that most of it lends itself to a compact pipe system: but that there is one part, perhaps a wing, an extension or the new cloakroom which used to be the laundry room, which stays obstinately outside any neat solution. If the system has to be extended to run hot water to a basin or shower it will mean a long pipe run, hot and cold, with nothing else on the way. So there is the cost of pipe and labour, the inconvenience, the continuing heat loss, the long dead leg, and particularly due to the last, a not very satisfactory service. This is a clear case for not extending the system, but for treating this outlet on its own, with saving of material, perpetual higher efficiency through less heat losses, and high user satisfaction.

It may be done in one of the following ways:

1. By single point instantaneous gas water heater, possibly balanced flue type since the presence of a convenient flue would be a coincidence. This would involve running one cold water pipe, from main or from cistern, and a gas pipe; or in a non-gas situation having a bottle of gas nearby. This type of installation is adequate for a sink or wash basin, or for a shower so long as the shower equipment is carefully chosen to complement the heater.

2. By electric storage heater of the smaller size, usually not more than 20 litres (5 gal) capacity. This may be of the free outlet type, to be situated above the outlet point; or it may be a pressurised heater which would stand under the floor, most usefully under the basin so that dead leg is almost nil.

Either of these heaters may be fed directly from mains or from the cold cistern supply. The free outlet or displacement type of heater is open topped and not itself under pressure. By opening a tap the user allows cold water to enter the heater, and this pushes out hot water. It must not have a control fitted to the outlet. The pressurised type of heater must first of all be bought for high pressure use. It must then be fitted either with an expansion pipe or with a pressure relief valve, and before undertaking to fit one of these the user should consult the local Electricity Board for detailed advice.

Up to the useful capacity, say 20 litres, either of these heaters may be used for a variety of purposes at any reasonable rate of flow. The free flow heater cannot be used for a shower since it must not have a mixing valve, a form of restriction, imposed upon its outlet.

The only services to be supplied are cold water and electricity, and perhaps in one case a vent pipe.

3. The third possibility, useful for little but a shower or a basin spray tap, is the instantaneous electric heater which

we have discussed already. It would usually need to be 6 kW loading. Its requirements are a cold water supply and electricity.

Maintenance

The domestic hot water supply is inescapably at the mercy of whatever the local water supply has in store for it. We have shown how to protect the primary circuits by the use of an indirect system, excluding contact with continuous raw water. The domestic system has to suffer it, whatever it is. Things are not generally as bad as that may suggest. Troubles due to soft acid waters are rare since copper tube came into general use. The effect upon lead was of course potentially dangerous. But hard waters are different, since they do not attack their surroundings but simply deposit their hardness as solid matter when heated. If by the use of a chemical additive such as Calgon these deposits can be kept as a sludge to be washed away, not allowed to adhere as hard scale, then trouble with heat exchangers and pipes is long deferred. If not, the time must come when those items have to be defurred, and if this can be done by chemical descaler it saves dismantling the system. Signs of trouble are that the hot water gets less hot, and/or that the flow rate decreases.

The least harmful but most annoying symptom is probably the slight stain or encrustation which develops, like a junior stalactite, on bath or basin if the tap has a tendency to drip, perhaps when being closed. If the bath or basin is wiped down *after* dripping stops this may be kept off indefinitely. But if it does occur, it will usually be removed by being wiped with a cloth on which is a little proprietary scale solvent solution, then rinsed with clean water. But ask the bath manufacturer before applying this treatment, if you have a new and perhaps plastic bath.

To attempt to sum up this chapter:

1.   Wet heating systems usually make provision in the size of heater to supply hot water as well as heating.

2. In terms of logic and efficiency this is not the best arrangement but is cheaper in first cost and takes less space than

3. The separation of hot water from heating by giving hot water its own heater.

4. A separate water heater cost is partly offset by needing a smaller heating boiler.

5. Means of providing hot water at about 3 kW rating include electric immersion heater, gas circulator; instantaneous gas water heater (higher ratings available).

6. Electric immersion heater goes with storage radiator system at off-peak rate.

7. Electric immersion heater may cost no more to run than a large boiler running at 3 kW load.

8. Hot water cylinder should always be well insulated.

9. The self-priming cylinder is a form of indirect cylinder.

10. Instantaneous multipoint heater may be fitted into a wet system for summer use on hot water service.

11. The use of a cylinder thermostat.

12. Avoidance of excessive 'dead leg'.

13. Domestic hot water for the remote part of the house.

14. Maintenance of the hot water side.

12 Choosing a System

You have decided (let us say) that you will go in for central heating; or that you will get rid of the old and worn out system you have, for a new one. On grounds of cost alone it is not a step to be taken lightly. But it is just at this point too that all the dreadful stories come to mind, of people beggared and bankrupted, made to wait two years for essential parts, driven to desperation — and all they started with was a simple wish to keep warm.

Well, no doubt about it, you must keep your wits about you, or else employ someone who can be fully trusted to do the caring on your behalf. For a start you can count those who will take a negative attitude to your job:

The local authority, who will want to increase your rates.
The local authority, who will want to see that their Building Regulations are not breached, by way of structure, or fire risks, or electrical details.
The water authority, watchful of their byelaws.
The Clean Air people if you burn coal or oil.
In certain circumstances you might even come up against Planning, e.g. if you want to put up an outhouse for a boiler.

But all on that list, and any we may have missed out, are really quite helpful if asked for help. What tends to upset them is having their rules broken without prior consultation which would have avoided it. So the first practical rule should be, to make a list of everyone who has a genuine need to know what you are doing, and to tell them.

No doubt you will then ask how do you know who these various authorities are? So we go one step back, to the chosen installer or to the fuel supplier who may be advising you about the new installation. He spends his working life in this area of activity and should know. He should know also any short cuts. This does not mean evasions. But suppose for instance that a national agreement has been made that a certain form of appliance detail is acceptable in spite of earlier precedent, then this need not be argued again. That kind of detail is for the fuel supplier or the appliance supplier to know.

The second practical rule is, therefore, to discuss the proposals in some detail with a representative of your local fuel supplier, Gas Region or Electricity Board, major oil company (Shell, Esso etc.) agent, or SFAS or NCB agent. The chosen one of these stands to make a continuing profit out of you, and this is your turn to get something besides fuel from him.

But, you may well say, we haven't yet decided which of these we will use. True. So go back yet another step, and see what is going to influence the decision between the kinds of heating which are outlined in this book. Here are just a few points which might be applicable.

(1) Age. Moving into retirement, do you seek simplicity and ease? Will you want to carry coal and ashes? Will you want to lie on the floor to light a blown out gas bypass flame? Or will you insist upon simple controls at reachable height all the time, and no humping?

(2) Physical disability creates the same conditions as age, above.

(3) Your premises, are they rented, owned, do you plan a long occupation or intend to sell and move in say five years? For a start you would not plough a lot of capital into a landlord's property unless there was a beneficial arrangement with the landlord. No need to go without heating, though. This is a situation suiting storage radiators, of which you can remove all but the circuit; or the hearth mounted oil fired unit which gives bulk warm air distributed around the house

by drift and perhaps an extract fan. It is *not* an occasion for running a pipe circuit or extensive ducts.

There may well be a different outlook towards the place in which you hope to spend the rest of your days, compared with one which you expect to move on from, as is common enough in these restless times. The case is however debatable. On the one hand it may be thought that to put in the best system available will bring its own reward in the price which the house will fetch eventually. On the other hand, pessimism or some other reason may dictate that you put in the cheapest form of system compatible with being able to describe it as central heating, and to enjoy it during occupation of the house.

(4) Geographical location. Fuel limitations sometimes apply. In quite a few places, usually smallish and quite a way from anywhere, there is no gas main. Such places almost always have a Calor gas agent. Only rarely do we find a place with no electricity — a cottage on the moor, perhaps. This is extremely limiting, because of the great reliance of so many other appliances upon electricity for their instrumentation and control. Possibilities coming readily to mind are a solid fuel boiler (but no circulating pump for a wet system); an oil fired hearth fitted heater as described in (3), in which the extract fan is not an essential part and is replaced by plenty of open doors. Pity the cottage-on-the-moor dweller if he is inaccessible to a supplier of solid or oil fuel. He has little left but wood, or peat, or solar heat, none of which come into this book. The portable paraffin stove is not an exciting prospect, since it gives off a gallon of water for every gallon of paraffin burned, and is a chief contributor to internal condensation.

(5) Household detail. This covers a good deal. It covers the flat which has no flue and no right of access to an upper floor, for which there is little choice beyond electric storage. It covers the new house built for the electric age, with no chimney, which does not prevent you from using gas fired balanced flue appliances; or from building a flue for yourself (subject to Building Regulations).

It covers the place which has no spare floor space, e.g. a 'bijou' kitchen, and the under stairs cannot possibly be connected to a flue. Electricity apart, there is the wall mounted gas boiler, and skirting heating to save the space taken by radiators. Or, given a hearth, there is the back boiler. Still under household detail we must think of places which have solid floors, and ask how will we run the pipes of a wet system. Perhaps tied to the same set of conditions will be a strong wish to keep all the 'engine room' details out of sight. The primaries of the hot water system can usually be accommodated in the core of the house, particularly if the hot water cylinder is vertically over the boiler position, as for good operation it should be. We have also drawn attention to the latest idea, in which the hot water cylinder is a part of the boiler and so primaries are done away with. But the heating system is different. It must run outwards to the heat emitters. This may be a case in which you use microbore, because the pipes are as inconspicuous as electric cable. It may also, remember, be the right place to make those economical runs, of back-to-back radiators or other heat emitters, which we have described.

(6) By no means least and by no means last comes personal preference. Nobody has to give a reason for not liking gas, detesting oil or having no use for solid fuel — like the lady who refuses to have electricity in the place, except for lighting and the Hoover (which she claims are different).

The likes and dislikes can be more penetrating than that. A typical case in heating, though not in central heating, concerns the gas fire. With unbelievable perversity many interior design conscious people seem to object to the modern designed exterior of most gas fires and to look longingly at the gas fired log effect unit, which is one of the worst things to happen to the gas industry in this decade.

Manufacturers of boilers for gas, oil and solid fuel went to endless trouble to dress their kitchen boilers in a manner which makes them almost indistinguishable from the washing machine, the fridge, the kitchen unit. While most people approved, there remained a market for the bizarre design, to the delight of the few who retained it.

Most people have by now grasped the point that modern manufacturing methods, upon which we depend for a product of competitive price, cannot leave any room for the one-off. A unit has only one height, or width, a choice of only three colours, a flue at the back only − and so on. If you want something else it is useless to look for a variant of that brand. The correct thing to do is to look at another brand, even another manufacturer, in the hope of finding what you want. The quicker thing to do may often be to accept and adapt to the item which is not too welcome.

A particular case in which shopping around might pay is in radiators. There is often very good reason for wanting a radiator of a particular height, one which will fit a space available. But a manufacturer whose radiators are, say, 14 and 19 and 24 inches high has no possible chance of turning out one at 18 or 25 inches. So forget him, and look for the one in whose range 18 or 25 are standard. You may not care for the profile as much, but this becomes a matter of priorities.

Helping Hands

Almost everyone without any special knowledge of the subject seeks impartial advice. This is a natural reaction to the pressures exerted by advertising, and in particular by the advertising of fuels in contexts which are popularised from time to time. But we give it as a long considered opinion, that there is no such thing as impartial advice. Also that it is not such an ideal proposition as may at first appear. Let's be honest and admit that whenever there is a choice partiality creeps in. When we vote at an election, for instance. What we usually do is to try to find out what the issues are, before making up our own minds. And in that may be summed up the purpose of this book. When choosing a central heating system we expect that you will make your own mind up. All we aim to do is to put the main facts before you, to let you see the issues on which your decision should be made.

While we are trying to destroy long held beliefs, let us add that there is hardly ever a best system, for you or for anyone else. There is a short list of systems which have the greater number of the features which suit you and suit your premises, and in the long run it will matter hardly at all which of that list you choose. Indeed, the more thoroughly you follow the advice to insulate, the less important does any form of heating become.

We have tried to give you pointers to strong and weak points in a number of systems, knowing that these are not usually available in the publicity material. Overall, we have aimed to put you on at least nodding terms with what is available, so that you may turn to the handouts with more confidence, ask significant questions and evaluate the answers. But that does not mean that you are now to be cast adrift entirely on your own resources. Below is a list of some of the organisations which exist for your good. If you should need the services which they represent, in most cases the first thing to do is to find and approach the local representative. But if that is not satisfactory do not hesitate to go to the headquarters.

Certifying Authorities

For all gas fired appliances: British Gas. The local showroom might not stock what you have in mind, but they have a current list of approvals. Never use a gas appliance which is without British Gas approval.

All oil fired appliances: DOBETA. Domestic Oil Burning Equipment Testing Association Ltd., 3 Savoy Place, Victoria Embankment, WC2R OBN. Do not buy an oil fired appliance without DOBETA approval.

All solid fuel appliances: The Solid Fuel Advisory Service and Solid Smokeless Fuels Federation issue jointly a list of Approved Domestic Solid Fuel Appliances. Avoid anything not on that list. Your SFAS agent should have a copy, or the SFAS region office, or at Hobart House, London, SW1X 7AE.

All electrical appliances: BEAMA or Electricity Council approval, usually the Kite Mark (BSI) as well. If in doubt try the Electricity Council at 1 Charing Cross, London, SW1, but the local electricity showroom should be able to give the answers.

Radiators, convectors: MARC (Manufacturer's Association of Radiators and Convectors) certify heat ratings, and membership of the Association will be clearly stated on makers' literature, if it has been gained.

Water valves etc: are usually accepted by the National Water Council. But the basis of such approval is a British Standard, and it should therefore be quite satisfactory to establish that valves and fittings conform to the appropriate BS.

There are more specialist bodies, most of them of concern to the professional. Outside of that list most items are likely to be covered by customer protection legislation: Trades Description Act, and Sale of Goods (Implied Terms) Act, which give the customer much more power than formerly to demand an instant replacement for goods which do not do what is claimed.

We have mentioned British Standard's Kite Mark only briefly. This is no oversight. The organisations mentioned above are specialist and their function is particular to their calling. The Kite Mark must always be respected as an extra badge of merit, which takes in such features as continuing surveillance of manufacture and the maintaining of high standards. To contact BSI direct, the address is 2 Park Street, London, W1A 2 BS.

Doing the Work

One of the most potent fears is of getting into the clutches of a 'cowboy' and finding out too late that he is incompetent, or insolvent, or both. At the height of the boom, and the worst excesses, the late Heating Centre tried to run an insurance scheme against such an eventuality, but being short of money they were obliged to get the customer to pay the premium, which put the trade in the worst possible light. Since then more appropriate safeguards have grown up, and any customer who feels in need of protection should be able to get it. The most likely deterrent is still ignorance of the availability of such schemes.

For gas fired appliances there is CORGI, the Confederation of Registered Gas Installers. Most gas showrooms carry a list of CORGI approved installers, and if themselves engaged in installation work no doubt also belong. It should be noted that the only tested competence of CORGI members is in relation to the gas burning appliances. They are not tested for wet or dry systems at present, though one may go some way in assuming a willingness to seek approval. It is desirable therefore to make sure that you choose a CORGI man who happens to be experienced in the type of system you intend to have.

For all types of system there is a service offered by HVCA, the Heating and Ventilating Contractors' Association, with a double guarantee for customers. In this case the contractor pays the premium and HVCA underwrites the guarantee, and will arbitrate in case of dispute, and take over if the contractor goes bankrupt. The wide net cast by HVCA enables them to have servicing organisations on their lists too.

The way to activate HVCA is to tell them the type of system you are thinking of putting in, for example a wet system with oil fired boiler. They will then let you have a short list of members in the region who specialise in that kind of work, from which you will select two, perhaps three, and ask for a tender and specification. The latter is important if you are to choose between tenders, since you need to know exactly what each is offering for the money. The address to contact HVCA is Esca House, 34 Palace Court, Bayswater, London, W2 4JG.

You have a part to play in constructing the specification. It is your decision whether to have full heating, or partial, or any one of the choices listed in the Introduction. The choice of maintained temperatures too is yours. Then you can listen to any arguments in favour of, say, radiators versus skirting heaters; plain versus thermostatic radiator valves; small bore versus microbore; and so on. Remember that the installer or contractor is, in his own way, far from impartial. If he has reached your house because he is a specialist in one branch of domestic heating he is quite clearly partial to it. So do not be afraid to argue with him on any but strictly technical matters.

Getting a trustworthy and competent installer is the most important part of all decision making. If you do this you can practically forget about the need to conform to Building Regulations and all the rest of the list set out earlier. Your man will be fully aware of what he can and cannot do, who wants to know about what, and so on. He will almost certainly know which fuel tariff, in case of choice, is best suited to your new needs. For cavity wall insulation choose a manu- facturer who belongs to the National Cavity Insulation Associa- tion, Bremar House, Sale Place, London W.2.

Costing

Although we have left this until last it is a very important factor in decision making, and the one which stays near the top of most people's lists. But in these troubled times we are not going to mention figures of any kind, but to draw comparisons and outline principles.

The question 'What will it cost?' is no more answerable than the other nonsensical 'How long is a piece of string?'. It depends upon almost everything. The proper objective for every house- holder is not to find out some fictitious datum cost but to make a determined effort to keep cost to a minimum com- patible with the achievement of comfort. This is a two-part exercise. It entails first using the maximum of good insulation (Chapter 10): then running the system in accordance with the rules set out in the Introduction about quantity, place and time of warming.

That is what the cost of running a system comprises, and it will clearly vary widely (even after maximum insulation) according to number in family; whether home loving or always out, particularly out all day at work; whether young and active, or elderly and chilly.

The *real cost* of an installation, ignoring the effects of infla- tion for a moment, must be the first cost, what it cost to buy and install, plus the cost of running over a standard period of time, which is taken by some to be five years, by others as ten years. We can illustrate our point by looking at both.

Using wholly hypothetical figures, let us consider two installations. System A cost £500 to put in, and costs £150 a year to run, while system B cost £800 but runs for £100 a year. Which is the better proposition?

Over five years the cost of A is	£
Capital	500
Running: 5 x £150	750
Total for 5 years	1250
Cost per year	£250
The cost of B is	
Capital	800
Running: 5 x 100	500
Total	1300
Cost per year	260

Now taking a ten year period, similar calculations show that the annual cost of A is £200, that of B is £180.

We can see, then, that the annual cost falls as the influence of the first cost diminishes; also that for the same reason the cheaper running cost wins out in the end. In certain circumstances no doubt people may wish to amortise, i.e. spread the capital, over only five years. But if as is more usual the period chosen is a notional life of the system, then ten years is by no means unrealistic, and certainly favours a system which may cost more to buy but promises less cost to run. Incidentally that is not to suggest that a system will have only a ten year life. Most systems keep going long after the technology they represent has become a bit old fashioned.

Section 5

Electric Wiring

POWER.
WATTS. = AMPS × VOLTS

1 Introduction

The purpose of electric wiring is to make available electrical energy whenever it is required:

(1) With maximum safety.
(2) With the capability of supplying the current for the usage required and for possible future extended usage.
(3) With maximum reliability.
(4) With maximum flexibility to provide for change in usage and extension.
(5) Economically.

Terminology

Terms used throughout this book include the following:

Wiring
The fixed installation of insulated electric cables between the intake point in a particular installation and the appliances that use the current (such as lamps, radiators, cookers, radio sets, etc.), including the fuses, switches, socket-outlets, lampholders and all other parts permanently fixed in the building.

Appliances
All current-consuming apparatus, whether fixed (such as a plumbed-in water heater), or portable (such as an electric iron).

Socket-outlet
A properly designed and permanently fixed device installed so that a portable appliance can be safely plugged in. (In Britain, although not in some other countries, all socket-outlets should be of the three-pin type, with two pins for the circuit connections and one for the earth connection.)

Area electricity board
In Britain, all electricity supplies are given by one or other of the twelve area electricity boards (in England and Wales) and equivalent authorities in Scotland. For the purposes of this book, the term 'area board' may be taken as referring to the electricity supply authority, whether it is a board, a power company, or any other body.

Series connection
A form of connection (Figure 1.1) in which all the current passes through the circuits or appliances one after the other.

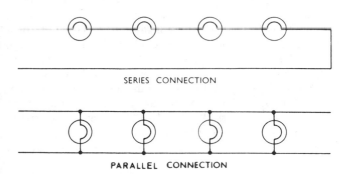

SERIES CONNECTION

PARALLEL CONNECTION

Figure 1.1. Series connection and parallel connection

Parallel connection
A form of connection in which all current-consuming parts of the circuit are individually connected across the two wires providing the supply.

INTRODUCTION

Power supply

The source of power
Electricity is generated in power stations where coal or oil is burnt to produce steam which turns a turbine coupled to an electrical generator. In Britain a number of nuclear power stations also providing power, the heat from the atomic reaction serving the same purpose as burning fuel in the furnace. In Britain there is a small proportion of power generated by falling water, driving a water wheel, or water turbine, but in some countries the majority of the power supply comes from this source.

The power is almost universally generated as alternating current, where the direction of flow of current changes fifty times a second (50 Hz (hertz)). In America and in some other parts of the world, the frequency is 60 Hz. Alternating current is used in preference to direct current mainly for ease of transforming from high to low voltage, and vice versa.

Obviously, the more current that is needed the larger the conductor necessary at a given pressure (voltage). This can be understood by reference to a water pipe system. To fill a given tank in a given time, either a high-pressure hose, of small diameter, can be employed, or else a low pressure and a large diameter hose. It is the same with electricity, where the pressure is represented by the voltage, and the flow by the current. To carry power from a power station to the point of consumption, perhaps fifty or one hundred miles away, overhead grid systems are used. It is impossible to increase the size of electrical conductor carried on pylons beyond a certain practical limit. The only way, then, to carry more power, is to increase the pressure, or voltage.

By the use of the transformer, which will be mentioned later in this book, alternating current can be transformed up or down in voltage, as required, and the voltage used for bulk transmission on the grid system is as high as 750,000 V.

This voltage is transformed down until it reaches the transformer at the end of one's own street, or somewhere on an industrial or housing estate site, at a voltage of 11,000 V; and the final transformation, to feed the power into the cables connected to the consumer's premises, is to a voltage of 415/240 V, 3-phase.

All alternating current power is generated on the 3-phase system. This means that the part of the generator where the rotating magnetic field sets up the current we ultimately use is divided into three equal sectors. The three separate windings, in which the power is generated, are brought out by means of six wires, one at the end of each winding, and one end of each winding has the wires connected to a common point, known as the neutral. The other ends – the free ends – are the supply mains, usually known as phases, and for ease of identification are called the red, yellow and blue phases.

The 3-phase system continues all the way to the transformer near to the consumer's premises, which we will call the local transformer, and on the low voltage side of this transformer we thus have four wires, the red, yellow and blue phases and the neutral. These wires are identified with red, yellow and blue markings, with black for neutral (*Figure* 1.2).

In the 3-phase system, two voltages exist. Between each phase and the neutral wire, on the low voltage side of the local transformer, the voltage is 240 V, the standard voltage in Britain (in other countries this may differ, and in America, for example, 110 V is commonly used). But between the red and yellow phases there is a voltage of 415 V, and 415 V also exists between the yellow and blue, and between the blue and red. This is the reason why the output voltage of the local transformer is given as 415/240 V.

The cables running out from the local transformer to the premises of the consumer (usually underground, but in rural districts overhead, on wooden poles) are tapped off, for each house, by taking a connection, say for the first house in the street from the red phase wire in the 3-phase cable and from the neutral, thus giving a 240 V supply to that house; for the second house, from the yellow phase wire and the neutral; and for the third house from the blue phase wire and the neutral.

This form of connection is made in order to balance the demand on the three phases, since the generator must ultimately supply a balanced load, and the varying demands of the

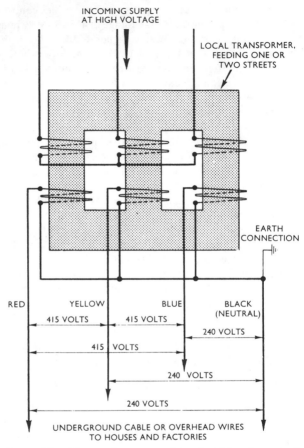

*Figure 1.2.   The transformer steps down the high voltage supply
from the power station and provides a 3-phase supply*

thousands of consumers that might be connected to any one
generator will balance out if connections are made in this way
Figure 1.3).

However, it is usual, where the demand in a particular
consumer's premises exceeds 15 kW, for a 3-phase supply to be

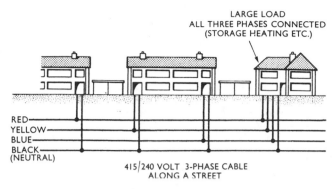

Figure 1.3. System of balancing the loads on the three phases in a suburban street

given, because the load would be too great to be balanced out properly if connected only to a single phase. Therefore more and more consumers, including private houses, are being fed with a 3-phase supply, as the loads grow.

At the local transformer, the neutral connection of the low voltage side, that feeds the consumers, is connected to earth. But this does not mean that the neutral wire can be considered as safe. There are circumstances under which it could become alive, and although in general the neutral (black) connection appears to be at the same voltage as the general mass of earth, it must at all times be treated as a live wire. The neutral wire is *not* the earth connection, to which reference will be made later, except in special circumstances, which will be mentioned later under protective multiple earthing (see p. 750).

The circuit

It is fundamental to electric current that there must be a circuit (see *Figure* 1.4). This means that the current must be able to flow from the point where it originates, at the local transformer, on,

SIMPLEST TYPE OF ELECTRICITY SUPPLY SYSTEM —
A BATTERY FEEDS A LAMP

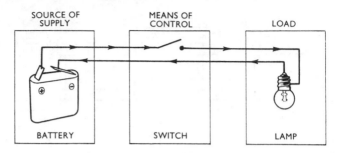

THE CIRCUIT IS FROM THE POSITIVE TERMINAL OF THE BATTERY,
THROUGH THE SWITCH, THROUGH THE LAMP,
BACK TO THE NEGATIVE TERMINAL.

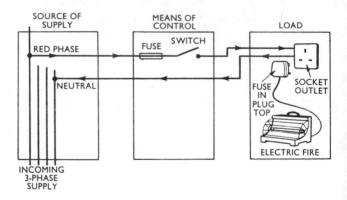

THE CIRCUIT IS FROM THE LIVE PHASE OF THE SUPPLY,
THROUGH THE FUSE AND THE SWITCH, THROUGH THE
LOAD, (ELECTRIC FIRE), VIA THE SOCKET OUTLET AND
BACK TO THE NEUTRAL CONDUCTOR OF THE SUPPLY MAIN.

*Figure 1.4.   The principle of the electric circuit: above, the simplest
electrical circuit; below, the normal alternating current circuit used
on domestic premises*

say, the red phase terminal, through the supply cable to the consumer's premises, through his wiring to the appliance, through the appliance, and back to the neutral connection and so back to the other end of the red phase wiring at the local transformer.

This is the fundamental point to be appreciated in all considerations of electrical wiring; there must be a circuit.

Fundamental considerations

Safety

Electricity is a good servant but a dangerous master. The lowest recorded voltage at which death occurred from an electric shock is 38 V. In general, 240 V seldom kills a fully dressed person wearing dry footwear (but may do so): but it is a fatal voltage for anyone wearing damp shoes, or perhaps with bare feet standing on a damp floor or touching earthed metal. The circuit, in this case, is from the live, or phase, conductor through the person's body and back to the earth point where the neutral connection is earthed in the local transformer. Since the whole mass of earth including all the buried metal and so on usually has very little resistance to the passage of current, the full current that could flow from the live wire through the person is limited only by the resistance offered by the person's body. Damp skin is a much better conductor than dry skin, and damp shoes offer very little insulation.

Anyone attempting to carry out electric wiring must at all times remember that he is dealing with a potentially lethal form of energy.

In Britain, it is still permissible for anyone to extend his or her electric wiring system, or to install new wiring, without special qualifications. In many countries this is not the case. It is a punishable offence, for example, in New Zealand, for anyone other than a registered and qualified electrician to install wiring of any kind.

However, if the work is undertaken with a full sense of responsibility, proper materials are used and proper methods employed, there is no reason why a safe installation should not result. *But the person installing wiring should always have in the front of his mind the possibility that he might have to give evidence at a coroner's court.*

The safety of electrical appliances and wiring is ensured, basically, in three ways. First, by *insulation*; secondly, by *earthing*; and thirdly, *by proper protection against fire risk.*

Insulation

Insulation is the method whereby the live electric wires or other equipment are covered in such a way that it is impossible for anyone to come into contact with live metal. Wiring, for example, is made up of copper conductors (sometimes aluminium conductors) covered with insulating material, and if the right type of cable is used, there can be no danger from touching the outside of the insulating covering.

Appliances of all kinds, if of proper design, have the live parts completely encased in porcelain or plastic materials so that it is impossible even for an inquiring child to insert its finger into any part that is live. Otherwise the live equipment is fitted inside a sealed part of the appliance, and access can only be obtained to it by deliberate interference.

Double insulation

Certain appliances are of what is known as the 'double-insulated' type. These appliances have first the normal functional insulation, as in all other appliances, and then a separate protective insulation enclosing all metal parts. Such appliances do not need an earth connection, but it must be borne in mind that no appliance can be considered as double insulated unless it complies with the Regulations and has been certified by the British Electrical Approvals Board.

Some (but not all) designs of shavers, hair dryers, dishwashers, clocks, blankets and similar appliances have been certified as double insulated, and thus need only the phase and the neutral connections to the mains.

Earthing

Earthing is the second line of defence. The whole mass of earth is obviously safe from the electrical point of view. Therefore if, say, a kettle has a wire connecting the body of the kettle, which can be touched, to the earth, then whatever happens to the live wires inside the kettle heating element, or in the connector

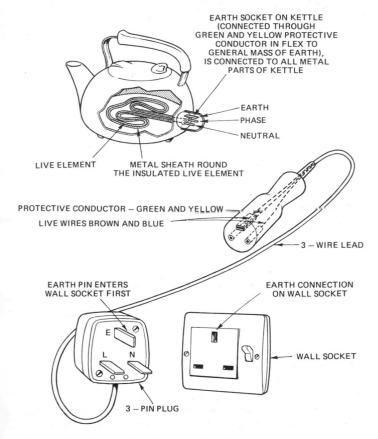

Figure 1.5. The earthing of a portable appliance, showing the connection through the 3-wire flexible lead to the earth point on the socket-outlet

feeding the appliance with current, the user is safe because any current finding its way to the body of the appliance would be short-circuited straight to earth (see *Figure* 1.5).

Metal parts of any kind of appliance in which electricity is used should always be earthed (with the exception of properly certified double-insulated appliances). With portable appliances, this is carried out, as will be seen later, by using a 3-core flexible cable and a proper plug and socket-outlet, the third pin of which, the earth pin (separate and different from phase and neutral pins) is properly connected to the earth. This is done by connecting the earth terminal in the socket-outlet on the wall to a proper earth point, which (by arrangement with the area electricity board only) may be earthed to the lead sheathing of the supply cables at the consumer's terminal point, or may be a special earth prepared properly and provided for this purpose.

At the appliance end, the connector or the cable termination (if it is a fixed termination) must be so arranged that every metal part of the appliance is properly connected to a terminal to which the third wire in the flexible – green and yellow – is connected, so that whatever leakage of current might take place, in whatever part of the appliance, the current will flow harmlessly to the earth point, through the green and yellow insulated protective conductor into the plug and to earth via the proper earth point.

Protection against fire risk
Protection against fire risk is secured by using properly dimensioned cables and fittings, and by protecting the circuits by means of the correct sizes and types of fuses or circuit-breakers.

Properly designed wiring
As well as the danger of shock, the supply of electric power from a large power station brings with it another danger.

When current passes through a wire, there is a certain resistance in the wire to be overcome. In overcoming this resistance, heat is generated in the wire. In the ordinary open-type electric radiator, this heating effect is usefully employed to give the heat we require from the radiator.

But heat is also being generated in the wiring itself. If the wiring is properly proportioned, the heating effect is small, but if the wire is too small, two problems arise. First, in extreme cases there is danger of fire from the wiring becoming too hot, and setting fire to adjacent materials with subsequent damage to the cable insulation, and secondly some of the voltage in the supply mains will be lost in the cable itself, and the appliance will not receive its full voltage, and thus, for example, lights may be dimmer than they should be.

This question of the proper dimensioning of the wiring installation in relation to the load to be fed with current applies not only to the wiring itself but to all the appliances used. Even the ordinary switch found on the wall of a living room must be suitable for its duty. Poorly designed switches, or switches that have become worn out, cannot carry the current they were intended to carry, or the increased current that wiring extensions have made possible for them to carry, mainly because the contact parts within the switch were never large enough, or have become twisted or bent or overheated so that they no longer make good contact. In consequence, there is too high a resistance within the switch, further heat is generated, and fire may result. This factor also applies to fuses, to junction boxes and to any part of the installation such as lampholders. There is a special aspect of the fire risk to be borne in mind when lampholders are considered.

People are becoming accustomed to higher and higher levels of lighting than were accepted in the past, and they have tended to add larger and larger lamps to existing lampholders. In addition, mushroom-shaped lamps are now available which give a high wattage, or power consumption, in a small volume, and lighting fittings are being made to accommodate lamps of a greater power than those for which they were designed.

A lamp gives out almost all its power in the form of heat. The overheating which may take place when oversized lamps are used may give rise to serious consequences, because the flexible or other wiring connected to the lampholder may become overheated to the stage where its insulation is damaged, and a short circuit may occur, which at the least may black out a number of lights, or at worst give rise to a fire.

Protection of the installation

The most commonly used type of protection is the fuse (*Figure* 1.6). A fuse is like a weak link in a chain, carefully designed to break when the maximum permissible load is exceeded, so that the crane, for example, to which a chain might be connected cannot be overloaded and perhaps overturned.

In the electric circuit, a fuse consists usually of a fine wire which has been carefully selected so that, when the maximum current which the circuit should carry is exceeded, the wire melts and effectively switches off the current, so saving the wiring itself and all the appliances on the circuit from damage.

Fuses are usually contained in fuseholders and installed in a consumer unit, in such a way that the designed overheating of the fuse and its ultimate rupture by melting cannot give rise to any fire risk or other serious consequences.

The circuits in the installation must be fused according to the Regulations mentioned later, and care must be taken to see that a blown fuse is replaced with a fuse of the proper type for the duty required, and not with a larger type which would invalidate the protection it gives to the circuit.

It is extremely unwise to repair a fuse that has blown without finding out why it blew. It might well happen that the danger still exists, for example if a flexible cord is frayed through it may have shorted its two conductors together sufficiently to have blown the fuse, and then left the bare copper exposed, so that a shock could result if the fuse is replaced. The faulty part of the installation should either be repaired or temporarily isolated, before replacing the fuse that has blown.

The miniature circuit breaker, or MCB as it is often referred to, may be used to protect a circuit. The MCB is a switch which operates automatically in the event of an overload or short circuit. It has the advantage that once installed, with the correct current rating for the circuit, its rating cannot be changed.

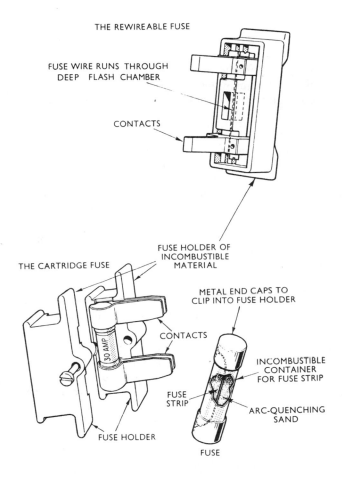

THE REWIREABLE FUSE

FUSE WIRE RUNS THROUGH
DEEP FLASH CHAMBER

CONTACTS

FUSE HOLDER OF
INCOMBUSTIBLE
MATERIAL

THE CARTRIDGE FUSE

METAL END CAPS TO
CLIP INTO FUSE HOLDER

CONTACTS

30 AMP

INCOMBUSTIBLE
CONTAINER
FOR FUSE STRIP

FUSE
STRIP

ARC-QUENCHING
SAND

FUSE HOLDER

FUSE

Figure 1.6.   Two types of fuse: above, the rewireable fuse; below,
the cartridge fuse

Reliability

Since most of us rely entirely on our electrical systems, anyone installing any kind of wiring must be careful to ensure that the wiring is absolutely reliable. This means that not only must it be properly designed but that it must be laid out in the building in such a way that it is not likely to be subjected to casual damage, and that any failure of wiring, or of appliances connected to any particular circuit, must not be allowed to give rise to wholesale blackouts and failures of supply in other parts of the building.

Flexibility

Wiring requirements are constantly changing. With the addition of more and more domestic appliances, and more and more electrical services in offices (for lighting, office machinery and every kind of electronic aid to office working), while in small factories and workshops additional electrical appliances are constantly being added, thought should be given to planning the installation so that it does not become overloaded. This may be effected by providing for growth of the installation by allocation of additional fuses etc.

Cost

There are many people who naturally feel that wiring must always be carried out as cheaply as possible. It is safe to say that good wiring pays for itself in peace of mind and in ease and convenience of usage. Money skimped on a wiring installation is money unwisely skimped. The minimum cost consideration should never be in the forefront of the mind of anyone planning or executing a wiring installation.

The electrician's responsibility

In every installation, the area electricity board or the electricity supply company or authority provides a service terminal point, on which all parts are sealed (*Figure* 1.7). This usually consists of a main fuse, or cut-out, and a meter. Some consumers take

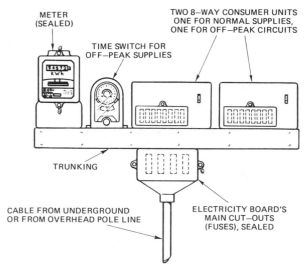

METER
(SEALED)

TIME SWITCH FOR
OFF–PEAK SUPPLIES

TWO 8–WAY CONSUMER UNITS
ONE FOR NORMAL SUPPLIES,
ONE FOR OFF–PEAK CIRCUITS

TRUNKING

CABLE FROM UNDERGROUND
OR FROM OVERHEAD POLE LINE

ELECTRICITY BOARD'S
MAIN CUT–OUTS
(FUSES), SEALED

*Figure 1.7. Consumer's terminal showing trunking to carry
wiring to meter, consumer units and time switch*

advantage of off-peak current, with the supply to the water-heating or space-heating circuits being restricted to the off-peak hours that occur during the night and sometimes during the afternoon period. If this type of usage is contemplated the area electricity board will provide, in addition, a time switch to adjust the hours of usage of the off-peak current (which is usually supplied at about half the price of normal current), and a separate meter.

All these appliances are the property of the area board, and must not be interfered with in any way by the electrician. To break the seal on the main fuses or any part of the metering circuit is to invite prosecution.

After the meter, the responsibility for the installation lies entirely with the consumer, and if it is a new installation, the electrician is therefore responsible for handing over to the consumer a proper wiring installation, which the electricity board will test, and if found in good order will connect up to the meters.

The electrician's bible

The main guidelines for electric wiring are the Regulations of the Institution of Electrical Engineers, known as the *Regulations for Electrical Installations*, and available from the Institution. These Regulations are constantly being amended, so that the user must make certain of providing himself with the latest copy.

These Regulations, although they are not part of the law of the land, are very nearly in the same category. For example, an insurance company, if it is asked to insure a building, will nearly always specify that the electric wiring must be in conformity with the practice laid down in the Regulations of the Institution. In cases where accidents occur, such as fires or electrical shocks, the best possible defence, on the part of the person who installed the wiring, is that it is in conformity with the Regulations. One would have a very poor defence indeed if the wiring did not conform to the Regulations.

Tests by electricity board

In addition, the area electricity board has the right to refuse to connect up an installation which it considers to be unsafe, and such an installation obviously does not comply with the Regulations. The tests the board's engineers will apply will be directed to ensuring that the Regulations have been properly carried out.

The electricity board also has the right to be notified when any alteration or addition is made to an installation, and may inspect the altered or added parts before they are connected to the main system.

Some definitions

Voltage

The pressure that forces the current round an electric circuit is measured in volts (V). The normal domestic supply (on systems with standard supplies) is at 240 V: a flashlamp bulb works at 1.5 V: most of the National Grid System works at 275,000 V, parts at 400,000 V. The voltage is equivalent to the head of water causing a flow along a pipe.

The following voltage levels are defined:

Extra-low voltage: below 50 V (120 V for d.c.) between conductors or to earth.

Low voltage: exceeding extra-low voltage but not exceeding 1000 V (1500 V for d.c.) between conductors, or 600 V (900 V d.c.) between any conductor and earth.

The electrician, dealing with domestic and small industrial installations, will therefore deal mainly with low-voltage supplies.

Current

The flow, or current, in a conductor is measured in amperes (A). A 1 kW fire needs a flow of about 4.16 A: a 100 W lamp needs about 0.4 A.

Resistance

When water flows through a thin pipe, it encounters a resistance to its flow. The larger the pipe, the less resistance. Also pipes differ, in resistance to flow, even at the same diameter. A smooth-bore pipe will offer less resistance than a rusted bore.

Similarly, with conductors of electricity, the thicker the wire, in general the less the resistance. Certain wires, like copper, silver and aluminium, have less resistance than similar-sized wires of steel or nickel alloy.

The effect of resistance

The effect of resistance in a conductor is to generate heat as the current passes, as mentioned earlier. In radiator elements, this is the desired effect, and the conductors used in these elements are designed to give a suitable resistance to generate the required amount of heat.

But in the conductors used for wiring a house, the aim should always be to reduce this heating effect to the minimum. Heat is not required in the wiring system: it will reduce the life of the insulation, and if excessive may even cause a fire.

Therefore care must always be taken to reduce the heating effect to the minimum by ensuring that all conductors used – the cables themselves, and all the fittings of every kind – are large enough to present a very low resistance to the current for which the circuit is to·be used.

Resistance is measured in ohms (Ω). As an example, a 100 W lamp has a resistance of about 600 Ω (though this varies a little as it heats up).

The resistance of the insulation used on electrical appliances is of course very high indeed – otherwise it would not be regarded as insulation. To give a typical example, the resistance of the insulation used in a good, new electric iron, measured between the live conductors in the element and the outer metal case of the iron, ought to be approximately 2,000,000 Ω known as 2 *megohms* ($M\Omega$).

The resistance of all parts of an electrical installation in a domestic dwelling – that is, the resistance of all the live conductors in the cables, the switches, the socket-outlets, and the consumer unit – measured against earth, must not be less than 1,000,000 Ω.

Later we shall see how this insulation resistance is tested.

Two simple formulae

There are two very simple and fundamental formulae that must be understood in relation to all electric circuits.

The ability of an appliance of any kind to consume electricity is measured in watts (W). A thousand watts equals one *kilowatt* (kW).

An appliance that is so designed that its resistance allows 1 A of current to flow when the appliance is connected to a voltage of 1 V is said to have a power rating of 1 W.

Therefore

$$\text{power (W)} = \text{current (A)} \times \text{voltage (V)}$$

As an example, a one-bar radiator with an element of 1000 W (1 kW) rating would take current of 4.16 A if connected to a 240 V circuit:

$$\text{power (W)} = \text{current (A)} \times \text{voltage (V)}$$
$$1000 = 4.16 \times 240$$

If you know any two of these three figures, you can calculate the other.

Often it is desired to know what current will be needed to feed a certain appliance, say a television set with a nameplate that says 200 W. We proceed as follows, assuming the set is to be connected to the 240 V supply mains:

$$\text{power (W)} = \text{current (A)} \times \text{voltage (V)}$$

Therefore:

$$\frac{\text{power (W)}}{\text{voltage (V)}} = \text{current (A)}$$

so,

$$\frac{200}{240} = \text{⅚ of an ampere, or } 0.83 \text{ A}$$

Ohm's law

The relation between the voltage and the current, in a simple circuit that has a certain resistance, is as follows:

$$\text{current (A)} = \frac{\text{voltage (V)}}{\text{resistance } (\Omega)}$$

To give a simple example, a kettle of 3 kW rating will have a resistance (in its heating element) calculated as follows:

$$\text{power (W)} = \text{current (A)} \times \text{voltage (V)}$$

Therefore:

$$\frac{\text{power (W)}}{\text{voltage (V)}} = \text{current (A)}$$

$$\frac{3000}{240} = 12.5 \text{ A}$$

From Ohm's law:

$$12.5 \text{ A} = \frac{\text{voltage (V) (240)}}{\text{resistance } (\Omega)}$$

Therefore:

$$\text{resistance } (\Omega) = \frac{240}{12.5} = 19.2 \, \Omega$$

Note: These simple but fundamental formulae apply to direct current and ordinary alternating current circuits in which the appliances used – radiators, immersion heaters, filament lamps, and the like – are mainly users of electricity by means of resistance wires that grow hot when current flows. When appliances that use motors and such devices as the electromagnetic choke coils in fluorescent lamps are considered, the formulae have to be modified to take into account the electromagnetic effects of the current: but the modifications needed for domestic and similar installations are usually so small that they can be ignored. They only become significant where larger industrial installations are concerned.

The unit of electricity

Although not strictly a matter concerning the electrical installation itself, it is as well to complete the picture by mentioning the current usage of various appliances.

An appliance – say, a one-bar electric fire – is designed so that when it is connected to the usual 240 V mains, it will use 1000 W, that is 1 kW.

If such a 1 kW fire is switched on for exactly 1 hour, it will draw 1 kilowatt-hour of energy from the mains.

One kilowatt-hour is the standard unit of electricity consumption.

You can use one unit of electricity by:

> burning a 1 kW fire for 1 hour,
> burning a ½ kW fire for 2 hours,
> burning a 2 kW fire for ½ hour.

To take another example, a 25 W lamp used for 1 hour:

$$25\,W \times 1\ hour = 25\,Wh = \tfrac{1}{40}th\ of\ 1000\,Wh = \tfrac{1}{40}th\ of\ a\ unit$$

or,

$$25\,W\ for\ 40\ hours = 25 \times 40\,Wh = 1000\,Wh = 1\ unit.$$

One further example: a cooker hotplate has a capacity, or loading, of 2 kW.

$$2\,kW\ (=2000\,W)\ for\ 1\ hour = 2\,kWh = 2\ units.$$

2 Materials for Wiring Installations

Wiring: general

Wiring may be carried out in several ways, which are conveniently discussed under four headings:

> the conductor
> the insulation
> the sheath
> the enclosure.

The conductor

In the majority of cases the conductors used in domestic or small commercial wiring installations are made of high conductivity copper, sometimes covered with a coating of tin to assist in preventing corrosion. In some cases, however, aluminium conductors are used.

Often, a single strand of conductor is used but to give more flexibility to heavier duty cables a number of small wires are stranded (twisted) together to make a larger conductor.

The important aspect of the conductor is of course the total cross-sectional area of the metal, since the larger the metal area, the greater the current-carrying capacity (subject to certain other factors). For example, a wire size very commonly used is known as $2.5\,\mathrm{mm}^2$. This means that the conductor has a cross-section area of $2.5\,\mathrm{mm}^2$.

The insulation

To insulate the live conductors, various methods are used.

Plastic insulation

There are several forms of plastic materials that are commonly used to insulate wiring conductors. First there is polyvinyl chloride (PVC) which is extremely tough, will not support combustion, and is not affected by water, oil, or most chemicals. It has however a definite temperature limit, above which it will melt and leave the conductor bare.

Then there is polythene insulation, made from a different type of plastic, with a lower safe temperature rating.

PVC/SWA cable uses PVC insulation, but is enclosed in a protective wrapping of steel wires, to form an 'armouring' or protective covering. This type of cable is normally used where a high degree of mechanical protection is required, such as underground between buildings.

Rubber insulation

This is the oldest form of insulation, and is still used, but is largely superseded by plastic materials for all but special applications.

Rubber is very flexible, but has a number of disadvantages. It burns easily, and it can be attacked by chemicals and by oil. It is to some extent absorbent to water. Direct sunlight soon causes rubber to deteriorate, so unprotected rubber cables should never be used outdoors. It is also attacked by certain insects, and in any case it ages and tends to become brittle.

The sheath

The insulated conductor is more often than not grouped with others within an insulated sheath, to form a *cable*. A cable may have two or more *cores* – each core being a separately insulated conductor, except where the earth connection (protective conductor) is also carried within the sheath. A common form of cable consists of two cores and earth – a red-coloured insulated conductor for connection to the phase wire, and a black-coloured insulated conductor for connection to the neutral wire, together with an uninsulated (bare) protective conductor (*Figure 2.1*).

These three cores are usually laid in a flat formation surrounded by a sheath or outer casing, for protection.

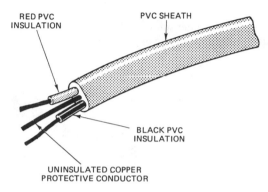

RED PVC INSULATION

PVC SHEATH

BLACK PVC INSULATION

UNINSULATED COPPER PROTECTIVE CONDUCTOR

Figure 2.1.   The protective conductor commonly incorporated in sheathed cable

The cable may be made up with a single core, which still has an outer sheath for protection against mechanical damage, or with any number of cores. For 3-phase circuits there will be three phase conductors, each coloured brown, and a neutral conductor, coloured blue, all within the sheath.

Sheaths may be made up as follows:

Plastic sheathing
For PVC-insulated cores a PVC sheath is most often used. A variant is a polythene-insulated core or cores covered with a PVC sheath.

Tough rubber
Older cables are known as TRS (tough rubber sheathed). Rubber sheathing is usually employed with rubber-insulated cores.

Mineral-insulated (MI) cables

These cables, though more expensive than the flexible sheathed type mentioned above, are capable of being used in situations where no other cable could be employed.

Single-strand copper wires are embedded in a tightly compressed white powder insulation within a copper or aluminium sheath. The powder is made of magnesium oxide (see *Figure 2.2*).

The MI cable can be subjected to the full heat of a blowlamp without damage. With an overall covering of PVC the cable may even be buried direct in the ground.

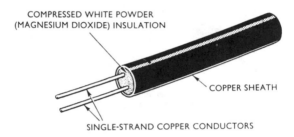

COMPRESSED WHITE POWDER
(MAGNESIUM DIOXIDE) INSULATION

COPPER SHEATH

SINGLE-STRAND COPPER CONDUCTORS

Figure 2.2.   Mineral-insulated copper-sheathed cable

The only disadvantage (apart from cost) of the MI cable is that great care must be taken when it is cut and made off into a terminal. This is because the magnesium oxide is hygroscopic – in effect, it attracts moisture, which can reduce the insulation value. Therefore the ends of any MI cable must at all times be kept properly sealed, using the special sealing equipment supplied by the manufacturers. When the cable is cut and made off, the simple instructions supplied by the makers must always be carefully followed.

The enclosure

Electric wiring is best protected against mechanical damage by being inserted in a suitable enclosure.

MATERIALS FOR WIRING INSTALLATIONS

Heavy gauge, steel screwed conduit
In this system, a complete enclosure made of screwed piping, and including all termination boxes and joint boxes, is provided. The steel conduit is cut to length, bent if necessary, and screwed so that it provides a perfect seal where it enters a termination box or where it is jointed (*Figure* 2.3).

The conduit system means the use of a considerable number of special tools such as dies, bending machines, pipe vices, and

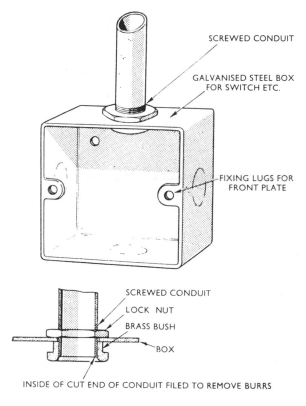

INSIDE OF CUT END OF CONDUIT FILED TO REMOVE BURRS

Figure 2.3. Typical box for the mounting of the switch or other fitment on a conduit system

saws. It is costly, and although it should always be designed in accordance with the Regulations so that the conduits are not tightly packed with wire, and draw-in points should be accessible, it is nevertheless not always easy to alter or extend a conduit system. A certain degree of skill and experience is needed before a conduit system is embarked upon, although there are no insuperable difficulties that could not be overcome by anyone used to handling metal-working tools.

Other types of conduit

Aluminium alloy conduits are sometimes used, and these must be screwed at joints and installed in the same way as steel conduits. They are subject to corrosion when embedded in cement and plaster, but may be protected by bitumastic paint.

Non-metallic conduit systems are also widely employed. These are made from a plastic tube which can be bent round corners. Some systems use screwed ends to fit into joints and terminal boxes, other systems employ cemented joints. This system is particularly suitable for installation where there is a strong possibility of corrosion, but where mechanical damage is not likely. Each circuit wired via this conduit must be connected to earth by a separate wire (protective conductor), with a covering of green/yellow PVC pulled in with the current carrying cables.

Protective channelling

While the conduit systems mentioned previously are used for the highest class of work and enclose single-core PVC cables to the required number, many domestic installations employ PVC sheathed cable, run on the surface where it is safe from damage, but protected when immersed in plaster by means of shaped metal channelling, or by short lengths of round or oval plastic tubing (*Figure* 2.4).

Steel and plastic trunking

Where a large number of cables have to be run in one direction, steel or plastic trunking, often of square section with a screwed-down or clipped removable lid is used (*Figure* 2.5). Steel

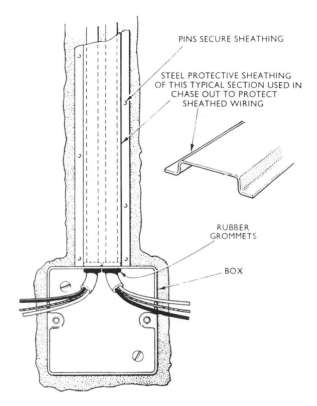

PINS SECURE SHEATHING

STEEL PROTECTIVE SHEATHING
OF THIS TYPICAL SECTION USED IN
CHASE OUT TO PROTECT
SHEATHED WIRING

RUBBER
GROMMETS

BOX

*Figure 2.4. Installing sheathed cable beneath plaster, with
protective metal channelling*

trunking must be electrically continuous and bonded securely to
earth. Plastic trunking must have an insulated protective conductor (formerly known as earth wire) coloured green and yellow
between all apparatus connected to the system.

Trunking is a very flexible system of installation. Suppose, for
instance, a small business were started in a workshop, where
initially only a few lights and one or two machines were required.

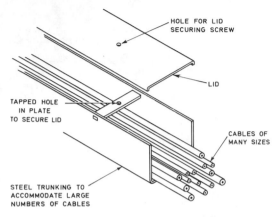

Figure 2.5.   Where a number of cables follow the same route, steel or plastic trunking may be used to protect them, but the number of cables in each run is limited by the Regulations

This installation could be completed using PVC cables in conduit, at moderate cost. If trunking were used, run at a high level on the walls around the room, the positions of lights, switches and machines could be fed using conduits, connected to the trunking and run down the walls to each position.

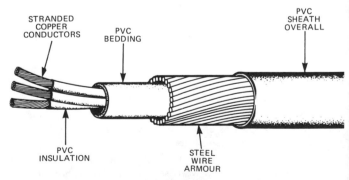

Figure 2.6.   PVC steel wire armoured PVC cable

Though much of the installation would be superfluous at first, there would be plenty of room in the trunking for future additional wiring in the case of business expansion, requiring extra lights and machines, sockets, etc.

PVC steel wire armoured PVC
This cable has stranded copper (or sometimes aluminium) conductors with PVC insulation, enclosed in galvanised steel wire armouring and an outer covering of PVC (*Figure* 2.6). It is

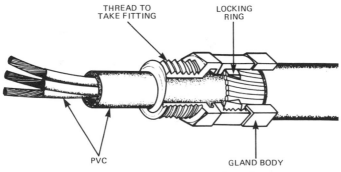

THREAD TO
TAKE FITTING

LOCKING
RING

PVC

GLAND BODY

Figure 2.7.   PVC/SWA/PVC gland

often used for underground supplies to outbuildings, laid in fine earth or sand and covered with protective tiles. The cable may be fixed onto most surfaces using plastic clips; terminations require glands which are simple and quickly made off to the cable ends (*Figure* 2.7)

3 The Electrical Layout

As mentioned earlier, all electrical systems depend on there being a complete circuit from the sources of supply to the appliance, such as a lamp, that is to be fed with current.

In an installation supplied in the ordinary way from the electricity board's mains, the source of supply is the supply terminals on the consumer's fuseboard.

Every circuit must start from the phase fuse terminal and return to the neutral terminal.

Circuits are interrupted so that the power may be controlled by:

> switches
> fuses
> miniature circuit breakers (MCBs)
> contactors and relays
> time switches
> thermostats

Switches

The simplest circuit consists of a pair of wires from the mains terminals supplying one appliance, say a lamp.

In this circuit there must be a switch, and that switch must be situated in the phase wire, as shown in *Figure* 3.1.(a), not in the neutral wire.

This requirement, which is of course part of the Regulations, is especially important. If an appliance, for example, a vacuum

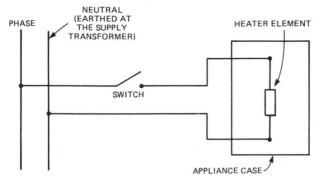

WHEN PROPERLY CONNECTED AS ABOVE, OPENING THE
SWITCH REMOVES ALL POSSIBILITY OF SHOCK

(a)

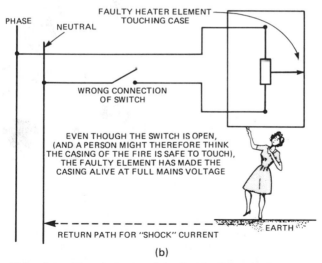

(b)

*Figure 3.1.   The switch must always be installed in the phase wire,
and not in the neutral. The lower diagram shows what happens if
the switch is wrongly installed and an appliance becomes faulty*

cleaner, is connected to a switched socket-outlet, and the plug is left inserted, the appliance may not be in operation because the switch is off, and therefore any uninstructed person, or perhaps a child, might start to tinker with it, thinking that because it is not running, it is dead. But if the switch were placed so that it interrupted the neutral (black) wire and not the phase (red) wire, the live phase of the supply would be carried through the flexible cable to the appliance, even if it is not running, and a fatal shock might result from anyone interfering with the appliance.

The next variant of the simple one-lamp circuit is the two-way switch, shown in *Figure* 3.2, used for example on staircases so that a person can switch off the upstairs light after going downstairs.

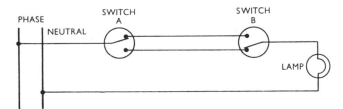

Figure 3.2. The two-way switch

In this circuit, the switches can have two positions, either of which can light the lamp. Suppose switch *A* is in the upper position, and switch *B* is in the lower position as in the figure. There is no circuit, so the lamp is out.

Now imagine a person near switch *B* turns that switch to the upper position. A circuit is established, and the lamp lights. He goes downstairs and reaches switch *A*, and wishes to turn the lamp out. He brings switch *A* to the lower position, and the lamp is extinguished. A second person, at switch *B*, has only to move his switch to the lower position for the lamp to light once more.

Many switches, notably those of the rocker type (i.e. with a rocking bar in place of the simple knob protruding from a hole in the cover), are often made only as two-way switches and care must be taken when necessary to see that the two-way design is bought. Any two-way switch can be used as a single-way switch, if needed.

Suppose now that on a long staircase, for example, with several landings, it is desired to arrange for the light to be switched on and off at several points. In this case intermediate switches are used.

The two wires between the switches *A* and *B* in *Figure* 3.2 are called the strapping wires. If, in the case shown, the wires were to be reversed, a circuit would be established and the lamp would light.

The intermediate switch shown in *Figure* 3.3 carries out this reversal of the strapping wires, and any number of intermediate switches may be installed.

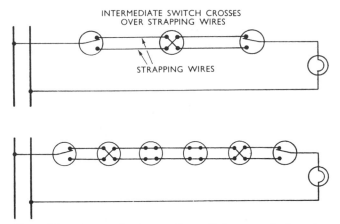

Figure 3.3.   The use of an intermediate switch to control a lamp (or other load) from a number of positions

In *Figure* 3.3 the upper diagram shows a single intermediate switch but in the lower diagram there are four such switches. The two positions of the switch contacts can be seen from the two diagrams. In the circuit shown in the lower diagram, the lamp can be turned off and on from six positions.

Fuses

Fuses are found on domestic installations at three points.

It should be made clear that with normal, standard supplies only the phase wire is fused. The neutral connection simply has a link. It is totally incorrect, and in contravention of the Regulations, to fuse the neutral side.

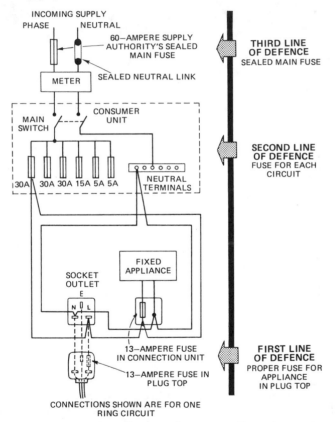

Figure 3.4. Fused protection on a domestic installation showing the three lines of defence against the consequences of faulty apparatus

There are the board's main fuses, or cut-outs as they are called (*Figure* 3.4). They are the third line of defence. These are sealed, and must not be interfered with. If the main fuse blows, the electricity board's engineers must be called out to replace it.

Secondly, there is the consumer's unit, with a fuse or MCB for each circuit or group of circuits, and a main switch for that fuseboard. (*Note:* this is the only switch provided. The electricity board no longer provides a main switch for the whole installation. To switch everything off, it is necessary to switch off the main switches on each consumer unit, if there is more than one. But it should not be forgotten that inside each, the wires from the board's meter are still alive.)

The fuses used in the consumer's unit may be of one of two types: rewireable fuses, or cartridge fuses (*Figure* 1.6).

Rewireable fuses
Rewireable fuses are perhaps the most commonly used. A fuse bridge, or fuseholder, of non-flammable material, is equipped with screws for holding a suitable length of fuse wire. This wire is usually threaded through a ceramic tube, or otherwise held in some way that will ensure that if the wire gets hot and ultimately melts or fuses, no fire damage can result.

The rewireable fuse is convenient in the sense that if a reel of fuse wire is handy a blown fuse can be rapidly replaced at any time, provided the faulty appliance or section of wiring has been repaired or isolated from the mains.

Perhaps the rewireable fuse may sometimes be considered as too convenient, because it is easy for unwise people to replace a blown fuse wire with a wire of the wrong size.

If a 30 A circuit is properly fused, the fuse will blow if the current exceeds 30 A for any length of time, and if all parts of the circuit wiring are correctly chosen, no harm will result. But if the fuseholder is renewed with thicker fuse wire, which will allow, say a 50 A current to flow continuously, some part of the circuit – perhaps a switch, or a flexible cable, or a socket-outlet – may become overheated and a fire could possibly result.

When replacing a fuse wire, always make sure that the screws are properly tight, but not too tight to damage the wire and reduce its current-carrying capacity. Check that the wire is properly fitted into the safety tube or path through the fuseholder. Do not strain the wire too tightly between the terminals, as tightening up may stretch it and reduce the copper section.

Fuseholders are usually marked with the *maximum* size of fuse wire they should carry. This figure should never be exceeded.

Cartridge fuses

The best type of fuse is one in which the actual fusible element is enclosed in a flame-proof cartridge. In some cases the cartridge is filled with a type of sand intended to extinguish any flame that might result from a fuse blowing as a result of a heavy excess of current.

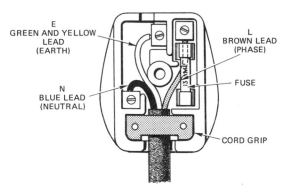

Figure 3.5. The fused plug top and the method of connection

The cartridge fuse is made in various sizes, such as 5, 10, 15, 20, 30, 60 A and so on.

It is slightly more expensive than the rewireable type, and there is always the problem of being caught with no spare cartridge of the correct size. Do not try to repair a blown cartridge fuse.

The best consumer's intake point installation will consist of cartridge equipment, each circuit being properly labelled as to its destination and the size of fuse needed, with an adequate supply of cartridge fuses in a convenient spot nearby.

The first line of defence in the household wiring system is the fuse to be found in the plug top in the 13 A plug shown in *Figure* 3.5.

This plug, now the recognised standard (British Standard 1363) has three 'square' pins (rectangular, to be precise) and the phase side is connected through a fuse. The fuses commonly available are: 3 A, red; 13 A, brown.

Care should always be taken to ensure that the correct size of fuse is inserted in the plug to suit the appliance to which it is connected.

Miniature circuit-breakers

As an alternative to fuses, small automatic circuit-breakers are now available, which are much the same size as the equivalent fuse (*Figure* 3.6).

A circuit-breaker is an automatic switch. It is so arranged that if a current of greater value than that for which it is set should pass through the device, the switch will open automatically and cut off the circuit, so preventing damage in the same way as a fuse.

The automatic operation of a circuit-breaker is known as 'tripping' – the switch trips a catch that holds it in. Trip mechanisms take two forms, both of which may be used on the same switch. An electromagnet – a coil of wire wound on an iron frame – has a mechanical pull that corresponds to the current passing through its coil. The current through the switch is taken through such a coil, arranged with an arm, attracted by the magnet, that can flick the switch to the off position if the current is too great.

In the second type of trip mechanism, a bimetal strip is used. All metals expand when heated, some more than others. If two strips of metal, one with a high rate of expansion with heat, and the other with a low rate, are joined only at their ends, when heat is applied the combined strip will bow, or bend, as the different rates of expansion come into play. Inside the switch there is a very small heater element that carries the main current. If the current is excessive, this element gets hot and causes the nearby bimetal strip to bend, and a linkage then trips the switch.

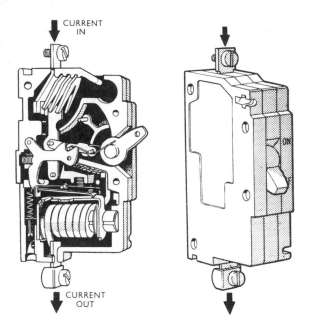

Figure 3.6. The miniature circuit-breaker, sometimes used in preference to a fuse (reproduction of a Crabtree design)

With the electromagnetic type of trip, the switch can be closed again immediately it has tripped. (It may trip again if the cause is still there.) But with the thermal, or bi-metal strip type, the switch cannot be closed again for a minute or two, as the heater element and the bi-metal strip have first to cool down.

724

Time switches

A time switch is often used for controlling such circuits as shop-window lighting and central heating. Like all other switches, the actual contacts of the time switch must be wired into the phase side of the circuit, and not into the neutral, and care must be taken that the rating of the time-switch contacts – for example, 10 A, as indicated on the nameplate – is not exceeded by the appliances on its circuit.

Time switches may be of several kinds. In some, known as the spring-rewind type, an electric motor winds a clockwork system, so that if the supply should fail, the clock will continue to run, and will open and close the contacts at the proper time, for a period which may be a few hours or a few days. In other designs, the clock is electrically operated, and will stop if the mains supply fails; it must be set to the correct time when the supply is resumed.

In both cases, there must be a separate, fuse-protected circuit to the clock motor. Some clocks have the motor-circuit fuse incorporated in the case. In other instances, it is necessary to provide a 2 A fuse and a separate connection.

Thermostats

Thermostats are temperature-operated switches, which are arranged to open or close a circuit as the temperature rises or falls. For room heating control, they may work in the range of 10°C to 20°C, while for refrigerator applications they may operate in the range of 0°C to −20°C.

In many cases, bimetal strips, mentioned earlier, are used. As the temperature rises, the bimetal strip heats and bends (*Figure 3.7*) so that ultimately the contact is broken and the heater circuit switched off. To prevent the contacts 'dithering' and consequently arcing, the contact piece is usually equipped with a small magnet, and as the bi-metal strip slowly bends it is

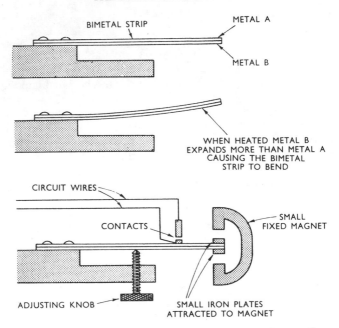

BIMETAL STRIP

METAL A

METAL B

WHEN HEATED METAL B
EXPANDS MORE THAN METAL A
CAUSING THE BIMETAL
STRIP TO BEND

CIRCUIT WIRES

CONTACTS

SMALL
FIXED MAGNET

ADJUSTING KNOB

SMALL IRON PLATES
ATTRACTED TO MAGNET

Figure 3.7. A refrigerator thermostat – the unit switches on as the temperature increases

suddenly snapped to the open or closed position, as the case may be, thus giving a clean break.

Thermostats should always be wired into the phase side of the circuit, and again the current rating of the contacts should never be exceeded.

Relays and contactors

Devices such as time switches and thermostats have switching contacts that are limited in their capacity, usually to circuits of about 3 kW. If the time switch, for example, is to be used for larger circuits, some auxiliary device is necessary. Small devices of this kind are called relays, larger examples are known as contactors.

An electromagnetic coil is supplied with current by the closing of the time-switch contact, and when this coil is energised it attracts an armature that in turn closes much larger contacts than those with which a time switch could be fitted: in fact, a contactor could control a load of 100 kW or more (see *Figure 3.8*).

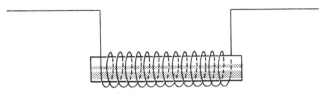

PRINCIPLE OF THE ELECTRO MAGNET. WHEN CURRENT PASSES THROUGH THE COIL WOUND ROUND THE IRON CORE THE IRON BECOMES MAGNETISED

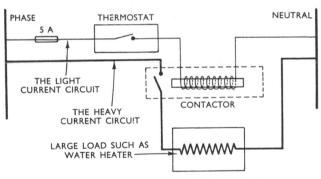

SCHEMATIC DIAGRAM OF A CONTACTOR IN A TYPICAL CIRCUIT. THE SMALL CONTACTS ON THE THERMOSTAT CAN CONTROL A FINAL CIRCUIT OF ANY SIZE

Figure 3.8.   The principle of the contactor

A relay is a smaller version of the contactor, and is usually of the type where the originating current is very small, such as the output from photoelectric cells which automatically switch on lighting equipment at dusk.

In connecting up contactors and relays, care must be taken to fuse the control circuit with a light fuse (a 5 A fuse is usually sufficient) and then to see that the fusing on the main circuit is adequate.

Both the control circuit and the main circuit switches must be wired into the phase side, as for all switches or circuit-breaking devices.

The circuit layout

We can now consider the circuit layout for a typical installation, for example, a four-bedroomed house.

Bearing in mind the first principle that each circuit must have proper protection by being adequately fused, one's mind must first turn to a system whereby every light, every appliance (such as a fixed radiator or cooker or refrigerator) and every socket-outlet had its own separate cable back to the main consumer's fuseboard, and was individually connected to a separate fuse of the appropriate size.

This would indeed be the perfect and ideal system, but would be extremely expensive on account of the lengths of cable needed and the number of fuses required. It is also unnecessary.

To consider the extreme alternative, suppose an installation had only one main fuse, to which all the circuits were connected. If this fuse blew, through a fault of any one appliance, such as a desk lamp, the whole house would be plunged in darkness. In any case, proper *graded* protection for the various circuits could not be provided in this way.

The practical solution obviously lies somewhere between these two extremes.

The number of circuits that may be grouped together on one fuse depends on the total demand on the circuit, evolved according to certain rules. For example, consider a lighting circuit. This might well originate at a 5 A fuse in the consumer's unit. It is laid down that each fixed lampholder must be assumed to carry a 100 W lamp. Now a 100 W lamp consumes 0.416 A. So 12 lampholders could legitimately be supplied from a single 5 A lighting circuit – *providing the correct size of cabling was used throughout the circuit.*

But this would not be practicable in the house we are discussing, since the wiring would become somewhat cumbersome and in any case it would be undesirable for every light in the house to go out if a single lampholder developed a fault.

A commonly used system would be to have two 5 A lighting circuits, one for the first floor and one for the ground floor, with perhaps ten or so lampholders wired to each. In this way there would be some light left in the house if one lampholder failed, and in addition the circuits would be a little underloaded so that extensions would always be possible.

Turning now to fixed appliances – cookers, water heaters, fixed radiators, and refrigerators – some of these (except perhaps refrigerators) are heavily loaded appliances, often calling for 12 kW or more in the case of cookers, 3 kW for water heaters, and so on.

There should be a separate final circuit for every appliance rated at 15 A and above, except in the special circumstances mentioned later when the ring circuit is discussed.

Therefore each of these larger fixed appliances should in fact have a separate circuit back to its own fuse, of appropriate size, in the consumer unit. Even if some appliances, such as a particular fixed radiator, do not initially require more than 2 kW (8½ A) it is strongly recommended that the circuit should be wired back to the consumer unit on the basis of a single feed of 15 A capacity: no one can tell if at some time in the future a larger radiator may not be needed at that point. Experience shows that the usage of electricity steadily grows, not only for installing *more* appliances but in substituting new, more heavily loaded appliances for older ones. For example – to mention a portable appliance – the elements fitted to electric kettles have grown in loading from the initial 600 W, and have now reached 3000 W or even more.

The ring circuit

Anyone who thinks carefully about the circuit arrangements set out above will soon reach the conclusion that there is some inevitable wastage of copper – that is, there is more current-carrying capacity than is needed *for most of the time*.

On the whole, it is better to have a little extra capacity in the circuits, to allow for extension. But there is a very widely used system that allows much fuller use to be made of the current-carrying capacity of the circuits installed.

This system is called the ring circuit (*Figure* 3.9), and it is based on the application of what is called the principle of 'diversity'.

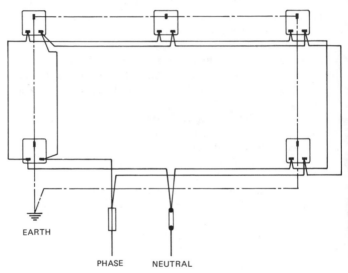

Figure 3.9. The principle of the ring circuit

Take any ordinary house, and consider the time and place at which various appliances are used.

The largest portable electricity-consuming appliance commonly used in domestic premises is the 3 kW fire. It is extremely unlikely that more than three such fires will be in use, at full load, at the same time, even in the coldest weather, at any rate on the ground floor.

Therefore, if there are, say, eight socket-outlets on the ground floor, each of 13 A capacity (thus capable of taking the 3 kW fire) it would be extremely generous in copper to wire each one separately back to the consumer unit. When the three large fires are in use, the remaining five sockets on the ground floor are likely to be used only for very light current appliances like lamps, radio and television sets.

Now suppose all the 13 A standard socket-outlets on the ground floor were connected in a ring. That is, a pair of 2.5 mm² wires starts at one 30 A fuse at the consumer unit and runs to the first socket, on to the second, the third, and so on, and then back to the *same* 30 A fuse (see *Figure* 3.10).

The ring circuit is based on the employment of a standard socket-outlet, of 13 A capacity, and having a fuse in the plug top. This socket-outlet will allow for an appliance up to 3 kW being connected, as such an appliance will need 12.48 A.

In this system, each 13 A socket has two routes back to the mains. The *maximum* use is made of the *minimum* amount of copper in the cables: that is, the minimum length of cabling is employed for a given number of socket-outlets.

The use of the ring circuit, as mentioned above, is only possible because of the diversity of usage that naturally evolves. In an ordinary dining room, where there might be perhaps six 13 A standard socket-outlets, it is very unlikely that more than two 3 kW fires would be in use at the same time, even under arctic conditions. Fires, as mentioned earlier, are the largest portable current-consuming appliances likely to be used in domestic premises. Any other appliances use so much less current that they do not need to be taken into account here.

The Regulations regarding the use of the ring circuit are:

If the floor area concerned does not exceed 100 square metres there can be an unlimited number of 13 A standard socket-outlets on the ring, which must consist of 2.5 mm² conductors and must terminate in a 30 A fuse.

Note: In practice, in domestic premises, the requirement mentioned above may mean that two separate rings are needed. A convenient division is to have a downstairs ring and an upstairs ring (see *Figure* 3.11). The more the rooms embraced by the ring, the greater the diversity. (People do not, in general, use all

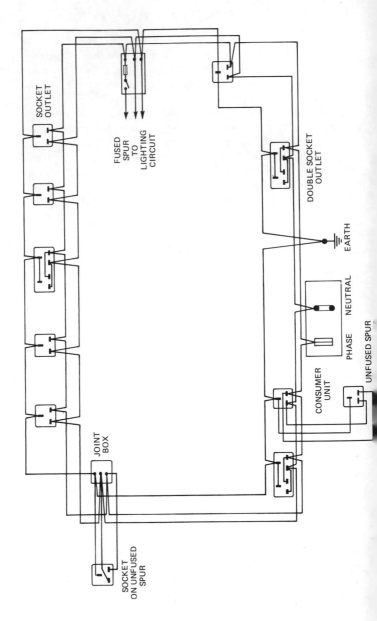

SOCKET OUTLET

FUSED SPUR TO LIGHTING CIRCUIT

DOUBLE SOCKET OUTLET

EARTH

PHASE   NEUTRAL

CONSUMER UNIT

UNFUSED SPUR

JOINT BOX

SOCKET ON UNFUSED SPUR

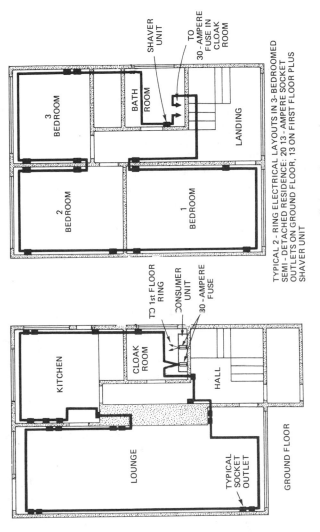

Figure 3.11. A practical ring circuit installation, using two rings

Left diagram (GROUND FLOOR):

KITCHEN

CLOAK ROOM

HALL

LOUNGE

TO 1st FLOOR RING

CONSUMER UNIT

30-AMPERE FUSE

TYPICAL SOCKET OUTLET

GROUND FLOOR

Right diagram (first floor):

BEDROOM 3

BEDROOM 2

BEDROOM 1

BATH ROOM

LANDING

SHAVER UNIT

TO 30-AMPERE FUSE IN CLOAK ROOM

TYPICAL 2-RING ELECTRICAL LAYOUTS IN 3-BEDROOMED SEMI-DETACHED RESIDENCE: 20 13-AMPERE SOCKET OUTLETS ON GROUND FLOOR, 13 ON FIRST FLOOR PLUS SHAVER UNIT

the rooms in a house at the same time, and even if they did, their current-using habits do not coincide.)

There are several additional features of the ring circuit to be mentioned. In addition to the main 13 A socket-outlets, it is possible to install any number of specially designed connections for very small current appliances such as shaver supplies, *providing* each connection is made by means of the proper fused connector designed for the purpose, complying with British Standard 3052.

Although the rule still holds good that appliances consuming above 3 kW, such as cookers and large immersion heaters, should be wired back separately and individually to appropriate fuses in the consumer unit, nevertheless there is a strong tendency, in domestic wiring practice, for more and more fixed appliances (each one not exceeding 3 kW) to be wired into the ring, to secure the maximum economy in the use of cable.

It should be noted that special regulations, to be mentioned later, apply to the method of connection of certain fixed appliances to the ring.

Spur connections
There are two types of spur connection ('tap off' or 'tee' connections) that may be made to a ring circuit – unfused spurs and fused spurs. This avoids the need to run two wires to an isolated area, providing the following points are observed:

When spurs supplying outlying socket-outlets (unfused spurs) are connected to a ring circuit (*Figure* 3.12), not more than one single socket, or one twin socket, or one fixed appliance shall be fed from each, and the total number of unfused spurs shall not exceed the total number of socket-outlets and stationary appliances connected directly to the ring. Unfused spurs shall be connected to a ring circuit at socket-outlets, or in suitable joint boxes.

The conductors supplying the unfused spur shall not be smaller than those forming the ring itself.

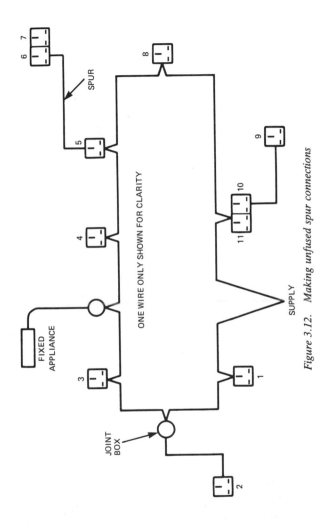

ONE WIRE ONLY SHOWN FOR CLARITY

SPUR

SUPPLY

FIXED APPLIANCE

JOINT BOX

Figure 3.12. Making unfused spur connections

The fused spur (*Figure* 3.13) is connected to the ring via a fused connection unit, the rating of the fuse in the unit not exceeding that of the cable forming the spur, and in any event not exceeding 13 A. The connection unit is provided with a cartridge fuse which can be replaced easily, usually from the front of the box. It is useful in cases where an isolated lighting circuit, made up of fixed lampholders, needs to be supplied. The use of this unit, fitted, say, with a 3 A fuse, obviates the need for a special wiring run back to the consumer unit to supply one or

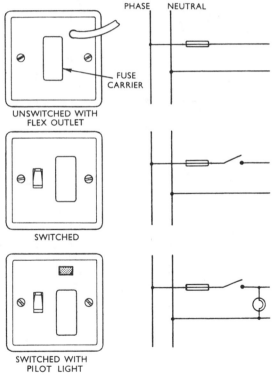

PHASE   NEUTRAL

FUSE CARRIER

UNSWITCHED WITH FLEX OUTLET

SWITCHED

SWITCHED WITH PILOT LIGHT

Figure 3.13.   Typical fused spurs made via fused connection units, switched and unswitched, showing the connections

two lighting points. In this case, the conductors on the spur need only be of a size suitable for the fuse fitted within the connection unit, except that if the spur supplies a socket the cable must be a minimum of $1.5\,mm^2$.

Radial circuits
Radial circuits are circuits which also utilise 13 A flat pin sockets, to British Standard 1363, except that the circuit is not wired in the form of a ring. There are two types of radial circuit, as shown

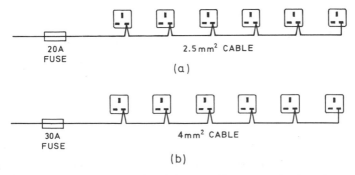

Figure 3.14. Two types of radial circuit (live wire only shown); (a) unlimited socket-outlets serving $20\,m^2$; (b) unlimited socket-outlets serving $50\,m^2$

in *Figure* 3.14. Radial circuits may supply an unlimited number of socket-outlets, providing the floor area served by the circuit does not exceed:

(a) Sercing one room only, which is not a kitchen, and is less than $30\,m^2$ floor area – $4\,mm^2$ conductors protected by 20A fuse or miniature circuit breaker supplying up to six outlets none of which supplies a fixed water heating appliance.
(b) Serving rooms other than above a radial final circuit – $2.5\,mm^2$ conductors protected by a 20A fuse or miniature circuit breaker supplying two socket outlets, or fixed appliances.

Immersion heaters supplying vessels in excess of 15 litres capacity, or heating appliances which are permanently connected and form part of a space heating installation, should NOT be connected to ring circuits. Provided that in total they do not exceed the circuit rating they may be connected to radial circuits in accordance with (a) and (b) above.

Off-peak circuits

In this system, the area electricity board provides a time switch to allow the off-peak supply to be taken at the specified hours only. Sometimes there may be provided, in addition, a contactor to switch on the off-peak circuits, since the time-switch contacts may not be of large enough current-handling capacity. The consumer himself has to supply the extra consumer unit, allowing for the required number of fuses (often termed 'ways'), and the requisite off-peak circuits.

Off-peak supplies are generally used in three ways: for thermal storage heaters, under-floor warming, storage water heating.

In addition, battery chargers are sometimes fed on the off-peak system.

Until 1970, *no* other circuits could be connected to the off-peak system. However, with White Meter and now Economy 7 tariffs, all the house circuits are connected for cheap night rate electricity.

Each off-peak circuit is wired back to the off-peak consumer unit. The termination points may be in the form of fused spur units – that is an outlet fitted with replaceable cartridge fuses and the connections being permanently made (see *Figure* 3.15).

White Meter and Economy 7

These are now the only methods of providing domestic cheap off-peak rates. Using a special meter these systems allow the same appliances to be used both on and off peak. At the beginning of the off-peak period a sealed time switch energises a relay in the meter which transfers the meter drive from one set of recording dials to another. At the end of the period the time

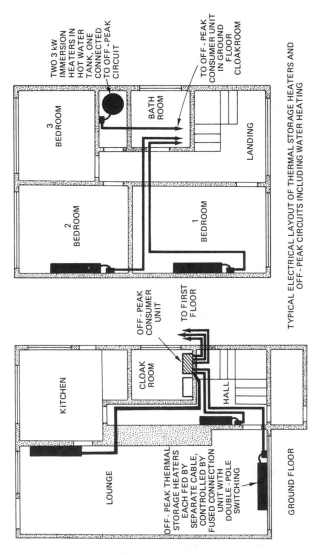

TWO 3 kW IMMERSION HEATERS IN HOT WATER TANK, ONE CONNECTED TO OFF-PEAK CIRCUIT

BEDROOM 3

BEDROOM 2

BATH ROOM

BEDROOM 1

TO OFF-PEAK CONSUMER UNIT IN GROUND FLOOR CLOAKROOM

LANDING

KITCHEN

LOUNGE

CLOAK ROOM

OFF-PEAK CONSUMER UNIT

TO FIRST FLOOR

HALL

OFF-PEAK THERMAL STORAGE HEATERS EACH FED BY SEPARATE CABLE, CONTROLLED BY FUSED CONNECTION UNIT WITH DOUBLE-POLE SWITCHING

GROUND FLOOR

TYPICAL ELECTRICAL LAYOUT OF THERMAL STORAGE HEATERS AND OFF-PEAK CIRCUITS INCLUDING WATER HEATING

Figure 3.15. Layout of off-peak circuits for storage heating and water heating supplies in domestic premises

switch de-energises the relay, switching the meter dials back to their daytime recording positions.

In the Economy 7 tariff the 'off-peak' period is seven hours, and in the White Meter it is eight hours, both of which occur during the night. It will often be necessary for the heating appliances to be wired to their own consumer unit or fuseboard. For convenience of control, the consumer may use an additional time switch of his own, this time switch being the responsibility of the consumer, as it is quite permissible for the heating appliances to be used at any time of the day, however a higher rate will be charged during the 'normal' period. For the above reason, it is in the consumer's interest to use electricity during the night and it will be cheaper to use, say an automatic washing machine connected by a time clock, in this period.

Summary

To sum up, the circuit layout in a typical house comes under the following headings:

Fixed appliances
(a) Cookers and immersion heaters, and any other fixed appliances using 3 kW or above (large current-consuming appliances).
   Each appliance usually wired directly and individually back to the consumer unit.
(b) Other fixed appliances may be connected to a ring circuit.
(c) Lighting circuits for fixed lamps (light current-consuming appliances).
   Grouped in circuits, each circuit wired back to the consumer unit.
(d) Off-peak circuits, for storage heaters, floor heating, immersion water heaters.
   Each appliance wired singly or in groups back to the consumer unit on separate circuits controlled by a time switch.

THE ELECTRICAL LAYOUT

Socket-outlets for portable appliances
The ring circuit is used, with unfused spurs as required.

Earthing

As mentioned earlier, earthing is a means of ensuring electrical safety. All metal parts of all appliances used in the installation should be connected solidly to earth at all times that the appliance is connected to live electric mains.

For fixed appliances, earthing is ensured by a permanent earth connection, which must be solidly connected to an earth point, a feature to be mentioned later. The connection must be made by means of (*a*) the steel conduit, if such a system is properly installed, or (*b*) a protective conductor of suitable size.

For portable appliances, fed by means of socket-outlets, the earth connection is ensured by means of the earth pin in the plug. The earth socket, into which this pin enters, must be connected to the earth point by proper permanent means, as in the case of fixed appliances.

In the majority of cases in domestic premises the earth socket is connected to the earth point by means of the uninsulated protective conductor in the sheathed cable itself.

If the existing cable has no protective conductor, the question arises as to how to provide an earth connection, if a new socket-outlet is being installed.

The earth connection
This raises the question as to what is an 'earth' connection. A wire buried in the earth itself forms a kind of earth connection, but an earth electrode of this kind has to be very carefully designed so that it will not corrode or, for example, find the earth around it becoming so dry that the electrode becomes insulating instead of conducting.

Wherever practicable, the earth terminal is nearly always provided by the area electricity board, although this is not obligatory. In the case of an underground service the incoming supply cable has a lead sheath and steel armouring which is connected to the carefully designed earth electrode at the

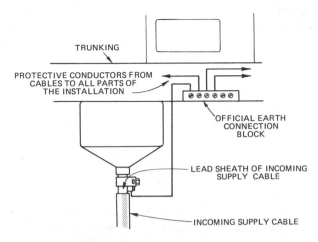

Figure 3.16. Earthing terminal at the consumer's intake point. Note: this terminal is not always provided by the electricity board, particularly in rural areas where the supply enters the house from an overhead power line

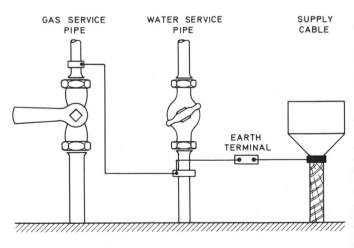

Figure 3.17. Bonding of services

substation. This sheath is usually provided, at the consumer's metering point, with a connection to an earthing terminal. All the earthing points of the whole installation should be connected back to this earthing terminal, which is the official earth point (*Figure* 3.16).

But if such a terminal does not exist, what can be done? In any case, overhead supplies, such as those provided in many rural areas, do not allow for the provision of an 'official' earth point.

The cold water system (*never* the hot water water pipes, these may be discontinuous) has often been used as the protective conductor system, however, this is insufficient for the sole means of earthing of an installation as modern systems often use plastic pipes, and a separate earth electrode *must* be provided.

The regulations state that gas, water and electricity services must be bonded together for safety as shown in *Figure* 3.17. The purpose of bonding the services is to ensure that all metal work within the premises is at the same potential, so reducing the risk of electrical shock.

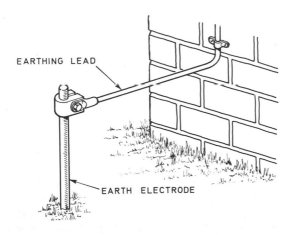

EARTHING LEAD

EARTH ELECTRODE

Figure 3.18.   A typical earth electrode providing an earth point where no other is avilable

An earth electrode is a metal rod or rods, or even plates, set in the ground providing an effective connection with the general mass of earth. The size of the earth electrode, and of the earthing conductor which makes the connection from the electrode to the earthing terminal, should be of the correct size, calculated according to IEE Regulation 542-16 (*Figures* 3.18 and 3.19).

But even with this arrangement, we are not out of all our earthing difficulties where no 'official' earthing point is provided. The ground near the installation may be rocky, or exceptionally dry, or there may be some other condition that leads to a high resistance between the earth electrode and the general mass of earth.

This could give rise to dangerous conditions. The whole ground might become alive, in the neighbourhood of the earth electrode, at the time of a fault, and a child, for example, touching perhaps a rainwater down-pipe with a water flow into a gutter, could be killed by electrocution, the current passing *from the ground* through his body, to the rainwater pipe (*Figure* 3.20).

Earth leakage circuit-breakers

The problem of providing proper earthing facilities under these conditions is solved by the use of the earth leakage circuit-breaker (ELCB).

Suppose an earth spike, or electrode, is provided. Assume also that very dry or rocky ground means that its resistance to the general body of earth is rather high – say up to $100\,\Omega$, instead of much less than $1\,\Omega$, as it should be.

Now imagine a wire connected from the earth terminal of the wiring installation as a whole to this electrode. If then an appliance fails – say an electric iron becomes faulty internally – the phase wire will become connected to the earth electrode, through the green and yellow protective conductor on the iron.

Under ideal conditions this occurrence would immediately cause enough current to flow to blow the fuse, and any danger to the person using the iron would be averted.

SAFETY ELECTRICAL EARTH
DO NOT REMOVE

Figure 3.19.   Label to be fitted to earthing lead. Lettering not less than 4.75 mm high

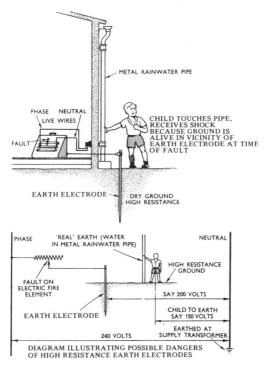

METAL RAINWATER PIPE

PHASE   NEUTRAL
LIVE WIRES

FAULT

CHILD TOUCHES PIPE, RECEIVES SHOCK BECAUSE GROUND IS ALIVE IN VICINITY OF EARTH ELECTRODE AT TIME OF FAULT

EARTH ELECTRODE

DRY GROUND HIGH RESISTANCE

PHASE

'REAL' EARTH (WATER IN METAL RAINWATER PIPE)

NEUTRAL

HIGH RESISTANCE GROUND

FAULT ON ELECTRIC FIRE ELEMENT

SAY 200 VOLTS

CHILD TO EARTH SAY 150 VOLTS

EARTH ELECTRODE

EARTHED AT SUPPLY TRANSFORMER

240 VOLTS

DIAGRAM ILLUSTRATING POSSIBLE DANGERS OF HIGH RESISTANCE EARTH ELECTRODES

Figure 3.20.   If the earth electrode is in dry ground having a high resistance, it is possible that a child or other person touching the metal rainwater pipe through which water is flowing to earth might receive a shock when there is a fault on an electrical appliance, unless measures such as the installation of earth leakage circuit-breakers prevent this danger from arising

THE ELECTRICAL LAYOUT

But with our high-resistance earth electrode, enough current does *not* flow to blow the fuse. The body of the iron remains alive.

However, *some* current does flow, and it is this current that is used to safeguard the installation.

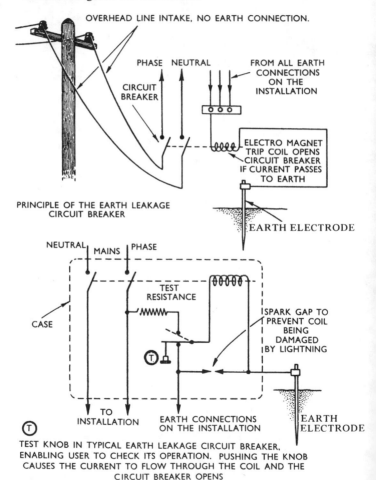

Figure 3.21. The principle of the earth leakage circuit-breaker

746

The connection between the earth terminal of the whole installation and the earth electrode is taken through an electro-magnetic coil attached to a circuit-breaker, or automatic switch, that is connected in series with the main fuse. Any current flowing through this coil will cause the switch to trip, or open, so disconnecting the mains, and removing all source of danger (see *Figure* 3.21).

Earth leakage circuit-breakers can be made to operate on several thousandths of an ampere, so that despite a high resistance at the earth electrode, the circuit-breaker will operate. It should be realised, however, that unlike a fuse it will cut off the whole supply and not only the faulty section.

More than one type of earth leakage circuit-breaker is avail-able. Some – as mentioned above – operate through the passage of the leakage circuit through the trip coil. That is the type must commonly employed, since it is the cheapest. It is referred to as a 'voltage-operated earth leakage circuit-breaker'.

It has one or two disadvantages. First, the current path through which the fault current must flow, to earth, may be paralleled somewhere else on the system, as for example in an immersion heater, where the water piping may well provide a second earth path for the fault current, in addition to the path provided by the proper protective conductor. This may affect (but not entirely nullify) the sensitivity of the earth leakage circuit-breakers (see *Figure* 3.22).

Secondly, it has to be realised that any fault anywhere on the installation will cause the earth leakage circuit-breaker to trip and so cut off the whole installation. Unlike normal fusing arrangements, there is no selectivity.

The first of these problems can be solved by the use of the somewhat more expensive current balance earth leakage circuit-breaker.

The current in the phase wire, in any normal circuit, must at all times exactly equal the return current in the neutral wire. If some current is passing from the phase wire to earth, these two currents no longer balance.

The current balance ELCB uses this condition, by employing in effect two coils, one carrying the phase current and the other the neutral, and so arranging the mechanical parts that if the force exerted by these two coils becomes unequal, the circuit-breaker will trip. This type of device is referred to as a 'current-operated earth leakage circuit-breaker'.

The second problem, the lack of selectivity, can be solved only by splitting the installation up into sections that are entirely separate electrically, each being fitted with a separate ELCB,

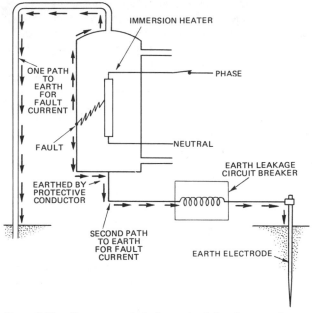

Figure 3.22. How an earth leakage circuit-breaker may become inoperative if the faulty appliance has a parallel path to earth, for the fault current, for example through water piping

whatever type may be used. The circuit-breakers all have a common earthing point, but on the installation side the protective conductors must be kept completely separate from each other (*Figure* 3.23). If this separation is carried out, the occurrence of a fault will result in only one circuit-breaker tripping, leaving the remainder of the installation in service.

748

THE ELECTRICAL LAYOUT

All ELCBs are provided with a test knob, so that the user can make sure that his essential protection against shock is in working order. Even the best earth leakage circuit-breakers, after some years of installation without faults occurring, may tend to stick, if not regularly tested.

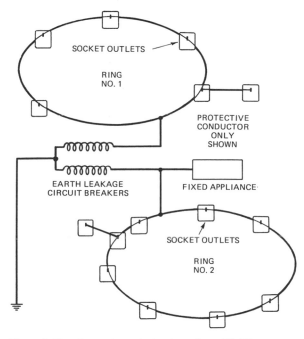

Figure 3.23. Separation of circuits, where ELCBs are employed, to allow for selective operation, so that only one portion of the installation is cut off should a fault develop on any part of the wiring or the appliances

This matter of earth leakage protection should be discussed with the electricity board in each individual case. Their engineers will probably have carried out extensive earth resistance tests in the area concerned, and will be able to advise on the most suitable kind of ELCB to install.

Protective multiple earthing (PME)

Another solution to the problem of satisfactory and safe earthing where difficulties are encountered is protective multiple earthing (*Figure* 3.24), but this is not a system that can be used by the electrician himself.

As we have seen earlier, the normal system of supply has the neutral conductor earthed at the supply transformer only. Normally, this neutral conductor must not be earthed anywhere else,

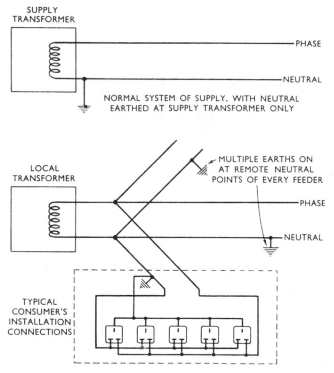

Figure 3.24. The principle of protective multiple earthing, which can only be used in areas where approval of the supply authority and of the appropriate minister has been obtained

because this could cause stray currents to flow in such other services as telephone cables.

However, sanction from the appropriate ministry is required before one can apply PME in a particular area. In this case, the neutral conductor is connected (by the electricity board) to the earth connection at each consumer.

When this PME system is applied, the neutral conductor on each installation becomes the earth point, and all the protective conductor connections are joined to the neutral, at the supply intake position.

The electrician should consult the electricity board about earth connection made in an area in which PME is being employed. He can learn about this likelihood by consulting the electricity board before any installation work commences.

4 Physical Plan of the Installation

The layout plan

Position of intake point

An important factor to consider is the situation of the intake point (which must incidentally be agreed with the electricity board). One place to avoid is the cupboard under the stairs, which is likely to get filled with things like pushchairs and tennis racquets, so that (1) the meter reader has great difficulty in getting to the meter, and (2) if a fuse blows, confusion in the resulting darkness may become even greater as the householder first has to force his way through old trunks and then fumble around with fusewire.

It should be realised that the area electricity boards only allow a certain distance of 'free' cable, from the mains in the street, or from the pole line, to the supply point. This is often of the order of 10 metres. If a supply point position is chosen so that this distance is exceeded, the consumer must be prepared to pay for the extra cable involved.

A garage is often found to be a convenient place for the intake point, but care must be taken (1) to situate the fuses, etc., in a position agreed with the area electricity board, and (2) to allow ample room for cabling runs to the rest of the house, *and* for extensions to the consumer unit assembly.

Many new houses are fitted with a cloakroom or lavatory adjacent to the hall, and this is another place where the intake point may conveniently be situated, perhaps in a cupboard. A new development is the placing of meters on the outside wall of

PHYSICAL PLAN OF THE INSTALLATION

the premises in a special lockable cabinet, so that the meter reader can take the readings even when the household is unoccupied.

How many socket-outlets are needed?

The number of socket-outlets to be installed, and their positions, must be a matter for the owner of the installation, but the electrician should try and persuade him to be as generous as possible with outlets. In every household the usage of electrical appliances is always increasing.

A reasonable number of socket-outlets for a three-bedroomed semi-detached house is indicated in *Figure* 3.11.

In general socket-outlets should be installed in living rooms at about 500 mm from the floor level, to obviate the need to stoop down to insert the plug. In the kitchen, socket-outlets may be at table-top level, for convenience in using irons, food mixers, kettles and the like.

It is desirable to install at least one socket-outlet on the landing and another in the hall, so that vacuum-cleaner connections may be made without difficulty.

It should always be remembered that much time and material can be saved by careful planning and measuring-up before commencing work. The frenzied rush to the electrical shop for one more reel of cable, just as it closes, is a sign of bad planning.

There is another advantage in taking great care to prepare a drawn-out plan of the installation. It is almost inevitable that extensions will be needed some time in the future, and it is of course not impossible that a fault will occur in some part of the wiring. If the original wiring plan is available, both the work of extension and that of tracing and rectifying a fault will be greatly simplified.

Identifying tags attached to cables under floors and behind consumer units will be found useful if work is to be carried out in the future.

Size of cable

Having decided on the circuit layout, the next problem relates to the physical installation of the wiring.

753

The first point to decide is the size and type of the cabling. The size of cable to be used is determined by several factors.

Lighting circuits

Each lampholder or fluorescent lighting fitting is usually taken as consuming 100 W. So if there are six lighting points on a circuit, the power that must be allowed for is 600 W. This is equivalent to 2.5 A, at 240 V.

For lighting circuits it is usual to arrange the points so that the circuits are wired using $1.00\,mm^2$ (one square millimetre in cross-sectional area) cable with PVC insulation, in the form of twin sheathed PVC cable with protective conductor included. These circuits are controlled by 5 A fuses (in domestic premises), and care should be taken to ensure that this current is not exceeded.

Permanently connected appliances such as cookers, water heaters and radiators

For appliances that consume a considerable amount of current, for example a cooker, the total wattage of the appliance must first be ascertained – that is, the loading with all parts switched on to their highest loadings.

Suppose this comes to 6 kW. The current necessary is therefore 25 A.

According to the wire tables published in the *Regulations for Electrical Installations*, where twin sheathed cable is used, the $6\,mm^2$ conductor size is suitable, when supplied from a 30 A fuse or MCB. But when considering appliances like cookers, it should always be realised that loadings continually increase, and when a new cooker is installed it may be very costly and inconvenient to have to rewire the circuit. Therefore it may pay to allow for a larger loading than is strictly necessary.

Investigations into the usage of cookers and other heavy-current appliances have shown that in normal domestic use a diversity factor may be applied. For example, a cooker whose total loading, with all plates and oven elements switched on full, is 13 kW, needing about 54 A, may in fact be connected by means of a 6 mm^2 cable, protected by a 30 A fuse because diversity is applied to take into account the fact that all the load will not be used at the same time.

The operation of diversity of demand is such that most cookers used in domestic premises may be supplied from a 30 A fuse, that allows for over 7 kW of load, however a 45 A fuse is available should a very large double oven cooker be used.

Ring circuit

The ring circuit is permitted, under the Regulations, only for use with 13 A socket-outlets fitted with fused plugs. The number of socket-outlets that may be connected has been set out earlier in Chapter 3.

Mineral-insulated cables

Mineral-insulated copper-sheathed cables employ single wires, not stranded conductors, and since the current-carrying capacity of any conductor is related to the heating effect caused by the passage of the current, and the mineral insulation differs from the PVC type of insulation in regard to its heat resisting properties, higher operating temperature and the ability to dissipate heat, different cable size rules apply. *Table* 4 1 shows the ratings of the sizes most commonly used.

Flexible cords

Flexible cords should always be used as little as possible and should be kept as short as possible. They should never be used for permanent wiring.

Four types of flexible cord are commonly used:

> for light-current work
> for heavy-current work
> for portable tools, etc.
> for the connection of hot appliances.

For light-current work such as suspending lamps and connecting up lighting fittings and radio sets, where the current does not exceed 3 A, the type of flexible cord generally used is twin, plastic-insulated cord, with 0.5 mm^2 conductors.

For heavy-current appliances such as radiators, three-core plastic-insulated cord, sheathed or covered with braiding, is used, with $1.5\,mm^2$ conductors.

For portable tools, a three-core, plastic-insulated cable, with $1.5\,mm^2$ conductors, is suitable.

For connections to such appliances as irons, water heaters and any other appliance that can become hot, a butyl rubber or silicone rubber cable, of three-core construction, with special heat-resisting qualities, and conductors of $1.5\,mm^2$ size, is used.

Table 4.1 Current rating of mineral-insulated cables

Nominal cross-section area of conductor (mm^2)	Single-core cables (A)	Twin cables (A)
1.0	22	17
1.5	27	22
2.5	36	29
4.0	46	38

Based on information contained in the *Regulations for Electrical Installations*, 15th edition.

Table 4.2 Flexible cords

Size (mm^2)	Current ratings (A)	Maximum permissible weight that a twin cable should support (kg)
0.5	3	2
0.75	6	3
1.0	10	5
1.5	15	5

Based on information contained in the *Regulations for Electrical Installations*, 15th edition.

Table 4.3 Current rating of single-core
PVC insulated cables bunched and
enclosed in conduit

Size of cable (mm²)	Two cables (A)
1.0	10
1.5	12
2.5	17
4	23
6	30
10	40
16	54

Based on information contained in the
Regulations for Electrical Installations,
15th edition.

Table 4.4 Current rating of twin and multi-core
sheathed PVC insulated cables

Size of cable (mm²)	One twin core cable (A)
1.0	12
1.5	15
2.5	20
4	26
6	33
10	46

Based on information contained in the
Regulations for Electrical Installations, 15th
edition.

Note: In using these tables, it is important to note that they are
not extracts from the Regulations but are derived from them and
are intended for approximate guidance only, the full text of the
Regulations for Electrical Installations should be consulted before they are applied to anything but the simplest domestic
installation. There are important qualifications in the Regulations that must be observed in certain cases; for example the

cables must be derated (allotted a lower current-carrying capacity) if the ambient air temperature is over 30°C. Conversely the ratings may be increased if the ambient temperature is below 30°C.

Wire tables

Table 4.2 shows the current-carrying capacities and weight-supporting loadings applicable to commonly used flexible cables used in domestic and small industrial installations.

Type of cabling

The conduit system

If the heavy gauge steel conduit system is adopted, the system must be electrically continuous throughout: that means that all sections of conduit (piping) must be screwed together, with screwed sleeves to join each section of straight pipe, and properly screwed and terminated lengths running into metal junction boxes and the boxes that receive switches, ceiling roses, socket-outlets, clock connector boxes and all other fittings.

The conduit must be carefully measured before screwing, and after the thread has been cut with the proper dies, the ends must be reamered out to remove all sharp edges.

Steel conduit is made in various sizes, and *Table* 4.5 gives the mechanical characteristics of the sizes most commonly used in domestic installations.

It is laid down in the Regulations that all conduit installations must be completely erected before any wires are drawn in.

In deciding how many wires can be pulled into conduit systems, it must be realised that the friction caused by the pulling in of wires running close together can damage the PVC insulation.

The *Regulations for Electrical Installations* lay down the number of separate single-core cables that can be drawn into various sizes of conduit, and it is assumed that the reader who contemplates installing a system of this kind will have consulted the Regulations.

The method used to determine the cable capacities of conduits is described in Regulation 529-7 and Appendix 12. Each cable size is allocated a factor. The sum of all factors for the cables

Table 4.5 Steel conduit sizes

Conduit external diameter (mm)	Pitch (mm)	Tapping drill (mm)	Clearance drill (mm)
16	1.5	14.5	18
20	1.5	18.5	22
25	1.5	23.5	27
32	1.5	30.5	34

intended to be run in the same conduit is compared with a Table, and a suitable size of conduit is selected, this takes into account any bends or sets that are to be included in the installation.

Installing conduit

If conduit wiring is to be installed in a new house, the conduit must be placed in position at exactly the right time in relation to the other building work, or else there will be a great deal of expensive reinstatement of plaster work that has had to be cut into to run the conduit. This stage is usually called the carcassing stage.

When the the shell of the house is built, and the roof is on, but before the floorboards are laid and of course before plastering commences, the electrician has the ideal conditions for his work.

For extensions to existing installations it is usually necessary to chase out a trough in the plaster and bricks for the conduit to lie partly below the surface, otherwise, with a plaster depth of only 10 mm, the conduit would stand proud of the wall. For the outlet boxes, into which the actual socket-outlets are to be fitted, a deeper hole must be cut in the wall.

Right-angle elbows should be avoided wherever possible, because of the obstacle they provide to easy drawing-in of the wires. Bends are preferred, and these should have an internal radius of not less than 2.5 times the overall diameter of the conduit, e.g. overall diameter of conduit $= 16\text{mm}$, minimum internal radius of bend $= 16 \times 2.5 = 40\text{mm}$.

Although a conduit system is in theory completely sealed, from end to end, air can gain access at the socket-outlets and switches, and moisture-carrying air brings with it the danger of condensation. This could mean that small quantities of water could run down into switches and other fittings, and give rise to corrosion. To prevent this, conduit systems should have drain holes situated at low points (in boxes).

Conduit runs should always be kept clear of gas pipes, water pipes, and any other wiring. This is because of the possible dangers of bimetallic corrosion through contact betwen different metals, and also because of possible sparking dangers, if a fault should occur on the electrical installation and fault current flows through the conduit itself.

As erection proceeds, draw wires should be inserted from junction box to junction box. These wires (or flat steel tapes) will greatly facilitate drawing-in. The Regulations state that all the conduit must be complete before any wires are drawn in.

When pulling in the cables, the best method is to bare all the ends of the conductors, twist them together and bend them over to form an eye and attach the end of the fish wire or tape to this eye. The procedure is shown in *Figure* 4.1. Care must be taken later to cut away the whole of the conductors used for this purpose, as they may have become damaged, before making them off into the fittings.

Always make certain that enough cable is pulled through. It is very unwise to leave only the bare minimum protruding from the box in the wall. If any slight slip is made during making off, there will be an extremely arduous business of pulling new wire in.

As a general rule, always try to avoid joints, even though they can be made in proper joint boxes, if there is no alternative. This

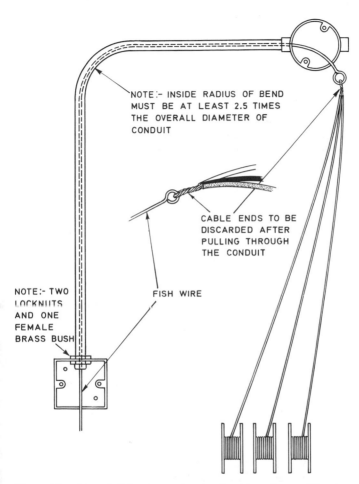

NOTE:- INSIDE RADIUS OF BEND MUST BE AT LEAST 2.5 TIMES THE OVERALL DIAMETER OF CONDUIT

CABLE ENDS TO BE DISCARDED AFTER PULLING THROUGH THE CONDUIT

NOTE:- TWO LOCKNUTS AND ONE FEMALE BRASS BUSH

FISH WIRE

Figure 4.1. Use of fish wire and twisted cables when pulling into conduit. The twisted end must be discarded before connecting up, as it may become damaged

761

means, of course, that short lengths of cable will get left on drums, and the electrician may think he has been wasteful. But he will have the satisfaction of knowing he has provided a sound job, and he will have avoided the laborious business of making joints in joint boxes which may – and often do – find themselves in difficult positions.

When it is necessary to pull in a number of cables, nasty kinks and knots may be avoided by 'combing' the cables through a piece of wood or stiff cardboard, with an appropriate number of holes, before entering them into the conduit. This will ensure that the cables are reasonably straight and will ease the drawing in process.

Sheathed wiring systems

PVC insulated and sheathed cables are by far the most commonly used materials in domestic wiring systems, whether for new installations or for extensions to existing wiring.

All wiring systems, as we have seen, must have proper earthing arrangements. With properly screwed metal conduit the conduit itself may act as the protective conductor, but where sheathed cable is used there is usually an uninsulated (bare) wire lying between the red and black wires within the sheath, to provide earth continuity.

The main points to watch when installing sheathed wiring systems are these:

(1) The greatest possible care must be taken to ensure that the cables are protected against mechanical damage.
(2) The cables have only a limited ability to resist heat, and must not be installed, for example, in the close vicinity of hot-water pipes or near flues.

If cabling has to be run in hot situations, the best choice is mineral-insulated copper-sheathed cable.

Preventing mechanical damage

Returning to the question of preventing mechanical damage, the installer must always try to visualise what *might* happen: for example, running cable in a trough cut into the plaster down a wall to reach a switch may be all right while the present occupier inhabits the room, but some future occupier might easily decide to fit a bookcase or a mirror on that part of the wall and drive nails or fixing screws right through the wire.

The best way of running sheathed wiring in plaster is to install a round or oval conduit for all runs, or at the least to chase out a trough for the wiring so that it can be covered with a metal channel. The use of conduit for runs to socket-outlets and switches has the advantage of enabling the cable to be pulled out if it has to be replaced, without breaking away the wall.

Alternatively, metal channelling fitted above the cable before making good the plaster will partly protect the cable, although complete protection is not ensured. A cautious person driving a nail or drilling for a wall plug would probably detect the metallic contact, if the channelling was in the line of fixing. The channelling will also protect the cable during plastering.

Similarly, if the floorboards are removed to run cabling beneath, it is rather tempting, when running at right angles to the joists, to cut a nick or groove in each joist, and run the cable across them in this way, afterwards replacing the floorboards. But some future occupier, not knowing the run of the cables, might well drive nails or screws into the floor, so penetrating the cable and even causing a fire (see *Figure* 4.2).

The proper method is to drill generously sized holes in the joist, at least 50 mm down each joist, and thread the cable through. 20 mm holes will allow three 2.5 mm^2 cables to pass through.

In general, if it is difficult to conceal the cables by running through confined spaces, or where thick stone walls are encountered, or if it is very difficult or impossible to obtain access below floors, it is better to run the cabling on the surface. People are not likely to damage a cable they can see. It is quite possible to run the usual cables in domestic premises so neatly that when painted to match the surroundings they become almost invisible, but are still apparent to anyone proposing to drill or drive nails.

Where the wiring need not be covered for aesthetic reasons, such as in a garage, it is better to run it in such a way that it can

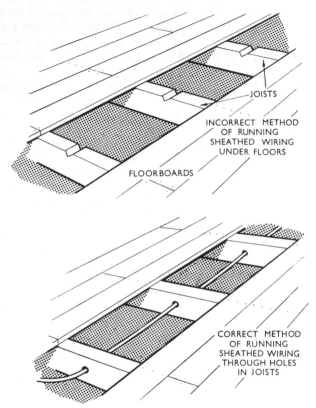

Figure 4.2. Running cable (or conduit) across joists: it is incorrect to run across the top of the joists in nicks, since nails driven through the floorboards could penetrate the pipe or sheathed cable and cause a fault. This method will also weaken the joists

be clearly seen (*Figure* 4.3). By using this method damage to the wiring will be less likely than if it is indifferently concealed.

Cables must always be supported by some form of clasp, usually taking the form of plastic clips (*Figure* 4.4) or buckle clips, the normal spacing being 250 mm apart. Saddles may be used to embrace several cables (*Figure* 4.9).

Where a number of cables run *along* a joist, half-way down, an easy way of fixing is to use saddles from old sheath ends, secured with tacks of at least 15 mm in length.

Sheathed cables should never be allowed to run unsupported for a distance much exceeding 300 mm. The reason for this is that if they are at any time subjected to overheating – and this may be

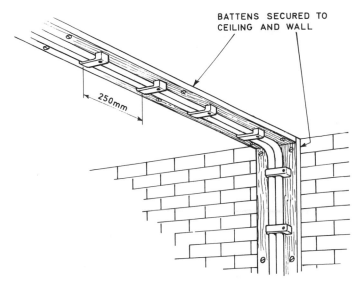

BATTENS SECURED TO
CEILING AND WALL

250mm

Figure 4.3. Sheathed wiring run bare on battens

due not only to the passage of excess current, but also through the proximity of a flue, or a hot-water pipe – the sagging cable may become distorted so that the PVC insulation tends to drop away from the conductors, and might even leave them bare.

It is always bad practice to tie or tape sheathed cables to existing water or gas pipes – especially the latter. Wood battens should be run along the path to be taken by the cables, well removed from the piping, and the cables secured by means of saddle clips.

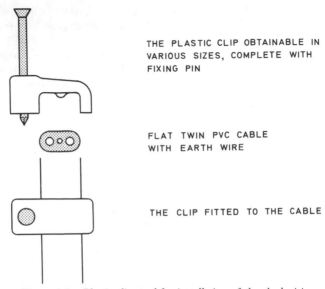

THE PLASTIC CLIP OBTAINABLE IN VARIOUS SIZES, COMPLETE WITH FIXING PIN

FLAT TWIN PVC CABLE WITH EARTH WIRE

THE CLIP FITTED TO THE CABLE

Figure 4.4. Plastic clip used for installation of sheathed wiring

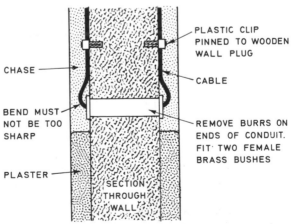

PLASTIC CLIP PINNED TO WOODEN WALL PLUG

CHASE

CABLE

BEND MUST NOT BE TOO SHARP

REMOVE BURRS ON ENDS OF CONDUIT. FIT TWO FEMALE BRASS BUSHES

PLASTER

SECTION THROUGH WALL

Figure 4.5. Running sheathed cable through walls: protective conduit should be employed, it need not be earthed

Where sheathed cables have to pass through a wall, or through any partition, the best method is to use some lengths of protective conduit (see *Figure* 4.5).

Running out the cable

The best system to employ, when running out sheathed cables, is to arrange some sort of spindle for the drums, such as a broomstick supported on wooden frames. If the cable runs off the drum as it lies flat on the floor, there will be a danger of producing a twisted mess of cable that will take much time to disentangle and may in any case result in kinks and untidy twists in the cable, preventing a neat appearance in the finished job.

To secure the neatest job, experiment with two short lengths of cable, say 300 mm each, on a piece of wood. See how near to each other the cables will lie, and then apply two sets of plastic clips, 250 mm apart. If the cables are now clipped in, and lie as close together as possible, measure the spacing between the clips at each point, and adopt that measurement along the runs of cable where more than one circuit is to be laid. Nothing looks worse than wiring with two or three cables untidily running along at varying distances apart.

When running out sheathed cable, which comes in 50 or 100 m drums, great care must be taken to avoid twists and kinks, as mentioned earlier. These may harm the cable if, when kinked, it is pulled too tight. The best way of smoothing out the cable is to clamp a smooth round object, of at least 30 mm diameter, in a vice and pull the cable tightly round it, one hand opposing the other.

PVC sheathed cable tends to be stiff to handle in cold weather. This problem can be overcome to some extent by storing the reels in a warm room before operations commence.

Assuming the installation (or extension) is to use sheathed cable run beneath the plaster, the first process is to mark out, as accurately as possible, the cable runs.

The cable could be covered with steel channelling (although this is not essential), and this comes in standard sizes. A run commonly used is two 2.5 mm^2 cables, as employed on a ring circuit, and is about 45 mm wide overall. If this size of channelling is used, a chase, or trough, about 50 mm wide needs to be cut in the plaster.

The best way to cut the plaster without bringing away more surface than is required is to employ a wide flat chisel and cut

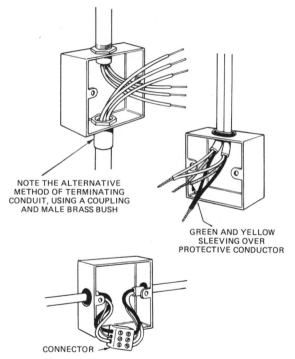

NOTE THE ALTERNATIVE
METHOD OF TERMINATING
CONDUIT, USING A COUPLING
AND MALE BRASS BUSH

GREEN AND YELLOW
SLEEVING OVER
PROTECTIVE CONDUCTOR

CONNECTOR

Figure 4.6. Types of box used both on conduit and sheathed wiring systems showing details and method of baring and twisting the conductors

diagonally inwards at both sides of the chase. The plaster can then be levered out with a knife.

The cable will terminate in a box, on which will be mounted the switch or socket-outlet.

Fitting steel boxes

Steel boxes (*Figure* 4.6) are made in different depths. The shallow boxes are 16 mm deep, and do not allow much room for more than one cable and the resultant interconnecting wiring. These are eminently suitable for switches. A deeper box is 47 mm deep, and allows ample room for PVC connectors, when a joint has to be made in a cable, or for the three sets of wires that result, say, from the entry and exit of ring circuit connections and also the departure of a spur connection.

These boxes have knockouts on all sides, and when the knockout has been removed, a rubber grommet must be inserted in the hole.

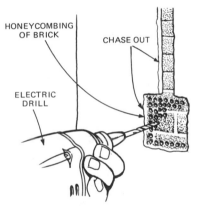

Figure 4.7. Using the electric drill to prepare the brickwork for the large hole needed for a deep box

The brickwork must be cut away to receive the deeper type of box. Over the whole area to be cut away (80 mm square for a one-way box, 80 mm by 160 mm for a two-way, and so on) holes are drilled in the brick with a size 10 or 12 masonry drill, and then a sharp chisel will soon clear away the honeycombed brick (see *Figure* 4.7).

The box must be sunk in so that its top edge is about 5 mm below the general plaster level of the wall.

Holes for screws will be found in the base of the box, two of them usually being oval to allow for adjustment. Holes must now be drilled in the wall (a size 8 woodscrew is usually used, so an appropriate drill or bit must be used), a wall plug inserted, and the box screwed firmly to the brick.

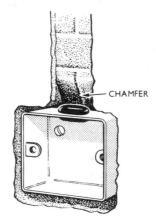

— CHAMFER

Figure 4.8. Chamfering brickwork to allow easy cable entry into box

At this point a small spirit-level is useful, because the levelling of the box will ensure that the front plate of the switch or socket-outlet will also come exactly level. If one switch-plate slopes one way and an adjacent switch slopes in the opposite direction, the result clearly indicates bad workmanship. The spirit-level may be used to level the box, using the tolerance provided by the oval holes, before the screws are finally tightened.

On any side of the box where cables are to enter, the brickwork should be chamfered away as shown in *Figure* 4.8, so that there is a smooth slope and not a sharp edge.

Fitting cables and channelling

The next step is to run the cables in the chase cut in the plaster. The cables are naturally springy, and it is not easy to get them to be flat ready to receive the metal channelling. It has been found worthwhile to plug the brick in one or two places (easily accomplished with an electric drill) and to fit a few clips along the run to hold the cables in position as shown in *Figure* 4.9.

The channelling may be secured by tacks or screws. Sometimes a satisfactory fixing (bearing in mind the plaster will soon hold the channelling firmly) may be secured by tacks driven into

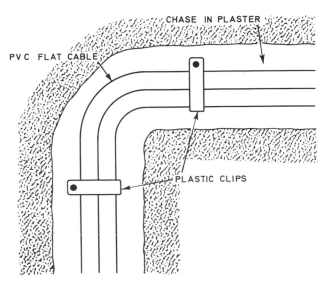

Figure 4.9. When installing metal channelling, keep the cable flat against the wall by using plastic clips under the channelling. Note: the radius of the sharpest bend must be at least four times the overall diameter of the cable (too tight a bend will damage the PVC). Also, all hidden cable should be run either vertically or horizontally, to give indication of run

the crevices between bricks. But the springy nature of PVC-insulated cable, especially, will often mean that screws, driven into proper plugged holes, say every 300 mm along each edge of the channelling, will have to be employed to secure a neat job in which the channelling is properly sunk well below the plaster level.

The channelling should be cut so that it forms a continuous cover for the cable. This means that it comes right up to each box. Sharp edges should be filed so that there is no danger of subsequent pressure accidentally cutting through the insulation.

Making good

The cables cannot be made off into the boxes before the wall is 'made good' – plastered and painted. Otherwise the switches and other fittings could become covered in paint.

The next step is to make good the plaster. The best method is to use first a cement and sand mixture (half cement, half sand) to fill in the main part of the trough containing the cables and their protective channelling, right up to the normal plaster surface layer.

An important point to remember here is that if the cement is allowed to harden for too long, it will be difficult to rake away the top layer to allow for subsequent plastering to restore the smooth unbroken surface of the original wall. Therefore the cement layer should be given, say, not more than 2 days to set, and then the surface should be scraped so that it lies about 5 mm below the normal wall level. The final finishing coat of plaster can then be applied. Priming and final painting can follow when the plaster has fully dried out.

Making off the cable ends

Perhaps the most likely source of trouble in an electrical installation lies in bad workmanship when making off cable ends.

When baring the insulation from the conductors, savage tearing with a sharp knife may easily cut through or nick one or more strands of wire, and these loose pieces of wire may come adrift and cause short-circuits, or may reduce the current-carrying capacity at the terminal, and so cause overheating. The best practice is to use a cable stripping tool (*Figure* 4.10).

When bringing two (or more) conductors into a terminal, enough insulation should be bared from each to allow the wires to be twisted together, with only enough bare copper showing for proper insertion in the terminal. The wires may be twisted with flat-nosed pliers, and the twisted ends cut off neatly with side cutters.

Only practice and experience will show exactly how much length of single conductor should be left outside the cable sheath, and of this, how much should be bared to make the connection. If too much wire is bared, there is a danger that as the box is closed up, the wires may become twisted or compressed against each other so that short-circuits occur. If on the other hand too little 'tail' wire (wire outside the sheath) is made available, making off may be difficult, and this may lead to the physical impossibility of tightening all the terminals as they should be tightened.

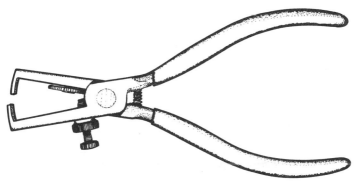

Figure 4.10. Cable stripping tool

Loosely tightened terminals can easily cause internal sparking and overheating. A high resistance is introduced into the circuit at this point, and insulation may become charred and dangerous, and springs in switch contacts may become overheated and lose their tension, and so provoke further trouble.

As each fitting – switch, ceiling rose, or socket-outlet – is completed, it should be *gently* pushed into position, the electrician taking every opportunity to make absolutely certain that as the fitting goes into its box none of the wires is being twisted too sharply, or compressed against a sharp edge, or brought into contact with the live terminals.

5 Accessories and Fittings

The consumer unit

Starting at the consumer unit (*Figure* 5.1) where the installer's responsibility commences, this component should be chosen with considerable care with two viewpoints in mind:

(1) Ease of installation of the original wiring.
(2) Ease of adding new wiring when the occasion demands.

For an average domestic installation, the consumer unit might well include eight fuseways, allocated as follows:

> two for the two ring circuits, 30 A each;
> one for the cooker circuit, 30 A;
> one for the main water-heating immersion heater, 15 A;
> one for a 3 kW fixed radiator in the living room, 15 A;
> two for lighting circuits, 5 A each;
> one spare.

But there will be many variations on this.

As mentioned earlier in this book, careful studies concerning diversity of use, carried out over many years in many different types of household using various kinds of appliance, have shown that it is safe to allow for considerable diversity: in other words, to plan the wiring and fuses and other appliances on the basis that not all the potential, or possible, loading will occur at the same time.

For example, in the *Regulations for Electrical Installations*, for individual domestic installations, the *suggested* diversity factor

ACCESSORIES AND FITTINGS

that can be applied for example, to fixed heating and power appliances other than motors, cookers and water heaters, is 100% full load up to 10 A, plus 50% of any load in excess of 10 A.

Taking this suggestion as a guide, if in a four-bedroomed house there are 2 kW fixed electric fires in each bedroom, the total potential loading would be $4 \times 2 = 8\,kW = 33.28\,A$. But the diversity factor suggested means that the cable size could be proportioned for the first 10 A plus 50% of the remaining current

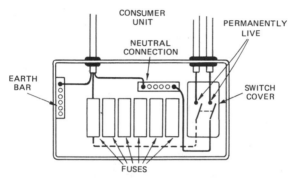

Figure 5.1. The interior of a typical consumer unit, showing phase (live) connection, neutral connection, earth bar and the cover over the switch, whose terminals remain alive even when the switch is off

$(33.28 - 10 = 23.28\,A)$ or 11.64 A. In total, therefore, the current that should be allowed for is $10 + 11.64 = 21.64\,A$, instead of 33.28 A. This also applies to the fuses and the other fittings on the mains side of the installation but *not* to the final circuits.

However, it must be emphasised that this (and other suggested diversity factors) are only guides. The person responsible for the installation must make his own judgement.

For example, while for a cooker the same kind of diversity is suggested, if this cooker is installed, say, in a nursing home where special meals are prepared, or in a large house where a large family lives, or perhaps in a small café, then diversity does not necessarily apply.

The worst that can happen if too *large* a cable and consumer unit are installed is some small, *apparently* unnecessary expense at the time of installation.

The worst that can happen if too *small* a cable and consumer unit are installed is overheating (with possible fire danger), frequent blowing of fuses, and a probable need to embark on a costly and inconvenient programme of rewiring.

Each consumer unit will have its own main switch, fuseholders for each way, and neutral terminals and earth terminals.

There are metalclad and insulated enclosures for consumer units. If a conduit system is being installed, a metalclad type will be used. For sheathed cable systems, the insulated enclosure is more usual, but the metalclad type may be used if desired, care of course being taken to ensure that the metal enclosure is properly earthed.

All types are provided with knockouts. These are either sheet-metal plugs, pressed into holes appropriate for conduit or wire entry, or else (in plastic boxes) clearly defined thin places in the plastic case, which can be tapped out by a careful tap with a hammer.

The Regulations state that all enclosures surrounding live parts must be completely closed. This is required to prevent the ingress of moisture, insects, and dust. So if any knockouts are not required for wiring they must be left intact, or if already knocked out, closed by means of rubber plugs.

Where conduit enters a consumer unit it must be fitted with a smooth brass bush at its end, to prevent the wires being damaged on the rough edges of the pipe. When bringing sheathed wiring in, close-fitting rubber grommets must always be used. These grommets have the dual purpose of protecting the wiring from damage when passing through the rough edges of the hole, and also blocking the hole around the wiring to seal the interior of the box.

Consumer units may be installed straight on to a brick or concrete wall, but there are several disadvantages if this method is used. First, brick walls may be damp, and this will ultimately cause rusting, even on the best galvanised boxes. Secondly, to obtain the neatest wiring layout, particularly with sheathed wiring, it is desirable to bring the wiring in from the back, and this is not possible if the boxes are flush against the wall (for conduit wiring, top entry is usually more convenient).

The ideal method is to make up (or obtain ready-made) a strong wooden board, of not less than 13 mm timber, supported

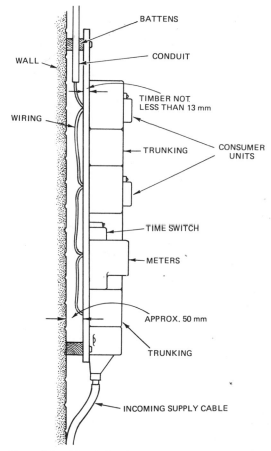

Figure 5.2. Sheathed cable entering from behind con-sumer unit

777

on battens at either side so that it stands about 50 mm away from the wall (see *Figure* 5.2). This board is then firmly fixed to the wall at its left and right edges. The sheathed wiring, brought in from above on battens, can then be taken into the consumer unit through holes of generous size (not less than 20 mm diameter) drilled in the board at points carefully measured out to coincide with the back knockouts.

With ample space behind the wooden board, the wiring will not be unduly pinched up, so avoiding the possibility of damage and overheating. Moreover, new wiring can easily be added. Further holes can be drilled in the baseboard by removing the fixing screws of any one consumer unit, and – if proper slack has been left in the wiring behind the board – slightly moving it out of place so that the hole can be drilled and the new wire brought through.

For larger installations, the area electricity board often provide a consumer's termination unit in which the supply cable sealing box, the main fuses, and the meter are mounted in such a way that a trunking connection may be made directly, with the unit mounted, as it were, on top of the trunking, see *Figure* 1.7.

It should always be remembered that space should be provided on the baseboard for possible additional consumer units. For example, if off-peak storage heating is to be added, not only will an extra unit be needed, but a time-switch and possibly a contactor will have to be installed.

Again, if the size of the installation grows so that a 3-phase supply mains has to be brought in, there will be the need for separate consumer units for each phase; and if this move has been necessitated by the installation of off-peak storage heating, there will have to be units for the red, yellow and blue phases on-peak, and for the red, yellow and blue phases off-peak, making six in all.

Wiring accessories

In running out the wiring from the consumer unit, one cardinal principle must always be observed. There should be no joints in the wiring runs other·than those made at proper fittings, using screw-down terminals of suitable size.

Care must always be taken to avoid what is unfortunately a common device for fixing more wires into a terminal than it will properly hold, or wires larger than those for which it was designed. Many amateurs have been known to cut away several of the bared strands of the conductors, to make them fit into the terminal. *This practice is entirely wrong, and may well be highly dangerous.* The reduced copper section at this one point may well give rise to considerable overheating, without blowing any fuse, and it could therefore happen that a fire is caused through a switch or socket-outlet becoming overheated.

Joint boxes

With sheathed wiring systems, round joint boxes are available. The electrician must be certain that the terminals are large enough to contain the required number of wires of the size to be used.

It should be mentioned, however, that many of these boxes are only suitable for use with the smaller sizes of cables, usually less than the 2.5 mm² size. Some boxes are specially made to take three 2.5 mm² conductors, for example where a tee-off is required.

The best practice is to avoid boxes wherever possible. Lighting circuits may be looped in, using four-plate ceiling roses, to avoid the necessity for joints (as mentioned later in this chapter) and, on ring circuits, any spur connections ought if possible to be made at socket-outlets, since the terminals on these units are capable of carrying three 2.5 mm² conductors.

Joint boxes are designed with knockout sections, and these should be broken out in such a way that the cable fits snugly and does not allow empty spaces around it where dust and insects may penetrate.

Where there is considerable likelihood that moisture or fumes or dust will penetrate, the proper box to use is a conduit type with sealing glands (that can be bought from the cable suppliers) so that the cable is properly sealed in to the box entry holes.

Metal boxes for switches, socket-outlets, etc., should be used with sheathed wiring systems, although plastic-type boxes are available. The protective conductor brought in with the cable must make proper connection with the box itself. An earthing screw is sometimes provided for this purpose, but the socket-outlet or other device usually has an internal arrangement whereby the earth connection terminal on the socket-outlet body has a metal strap connecting it to the screws used to fix the device on to the box, thus providing an earth connection when the socket-outlet is assembled.

A short cut sometimes adopted by amateurs, where they wish to earth a metal box, is to trap the earth wire beneath the lid of the box, holding it tight by means of the fixing screws. This means that a gap is left, through which moisture may penetrate. This short cut should not be employed.

Where plastic boxes are used, care must be taken to see that holes are not left in such a way that subsequent plastering will fill the box with liquid plaster.

Whatever type of box is used, it should be chosen so that there is ample room for all the wiring, and that when the switch or other fitting is applied, the wiring will not be squeezed up so tight that there is danger of a sharp point on the back of the switch pressing the wires against the metal part, with the possibility of ultimate breakdown of the insulation.

There is another danger that must be carefully avoided, and that is of cutting off the ends of the cable a fraction too short, so that when the switch is pressed home and the retaining screws are tightened, one or other of the connections is being gradually strained either to breaking point or is pulled out of the terminal.

Only experiment and practice on a dummy circuit, using some scrap cable, will show how much cable should be left.

All fittings – boxes, surface switches, socket-outlets – must allow for the outer sheath of the cable, in sheathed cable systems, to be brought well inside the protection of the box – in other words, the unprotected cores of the cable, even with their normal insulation, must never be accessible outside an area protected by some form of box.

Ceiling roses and connectors

Ceiling roses, for pendant lamps, are plastic with non-flammable back plates, called patresses.

These ceiling roses often have four terminals instead of the three that might be expected. This is because many electricians use the loop-in system (*Figure* 5.3), which uses a little more wire but involves less labour than the alternative.

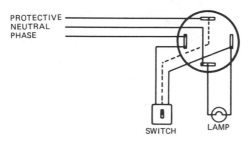

Figure 5.3. The loop-in system for ceiling rose wiring

The loop-in system has the advantage of not requiring a joint box as was necessary with older systems (see *Figure* 5.3). If, however, there is some good reason for using the joint box, care should be taken to ensure that no bare conductors are exposed. The conductors must 'fill' the terminals, which may require the conductors to be doubled back on themselves and that the terminal screws are tight (*Figure* 5.4).

Connection of fixed appliances

Most fixed appliances, with sheathed cable systems, are connected via a fused spur to the ring.

Other appliances such as fluorescent lamp fittings and towel rails are generally provided with bases of such a type that either they will fit directly on to the standard galvanised steel conduit termination box, or else they fit on to the wall or ceiling in such a way that they form a complete enclosure over the properly

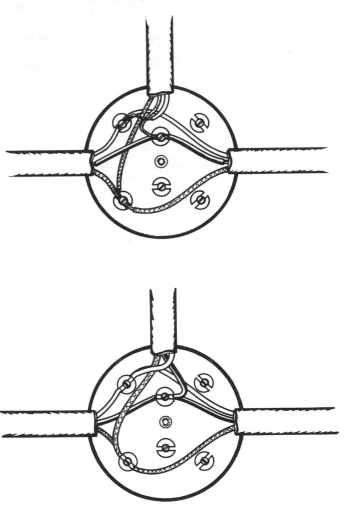

Figure 5.4.   (a) Joint box showing poor workmanship – excessive insulation removed, and sleeving omitted from protective conductor; (b) correct termination with green/yellow sleeve over protective conductor

bushed end of the conduit, or of the protected end of the sheathed cable, *and* at the same time are provided with proper means for securing the protective conductor connections. Fixed floor standing heaters are wired to a connection unit via flexible heat resisting cable.

On ring circuits, the number of fused spurs is unlimited, but the number of unfused spurs must not exceed the total number of socket-outlets and items of stationary equipment connected directly in the circuit. Both types of spur are connected to the ring via connection units or into the backs of socket outlets. The fused connection unit is available in flush or surface type, and can be mounted in standard conduit boxes.

Special fittings

Clock connectors
For clocks, where the current consumption is very small indeed, special fused clock connectors should be used. These moulded plastic accessories are neat and small, and are often connected into a convenient lighting circuit. A 2 A fuse is incorporated.

Outlets for fixed storage heaters
As socket-outlets are not permitted on off-peak circuits for storage heaters a switch unit with a flex outlet is used, and may be obtained with a flush or surface mounting.

A special problem may arise in connection with those storage heaters that are fitted with fans to boost the heat output when needed. Since the boost is needed at on-peak times as well as during off-peak hours these fans must obviously operate from a normal, or on-peak circuit. Special fittings are available, whereby the heater and fan can be connected to a single unit, designed to allow two circuits to be used, each isolated from each other (*Figure* 5.5). This type of fitting is not now required when White Meter 8 and Economy 7 tariffs are used.

But for installations that are fed on the 3-phase system, it is necessary to ensure that two different phase connections are not brought near to each other in the same room. This would mean that a voltage above low voltage could exist, and the possibility of a fatal shock would be increased.

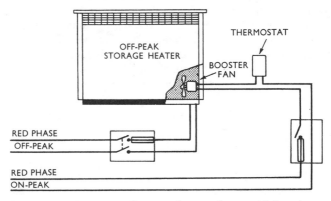

Figure 5.5. Connection diagram of storage heater with fan, showing the need to connect both the storage heater circuit and the fan circuit to the same phase, although not to the same consumer unit. The two switches should be mechanically interlinked, so that the heater is completely isolated in one operation

This requirement means that when the off-peak storage heating is installed the electrical layout of the installation as a whole must be considered. It may not be found very difficult to rearrange the main circuits at the consumer unit so that, for example, the two storage heaters that are situated on the ground floor are both fed from the red phase off-peak circuit, while the ground floor ring for on-peak socket-outlets is also fed from the red phase. On the first floor, the blue phase may be used both for the first floor ring and for the off-peak storage heaters.

Floor-mounted socket-outlets
Many manufacturers provide a special type of floor socket-outlet, fitted with a strong cover that may be screwed into place

when the plug is not in use, so that no dust or moisture can find its way into the fitting, and furniture can be confidently allowed to stand on it. Such a special fitting should always be used when the circumstances make it necessary.

Outdoor fittings

To prevent ingress of rain, and condensation inside, specially designed weatherproof switches, socket-outlets, lampholders and all other fittings should always be used outdoors.

Galvanised steel conduit boxes should be used, even if conduit is not being employed, since sheathed cable can be brought into these boxes, in a watertight fashion, by means of the special glands supplied by the manufacturers. If there is any doubt about watertightness, most cable manufacturers supply a type of plastic compound that remains flexible indefinitely to plug the intake ends of the cable coming into outdoor-mounted fittings.

Switches should be weatherproof, mounted in metal boxes. Great care must be taken in bringing in either conduit or sheathed cable (with glands) to see (1) that earthing continuity is carefully preserved, and (2) that no moisture can enter, whatever the direction of the rain.

Bathroom switches

It is contrary to the Regulations that there should be any portable electrical appliance or socket-outlet (except shaver sockets to BS 3052) or switch other than that of the ceiling type in a bathroom, and all electrical fittings must be of the all-insulated type: that is, the outer body must contain no metal parts at all. All lampholders used in bathrooms must be of the all-insulated type, and must be fitted with a protective skirt, as illustrated in *Figure* 5.6.

The two most commonly used special fittings for bathrooms are the shaver socket and the ceiling switch.

Shaver sockets

To ensure that no user of an electric shaver could receive a shock while shaving in wet conditions, specially designed shaver sockets must be used in bathrooms.

Shaver sockets use a small transformer, the secondary side of which – the side that supplies the shaver itself – is entirely isolated from earth, so that no one touching any part of this circuit could receive an electric shock, as there would be no return path to earth.

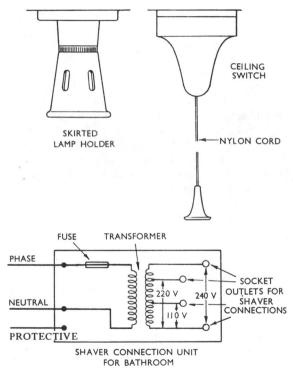

Figure 5.6. Bathroom fittings. Comprising special shaver socket, lampholder with skirt, and ceiling switch

Only shaver sockets which comply with British Standard 3052 (which lays down the standard of insulation between the primary and secondary windings of the isolation transformer, and specifies other safety precautions) may be used in bathrooms, and they must be properly earthed; however, shaver sockets without a transformer may be used in any other room.

Ceiling switches

For bathrooms one way of complying with the Regulations is to place the lighting switches outside the room altogether, and this practice is often adopted. A single light may be switched in this way, and another light, say over a mirror, may well be switched by means of a ceiling switch. This type of switch is mounted on the ceiling and operated by means of a pull cord, usually of nylon. Some such switches have an indicator light, so they may be found in the dark.

Apparatus installed in flammable atmospheres

If electrical apparatus is to be brought anywhere near an area where petrol, paraffin, butane gas, or any flammable substance is used, or where the vapour that rises from such substances may persist, then various regulations made by local authorities must be obeyed, and these regulations, added to the *Regulations for Electrical Installations*, impose a very high standard of practice in such situations.

To start with, specially designed flameproof gear must be used. It is rigidly tested to ensure not only that sparks cannot escape and cause explosions, but in addition it is so arranged that if flammable gases are trapped inside the conduits or boxes, and an internal explosion occurs, the metal parts will resist it and will not cause bare electrical wires to be exposed.

The beginner is advised not to contemplate the installation of flameproof gear unless he has professional advice available, and in addition he must be sure that he has studied – and complied with – the stringent regulations that apply.

Bell transformers

We shall see later that all extra low voltage circuits, television and sound radio, aerials, loudspeaker connections, and telephone wiring – must be kept quite separate from power wiring, and must not be run in the same conduit or trunking.

There is however one point where the extra low voltage and standard systems meet. Electrical bells and chimes are often supplied at 12 V by means of small transformers, fed from the mains.

Such transformers are usually supplied by fused spur connections from a convenient lighting circuit, and may be fused at 2 A. Some bell transformers have their own fuses inside the case. Care must be taken to ensure that the low-voltage circuit wires cannot possibly come into contact with the 240 V mains circuit unless the bell circuit is insulated for the higher voltage. Auto-transformers (mentioned under 'Transformers', p. 827) must not be employed.

Double-pole switches

We have seen earlier that with the phase and neutral supply system the switches used (other than the main switches) should be of the single-pole type – that is, they break the phase conductor only, and not the neutral.

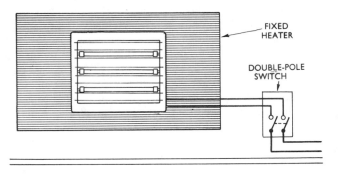

Figure 5.7. Double-pole switch used for heating appliances where element could possibly be touched

But there are some exceptions to this rule. In the case of immersion heaters the Regulations lay down that double-pole switches shall be used; and for any *fixed* heating appliance *where the heating elements could possibly be touched*, both conductors feeding the appliance must be interrupted by a switch placed near the appliance (see *Figure* 5.7). (This would apply for example, to a glowing-bar type radiator permanently installed on a wall, which must have a wire screen to prevent a coat or dress blowing up against it, but where the elements could be touched by inquiring childish fingers when the fire appears to be safe as it is not glowing.)

Double-pole switches are available from all manufacturers for these special applications, and will mostly fit into the same boxes (or occupy the same space as surface units) as their single-pole counterparts.

6 Extensions to Old Installations and Temporary Wiring

Extensions to old installations

Extensions to old installations are a frequent requirement.

The electricity board reserves the right to be notified of any proposed addition to an existing installation, for a number of reasons. First, they must be satisfied that their service cable and meter will not become overloaded. Secondly, they must ensure that any additional connections do not disturb the service to other consumers. (For example, a heavy load, suddenly imposed or removed on a single-phase supply at the end of a long main cable, might cause severe flicker on the lighting systems of all the nearby consumers. Finally, they must test the extension, to ensure that it is safe in every way.)

Extending or repairing old installations may offer many more traps than new work, and the first thing to check is the condition of the existing wiring.

In a later section on testing we shall discuss this matter more fully, but it may be mentioned here that the first test is to see that the consumer unit is not already overloaded, according to the principles set out in an earlier chapter about the loading of the various circuits; and then the insulation of the existing wiring and its earthing condition must be checked carefully.

Too often, in old houses, the wiring (perhaps 30 or 40 years old, and carried out in rubber-insulated wire) has severely deteriorated. The rubber insulation has become brittle and broken in places, and where overheating has occurred (especially at such places as ceiling roses where larger and larger lamps have continually been employed, over the years), the insulation may be in a very poor condition. This may not always be fully revealed with the 'Megger' test for insulation (see chapter on

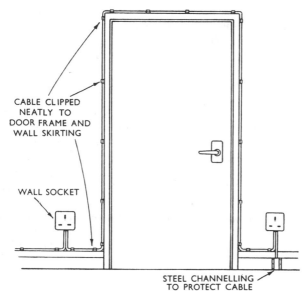

CABLE CLIPPED NEATLY TO DOOR FRAME AND WALL SKIRTING

WALL SOCKET

STEEL CHANNELLING TO PROTECT CABLE

Figure 6.1. Neat arrangement of surface wiring around the doorway and along skirting board, with protection where the wire enters the floor. Bends must conform to Table 6.1 (see IEE Table 52C)

testing), but such a test should be accompanied by a visual inspection of the wiring in a typical fitting. In such cases, no extensions should be added to such wiring.

Extensions to existing wiring, where they may be safely carried out, may conveniently be made in sheathed wiring, often run on the surface to avoid disturbance to decorations.

This surface wiring is a legitimate method, providing great care is taken to see that the cables are either protected from damage by means of a suitable metal cover, or else run in such a way that they can be clearly seen. A very neat job, with PVC sheathed cable, can be carried out by running the cable along the top of a skirting board, and round a door frame, as shown in *Figure* 6.1. If the cable is subsequently painted to match the woodwork it will scarcely be noticed by the casual eye, yet it is sufficiently obvious to avoid the danger that someone will knock nails right through it.

A point where special care is necessary is where sheathed cable enters a floor. Here it is especially vulnerable. Half round or oval metal channelling should always be fitted at this point, to prevent accidental damage.

Surface-type fittings are usually employed in such work. These fittings have knockouts all round the box, and care must be taken (1) to knock out only the minimum area needed to accommodate the cable, (2) to see that all unused knockouts are left in position, to prevent the intrusion of dust, and (3) that the wires, as made off, are not pinched when the box is screwed to the wall.

When in doubt about the state of an old installation (and tracing wiring runs may be very difficult in old buildings) it is better to run the new circuits straight back to the consumer unit, and then to ask the electricity board to connect them up.

Conversion to ring circuit

It is often possible to convert an old wiring system which is still in good order into a ring system, but of course this can only be done if the size of conductor originally used is sufficient to satisfy the Regulations: i.e. it must not be less than $2.5\,\text{mm}^2$.

For example, suppose a house has a $2.5\,\text{mm}^2$ (or the original 7/.029) feed straight from the consumer unit to a 15 A socket-outlet in the sitting room, and another similar feed to another 15 A socket in the dining room (*Figure* 6.2). If these two feeds can be clearly traced at the consumer unit, they can be taken as the two ends of a ring, and brought into one 30 A fuse at the consumer unit.

EXTENSIONS TO OLD INSTALLATIONS

Table 6.1 Minimum internal radii of bends in cables for fixed wiring

Insulation	Finish	Overall diameter for flat twin cable across the widest part	Factor to be applied to overall diameter of cable to determine minimum internal radius of bend
		not exceeding 10 mm	3
PVC or rubber	non-armoured	exceeding 10 mm but not exceeding 25 mm	4
		exceeding 25 mm	6

Abridged from the *Regulations for Electrical Installations, Table* 52C.

Example: If a 1.5 mm^2 twin sheathed PVC cable with a major diameter of 8 mm were used then:

minimum *internal* radius bend = 8 × 3 = 24 mm.

At the remote ends, surface wiring can be taken from the socket-outlet in one room, all round that room, to feed as many 13 A socket-outlets as desired, and then through the dividing wall into the other room, to feed further socket-outlets in that room, terminating at the second original 15 A socket-outlet position.

A problem often facing those called on to extend old installations is the need to provide an earth connection, when the original installation employed only two-pin socket-outlets, with no earth. In this case, there is no alternative, when installing the 13 A socket-outlets that must be used, to running an earth connection (protective conductor) right back to the earthing point at the consumer's terminal. The size of this conductor must be as laid down in the Regulations, but it must not be smaller than 1.5 mm^2. The temptation to provide a local earth, near to the socket-outlet concerned, by making a connection to any nearby water pipe must be resisted, since the installation must never have more than one earthing point. If protective conductors are added they must be insulated conductors, coloured

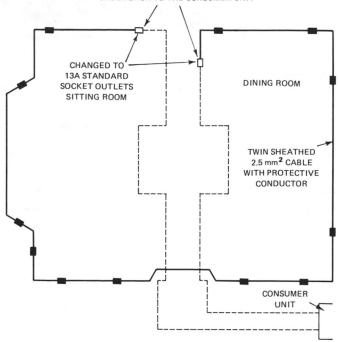

ORIGINAL 3 PIN 15A SOCKET OUTLETS
EACH WIRED WITH 7/.029
(EQUIVALENT TO 2.5 mm² APPROX.)
CABLE BACK TO THE CONSUMER UNIT

CHANGED TO
13A STANDARD
SOCKET OUTLETS
SITTING ROOM

DINING ROOM

TWIN SHEATHED
2.5 mm² CABLE
WITH PROTECTIVE
CONDUCTOR

CONSUMER
UNIT

Figure 6.2. Conversion of old wiring to ring circuit by using the existing feeds to socket-outlets.
Note: the existing wiring must be at least 2.5 mm² in size (or the old equivalent of 7/.029), and it is assumed that the original socket-outlets are correctly earthed with conductor of 1.5 mm² minimum

green and yellow, and be properly clipped and protected throughout.

The tests that must be made before commencing any work on an old installation (see chapter on testing) may show that the wiring is faulty.

In rectifying a fault on the wiring it may be permissible to restore the faulty wiring to its original condition, with good workmanship and good materials.

794

EXTENSIONS TO OLD INSTALLATIONS

If non-standard wiring connections are found in an installation which is supplied on the standard 240 V a.c. phase and neutral system (e.g. fuseboards using fuses for live *and* neutral feeds), then one is well advised not to restore the faulty non-standard wiring, but to put in standard connections (single-pole fusing, and proper earthing) on a new circuit installed in place of the old. Do not perpetuate incorrect wiring, which is basically unsafe and could give rise to serious troubles, including electrocution incidents.

An example of this aspect of obsolete installation problems was recently mentioned to the author by a contractor. His men went to the house of an elderly widow, who had written to him to say that the electric fire in her bathroom would not work. They found an antique, unguarded bare-element 2 kW fire, plugged into a two-pin socket-outlet in the bathroom, obviously with no earth connection. Behind the socket, the rubber insulation on the wiring, installed in wooden troughing, had become so brittle that it had broken away, leaving the live wires bare. Some vibration had made them touch, and the fuse had blown. A nephew of the old lady had replaced the fuse with a much thicker wire, and this had also blown, burning his hand, so he left it alone.

The lady was most indignant when the contractor called on her and said that it would be impossible to effect a simple repair, and the socket-outlet should never have been fixed in the bathroom.

He was, of course, absolutely right in refusing to perpetuate a dangerous situation: but he learned later that a 'handyman' had 'done the job' for £5, and had simply taped up the insulation for a few inches, where the wire was accessible behind the old two-pin socket-outlet, and replaced the fuse. If the old lady had been electrocuted, he would have had much to answer for.

The contractor advised the electricity board that an unsafe installation existed, and they managed to convince the lady that rewiring was necessary.

Warning points to users of electrical installations
The users of an installation should be warned especially about the following points.

It is very unwise to use adapters if it is at all possible to avoid them. They tend to give rise to radio and television interference troubles through loose contacts, and they may well become overloaded, and in consequence overheated, and possibly

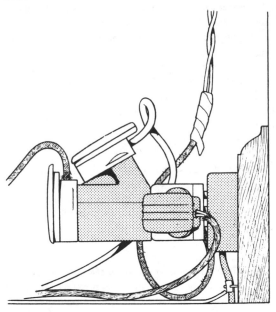

Figure 6.3. This arrangement is to be avoided. This illustrates a mass of adapters, which generally give rise to overheating, interference on radio and television, and the possibility of danger through tripping over flexible wires

dangerous (see *Figure* 6.3). They give rise to long lengths of flex, which may cause people to trip.

Never extend a flexible lead by simply joining extra flex on to the end and making a taped joint. This can easily pull out and give rise to live wires lying on the carpet for children to touch; and the joint, simply being twisted, is never satisfactory and may itself overheat.

Avoid loose flex wherever possible since it is liable to trip people up or to break or fray when stepped on, and it should never be run under carpets or linoleum, since any damage will not be seen.

Never run an extension by stapling flex on to a skirting board. Flex is not suitable for this type of installation as it has no protection against mechanical damage.

Temporary wiring

Before setting up a temporary installation, it is advisable to study the relevant section of the *Regulations for Electrical Installation*. In these Regulations, 'temporary' is defined as referring to wiring not expected to be in use for more than three months.

Briefly, some of the more important points to be observed include the requirement that all temporary installations shall be dismantled as soon as they are no longer required, and in any case shall be completely overhauled at three-monthly intervals.

Every temporary installation must be provided with protection against excess current (normally by means of fuses) and with a switch or other device that disconnects *all phases or poles of the supply* (*Figure* 6.4). Equipment that has been used on temporary installations, particularly those for outdoor use, should be thoroughly checked before being used again; corrosion may have rendered some items unsafe.

Except in private houses, temporary electrical installations must be in charge of a competent person, whose name and address must be clearly shown, close to the main switch.

Apart from these special points, all temporary installations must be properly tested and must have the correct values of insulation resistance, earth continuity, and correctness of polarity (that is, the switches must be in the phase wire and not in the neutral, and socket-outlets must be connected the right way round) exactly as these requirements apply to permanent installations.

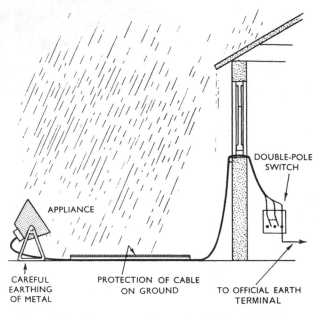

Figure 6.4. Temporary wiring needs double-pole isolation

For the purposes for which most temporary installations are required, PVC sheathed and insulated cable is usually suitable, but care must always be taken to ensure that temporary wiring is not inadvertently moved by other people so that, for example, wires lie in contact with a hot-steam pipe, or encounter similar hazards.

Temporary outdoor wiring
Outdoor wiring for such purposes as floodlighting must be carried out with special care, since driving rain may well penetrate any of the fittings, and give rise to danger of shock or short circuits and blown fuses.

Extreme care in earthing every metal part of every floodlight or switch is essential. Nothing should be taken for granted – a check should be made with a testing instrument (see chapter on testing) to make certain all metal parts are properly earthed. Temporary earth connections to nearby pipes or other ironwork must not be used. The protective conductor must be continuous back to the earth point of the installation from which the supply is taken.

The switches used on temporary outdoor installations (as well as themselves being earthed) must be of the double-pole type. When assembling the cables, the entry holes in the switches and other appliances (such as the floodlamps themselves, or fuse-boards) should either be provided with weatherproof glands, or else carefully filled with the proper type of semi-plastic compound supplied by fittings manufacturers for this purpose, to prevent the entry of moisture.

Where temporary outdoor cabling runs on the ground, it should be protected against damage by being covered with planking or some similar form of protection. Otherwise persons treading on the cable may drive sharp chippings through the insulation. It is usually better to suspend the cable overhead, if at all possible.

Stage lighting

A special case of temporary lighting often encountered relates to wiring for theatrical purposes in public halls.

If the supply is to be taken from 13 A socket-outlets (one of which is adequate for 3 kW of lighting – thirty 100 W lamps), care must be taken that double-pole isolating switches are provided for the circuits connected to each separate socket-outlet.

Dimmers

Dimming of stage lighting is often required. Dimmers using variable resistances are available, and must be of the rating needed for each circuit, otherwise they will be overloaded and could become dangerously hot. The easiest method of providing

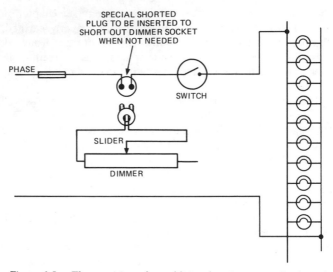

Figure 6.5. The provision of an additional socket, normally shorted out by a shorted plug top, so that a dimmer can be inserted when required, as in a village hall wiring system where stage lighting is occasionally needed

for dimmers is to install an additional two-pin socket-outlet in series with the phase wire and arrange for it to be controlled by a switch. The circuit is shown in *Figure* 6.5.

Floodlight and spotlight connections
When supplying floodlights and powerful spotlights, the proper method is to terminate the main wiring 2 m or more away from the floodlamp and then to feed the lamp, via the socket-outlet, with special heat-resistant cable.

7 Testing Electrical Installations

Testing electrical installations can be considered from three aspects: first there is the preliminary internal testing that must be carried out when an installation (or an addition to an installation) is completed, and before it is made alive; secondly, there are the official tests that are carried out by the electricity board before the installation is connected to the mains; and finally there is the testing necessary to find faults, or to ascertain the condition of an old installation.

Equipment needed
The basic instruments needed for testing and checking are illustrated in *Figure* 7.1. They comprise:

(1) A universal test meter.
(2) A bell and battery set for tracing wires.
(3) A 'Megger', combined with a protective conductor continuity tester.

The universal test meter
The universal test meter is a device whereby a single scale can read volts, amperes and ohms, by adjusting the knob with appropriate markings. An instrument of this kind can be invaluable for locating faults. It must be capable of reading up to 500 V a.c. or d.c., and the resistance range should be capable of reading down to less than one ohm.

The resistance range on such meters is operated by means of a small dry battery, inserted into the instrument in a similar fashion to that employed in portable transistorised radio receivers. To allow for variations in battery voltage, an adjusting knob is provided. When the two leads from the instrument are clipped together, obviously the resistance between them is practically

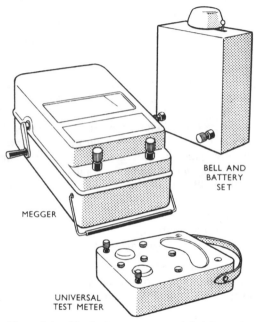

BELL AND
BATTERY
SET

MEGGER

UNIVERSAL
TEST METER

Figure 7.1.   The basic instruments needed for testing and checking: the universal test meter, the bell and battery set, and the 'Megger'

zero, and the adjusting knob is moved until the needle reads zero. This adjustment should be carried out before every set of resistance tests is undertaken.

The bell and battery set
For rapid checking of circuit connections, a bell and battery set is extremely useful. Two torch batteries are connected to a bell,

and the assembly is connected to two probes or clip leads, so that when the leads are joined together the circuit will be completed and the bell will ring. A long lead will enable circuits in all parts of a domestic installation to be checked out rapidly, or 'rung out'.

It must be remembered that a 'ringing out' test does not prove that the circuits are properly insulated, either between conductors or to earth, but only that there is a continuous conductor path from one point to another.

The 'Megger' test meter

The 'Megger' is a patented instrument which takes the form of a hand-driven generator that provides a voltage of 500 V at the terminals. It is used for measuring the insulation resistance of the installation.

The 'universal' type of instrument, mentioned earlier, is entirely unsuitable for insulation testing, except for rough preliminary checks. Such an instrument relies on a 1.5 V battery, and one can imagine many parts of an electrical installation where bad workmanship or defective fittings or appliances have resulted in two bare wires, phase and neutral, being wrongly situated, and so lying within a hair's breadth of each other. This gap will still show perfect insulation between them if a testing instrument using only 1.5 V is applied, and the result will be misleading and a dangerous situation on the installation may not be revealed. But the 500 V output of the 'Megger' will break down such a gap, and the fault will be revealed.

The 'Megger' has a scale that reads in thousands of ohms or in megohms (millions of ohms), and it is so arranged that once the turning of the handle has reached a certain speed, no increase in speed will affect the reading.

Some types of 'Megger' have a second instrument incorporated in the same case. This instrument measures the impedance of the earth loop at any point in the installation.

With alternating current, as mentioned earlier, there are factors other than pure resistance that affect the amount of current flowing through a circuit. Where coils are concerned, the electromagnetic effect may mean that there is greater opposition to the passage of the current than that due to resistance. The resulting combined opposition to the passage of current is called impedance, a term applicable to a.c. circuits only.

The impedance of the earth loop – that is, of all the conductors used to carry earth current from any one point on the installation to the general mass of earth – includes the resistance of the protective conductors in the installation, the resistance of the earth electrode or other earth connection to the general mass of earth, and the electromagnetic effects (which may arise in any part of this circuit) mentioned earlier.

In the section on earthing, in Chapter 3, we have seen that this earth loop impedance must not be greater than a certain value which depends on the type of protection provided. To check that it is below this impedance, a suitable instrument (which may be incorporated with the insulation-testing 'Megger') must be used.

Preliminary testing

These tests are *not* intended to be the 'official tests' of the installation, and are only intended as a guide to the condition of the wiring.

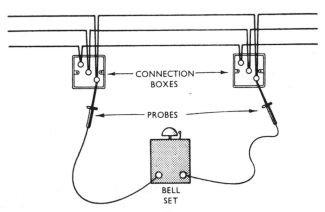

Figure 7.2.   Continuity test using bell set

All preliminary testing is carried out before the main fuses have been inserted.

Continuity test

The first test is a simple continuity test to ensure that all connections have been properly made. The bell set (*Figure* 7.2) can be used for this, and also to check the proper connection of the switches, thermostats, time switches and other devices, to ensure that they are all on the phase side of the circuit. This can be tested by checking continuity from the neutral connection of the circuit being tested, at the consumer unit right through the thermostat, switch, or other interrupting device, making sure that the switch breaks the phase wire and not the neutral wire.

Polarity test

Next there is the question of polarity – socket-outlets having their connections made the right way round. On the ordinary 13 A fused plug socket-outlet, looking at the face of the socket-outlet, the phase connection must be on the right, the neutral on the left and the earth at the top. A simple continuity check from each socket back to the phase fuse will ensure that this is correct (see *Figure* 7.3).

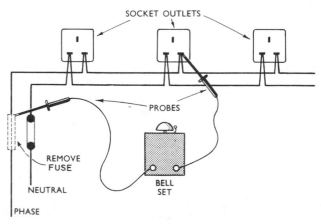

Figure 7.3. Polarity test with bell set

Protective conductor test

The next step is to check protective conductor continuity. For this purpose, an *approximate* check that no gross errors have occurred can be made by means of the universal testing instrument, arranged on its ohm-reading scale.

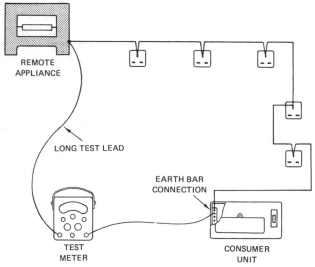

REMOTE
APPLIANCE

LONG TEST LEAD

EARTH BAR
CONNECTION

TEST
METER

CONSUMER
UNIT

Figure 7.4. Preliminary test of protective conductor resistance

It will be recalled from the section on earthing, that all exposed metal that can possibly become connected to a live circuit must be effectively earthed, in such a way that the resistance of the protective conductor is of low enough value, to carry fault currents without danger. As a guide, the resistance of the protective conductor should not be greater than $0.5\,\Omega$, or $1\,\Omega$ if the conductor is copper.

With one lead of the testing instrument on the earth point, and the other arranged as a probe that can be attached to all parts of the fixed appliances, or the portable equipment plugged into the socket-outlets, the protective conductor resistance can be checked with the universal instrument (*Figure* 7.4).

However, this cannot be taken as the full, official test. The reason for this again hinges on the fact that the universal instrument only has a 1.5 V battery. Suppose a connection was badly made, so that the wires were simply touching each other, very lightly. This would mean that a 1.5 V battery would show a good connection, but if a heavy current should pass through this circuit, the connection would obviously not be good enough: arcing and ultimate melting of the surfaces in contact would occur, with consequent fire danger.

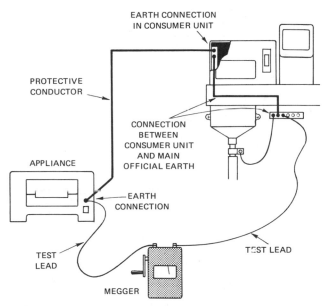

Figure 7.5. 'Megger' test on protective conductor continuity

In fact, the Regulations specify that when testing the protective conductor, alternating current of a magnitude approaching one and a half times the rating of the circuit under test shall be used, with a maximum of 25 A. As mentioned above, only a properly designed instrument can provide a test current of an appropriate value to make sure that the slightest defects in the protective conductor system are observed and can be detected (see *Figure* 7.5).

Insulation test

This test ensures that the insulation throughout the whole installation has not been damaged in any way, and for low voltage circuits, that is up to 1000 V a.c., the test has to be carried out, according to the Regulations, with a direct current voltage not less than twice that which will be normally applied to the installation, although it need not exceed 500 V, for installations rated up to 500 V.

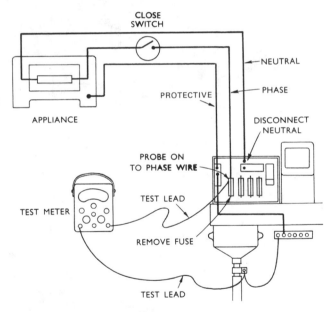

Figure 7.6.   Insulation to earth test circuit

The figure of 500 V is that which is usually used, with the aid of the 'Megger'.

Again, the universal type of instrument would not be suitable, even using its resistance scale. If, for example, the wire running through a conduit had been strained over a sharp edge incorrectly left at the end of a tube, the bare conductor might be within a tenth of a millimetre of the earthed metal, and yet the 1.5 V output of the instrument would not break down this gap and reveal the defect.

The insulation resistance is measured on each circuit by closing all switches on all appliances in circuit, and with the neutral connection disconnected (*Figure* 7.6). Under these conditions the circuit will be complete throughout the phase wire, the switch, the appliance, and the neutral wire back to the consumer unit.

The universal tester again may be used to provide a rough check. One lead should be clipped to the official earth point (or for a rough preliminary test) to a water pipe or other convenient earth, and the other lead to the phase wire. The reading on the ohm scale of the instrument should be of the order of 1 or 2 MΩ. This test is only suitable for finding major errors, such as the live wire firmly touching the protective conductor connection in a fitting or connection box.

But it must be emphasised that the only conclusive and official test is that carried out with the 500 V 'Megger'.

The bare minimum insulation resistance acceptable under the regulations is 1 MΩ, applying to the complete installation. This means that when all the phase wires at the consumer unit are connected together and to the testing instrument, all switches closed, all appliances inserted in the circuit, all neutral wires being left disconnected, and the other end of the 'Megger' is connected to earth, then there is a minimum of 1 MΩ between the whole of the installation taken together, and earth. A higher value should always be aimed at, and a good installation might well have an insulation resistance of well over 5 MΩ.

A second insulation test should be carried out between conductors (see *Figure* 7.7); for the purpose of this test all lamps and appliances are removed, or isolated by opening their local switch, and the test instruments' leads connected to the phase conductor and the neutral conductor, the minimum reading being 1 MΩ.

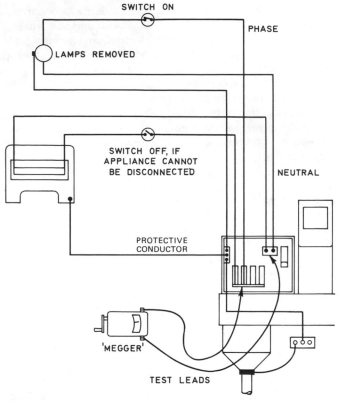

Figure 7.7. Insulation test between conductors

If for the purpose of either of the above tests, equipment is removed, then it should be tested in a similar manner separately, and in this case a minimum reading of ½ MΩ is permissible.

Official testing

The electricity board will test the installation for insulation resistance, for protective conductor continuity, for earth loop impedance back to the earthed neutral on the supply transformer, for correct connection of the final earthing point, and for adequate fusing. They will also check the quality of the wiring, and if an earth leakage circuit-breaker has been installed they will check the operation of this device, and the earth resistance of the electrode used.

They are not concerned with the internal connections of the installation itself and it is not their duty to see that the proper lamps light when the switch is closed, or that appliances such as water heaters and the like, installed by the electrician, operate correctly. They are, however, concerned with the safety aspect of ensuring that all socket-outlets are connected up the right way round, and this point will therefore be checked by the electricity board's engineers.

They will also check that there are no socket-outlets in bathrooms, and that other safety measures have been observed.

If off-peak storage heating circuits are installed, a check will be made to ensure that these circuits are all terminated directly on the storage heaters, and that no other socket-outlets or other connections exist on these circuits.

Tracing faults

Suppose now that the preliminary tests have revealed a fault on the system.

With the aid of a bell set, and a universal meter, the fault can be traced quite easily by splitting the installation up into sections.

Insulation fault
Let us suppose that the fault is an insulation fault – that means that the whole installation shows that the phase wire is in effect connected to earth, and therefore does not have the required insulation resistance of at least $1\,M\Omega$ with respect to earth.

The circuits comprising the installation can easily be separated out at the consumer unit. Taking one circuit at a time (the fuses, of course, still remaining withdrawn), disconnect the neutral wires and thus both ends of the circuit are clear of any other connection. Then, with all the switches closed and appliances connected, check each circuit under these conditions, until one (or more) is found on which there is a fault (see *Figure* 7.8).

Concentrating on this circuit (all others being healthy) first the appliances may be disconnected, one by one, until a possible

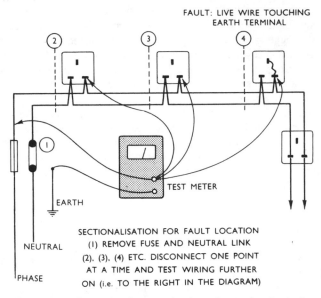

Figure 7.8. Principle of sectionalisation when testing for faults

faulty appliance shows up. If no appliance is faulty then proceed as follows:

Assume for the moment that there is only one fault in the circuit. Go to the first disconnection point on this circuit (which might be a joint box on the sheathed cable run), and disconnect both wires.

Return to the consumer unit and once again check both the phase and neutral wires for insulation to earth. Suppose that they are both 'good', the fault has thus been removed by this disconnection. It is obviously beyond the point of disconnection.

Transfer the testing instrument to the first joint box, which has already been opened, and proceed further to the next joint box or switch, the next break point on the circuit, and disconnect the wires in this second joint box.

Test again. If the fault is cleared, proceed further down the circuit. If it is not cleared, then obviously it lies in the section between the testing point (at this first disconnection point) and the further point at which the circuit has been broken.

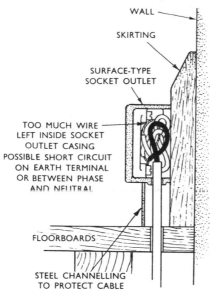

WALL

SKIRTING

SURFACE-TYPE
SOCKET OUTLET

TOO MUCH WIRE
LEFT INSIDE SOCKET
OUTLET CASING
POSSIBLE SHORT CIRCUIT
ON EARTH TERMINAL
OR BETWEEN PHASE
AND NEUTRAL

FLOORBOARDS

STEEL CHANNELLING
TO PROTECT CABLE

Figure 7.9. Common causes of faults on electrical systems

Suppose the fault *is* cleared, then proceed further and go beyond the switch (or second connection point) which may perhaps bring you to some fittings or socket-outlets. These must be methodically disconnected, one by one, testing after each disconnection, until the faulty unit is isolated. It must then be inspected to find where the fault lies.

One of the most common causes of faults in domestic installations is that the wiring behind a socket-outlet or a switch has been incorrectly made off, so that either too much bare conductor exists, and is touching the earthed metal or the neutral wire, or, on the other hand, the switch or other fitting may be incorrectly assembled, possibly so that two wires are incorrectly inserted into one terminal (see *Figure* 7.9).

Suppose the fault has been found to be in a run of cable. If the installation is carried out in conduit, it will not be very difficult to pull out the cable in that section and inspect it, and the fault will probably soon be found. It may well be due to the insulation being damaged as the cable was drawn into the conduit.

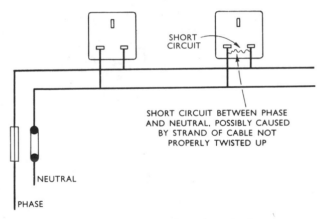

SHORT CIRCUIT

SHORT CIRCUIT BETWEEN PHASE
AND NEUTRAL, POSSIBLY CAUSED
BY STRAND OF CABLE NOT
PROPERLY TWISTED UP

NEUTRAL

PHASE

Figure 7.10.   Testing for a short circuit

If the installation is carried out in sheathed wiring embedded in plaster, then it will be necessary to break out the section containing the fault and replace with with new wire. It is unwise to attempt to locate the fault and to patch it up. New cable must be used.

Up to now it has been assumed that the fault is one of bad insulation. There are, however, two other kinds of faults.

Short circuit

First, there is a short circuit (*Figure* 7.10). Both the neutral and the phase wires may remain well insulated from earth, but are short-circuited to each other.

In the majority of cases this is due to incorrect connections in fuses, switches or fittings. It is unlikely that the wires within a conduit, or inside the sheath on a sheathed cable, have come into contact with each other without at the same time going down to earth, although this type of fault could not necessarily always be ruled out. A short circuit could occur if severe mechanical damage has occurred to sheathed cable, perhaps under a floor, where for example, a workman from another trade, such as a plumber fitting water pipes, or a gas fitter, has inadvertently severely manhandled the cable.

The short circuit can be isolated by the same methodical sectionalising test methods as those outlined above.

Open circuit

Another type of fault is the open circuit (*Figure* 7.11). Here again, in this case where there is no circuit between two points,

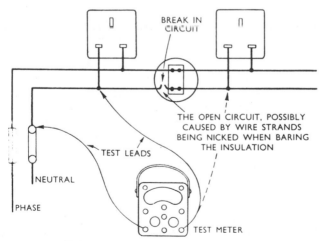

Figure 7.11.   Testing for an open circuit

the fault is most likely to lie in a switch or other fitting. There have been cases where open circuits have arisen when fittings have been incorrectly made off, and the electrician, roughly baring the ends of the wire, has nicked through all the strands, and then when the tension comes on the 'tail' which has been inserted into a switch or socket-outlet or some other fitting as the unit is screwed together, the weakened wires break away, leaving an open circuit.

Cables that have been badly kinked before installation could give rise to open circuits, as the kinking may have broken the copper conductors.

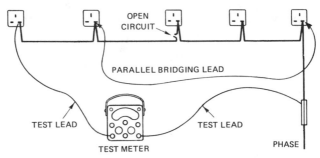

Figure 7.12.   Locating an open circuit by paralleling sections of the wiring with a long test lead

The open circuit may not be so easy to find, under certain circumstances, as the other types of fault, but with the aid of a long test lead, it is not difficult to parallel each installed wire by an external lead across the gap between, say, two junction boxes, or the consumer unit and a fitting, and if a complete circuit is obtained in this way, shorten the test lead until the section or fitting in which there is an open circuit (see *Figure* 7.12) is found.

Typical faults in installations

Incorrect system of fusing
Where the normal supplies of phase and neutral are concerned, double-pole fusing has frequently been found. This is most often found in a final circuit where there is a circuit distribution board.

Proximity of different phases

Small business installations are frequently fed by a 3-phase system, in which a voltage of 415 V exists between wires connected to different phases. In general all the conductors in one room should be connected to the same phase. There is an exception that allows points between which a voltage exceeding 240 V is present to exist in the same room if they are 2 m or more

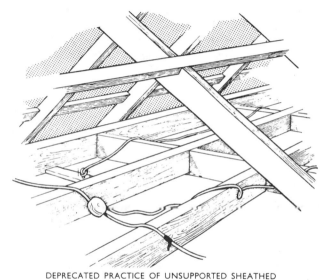

DEPRECATED PRACTICE OF UNSUPPORTED SHEATHED
WIRING IN LOFT, WITH JUNCTION BOX UNFIXED

Figure 7.13. Bad wiring in lofts and cellars is sometimes found, with the wiring unsupported, the junction boxes unsecured, and the cable unprotected

apart, but as mentioned earlier where storage heaters are installed (in which a fan is used to assist in the heat output and to provide a measure of control), very often it has been found that conductors of two different phases are used near together, since the storage heater is supplied independently from one circuit which may be connected to one phase, and the local control circuit for the fan is connected to another, which is not part of the off-peak system, since the fan may be needed to increase the output when the off-peak power is not available.

Insufficient protection for sheathed wiring
It is frequently found that when sheathed wiring is out of sight, it is also out of the electrician's mind, in the sense that he has not provided any protection at all. It is just as important that sheathed wiring should be protected from mechanical damage in such places as lofts and cellars, which are infrequently used, as it is in cases where the wiring is obviously visible (see *Figure* 7.13).

Conduit installation troubles
Insufficient attention is often given to the filing away of sharp edges on the ends of conduit piping, and the lack of the provision of bushes. This means that all cables drawn through this particular piping may well be damaged, and liable to subsequent failure.

Insufficient attention has often been paid to the protection of conduits, ducts, and trunking systems against the entry of water.

Overcrowding of cables in conduits and trunking
No more wires than those laid down in the various Regulations should be accommodated in a given circuit, and if these figures are exceeded there may be trouble due to overheating and possible failure, and in any case the cables will have to be derated (used at a lower current rating than normal).

Incorrect cable for heating appliances
Heat-resistant insulated cable should always be used for connections to immersion heaters, thermal storage heaters and indeed any appliance that gets hot. It has often been found that ordinary PVC insulated cable is employed.

TESTING ELECTRICAL INSTALLATIONS

Omission of any identification at the consumer unit
If the circuits are not identified and the type of fuses that are appropriate for each circuit clearly stated, it will be much more difficult to put right any trouble of any kind that may arise on the installation, now or in the future.

Failure to use flameproof or intrinsically safe equipment
In places where flammable liquids are stored, or where, for example, the gas bottles used for welding, or for domestic gas purposes in conection with caravans and the like are located, properly designed flameproof equipment and wiring are necessary.

Insufficient attention to the bonding of all metalwork to earth
Every piece of metal in any way associated with an electrical appliance should be bonded to earth, and it is often found that this is omitted.

Omission of protective shield or skirt to lampholder of bathroom, in lighting pendant or fittings
All lampholders in bathrooms must be insulated and fitted with a protective skirt.

General note on testing old installations

When rectifying a fault on old wiring, do not start by assuming that the supply is the usual single-phase and neutral 240 V a.c. system. Several other systems are still in use in remote parts of the country.

The first test, therefore, should be to find out the system in use. The nameplate on the meter, plus the information given on any lamp that may be in use, will provide a useful starting point. The meter will show if the system is a.c. or d.c., and the frequency employed, and probably the voltage as well, and in any case the lamp will show the voltage.

But the universal test instrument should be applied to check the voltage from each supply wire, separately, to earth.

It should always be assumed that the system is wired up wrongly: never take it for granted that single-pole fusing (as standard on modern installations) is used or that single-pole switches are placed in the phase conductor, or that the neutral wire is in fact at or near earth potential, or that any earth connection at all does in fact exist.

Test records
Keep a record of all tests, with the date and leave a copy with the installation. It will greatly assist anyone working on the installation at a later date.

Testing an installation after fire or water damage
If a fire has occurred in some part of a house, or if, for example, flooding has taken place, or if a tank in a loft has overflowed, a check should be initiated immediately before any current is used.

The main switches on the consumer unit should be opened at once, and the 'Megger' should be applied to each circuit to make two insulation tests. First, when the fuses are removed, access can be obtained to the phase end of each circuit and the neutral connections can be taken out one by one, and with all appliances disconnected but the switches on the circuits closed, an insulation test can be carried out between phase and neutral on each circuit. Then a similar insulation test is carried out between each conductor and earth.

With plastic wiring, heat may have caused considerable damage to the wiring and major renewal operations will have to be commenced. On the other hand, water damage will not have affected the insulation itself, but may have given rise to pockets of water in socket-outlet boxes, switches and other fittings. This means that each of these must be opened and dried carefully, and for this purpose an ordinary hair dryer fed from some circuit in another part of the house which is in good order, may conveniently be used. It is probable that at least one circuit may have escaped major damage.

8 Miscellaneous Aspects of Installation Practice

Outdoor wiring

Apart from underground wiring connections between buildings (which may be carried out by means of mineral-insulated or PVC/SWA/PVC cable, properly protected by means of bricks or concrete slabs), outdoor wiring should employ a catenary, or suspended system (*Figure* 8.1).

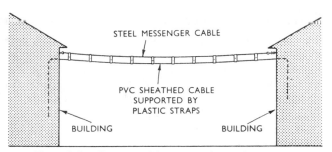

Figure 8.1.   Catenary wiring system for outdoor work

There are two methods of catenary suspension. In one method, a special cable is employed, using a chlorosulphonated polyethylene (CSP) sheathed cable with a built-in steel wire for suspension purposes. In the second method, a separate steel wire is employed, and the special outdoor cable is suspended from it by means of straps made from plastic material in ring or tape form.

It is permissible to span a gap of 3 m between adjacent buildings by means of a span of PVC sheathed and insulated cable, carefully clipped at each end to ensure that its own weight, and possible movement in the wind, will not cause the cable to be damaged at the clips.

Bell, television and telephone wiring

It should be clearly noted that wiring for the purposes of bell circuits, telephone circuits, television and radio circuits does not come within the scope of the *Regulations for Electrical Installations*, except in so far as the Regulations state that this wiring must be kept entirely separate from any wiring connected to circuits which are themselves joined to the mains. This is the first principle to be observed in regard to what we may now call auxiliary circuits.

Bell wiring

Bell wiring calls for little comment. Most bells or chimes are supplied from a bell transformer which must be properly fused with a 1 A fuse on the high voltage side. The first test should ensure that both windings are continuous and the second test should ensure that the insulation between the 240 V side, and the low-voltage side is in good order (see *Figure* 8.2).

Bell-circuit wiring is usually carried out in twin plastic flex, which may well be run in plastic conduit beneath the plaster, or may be neatly tacked with insulated staples on the surface in the case of existing installations. Joints in such wiring should preferably be soldered and taped, since it is desirable to make sure that there is minimum resistance at any jointing point, but ordinary mains-type plastic connectors may of course be used.

Telephone wiring

Telephone wiring may only be installed by the telephone authorities' own staff, but they like to be advised of new telephone connections that are to be required, as early as

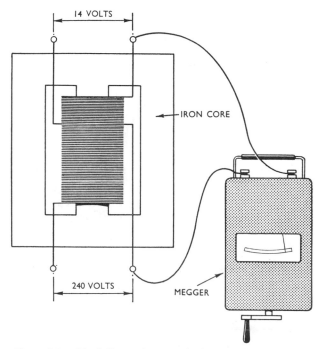

*Figure 8.2. The bell transformer, checking insulation between
high voltage and low voltage sides*

possible, and they are willing to provide polythene plastic
ducting to be built into the house, and to run to a suitable point
outside.

If this procedure is adopted, the telephone wiring can be
concealed as unobtrusively as the power wiring, and the appearance of unsightly telephone wires, stapled on top of the skirting
board and round the door frames, can be avoided.

Television and radio circuits
It is becoming increasingly common for television and VHF
aerial down-lead circuits to be installed as part of the wiring of a
building, and to terminate at high-frequency sockets which are

823

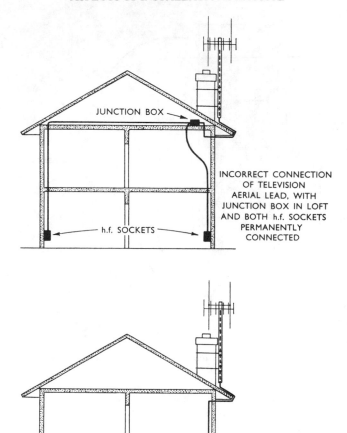

JUNCTION BOX

INCORRECT CONNECTION
OF TELEVISION
AERIAL LEAD, WITH
JUNCTION BOX IN LOFT
AND BOTH h.f. SOCKETS
PERMANENTLY
CONNECTED

h.f. SOCKETS

CORRECT CONNECTION.
EXTENSION TO
ROOM 2 PLUGGED
INTO h.f. SOCKET IN
ROOM 1 ONLY
WHEN NEEDED

ROOM 2

ROOM 1
h.f. SOCKET

*Figure 8.3. Incorrect and correct connections of television aerial
leads to high-frequency sockets in various rooms in the house*

themselves mounted on plates that fit standard wiring boxes, so that they may be sunk flush into the wall, enabling the television set aerial lead to be plugged in neatly.

Low-loss television cable may be used for two purposes: for the television connections, and for the VHF connections for FM radio reception. It is common to install such wiring below the plaster in plastic conduit, so that it can be pulled out if trouble develops.

There is no technical reason why this wiring, which is usually plastic covered, could not be installed directly in the plaster, but if so there is always the possibility that it may be damaged by nails driven into the wall. It will then become very difficult to replace, and any fault could necessitate breaking away plaster walls and subsequent redecoration.

There is a most important point to be watched in this connection. The method sometimes adopted is to bring the lead from the aerial on the chimney into the loft or other similar area, and then to join on to it, leads running to high-frequency sockets, in for example, the dining room, the sitting room, and possibly a bedroom as well. This means that the aerial lead has connected to it one socket which is in use for television reception and two other sockets which are not in use, and this frequency causes a 'mis-match', so that reception is impaired.

To avoid this, the lead from the aerial should be brought down to the point most likely to be used regularly, such as the sitting room, and then run to the next room, and from there to the third or other plug points that are to be provided (see *Figure* 8.3). At the termination in the sitting room a special high-frequency switch can be provided to switch in the additional television cable length into, say, the dining room, or else a neatly arranged lead can be left with a male socket on the end which can be plugged into the wall socket in place of the connection to the television set, and which has the effect of extending the aerial down-lead in series, into the dining room, and (with the same arrangement) on to a bedroom or other receiver point. In this way, the best reception will be obtained without troubles due to mis-matching.

Audio-frequency (sound) circuits

In some installations, sound recording enthusiasts (perhaps in connection with the making of sound films), may like to have facilities whereby one room can be used as a studio and the output from the microphone and amplifier taken to other rooms where recording can be carried out without the noise of the instruments disturbing the studio atmosphere.

This facility can be provided very easily if it is foreseen during the installation work. All that is needed is to use the same type of VHF television cable as used for the television circuit itself, and to provide links between the rooms, terminating in each case on a flush-type high-frequency socket-outlet inset in the wall, so that microphone or loudspeaker circuits can be plugged in as required without running very long leads (which may pick up hum or give rise to attenuation problems) through passages and under doors.

Motor circuits

Until the last decade most small motors, such as those used in domestic premises, and in small workshops, had to be provided with starting devices, but nowadays quite large motors, up to 3.5 kW or above, can be started by simply switching them on to the mains.

The types of motor used in such domestic devices as washing machines, vacuum cleaners, refrigerators and power drills do not involve any special problems. However, for motors approaching 750 W and larger (such as those used for lathes in small workshops), there is one factor that needs to be taken into account.

When a motor starts, it may well take ten or twelve times its normal operating current. This current rush at starting is of brief duration, but nevertheless may blow fuses unnecessarily, since the installation will not be harmed, nor the wiring overheated, by this excess current of very brief duration. To give an example, a 750 W single-phase motor at full load will take just over 3 A, but when starting it may take considerably more current than this and the makers recommend that a 10 A fuse should be used.

826

Motors that have to start very frequently may give rise to difficulties as the excess current during the starting period heats up the fuse more and more, and ultimately it may blow, but not because of any defect in the installation.

One method of avoiding this is to install a motor starting unit, which is usually available from the manufacturer of the motor, and comprises a pushbutton-operated starting switch. It is usually equipped with a special overload device to prevent damage to the motor or to the installation. These devices often take the form of a thermal overload. A small heating element, suitably proportioned, is connected into the motor circuit, and operates a bimetal strip in much the same way as the thermostat mentioned earlier, and the bimetal strip when it operates trips out the switch.

For domestic and small workshop applications, single-phase motors are the most commonly used. They present no problems in regard to their connection to the supply.

For larger drives, the 3-phase motor requires a special 3-phase socket, and a proper 3-phase isolation switch must be provided, even if the starting arrangements are incorporated within the machine to be driven.

Transformers

The transformer is a most useful static device, with no moving parts and therefore no need for maintenance, used to change one voltage to another. Basically, it has remained unchanged since it was first developed by Faraday in 1831.

The transformer consists of iron stampings made from thin plate, arranged in the form of a ring (*Figure* 8.4). On one side is a winding having, let us say, 2000 turns, and on the other side a winding having, say, 1000 turns.

If the 2000-turn winding (the primary winding) is now connected to a supply of alternating current, then a voltage will appear on the 1000-turn winding (the secondary winding) which is exactly one-half of that applied to other side. The voltage can be stepped up or down at will by changing the 'turns ratio', providing the coils are suitable for an application at the voltage desired.

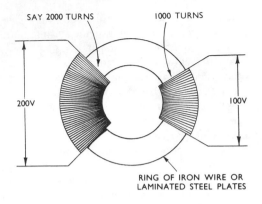

SAY 2000 TURNS   1000 TURNS

200V   100V

RING OF IRON WIRE OR
LAMINATED STEEL PLATES

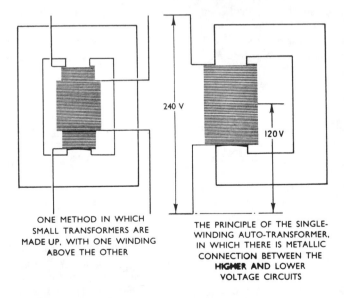

240 V   120 V

ONE METHOD IN WHICH
SMALL TRANSFORMERS ARE
MADE UP, WITH ONE WINDING
ABOVE THE OTHER

THE PRINCIPLE OF THE SINGLE-
WINDING AUTO-TRANSFORMER,
IN WHICH THERE IS METALLIC
CONNECTION BETWEEN THE
HIGHER AND LOWER
VOLTAGE CIRCUITS

Figure 8.4. The principle of the transformer: the two-winding transformer and the auto-transformer, which is not permitted for normal use in domestic premises

ASPECTS OF INSTALLATION PRACTICE

The most common example of the transformer found in domestic use is the bell transformer, giving a low voltage from the 240 V supply. In this case, it would obviously be very wrong to connect 240 V mains to the low-voltage terminal, as not only would the insulation of the low-voltage winding be insufficient for 240 V, but in addition a dangerously high voltage would be produced on the 240 V winding, and this too would flash over to earth and destroy the winding since its insulation would also be insufficient.

There are regulations concerning transformers which insist that the insulation between the two windings should be of at least as high a value as the insulation of the primary or 240 V winding to earth. This prevents the high voltage from penetrating to the low-voltage side.

There are, however, certain types of transformer known as auto-transformers, which must not be used for domestic purposes, although they have many applications in industry. In this type of transformer there is a single winding arranged on one side, as it were, of the iron ring, and the full mains voltage is applied across the winding. A tapping is taken from it, at, say, half-way down, to provide half the mains voltage. This means that there is physical connection between the 120 V circuit and the 240 V circuit, and a breakdown in the winding (which does happen from time to time on small transformers) could result in 240 V being applied to the 120 V circuit. This is the reason why the auto-transformer is not permitted in domestic premises.

Continental equipment

The marking of the wires connecting continental equipment to the mains is often different from that used in Britain, and care must be taken to ensure that the earth wire is correctly ascertained. Some continental machinery uses white earth wires, and many domestic appliances manufactured on the continent and in the Far East have no earth connection at all. In such cases, the two-core flex should therefore be removed and a three-core flex substituted, but there a further problem arises. Within the device itself – say, for example, a food mixer – it may not always be possible at first glance to see where to attach an earth connection in such a way that it ensures that all metal parts that can be touched are connected properly to the earth wire. This means some care and thought and perhaps the need to arrange some bonding wires within the appliance to make certain that all metal parts of all kinds within the appliance are in fact joined together and to earth. However, the appliance may be of the double-insulated type (see page 9), and this is then unnecessary.

Cupboard door switches
To provide an arrangement whereby when a cupboard door is opened a light within it is lit up can be done by means of a normally off switch specially provided for this purpose. These switches have a protruding knob which is arranged that it may be pressed by the back of the cupboard door as the door closes, and this action holds the switch open. As the door is opened the knob springs out and closes the circuit. These switches can be inserted into the frame of the door in a specially made hole, or they may be mounted inside the frame with a wooden block on the door carefully arranged to press on the knob and open the switch as the door closes.

Connections to gas appliances and oil-fired central heating plant
There may be a need to provide a supply for the equipment that is associated with central-heating equipment, either for lighting up the flame when a thermostat determines when it should be lit, or for increasing water flow in a central-heating water system circuit.

The supply to such devices may be made by a normal socket-outlet, but the cable used must be of the butyl heat-resistant type.

In certain larger installations, it may be necessary to use flameproof switches and other fittings in the room where the gas- or oil-heated boiler is situated. Consultation with the manufacturers may be necessary.

Connections to underfloor electric heating
For bungalows especially, underfloor electric heating is frequently employed. This form of heating may be carried out in

several ways, but it often consists of insulated electric wires buried in the floor and covered by a layer of concrete. Some systems employ plastic-coated mineral-insulated copper-sheathed cable, which may be safely operated at high temperatures, others employ special heating wires simply immersed in the concrete, while what is probably the best system uses a conduit buried in the cement of the floor and withdrawable heating cables.

For a room of 5 m by 4 m a floor heating loading of about 3 kW is necessary, and this is better supplied by means of a separate feed run directly back to the consumer unit. This is because a thermostat is needed in the circuit, to prevent undue consumption of current, and this would mean a wiring complication if the floor heating was supplied from the normal ring circuit.

In any case, such supplies should always be taken at off-peak periods, so that a separate feed is automatically needed.

The actual designing and installation of a floor-heating system requires specialist knowledge, and in any case must be carried out over a considerable period in close collaboration with the builder. Such a system can very rarely be installed in any but new buildings.

Warm-air central heating and air conditioning
Some houses are equipped with ducted air systems, so that air is warmed up at a central point (or at several points) by electric heaters, with fans to control the flow of air.

In providing supplies to these heaters, the only point the electrician has to observe is to ensure that the cables are of adequate size (since some heating elements exceed 3 kW in capacity) and that the necessary thermostat connections, as required by the makers, are incorporated into the wiring layout.

In many houses complete air conditioning is employed. This means that the air taken into the sealed, double-glazed and fully insulated interior of the house is cleaned, humidified if necessary, and heated in winter or cooled in summer, the air-conditioning plant being provided with both heating and refrigerating units.

Some of these air conditioners have complex thermostat and humidity-controlling devices, which need extensive wiring runs; and since the load on many of them is quite high – 12 kW is common for an ordinary three-bedroomed house – obviously special large current-carrying mains cables and appropriate fuses are needed.

Dimmers

To dim a domestic lighting circuit thyristors are widely used. The thyristor blocks the current for part of each cycle of alternation, the amount of blockage being controlled by the application of a control voltage to one of the electrodes of the thyristor by means of a variable resistor. Such a device is inserted in the lighting circuit and allows for full control, without the problem of heat loss, and in relatively small bulk.

Another commonly used method in the theatres and dance halls is to insert a variable resistance between the mains and the lamp circuits to be dimmed.

This resistance obviously carries the whole current of the lighting system, and so will develop heat. Moreover, until recently most resistance dimmers of this type were fairly bulky, and could not therefore be easily incorporated into the lighting circuits of, say, an ordinary lounge or dining room.

Nowadays, devices have been developed of a size not very much larger than a socket-outlet, which can be safely buried in the wall, and are arranged so that the heat is safely dissipated.

Delay switches

In buildings where there are a number of flats with access by stairways instead of lifts, delay switches are sometimes fitted, to allow for the lights to be switched on when entering the building at basement level, and for them to remain on for a given period of perhaps five minutes. They then switch themselves off to avoid current waste in lighting up the staircases and passages during the night, when no light is needed.

These delay switches take several forms. In some the pressure on the switch winds up a small spring, which then unwinds over a period and switches off the circuit. In another form a pneumatic piston is provided within the switch, which is lowered into its cylinder against the air pressure by the operation of switching on, and then as the air gradually escapes through a controlled orifice, the piston rises with the help of a spring and switches off the lamp. These devices can be purchased from most switch manufacturers.

Security devices
There are several patent burglar-alarm systems on the market, but many of them have the disadvantage that being widely advertised the burglars themselves are fully familiar with their requirements. The best system is undoubtedly one evolved specially for the installation concerned. Obviously all windows

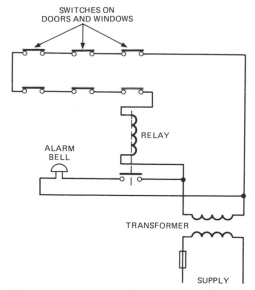

Figure 8.5. A burglar alarm circuit, using a relay, so that a broken wire or opened switch will cause an alarm bell to sound

and doors need some kind of protection, and small switches will have to be installed on every door and window to operate if the door or window is opened. A simple 'closed' circuit system may be wired so that even if the burglar sees the wiring and cuts it, the alarm still operates. This system is arranged as shown in *Figure* 8.5. Each door or window is fitted with a small switch so that if entry is attempted, the switch contacts will open. This will cause a relay to operate and close a bell circuit, giving an alarm. If wires are cut or break, the alarm will sound, thus the system is self-monitoring, against open circuits.

Emergency lighting

Emergency lighting can be provided in ordinary domestic premises, with moderate cost, by using a trickle charger suitable for a 12 V car battery, the battery itself, and a relay (see *Figure* 8.7).

The system requires a relay which will remain permanently energised as long as its coil is connected to the 240 V mains circuit. This relay should be properly protected on the mains side with a 2 A fuse, and should be enclosed to prevent damage.

The contacts, which remain permanently open when the relay is energised, may be connected to the battery and to a 12 V lighting circuit run as required in the house. Since this is not mains wiring, it is not subject to the normal regulations, but may be run in any desired method, providing these wires are not brought into contact with the mains. However, twin plastic cable run in plastic conduit will be quite satisfactory, but surface wiring neatly cleated is of course permissible.

Obviously emergency lighting is not required everywhere, but one 36 W car headlamp bulb in the sitting room, another in the kitchen and perhaps a 6 W type on the landing and a further 6 W bulb in a lavatory will be sufficient.

When the relay drops off through mains failure, all these lamps will be lit. As mains failure is usually of short duration, it may not matter if the lamps remain alight, even if all of them are not needed. In any case, the battery benefits by being discharged on occasion. If no failures occur for long periods, the battery may deteriorate.

When the mains supply is restored, the relay will automatically pick up and break the circuit, and the battery will at once begin to charge up once more.

The type of relay obtained may not necessarily have contacts that will carry the whole current for the emergency lighting

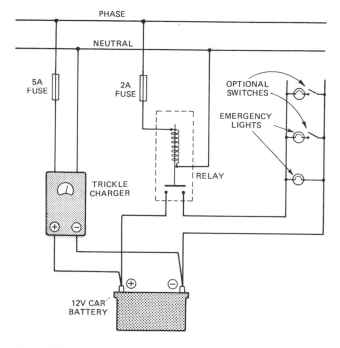

Figure 8.7.   An emergency lighting circuit, using a trickle-charged 12 V automobile-type battery as the main source of supply

circuit if all the lamps are in use, and it may be necessary to employ a second relay, operated from the battery, with contacts of greater capacity. The first, or main failure relay, simply operating a battery circuit for the coil of the second relay, whose contacts will carry the whole of the main current. This depends

835

on the type of relay obtained. The current for a 36 W car headlamp bulb at 12 V is 3 A and thus if two of these are in use plus two 6 W lamps, 7 A will be needed, and not all relay contacts will carry this current for any length of time.

Some relays have a number of contacts, designed originally for closing a number of circuits at once, and these contacts can be paralleled up so that the current is shared between them and they are all working within their rating.

Electricity in the greenhouse and the garden
Electricity may be used in a greenhouse for heating, for seed propagation, for raising cuttings and for soil sterilisation, and many other purposes. It may also be used in the garden to drive an electrically operated lawnmower or hedgecutter.

Great care should be taken when installing socket-outlets in greenhouses where damp and humid conditions often prevail, to ensure that all fittings are of the weatherproof type, and that the greatest care is taken to ensure proper earthing, since an electric shock obtained under these conditions would be especially dangerous.

Conduit systems, mineral-insulated copper-sheathed or PVC armoured cables, with metallic fittings are the best for this purpose, and if an outdoor socket for the lawnmower is provided, again this must be carefully installed so that corrosion effects are minimised. Weatherproof socket-outlets should be used. These are available with the added protection of earth leakage circuit-breakers (Chapter 3).

Section 6

Home Decorating

1 Tools and Materials

Home decorating is really easy and by doing it yourself a lot of money can be saved. Painting and wallpapering does need care, but not an exceptional amount of skill.

Careful planning beforehand will enable you to do the work in stages, so that a little can be done at a time if that is more convenient.

When decorating for the first time buy the best materials and tools you can afford, especially paint brushes, and you will be set up for a long time to come.

Basic tools

Basic decorating tools consist of the following: three sizes of paint brushes – 13 mm, 25 mm, 50 mm ($\frac{1}{2}$ in, 1 in, 2 in); a choice of either a larger brush, paint pad or paint roller for large areas of work, such as walls and ceilings; step ladder and trestles; builder's board; scrapers; putty knife; sanding block; blow-torch or chemical paint stripper; paperhanging brush; paste brush; scissors; plumb line; Stanley knife; metre rule; steel tape; seam roller; wire brush; filling knife.

Choosing the paper

There is a very wide choice of paper available. Papers with small patterns, completely plain, or with vertical stripes are the most economical, as there is less waste when matching the pattern of adjoining strips. A patterned paper will help to disguise unevenness in the surface of a wall.

Figure 1.1. The tools for paper hanging: Stanley knife; plumb line; scraper; scissors, filling knife; paste brush; paperhanging brush; steel tape; rule; sanding block; seam roller; wire brush

Vinyl papers are ideal for bathrooms and kitchens, as they have a plastic coating and are washable and pretty well steam-and water-proof. They are also good for stairways and passages where the walls are likely to get rubbed or marked by people passing.

Ready-pasted papers cost a little more than normal wallpaper, but you do not have to buy paste or a paste brush, or buy or borrow a pasting table. They save no end of time, and are the ideal thing to use if you only want to do a small section of your papering at one time. You can hang just one strip in, literally, a matter of minutes if you want to, and then call it a day, with hardly anything to clear up afterwards.

Your wallpaper supplier will tell you how many rolls of paper you should need if you give him the height of the room and the *total* distance round the room, taking in the window and door spaces.

Wallpaper pastes

There are two main types of pastes – the old-established cold water flour paste and cellulose paste – and both have their merits. Generally speaking, cellulose paste is less likely to stain than flour paste. On the other hand, flour paste is less likely to disturb the pattern of loosely bound pigmented papers and have less tendency to strike through from the back of the paper. It is always a good idea to ask the advice of the wallpaper supplier on this matter.

For hanging vinyl wallcoverings, a paste should be used which contains a fungicide, because the vinyl film is impervious and will not allow moisture to evaporate off.

Choosing the paint

After you have made your choice of colours, you have to decide what kind of paint you are going to use. So many brands, so many names. What do they all mean?

Gloss paints

These have a tough, hard, shiny finish. They are known as oil-based paints as linseed oil was used traditionally in their manufacture. Nowadays, synthetic resins such as polyurethane are used instead, making them even tougher and harder wearing.

Gloss paint is the one normally used for woodwork and metalwork, and for rooms like kitchens and bathrooms, where there is likely to be steam about. They are comparatively slow-drying and need to be left at least overnight before a second coat is applied (if this is necessary). A primer and probably an undercoat will be needed for previously unpainted surfaces.

Normally, oil-based paints come ready for use in the can, but they will need a thorough stirring to make certain that any pigment settled in the bottom of the tin is well mixed in. They should not need thinning, but if old paint in a tin has hardened up, use white spirit or turpentine.

Figure 1.2. The tools for painting and ceiling work: 13 mm, 25 mm and 50 mm ($\frac{1}{2}$ in, 1 in and 2 in) paint brushes; paint pad; stepladder and trestles; builder's board; paint roller and tray; blow-torch; sanding block; scrapers; filling knife

In addition to those of full gloss finish, oil-based paints can have satin, eggshell, silk and semi-gloss finishes, although all of these are slightly less hard-wearing.

Non-drip paints

Also known as one coat or jelly paints, these incorporate an undercoat and are available in both oil-based and water-borne paints. They are applied thicker than ordinary paints as they do not drip easily. Generally speaking, jelly paints do not appeal to the experienced painter as they cannot be brushed out to a very fine finish. On new work these paints can be adequate, but where a colour change is required, sometimes there is insufficient pigment to obliterate an under-colour without applying two coats. Non-drip paints have not replaced standard paints, but rather have supplemented them.

Emulsion paints

These are water-based and do not contain oil, which is a great advantage as the brushes or paint rollers can very easily be cleaned under a tap after use. Words like 'acrylic' and 'vinyl' used with emulsion refers to resins contained in them, which give them tough and hard-wearing surfaces, although they are not normally as tough as gloss paint.

Emulsions are nowadays made which can be used for outside painting and woodwork, but in general their main use is still for walls and ceilings, where a high gloss is not required. They are so quick-drying that after about two hours a second coat can be applied. Emulsions only require a primer on very porous surfaces but, thinned with water according to the maker's instructions on the tin, they will make their own primer.

Priming paints

Primers give both wood and metal a good surface for subsequent paintwork, but are really not needed inside the house, except on things like metal window frames. They waterproof the surface and help to prevent rust, and on outside woodwork which is subject to the weather they should be used.

Undercoating paints

The instructions on your paint tin will tell you whether an undercoat is needed. Undercoats give a good surface for a top coat of gloss to adhere to and are advisable if a really professional job is aimed at. Their greatest value is in covering up a dark colour if you want to paint over it with a lighter one. The dark colour might well show through if gloss alone were used.

2 Preparation

With any decorating job, adequate preparation is 90 per cent of the battle. Practically all faults and failures which are blamed on materials can be traced back to the fact that the surface upon which the material was placed had been poorly prepared.

Before you start work, cover the floor and any furniture still in the room with dust-sheets or a thick covering of newspapers.

You can quite safely paper over emulsion paint on a wall, but it must be washed down first using warm water with a little detergent in it to remove any grease or dirt. It is also possible to put new paper on top of old, but here the new paste may weaken the adhesive power of the old, resulting in bubbles or even the whole lot coming away.

But whether you decide to take a chance about this or not, you must remove any shelves which are screwed to the wall, wall light fittings, hooks and so on, and insert matchsticks into the screw holes before papering. When papering over the matchsticks, they will poke through the paper and you will not spend hours trying to find where the holes were. If you do disconnect light fittings, first turn off the current at the main and then bind the ends of each wire separately with insulating tape. If you have to switch the current on again, perhaps because someone is cooking the lunch in another part of the house, make absolutely sure that it is off once more before you start working in the area where the lights are. Wet paste is a good conductor of electricity.

Stripping off old paper

All in all it is much better to strip off the old paper, and you can buy special strippers for this. However, all but the most stubborn of

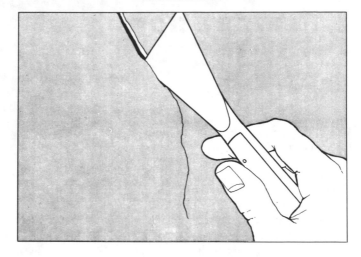

Figure 2.1. Undercut cracks so that the filling will stay in place

papers can be removed relatively easily simply by soaking them well with warm water, applied with a sponge over a fairly small area at a time, and then working the paper from the wall with a scraper. Quite large pieces may simply pull away without any great effort on your part. Take care not to dig into the plaster with the scraper or you will have a repair job to do later.

Heavy papers will take rather more soaking than others to come free, and vinyl ones will need their surface scratched with a wire brush or scored with a scraper, so that the water can penetrate through the plastic coating to the paste below. With some special vinyls the surface is designed to peel away, leaving the paper backing, which you can use as a base for your new paper.

Filling in cracks in walls

When the walls are down to bare plaster, examine them carefully. If they are sound and quite unmarked you will be extremely lucky, but it is more than likely that there will be cracks or small pieces of plaster chipped out here and there. If these cracks are ignored it is unlikely that the house will fall down, but they may get worse in time and they could quite easily show through the paper.

Small cracks and chips can be filled with a quick-drying, cellulose preparation like Polyfilla, or a plaster-like material such as Keene's cement. First, with a sharp, pointed knife, widen the crack just enough so that you can undercut the edges. This will hold the filler firmly in place when it hardens. Press the filler into the crack with a filling knife, leaving it a little proud of the wall surface. It will quickly dry, and when it has done so, rub it smooth and level with the wall with fine sandpaper. Any rough patches in the plaster should also be sanded smooth.

If you have done much sanding, leaving a porous surface, it is a good idea to give the whole wall a coat of wallpaper paste, thinned to a liquid consistency with water. This is called sizing and will seal the pores to give a good working surface.

Preparing ceilings

Brush down and wash the ceiling first of all. It may well have lining paper on it, possibly used to disguise a poor surface, for ceilings are subject to cracking more than solid walls. If the lining paper is adhering firmly, do not remove it, or you may find that you have major repair work to do. If, on the other hand, the ceiling is bare plaster, repair any small cracks just as you would on a wall, and size it with wallpaper paste.

Ceilings are often subject to a certain amount of movement, caused possibly by settlement of the house, or even by the shifting of heavy furniture in the room above. The repair of a bad crack can be given added strength as follows.

Fill it with either a cellulose or plaster-like filler, sand down when dry, and then paste a piece of lining paper over it so that it covers the crack and about 25 mm (1 in) of the ceiling all round it. There should be enough of the paper so that the edges, which should not be pasted, hang down all round. When the paper has dried and is firmly stuck, tear the edges away, pulling in towards the centre all the time, so that you are left with a feathered edge. Give this a thin coat of filler and lightly sand it smooth when it is dry. The repair will hardly be visible, but you can give it a coat of emulsion, which will blend it into the ceiling even more effectively.

Preparing paintwork

The first thing to do before tackling any painting job is to assess just what needs doing. If old paintwork is in good condition, it is unnecessary to strip it off. Odd patches of flaking may be found round door panels and window frames, but these can be sanded smooth and any cracks and crannies filled with a filler. Many modern paints take quite happily over old gloss paint without your having to do anything to the surface except wash it down. If this is so with the paint you choose, it should say so on the tin, but if in doubt a light sanding over the whole surface will give a key for the new paint to stick to. If you are painting over a very dark colour, an undercoat is advisable.

Should the old paint be in such a bad condition that it must be removed, the two easiest methods are burning it off or using a chemical stripper. The latter will be more costly over a large area.

A modern gas blow-torch makes burning off much simpler than trying to cope with the temperamental old-type blowlamps. The flame will soften the paint so that it is easily worked off with a scraper (or a wire brush for awkward mouldings which the scraper will not reach), but keep the torch moving so that you do not burn the wood.

There will be some areas where you cannot use a torch. If used on windows, the heat would be likely to crack the panes, so a chemical stripper is best here. The properties of strippers vary from make to make, so read the instructions very carefully before you start work. All should be applied with an old brush, which will not be any use for painting with afterwards. In general it can be said that strippers either soften the paint much as a blow-torch does, so that you use a scraper with them as before, or else at least partially dissolve it. Very careful washing down afterwards in line with the manufac-turerers instructions is needed so that no stripper is left in odd corners. Wear rubber gloves when working with strippers.

PREPARATION

Stripping paint can also be done by sanding, but except for very small areas, if this is done by hand it is a most tedious job. Mechanical sanders are much quicker, but they do create an incredible amount of dust.

After stripping, rub the surface down with M2 grade glasspaper, following the grain. Cracks should be filled with a proprietary wood filler, sanding smooth again afterwards.

New, unpainted wood should, after sanding, have the knots sealed with a knotting varnish, which will stop any resin seeping from them, and then a primer coat applied before the undercoat. Aluminium primer both seals knots and primes at the same time.

3 Painting

Oil-based gloss paint should be applied in smooth, even strokes. Do not have too much paint on your brush. Dipping it 25 mm (1 in) into your paint tin at the most is ample.

On a large area, working from the top, paint two vertical strips of a convenient width and depth for you to reach without having to move, leaving a gap of the same width between them. Then, with horizontal brush strokes, work the paint across the gap without putting any more on your brush. This should ensure that the paint over the whole area is not too thick, and prevent unsightly runs and sags.

Finish off with gentle vertical strokes of the brush, feathering the edges, and you should have no brush marks left when the paint is dry.

Work across the rest of the area in strips like this, and then move to a lower level and repeat the pattern. Keep going until the whole job is done, or the hard edge where you stopped work may show when the paint has dried.

With non-drip paints do not brush out in the same way. Concentrate on an even, not-too-thick coating in the first place and leave it at that.

Doors and windows

The most convenient order for painting doors and windows is shown in *Figures 3.1* and *3.2*, but make sure to remove all handles and catches first.

There are two points to bear in mind when painting windows. The first is that the paint must form a seal between the woodwork and the glass to prevent moisture from condensation seeping into

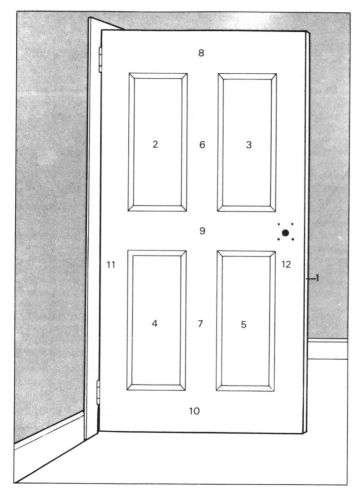

Figure 3.1. The best order for painting a panelled door

the wood and rotting it. To achieve this, when painting the window bars and main frame, the paint should also cover about 3 mm ($\frac{1}{8}$ in) of the glass all round. To ensure a neat job, place strips of masking tape all round each pane, leaving the suggested gap between its outer edge and the putty or wood. With a 12 mm or 25 mm ($\frac{1}{2}$ in or 1 in) brush, paint away, but peel off the masking tape almost at once afterwards. If you leave it until the paint is even partially dry, it may pull the paint away from the seal you have made.

The second point to note concerns sash windows. To avoid any possibility of the frames sticking, do not paint in the slots in which the window slides.

Metal windows

Some metal windows are made of alloys which need not be painted, although you may wish to do so to change the colour. Others may rust and must be painted.

Remove any rust before you start, using emery paper and/or a wire brush. A chromate primer should be used on iron and steel. Aluminium paint can also be used as a primer or as a final coat over metal primers because of the attractive finish it produces.

Painting radiators

There are few paints which will resist at least some colour change when used on radiators. This is particularly so with light shades. Aluminium paint stays as it is, even on the hottest radiator, but if you do not want a metallic finish, use a chromate primer, undercoat and gloss finish. Special, long-handled brushes with the bristles mounted at an angle can be bought for reaching awkward places behind radiators.

Use of paint rollers

Paint rollers are probably easier and quicker for a beginner to use for large areas such as ceilings and walls. They are suitable for either emulsion or gloss paints. Do not overfill the paint tray when using this method of painting. Rollers are particularly good for painting

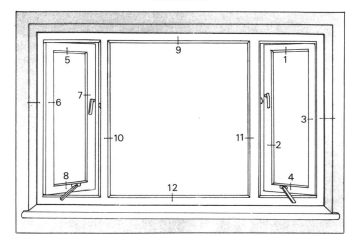

Figure 3.2. The best order for painting a multi-paned window

textured surfaces as the soft lambswool from which most good ones are made carries the paint into all the indentations without you having to work at it. Be prepared to touch up with a brush or paint pad in those places, such as corners and edges of ceilings, where the roller cannot reach.

Use of paint pads

Paint pads with mohair heads are best for large areas such as walls and ceilings, whether textured or plain. They are available in a wide range of sizes. Some have a hollow handle which will take a broom handle to extend your reach. For use with walls and ceilings a 100 mm (4 in) pad is recommended. Paint pads should not be left loaded with paint as the mohair is so fine that it soon hardens. Wash out the pads after each session; this will save a great deal of trouble later.

Estimating paint coverage

The table below of average quantities is based on one prepared by Dulux, but the following points should be borne in mind when using it. Porous and textured surfaces will take more paint than smooth ones. If you are using several coats on a surface, allow for this. If an emulsion paint is thinned, it will go further. The table is more suited for use when covering large areas, such as walls.

Average spreading rate per litre	*Square metre*	*Square yard*
Masonry sealer	12	14
Undercoat	11	13
Gloss	17	20
Non-drip gloss	12	14
Eggshell	16	19
Flat	16	19
Emulsion	14	17

4 Paper Hanging

After all painting has been carried out in the room, the paper can now be hung. If there is a plain wall, unbroken by doors, windows or a fireplace, this is the best place to start papering if you have not done any before. Find the centre of the wall by measuring from either end and make a small pencil mark on the spot.

Stand on a stepladder and suspend a plumb line from a drawing pin pushed into the wall at its highest point, so that the line runs through your mark on the wall. Make two or three other pencil marks along the line of the plumb and, using a long rule, join them up with a pencil line. This gives you a straight and vertical datum line to start your papering from.

The papering begins

Cut your first length of paper, allowing about 150 mm (6 in) on top of the wall height measurement for trimming and pattern matching. Spread out the paper face down, on the pasting table and paste half of it thoroughly with your paste brush, working outwards from the centre in a herring-bone pattern. Move the paper to one edge of the table and then the other as you paste that side, to prevent paste getting on to the table surface. Make sure the edges are well pasted, and then fold over the half you have done, paste side to paste side. Repeat the process for the other half. For heavy paper more paste is needed than for thin, and allow a minute or two for the paste to sink in.

Carrying the folded paper, mount the stepladder, release the top fold, and offer your right hand to the wall so that the paper edge lines up with the vertical pencil line, and half your trimming allowance is above the wall on the ceiling. Press the paper lightly to the wall with your right hand – still holding the left hand well away from the wall, then use your right hand to ensure the paper lines up with the pencil line. You will be able to slide the paper slightly, into position, if necessary. Allow your left hand to take the rest of the paper to the wall, then smooth out with either a paperhanging brush, clean paint roller or dry sponge, again working from the centre outwards. If while doing this a wrinkle appears, pull that section of paper back from the wall and smooth it back again.

With the back of your scissors, score along the line where the paper meets the ceiling, making a definite crease. Pull the top of the paper clear of the wall, cut along the crease mark and smooth the paper back on the wall. Do the same where the paper joins the skirting board, but allow an extra 3 mm ($\frac{3}{8}$ in) beyond the crease mark when cutting so that the paper will just turn on to the top of the skirting board. This will hide any cracks present between the wall and skirting board.

The subsequent lengths of paper are hung in a similar manner, butted up to the edge of the previous one, but you will have to slide them a little upwards or downwards until the pattern matches. Where the pattern is a very big one, you may have to leave more than the 150 mm trimming allowance to match the pattern. When each length is well butted up to the next, work gently up and down the seam with the seam roller to make sure the edges are well stuck. Lift and repaste any edges which will not stick down properly.

Getting round corners

When you come to a corner, it is most unlikely that the line of this will be absolutely straight or that it will be quite vertical all the way down. If it is not, and you try to fold more than a very narrow width of paper round it, you are almost certain to get creases which cannot be smoothed out, and the edge of the section which has gone round the corner may well be out of true. The length, if butted up to it, will then be out of true as well.

Test the corner with a plumb line if you like, and you may be lucky, but nine times out of ten it is better to cut your strip when approaching a corner so that no more than about 12 mm ($\frac{1}{2}$ in)

PAPER HANGING

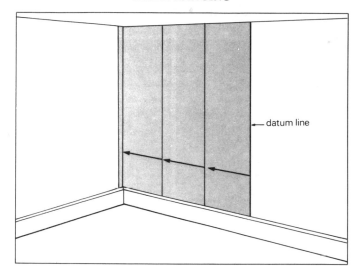

Figure 4.1. Working from a vertical centre line on the wall will ensure the paper strips are hung correctly. Where a corner is out of true, allow only about 12 mm to turn on to the new wall (see text)

actually makes the turn. Any creases in the 12 mm can be smoothed out quite easily after it is pasted into place.

Mark a vertical datum line on the new wall, at the appropriate width, and hang the cut-off piece (or a full-width strip, as the case may be) to abut the turn strip. If the edge of the 12 mm strip is not perfectly straight you cannot butt up to it, and you may have to overlap the new length slightly. Any slight pattern-matching discrepancy will not be really noticeable on a corner. If you overlap away from the light from a window, the join will not throw shadow and can be seen even less.

The same general principles should be followed when turning paper into a window recess. Turn only about 12 mm into the recess, and paper the recess itself with narrow strips, overlapping the turn in if need be.

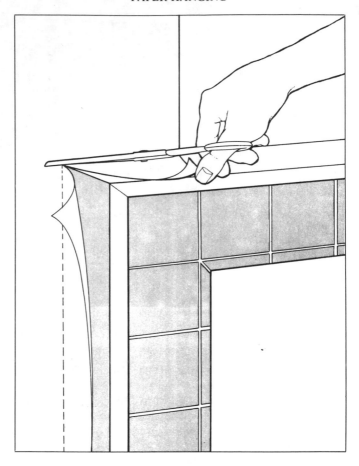

Figure 4.2. Cut into the paper at an angle, towards each corner of the fireplace and trim off surplus

Papering round fireplaces

If your room has a fireplace with recesses on each side of it and you have a fairly bold pattern, it is important that this pattern should be placed symmetrically on the chimney breast. Lack of symmetry will be more easily seen on a short section of wall. Your whole papering job in this case should really start here, but it is a little more tricky for a beginner as you will be into corners almost at once, and the paper has to be fitted round the fireplace itself. This probably sounds more difficult than it is.

Make your datum line in the centre of the chimney breast, and hang your first length of paper, down to the fireplace with a bit over at the bottom. Then, with your scissors, cut into the paper at an angle towards each corner or projection of the fireplace until you can crease the paper in to the point where it joins the wall, all along the fireplace's outline. Pull the paper back a section at a time, trim along the creases with scissors, and smooth the paper back well into the angle. Hang the remaining lengths.

Papering round light switches and plugs

For papering round these, let the paper fall loosely over the switch or plug, find the point approximately in its centre, and make scissor

Figure 4 3 Make scissor cuts towards each corner of the switch

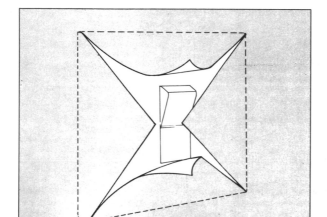

cuts outwards towards each corner. If the switch is round, make six or more radial cuts from the centre to its circumference. In either case, the paper can be creased in with the back of the scissors round the switch and the surplus neatly trimmed off.

With a recessed switch or plug, one can loosen the screws holding the cover and tuck the edges of the paper under it. This is the easiest way to achieve a really neat effect, but always switch off the electric current at the main (not just at the switch). Remember you are working with wet materials.

Ready-pasted wallpapers

As mentioned in the chapter on Tools and Materials, although these may be slightly more expensive, they save no end of time and trouble. A waterproofed cardboard trough is usually supplied with the paper.

Cover the floor under your working area before you start as you are almost bound to get some water spilled on it. Cut your length of paper and then roll it up loosely again, pattern side inwards. Submerge it in the water trough which should be placed under the spot where you are hanging the length. The instructions with the paper tell you how long to leave it in the water to soften the paste, which is usually between one and two minutes. The paste has a fungicide ready mixed into it.

Taking the paper by its top edge, lift it from the trough. It will unroll itself as you do this; leave the bottom end just over the trough for a few seconds for the surplus water to run off. Hang the paper in the normal way. If vinyl papers are being used and the odd corner has not stuck properly after the paper is dry, stick it down with a latex adhesive such as Copydex.

Papering a ceiling

Papering a ceiling is a little more difficult than papering walls, and parts of the job are easier if there is a second person there to help.

Start the papering at the window side of the room and hang it

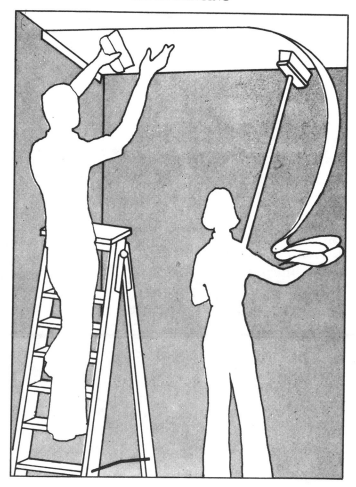

Figure 4.4. Tuck the end of the paper and the side edge well into the joint between the ceiling and the wall. A helper can support the paper for you with a broom head

parallel to the window wall. Find a point at each end of the ceiling the width of the paper, minus 12 mm (½ in) for trim, away from the wall. Insert a drawing pin or small nail at each of the two points and tie a chalked string from one pin to the other, close up against the ceiling. Use a coloured chalk for a white surface. Pull the string gently in the centre and then release it, so that a chalk line will be transferred to the ceiling. This is your guide line.

You will probably be dealing with longer strips of paper than you were for the walls and will have to fold over the ends more than once on the pasting table to enable you to carry them. The carrying can be made easier if you loop the centre of the folded paper over a roll of ceiling paper, allowing the folds to hang down on each side.

Standing comfortably with your face to the wall, tuck the end of the paper and the side edge well into the joint between the ceiling and the wall, lining the other edge up with your guide line. Then gradually work backwards, unfolding the paper as you go and smoothing it on with the paperhanging brush. If you do have a helper, the job will be much easier as he or she can support the other end of the length for you, standing on the floor – if there is no room on the platform – and using the (clean) head of a broom to hold it up. Care is needed with such long lengths that they are kept straight, both to avoid buckles caused by inadvertent stretching of the paper, and so that the next length will butt up properly. Finally trim the two ends and the side along the wall.

Should you have to contend with a ceiling rose, it pays to do some accurate measuring and mark the position on the dry piece of paper. Make a number of star cuts in the paper, then paste the whole piece in the normal way.

When you reach the ceiling rose, merely feed the flex through the hole, and ease the paper around the rose. Press the cut pieces to the rose base, then trim off with small scissors. You can allow a slight turn on to the rose so no gap is visible. Wipe paste off the rose before it hardens.

Carry on across the ceiling with the remaining lengths.

Appendix
Energy Saving

This chapter is extracted from *Beginner's Guide to Home Energy Saving*, published by Newnes Technical Books, Borough Green, Sevenoaks, Kent, TN15 9AR. Particulars of this book can be obtained from Newnes Technical Books.

This chapter explores possibilities for making fuel savings at no cost. Some of these were established habits a few decades ago, but have been largely forgotten in the age of push-button central heating. Others arise from modern theoretical knowledge, or involve the better use of modern appliances. Such techniques include:

- making the maximum use of sunshine throughout the heating season;
- studiously avoiding over-ventilation;
- choosing your use of rooms to make the greatest possible use of 'incidental heat';
- applying an understanding of comfort so as to be comfortable at lower energy cost;
- getting to know the outside temperature above which no space heating is needed;
- exploiting the 'thermal mass' of the house;
- exploiting the buoyancy of warm air;
- using appliances in a more efficient way;
- making full use of curtains to reduce heat loss from windows;
- making the most use of heat from cooking;
- pre-heating the cold water supply from ambient air to reduce hot water costs.

Using sunshine

You will be aware that even in mid-winter the sun can supply some useful heat to a house, but most modern houses are not designed or oriented to exploit it. Heating systems, too, are commonly designed to ignore solar gains, with the result that rooms into which the sun shines can overheat on sunny days unless you juggle with manual controls, or open a window to spill some heat (which often seems easier), or even draw the curtains. The former may be unnecessary or it may not. Both of the latter actions are needlessly wasteful.

The following paragraphs suggest how with a little thought and the minimum of effort you can make full use of such sunshine as you are lucky enough to get. They may make little impact on your fuel costs, but they could make an appreciable difference.

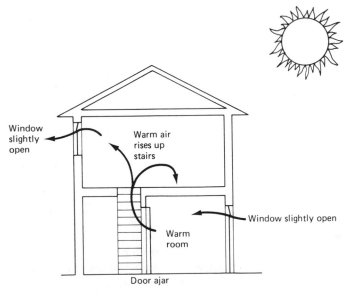

Fig. 5.1 Use of buoyant air movement to draw solar warmth through the house

Open the curtains of sunny rooms as early as possible in the day, and open them as widely as possible. Do not open the windows — that will let the heat escape. Even if you are not using such a room, open its door to let the heat percolate into the rest of the house. If there is a room heater or heat emitter (radiator or warm-air grille), shut it off while the sunshine lasts. Even if the room overheats a little, don't open windows or close curtains if you can avoid it. That way more heat will be stored up for later in the day when the sun has moved round or gone down.

Use only a minimum of ventilation throughout the house. The exception might be if, by ventilation, you can create a slight through draught to carry sun-warmed air through the house and distribute it (*Figure 5.1*). A first-floor window opened slightly on the shady side of the house may help, depending on wind conditions that day. If possible, transfer activities to sunny rooms, and if possible do without central heating. But remember that if you let the sunless parts of the house go cold, it will take time to warm them up again. Get to know what cunning you can employ with your own house to be comfortable without heating as often as possible.

Avoiding over-ventilation

With ventilation you have to strike a balance between insufficient air, leading to stuffiness and possibly condensation on walls, floors and ceilings, and over-ventilation, which is very wasteful of heat. Research has shown that British people tend to over-ventilate their houses in mild winter weather, when draughts are not so noticeable. If you habitually do this you will use a lot more heating fuel than necessary. One reason is that most windows when they are open at all let through far more air than is needed. If the outside temperature is as high as $13^{\circ}C$ ($55^{\circ}F$) you should not need heating at all, especially if there is any sunshine. Apart from sunshine, other incidental gains may well provide all the warmth you need to achieve comfort temperatures inside, if you do not waste it through ventilation.

If it is windy outside you probably need no windows open at all. Most houses have sufficient leakage, through other routes than the cracks you may be able to block up, to ventilate them adequately in windy weather. You must, of course, provide enough air to feed any fuel-burning appliance and remove pollution: failure to do so can be dangerous.

Remember that warm air rises, and windows left open upstairs will spill out vast quantities of valuable warm air – often causing cold draughts downstairs as well.

Using naturally warm rooms

Many houses have some rooms that receive more than their fair share of incidental heat gains. The kitchen is usually one of these, especially if it has a fridge and a central heating boiler in it. Consider whether it is possible to make more use of this heat by using such rooms more and not heating the rest of the house so much. A corner of a kitchen that is clean, well-decorated and attractively lit might easily double as a living room or homework room at such times. Many people have always arranged their lives around the warm places, so such advice may seem fatuous to them. But others, with full central heating, have come to see rooms as having distinct functions, and so use each one strictly for that function and add heat and light as necessary, because it is so easy to do so. There may be economies to be made from re-thinking such habits.

Understanding the nature of comfort

Most of us have become so used to simply turning up the heat in a room if we feel chilly in it that we do not consider whether we could be equally comfortable by another means without spending more on heating. Ask yourself whether you could improve the economy of using that room by:

● eliminating or avoiding a draught;

● improving where you sit in relation to radiant warmth, or keeping away from the coldest surfaces;

- reducing the tendency for warm air to rise to the ceiling and stay there — encourage it to circulate and mix by using a radiator shelf (*Figure 5.2*) or placing a small fan to push or pull warm air down from high level;
- preventing cold air pooling on the floor, avoiding sitting with your feet in it, or taking special measures to keep your feet warm;
- using items of furniture that maximise thermal comfort — for example, a dining chair with a blanket or jacket draped over the back for long hours of sedentary work, as protection against draughts or cold radiation; arranging furniture that people can snuggle into like cats do (who know all about comfort);

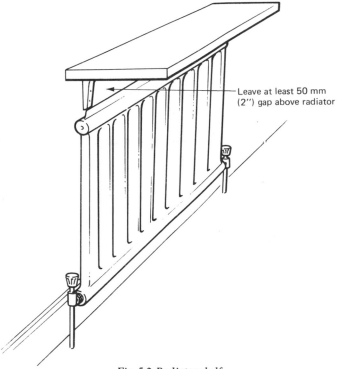

Leave at least 50 mm (2″) gap above radiator

Fig. 5.2 Radiator shelf

- shutting doors to contain the incidental heat gains from lights and/or a television set;
- making sure everyone in the room is equally well placed, or those most sensitive to cold sit in the warmest places.

Getting to know the 'no-heat' temperature

Keep an eye on the outside temperatures in mild winter weather, and get to know at what outside temperatures, in various conditions (of wind, sunshine and internal heat gains) you can be comfortable inside without adding extra heat. In some circumstances it may be a lot more economical to provide just a little heat in one room than to heat the whole house, even if you heat that one room with a relatively expensive fuel.

Exploiting the house's 'thermal mass'

If you only want a bit of warmth for a short period, it may be sensible in a 'massive' house to use a 'local' heat source rather than central heating if you have it, and to avoid having to heat up the whole structure.

If you have free heat from sunshine, realise that heat will stay in the room for a long while after the rays of the sun have gone, in a heavy structure. In such a room, even when the sun's heat is no longer enough for comfort, less extra heat will be needed in the evening than in rooms that have been cold all day.

At the end of the evening, switch off heating as early as possible before retiring – get to know how long it takes before the room becomes perceptibly chilly, at various outside temperatures and windspeeds. Make manual adjustments to heating at or before bedtime each night, to avoid leaving an extravagantly heated living room behind when you go to bed.

Exploiting the buoyancy of warm air

Use the fact that warm air rises to help distribute solar heat around the house, if you can usefully do so. In the evening, use the buoyancy of the warm air of living rooms to boost the temperature of bedrooms at bedtime: open the living-room doors at bedtime for this purpose. Conversely, remember that you can heat downstairs rooms more economically if you shut their doors: there is no point in heating unoccupied bedrooms, except of course to warm them up before using them, or when they are in use during waking hours.

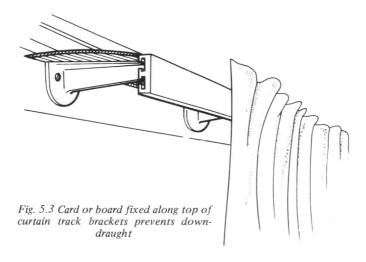

Fig. 5.3 Card or board fixed along top of curtain track brackets prevents down-draught

Making full use of curtains

Curtained windows, particularly if the curtains are close fitting and well lined, can be as good as or better than double-glazing at retaining heat. During the heating season, close all curtains as soon as it gets dark – or even sooner if you can bear it and there is no more sunshine around.

Some curtain tracks stand clear of the wall to which they are fixed. If possible fix hardboard or stiff card neatly across the top to reduce the flow of warm air down the face of the window (*Figure 5.3*). The traditional 'box pelmet' does this job admirably, and prevents air currents from causing warmth to be 'pumped' out of the room in this way.

Heat used in cooking

Some understanding of the heat output of the cooker is advisable, for three reasons:
- safety;
- having understood the safety aspect, you may be able to use heat from the cooker as a source of space heating, either regularly or in an emergency;
- you may be motivated to use it more economically.

It is necessary to consider gas and electric cookers separately, because they have important differences. A gas cooker has the same order of heat output as a central-heating system. For example, assume a typical central-heating/hot-water boiler burns gas at about 50 500 BTU/hour and the gas cooker (with the oven, four rings and a grill all on) burns about 53 700 BTU/hour (0.51 and 0.54 therms/hour or 14.8 and 15.7 kW, respectively). However, the central-heating boiler has a 'rated output' of 38 000 BTU/hour (i.e. it delivers this much useful heat), which is about 75 per cent of its rate of burning gas. Against this, the cooker delivers *all* the heat value of the gas it burns into the house, because it has no flue. So the cooker is a source of heat one-third more powerful, through being about 100 per cent efficient (at least as a producer of heat in the house).

It does seem rather illogical that the central-heating boiler has to have a flue while the cooker does not, especially as this flue disposes of a quarter of the power of the boiler. However, the boiler may be running continuously, while the cooker is only expected to be used for an hour or two at a time, and during waking hours. The room where the cooker is must be adequately ventilated, of course (as is the case for a central-heating boiler, except one with a balanced flue). But such ventilation does not prevent all the waste gases staying in the house. In fact it may well assist, because a strong current of hot air from the cooker, backed by a source of cool air from outside, is quite likely to pour into the rest of the house by 'stack effect', unless barred by a closed door.

Certain observations follow. Firstly, the cooker provides by far the biggest incidental heat gain in the house: even one large burner represents some 17 per cent of the cooker's output, equivalent to 9000 BTU/hour or about 2½ kW. Up to a point you probably have the choice as to whether to use this heat or forcefully to reject it, e.g. by a cooker hood or extract fan. To use it all would probably be unwise, as there may be potential lung irritants in the burned gases; in any case these gases usually carry dirt, grease and smell, and almost certainly water vapour. Such health risks as there are, are small: burned natural gas consists largely of carbon dioxide and water, but also traces of oxides of nitrogen, which, in quantity, can be harmful to lung sufferers. Some people of limited means consciously use gas cookers for space heating, perhaps without realising that, leaving all other considerations aside, they are using their gas in the most efficient way possible.

Given that the cooker provides so much heat, it also follows that it will pay to use it as efficiently as possible for cooking. This matters most outside the heating season, when the waste heat is of no other benefit. If, however, your heating system and the layout of the house do not make it possible to exploit the waste heat to help warm the house, then efficient use of the cooker is doubly important.

Gas cookers are limited in their scope for more efficient cooking. The use of broad-bottomed pans with lids, and especially of pressure cookers, no doubt helps. A gas overhead grill at about 3¼ kW is a very inefficient way of cooking — especially while it is warming up (an electric toaster of 1¾ kW will make toast a lot faster, but the fuel costs about five times as much as the lower gas tariff). It is certainly worthwhile, too, to cook as many dishes as possible simultaneously in the oven, which is in itself the most efficient part of the cooker (gas or electric) because of its retained heat and thermostatic control.

Electric cooking is inherently less wasteful of heat, partly because there are no burned gases to vent off, and partly because, where boiling rings are concerned, flat solid plates in contact with the bottoms of pans and kettles inevitably put more of the heat where it is required. The maximum heat output from electric cookers is typically up to 7 kW.

There is probably scope for better insulation of ovens of all types; present insulation standards are designed to keep outside surface temperatures within safe limits rather than to conserve heat for its own sake. The gas-cooker owner can experiment to find out which common processes normally done over gas might be done more economically by purpose-built electrical appliances. The improved cooking efficiency does not, however, outweigh the present differences in tariff. Typical annual consumptions for families are 60—80 therms of gas (£14—£18 at the *higher* rate of 22.8p/therm), as against 1000—1500 kW h of electricity (£29—£43 at 2.9p/ kW h).

The electric kettle is an exceedingly efficient way of boiling water, being both direct and very fast. The electric slow cooker, however, loses a great deal of heat simply because it takes so long.

Helping water heating with ambient energy in summer

The temperature of cold water entering the house through the main (normally well below outside air temperature) will usually vary through the seasons, but also depends on the source from which the water is drawn. The warmer the supply to the hot water system, the less your hot water will cost. If, as is usual, the water stands in a large tank in the loft before it is used, it will warm up to something approaching air temperature, especially if the loftspace is heated by the sun. Hence, for example, if by this means you can warm the cold water supply from $10°C$ to $15°C$, it will take 12½ per cent less heat to raise its temperature to $50°C$ in the hot water system. Such a saving is unlikely to be dramatic, but would nevertheless justify removing the insulation from the cold-water tank at the start of the summer. Don't forget to put it back when the heating season starts again.

None of the suggestions listed in this chapter is likely to make on its own a large difference to your consumption, but the sum of all of them might easily equal the yield from a fairly expensive modification to the house, whereas most of them will have cost nothing at all.

Index

INDEX

INDEX